FOUNDATIONS OF EDUCATION

TWELFTH EDITION

FOUNDATIONS OF EDUCATION

Allan C. Ornstein
St. John's University

Daniel U. Levine
Emeritus, University of Missouri at Kansas City
and University of Nebraska at Omaha

Gerald L. Gutek
Emeritus, Loyola University Chicago

David E. Vocke
Towson University

WADSWORTH
CENGAGE Learning

Australia • Brazil • Japan • Korea • Mexico • Singapore • Spain • United Kingdom • United States

Foundations of Education, Twelfth Edition
Allan C. Ornstein, Daniel U. Levine,
Gerald L. Gutek, David E. Vocke

Editor-in-Chief: Linda Ganster

Executive Editor: Mark Kerr

Managing Development Editor: Lisa Mafrici

Freelance Development Editor: Melissa Kelleher

Editorial Assistant: Greta Lindquist

Media Editor: Elizabeth Momb

Senior Media Editor: Ashley Cronin

Brand Manager: Melissa Larmon

Senior Market Development Manager:
Kara Kindstrom

Content Project Manager: Samen Iqbal

Art Director: Jennifer Wahi

Manufacturing Planner: Doug Bertke

Rights Acquisitions Specialist: Roberta Broyer

Production Service: Teresa Christie, MPS

Photo Researcher: Corey Geissler

Text Researcher: Sarah Carey

Copy Editor: Julie McNamee

Text Designer: Roy Neuhaus

Cover Designer: CMB Design

Cover Image: GettyImages bldaro70505392,
© Andersen Ross

Compositor: MPS

For product information and technology assistance, contact us at
Cengage Learning Customer & Sales Support, 1-800-354-9706.
For permission to use material from this text or product,
submit all requests online at **www.cengage.com/permissions**.
Further permissions questions can be e-mailed to
permissionrequest@cengage.com.

Library of Congress Control Number: 2012943668

Student Edition:
ISBN-13: 978-1-133-58985-3
ISBN-10: 1-133-58985-5

Loose-leaf Edition:
ISBN-13: 978-1-133-94080-7
ISBN-10: 1-133-94080-3

Wadsworth
20 Davis Drive
Belmont, CA 94002-3098
USA

Cengage Learning is a leading provider of customized learning solutions with office locations around the globe, including Singapore, the United Kingdom, Australia, Mexico, Brazil, and Japan. Locate your local office at **www.cengage.com/global**.

Cengage Learning products are represented in Canada by Nelson Education, Ltd.

To learn more about Wadsworth, visit **www.cengage.com/wadsworth**
Purchase any of our products at your local college store or at our preferred online store **www.CengageBrain.com**.

Printed in the United States of America
1 2 3 4 5 6 7 16 15 14 13 12

Brief Contents

Contents

PART FIVE
Curricular Foundations 399

Preface

We are dedicated to the professional preparation of educators. To achieve this goal, we provide quality content, technology, and services to ensure that new teachers are prepared for the realities of the classroom. Our aim is to connect preservice to practice to foster teachers' lifelong career success.

Goals and Themes of This Edition

As *Foundations of Education* enters its Twelfth Edition, three goals continued to be central in revising and updating the book:

Goal #1. Include contemporary and substantive subject matter To meet this goal, we have worked to refine and update the themes that recur throughout the book:

- **Diversity:** We continue to place emphasis, throughout this revision, on addressing educational issues involving or influenced by cultural diversity.

- **Standards and Accountability:** We have added new information to several chapters that addresses the growing emphasis on holding students, teachers, and schools accountable for performing at levels specified by local, state, and national standards.

- **Technology:** We have systematically placed emphasis on the growing role of technology in education. This emphasis includes sections on the history of technology in education, the place of technology in school reform, the expanding reach of new technological literacies such as social networking, and the effects of digital technologies on children.

- **Developing Your Own History, Autobiography, and Philosophy of Education:** This edition, especially Part Two, Historical and Philosophical Foundations, emphasizes the relevance of reflecting on and writing your history of education, your own educational autobiography, and your own philosophy of education to your professional development as an educator.

- **Continuity and Change:** This edition now emphasizes the areas in which the landscape of education is changing. A marginal icon identifies sections of the narrative where this theme is explicitly addressed.

New content coverage in the Twelfth Edition includes the following:

> **Chapter 1: New** sections on Teacher Residency; on the Adequacy of Preparation Programs; on Teacher-Quality Components of No Child Left Behind and Race to the Top; and on Professional Learning Communities.

> **Chapter 2: Updated** information on NCATE's—recently renamed The Council for the Accreditation of Educator Preparation (CAEP)—influence on teacher-preparation programs. A discussion of the attempts under way in several states to curtail the bargaining rights of teachers, an extended look at induction programs, and an updated focus on professional development opportunities for teachers.

New material on pay-for-performance plans, especially those being encouraged by the federal government through Race to the Top initiatives. A **new** section on Professional Learning Communities. (Thanks to Ron Thomas of Towson University for his assistance with this section.)

Chapter 3: New time lines on ancient China, ancient Egypt, ancient Israel, ancient Greece, ancient Rome, Islam, the Middle Ages, the Renaissance, the Reformation, and the Enlightenment.

Chapter 4: New time lines on Johann Amos Comenius, Jean-Jacques Rousseau, Johann Heinrich Pestalozzi, Johann Friedrich Herbart, Friedrich Froebel, Herbert Spencer, John Dewey, Jane Addams, Maria Montessori, Jean Piaget, and Paulo Freire. A new TeachSource Video Activity on Piaget's stages of development is keyed to the chapter's narrative.

Chapter 5: New time lines on Benjamin Franklin, Thomas Jefferson, Benjamin Rush, Noah Webster, Horace Mann, Catharine Beecher, Booker T. Washington, and W. E. B. Du Bois.

Chapter 6: The "From Preservice to Practice" activity features a new primary source from Dewey's *Democracy and Education* on the purpose of the school. The new TeachSource Video activity features four philosophies of education in action. The Technology @ School and Certification Connection activities focus on the Common State Standards and 21st Century Themes initiatives.

Chapter 7: New data on state and local school boards. An expanded discussion on the impact of accountability measures on school district personnel. A **new** TeachSource Video Case spotlights the Bronx Engineering and Technology Academy to illustrate the small school concept.

Chapter 8: New, updated statistics on revenues and expenditures throughout the chapter. Extensive material on the impact of the economic downturn on state and local school districts. Updated discussion on the expansion of school choice, charter schools, and educational vouchers. A **new** TeachSource Video Case examines the issue of educational equity. An examination of the Race to the Top funding initiatives from the Obama administration.

Chapter 9: New sections on Copyright Policy and New Media; and on Cyberbullying and Other Electronic Misdeeds, with subsections on Cyberbullying, Disparagement of School or Staff, Gaining Access to Prohibited Materials, and Sexting.

Chapter 10: New sections on Cohabitation Increase and Effects; on Adolescent Subculture as a Determinant of Later Success, or Not; and on The Increasing Plight of Working-Class and Low-Skilled, Middle-Class Men.

Chapter 12: New sections on Movement to Charter Schools Reinforcing Segregation; on The Status of NCLB and Movement toward Waivers; and on Increase in Autism.

Chapter 13: A new TeachSource Video Activity and Taking Issue section on the Common Core State Standards. Additionally, the role played by the Common Core State Standards in shaping curriculum and ultimately classroom instruction threaded throughout the chapter. Discussion of changes made to adjust NCLB by the Obama administration.

Chapter 14: Additions to the chapter emphasize the influence of the Common Core State Standards on school curriculum. Updated information and statistics incorporated in material on differentiated instruction, twenty-first century skills, technology-enhanced instruction, importance of the arts, education of English language learners, education for healthy youth, and green education.

Chapter 15: New sections on Curriculum Content, Instructional Emphases, and Approaches to Teacher Preparation; and on Teacher Training in Finland.

Chapter 16: New sections on The Harlem Children's Zone (HCZ) and Purpose Built Communities (PBC); on Research on Technology Achievement Effects; on Success at Online Schools?; on Blended Learning Approaches and Flipped Classrooms; on One-to-One Provision of Computers to Students; and on Mobile Learning.

Other current and important topics that continue to receive particular emphasis in the Twelfth Edition include professional development, the history of education in China, legal protections regarding assaults on teachers and students, problems with and prospects for federal legislation, school choice and charter schools, curriculum and testing standards, promising instructional innovations and interventions, approaches for helping students from low-income families and for equalizing educational opportunity, and international achievement patterns. Unique to this text, you'll find that footnotes not only point to up-to-date sources but also lend themselves to helping students explore topics that particularly interest them. The wide range of sources cited also provides students with access to a wealth of resources for future study of educational issues.

Goal #2. Increase the effectiveness of the text for student learning and provide material that instructors need when preparing their students for teaching careers   The Twelfth Edition of *Foundations of Education* includes many special features designed to help students easily understand and master the material in the text and provide professors with the tools to create in-depth and lively classroom discussions.

- **Time lines** have been added to the history and philosophy chapters in Part Two to mark milestones in education.

- **TeachSource Video Activity** boxes refer to the award-winning online Video Cases (available on Education CourseMate) and provide questions to help students relate key chapter topics to video content, to certification exams, and to their own practice as teachers. Two or more video activity boxes are now available for nearly every chapter.

- **Focus and Refocus Questions** are included in every chapter. Focus Questions appear at the beginning of each chapter to provide students with an advance organizer of chapter material. Refocus Questions, which appear after major sections of chapters, are designed to help students reinforce their comprehension by connecting the concepts discussed in the book to their own personal situations.

- The **From Preservice to Practice** feature helps students both apply and think critically about concepts discussed in each chapter. In these boxed inserts, students read vignettes that describe situations in which new teachers might find themselves and answer case questions that encourage critical and applied thinking about how they might best respond in each situation.

- **Topical overview charts,** found in every chapter of the text, summarize and compare key topics, giving students a concise tool for reviewing important chapter concepts.

- **Technology @ School** features keep students up to date on relevant developments regarding educational technology and provide access to websites that will be valuable resources as they progress through their teaching careers. Some examples of this feature include Helping Students Develop Media Literacy (Chapter 10) and Safety Issues and New Technologies on the Internet (Chapter 14).

- **Taking Issue** features present controversial issues in the field of education, offering arguments on both sides of a question so that students can understand why the topic is important and how it affects contemporary schools. Updated for the Twelfth Edition, this feature now asks students to also answer, "What is Your Stand?" and covers issues such as alternative certification, merit pay, magnet schools, and high-stakes exams for graduation. New topics for the Twelfth Edition include social justice (Chapter 4), immigration (Chapter 5), teacher objectivity (Chapter 6), and Common Core State Standards (Chapter 13). Instructors may want to use these features as the basis for class discussion or essay assignments.

- **Certification Connection Activities** are end-of-chapter features that link chapter content to the Praxis Exam and other certification exams.

In addition, other key pedagogic features and study aids have been retained, including the following:

- **Marginal notations** reinforce central points throughout the text.

- **End-of-chapter features** include **summary lists** that facilitate understanding and analysis of content, a **list of key terms**, annotated lists of selected **print and electronic resources for further learning** that may be of special interest to readers, **discussion questions** to stimulate class participation in examining text material, and suggested **projects for professional development**.

- **An extensive glossary** at the end of the book defines important terms and concepts.

Goal #3. Draw on the Internet and other electronic media to enhance learning   Our updating has drawn, to a considerable extent, on resources available on the Internet. Students may explore areas of personal interest by scrutinizing the printed versions of many sources we cite—including news sources such as the *New York Times* and *Education Week* and journal sources such as the *American School Board Journal* and *Educational Leadership*. But, in general, most of our citations are available to students on the Internet and can be accessed easily by searching with university library resources such as EBSCO Academic Search Premier.

To facilitate access, we frequently provide URLs to websites that were active at the time we prepared this text. For many scholarly papers and for articles in periodicals, we provide initial URLs; the reader then can click on "Archives" or "Back Issues" (or similar terms) on the first screen to find the designated issue, or can use a search function provided in the initial screen. On controversial issues, we try to encourage use of sites that represent a variety of points of view. All websites mentioned in the text are links on Education CourseMate.

Organization

The text consists of sixteen chapters divided into the following six parts:

- **Part One (Understanding the Teaching Profession)** considers the climate in which teachers work today and its impact on teaching. Changes in the job market and in the status of the profession and issues such as teacher empowerment, professional learning communities, and alternative certification are treated in some detail.

- The four chapters in **Part Two (Historical and Philosophical Foundations)** provide historical and philosophical contexts for understanding current educational practices and trends by examining the events and ideas that have influenced the development of education in the United States. These chapters provide a historical and philosophical perspective needed by professionals in education, encourage students to develop a philosophical understanding early in the course, and establish a knowledge base that will help them comprehend and think critically about the discussion of the contemporary foundations that occur later in the text.

- **Part Three (Political, Economic, and Legal Foundations)** presents an overview of the organization, governance, and administration of elementary and secondary education; the financing of public education; and the legal aspects of education.

- **Part Four (Social Foundations)** examines the relationships between society and the schools that society has established to serve its needs. The three chapters in this part discuss culture and socialization; the complex relationship between social class, race, and educational achievement; and the various programs aimed at providing equal educational opportunities for all students.

■ **Part Five (Curricular Foundations)** examines the ways in which changes in societies have led to changes in educational goals, curriculum, and instructional methods. Throughout these chapters, we explicitly point out how the particular philosophical ideas discussed in Chapter 4 are linked to goals, standards, curriculum, and other facets of contemporary education. This section concludes with a look at emerging curriculum trends.

■ **Part Six (Effective Education: International and American Perspectives)** provides a comparative look at schools and their development throughout the world and an in-depth analysis of current efforts to improve school effectiveness in the United States.

Teaching and Learning Supplements

Accompanying the text are the following ancillaries:

■ **Online Instructor's Manual and Test Bank.** The Instructor's Manual has been thoroughly updated and revised to reflect new text content; it offers for each chapter of the text a chapter outline, a chapter overview, student objectives, lecture and discussion topics, student projects, selected resources, a transition guide, and model syllabi. The Test Bank contains hundreds of test items, developed according to sound principles and standards of test construction.

■ **Microsoft PowerPoint® Slides.** These vibrant PowerPoint lecture slides for each chapter assist you with your lecture by providing concept coverage using images, figures, and tables directly from the textbook.

■ **ExamView® Test Bank.** Available for download from the instructor website, ExamView testing software includes all of the test items from the printed Test Bank in electronic format, enabling you to create customized tests in print or online.

■ **Education CourseMate**

   • For instructors, Cengage Learning's Education CourseMate includes **EngagementTracker**, a first-of-its-kind tool that monitors student engagement in the course. The accompanying instructor website, available through **login .cengage.com**, offers access to password-protected resources such as an electronic version of the instructor's manual, test bank files, and PowerPoint slides. CourseMate can be bundled with the student text. (Contact your Cengage sales representative for information on getting access to CourseMate.)

   • For students, **Education CourseMate** brings course concepts to life with interactive learning, study, and exam preparation tools that support the printed textbook. Students have access to an integrated E-book, learning tools such as glossaries, flashcards, quizzes, time line activities, award-winning TeachSource Video Cases, and more. The TeachSource Video Cases are video modules presenting actual classroom scenarios supported by viewing questions, teacher interviews, artifacts, and bonus videos. These modules allow preservice teachers to realistically and thoroughly analyze the problems and opportunities in the case and experience the complex and multiple dimensions of true classroom dilemmas that teachers face every day. Go to **CengageBrain.com** to register or purchase access.

   • Access to Education CourseMate includes access to **Infotrac® College Edition**, an Online Research and Learning Center featuring 24/7 access to more than 20 million full-text articles from nearly 6,000 journals. Covering a broad spectrum of disciplines and topics, this online library is ideal for every type of research.

- **WebTutor™ for Blackboard and WebCT.** Jumpstart your course with customizable, rich, text-specific content within your Course Management System. Whether you want to Web-enable your class or put an entire course online, WebTutor delivers. WebTutor offers a wide array of resources, including access to the E-book, glossaries, flashcards, quizzes, time line activities, TeachSource Video Cases, and more.

Acknowledgments

The Twelfth Edition would not have been possible without contributions and feedback from many individuals. In particular, David Vocke, Professor of Education at Towson University, planned and implemented many substantial revisions in Chapters 2, 7, 8, 13, and 14. His outstanding contributions to this volume are in themselves a testimonial to the breadth of his knowledge and the acuity of his insight as an educator dedicated to improving professional preparation. Gerald Gutek, Professor Emeritus of Education and History at Loyola University of Chicago, has also made an outstanding contribution to the book as the author of Chapters 3, 4, 5, and 6, which he thoroughly revised and updated for this edition.

A number of reviewers made useful suggestions and provided thoughtful reactions that guided us in every edition. We thank the following individuals for their conscientiousness and for their contributions to the content of this edition:

James Brown, *Southern University at Shreveport*
Robert Ceglie, *Mercer University*
Evyonne Hawkins, *Richland Community College*
Sheila Ingle, *Gardner Webb University*
Bridget Ingram, *Clark State Community College*
Denise Simard, *SUNY Plattsburgh*
Mary Ware, *SUNY Cortland*
Amy Williamson, *Angelo State University*

In addition, we thank the numerous reviewers who have contributed to prior editions:
H. Rose Adesiyan, *Purdue University, Calumet*
Louis Alfonso, *Rhode Island College*
Terryl J. Anderson, *The University of Texas of the Permian Basin*
Mario L. M. Baca, *California State University, Fresno*
Harold B. Bickel, *University of South Alabama*
Nancy A. Blair, *Ball State University*
Les Bolt, *James Madison University*
John A. Bucci, *Rhode Island College*
Patricia Burdell, *Central Michigan University*
Paul R. Burden, *Kansas State University*
Darilyn Butler, *Queens University of Charlotte*
John Caruso, Jr., *West Connecticut State University*
Donna Lynn Ciampa, *Suffolk County Community College*

Gary K. Clabaugh, *La Salle University*
Charles R. Colvin, *SUNY Fredonia*
Jack Conklin, *North Adams State*
James F. Cummings, *Newberry College*
Arnold Danzig, *Northern Arizona University*
Donald C. Edinger, *Grand Valley State College*
Virden Evans, *Florida A&M University*
Jerry R. Franklin, *Morehead State University*
Kate Friesner, *The College of Santa Fe*
Sherell M. Fuller, *University of North Carolina at Charlotte*
F. H. George, *Southeastern Oklahoma State University*
Judith A. Green, *Kansas State University*
Pam E. Green, *Southwestern College*
Leslie Griffin, *Delta State University*
Thomas W. Gwaltney, Jr., *Eastern Michigan University*
Carole Wylie Hancock, *Washington State Community College*
Dwight Hare, *Northeast Louisiana University*
JoAnn Hatchman, *California State University, Hayward*
Samuel Hinton, *Eastern Kentucky University*
Patrick B. Johnson, *Dowling College*
Ralph R. Karst, *Northeast Louisiana University*
Kelly Kolodny, *Framingham State College*
James Lawlor, *Towson University*
Edith Lombardo, *West Virginia State College*

Joseph Matthews, *Brigham Young University*

Derwyn McElroy, *Auburn University, Montgomery*

Colleen A. Moore, *Central Michigan University*

William Phillips, *Fairmont State College*

Richard R. Renner, *University of Florida*

Maureen A. Reynolds, *Indiana University, Kokomo*

Patrick Socoski, *West Chester University*

Jack Stirton, *San Joaquin Delta Community College*

John P. Strouse, *Ball State University*

T. Lavon Talley, *Oglethorpe University*

Margaret Tannenbaum, *Rowan University*

Sevan G. Terzian, *University of Florida*

Roderick M. Thronson, *Carroll College*

Rosita Tormala-Nita, *University of Wisconsin at Milwaukee*

Cheryl Valdez, *Chapman University, California*

Innes J. Villalpando, *Southwestern College*

Guy O. Wall, *Indiana University Southeast*

J. W. Weatherford, *University of Central Oklahoma*

Lowell E. Whiteside, *Central Missouri State University*

Jody Messinger Wolfe, *West Virginia University*

We also want to acknowledge and express appreciation to Development Editor Melissa Kelleher for her assistance. In addition to providing leadership and guidance in all aspects of development, Melissa performed numerous related functions such as preliminary copy editing, assurance of consistency, and verification of sources. Other important contributions at Cengage Learning were made by Mark Kerr, Executive Editor; Ashley Cronin, Senior Media Editor; Kara Kindstrom, Senior Marketing Manager; Samen Iqbal, Content Project Manager; Teresa Christie; Copy Editor, Julie McNamee.

PART ONE

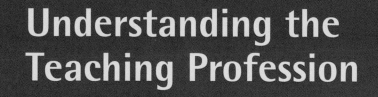

Vstock LLC/Jupiter Images

Understanding the Teaching Profession

Motivation, Preparation, and Conditions for the Entering Teacher

You probably have been wondering whether teaching is the right career for you and whether you will be entering a profession with good opportunities for personal and professional growth. Even if your goal has long been to teach, you might be wondering about the difficulties and rewards of the field you have chosen or are considering. Is your desire to be a teacher strong enough to withstand the challenges you are likely to meet? What can you expect to encounter in your preparation program, and what lies ahead after you become a teacher? This chapter (and subsequent chapters) will examine such topics, including motivations for becoming a teacher, teacher supply and demand, pay scales, career preparation, and efforts to improve the teaching workforce and to give teachers more decision-making power. To help focus your thoughts, keep the following questions in mind:

FOCUS QUESTIONS

■ What are the usual reasons for becoming a teacher, and how do your reasons compare?

■ What are the current employment trends for teachers?

■ What salaries and benefits do teachers earn? How do these compare with other occupations?

■ How are teachers prepared? How are they certified?

■ What are the current trends in teacher education?

■ What do teachers find satisfying and dissatisfying about their work?

■ What are some current developments in teacher workforce quality and teaching conditions?

---

*This chapter was revised by Dan Levine.

Choosing a Career in Teaching

The path to becoming a teacher begins when you choose teaching as a career. In this section, we'll review some motives for choosing a teaching career and the challenges that accompany this choice. We'll also examine the growing concern that too few minority college students are becoming teachers.

Motivations for Choosing Teaching

Reasons for teaching

We have many motives, both idealistic and practical, for choosing a career in teaching. Often, a person's reasons for wanting to teach stem from his or her *personal philosophy of education,* a topic we will revisit throughout this book. If you are thinking of entering the teaching profession, ask yourself why. Your motives may include (1) love of children, (2) desire to impart knowledge, (3) interest in and excitement about teaching, and (4) desire to perform a valuable service to society. Perhaps you hope for job security, pension benefits, and relative ease in preparing for teaching compared with the training required by some other professions.

Reasons for entering the profession

One study asked future teachers from a representative sample of seventy-six schools and colleges of teacher education to state their reasons for selecting the teaching profession. Ninety percent of the respondents cited "helping children grow and learn" as a reason. Next highest was "seems to be a challenging field" (63 percent), followed closely by "like work conditions" (54 percent), "inspired by favorite teachers" (53 percent), and "sense of vocation and honor of teaching" (52 percent). These reasons also were cited in several other recent studies. Some of these studies further found that admiration for one's elementary and secondary teachers often shapes decisions to become a teacher.[1] This chapter's From Preservice to Practice box also looks at the reasons people decide to become teachers.

> **REFOCUS** How do your reasons for becoming a teacher compare with those of the teachers surveyed? Does your list rank the reasons in the same order? What other reasons might you add to this list?

The Challenge of Teaching All Students

You probably are strongly motivated to perform effectively when you anticipate becoming a teacher, but you are likely to encounter some difficulties in achieving this goal after you actually begin teaching. As we point out in this section and in subsequent chapters, there will be numerous jobs open in the schools, but many will require teaching disadvantaged students who live in difficult circumstances with which you may be unfamiliar.

Challenges in teaching all students

Many of these jobs will involve working with special-education populations, students who are just learning English, and/or distinctive racial or ethnic minority groups with whom you may have had little contact. You probably will be well prepared to teach subject matter in your chosen field, but many of the students you are assigned will be performing poorly in reading comprehension and will need much help to improve their understanding and learn how to learn.

Despite the difficulties inherent or implicit in these kinds of situations, you will be expected to help make sure that *all* students perform at an adequate level in accordance with national and state laws. Although historically there have been few schools and classrooms with significant numbers of hard-to-teach students in which many or most of them are performing adequately, the number has been growing in recent years. We devote attention to these schools and classrooms in subsequent material dealing with effective teaching and with unusually effective schools.

---

[1]Paul E. Barton, "The Closing of the Education Frontier," 2002 report prepared for the Education Testing Service, available at **www.ets.org/research/pic**; "The Importance of Schools in Rural Communities," *ASCD Research Brief*, January 18, 2005; Daniel Gross, "The Education Factor," *Education Next* (Spring 2009), available at **www.educationnext.org**; "Engaging the World Anew Conference," 2011 speech by U.S. Secretary of Education Arne Duncan, available at **www.ed.gov**; and "Obama Requests Funding to Help Math, Science Teacher Preparation," *eSchool News*, February 8, 2012, available at **www.eschoolnews.com**.

FROM PRESERVICE TO PRACTICE

Considerations

"Are each of you certain that you want to enter the teaching profession?" Professor Johnson asked. "Remember, the challenges of the profession often become stressors. About half of the teachers who enter the profession leave within a few years. So, tell me why you want to become a teacher, Jennifer."

"My grandmother was a teacher, and my mother is a teacher. Both of them have told me how rewarding the career can be. I like children. I've loved my experiences with children in summer camps, so now I'm choosing elementary school teaching."

"I want to coach and teach," said Mark. "Some of the best times in my life have been when I played basketball or tennis. The coaches made it their business to see that I followed their discipline and that I paid attention to academics, too. These experiences taught me new values and new disciplines and gave me a vision for what I want to do with my life. I want to work at the high-school level."

"I don't have any great yearning to teach," said Caitlin. "I have to support myself after I graduate—my parents made it plain that I'm on my own financially after next year. I want to be an artist, and I think I can do that if at first I support myself by teaching. There are several galleries in the area, and if I could

get a job teaching junior or senior high, maybe I could get some work shown locally, earn a few commissions, and be on my way."

"I know I won't get rich," said Peter, "but there is something compelling about watching the 'aha' experience in a student's face. I've taught swimming and diving during the summers. When a skill finally clicks in, the triumph of that young boy or girl makes it all worthwhile. I want to teach physical education in an elementary school."

Professor Johnson replied, "Each of you seems to have considered this choice for some time. I will share a few other reasons mentioned by other students. Teaching is one profession you can use to travel the world. International schools and foreign private schools search regularly for people such as you. Teaching English as a second language has given many a free ticket to China, Japan, and Korea. Or you can teach as a missionary in church schools.

"Another primary consideration is that state retirement systems usually provide fairly secure long-term benefits. That kind of security can be hard to find in the business world today.

"As a follow-up to this discussion, write a reflection paper about the discussion and your reasons for choosing education. Bring it to class next week."

Case Questions

1. Why is it important that preservice teachers reflect on their motivations for selecting the teaching profession?
2. Why are you choosing the teaching profession?
3. Geographically, where do you think you might want to teach? Why? What are the projected job opportunities in that area at the time you finish your education?

Teaching Force Diversity: A Growing Concern

Although the U.S. school population is becoming increasingly diverse, the teaching force has not kept pace. For example, African American, Asian American, and Hispanic American students make up more than 40 percent of the public-school student population, but the proportion of elementary and secondary teachers from these minority groups is generally estimated at 17 percent or less. Although the number of minority public-school teachers has about doubled in the past twenty years, the number of minority students has increased about 75 percent, thus maintaining a wide shortfall in minority teachers. The disparity is particularly acute in the largest urban districts, where minority students sometimes comprise 90 percent or more of enrollment.[2]

[2]Rona F. Flippo and Julie G. Caniff, "Who Is Not Teaching Our Children?" *Multicultural Perspectives* (Issue 2, 2003); Ulrich Boser, "Teacher Diversity Matters," 2011 report posted by the Center for American Progress, available at **www.americanprogress.org**; and Richard M. Ingersoll and Henry May, "The Minority Teacher Shortage," *Phi Delta Kappan* (September 2011), available at **www.kappanmagazine.org**.

OVERVIEW 1.1

Ways to Improve Your Employment Prospects

Advance Preparation	Scouting and Planning	Assembling Materials	Applying for a Job	Preparing for an Interview
Check your state's certification requirements and follow them correctly. Acquire adjunct skills that make you multidimensional, ready to assist in activities such as coaching or supervising the student newspaper. Maintain an up-to-date file listing all your professional activities, accomplishments, and awards. Keep well-organized notes on what you learn from classroom observations. Begin a journal specifically related to teaching concerns. Use it to reflect on what you see and hear and to develop your own ideas.	Collect information on school districts that have vacant positions. Possible sources of information include your career planning or placement office and the state education department's office of teacher employment. Look into computerized job banks operated by professional organizations or available elsewhere on the Internet. Visit, call, or write to school districts in which you are particularly interested. Plan your application strategy in advance.	Prepare a neat, accurate, and clear resume. Prepare a professional portfolio that includes lesson plans, peer critiques, descriptions of relevant experience, supervisors' evaluations, and, if possible, a video of you teaching. Ask your career planning or placement office for advice on other materials to include with the credentials you will submit.	Begin applying for teaching jobs as soon as possible. Apply for several vacancies at once.	Take time to clarify your philosophy of education and learning. Know what you believe, and be able to explain it. Be prepared for other interview questions as well. In particular, anticipate questions that deal with classroom management, lesson design, and your employment history. Learn as much as you can about the school district before the interview: for instance, organization, levels of teaching positions, types of schools, and use of technology

Reasons to increase teacher diversity

Proposals for promoting diversity

> **REFOCUS** What do you think might make teaching a more attractive career option for today's college students, minority and nonminority? If you are a member of a minority group, what attracts you to teaching? How will you prepare to work with students who may have a different ethnic or socioeconomic background from your own?

Increasing teaching force diversity to better reflect the student population is widely viewed as an important goal. For one thing, teachers from a cultural or ethnic minority group generally are in a better position than are nonminority teachers to serve as positive role models for minority students. In many cases, minority teachers also may have a better understanding of minority students' expectations and learning styles (see Chapter 11, Social Class, Race, and School Achievement, and Chapter 12, Providing Equal Educational Opportunity), particularly if minority teachers working with low-income students grew up in working-class homes themselves. For example, Lisa Delpit and other analysts have pointed out that many African American teachers may be less prone than nonminority teachers to mistakenly assume that black students will respond well to a teacher who is friendly in the classroom. In addition, teachers from Asian American, Latino, and other minority groups are in demand for working with students who have limited English skills.[3]

Officials of the American Association of Colleges for Teacher Education (AACTE) have stated that data on the low proportion of minority teachers constitute a "devastating" crisis. Along with other organizations, the AACTE has proposed and helped

[3]Lisa Delpit, "The Silenced Dialogue," *Harvard Educational Review* (August 1988), pp. 280–298; Marona A. L. Graham-Bailey, "An Incomplete Identity," *Rethinking Schools* (Fall 2008), available at **www.rethinkingschools.org**; Jennifer Rokosa, "More Diverse Teachers for More Diverse Schools," 2011 paper posted by the Center for American Progress, available at **www.americanprogress .org**; and Lisa Delpit, *"Multiplication Is for White People"* (New York: The New Press, 2012).

initiate legislation for various new programs to increase the number of minority teachers: increasing financial aid for prospective minority teachers, enhancing recruitment of minority candidates, and initiating precollegiate programs to attract minority students.[4]

Supply/Demand and Salaries

Will you find work as a teacher? How much money will you earn? These two questions are related, following the economic principle of **supply and demand**. When teacher supply exceeds demand, salaries tend to decline. Conversely, high demand and low supply tend to increase salaries. As discussed in Chapter 2, The Teaching Profession, supply and demand also affects the social status and prestige accorded to a particular occupation.

Job Opportunities

Interest in teaching careers increases

In the 1960s and 1970s, a falling birth rate resulted in a teacher surplus. As college students and teacher educators recognized the substantial oversupply, enrollment in teacher-education programs decreased. The percentage of college freshmen interested in becoming teachers declined from 23 percent in 1968 to 5 percent in 1982. Since then, the trend has reversed. The percentage of college students interested in teaching rose by nearly 100 percent during the late 1980s and 1990s and has remained relatively high since then. In addition, many community colleges are now participating in teacher preparation, and the economic recession appears to be encouraging more individuals to apply for entry into preparation programs for teachers.[5]

Reasons to expect a teacher shortage

Analysts predict many candidates in upcoming years but also many teaching jobs. Several million new teachers will be needed in the next decade for the following reasons:[6]

1. When the post–World War II baby boom generation began to produce its own children, a mini baby boom developed. Most of those children now attend K–12 schools. In addition, many immigrant families have entered the United States in recent years. As a result, school enrollment has been increasing (see Table 1.1).

2. A significant proportion of the current teaching force will reach retirement age in the coming decade.

3. Educational reformers are attempting to reduce class size, expand preschool education, place greater emphasis on science and mathematics, and introduce other changes that require more teachers.

4. Higher standards for becoming a teacher are limiting the supply.

5. New charter schools are being established in many locations.

6. Employed teachers continue to leave the classroom and/or the profession at a substantial rate.

---

[4]*Minority Teacher Supply and Demand* (Washington, D.C.: American Association of Colleges for Teacher Education, 1990), p. 3. See also Paul E. Barton and Richard J. Coley, "Parsing the Achievement Gap Part II," 2009 report prepared for the Educational Testing Service, available at **www.ets.org**; and Saba Bireda and Robin Chait, "Increasing Teacher Diversity," 2011 report posted by the Center for American Progress, available at **www.americanprogress.org**.
[5]Debra D. Bragg, "Teacher Pipelines," *Community College Review* (July 2007), pp. 10–29; and "Preparing and Credentialing the Nation's Teachers" (Washington, D.C.: U.S. Department of Education, 2011), available at **www.ed.gov**.
[6]Gene A. Budig, "A Perfect Storm," *Phi Delta Kappan* (October 2006), pp. 114–116; Geoffrey Borman and N. Maritza Dowling, "Teacher Attrition and Retention," *Review of Educational Research* (September 2008), pp. 367–409; Barbara Miner, "Teaching's Revolving Door," *Rethinking Schools* (Winter 2008/2009), available at **www.rethinkingschools.org**; and Joe Mathews, "What Teacher Shortage?" 2011 posting by NBC Bay Area, available at **www.nbcbayarea.com**.

Table 1.1	Public- and Private-School Kindergarten through Grade 12 Enrollments, 1992 to 2020 (in Millions)			
	Total	Public	Private	Private as Percentage of Total
1992	48.5	42.8	5.7	11.8
2000	53.4	47.2	6.2	11.6
2020 (projected)	57.9	52.7	5.3	9.1

Note: Data include most kindergarten and some prekindergarten students. Projected sum differs from 100 percent due to rounding.

Source: William J. Hussar and Tabitha M. Bailey, *Projections of Education Statistics to 2020* (Washington, D.C.: U.S. Government Printing Office, 2012), Table 1.

✓ Standards & Assessment

■ Reasons to expect no shortage

■ Shortages in special-needs fields

Other educators, however, insist that the chances are slim of a widespread shortage of teachers in the upcoming decade. For one thing, recent shortages have mainly involved large urban districts and specialized fields such as math and science; many districts have reported no general shortage of potential teachers. In addition, it may be that fewer teachers are leaving the profession than in earlier years, and increased enrollment of students may be leveling off. Improved salaries may also bring ex-teachers back to the schools and attract people who trained as teachers but did not enter the profession.[7]

Given the arguments on each side of the issue, it is difficult to determine whether major teacher shortages will be widespread in the next decade. However, shortages certainly will continue to exist in special-needs fields such as education of students with disabilities, remedial education, bilingual education, science and mathematics, and foreign languages. In addition, teachers will remain in short supply in many rural areas and in some city and suburban communities that register significant population growth, particularly in the South and Southwest.

■ Upgraded programs

Opportunities in Nonpublic Schools   Prospective teachers may find numerous job opportunities in nonpublic schools during the next decade. As Table 1.1 shows, private schools enroll about 10 percent of the nation's elementary and secondary students. Like the public schools, many private schools are upgrading their instructional programs, often by hiring more teachers who specialize in such areas as science, math, computers, educating children with disabilities, and bilingual education.

■ Changing enrollment patterns

In the past three decades, Catholic school enrollment has declined, but many other nonpublic schools have been established. Enrollment has increased most in the independent (nonreligious) sector and in schools sponsored by evangelical and fundamentalist church groups. Moreover, many Catholic schools have been increasing the percentage of lay teachers on their faculties, and this trend is likely to continue. Furthermore, some Catholic schools have been or are being converted to charter schools with increased staffing by personnel not part of the church hierarchy.[8]

■ **REFOCUS** Are you preparing to enter a high-demand teaching specialty? If not, what can you do to improve your employment prospects?

Regardless of whether a large teacher shortage does or does not develop in the next ten years, astute prospective teachers will take certain steps to enhance their opportunities for rewarding employment. Some of these were outlined in Overview 1.1.

---

[7]Patrick Murphy and Michael DeArmond, "A National Crisis or Localized Problems?" *Education Policy Analysis Archives* (July 31, 2003), available at **http://epaa.asu.edu**; Donald Boyd et al., "Who Leaves?" 2008 paper prepared for the National Bureau of Economic Research, abstract available at **www.nber.org**; and Eamonn O'Donovan, "Is There a Teacher Shortage on the Horizon?" *District Administration* (March 2011), available at **www.districtadministration.com**.
[8]Roseanne L. Williby, "Hiring and Retaining High-Quality Teachers," *Catholic Education* (December 2004), pp. 175–193; Paul Vitello and Winnie Hu, "For Catholic Schools, Crisis and Catharsis," *New York Times*, January 17, 2009; and Dale McDonald and Margaret M. Schultz, "Catholic School Data," 2011 report prepared for the National Catholic Schools Association.

| Figure 1.1 | Average Teacher Salaries in the United States, by State Quintiles |

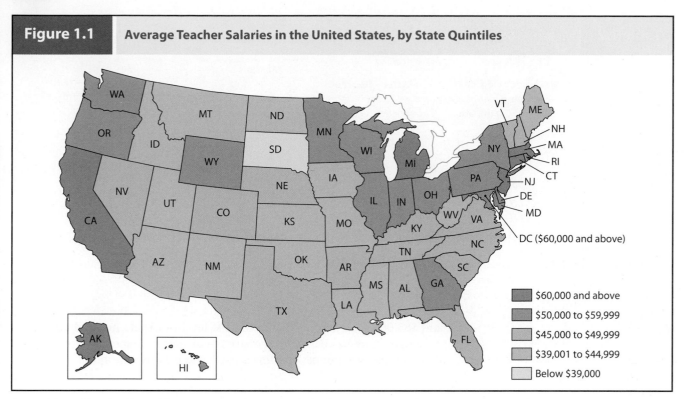

DC ($60,000 and above)

- ■ $60,000 and above
- ■ $50,000 to $59,999
- ▨ $45,000 to $49,999
- ▨ $39,001 to $44,999
- □ Below $39,000

Source: Adapted from *Rankings of the States 2008 and Estimates of School Statistics 2009* (Washington, D.C.: National Education Association, 2008), Table 16.1.

Pay Scales and Trends

Increase in salaries

Traditionally, teachers have received relatively low salaries. In 1963, for example, the average teacher salary in today's dollars was less than $40,000. Now, this figure is about $55,000, and experienced teachers in wealthy school districts frequently earn $80,000 to $100,000. Moreover, teachers have opportunities to supplement their income by supervising after-school programs, athletics, drama, and other extracurricular activities. Some teachers advance to administrative positions with annual salaries of well over $100,000. In addition, keep in mind that public-school teachers usually take advantage of benefits (such as pensions and health insurance) that are excellent compared to those of workers in other professions.[9]

Differences among states

Teaching pay varies considerably among and within states. Figure 1.1 shows the range of variation. Average overall salaries in the three highest-paying states (California, Connecticut, and New Jersey) are much higher than those in the three lowest-paying states (Montana, North Dakota, and South Dakota). Of course, we must take into account comparative living costs. It is much more expensive to live in New York, for example, than to live in the northern plains states. Salaries differ widely within states, too, where average state pay scales are high. Salary schedules in wealthy suburban districts generally are substantially higher than those in most other school districts.

Salaries vary with experience and education

The greatest variation in salaries relates to years of experience and education. Teachers with more experience and more education earn more than those with less of either. Table 1.2 shows the range based on years of experience and additional education in a typical salary schedule for the public schools of St. Mary's County, Maryland. The salary schedule provides $44,018 for a first-year teacher with a standard certificate

---

[9]Jay Chambers and Sharon Bobbitt, *The Patterns of Teacher Compensation* (Washington, D.C.: U.S. Department of Education, 1996); *Rankings of the States 2008 and Estimates of School Statistics 2009* (Washington, D.C.: National Education Association, 2008), available at **www.nea.org**; and "In Illinois, Some Teachers Earn Six-Figure Salaries," *Education News*, June 1, 2011.

Table 1.2	Selected Steps in the Salary Schedule for St. Mary's County, Maryland, Schools			
	Bachelor's Degree and Standard Certificate	Master's Degree or Advanced Certificate	Master's Degree and Advanced Certificate + 15 Approved Hours	Master's Degree and Advanced Certificate + 51 Approved Hours
First year	$44,018	$46,452	$47,679	$50,121
Fifth year	46,247	50,031	51,920	57,720
Tenth year	55,820	58,339	61,555	67,300
Thirtieth year	60,062	77,567	79,315	85,008

Note: All teachers must earn an advanced certificate within ten years of initial state certification. Teachers on an eleven-month contract typically earn $4000 to $8000 more.

Source: Internet site of the St. Mary's County, Maryland, Public Schools at **www.smcps.org.**

REFOCUS What salary do you expect to earn in your first teaching position?

and $85,008 for a teacher at the highest level of experience and education. Although numbers change from district to district and state to state, the wide difference between upper and lower pay levels is fairly common.

Preparing Teachers

Continuity & Change

Evolution of teacher training

During the U.S. colonial period and well into the early nineteenth century, anyone who wanted to become a teacher usually obtained approval from a local minister or a board of trustees associated with a religious institution. A high school or college diploma was considered unnecessary. If you could read, write, and spell and were of good moral character, you could teach school. By the 1820s, future teachers had begun attending normal schools (discussed in Chapter 5, Historical Development of American Education), although formal certification remained unnecessary. Eventually, the normal schools became teacher colleges, and most of the teacher colleges are now diversified colleges and universities. Today, all public-school teachers must be certified. Except for alternative certification or temporary certification, all states require a bachelor's degree or five years of college work for entrance into teaching.

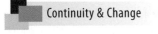 Standards & Assessment

Requirements for certification

Certification

Prospective teachers who want to teach in a U.S. public school must be certified by the state in their chosen subject areas or grade levels. At one time, most states granted **certification** based on documentation that the candidate possessed appropriate professional preparation and good moral character. However, increasing public dissatisfaction with the quality of education led to changes in certification practices.[10]

In past decades, teaching certificates usually were issued for life. Currently, by contrast, some states issue certificates valid for only three to five years. Although teachers currently holding life certificates are unaffected, those with renewable certificates usually must furnish proof of positive evaluations or university course work to have their certificates renewed.

---

[10]Elizabeth A. Kaye, ed., *Requirements for Certification of Teachers, Counselors, Librarians, and Administrators of Elementary and Secondary Schools, 2011–2012*, 76th ed. (Chicago: University of Chicago Press, 2011).

Wide differences among states

Variation in Certification Requirements Certification requirements vary widely from state to state. The resulting variance in teacher-preparation programs leads to problems in determining how well prepared entering teachers actually are. The required semester hours in general education (that is, arts and sciences) for a secondary certificate varies nationwide from about thirty hours to about seventy-five hours. The minimum hours required in professional teacher-education courses and the number of semester or quarter hours needed to teach an academic subject also vary in accordance with state requirements. Add to this the fact that courses with the same title may have drastically different content from one institution to another, and you'll see why state and institutional requirements, even when taken together, do not guarantee that teachers have studied a uniform set of skills and concepts.

Interstate movement of teachers

Reciprocity of Teacher Certificates Differences in certification requirements between states have also traditionally inhibited the movement of teachers throughout the country. If you were certified to teach in New York, for example, you might not meet the requirements for teaching in Illinois. Organizations concerned with educational quality generally have criticized this lack of reciprocity among states. Many educators have argued that easing interstate movement of teachers would help (1) balance teacher supply and demand, (2) improve opportunities for teachers, (3) reduce inbreeding and provincialism in local school systems, and (4) increase morale among teachers.

REFOCUS Does your state participate in regional teacher-education agreements with other states? If yes, are graduates of your institution automatically qualified to apply for teaching positions in cooperating states? If not, in which nearby states could you most easily obtain a teaching certificate?

Reciprocity compacts of varying success were established between some states as early as 1900. In recent years, regional agreements have developed that recognize preparation requirements across states. Most states have signed interstate contracts in which they agree to issue comparable certificates or licenses to teachers who have completed a state-approved program at an institution accredited by the region covered in the contract. In addition, various organizations are developing nationwide approaches to improve teachers' geographic mobility.[11]

Regional certificates

Nontraditional preparation

Alternative Certification Most states have introduced **alternative certification** programs, partly to attract more talented candidates to teaching and partly in reaction to current or anticipated shortages in teaching fields such as science and math. These programs help prospective teachers pursue certification without following the traditional preparation path at schools and colleges of education. A New Jersey program, for example, seeks to attract "talented persons who did not study education in college." Nationwide, hundreds of thousands of teachers have been certified through alternative certification programs. Many new teachers within this group pursue teaching careers after leaving the armed forces.[12]

Critiques of alternative certification

Alternative certification programs promote intense supervision and compressed formal course work during the first few years of the teaching assignment. Such programs almost always require professional development activities and courses while learning to teach. Several systematic examinations of alternative certification programs have provided encouraging indications that some attract well-educated individuals and may be meeting their goal of intense supervision. However, there appears to be great variation in both requirements and outputs among the many programs being implemented, and some assessments have raised questions. For example, data on

[11]Jane G. Coggshall and Susan K. Sexton, "Teachers on the Move," 2008 report prepared for the National Association of State Directors of Teacher Education Certification (NASDTEC), available at **www.nasdtec.org**; and "The NASDTEC Interstate Agreement Facilitating Mobility of Educational Personnel," 2011 posting by NASDTEC, available at **www.nasdtec.org/agreement.php**. The organizations include NASDTEC, the Council of Chief State School Officers, and the Educational Testing Service.
[12]Paul E. Pederson and Daniel Nadler, "What Happens When States Have Genuine Alternative Certification?" *Education Next* (Winter 2009), available at **www.educationnext.org**; C. Emily Feistritzer, "Alternative Teacher Certification: A State-by-State Analysis," 2010, summary available at **www.teach-now.org**; and Elizabeth Olson, "Teaching as a Second, or Even Third, Career," *New York Times*, September 15, 2011.

several alternative certification programs indicate that many participants received little or none of the training or supervision that school districts were supposed to provide. In several cases, participants acquired large debts and were unable to find teaching jobs afterward. In addition, mentoring for alternatively certified teachers can place a heavy burden on school districts.[13]

Continuity & Change

Teach for America

Probably the best-known alternative certification program is a national effort called Teach for America (TFA). Designed to attract recent graduates from colleges at which students have high achievement scores, Teach for America has spent tens of millions of dollars to recruit potential teachers, train them intensively for eight weeks, and place them in school districts with severe urban problems. Some initial reports were promising. For example, in some years, more than one-quarter of the participants were minority individuals, and many of the secondary-school participants had much-needed skills in math or science. Tens of thousands of teachers have been trained, and many are still teaching or hold other jobs in school districts. Several studies have reported promising results regarding the contributions of TFA participants. But other studies indicated that many of these potential new teachers were frustrated by conditions in difficult schools and/or withdrew before completing their teaching assignments.[14]

Despite the growing popularity of alternative certification programs, most teachers attend more traditional teacher-education programs. The Taking Issue box presents some arguments for and against alternative certification programs.

Between traditional and alternative

Teacher Residency   The Teacher Residency approach lies somewhere between the traditional route to certification and alternative certification. On the one hand, this approach recruits motivated but untrained candidates, as do many alternative programs.

REFOCUS   What are the certification requirements in the state where you want to teach? How can you find out? How might you prepare yourself for geographic mobility during your teaching career?

On the other hand, it places candidates in a full-year residency under the supervision of experienced teachers, where they have time and help to begin and to complete a master's degree approaching the depth frequently found in traditional preparation programs. Carried out cooperatively by school districts and institutions of higher education, a Teacher Residency program can help districts obtain new teachers who are able to function successfully in difficult situations. Furthermore, the program can help universities or colleges meet their obligations to prepare and place outstanding teachers in urban schools.[15]

Among the first Teacher Residency programs were three established in Boston (**www.bostonteacherresidency.org**), Chicago (**www.ausl-chicago.org**), and Denver (**www.denverteacherresidency.org**), respectively. Early research has indicated that retention rates in teaching are unusually strong. Substantial funds for Teacher Residency programs have been made available through the Higher Education Opportunity Act, and numerous institutions are planning or exploring how to participate in establishing them.

---

[13]Sharilyn C. Steadman and John S. Simmons, "The Cost of Mentoring Non-University-Certified Teachers," *Phi Delta Kappan* (January 2007), pp. 364–368; Daniel C. Humphrey, Marjorie E. Wechsler, and Heather J. Hough, "Characteristics of Effective Alternative Teacher Certification Programs," *Teachers College Record* (January 2008), pp. 1–63; "An Evaluation of Teachers Trained Through Different Routes to Certification," 2009 report prepared for the Institute of Education Sciences, available at **http://ies.ed.gov**; and Carlyn Ludlow, "Alternative Certification Pathways," *Education and Urban Society* (July 2011).

[14]Ildiko Laczko-Kerr and David C. Berliner, "The Effectiveness of 'Teach for America' and Other Under-Certified Teachers on Student Academic Achievement," *Education Policy Analysis Archives*, September 6, 2003, available at **http://epaa.asu.edu**; Julie Mikuta and Arthur Wise, "Teachers for America," *Education Next* (Spring 2008), available at **www.educationnext.org**; Christine Amario, "Teach for America Met with Big Questions in Face of Expansion," *Huffington Post*, November 27, 2011, available at **www.huffingtonpost.com**; and Valerie Strauss, "Has the NEA Warmed Up to Teach for America?" *Washington Post*, January 5, 2012.

[15]Barnett Berry et al., "Creating and Sustaining Urban Teacher Residencies," 2008 paper prepared for the Aspen Institute and the Center for Teaching Quality, available at **www.teachingquality .org**; Geoff Decker, "To Transform Failing Schools, New Teachers Take Up Residence," 2011 posting by Gotham Schools, available at **http://gothamschools.org**; Amy MacKown and Kate Walsh, "The Clinical Immersion Model of Teacher Prep," 2012 posting by the National Council on Teacher Quality, available at **www.nctq.org**; and information at **www.utrunited.org**.

TAKING ISSUE

Read the brief introduction below, as well as the Question and the pros and cons list that follows. Then, answer the question using your own words and position.

Alternative Certification

Many states have introduced alternative certification programs that bypass traditional teacher-education requirements. In general, these programs help orient college graduates to the teaching experience. They then place graduates in full-time teaching positions, where they receive training that leads to certification while they learn about teaching and education.

Question

Should we encourage alternative certification programs that bypass traditional teacher-education requirements? (Think about this question as you read the PRO and CON arguments listed here. What is *your* take on this issue?)

Arguments PRO

1. Learning to teach on the job can provide better opportunities to determine what does and doesn't work in the actual world and to talk with, observe, and emulate successful teachers.

2. Professional studies integrated with full-time teaching are likely to be more meaningful and practical than studies presented in largely theoretical college courses.

3. Alternative programs, which avoid years of study for certification, can attract teacher candidates to shortage areas such as mathematics, science, and bilingual education.

4. Alternative programs help attract minority teachers, retired persons with special skills in technical subjects, and other candidates who can make important contributions in improving the education system.

5. Competing alternative programs will stimulate colleges and universities to improve their teacher-training programs.

Arguments CON

1. Learning to teach on the job frequently proves unsuccessful because many participants find the immediate demands overwhelming and fail to develop and hone their skills adequately.

2. Initial data on several alternative certification programs show that, in practice, school districts either lack sufficient resources to provide professional studies for participants or have other priorities.

3. These programs offer short-term relief only. Many participants realize they are unsuited for or not interested in the work and withdraw during or soon after the first year.

4. Alternative certification reinforces inequity in education because it often places inexperienced persons at inner-city schools, which have high turnover and the most need for well-trained and experienced faculty.

5. Competing alternative programs may distract colleges and universities from offering training that develops the understanding and skills of reflective teachers over several years of study.

Question Reprise: What Is Your Stand?

Reflect again on the following question by explaining *your* stand about this issue: Should we encourage alternative certification programs that bypass traditional teacher-education requirements?

Trends in Preservice Education

In recent years, major developments in preservice teacher education have included increased emphasis on producing "reflective" teachers; growing use of computers and other technology; requirements that future teachers learn about methods for teaching students with disabilities and other special populations; and programs to prepare teaching candidates for the diverse cultural and ethnic settings of contemporary U.S. schools.

Thoughtful practitioners

Reflective Teaching   In accordance with recent emphasis on improving students' thinking and comprehension skills, many institutions emphasize **reflective teaching** as a central theme in teacher education. Reflective teachers frequently observe and think about the results of their teaching and adjust their methods accordingly. Closely related terms such as *inquiry-oriented teacher education, expert decision making,* and *higher-order self-reflection* also describe this concept. Hundreds of schools of education have reorganized their programs to prepare reflective teachers, but the programs are diverse and show little agreement on what reflective teaching should mean.[16]

Technology training for teachers

Computer and Technology Use   Most likely, your teacher-education program offers you some training and access to a computer lab. National surveys of teacher-education programs indicate that more than 90 percent have established computer or technology laboratories. These laboratories encompass a wide variety of activities and objectives, such as orienting future teachers in computer use, introducing hardware and software developed for elementary and secondary schools, and strengthening interest and capability in technology for lesson design or delivery. Many institutions have begun to emphasize the use of technology and electronic media to help teachers advance their students' critical thinking, social and civic development, and digital and visual literacy. Usually, one purpose of this aspect of teacher education is to reduce the possibility that future teachers will become overwhelmed when encountering students who are acquainted with and even adept at the latest technologies.[17]

✓ Standards & Assessment

 Continuity & Change

Preparation for main-streaming and inclusion

Typical requirements

Requirements for Teaching Students with Disabilities   Many states and teacher-training institutions now require that all future teachers receive some preparation in working with students who have significant disabilities. As a teacher, you will likely have students with special needs in your classes. The law demands that students with disabilities be *mainstreamed* in regular classes as much as is possible and feasible, and the growing trend is toward full *inclusion* of disabled students no matter how extensive their special needs. (See Chapter 12, Providing Equal Educational Opportunity, for information about mainstreaming, inclusion, and related topics.) As a consequence, most teachers can expect certain responsibilities for working with students with special needs. Typical teacher-training requirements involve the following:[18]

- Cooperative, interdisciplinary efforts in which both higher-education faculty and knowledgeable field educators help future teachers learn approaches to working with students with disabilities

- Requirements in many states that all future teachers complete one or more courses in education for students with special needs and/or that existing courses incorporate substantial amounts of material on the subject

---

[16]Victoria J. Risko, Carol Vukelich, and Kathleen Roskos, "Preparing Teachers for Reflective Practice," *Language Arts* (November 2002), pp. 134–145; Lana M. Danielson, "Fostering Reflection," *Educational Leadership* (February 2009); Beth Berghoff, Sue Blackwell, and Randy Wisehart, "Using Critical Reflection to Improve Urban Teacher Preparation," *Perspectives on Urban Education* (Spring 2011), available at **www.urbanedjournal.org**; and Janneke van de Pol, Monique Volman, and Jos Beishuizen, "Promoting Teacher Scaffolding in Small-Group Work," *Teaching & Teacher Education* (February 2012), pp. 193–205.
[17]American Association of Colleges for Teacher Education, *Log On or Lose Out* (Washington, D.C.: AACTE, 2000); Phyllis K. Adcock, "Evolution of Teaching and Learning through Technology," *Delta Kappa Gamma Bulletin* (Summer 2008), pp. 37–41; and Sara Bernard, "Five Progressive Schools of Education," 2011 posting by MindShift, available at **http://blogs.kqed.org/mindshift/**.
[18]Tamara J. Arthaud et al., "Developing Collaboration Skills in Pre-Service Teachers," *Teacher Education and Special Education* (Winter 2007), pp. 1–12; and Chris Folin and Dianne Chambers, "Teacher Preparation for Inclusive Education," *Asia-Pacific Journal of Teacher Education* (February 2011), pp. 17–32.

Preparation for Teaching in Diverse Settings   Increasing enrollment of racial and ethnic minority students in U.S. schools is prompting programs to prepare future teachers by adding components to help candidates function successfully in diverse settings. Similar efforts are underway in teacher licensing. For example, the Praxis III teacher performance assessment approach, developed by the Educational Testing Service (ETS), specifies that a candidate for a teaching license should be able to demonstrate a "comprehensive understanding" of why it is important to become familiar with students' background knowledge and experiences.[19]

Adequacy of Preparation Programs

It is difficult, if not impossible, to characterize the overall adequacy and effectiveness of the myriad teacher-preparation programs in the United States. They range from very large to tiny, from relatively well funded to financially skimpy, and from brand new to nearly a century old. Moreover, they all offer widely varying definitions of what it means to be the quality teacher they are trying to produce. Nevertheless, analysts are trying to evaluate them.

For example, a group of business and civic leaders called the Teaching Commission examined various aspects of teacher quality and issued a major report titled "Teaching at Risk." Regarding a perceived need to reinvent teacher-preparation programs, the Commission assigned a grade of C for effort and a grade of D for results. Among other findings, it concluded that too many teachers have too little knowledge of mathematics, science, or other subjects they teach, and that the training of future teachers "adds far too little value" to their skills and capabilities. An organization named the Education Schools Project subsequently released the results of a five-year study of teacher-education programs. Its report, titled "Educating School Teachers," concluded that as many as one-quarter to one-third do an excellent job, but that most future teachers are being prepared in programs that too often have inadequate curricula, low standards, and faculty out of touch with the schools. Five years later, the National Council on Teacher Quality reported that although there were many positive aspects of student-teaching assignments in its national study, many programs followed questionable practices such as lack of rigor in selecting cooperating teachers as mentors.[20]

As indicated in the preceding paragraphs, critics of teacher education generally admit that there are many excellent programs and training components among the more than one thousand institutions that prepare teachers in the United States. Some descriptions and analyses of excellent programs and promising practices can be found at the websites of the Rand Corporation (**www.rand.org/pubs/monographs /MG506**) and the Education Schools Project (**www.edschools.org/pdf /Educating_Teachers_Report.pdf**). A former president of the American Educational Research Association has identified ten encouraging emerging trends that typify exemplary programs, including viewing teacher-preparation as an all-university responsibility; recognizing multiple pathways into teaching; using research to guide the curriculum; and going beyond test scores to measure program effectiveness.[21]

REFOCUS   What trends listed here especially describe your teacher-education program? Do any of the trends describe directions in which you *wish* your program would head?

---

[19]Nancy L. Commins and Ofelia B. Miramontes, "Addressing Linguistic Diversity from the Outset," *Journal of Teacher Education* (May/June 2006), pp. 240–246; and Arnetha F. Ball and Cynthia A. Tyson, eds., *Studying Diversity in Teacher Education* (Washington, D.C.: American Educational Research Association, 2011).
[20]Louis V. Gerstner, Jr., et al., *Teaching at Risk* (New York: The Teaching Commission, 2006); Arthur Levine, *Educating School Teachers* (Washington, D.C.: Education Schools Project, 2006), available at **www.edschools.org**; Julie Greenberg, Laura Pomerance, and Kate Walsh, "Student Teaching in the United States," 2011 report prepared for the National Council on Teacher Quality, available at **www.nctq.org**; and "National Review of Teacher Prep," 2012 report prepared for the National Council on Teacher Quality, available at **www.nctq.org**.
[21]Marilyn Cochran-Smith, "Ten Promising Trends (and Three Big Worries)," *Educational Leadership* (March 2006); and Marilyn Cochran-Smith et al., "Teachers' Education, Teaching Practice, and Retention," *Journal of Education* (No. 2, 2011), pp.19–31.

Prospective Teachers: Abilities and Testing

Standards & Assessment

In recent years, much discussion has centered on improving the quality of the teaching workforce, particularly on improving the abilities of prospective teachers and on testing their competence for teaching.

Teacher Abilities

Standardized test scores

Discussions of the quality of the teaching workforce frequently focus on ability scores derived from standardized tests such as the Scholastic Assessment Test (SAT) and the American College Test (ACT). Among potential teachers, such test scores declined in the 1970s, as they did for students majoring in business and numerous other subjects. For example, between 1973 and 1981, the average SAT verbal score of college students intending to teach fell from 418 to 397. Since 1982, however, test scores of college students who say they intend to become teachers have appreciably increased and generally resemble those of students majoring in business, psychology, and the health professions. In addition, some recent studies have found that teachers' average test scores are about the same as those of other college-educated adults.[22]

Testing Teachers

Testing basic skills

Some efforts to improve the teaching force focus on **basic skills testing** of preservice teachers, new teachers, and sometimes experienced teachers. Drawing on the argument that teachers whose scores are low in reading, mathematics, communications, and/or professional knowledge probably are ineffective in their teaching, many states have introduced requirements that prospective teachers pass some form of minimum skills test in reading and language, math, subject-area specialty, and/or professional knowledge. More than forty states now use the Praxis test developed by the Educational Testing Service for this purpose. To become a certified teacher, you likely will need to pass a series of Praxis exams.

Praxis examination

Criticisms of testing

Testing of prospective and current teachers remains a controversial topic. Many political leaders see testing as one of the few feasible steps they can take to improve public confidence in the teaching force. Opponents argue that the process unjustifiably excludes people who do poorly on paper-and-pencil tests. Many opponents believe that existing tests are biased against minorities and other candidates not from the cultural mainstream. Critics also cite data indicating that scores on standardized tests taken by future teachers correlate poorly with subsequent on-the-job measures of teaching effectiveness.[23]

In support of testing

Proponents of testing generally counter that all or nearly all teachers must be able to demonstrate that they can function at least at the seventh- or eighth-grade level in reading, writing, and math—the minimum level currently specified on some tests—to perform effectively in their jobs. Many proponents also argue that research

---

[22]Barbara A. Brusch and Richard J. Coley, *How Teachers Compare* (Princeton, N.J.: Educational Testing Service, 2000), available at **www.ets.org**; Drew H. Gitomer, *Teacher Quality in a Changing Policy Landscape* (Princeton, N.J.: Educational Testing Service, 2007), available at **www.ets. org**; "Quality of Teaching Pool Improving," *Reading Today* (February/March 2008); and Matthew Di Carlo, "Do Teachers Really Come from the 'Bottom Third' of College Graduates?" 2011 posting by the Shanker Blog, available at **www.shankerblog.org**.
[23]Cassandra M. Guarino, Lucrecia Santibanez, and Glenn A. Daley, "Teacher Recruitment and Retention," *Review of Educational Research* (Summer 2006), pp. 173–208; Joshua D. Angrist and Linda Tyler, "Toward Increasing Teacher Diversity," 2011 report prepared for the Educational Teaching Service, available at **www.ets.org**.

REFOCUS Are teachers in your state required to pass a test? If yes, what are the requirements? What are the passing and failing rates in your state and at your institution?

has provided enough information to justify minimum standards and to allow for the creation of more valid exams.[24] In any case, testing remains highly popular, and you should make sure that your teacher-preparation program and general studies help you prepare to pass any exams that you must take.

Job Satisfaction and Dissatisfaction

Are people who become teachers generally satisfied with their work? Job conditions strongly affect satisfaction, and, as we'll see in this section, job conditions are changing in response to many calls for educational reform. Several of these changes seem likely to improve teachers' job satisfaction.

Teacher Satisfaction

Continuity & Change

■ National surveys

In polls conducted for the Metropolitan Life Insurance Company, teachers have been asked, "All in all, how satisfied would you say you are with teaching as a career?" Most of the respondents have answered either "very satisfied" or "somewhat satisfied." About half have reported that they were more enthusiastic about teaching than when they began their careers. Furthermore, the percentage of satisfied teachers has increased from 40 percent in 1984 to 62 percent in 2008. Similar but sometimes even more positive results have been documented in several other recent polls. Additional information about teacher satisfaction is provided in Chapter 2, The Teaching Profession.[25]

■ Reasons for dissatisfaction

Many teachers do, however, report dissatisfaction with their work. Nationwide surveys show that significant percentages believe they have insufficient time for counseling students, planning lessons, and other instructional functions. Other complaints include ambiguity in supervisors' expectations; negative student behaviors; unresponsive administrators; decrepit facilities; obligations to participate in staff development perceived as irrelevant or ineffective; inadequate salaries; lack of supplies and equipment; forced concentration on teaching low-level skills; extensive paperwork and record keeping; and insufficient input on organizational decisions. Perceived overemphasis on pedestrian instruction as well as low-level tests as part of responses to federal legislation has become an important aspect of teacher dissatisfaction in recent years.[26]

State and District Standards and Teacher Stress

✓ Standards & Assessment

■ High-stakes tests

Teaching is a difficult profession that usually involves significant stress. In recent years, the introduction of state and district standards for student performance has substantially increased this stress. Standards are often accompanied by accountability mechanisms involving standardized testing and publication of achievement scores for schools and, sometimes, individual classrooms. All states now require some degree of uniform testing in all school districts. Many of these tests carry high stakes, such as whether students pass from one grade to another, become eligible to graduate, or must

---

[24]Richard J. Murname, "The Case for Performance-Based Licensing," *Phi Delta Kappan* (October 1991), pp. 137–142; Peter Youngs, Allan Odden, and Andrew C. Porter, "State Policy Related to Teacher Licensure," *Educational Policy* (May 2003), pp. 217–236; and National Research Council, *Preparing Teachers* (Washington, D.C.: The National Academies Press, 2010).

[25]Andrew S. Latham, "Teacher Satisfaction," *Educational Leadership* (February 1998), pp. 82–83; *Metlife Survey of the American Teacher: Past, Present and Future* (New York: Metropolitan Life, 2008), available at **www.metlife.com**; and C. Emily Feistritzer, *Profile of Teachers in the U.S. 2011* (Washington, D.C.: National Center for Education Information, 2011), available at **www.ncei.com**.

[26]Cynthia Kopkowski, "Why They Leave," *NEA Today* (April 2008), available at **www.nea.org /neatoday**; "What Keeps Good Teachers in the Classroom?" *Issue Brief* (February 2008), available at **www.all4ed.org**; and Daniel I. Rubin, "The Disheartened Teacher," *Changing English* (December 2011), pp. 407–416.

attend summer school, and whether or not schools may be closed or intensely scrutinized because of low test scores.

Teaching to the tests

With such consequences, many teachers feel severe pressure to improve their students' test scores. This reaction is particularly prevalent at low-performing schools, but it also occurs even at some high-performing schools in locations where states or districts set high requirements for improved performance every year. Faculty in many schools wind up devoting much of the school year to preparing for tests and to emphasizing test-preparation materials in obtaining and using teaching resources, practices known collectively as "teaching to the test." As we point out elsewhere in this book, this situation has raised controversial questions as to whether the standards movement facilitates or impedes improvements in student performance, as teachers narrow their instructional focus to the tested skills. Although some teachers report finding ways to provide engaging, quality instruction within frameworks that require continuous attention to the many learning objectives specified on state and district tests, even these teachers typically experience high-level stress as they learn to function effectively within such frameworks.[27]

Coping with Stress

Teaching can be stressful

As we've seen, teaching has its difficult moments. Research also indicates that elementary and secondary teaching has become more stressful in recent years. In response, many professional organizations and school districts offer courses or workshops emphasizing coping techniques and other stress-reduction approaches.

Coping techniques

Counselors point out that exercise, rest, hobbies, good nutrition, meditation or other relaxation techniques, vacations, and efficient scheduling of personal affairs can

[27]Stuart S. Yeh, "Limiting the Unintended Consequences of High-Stakes Testing," *Educational Policy Analysis Archives,* October 28, 2005, available at **http://epaa.asu.edu/ojs**; "Testing the Joy Out of Education," *American Teacher* (October 2008), available at **www.aft.org**; Dana Goldstein, "The Test Generation," *American Prospect* (April 4, 2011), available at **www.prospect.org**; and Lisa Guisbond, "NCLB's Lost Decade for Educational Progress," 2012 report prepared for Fair Test, available at **www.fairtest.org**.

TECHNOLOGY @ SCHOOL

An Internet Resource for Prospective Teachers

"Survival Guide for New Teachers" (available at **www2.ed. gov/teachers/become/about/survivalguide**) offers a "collection of reflections by award-winning first-year teachers." Sections in this document advise you on how to work with veteran teachers, parents, and principals. The following is an excerpt from the introductory message.

What Does "Sink or Swim" Mean?

To start with, first-year teachers are still liable to be assigned the most challenging courses—the ones with a heavy developmental emphasis and students who need additional expertise to teach. Moreover, many new teachers receive little more than a quick orientation on school policies and procedures before they start their jobs. And there is often no time in the day—or week, for that matter—allotted for sitting down with colleagues to discuss pedagogical methods, daily dilemmas like time and classroom management, and coping strategies ....

Fortunately, some promising new initiatives are already under way. For example, 100 percent of the graduates of a program for first-year teachers from Texas A&M University–Corpus Christi, Texas, have stayed on the job after five years of teaching. Meanwhile, the statewide retention rate is about 50 percent after five years, according to the university.

Texas's Induction Year Program is designed to provide support and instruction to first-year teachers while getting them started toward master's-level professional development. The program focuses on practical issues such as classroom management, communication skills, and discipline. Also, faculty members regularly visit participants' classrooms to evaluate the teacher's performance.

In addition to university teacher-preparation programs, school districts are doing more to make first-year teaching a success. Districts from Wilmington, Delaware, to Columbus, Ohio, to Omaha, Nebraska, have instituted induction programs for new teachers that include mentoring, peer assistance, and other forms of guidance and support.

help individuals cope with high-stress jobs. You may also reduce stress if you participate in professional renewal activities or support groups, separate your job from your home life, and keep an open-minded attitude toward change. First-year teachers experience unique stress as they enter new teaching jobs. For this reason, professional organizations, school districts, and even the U.S. Department of Education offer supportive programs. The Technology @ School box in this chapter describes one such effort.

Reforming Schools by Improving Teacher Qualifications and Functioning

As you see, most teachers are motivated by a desire to work with young people and to enter a challenging and honorable field. Most are satisfied with most aspects of their jobs. Some dissatisfaction arises, however, mostly with various nonteaching considerations and with the demands imposed by the contemporary movement to raise performance standards. As we will see next, nationwide efforts are under way to address some of the conditions that teachers find difficult and to reform schools by improving teachers' qualifications and functioning.

National Reports

Among many calls for educational reform over the past two decades, the most widely known come from a series of **national reports** on the state of education in the United States. One of the most prominent reform efforts is the federal No Child Left Behind Act. This and other reform efforts that we describe here have changed, and will continue to change, job conditions for teachers in fundamental ways.

Problems identified in *A Nation at Risk*

Since the mid-1980s, numerous reports have focused on problems of education in the United States. *A Nation at Risk* (1983), the best known and most influential of the national reports, was prepared by the National Commission on Excellence in Education sponsored by the U.S. Department of Education. Arguing that the United States is "at risk" in the sense that "its once unchallenged preeminence in commerce, industry, service, and technological innovation is being overtaken by competitors throughout the world," the commission concluded that one major aspect of decline has been a "rising tide of mediocrity" in the schools. Here, we should note the report's suggestions for making teaching a more rewarding and respected profession:[28]

Proposals for the teaching profession

- Set higher standards for entry into the profession.
- Improve teacher salaries so they are "professionally competitive, market-sensitive, and performance-based," thus making them part of a system that rewards superior teachers (in other words, institute merit pay, a practice discussed in Chapter 2, The Teaching Profession).
- Add an additional month of teacher employment with pay.
- Institute a *career ladder* so that qualified people progress from beginning teacher to experienced teacher and finally to the level of *master* teacher.
- Involve master teachers in preparing and supervising probationary teachers.

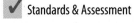 Standards & Assessment

Teacher–Quality Components of No Child Left Behind and Race to the Top

During the past two decades, teacher quality has increasingly been recognized as a prominent determinant of students' performance, even after account is taken of their family background and previous achievement. Acknowledging the central importance of teachers, reformers have designated improvement in teacher quality as a centerpiece of two major national programs, No Child Left Behind and **Race to the Top**.

The No Child Left Behind Act Teacher Quality Components In 2001, teacher-quality improvement activities became an integral part of the national school reform movement with passage of the **No Child Left Behind Act (NCLB)**. We will discuss major components of NCLB dealing with student achievement elsewhere, particularly in Chapter 12, Providing Equal Educational Opportunity. Here we review the key sections dealing with requirements that teachers in school districts receiving federal funding must be "highly qualified."

Highly qualified teachers

Requirements in these sections were explained in a 2004 U.S. Department of Education document (see "A Toolkit for Teachers," available at **www.ed.gov/teachers/nclbguide/nclb-teachers-toolkit.pdf**). The document notes that the NCLB "represents a sweeping overhaul of federal efforts to support elementary and secondary education" and "sets the goal of having every child making the grade on state-defined education standards by the end of the 2013–14 school year." As part of the overhaul, NCLB "outlines the minimum qualifications needed by teachers and paraprofessionals who work on any facet of classroom instruction. It requires that states develop plans to achieve the goal that all teachers of core academic subjects be highly qualified by the end of the 2005–06 school year."

Three requirements

Under NCLB, a **"highly qualified teacher"** must have (1) a bachelor's degree, (2) full state certification and licensure as defined by the state, and

---

[28]National Commission on Excellence in Education, *A Nation at Risk* (Washington, D.C.: U.S. Department of Education, 1983), p. 5. See also Richard Rothstein, "A Nation at Risk Twenty-Five Years Later," *Cato Unbound*, April 7, 2008, available at **www.cato.org**; Margaret Spellings, *A Nation Accountable* (Washington, D.C.: U.S. Department of Education, 2008), available at **www.ed.gov**; and Megan Erickson, "A Nation of Little Lebowski Urban Achievers," *Jacobin* (Winter 2012), available at **http://jacobinmag.com**.

(3) "demonstrated competency as defined by the state in each core academic subject he or she teaches."

Defining competency

New elementary teachers can demonstrate competency by "passing a rigorous state test on subject knowledge and teaching skills in reading or language arts, writing, mathematics and other areas of the basic elementary school curriculum." New middle- and high-school teachers can demonstrate competency "either by passing a rigorous state test in each subject they teach, or by holding an academic major or course work equivalent to an academic major, an advanced degree or advanced certification or credentials." Those already employed as teachers at any level can demonstrate competency by meeting the requirements for new teachers or by meeting a state-defined "high, objective, uniform state standard of evaluation (HOUSSE)." States have defined and established their HOUSSE standards for competency among current teachers. Many are using point systems that allow teachers to count a combination of years of successful classroom experience, participation in high-quality professional development that evaluates what the teacher has learned, service on curriculum development teams, and other activities related to developing knowledge in an academic area.

Developments with respect to implementation of NCLB teacher-quality goals have included the following:[29]

Federally funded activities

■ The federal government has been distributing millions of dollars for activities such as devising and implementing alternative certification programs for teachers and administrators, establishing teacher merit-pay programs, providing bonus pay for teaching in high-need subjects and high-poverty schools, testing teachers in their subjects, and forming a Teacher Assistance Corps to help states carry out their quality-improvement initiatives.

Controversy over data

■ Much controversy has arisen regarding state progress toward ensuring highly qualified teachers in all classrooms. For example, although many states have reported that more than 90 percent of courses are taught by highly qualified teachers, some observers have cited various data indicating that numerous staff teaching science, math, and other specialty subjects were working "out-of-field," or teaching in areas where they had not demonstrated competency, particularly in high-poverty schools. They have concluded that either the state data were incorrect or criteria for defining "highly qualified" had been set very low, or both. In addition, most analysts believe that major problems still generally exist with respect to providing highly qualified teachers and support for teachers in high-poverty urban districts, in many rural districts, and in certain teaching areas such as special education and instruction for English language learners.

Race to the Top Teacher–Quality Components   The **Race to the Top (RTTT)** program was initiated in 2009 to provide competitive grants for projects and approaches that reform educational systems and improve student achievement. By 2012, nearly $4.5 billion had been awarded to twenty-one states and the District of Columbia, and billions of dollars more were scheduled to be given to these and other jurisdictions thereafter for subsequent and related innovative efforts. Major areas of reform and innovation involve awards to grantees to improve standards and assessments; support early-childhood learning; recruit, reward, and retain effective teachers

---

[29]Michael A. Rebell and Molly A. Hunter, "'Highly Qualified' Teachers," *Phi Delta Kappan* (May 2004), pp. 690–696; Mary M. Kennedy, "Sorting Out Teacher Quality," *Phi Delta Kappan* (September 2008), pp. 59–63; Margaret Spellings, "Key Policy Letters Signed by the Education Secretary or Deputy Secretary," 2008 letter published by the U.S. Department of Education, available at **www.ed.gov**; and "Do Low-Income Students Have Equal Access to the Highest-Performing Teachers," *NCEE Evaluation Brief* (April 2011).

and principals; build data systems that help educators improve their practice; substantially improve achievement at low-performing schools; and improve teacher quality. Grants awarded for the purpose of improving teacher quality require funded states to do the following:[30]

- Link data on students' achievement level and growth in performance to their teachers.
- Relate this information to the in-state programs that prepare teachers.
- Publicly report these and other data on program effectiveness for each preparation program in the state.
- Expand teacher-preparation programs and credentialing options that are successful in producing licensed teachers whose students score well.

Several of the states receiving initial grants went beyond the minimum requirement of agreeing to tie students' achievement data to their teachers and to teacher-preparation programs, promising such further actions as collecting data on graduates' job placement and their persistence in teaching. Several also planned to close or reduce teacher-preparation programs scored as weak or inadequate. A few of the grantees further stated the intention to redesign their teacher-testing arrangements. Government officials hope that knowledge and experience gained in these initiatives will provide information and examples on how to strengthen systems for collecting and using data and on how to increase accountability involving teacher-preparation elsewhere.

The Holmes Partnership and Other Groups

Holmes Partnership recommendations

We already have mentioned the reports of the Teaching Commission and the Education Schools Project. Since 1986, teaching reform also has been a primary concern of the Holmes Group, a consortium of deans of education at major research universities. Renamed the Holmes Partnership in 1996, Holmes commissioned a series of reports, including *Tomorrow's Teachers* (1986), *Tomorrow's Schools* (1990), and *Tomorrow's Schools of Education* (1995). In line with reforms emphasized in other reports, the Holmes Partnership has stressed the need for teacher-education students to have early experience in schools. Consequently, the group has focused on the creation of **professional development schools (PDSs)**. Like a traditional laboratory school, the PDS is designed to link a local school district with a college or school of education but in a more comprehensive and systematic fashion. College faculty members function as classroom teachers and serve as mentors for new teachers. According to advocates, PDSs allow experienced teachers, beginning teachers, teacher educators, and administrators to work together to create a community of learners and to improve educational opportunities for low-achieving students. There are now more than a thousand professional-development schools.[31]

In support of PDSs

Other groups, including the American Federation of Teachers (AFT), the American Association of Colleges for Teacher Education (AACTE), and the National Education Association (NEA), have been working to establish plans for schools similar to PDSs.

---

[30]Stephen Sawchuck, "Teacher Elements of Final Race to the Top Guidelines," *Education Week*, November 12, 2009; Edward Crowe, "Race to the Top and Teacher Preparation," 2011 posting by the Center for American Progress, available at **www.americanprogress.org**; and Michele McNeil, "Race to Top Winners Under Gun to Keep Commitments," *Education Week*, January 11, 2012.

[31]*The Holmes Partnership Trilogy* (New York: Peter Lang, 2007); Roberta Trachtman, "Inquiry and Accountability in Professional Development Schools," *Journal of Educational Research* (March 2007), pp. 197–203; Gini Doolittle, Maria Sudeck, and Peter Rattigan, "Creating Professional Learning Communities," *Theory into Practice* (Fall 2008), pp. 303–310; and Lisa J. Vernon-Dotson and Loury O. Floyd, "Building Leadership Capacity via School Partnerships and Teacher Teams," *Clearing House* (January 2012), pp. 38–49.

Surveys indicate that many schools and colleges of education are cooperating with professional development schools or similar institutions. However, progress has been hampered by lack of funds and other obstacles to collaboration among both school districts and higher-education institutions.[32]

Renaissance Group proposals

Additional support for teaching profession reform has come from the Renaissance Group, a consortium of higher-education institutions composed primarily of former teacher-training colleges. The Renaissance Group contends that teacher training should be integrated throughout a student's university experience rather than reserved for the student's final year and should incorporate extensive, sequenced field and clinical experience.[33]

School Reform and Teacher Empowerment

Some reform efforts deal specifically with **teacher-empowerment activities**, which can range from increasing the role of teachers in school-wide decision making to providing teachers with more autonomy in the classroom. Important efforts that involve empowering teachers include the following activities and functions.

Definition of professional learning communities

Professional Learning Communities   Although there is no universally agreed-on definition of **Professional Learning Communities (PLCs)**, they generally are defined in terms of a group of teachers and other colleagues working together to share good ideas, figure out how to improve instruction for their students, and coordinate activities to enhance learning throughout their schools and classrooms. For example, much of the in-service training in many schools is now designed and even delivered by the teachers themselves. Moreover, teachers in many schools and districts collaborate in selecting curriculum standards to emphasize and the sequence to be followed to attain prescribed standards for student performance.

Using a more expansive definition, PLCs sometimes are defined to include any group of educators working together to explore educational and organizational issues. Here the definition has been broadened to include members of professional associations and study groups, active supporters of instructional programs and proposals, and other groupings beyond educators seeking to address specific issues in particular schools and districts.

Supporting elements for PLCs

Because there has been rapid growth in the formation and functioning of PLCs, many analysts view them as an increasingly important component to improve achievement and other aspects of our educational systems. Accompanying the increased prominence of PLCs, there has been growing recognition of the supporting elements required to ensure their effectiveness. These elements include the following:[34]

- Sufficient time and other resources to meet and follow up on suggested improvements
- Critical facilitation by formal and informal school leaders

---

[32]Anne Lieberman and Lynne Miller, "Teacher Development in Professional Practice Schools," *Teachers College Record* (Fall 1990), pp. 105–122; "Welcome to the Professional Development Schools Website," 2010 posting by NCATE, available at **www.ncate.org**; information at **www.napds.org**; and Juliana Taymans et al., "Opening the Black Box," *Urban Education* (January 2012), pp. 224–249.

[33]Information about the Renaissance Group is available at **www.csufresno.edu/renaissancegroup**.

[34]Richard DuFour, "Schools as Learning Communities," *Educational Leadership* (May 2004); "Professional Learning Communities," 2009 posting by The Center for Comprehensive School Reform and Improvement, available at **www.centerforcsri.org**; Bracken Reed, "Creating a Leadership Culture," *Education Northwest* (Fall-Winter 2011), available at **www.educationnorthwest.org/edunw-magazine**; Elizabeth A. van Es, "Examining the Development of a Teacher Learning Community," *Teaching & Teacher Education* (February 2012), pp. 182–192; and information at **www.allthingsplc.info**.

►ǁ TEACHSOURCE VIDEO ACTIVITY

Teaching as a Profession: Collaboration with Colleagues

After reading this section, go to the Education CourseMate website to access the video entitled "Teaching as a Profession: Collaboration with Colleagues." This video provides examples of the difficulties but also the potential rewards of collaboration. After watching the video, answer the following questions:

1 What might school officials do to enhance and facilitate productive collaboration?

2 What can you as a teacher do to promote successful collaboration?

- Access to data and personnel relevant to identifying and solving existing or potential problems and planning to overcome them
- Knowledge about and assistance in collaborating effectively

Varied terms and arrangements

School-Based Management   Agreements reached between employees and school boards in many districts have given teachers a larger role in determining school policies and practices. Variously known as **school-based management**, site-based decision making, self-managing schools, and by similar or related terms, arrangements initiated by these agreements frequently give faculties opportunities to help select instructional methods and materials and to determine how funds are to be spent in their schools.

The first wave of school-based management activities in the 1970s and 1980s typically provided for the establishment of school councils representing teachers, administrators, and, in some cases, parents and other community members, while also providing for the preparation of school-improvement plans shaped by the councils and their constituents. When these efforts frequently did little to improve student achievement, many districts delegated more authority to school councils. For example, some Dade County, Florida, schools adopted a self-governance approach in which teachers and administrators work together to fundamentally redesign the educational programs in their schools. As part of this project, the board of education suspended requirements in such areas as maximum class size, length of the school day, and number of minutes per subject.[35]

Structure and support for School-Based Management

In addition, leading districts emphasizing school-based management sometimes moved to give decision-making councils greater structure and support, such as full-time facilitators, greater time for meeting and planning, and other elements enumerated earlier as essential to the functioning of internal learning communities. Although such support and resources have become more difficult to provide due to difficult economic conditions in most school districts, the goals of school-based management and efforts to implement it in practice still function to increase opportunities for teachers to be more empowered and successful in their chosen profession.

 Continuity & Change

Numerous titles and activities

Instructional Support Positions   For many years, school systems have employed instructional personnel such as instructional coaches, mentors for inexperienced staff and for teachers implementing new or experimental approaches, coordinators for

---

[35]Peter J. Cistone, Joseph A. Fernandez, and Pat L. Tornillo, "School-Based Management! Shared Decision Making in Dade County (Miami)," *Education and Urban Society* (April 1989); Brian Caldwell, "Reconceptualizing the Self-Managing School," *Educational Management Administration & Leadership* (April 2008), pp. 235–252; Hon K. Yeung and Alison L. F. Cheng, "The Role of Staff Development in School-Based Management," *Academic Leadership* (Winter 2011), available at **www.academicleadership.org**; and Agustinus Bandur, "School-Based Management Developments and Partnership," *International Journal of Educational Development* (March 2012), pp. 328–344.

innovative programs or major initiatives, facilitators for professional learning groups, and teacher leaders to assist administrators in introducing improvements and refinements in curriculum and instruction. All these and related positions can be full time or part time, and they all provide opportunities for classroom teachers to play an expanded role in carrying out their schools' and districts' basic functions and missions.[36]

Instructional support positions reflect improvement demands

Opportunities of these sorts have been increasing and seem likely to multiply still more in the future. School districts are undertaking complicated reforms, partly to satisfy federal and state mandates, and concerned citizens are demanding large improvements in graduation rates and in science and math achievement as well as reduction of disparities by social class and race. In addition, increased emphasis is being placed on mentoring new teachers, particularly those who are graduates of alternative programs that required relatively little pedagogical knowledge or classroom experience. Taken together, these forces point toward trends to expand opportunities for teachers to fill positions that provide substantial instructional support for their colleagues.

Continuity & Change

REFOCUS Which of the reform efforts just described would you most like to participate in when you begin teaching? Which of the reforms do you think might prove particularly rewarding, and which may prove somewhat frustrating? Why?

Outlook for Teaching

Bright prospects for teachers

Until the school reform movement of the 1980s, college students majoring in education confronted a buyer's market for teachers, and many questioned the wisdom of entering a field apparently declining in salary and public esteem. Since then, attention increasingly has focused on education, and there has been good news regarding teachers' prospects. The pattern of teacher oversupply has been alleviated, and governments at all levels are acting to improve teacher recruitment and preparation, working conditions, and professional responsibility. Individuals dedicated to helping young people learn and grow in school should have considerable opportunities to realize their ambitions. In years to come, the teaching profession should continue to experience a renewed excitement and an even greater sense that the work is of vital importance to American society.

Summing Up

1. Although we see many reasons for entering the teaching profession, research indicates that most teachers do so to help young children and to provide a service to society.

2. Many educators are focusing on ways to increase diversity in the teaching workforce to better reflect the student population.

3. Demand for new teachers will likely continue.

4. Teacher salaries have improved in recent years.

5. Requirements for teacher certification vary from state to state and among institutions of higher learning.

6. Trends in teacher education include an emphasis on developing reflective teachers. Teachers also are increas-

ingly prepared to use up-to-date technology, to work with students who have special needs, and to teach in widely diverse settings.

7. Although admitting that it is not possible to generalize about myriads of teacher-preparation programs, several major reports have concluded that many programs are not doing an adequate job in training future teachers.

8. Most teachers are satisfied with most aspects of their jobs, despite some dissatisfaction with starting salaries and certain other aspects of the profession.

9. Concern remains widespread over the quality of the teaching workforce. Major national reports on education as well

---

[36]Rhonda Davis, "Instructional Coaching," *Education Update* (November–December 2011), available at **www.educationupdate.com**; Liana Heitin, "Doctor's Orders," *Education Week*, September 28, 2011; Sara Stoelinga and Melinda Magin, "Peer? Expert? Teacher Leaders Struggle to Gain Trust While Establishing Their Expertise," 2011 posting by the Urban Education Institute, available at **www.uchicago.edu**; and Corinne van Velzen, et al., "Guided Work-Based Learning," *Teaching & Teacher Education* (February 2012), pp. 229–239.

as the No Child Left Behind Act have led to higher standards for licensing.

10 Many school districts are working out approaches for empowering teachers to make schools more effective.

11 Increasing public concern for education, changes occurring in the schools, and improvements in the outlook for teachers are bringing new excitement and importance to the role of the teacher.

Key Terms

The numbers indicate the pages where explanations of the key terms can be found.

supply and demand 6
certification 9
alternative certification 10
reflective teaching 13
basic skills testing 15
national reports 18

No Child Left Behind Act (NCLB) 19
highly qualified teacher 19
Race to the Top (RTTT)
   program 20
professional development school
   (PDS) 21

teacher-empowerment activities 22
Professional Learning Community
   (PLC) 22
school-based management 23

Certification Connection Activity

This chapter introduces the teacher candidate to the career of teaching. Consider that as you mature as a teacher, reflective practice becomes a mechanism for the change and improvement of your own teaching. In most cases, teachers reflect daily on what the students learn and how the students engage with the classroom learning processes. The process helps teachers to improve instruction and become more self-reliant as their teaching matures.

As an exercise to prepare you for writing short answers on the Praxis II examination, think about your most recent classroom experience. Reflect on your interactions with the students and what motivation you provided that encouraged them to learn. As you reflect, think about what you could do differently. Sometimes, teachers find it helpful to ask, "If I could do this over, what would I do differently?" A second question that might help you to reflect is, "What did the students learn from this experience?"

Discussion Questions

1 Are difficult economic conditions and widespread controversies involving education likely to cause a decline in teacher satisfaction in the future? If not, what might help generate further improvements?

2 Have your reasons for becoming a teacher changed over time? If so, what caused the change or changes? What might be most likely to change your motivation in the future?

3 Do you believe that the trends in teacher education identified in this chapter are desirable? Do you think they will improve education in the schools? What conditions are necessary to make them effective?

4 What jobs other than teaching in elementary or secondary schools may be open to persons with a teaching certificate? What additional preparation might be necessary or helpful in obtaining such jobs?

Suggested Projects for Professional Development

1 Collect and analyze information on teacher-salary schedules in several nearby school districts. Compare your data with the information that other members of your class acquire from additional districts. What patterns do you see? What might be the advantages and disadvantages of teaching in these districts?

2 Investigate funding for teacher education at your campus. Does your school or college of education serve as a cash cow that provides substantial funding for other campus units?

3 Interview an elementary-school teacher and a high-school teacher about their satisfaction with their work and their reasons for being satisfied or dissatisfied. Compare your findings with those of other students in your class.

4 Individually or as a team member, prepare a report on projects and organizations that work to ensure that teachers possess a high level of preparation for their jobs. You might, for example, research the Interstate Teacher Assessment and Support Consortium and the National Board for Professional Teaching Standards by looking at their websites.

⑤ Find out what your state has done with respect to review-ing and modifying certification requirements. Find out how your state defines competency of new and employed teach-ers in response to the No Child Left Behind Act of 2001. Have these actions produced changes in your preparation program? Are they raising issues for beginning teachers or controversies regarding the status of current teachers in your state? (Information may be available at your state department of education's website.)

Suggested Resources

Internet Resources

The federal government maintains various websites. Many topics in this chapter (and in this book) can be explored at **www.ed.gov** and **www.eric.ed.gov**. Various profes-sional organizations, such as the Association for Supervision and Curriculum Development (**www.ascd.org**) and Phi Delta Kappa (**www.pdkintl.org**), also sponsor relevant sites.

Teacher Quality Bulletin is a weekly publication available by e-mail or online from the Teacher Quality Clearinghouse at **www.nctq.org**.

The theme of the October 2011, issue of *Educational Leadership* (**www.ascd.org**) is "Coaches: The New Leadership Skill."

Many reports dealing with issues considered in this chapter are published by the National Comprehensive Center for Teacher Quality at **www.tqsource.org**.

The January 2012 issue of the *School Administrator* (**www.aasa.org**.) is devoted to the theme "Culture of Collaboration" and includes several articles dealing with Professional Learning Communities.

To find your state department of education's website, access the first screen at **www.ccsso.org**.

Publications

Barnett, Berry, and Teachersolutions 2030 Team. *Teaching 2030*. New York: Teachers College Press, 2011. *A group of accom-plished teachers and educational leaders consider issues the writers expect to become or remain important in the future.*

Cochran-Smith, Marilyn, and Kenneth M. Zeichner. *Studying Teacher Education*. Mahwah, N.J.: Lawrence Erlbaum As-sociates, 2005. *Subtitled "The Report of the AERA Panel on Research and Teacher Education," this volume describes results of research on teacher characteristics, preparation, job condi-tions and satisfaction, and related topics.*

Falk, Joni K., and Brian Drayton, eds. *Creating and Sustaining Online Professional Learning Communities*. New York: Teachers College Press, 2009. *Discusses ways to build online communities and how they can contribute to professional development and growth.*

Herndon, Joseph. *The Way It Spozed to* Be. New York: Bantam, 1968. *A classic when it was published,* this *book, which describes the satisfactions and difficulties of teaching in the inner city, remains relevant in the new millennium.*

Mitchell, Antoinette, Sheila Allen, and Pamela Ehrenberg. *Spotlight on Schools of Education*. Washington D.C.: National Council on Accreditation of Teacher Education, 2005. *Based on a review of fifty-eight accreditation reports, this volume re-ports on the ways schools of education approach curriculum, assessment, and continuous improvement. It is available from* **www.ncate.org**.

Additional resources for this chapter, including the TeachSource Videos, can be found on the Education CourseMate website. Go to **CengageBrain.com** to access the site.

The Teaching Profession

Until the twentieth century, teachers received relatively little preparation and had little say in the terms of their employment. Formal teacher training consisted of one or two years at a normal school or teacher's college, and after they were employed in a local school, teachers had to follow strict rules and regulations that monitored their behavior outside school. Unorganized and isolated from one another in small schools and districts, teachers could be summarily dismissed by a local board of education. Many were told they could not teach material that a community member might find objectionable.

Times have changed. Today, teachers strive to be professionals with expert knowledge concerning instruction, content, and assessment in their particular fields. In addition, they are well organized as a group and have gained greater rights to be judged on their work performance rather than on their behavior outside school. Often, too, they participate in decision making about work conditions. In many cases, they are forging stronger links with school administrators, university researchers, government officials, and the communities they serve. The first part of this chapter describes ways in which teachers are striving for full professional status, and the second part discusses how teacher organizations have grown in power and prominence. As you read this chapter, think about the following questions:

FOCUS QUESTIONS
■ What trends suggest that teaching is moving toward a full-fledged profession?

- In what ways is teaching not fully a profession?
- Does pay for performance help or hinder the teaching profession?
- What are the goals and activities of the two main professional organizations, the NEA and the AFT?
- What are other important professional organizations for teachers?
- What professional organizations might education students and beginning teachers join?

---

*This chapter was revised by Dr. David E. Vocke, Towson University.

Is Teaching a Profession?

Continuity & Change

Characteristics of a profession

The question of whether or not teaching is a true profession has been debated for decades. Some have tried to identify the ideal characteristics of professions and, by rating teachers on these items, determine whether teaching is a profession. The following are characteristics of a full **profession**, based on the works of noted authorities during the latter half of the twentieth century.[1]

1. A sense of public service; a lifetime commitment to career
2. A defined body of knowledge and skills beyond that grasped by laypeople
3. A lengthy period of specialized training
4. Control over licensing standards and/or entry requirements
5. Autonomy in making decisions about selected spheres of work
6. An acceptance of responsibility for judgments made and acts performed related to services rendered; a set of performance standards
7. A self-governing organization composed of members of the profession
8. Professional associations and/or elite groups to provide recognition for individual achievements
9. A code of ethics to help clarify ambiguous matters or doubtful points related to services rendered
10. High prestige and economic standing

Teaching as an emerging profession

Critics claim that teaching is not a profession in the fullest sense because it lacks some of the previously listed characteristics, but it may be viewed as a "semi-profession" or an "emerging profession" in the process of achieving these characteristics. Several sociologists contend that nursing and social work are also semi-professions.[2]

In particular, teaching seems to lag behind professions such as law and medicine in four important areas: (1) a defined body of knowledge and skills beyond that grasped

---

[1]Ronald G. Corwin, *Sociology of Education* (New York: Appleton-Century-Crofts, 1965); Robert B. Howsam et al., *Educating a Profession* (Washington, D.C.: American Association of Colleges for Teacher Education, 1976); Susan J. Rosenholtz, *Teachers' Workplace: The Social Organization of Schools* (New York: Longman, 1989); and Kathryn Riley, "Redefining the Profession—Teachers with Attitude," *Education Review* (2003), pp.19–27.

[2]Amitai Etzioni, *The Semiprofessions and Their Organizations: Teachers, Nurses, and Social Workers* (New York: Free Press, 1969), p. v; Steve McNally, "If Nursing's Profile Is to Be Raised It Must Be Assertive," *British Journal of Nursing* (September 26, 2002), p. 1114; and Richard Ingersoll and David Perda, "The Status of Teaching as a Profession," in Jeanne H. Ballantine and Joan Z. Spade, eds., *Schools and Society: A Sociological Approach to Education* (Thousand Oaks, CA: Sage Publication, 2008).

by laypeople, (2) control over licensing standards and/or entry requirements, (3) autonomy in making decisions about selected work spheres, and (4) high prestige and economic standing. In the following sections, we explore these four aspects of teaching.

A Defined Body of Knowledge

No agreed-upon knowledge

All professions have a monopoly on certain knowledge that separates their members from the general public and allows them to exercise control over the vocation. Members of the profession establish their expertise by mastering this defined body of knowledge, and they protect the public from untrained amateurs by denying membership to those who have not mastered it. In the past, "education" or "teaching" has established no agreed-upon, specialized body of knowledge.[3] Nor has teaching been guided by the extensive rules of procedure and established methodologies found in professions such as medicine or engineering. As a result, too many people, especially the public and politicians, talk about education as if they were experts—the cause of much conflicting and sometimes negative conversation.[4]

Major components of preservice preparation

A developing body of knowledge also allows teacher-education course content to vary from state to state and even among teacher-training institutions within a given state. Teacher preparation usually consists of three major components: (1) liberal (or general) education, (2) specialized subject-field education—the student's major or minor, and (3) professional education. Almost all educators agree that preparing good teachers rests on these three components. Arguments arise, however, over the relative emphasis that each component should receive. How much course work, for example, should the education program require from liberal-education courses versus courses in a specialized subject field and professional education? Viewpoints also differ concerning the extent to which clinical experience, which involves actual practice in school settings, should be incorporated in professional education courses. Thus, your teacher-education program may differ from one at another college or university.[5]

In the 1960s, James Koerner and James Bryant Conant described the problem in highly critical books, and their criticism from several decades ago can still be heard today. Koerner argued that by requiring too many education courses—as many as sixty hours at some state teacher colleges—and by making these courses too soft, colleges of education were producing teachers versed in pedagogy at the expense of academic content.[6] In 2002, then-Secretary of Education Rod Paige called for a de-emphasis on education course work in the preparation of teachers. Critics today continue to advocate for a reduction in required education courses and challenge the notion that teacher preparation is linked to teacher performance.[7]

Standards & Assessment

NCATE standards

Members of the education profession are taking steps to change this situation and incorporate a developing professional knowledge base into a set of national performance standards that will be used to hold teacher-education institutions

---

[3]John Loughran, "Is Teaching a Discipline?" *Teacher and Teaching: Theory and Practice* (April 2009), pp. 189–203; and Darrel Drury, "The Professionalization of Teaching—What NEA Surveys Tell Us about a Common Knowledge Base," *Education Week* (June 30, 2011).

[4]Jonathan Saphier, *Bonfires and Magic Bullets: Making Teaching a True Profession* (Carlisle, MA: Research for Better Teaching, 1995); Valeri R. Helterbran, "Professionalism: Teachers Taking the Reins," *Clearing House* (January 2008), pp. 123–127; and Trip Gabriel, "Teachers Wonder, Why the Heapings of Scorn?" *New York Times,* March 3, 2011, p. A1.

[5]Arthur Levine, "Are Schools of Education in Urgent Need of Reform?" *Trusteeship* (January 2007), p. 40; and National Council for Accreditation of Teacher, Education, "Transforming Teacher Education through Clinical Practice: A National Strategy to Prepare Effective Teachers," Report of the Blue Ribbon Panel on Clinical Preparation and Partnerships for Improved Student Learning, *National Council for Accreditation of Teacher Education* (November 1, 2010): *ERIC*, EBSCO*host* (accessed September 23, 2011).

[6]James D. Koerner, *The Miseducation of American Teachers* (Boston: Houghton Mifflin, 1963); James Bryant Conant, *The Education of American Teachers* (New York: McGraw-Hill, 1963); and George Will, "Ed Schools vs. Education," *Newsweek,* January 16, 2006.

[7]Piper Fogg, "Report Blasts Teacher-Education Programs as Outdated and Low Quality," *Chronicle of Higher Education* (September 29, 2006), p. 10; and Linda Darling-Hammond, "Teacher Education and the American Future," *Journal of Teacher Education* (January 2010), pp. 35–47.

accountable. The **National Council for Accreditation of Teacher Education (NCATE)** (recently renamed the Council for the Accreditation of Educator Preparation [CAEP]) has set standards that determine which teacher-education programs meet national standards in the preparation of teaching candidates and specialists about to enter the classroom. As recently as 2011, 40 percent of the 1,200 colleges involved in training teachers were not accredited by NCATE. However, most NCATE members have worked diligently to meet NCATE standards, and approximately 726 teacher-education programs are either accredited or are being considered for accreditation. Most of the remaining 500 teacher-education institutions use NCATE standards to conduct state-level evaluations. Thus, by 2009, twenty-five states had adopted or adapted NCATE unit standards for state evaluation of teacher-education programs, and forty-eight states had started working in partnership with the organization to conduct rigorous program review. NCATE standards are increasingly the norm in teacher preparation.[8] Moreover, the American Association of Colleges for Teacher Education (AACTE) promotes the pursuit of NCATE accreditation. To further this end, AACTE offers technical assistance, such as consultants to nonaccredited institutions, during the accreditation process.[9]

> **REFOCUS** Is your institution accredited by NCATE? Find out and learn more about the NCATE standards at their website, www.ncate.org.

Controlling Requirements for Entry and Licensing

Variations in certification

Whereas most professions have uniform requirements for entry and licensing, teaching historically has lacked such requirements. Each of the fifty states sets its own certification requirements, which vary from state to state. As indicated in Chapter 1, Motivation, Preparation, and Conditions for the Entering Teacher, prospective teachers in most states are required to pass minimum competency tests in reading, writing, and math. Furthermore, National Board Certification has been implemented through the independent National Board for Professional Teaching Standards for the purpose of awarding additional teaching certification to master teachers. You might want to research the qualifications and testing required for certification in your state to compare with others nearby.

Standards & Assessment

Unfortunately, some reports suggest a significant number of secondary-school teachers appear to be teaching out of license—in other words, outside their recognized areas of expertise. This problem is especially critical in the core academic subjects—English, social studies, science, and mathematics—where, in 2007–2008, 15.6 percent of classes were taught by an out-of-field teacher. The problem is more pronounced in high-poverty schools, where 21.9 percent of core classes were taught by an out-of-field teacher.[10]

Debate about alternative certification

The outlook is further clouded by the trend toward alternative certification, discussed in Chapter 1, Motivation, Preparation, and Conditions for the Entering Teacher. This process—by which teachers are recruited from the ranks of experienced college graduates seeking second careers—is intended to be an expedited route to eliminate teacher shortages in certain subject areas such as mathematics, science, and special education or to upgrade the quality of new teachers. It has also been seen as a way to meet the highly qualified teacher requirement of the No Child Left Behind Act (NCLB).[11] Alternative certification is often praised as practical and innovative by laypeople and school board members. Most teacher-preparation organizations, on the other hand, see alternative

---

[8]"Quick Facts about NCATE" at **www.ncate.org/Public/AboutNCATE/QuickFacts /tabid/343/Default.aspx** (2011).
[9]AACTE, "AACTE Endorses NCATE Blue Ribbon Panel Report on Clinical Preparation" at **http://aacte.org/index.php?/Media-Center/Press-Releases/aacte-endorses-ncate -blue-ribbon-panel-report-on-clinical-preparation.html** (November 2010); and see "Accreditation Issues" at **http://aacte.org/index.php?/Accreditation-Issues/NCATE -Accreditation-Consulting-Service** (September 2011).
[10]Daniel C. Humphrey and Marjorie E. Wechsler, "Insights into Alternative Certification: Initial Findings from a National Study," *Teachers College Record* (March 2007), pp. 483–530; Vaishali Honawar, "Teachers Achieving 'Highly Qualified' Status on the Rise," *Education Week* (June 11, 2008), pp. 14–15; and Sarah Almy and Christina Theokas, *Not Prepared for Class: High-Poverty Schools Continue to Have Fewer In-Field Teachers* (Washington, D.C.: The Education Trust, November 2010).
[11]Melanie Shaw, "The Impact of Alternative Teacher Certification Programs on Teacher Shortages," *International Journal of Learning* (July 2008), pp. 89–97.

certification as a threat to the profession. There is a growing body of research that suggests new teachers who avoid traditional teacher-preparation programs have attrition rates that are significantly higher than traditionally certified teachers.[12] The AACTE is an outspoken critic of alternative certification programs and believes teachers should only be placed in classrooms after they complete a high-quality preparation program.[13]

Whatever teachers might think about differing requirements for certification, they traditionally have had little to say in these matters. However, teacher organizations are lobbying state legislatures, departments of education, **professional practice boards** (discussed later in this chapter), and independent organizations to implement rigorous licensure standards for entry into the teaching profession. The more input teachers have—that is, the more control they exercise over their own licensing procedures—the more teaching will be recognized as a full profession.

Involvement of teacher organizations

Autonomy in Determining Spheres of Work

Professional control versus lay control

In a profession, every member of the group, but no outsider, is assumed to be qualified to make professional judgments on the nature of the work involved. In fact, control by laypeople is considered the natural enemy of a profession; it limits a professional's power and opens the door to outside interference. Professionals usually establish rules and customs that give them exclusive jurisdiction over their area of competence and their relationships with clients; professional autonomy is characterized by a high degree of self-determination.

Traditional lack of teacher input

Teachers, in contrast, have traditionally had little input in curriculum decisions, and they are vulnerable when they seek to introduce textbooks or discuss topics that pressure groups consider controversial. Many times, school officials often hire outside "experts" with little teaching experience to help them select books, write grant proposals, or resolve local school-community issues. Most often, school reform initiatives come from government officials, business leaders, and civic groups rather than from teachers. There are those who contend that the accountability measures that accompanied the federal NCLB mandates undermined teachers' autonomy, thus negatively impacting the quality of teaching.[14]

High Prestige and Economic Standing

High-prestige occupations

Occupational prestige refers to the esteem a particular society bestows on an occupation. Do you consider teaching a high-prestige occupation? Occupations rate high in prestige if they are generally perceived as making an especially valuable contribution to society. Occupations that require a high level of education or skill and little manual or physical labor also tend to be prestigious. On these aspects of social status, the job of elementary or secondary teacher historically has ranked relatively high.

Teacher prestige

Perhaps the best-known studies of occupational prestige have been those conducted by the National Opinion Research Center (NORC), beginning in 1947. In these studies of more than 500 occupations, the highest average score for a major occupation was eighty-two for physicians and surgeons, and the lowest was nine for shoe shiners. Elementary-school teachers were rated at sixty, and secondary-school teachers at

---

[12]Christopher Nagy and Ning Wang, "The Alternate Route: Teachers Transition to the Classroom," Online Submission, Annual Meeting of AERA, March 9, 2006; Linda Darling-Hammond, "Teacher Education and the American Future," *Journal of Teacher Education* (January 2010), pp. 35–47; and Richard Ingersoll, Lisa Merrill, and Henry May, "What Are the Effects of Teacher Education and Preparation on Beginning Math and Science Teacher Attrition," a paper presented at the Annual Meeting of AERA, April 8–11, 2011.
[13]Richard M. Ingersoll, "Short on Power, Long on Responsibility," *Educational Leadership* (September 2007), pp. 20–25; and Stephen Sawchuk, "Higher Education Groups Oppose Teacher-Training Bill," *Education Week* (July 26, 2011) at **http://blogs.edweek.org/edweek/ teacherbeat/2011/07/higher_ed_groups_line_up_again.html**.
[14]Emery J. Hyslop-Margison and Alan M. Sears, "Enhancing Teacher Performance: The Role of Professional Autonomy," *Interchange* (January 2010), pp.1–15.

Figure 2.1	Occupations of Very Great Prestige—The Public's Perception

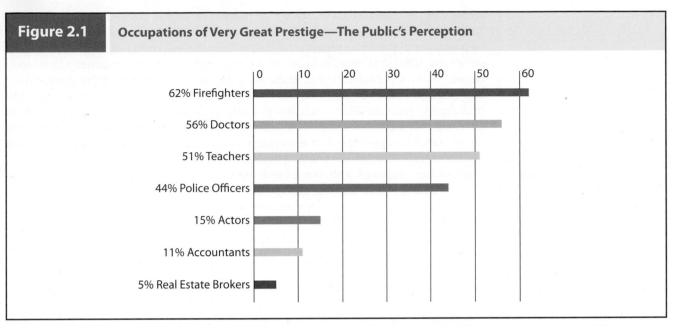

Source: "Firefighters, Scientists and Doctors Seen as Most Prestigious Occupations," *The Harris Poll* (Harris Interactive, Inc., August 4, 2009) at **http://harrisinteractive.com/vault/Harris-Interactive-Poll-Research-Pres-Occupations-2009-08.pdf**.

sixty-three—both above the ninetieth percentile.[15] In a 2009 Harris Poll, 51 percent of respondents indicated that teaching was a job with "very great prestige"; firefighters were at the top of the scale with 62 percent, and real estate agents were at the bottom of the rankings at 5 percent. (See Figure 2.1.)[16]

Continuity & Change

▌ Prestige derived from complex work

One reason teachers have maintained or even increased their favorable rating on surveys of occupational prestige is that their average education level has risen greatly over the past century. Another reason for the continued favorable rating might be the complex nature of teaching. Brian Rowan, comparing teachers' work with other occupations, found that work complexity related directly to occupational prestige. Teaching, more complex than 75 percent of all other occupations, ranked quite high in prestige. The complexity of teachers' work is manifested in their need to apply principles of logical or scientific thinking to define problems, collect data, establish facts, and draw conclusions. To be a teacher, you must be highly proficient in language (reading, writing, and speaking), and, most of all, you must work effectively with many kinds of people— children, adolescents, parents, colleagues, and superiors. Additional studies remind us that the work of teachers is multidimensional. However, society accords higher prestige (and, of course, higher pay) to professionals such as physicians, lawyers, and engineers, mainly because they must deal with information generally regarded as more abstract (complex) and because these fields currently require more rigorous academic preparation and licensure.[17]

▌ Salary trends

Although teachers' salaries since 1930 have increased more than those of the average manufacturing-industry worker (as discussed in the previous chapter), teacher pay remains lower than that of the comparable college graduate, such as an architect, registered nurse,

---

[15]C. C. North and Paul K. Hatt, "Jobs and Occupation: A Popular Evaluation," *Opinion News,* (September 1, 1947), pp. 3–13; Robert W. Hodge, Paul M. Siegel, and Peter H. Rossi, "Occupational Prestige in the United States, 1925–63," *American Journal of Sociology* (November 1964), pp. 286–302; and Donald J. Treiman, *Occupational Prestige in Comparative Perspective* (New York: Academic Press, 1977).

[16]"Firefighters, Scientists and Doctors Seen as Most Prestigious Occupations," *The Harris Poll* (Harris Interactive, Inc., August 4, 2009) at **www.harrisinteractive.com/vault/Harris-Interactive-Poll-Research-Pres-Occupations-2009-08.pdf**.

[17]Brian Rowan, "Comparing Teachers' Work with Work in Other Occupations," *Educational Researcher* (1994), pp. 4–17; and Anthony Milanowski, *Using Occupational Characteristics Information for O*NET to Identify Occupations for Compensation Comparisons with K-12 Teaching* (Madison, WI: Wisconsin Center for Education Research, June 2008).

accountant, or occupational therapist.[18] In two recent studies, researchers found that the "average weekly pay of teachers in 2003 was nearly 14% below that of workers with similar education and work experience" and that "[a]n analysis of trends in weekly earnings shows that public school teachers in 2006 earned 15% lower weekly earnings than comparable workers[.]"[19] Education officials and researchers have suggested that substantially raising the salaries of teachers may be the way to enhance the profession's prestige and thus attract better qualified candidates to teaching. Secretary of Education Arne Duncan indicated that society should look at teaching as it does the profession of law, medicine, and engineering.[20] It is interesting to note that the results of the most recent *MetLife Survey of the American Teacher* found that 62 percent of teachers polled are "very satisfied" with their careers, a twenty-year high, but only 16 percent "agree strongly" that teaching allows them the opportunity to earn a decent salary.[21]

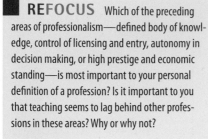

REFOCUS Which of the preceding areas of professionalism—defined body of knowledge, control of licensing and entry, autonomy in decision making, or high prestige and economic standing—is most important to your personal definition of a profession? Is it important to you that teaching seems to lag behind other professions in these areas? Why or why not?

To its credit, the educational reform movement of the 1980s and 1990s put teachers in the limelight and brought pressure on school districts to increase salaries. Unfortunately, the gains of the last two decades of the twentieth century have not been sustained during the first decade of the twenty-first. In spite of this salary stagnation, teachers continue to maintain a relatively high sense of job satisfaction and occupational prestige.

Trends toward Professionalism

Although teaching, as we have seen, may not yet be considered a fully professionalized occupation, certain trends have helped it move in that direction. **Collective bargaining**, for example, can enhance teachers' capacity to make decisions about their classroom work. Let's look at several other major aspects of a long-range trend toward professionalizing teaching.

The Scope of Collective Bargaining

In the United States today, more than 80 percent of teachers have their representatives formally bargain with their employers, the school board. In thirty-four states and Washington D.C., school districts are legally required to bargain with teachers, while in eleven states, collective bargaining is permissible. Five states prohibit teachers from collective bargaining. The extent and nature of collective bargaining varies from negotiations conducted in the absence of a law allowing or forbidding it, to full-scale contract bargaining backed by the right to strike.[22] In contrast, the private-school sector has no collective bargaining.

Is collective bargaining professional?

In some ways, collective bargaining may be considered a nonprofessional or even antiprofessional activity. In law, medicine, or the ministry, for example, few professionals work in organizations in which collective bargaining determines employment terms. Collective bargaining, however, can significantly improve teaching professionalism by

---

[18]Steven L. Denlinger, "A Look at the Problem of Teacher Deficits," *Clearing House* (January–February 2002), pp. 116–117; Dan Goldhaber and Daniel Player, "What Different Benchmarks Suggest about How Financially Attractive It Is to Teach in Public Schools," *Journal of Education Finance* (Winter 2005), pp. 211–230; and John M. Krieg, "Book Review—How Does Teacher Pay Compare?" *Economics of Education Review* (2007), pp. 265–266.

[19]Sylvia A. Allegretto, Sean P. Corcoran, and Lawrence Mishel, *The Teaching Penalty: Teacher Pay Losing Ground* (Washington, D.C.: Economic Policy Institute, 2009).

[20]Stephen Paine, *What the U.S. Can Learn for the World's Most Successful Education Reform Efforts* (New York: McGraw-Hill Research Foundation March 2011); and Kelly Ni, "Education Head Wants Prestige for Teachers," *Epoch Times* (July 30, 2011).

[21]MetLife, Inc., *The MetLife Survey of the American Teacher: Expectations and Experiences* (2008) at **www.eric.ed.gov/PDFS/ED504457.pdf**.

[22]Barbara Hornick-Lockard, "Collective Bargaining and Teachers' Unions," *Research Starters Education* (Ipswich, MA: Research Starters—Education, 2008); and Stephen Sawchuk, "States Eye Curbs on Collective Bargaining by Teachers," *Education Week* (February 9, 2011), pp. 1–20.

giving teachers greater authority to influence their work conditions and their effectiveness as teachers in the classroom.

Collective Bargaining Under Attack

■ Collective bargaining facing challenges

Today, collective bargaining is under attack in several states. Wisconsin, Idaho, Tennessee, and Indiana are among the states that have had legislation introduced to limit the scope of collective bargaining. Teacher evaluation, salaries, and tenure are but a few of the issues that some state lawmakers and governors want removed from the collective bargaining table.[23] Movements toward school reform, school restructuring, and teacher empowerment, where collective bargaining remains intact, can give teachers more professional autonomy, union strength, and higher salaries in exchange for greater accountability and reduced adversarial bargaining. Continuing in this vein, collective bargaining can go beyond resolving conflicts between school boards and teachers and potentially raise the overall status of the profession.[24]

✓ Standards & Assessment

■ Setting professional standards

Educators are unlikely to achieve complete autonomy in setting professional practice standards, but their role has increased. Today, nearly all states have professional standards boards, but they vary in the powers they possess. Among their responsibilities may be the authority to issue, renew, suspend, and revoke certificates for teachers and administrators. In twenty-eight states, these boards act in an advisory capacity; in three states, their decisions are reviewed by the states board of education; while in eleven states, they have the power to make independent decisions.[25]

■ A national board

The concept of rigorous licensure standards and independent professional practice boards has been endorsed by the American Federation of Teachers (AFT) and the National Education Association (NEA), which together represent the vast majority of teachers in the United States. The Carnegie Task Force on Teaching as a Profession was instrumental in the founding of the **National Board for Professional Teaching Standards (NBPTS)** in 1987. Many educators see the NBPTS as a professional board implementing meaningful standards that lead to the awarding of advanced teacher certification. Both major teacher organization presidents sit on the NBPTS board of directors, and a majority of the board members are from the teaching profession.[26] Currently, the NBPTS has granted national certification to more than 91,000 master teachers, teachers who have demonstrated the skills of an expert by passing a series of rigorous assessments, in twenty-five certificate fields.[27] Although NBPTS certification is voluntary and cannot be required as a condition of hiring, many state boards of education, local school boards, and superintendents have developed incentives to encourage teachers to seek national certification. All fifty states have already initiated support in the form of certification fee reimbursement or salary supplements.[28] For more information on national board standards and certification areas, see **www.nbpts.org**.

Mediated Entry

Mediated entry refers to the practice of inducting people into a profession through carefully supervised stages that help them learn how to apply professional

---

[23]Louis Fischer, David Schimmel, and Leslie Stellman, *Teachers and the Law* (New York: Longman, 2007), pp. 44–56; Sean Cavanagh, "Labor-Curb Plan Eyed Warily," *Education Week* (March 9, 2011), pp. 1, 21; and Sean Cavanagh, "New Laws Curbing Public-Worker Bargaining Besieged," *Education Week* (April 20, 2011), pp.26–28.
[24]Perry A. Zirkel, "Striking Results," *Phi Delta Kappan* (February 2003), pp. 478–479; and Susan Black, "Bargaining: It's in Your Best Interest," *American School Board Journal* (April 2008), pp. 52–53.
[25]Paul Manna and K. C. Tydgat, "Gatekeepers to the Classroom: The Emergence and Influence of State Teacher Professional Standards Boards," *Conference Papers – Southern Political Science Association* (January 2008).
[26]Albert Shanker, "Quality Assurance: What Must Be Done to Strengthen the Teaching Profession," *Phi Delta Kappan* (November 1996), pp. 220–224; and see "National Board for Professional Teaching Standards" at **www.nbpts.org/about_us/board_of_directors** (2011).
[27]See "A Guide to Understanding," **www.nbpts.org/for_candidates/certificate_areas1** (2011).
[28]Rick Allen, "National Board Certified Teachers: Putting in the Time, Energy, and Money to Improve Teaching," *Education Update* (2010), pp.1–5; and see "The Benefits" at **www.nbpts.org/become_a_candidate/the_benefits** (2011).

▶ ‖ **TEACHSOURCE VIDEO ACTIVITY**

Mentoring First-Year Teachers: Keys to Professional Success

After reading this section, go to the Education CourseMate website to access the video entitled "Mentoring First-Year Teachers: Keys to Professional Success." In this video, you'll see new teacher Dania Diaz working with her mentor teacher, Abdi Ali. How do you relate to Dania and her experiences as a new teacher (see Interview Transcript #2)? After watching the video, answer the following questions:

1 How does this video illustrate the concept of an induction program described in the chapter?

2 In your opinion, what insights has Dania gained about teaching as a result of being mentored by Mr. Ali?

This video reinforces key concepts found in Section IV: Profession and Community of the Praxis II exam.

knowledge successfully in working environments. For example, aspiring physicians serve one or more years as interns and then as residents before being considered full-fledged professionals.

▍ Lack of assistance for new teachers

Dan Lortie's classic study of the teacher's job from a sociological perspective concluded that teaching ranks between occupations characterized by casual entry and those that place difficult demands on would-be members. For example, secretarial knowledge and skills are significantly less demanding than those of a medical doctor.[29] Too often, novice teachers report learning to teach in isolation through trial and error in the classroom. They also report that the beginning years of teaching can be a period of anxiety, frustration, and fear—even of trauma. Perhaps as a result, 14 percent of new teachers leave the profession at the end of their first year of teaching.[30] Although almost any occupation or profession produces problems and anxieties at first, a more systematic mediated entry would likely lessen the high attrition rate of beginning teachers.

▍ Professional development schools as clinical settings

In recent years, more colleges and universities have been using professional development schools (PDSs) (described in Chapter 1, Motivation, Preparation, and Conditions for the Entering Teacher) as clinical settings where aspiring teachers gain more extended and intensive classroom experiences before beginning their student teaching (residencies). This multisemester approach—in actual classrooms, under the guidance of experienced teachers and university professors—provides a more methodical **induction** into the teaching profession. Thus, there is better retention of new teachers as they begin their careers.[31]

▍ Establishing a transition period

The teaching profession now recognizes the need to develop a period of induction and transition into teaching, especially given that approximately 45 percent of new teachers leave the profession by the end of year five. As a result of this realization, the number of beginning teachers participating in induction programs has increased from 40 percent in 1990 to 91 percent in 2008, and twenty-two states and numerous local school districts fund more systematic efforts to transition into the

---

[29]Dan C. Lortie, *Schoolteacher: A Sociological Study* (Chicago: University of Chicago Press, 1975).
[30]Kathy Wiebke and Joe Bardin, "New Teacher Support," *Journal of Staff Development* (Winter 2009), pp. 34–38; and Vicki Luther and Laila J. Richman, "Teacher Attrition: Listening to Teachers to Find a Solution," *Academic Leadership* (Fall 2009), p. 29.
[31]Sharon Castle, "Do Professional Development Schools (PDS) Make a Difference?" *Journal of Teacher Education* (January/February 2006), pp. 65–80; and Nancy I. Latham and W. Paul Vogt, "Do Professional Development Schools Reduce Teacher Attrition?" *Journal of Teacher Education* (March/April 2007), pp. 153–167.

profession.[32] This growing effort to support induction programs addresses beginning teachers' primary concern that leads them to abandon the profession: the lack of adequate support from school administration. Studies suggest that there is wide variety in the continuum of services provided in induction programs, but the more multifaceted a program is, the more success there tends to be in counteracting the "sink-or-swim" approach to induction. Comprehensive programs that include mentoring by experienced teachers, shared planning time, new teacher workshops, and reduced teaching loads are more likely to lead to increased teacher learning and thus better retention and increased student learning.[33] Overall, the trend toward more carefully mediated entry is likely to continue; major teacher unions and several education reform groups support it, as does federal legislation, which mandates "highly qualified teachers."[34] (We define and discuss *highly qualified* in Chapter 1, Motivation, Preparation, and Conditions for the Entering Teacher.)

Professional Development

Keeping up to date

Your teacher training does not end when you begin teaching full time. Teaching demands rigorous and continuous training, which is often referred to as **professional development**. Effective professional development should develop a teacher's knowledge and skills with the goal of improving student achievement. To stay up to date in their preparation and to acquire new classroom skills, teachers are expected to participate in various forms of workshops, local or national conferences, college courses, or online courses. In most states, completion of a master's degree, either in a content field or in professional education course work, is a mandated form of professional development required to maintain one's certification.[35]

Rising importance of professional development

The ultimate goal of professional development is to improve teaching and learning. A number of recent studies examining professional development trends in the United States conclude that the most effective training programs for positively impacting student achievement were those that incorporate thirty to one hundred hours of teacher-engaged time over a period of six months to one year. Those staff-development efforts lasting fewer than fourteen hours had little effect on student achievement. These findings coincide with international comparisons of professional-development efforts in top-performing industrialized nations and the United States. In the countries that perform well on international achievement tests, teachers spend significantly more time meeting together to share ways of improving classroom instruction than teachers in the United States. Teachers are using this research to make the case for more sustained, cohesive professional-development training.[36]

Continuity & Change

Both the NEA and the AFT support the concept of staff development as integral to a teacher's professional growth. The AFT has developed its Educational Research and Dissemination (ER&D) program to expose teachers to the growing body of important education research findings. A series of collegial workshops explore the latest research and practical classroom applications. Universities have trained teachers to act as workshop

---

[32]Richard M. Ingersoll and Michael Strong, "The Impact of Induction and Mentoring Programs for Beginning Teachers: A Critical Review of the Research," *Review of Educational Research* (April 2011), pp. 201–233; and Richard M. Ingersoll, "Beginning Teacher Induction: What the Data Tell Us," *Phi Delta Kappan* (May 2012), pp. 47–51.
[33]Lora Bartlett and Lisa S. Johnson, "The Evolution of New Teacher Induction Policy," *Educational Policy* (November 2010), pp. 847–871; and Sheryn Waterman and Ye He, "Effects of Mentoring Programs on New Teacher Retention: A Literature Review," *Mentoring & Tutoring: Partnership in Learning* (May 2011), pp. 139–156.
[34]Alliance for Excellent Education, "Understanding and Reducing Teacher Turnover," *Education Digest* (May 2008), pp. 22–26; and Kathy Wiebke and Joe Bardin, "New Teacher Support," *Journal of Staff Development* (Winter 2009), pp. 34–38.
[35]Laura Desimone, "A Primer on Effective Professional Development," *Must Reads from Kappan* (Summer 2010–2011), pp. 28–31.
[36]Steven Sawchuk, "Staff Development for Teachers Deemed Fragmented," *Education Week* (February 11, 2009).

TECHNOLOGY @ SCHOOL

Professional Development Opportunities on the Internet

Whether you are preparing to teach, experiencing your first year in the classroom, or a veteran teacher, professional growth and development are critical to your teaching success. The Internet provides a rich array of technology resources for novice and veteran teachers to assist in their development as effective classroom teachers.

New teachers especially need assistance with job search information. Teachers-Teachers.com (**www.teachers-teachers.com**) is a free teacher-recruitment service that provides candidates with the opportunity to complete online applications and cover letters for openings that are posted on the site that match their preferences. Teachers.net also has a "Teacher Job Center" page on its site (**http://jobs.teachers.net**).

A site that has consistently provided useful resources for teachers is Kathy Schrock's Guide for Educators (**http://school.discoveryeducation.com/schrockguide**), where you will find a wide range of Internet resources, such as teacher helpers, search tools, new sites of the day/month, teaching tools, homework helpers, and classroom lessons/activities supporting subject-specific curriculum topics.

Beginning and veteran teachers can find Internet resources in just about any subject area at a variety of websites, and each site is likely to have links to additional web resources. Scholastic Inc. sponsors a site (**http://teacher.scholastic.com/newteacher**) for teachers that includes a series of articles with insightful advice for surviving the first year of teaching, in addition to useful classroom materials for the beginning teacher.

Although the Internet contains thousands of sites that address the professional-development needs of educators, a few are typical of the comprehensive reach these sites have. New Teacher Survival Central (**www.discoveryeducation.com/survival/index.cfm**) includes information on utilizing cutting-edge technology and provides access to new teacher blogs. PBS Teachers (**www.pbs.org/teachers**) provides links to standards-based curriculum resources as well as professional-development activities. Edutopia (**www.edutopia.org**) contains "diverse and innovative media resources" that are easily accessible; the video library is impressive. Education World (**www.educationworld.com**) includes pages on technology integration and lifestyle issues.

Finally, all of the sites are now featuring teachers' blogs, wikis, Twitter, or Facebook pages that are designed to provide advice to the new teacher as well as the opportunity to pose questions about specific problems in forum discussions.

leaders, and the program continues to grow.[37] The NEA has developed the *NEA Academy*, a repository for online courses that have been peer-reviewed for content and rigor. Teachers are encouraged to collaborate with colleagues in taking the courses to develop a community of learners.[38] As the Technology @ School box describes, teachers have numerous opportunities to use the Internet for professional development.

New varieties of staff-development programs are giving teachers a major voice in decisions that affect their professional careers. These programs also help to establish the concept that teaching, like other full-fledged professions, requires lengthy and ongoing training.

Merit Pay

Critiques of merit pay

Real changes in teacher remuneration are being implemented in a growing number of school districts throughout the United States. School officials are questioning the effectiveness of the single salary schedule to compensate teachers and are implementing various forms of **merit pay** (a supplement to a teacher's base salary to reward superior performance). Proponents contend that such incentive systems are necessary to improve overall teacher quality by motivating classroom teachers

[37]AFT, "Professional Development for Teachers," at **www.aft.org/issues/teaching/profdevel/#content** (September 2011); and *AFT ER&D: A Professional Development Program* at **www.aft.org/issues/teaching/profdevel/examples.cfm** (September 2011).
[38]Steven Sawchuk, "The Online Option," *Education Week: Spotlight on Reinventing Professional Development* (October 1, 2009); and NEA Foundation, Learning and Leadership Grants at **www.neafoundation.org/pages/educators/grant-programs/grant-application/learning-and-leadership** (September 2011).

TAKING ISSUE

Read the brief introduction below, as well as the Question and the pros and cons list that follows. Then, answer the question using your own words and position.

Merit Pay

Traditionally, teachers have earned salaries based on their years in teaching and their highest degree obtained. Recent alternative pay plans, however, offer rewards to teachers considered above average in teaching skills or increasing student achievement as measured on achievement tests.

Question

Should individual teachers receive special pay increases based on "merit"? (Think about this question as you read the PRO and CON arguments listed below. What would be YOUR take on this issue?)

Arguments PRO

1. Teachers whose students consistently score high on assessments must be outstanding teachers. Such teachers merit extra compensation for their work.

2. There is a growing body of research that suggests individual teachers can impact a student's learning. If such statistical evidence exists, teachers should be rewarded for positive student performance.

3. Performance-pay programs encourage teachers to focus on teaching the established curriculum because that is what the assessments are designed to measure. This ensures that students throughout the district are learning the same information and skills.

4. Without opportunities to earn performance pay, capable and ambitious people will choose incentive-producing careers such as business; thus, the best candidates will not be attracted to teaching, and high-quality teachers will be inclined to leave teaching.

5. Merit pay promotes excellence in teaching by acting as an incentive for teachers to improve their performance. Each teacher is encouraged to develop better teaching behaviors to increase student performance. Business and most other professions offer such motivators, so why not teaching?

Arguments CON

1. Factors related to achievement are so diverse that it is impossible to differentiate the teacher's contribution from home, social-class, and peer-group influences.

2. At this time, pay-for-performance plans will only reward teachers in the core subject areas because that is what is currently being assessed. Hard work can perhaps be measured, but many creative activities do not necessarily correlate with good teaching. If creativity is a criterion, merit pay may be rewarded more for the teacher's apparent inventiveness than for students' learning.

3. If student results on mandated assessments are the primary evidence of performance, teachers will only teach to the test, thus narrowing the educational experience for students.

4. Businesses can offset extensive merit pay rewards by raising prices, but schools must rely on taxes. Taxpayers often will not or cannot support financial incentives significant enough to support a fair merit-pay system.

5. Incentive pay, by definition, goes to only a few. Such a plan penalizes equally qualified teachers who miss out for lack of enough positions. Moreover, competition for merit pay pits one teacher against another, encourages political games, and destroys the collegial cooperation essential to good education.

Question Reprise: What Is Your Stand?

Reflect again on the following question by explaining YOUR stand about this issue: Should individual teachers receive special pay increases based on "merit"?

and encouraging high-quality people to enter and stay in the profession.[39] Although polls show 71 percent of the public supports the concept of merit pay, teachers have historically expressed reservations about such plans. Some argue that teachers' work is complicated and difficult to measure and that assessments of merit are too often

---

[39]Nancy Protheroe, "Performance Pay for Teachers," *Principal* (March 2011), pp. 28–34.

subjective, especially when left in the hands of a single person—the school principal.[40] Teachers and their professional organizations feel more comfortable with peer evaluations. Where merit plans have been implemented, according to some reports, teachers have often believed that the wrong people were selected for preferential pay. Some observers fear that such rewards go to relatively few teachers at the expense of many others and threaten unity and collegiality among educators.[41] The need, critics say, is to involve teachers in the design and implementation of a compensation-reform plan that focuses on helping teachers become more successful in the classroom.[42] The Taking Issue box presents some arguments for and against merit pay.

 Pay-for-performance plans

Even as arguments continue, merit-pay plans are being developed for implementation in school districts across the United States. The Obama administration is supporting these efforts through programs such as the Teacher Incentive Fund (TIF) and Race to the Top (RTTT); through the TIF alone, $1.2 billion has been awarded to sixty-two school districts, nonprofit organizations, and state departments of education in twenty-seven states. A key element in the design of these plans is that they must support performance-based approaches to recruiting, retaining, and rewarding "highly effective teachers." *Pay-for-performance* plans that tie salary incentives to the use of student achievement data to evaluate teachers was a major factor for the eleven states that were awarded RTTT grants. Even the NEA and AFT have recently participated in the design and implementation of performance-pay plans in Denver, Nashville, and New York City.[43] Overall, the trend toward raising the ceiling on teachers' salaries and making distinctions based on merit should attract brighter students into the profession and keep good teachers from leaving classrooms for more competitive salaries in other fields.

Professional Learning Communities

Continuity & Change

Decision making at the school level

Teachers as experts

Many educational reforms, as we have seen, involve a movement toward teacher empowerment—increasing teachers' participation in decisions that affect their own work and careers. One such reform is the **Professional Learning Community (PLC)**, a collaborative effort among a school's teachers and staff to improve student learning. PLCs use available school and district assessment data and student work to analyze results and establish goals for student progress. Collectively, they identify instructional strategies and best practices to incorporate into instruction in a systematic effort to enhance student achievement. Success of the PLC in enhancing student achievement depends on the commitment and persistence of the educators' collaborative effort.[44]

The assumption underlying PLCs is that teams of teachers are best suited to apply their professional expertise in the areas of data analysis, content knowledge, teaching skills, research, and reflection to improve student learning.[45] Teachers are able to use their professional knowledge and experience in the school setting to collectively plan to change the educational environment. Dufour, a leading expert on PLCs, contends

[40]William Bushaw and Shane Lopez, "A Time for Change: The 42nd Annual Phi Delta Kappa/Gallup Poll of the Public's Attitudes Toward the Public School," *Phi Delta Kappan* (September 2010), pp. 9–26; and Al Ramirez, "Merit Pay Misfires," *Educational Leadership* (December 2010), pp. 58–55.
[41]Jay Mathews, "Merit Pay Could Ruin Teacher Teamwork," *The Washington Post,* October 6, 2008, p. B2.
[42]Nora Carr, "The Pay-for-Performance Pitfall," *American School Board Journal* (February 2008), pp. 38–39; and Gary W. Ritter and Nathan C. Jensen, "The Delicate Task of Developing an Attractive Merit Pay Plan for Teachers," *Phi Delta Kappan* (May 2010), pp. 32–37.
[43]Matthew G. Springer and Catherine D. Gardner, "Teacher Pay for Performance," *Phi Delta Kappan* (May 2010), pp. 8–15; Theresa A. Quigney, "ESEA's Proposed Pay-for-Performance Option: Potential Issues Regarding the Evaluation of Special Educators," *Academic Leadership: The Online Journal* (Fall 2010); Elizabeth Duffrin, "What's the Value in Value-Added?" *District Administration* (January 2011), pp. 48–52; and Donald B. Gratz, "Performance Pay Path to Improvement," *Kappa Delta Pi Record* (Summer 2011), pp. 156–161.
[44]*What Is a PLC* (2009) at **www.centerforcsri.org/plc/program.html** (April 2012).
[45]Rebecca A. Thessin and Joshua P. Starr, "Supporting the Growth of Effective Professional Learning Communities Districtwide," *Phi Delta Kappan* (March 2011), pp. 48–54; and Anne Kennedy, Angie Deuel, Tamara Holmlund Nelson, and David Slavit "Requiring Collaboration or Distributing Leadership?" *Phi Delta Kappan* (May 2011), pp. 20–24.

► ❙❙ **TEACHSOURCE VIDEO ACTIVITY**

Teaching as a Profession: Collaboration with Colleagues

G o to the Education CourseMate website to access the video entitled "Teaching as a Profession: Collaboration with Colleagues," and think about what collaboration as a teacher means to you. What do you think are the challenges and rewards associated with collaboration? After watching the video, answer the following questions:

1 Explain how the teachers in this video exemplify the concepts of *teacher empowerment* and PLCs that are described in this chapter.

2 In this video, we meet a group of teachers who are trying to address an important issue related to the school's math curriculum. Is their collaboration successful? Why or why not?

_____

This video reinforces key concepts found in Section IV: Profession and Community of the Praxis II exam.

that most professions require such collaboration with colleagues, and PLCs provide a platform where teachers can collaborate in a coordinated and systematic effort to support the students they serve.[46]

■ Willingness to get involved

The fate of PLCs requires that teachers are able to overcome the traditional school culture that fosters isolation. Teachers must be willing to take responsibility for directing their own behavior and invest the extra time necessary for an effective, collaborative PLC. To support this, school leaders must provide training in the skills necessary to make PLCs function and provide time in the teachers' schedules.[47] Advocates of PLCs claim that teachers welcome the increased involvement because when they are implemented correctly, PLCs are the best hope for school improvement.

Critics contend that PLCs actually challenge teacher autonomy and the traditional culture of schools by requiring collaboration with others. From this perspective, teachers should be able to act on their own with regard to what works in the classroom to improve student achievement. Considerable time, they say, is devoted to analyzing data, discussing remedies, and experimenting with instructional strategies.[48]

Expanding PLCs will require patience and a willingness to work collaboratively with others in the profession. Once in practice, however, upgrades in the instructional program should improve academic achievement and further enhance teachers' professional status.

REFOCUS How do you believe movements toward increasing professionalism in teaching will affect you? Will you look for a position in a school that makes a strong effort to help new teachers? Would you prefer a mediated-entry program similar to that in the medical profession, with intern and resident teacher levels, before you become a full-fledged professional teacher? How can you prepare yourself to effectively carry out the shared responsibilities of PLCs?

Teacher Organizations

■ NEA and AFT

Although today's working conditions need improvement, they sharply contrast with the restrictions teachers once endured. For example, a Wisconsin teacher's contract for 1922 prohibited a woman teacher from dating, marrying, staying out past 8 p.m.,

_____

[46]Rick Dufour, "Work Together—But Only if You Want To," *Phi Delta Kappan* (February 2011), pp. 57–61.
[47]James F. Kilbane Jr., "Factors in Sustaining Professional Learning Community," *NASSP Bulletin* (September 2009), pp.184–205; and Rebecca A. Thessin and Joshua P. Starr, "Supporting the Growth of Effective Professional Learning Communities Districtwide," *Phi Delta Kappan* (March 2011), pp. 48–54.
[48]Richard Dufour, "Professional Learning Communities: A Bandwagon, an Idea Worth Considering, or Our Best Hope for High Levels of Learning?" *Middle School Journal* (September 2007), pp. 4–8; and Karen Seashore Louis and Kyla Ahlstrom, "Principals as Cultural Leaders," *Phi Delta Kappan* (February 2011), pp. 52–56.

FROM PRESERVICE TO PRACTICE

A Professional Learning Community

During a break in the teachers' lounge, Anna Solemini, a first-year teacher, listened to her colleagues talk about the recent state achievement data that had just been released from the state assessment office. Detailed data were not yet available, but teachers knew that scores for the sixth and eighth graders were up in math and reading, while there was a slight dip in the scores of seventh graders on both assessments. The teachers in the room were still unclear as to whether they had made Adequate Yearly Progress based on the state assessments, though they believed they were "safe" from what they were hearing. As a new teacher, Anna knew the results were important but was unsure what they meant for her and her colleagues.

During the next several weeks, Anna discovered the impact the scores would have on her school. At each grade level, she was aware that there were groups of teachers organized into three PLCs. Each PLC was comprised of content teachers representing a given grade level. Prior to forming the PLCs, some had lobbied that they be structured according to content area, but after much deliberation, the collaborative decision was made that interdisciplinary teams at each grade level would be more reflective of the middle school philosophy and be more likely to meet the needs of the school's students. Members of the PLCs and teachers who took on the role of team leaders received extensive training in how to work effectively in such a collective endeavor.

Each PLC not only reviewed the scores from the state assessments but also examined data from formative assessments that had been administered to students the two previous grading cycles. One of the discoveries they made as they analyzed the data was that there had to be a realignment of literacy and math instructional objectives, especially at the seventh grade level. After they were satisfied that the objectives were properly aligned with the assessment, they began work on improving the instructional plan to meet the needs of all learners. The PLCs investigated strategies designed to engage middle-level learners through a literature review and consultations with a local university professor who was affiliated with the professional-development school network. Their research and investigation led them to conclude that literacy and math skills at all three grade levels needed to be incorporated into an interdisciplinary approach to reinforce the state curriculum standards. They were able to implement the use of multiple texts and collaborative learning strategies to differentiate instruction to meet the needs of all students. Convinced they were on the right track to enhance student learning, the PLCs systematically monitored the reforms to determine if they would yield the desired results.

Anna was impressed with the efforts of the PLCs. She was proud of the way her fellow teachers collaborated to improve the educational environment of her school. She is looking forward to the possibility of becoming a member of the professional learning team so she can take a more active role in making a difference for all students in her school.

Case Questions

1. What further information should Anna seek before trying to join the school's PLC?
2. How does the concept of the PLC support the position that teaching is a profession?
3. Why might some teachers object to serving on a PLC?
4. Would you support Anna's quest to join the PLC?

smoking, drinking, loitering in ice cream parlors, dyeing her hair, and using mascara or lipstick.[49] A critical factor in the development of teaching as a profession has been the growth of professional organizations for teachers. The **National Education Association (NEA)** and the **American Federation of Teachers (AFT)**, the two most important, have been considered rivals, competing for members, recognition, and power. Overview 2.1 sums up the major differences between the two organizations. Although some educators believe that this division produces healthy professional competition, others consider it detrimental to the teaching profession—a splitting of power and a waste of resources. Still others argue that teachers will not attain full professional status until one unified voice speaks for them. As a result of these criticisms,

---

[49]*Chicago Tribune*, September 28, 1975, sect. 1, p.3.

OVERVIEW 2.1

Comparison of the National Education Association (NEA) and the American Federation of Teachers (AFT)

	NEA	AFT
Total membership (2011)	3,200,000	1,500,000
Members who are classroom teachers	2,150,000	850,000
President	Dennis Van Roekel	Randi Weingarten
President's term	3 years (maximum 6 years per person)	2 years (no maximum)
Organizational view	Professional association	Union affiliation with AFL-CIO
Geographic strength	Suburban and rural areas	Large and medium-size cities

in 2000, the NEA-AFT Partnership was formed in an effort to collaborate on projects that are committed to "nurturing and improving public education."[50] Although collaboration is the goal of the partnership, each organization states it is free to conduct its work separately and independently.

Benefits of organizational membership

Regardless of which teacher organization you prefer or are inclined to join, the important step is to make a commitment and to be an active member. Organizational membership will increase your own professionalism and gain you collegial relationships. Your support also helps to improve salary, working conditions, and benefits for many teachers. In addition, reading the journals, magazines, or newsletters that most professional organizations publish, as well as visiting their websites, will keep you abreast of the latest developments in the field. See the Suggested Resources section at the end of this chapter for resources provided by each organization.

National Education Association (NEA)

The NEA is a complex, multifaceted organization involved in education on many local, state, and national levels. Unlike the AFT, the NEA includes both teachers and administrators at the national level. As shown in Table 2.1, in 2011, membership totaled 3.2 million.[51] Among NEA members in 2011, more than 2.15 million were classroom teachers.[52] More than two-thirds of the nation's 3.2 million public-school teachers are NEA members.[53] Primarily suburban and rural in its membership, the NEA is one of the top lobbying forces in the country. Its fifty state affiliates, along with more than 14,000 local affiliates, are among the most influential state-level education lobbies.[54] Finally, the NEA only supports teachers going on strike as a last resort to settling disputes, whereas the AFT more readily endorses this tactic for dispute resolution. The NEA offers a wide range of professional services. Individual benefits include savings on optional insurance programs, financial services, and member discounts on various services. The research division conducts annual studies on the profession's status; it also publishes research memos and opinion surveys

NEA membership

NEA services

---

[50]See "NEA-AFT Partnership" at **www.nea.org/home/11204.htm** (2011).
[51]See **www.nea.org/home/1594.htm** (2011).
[52]See **www.nea.org/home/1594.htm** (2011); telephone conversations with Amy Buffenbarger, NEA Media Research and Content Analyst, January 13, 2009.
[53]See **http://nces.ed.gov/programs/digest/d10/tables/dt10_004.asp?referrer=list** (2011).
[54]See **www.nea.org/home/LegislativeActionCenter.html** (2011).

Table 2.1	Membership in the NEA and AFT	
Year	NEA Membership	AFT Membership
1960	714,000	59,000
1970	1,100,000	205,000
1980	1,650,000	550,000
1990	2,050,000	750,000
1995	2,200,000	875,000
1998	2,300,000	950,000
2003	2,700,000	1,000,000
2011	3,200,000	1,500,000

Source: "The AFT Soars," *The 1988–90 Report of the Officers of the American Federation of Teachers* (Washington, D.C.: AFT, 1990), p. 15; *NEA Handbook, 1986–87* (Washington, D.C.: NEA, 1986), Table 4, p. 142; *NEA Handbook, 1994–95* (Washington, D.C.: NEA, 1995), Table 1, p. 164; and *NEA Handbook, 1997–98,* Table 1, p. 166; also see **www.nea.org/home/1594.htm** (2009) and **www.aft.org/join/index.cfm** (2011).

REFOCUS Which goals and activities seem more appealing to you, those of the NEA or those of the AFT? Why?

on an annual basis. The NEA's major publication is a monthly newspaper, *NEA Today*. Most of the fifty state affiliates also publish monthly magazines.

American Federation of Teachers (AFT)

AFT membership

Formed in 1916, the AFT is affiliated with the American Federation of Labor and Congress of Industrial Organizations (AFL-CIO) labor union. The AFT was originally open only to classroom teachers. In 1976, however, to increase membership, the AFT targeted professional employees such as higher-education faculty, nurses, health-care professionals, government employees, and school-related personnel such as paraprofessionals and cafeteria, custodial, maintenance, and transportation workers. Membership in 2011 stood at just over 1.5 million (Table 2.1), of whom 850,000 were teachers.

AFT services

The AFT publishes a quarterly professional magazine, *American Educator*, and a monthly newspaper, *American Teacher*. In addition, local affiliates each produce a bimonthly bulletin. Members have access to resources on the AFT website that are designed to enhance classroom teaching and learning. The AFT also provides individual benefits to members similar to those of the NEA, such as access to legal services and insurance programs. Unlike the NEA, the AFT has always required its members to join the local (3,000 affiliates), state (forty-three states), and national organizations simultaneously.[55]

The AFT and teacher militancy

The AFT expanded rapidly in the 1960s and 1970s when its affiliates spearheaded a dramatic increase in teacher strikes and other militant actions. Subsequently, the AFT became the dominant teacher organization in many large urban centers where unions have traditionally flourished, where militant tactics were common, and where teachers in general have wanted a powerful organization to represent them. In rural and suburban areas, where union tactics have received less support, the NEA remains dominant.

In addition to the NEA and AFT, several hundred other educational organizations exist.[56] The U.S. Department of Education provides an easily searchable database

[55]See "About AFT Teachers" at **www.aft.org/yourwork/teachers/about.cfm** (2011); "American Federation of Teachers, AFL-CIO" at **www.aft.org/about** (2011); "Tools for Teachers" at **www.aft.org/yourwork/tools4teachers/index.cfm** (2011).
[56]See *Education Resource Organizations Directory* (EROD—U.S. Department of Education) at **http://wdcrobcolp01.ed.gov/Programs/EROD**.

to find an organization that is likely to meet your needs at the Education Resource Organization Directory (EROD). In the following sections, we describe some of the basic types of organizations that could be helpful to a new teacher.

Specialized Professional Organizations

Subject-related associations

At the working level of the classroom, the professional organization that best serves teachers (and education students) usually focuses on their major field. A subject-centered professional association provides a meeting ground for teachers who share similar interests. These professional organizations customarily provide regional and national meetings and professional journals that offer current teaching tips, enumerate current issues in the discipline, and summarize current research and its relationship to practice. The first column of Overview 2.2 lists fifteen major organizations that focus on specific subject matter.

Student-related organizations

Other organizations, also national in scope, focus on the needs and rights of particular kinds of students, ensuring that these children and youth are served by well-prepared school personnel. Several such organizations are listed in the second column of Overview 2.2. These associations hold regional and national meetings and publish monthly or quarterly journals.

Other professional associations

Still another type of organization is the professional organization whose members cut across various subjects and student types, such as the Association for Supervision and Curriculum Development (ASCD) and Phi Delta Kappa (PDK), also listed in the second column of Overview 2.2. These organizations tend to highlight general innovative teaching practices, describe new trends and policies affecting the entire field

OVERVIEW 2.2

Major Specialized Professional Organizations for Teachers

Organizations That Focus on Specific Subject Matter

1. American Alliance for Health, Physical Education, Recreation and Dance
2. American Council on the Teaching of Foreign Languages
3. American School Health Association
4. The Association for Career and Technical Education
5. Association for Education in Journalism
6. International Reading Association
7. International Technology and Engineering Educators Association
8. Modern Language Association
9. Music Teachers National Association
10. National Art Education Association
11. National Business Education Association
12. National Council for the Social Studies
13. National Council of Teachers of English
14. National Council of Teachers of Mathematics
15. National Science Teachers Association

Organizations That Focus on Students and General Education Issues

1. American Association for Gifted Children
2. American Montessori Society
3. Association for Childhood Education International
4. Association for Experiential Education
5. Association for Middle Level Education
6. Association for Supervision and Curriculum Development
7. Council for Exceptional Children
8. Learning Disabilities Association of America
9. National Association for the Education of Young Children
10. Phi Delta Kappa
11. Teachers of English to Speakers of Other Languages

of education, have a wide range of membership, and work to advance the teaching profession *in general*. Each organization publishes a well-respected journal: *Educational Leadership* by ASCD, and the *Phi Delta Kappan* by PDK.

Religious Education Organizations

As of 2011, in grades K–12, there are approximately 464,000 non–public-school teachers, of whom 135,000 belong to religious education associations. One of the largest religious education organizations is the National Association of Catholic School Teachers (NACST), founded in 1978. It currently comprises more than 4,500 lay teachers, mainly from large cities. Few Catholic K–12 school teachers belong to either the NEA or the AFT.[57]

The largest and oldest Catholic education organization is the National Catholic Education Association, comprising 200,000 Catholic educators. Most members are administrators who serve as principals, supervisors, or superintendents of their respective schools. It is estimated that there are currently more than 2.1 million students in approximately 7,094 Catholic elementary and secondary schools in the United States.[58]

Parent–Teacher Groups

PTA membership

Parent-teacher groups provide forums for parents and teachers to work together in creating positive learning environments in schools across the nation. As a teacher, you can take an active part in these associations and work with parents on curriculum and instructional programs, student policy, and school-community relations.

Founded in 1897, the **Parent-Teacher Association (PTA)**—the most prominent of the groups—is a loose confederation of fifty-four state congresses and more than 26,000 local units in all fifty states, with more than 5.1 million members in 2011. Every PTA unit devises its own pattern of organization and service to fit its school and neighborhood. PTA membership is open to anyone interested in promoting the welfare of children and youth, working with teachers and schools, and supporting PTA goals.[59] It maintains open lines of communication through Facebook, Twitter, and its official blog, "OneVoice." *Our Children* is the official print publication of the association.[60] The PTA website also offers an online newsroom (go to **www.pta.org** and click on "Newsroom") as a source for legislative information and current news of interest to the organization.

National PTA activities

As the nation's largest child-advocacy organization, the National PTA is constantly assessing children's welfare to respond to changes in society and in children's needs. The National PTA has recently lobbied to encourage parental monitoring of the implementation of the Common Core State Standards, increase federal funding for education, include the arts in education, enhance child nutrition programs, and provide health care for children and families in poverty.[61]

Organizations for Prospective Teachers

Help in understanding the profession

Students considering teaching careers may also join professional organizations. These organizations can help you answer questions; investigate the profession; form ideals of

[57]"Number of teachers in elementary and secondary schools, and instructional staff in postsecondary degree-granting institutions, by control of institution: Selected years, fall 1970 through fall 2019," Digest of Education Statistics: 2010, at **http://nces.ed.gov/programs/digest/d10/tables/dt10_004.asp?referrer=list**; telephone conversation with Virginia Crowther, office manager-membership, National Association of Catholic School Teachers, September 19, 2011.
[58]See **www.ncea.org/news/AnnualDataReport.asp** (September 19, 2011).
[59]Susan Ludwig, "Education Interest Groups," *Research Starters Education: Education Interest Groups* (June 2008), p. 1; see "Mission, Vision, and Values" at **http://pta.org/1162.asp** (September 13, 2011).
[60]See **http://pta.org/pta_magazine.asp** (September 15, 2011).
[61]See "Public Policy" at **http://pta.org/public_policy.asp** (September 15, 2011).

OVERVIEW 2.3

Professional Organizations Students Can Join

Name and Location	Membership Profile	Focus	Major Publications
National Education Association Student Program, Washington, D.C. **www.nea.org**	Undergraduate and graduate students (60,000) 1,100 college/university chapters	Future teachers, understanding the profession, liability coverage	*Tomorrow's Teachers* (annual), NEA Student Program Facebook Page **www.facebook.com/ neastudentprogram**
Pi Lambda Theta, Bloomington, Ind. **http://pilambda.org**	Undergraduate and graduate students, and professional educators (11,000)	International honor society, promotes professionalism	*Educational Horizons* (quarterly)
Phi Delta Kappa Bloomington, Ind. **www.pdkintl.org**	Undergraduate and graduate students, teachers, administrators, and professors (33,000)	Professional association; research; service, leadership, and teaching; issues, trends, and policies	*Phi Delta Kappan* (monthly), PDK blog, Classroom Tips (digital)
Kappa Delta Pi, Lafayette, Ind. **www.kdp.org**	Graduate students, undergraduate students, teachers, administrators, and professors (45,000)	International honor society, teaching, professional growth	*The Educational Forum* (quarterly), *New Teacher Advocate* (quarterly), *Kappa Delta Pi Record* (quarterly), Electronic publications: Solutions, Novice Notes, Ideas to Know, Resources Roundup
American Educational Research Association, Washington, D.C. **http://aera.net**	Graduate students and professors (25,000)	Research and its application to education	*Educational Researcher* (monthly), *American Educational Research Journal* (quarterly), *Review of Educational Research* (quarterly), *Educational Evaluation and Policy Analysis* (quarterly)

Sources: **www.nea.org/home/1600.htm** (2011); **www.pilambda.org** (2011); **www.pdkintl.org** (2011); **www.kdp.org/aboutkdp** (2011); **http://aera.net** (2011).

REFOCUS

- Which of the professional organizations listed in this chapter hold the most interest for you? Which might be useful to join later in your career?
- How can you find out more information about professional organizations that interest you?

professional ethics, standards, and training; meet other students and educators at local and national meetings; and keep up with current trends in the profession.

Overview 2.3 lists professional organizations that offer specific services for student members. Ask your professors for appropriate information if you are interested in joining any of these organizations. Most of the professional organizations offer discounted student membership rates. Search the Internet for any of the organizations listed to find out more about becoming a member.

Summing Up

1 It is generally agreed that teaching, although not yet a full profession, is moving toward becoming one.

2 Collective bargaining is an integral part of the teaching profession, giving teachers greater authority to determine working conditions and their effectiveness as teachers.

3 Many education trends are raising the level of teacher professionalism. State professional practice boards and the National Board Certification, for example, enable teachers to participate in setting criteria for entering the profession. Induction and professional development programs help establish the idea that teaching is a full-fledged profession requiring lengthy and continued training. Merit pay and Professional Learning Communities (PLCs) provide opportunities for increased salaries and more professional responsibilities designed to enhance student learning.

4 The NEA and AFT represent the majority of classroom teachers; these organizations have improved teachers' salaries and working conditions and have gained them a greater voice in decisions that affect teaching and learning in schools.

5 Many professional organizations are open to undergraduate students or to graduate students and teachers. All provide valuable information and services to educators at different career levels.

Key Terms

The numbers indicate the pages where explanations of the key terms can be found.

profession 28
National Council for Accreditation of Teacher Education (NCATE) 30
professional practice boards 31
occupational prestige 31
collective bargaining 33

National Board for Professional Teaching Standards (NBPTS) 34
mediated entry 34
induction 35
professional development 36
merit pay 37

Professional Learning Community (PLC) 39
National Education Association (NEA) 41
American Federation of Teachers (AFT) 41
parent-teacher groups 45
Parent-Teacher Association (PTA) 45

Certification Connection Activity

This chapter introduces teaching as a profession. A professional is a lifelong learner, one that continues to learn outside of the university. One of the main ways that a professional learns is from professional journals. To prepare for the Praxis II questions about teacher professionalism, go to your library and find the journal that best fits your major. Read one article on current research in your subject or area of certification. In your journal, reflect on how that practice or research might affect your teaching as practice for the Praxis II.

Discussion Questions

1 In your opinion, is teaching a profession or not? What changes might make teaching a true profession? What does teacher professionalism mean to you?

2 What special relationships does your college of education have with area school districts and schools? How do these relationships enhance your preparation as well as the work of the teachers and administrators? How could these be improved?

3 Are professional-development programs essential for maintaining high-quality teaching? If so, what should their main focus be? Who should design these programs and how?

4 Do you agree with proponents of PLCs that teachers should have a greater role in directing the instructional program of schools? As a teacher, what do you see as the benefits of PLCs? What do you see as their drawbacks?

Suggested Projects for Professional Development

1 Examine the National Board for Professional Teaching Standards (NBPTS) website to develop a profile of National Board Certified (NBC) teachers in your state. Then answer these questions: How many teachers are there? Where are most located? Which teaching field is most prominent? Contact and invite a local NBC teacher to address your class about national certification. Be sure to prepare a list of questions prior to the class presentation.

2 Survey local public-school teachers and your education faculty regarding their views on merit pay. Compare and contrast your results with the views expressed in the Taking Issue feature. What is your opinion? What are you uncertain about? How can you find more information to clear up these uncertainties?

3 Either by telephone or over the Internet, contact your local NEA and AFT affiliates, and ask for information on membership costs, benefits, and services, as well as position statements on key educational issues. Talk with teachers in the schools you visit, asking them which of the organizations tend to represent teachers in your area and why. Make a chart to display your information, and share it with the class.

4 Talk with your education professors and with teachers in the schools you visit to find out which professional organizations they belong to—and why. Review the list of specialized professional organizations in Overview 2.2, and select two or three that most interest you. Using their Internet sites, contact these organizations to find out student membership costs, special benefits, publications, and special programs.

Suggested Resources

Internet Resources

Information about many of the organizations discussed in this chapter can be found on the Internet. For example, the NEA maintains a home page at **www.nea.org**; the AFT can be found at **www.aft.org**; and the National PTA can be found at **www.pta.org**. In exploring specific topics such as professional development and educational technology, the biggest problem often is deciding which of the many good sites to visit first. A general Internet search will provide a good start. For professional development, try the Learning Forward website at **www.learningforward.org/index.cfm**. For educational technology, visit the website of the International Society for Technology in Education (ISTE) at **www.iste.org**. For information on national board certification, consult the NBPTS site at **www.nbpts.org**.

Publications

Baines, Lawrence. *The Teachers We Need vs. the Teachers We Have: Realities and the Possibilities*. Lanham, MD: Rowman & Littlefield Education, 2010. *Describes the educational and economic situation that has fostered the development of nonaccredited teacher-preparation programs and argues that standardized testing does not differentiate good teachers from poor teachers.*

Beck, Clive, and Clare Kosnik. *Innovations in Teacher Education: A Social Constructivist Approach*. Albany: State University of New York Press, 2006. *Examines teacher-education programs in Australia, Canada, and the United States and suggests that the constructivist approach can lead to effective teacher-education programs.*

Cochran-Smith, Marilyn, Sharon Feiman-Nemser, D. John McIntyre, and Kelly E. Demers, eds. *Handbook of Research on Teacher Education: Enduring Questions in Changing Contexts. 3d ed*. New York: Routledge; [Manassas, VA]: Co-published by the Association of Teacher Educators, 2008. *Reviews recent research in the field and examines such current issues as the professional knowledge base, diversity, field placements, and educators' qualifications.*

Conant, James B. *The Education of American Teachers*. New York: McGraw-Hill, 1964. *A classic text on improving teacher education and teacher professionalism.*

Darling-Hammond, Linda, and John Bransford, eds. *Preparing Teachers for a Changing World: What Teachers Should Learn and Be Able to Do*. San Francisco, CA: Jossey-Bass, 2005. *Sponsored by the National Academy of Education, this book informs teacher educators and policy makers about the most effective ways to prepare teachers who will meet the needs of the nation's schoolchildren.*

Drury, Darrel, and Justin Baer. *The American Public School Teacher: Past, Present and Future*. Boston: Harvard Education Press, 2011. *Reflects on the NEA surveys that are conducted every five years.*

Feistritzer, C. Emily, and Charlene K. Haar. *Alternate Routes to Teaching*. Upper Saddle River, NJ: Pearson/Merrill/Prentice Hall, 2008. *The authors survey teachers to examine alternative certification programs across the country.*

Fogarty, Robin, and Brian Pete. *From Staff Room to Classroom: A Guide for Planning and Coaching Professional Development*. Thousand Oaks, CA: Corwin Press, 2007. *A practical look at providing professional development for enhancing classroom teaching and assessment aimed at improving student learning.*

Glatthorn, Allan A., Brenda K. Jones, and Ann Adams Bullock. *Developing Highly Qualified Teachers: A Handbook for School Leaders.* Thousand Oaks, CA: Corwin Press, 2006. *Defines the concept of "highly qualified teachers" and then describes methods of attracting, developing, and retaining such professionals.*

Hannaway, Jane, and Andrew Rotherham. *Collective Bargaining in Education: Negotiating Change in Today's Schools.* Boston: Harvard Educational Publications Group, 2006. *A well-written and fair look at the collective bargaining process and its impact on educational change.*

Johnson, Susan Moore. *The Workplace Matters: Teacher Quality, Retention and Effectiveness.* Washington, D.C.: NEA, 2006. *Workplace conditions make a difference in retaining teachers; this work examines current research.*

Kahlenberg, Richard D. *Tough Liberal: Albert Shanker and the Battles over Schools, Unions, Race, and Democracy.* New York: Columbia University Press, 2007. *In writing this biography of the long-time AFT president, Albert Shanker, the author describes the recent history of the teacher's union in the United States.*

Laine, Sabrina, Ellen Behrstock-Sherratt, and Molly Lasagna. *Improving Teacher Quality: A Guide for Education Leaders.* San Francisco: Jossey-Bass, 2011. *Reviews the most current research on improving teacher quality. Innovative best practice strategies are highlighted that are based on the principles of collaboration.*

Lieberman, Ann, and Lynne Miller, eds. *Teachers in Professional Communities: Improving Teaching and Learning.* New York: Teachers College Press, 2008. *Professional communities as an approach to professional development are described, and recommendations are made for incorporating them into the school setting.*

Moe, Terry M. *Special Interest: Teachers Unions and America's Public Schools.* Washington, D.C.: Brookings Institution Press, 2011. *Examines teacher unions and their influence on public schools from a conservative perspective.*

Neapolitan, Jane E., and Terry R. Berkeley, eds. *Where Do We Go from Here? Issues in the Sustainability of Professional Development School Partnerships.* New York: Peter Lang, 2006. *Looks at suggestions for improving PDS partnerships in the future.*

Skinner, Elizabeth A., Maria Teresa Garreton, and Brian D. Schultz. *Grow Your Own Teachers: Grassroots Change for Teacher Education: Teaching for Social Justice.* New York: Teachers College Press, 2011. *This book examines the school reform movement in Chicago, especially teacher-preparation efforts.*

Additional resources for this chapter, including the TeachSource Videos, can be found on the Education CourseMate website. Go to **CengageBrain.com** to access the site.

PART TWO

Historical and Philosophical Foundations

3

Global Origins of American Education

As a global process, education is not limited to one place and time. Although it has unique features, American education did not develop in isolation from other cultures and societies. By looking back through time, we can gain a global historical perspective that illuminates education in our time. This chapter explores education in preliterate Chinese, Egyptian, Hebraic, Arabic, and European cultures. By reflecting on our past, we can gain a perspective on our present and develop strategies for our future.

As you read this chapter, consider the following questions:

FOCUS QUESTIONS

- How were knowledge, education, schooling, teaching, and learning defined in the past?
- How did curricula (the content of education) and teaching methods develop over time?
- When and how have schools been used to maintain cultural continuity or to generate cultural change?
- How did racial, gender, and socioeconomic class affect cultural diversity and privilege in the past?
- How did teaching develop from a craft into a profession?
- Who set educational standards?
- How did schools respond to technological innovations?

Constructing Your Own History or Autobiography of Education

Studying the history of education provides an opportunity for you to construct your own history of education by writing your educational autobiography. This examination of the origin of your ideas about education relates closely to your construction of your own philosophy of education. You can trace the roots of your ideas and beliefs about education by looking into your grandparents' and parents' educations as well as your own. As you find your own educational origins, you can build a bridge between your experiences and the broader historical developments discussed in this chapter. To begin to construct your educational autobiography, you might (1) interview your grandparents, parents, and others about their educations; (2) identify and examine family artifacts, photographs, records, and other memorabilia that relate to attending and graduating from school; (3) think deeply and reflectively about your own educational experiences. Then, you can record your findings and begin to write your own autobiography. As you proceed through the chapter, you will encounter ideas to prompt you to add to or revise your educational autobiography.

―――――――――
*This chapter was revised by Gerald L. Gutek.

Education in Preliterate Societies

 Cultural transmissions

Continuity & Change

Our narrative begins in preliterate times, before the invention of reading and writing, when our ancestors transmitted their culture orally, through songs and stories, from one generation to the next. We can find the origins of informal learning in our own family's stories and come to understand why storytelling remains so powerful today. Although we live in a time when information is transmitted almost instantaneously by electronic means, studying preliterate education can help us understand why so much of the school curriculum continues to focus on teaching traditional skills rather than educating for cultural and technological change.

Preliterate people faced the almost overwhelming problems of surviving in an environment that pitted them against drought and floods, wild animals, and attacks from hostile groups. By trial and error, they developed survival skills that over time became cultural patterns.

For culture to continue, it must be transmitted from adults to children. By **enculturation**, children learn the group's language and skills and assimilate its moral and religious values.

Survival skills and values

The transmission of survival skills from the adults to the children was done by teaching them what they needed to survive and by instilling the group's values through special commemorative events. The survival skills included hunting, fishing, food gathering, building shelters, and preparing food. The young learned these skills by imitating what adults did. The skills became identified with gender. From their fathers and the older men, boys learned to how to hunt, fish, and defend the group from enemies. From their mothers and older women, girls learned how to gather and prepare food.

 Continuity & Change

Thus, even as early as preliterate society, the group's gender patterns designated some activities as appropriate for males and others for females. These gender-specific patterns had an impact on education that continued to the contemporary period and have been slow to change.

While skill learning in preliterate societies was based on doing what was actually needed for individual and group survival, the more general values—the moral codes—that related to survival were marked by dramatic ceremonies that celebrated the individual's passage from childhood to adulthood. These rites of passage were celebrated with ritual dancing, music, and dramatic acting that endowed the event with a

FROM PRESERVICE TO PRACTICE

Learning National Identity through Patriotic Programs

In this vignette, Dr. Gutek, the chapter's author, reflects on his observation of an elementary school program.

Throughout the chapters on the history and philosophy of education, I encourage you to reflect on your educational experiences and to use these reflections to construct your own history and philosophy of education. Here, I reflect on my experience of attending a program about "Freedom," presented by the first-grade class at a local public school. The program was part of the school's celebration of President's Day.

The children filed on to the stage, which displayed a large American flag and, in unison, recited "I pledge allegiance to the flag of the United States of America…" They then sang patriotic songs, such as "This is My Flag," "America," and "This Land is My Land." One boy, costumed as George Washington, recounted the well-known story about how he told the truth

to his father that he had chopped down the cherry tree. Another boy was dressed as Abraham Lincoln.

As a historian of education, the performance led me to reflect on its educational and cultural meaning. I thought about the use of stories (oral traditions) and celebratory performances in education, especially how stories, songs, and symbols are used to construct a group's identity and values. The large flag, the songs, and the costumes all built a sense of American identity in the children. The proverbial but most likely mythical story of George Washington and the cherry tree reinforced the values of honesty and truthfulness. I thought about how significant adults, such as the music director and the teachers, had planned and orchestrated the program. I am sure that many of you have either participated in or observed a program like the one I described.

Case Questions

1. How does this contemporary school performance resemble the oral tradition in preliterate societies?

2. How do songs and stories construct children's sense of group identity?

3. How do educational episodes, like the one just described, relate to cultural identity and cultural diversity?

4. Reflect on similar school programs in your own education, and relate them to your educational autobiography and philosophy.

---

powerful supernatural meaning evoking moral and religious responses. Thus children learned the group's prescriptions (acceptable behaviors) as well as its proscriptions or taboos (forbidden behaviors).

Continuity & Change

Both informal education and formal education in schools remains laden with what children should or should not do. Positive behavior is reinforced by praise and rewards, and inappropriate behavior with sanctions, "time outs," and suspensions.

While parents and adults taught skills, tribal elders, such as priests and chiefs, transmitted the group's culture, especially its religious beliefs and moral values, to the young. For these early teachers, the purpose of education was to preserve and maintain the culture. They feared that any change might disrupt the group's survival.

Oral tradition

Without writing to record their histories, preliterate societies relied on oral tradition—storytelling—to transmit their cultural heritage. Elders or priests, often gifted storytellers, sang or recited poems and stories that commemorated events in the group's past. Combining myths and actual historical events, the oral tradition developed the group's collective memory and identity by telling young people about the group's heroes and victories. These songs and stories helped the young learn the group's spoken language, traditions, and values.

Storytelling continues to be an engaging teaching strategy today, especially in preschools and primary grades. Often adults, such as military veterans and artists from the school's community, will visit the classroom to tell their stories. Through stories, children meet their culture and its heroes, legends, and history.

As toolmakers, humans improvised and used spears, axes, hooks, and other tools—the earliest examples of technology. Similarly, as language users, they created

▶❚❚ TEACHSOURCE VIDEO ACTIVITY

Diversity: Teaching in a Multiethnic Classroom

Go to the Education CourseMate website to access the video entitled, "Diversity: Teaching in a Multiethnic Classroom." In this video, second-grade students are working on a project to create Japanese Kamishibai books. The project connects the students to the history and culture of ancient Japan. Answer the following questions:

❶ How did the project connect the students to Japanese culture?

❷ How did the project illustrate this chapter's thesis that education is a global historical process?

❸ How did the project connect the past to contemporary multicultural education?

pictographs and then developed symbols that represented people, animals, and natural phenomena. These early beginnings of expression and communication in signs, pictographs, and then letters signified the great cultural leap to literacy—and then to schooling. After writing was invented, a people could record their group's story or history, which led to the need for children to be taught to read and write.

In certain places around the world, groups developed their own written languages, which supplemented the earlier oral traditions of prehistory. To illustrate the development of education, we look at three great ancient cultures: the Chinese, the Egyptian, and the Hebraic. We see them first in their own cultural contexts and then consider their contributions to our life and times.

Education in Ancient Chinese Civilization

Our exploration of education's global roots begins with China, which has 4,000 years of continuous history and is one of the world's most enduring civilizations. Ancient China influenced the cultures of Japan, Korea, and Vietnam. While Chinese culture is significant in ancient history, modern China (the People's Republic of China—PRC) is an important contemporary world power. With more than 1.3 billion people, China has the largest population of any country in the world. Its economy is exceeded only by that of the United States.

As a great empire, Chinese civilization reached high pinnacles of political, social, and educational development. The empire, ruled by a series of dynasties, spanned more than forty centuries, from 2200 BCE to 1912 CE.[1]

Educational philosophies, especially Confucianism, which originated in imperial China, still influence culture and education today. (See Overview 3.1 for key periods relating to education in China and other countries.)

Continuity & Change

China's history illustrates how the processes of continuity and change affect education. Like other peoples, such as the ancient Greeks, the Chinese, who called their empire the "Middle Kingdom," held their culture in such high esteem that they saw it as the center of civilization. Believing that their language and culture were superior to all others, they looked down on foreigners as barbarians.[2] Seeking to avoid the influences of other peoples and cultures, the Chinese sought to isolate themselves. This ethnocentric attitude, which emphasized continuity with the past and especially tradition, was fearful of cultural diversity and change.

---

[1]John Keay, *China: A History* (New York: Basic Books), 2009.
[2]W. Scott Mouton and Charlton M. Lewis, *China: Its History and Culture* (New York: McGraw-Hill, 2005), pp. 22–40.

Although the ancient Chinese invented paper, printing, gun powder, the propeller, the crossbow, and the cannon, they tended to regard technological innovations as novelties rather than as important agents of material and economic change. Eventually, imperial China's reluctance to adapt technology from other cultures isolated and weakened it and, by the nineteenth century, made it vulnerable to foreign exploitation. At the end of the twentieth and into the twenty-first century, China made a dramatic change in its attitude and embarked on a concerted policy of modernization.

How imperial China dealt with the issue of continuity and change and with technology raises several important issues for educators today. The challenge of how to adapt to new ideas from other cultures, especially in science and technology, and still maintain one's own cultural identity remains an important educational issue in China and in other countries. This issue raises such questions about the purposes of education as: (1) Should schools emphasize a cultural core that builds a sense of cultural identity or should they encourage cultural diversity? (2) How should schools integrate technology into the culture? (3) Should schools be open or guarded about new ideas from other cultures? (4) What is the relationship between cultural continuity and change, and how does education promote one or the other?

Confucian Education

Unlike the Egyptian and Judaic cultures discussed later in the chapter, Chinese philosophy was more concerned about living here and now than with universal questions about the afterlife and immortality of the soul. To examine Chinese education's origins, we go back to the third century BCE, when China was beset by political and cultural turmoil.

During periods of social and political crisis, the major question is whether education should emphasize cultural continuity by reviving the traditions of the past to restore social and political harmony, or should it develop strategies for social change? In answering this question, three philosophies—Legalism, Taoism, and Confucianism—proposed different paths or purposes for education in China.

During the Ch'in dynasty, Legalism, developed by the scholar, Shih Huang Ti, was decreed as imperial China's official philosophy. Arguing that the emperor's edicts were unquestioned law, Legalism advocated a highly disciplined authoritarian government that would ruthlessly maintain order. Fearing dissent, Legalists imposed a strict censorship to repress alternative philosophies such as Taoism and Confucianism. The Legalists used education to impose their definition of Chinese culture through indoctrination.

Taoism, developed by Lao Tzu, a philosopher who lived in the sixth century BCE, still influences Chinese culture and education. Taoism presented an alternative to Legalism. In his *Tao Te Ching*, translated as "The Way and Virtue," Lao Tzu began a philosophical journey to find the path to the true reality, which is often hidden by misinformation. All things, Lao Tzu claimed, come from and follow an unseen, underlying, unifying force that moves through the world. Unlike the Legalists, who wanted to control others, Lao Tzu advised people to stop trying to control other people and events, go with the stream of life, and live simply and spontaneously.[3] In Taoism, education's purpose is to encourage the self-reflection needed to find one's true self and to take the path to truth.

When the Han dynasty came to power in 207 BCE, the Han emperors rejected Legalism and made Confucianism China's official philosophy. Unlike Western philosophers, Confucius (551–479 BCE) was not concerned with theological or metaphysical issues about the human being's relationship to God or the universe. He believed it was more important to establish the standards needed to create an ethical society than to ponder unanswerable questions. Unlike the authoritarian Legalists and the politically disengaged Taoists, **Confucius** based his educational philosophy on an ethical hierarchy of responsibilities that began with the emperor and flowed downward, touching everyone in society. His ideal of hierarchical relationships can be depicted

Continuity & Change

Continuity & Change

Need for harmony

Standards & Assessment

---

[3]Chung-Yuan Chang, *Creativity and Taoism: A Study of Chinese Philosophy, Art, and Poetry* (New York: Jessica Kingsley Publishers, 2011), pp. 81–100.

as an ethical ladder on which the person standing on each rung is connected to the people standing above and below. Education's major purpose is to create and maintain a harmonious society in which everyone clearly knows her or his status, duties, and responsibilities, and the appropriate way of behaving toward others.

 Rituals and manners

The Confucian system of character education set standards for civility—polite, correct, and appropriate behavior. Endorsing the ideal of the teacher as a mentor, he believed that children learn to behave ethically when they have a clear model of appropriate behavior to emulate. Teachers need to personify this model of civility and require their students to follow it in the school.

Standards & Assessment

Confucius believed a correct or appropriate standard of behavior exists for every situation and that everyone should be expected to observe that standard. Children learn appropriate behavior as a set of rituals or patterns that follow the correct procedures all people are expected to perform. The Confucian model of character formation removes the chance element from behavior presented when unexpected situations arise.

Because the Confucian hierarchy defines a person as a father, mother, brother, sister, ruler, or subject, the purpose of character education is to learn how to correctly perform the appropriate behavior for one's designated role and rank.

Continuity & Change

Living during a period of cultural and political instability, Confucius's goal was to restore social harmony, which he believed resulted from maintaining the culture's continuity rather than changing it.

Confucius established an academy to prepare students as officials in China's imperial government. Wanting to attract only highly motivated students, he set high admission standards for entry to his school. He designed a curriculum that included the Chinese classics, music, poetry, diplomacy, and the rituals of polite behavior and ceremonial court etiquette. Believing that all future officials should study the same general subjects, he established a core curriculum of selected great books such as the *Classics of Change, Of Documents, Of Poetry, Of Rites*, and the *Spring* and *Autumn Annals*. These Confucian texts were used in Chinese education from 1313 BCE to 1905 CE.[4]

Like other effective teachers, Confucius developed a well-defined system of classroom management. He held high expectations for his students. As a mentor, he maintained a proper distance from his students but was approachable to them. He corrected and criticized his students in a positive and constructive way. His students respected their teacher as "the master." In China, teacher–student relationships, like other relationships, were well known and followed with precision. The Confucian teacher is entrusted with guarding and transmitting the traditional heritage to maintain cultural continuity and social stability.[5] As Confucius said, "A man worthy of being a teacher gets to know what is new by keeping fresh in his mind what he is already familiar with."[6]

Hierarchy

The Confucian concept of hierarchical ethical relationships has important educational implications, especially for character formation and civility. The Confucian concept of hierarchical relationships, which positions individuals into superior and subordinate rankings, differs significantly from the American idea of equal and flexible relationships. In the Confucian system, it is more important to keep old friends than to make new ones. Making new friends might bring change that upsets the established social pattern.

In situations where relationships are equal and flexible, individuals are constantly moving from old to new relationships. They are continually redefining their relationships and creating new openings or boundaries for old and new friends. Character

[4]Jennifer Oldstone-Moore, *Confucianism* (Oxford and New York: Oxford University Press, 2002), pp. 35–37; and Daniel K. Gardner, *The Four Books: The Basic Teachings of the Later Confucian Tradition* (Indianapolis: Hackett Publishing Co., 2007). For a biography of Confucius, see Annping Chin, *The Authentic Confucius: A Life of Thought and Politics* (New York: Oxford University Press, 2007).
[5]Bryan W. Van Norden, *Introduction to Classical Chinese Philosophy* (Indianapolis, IN: Hackett Publishing Co., 2011), pp. 18–30 and 34–44.
[6]Confucius, *The Analects*, Book II, in D. C. Lau, "Introduction," *The Analects*, trans. D. C. Lau (New York: Penguin Books, 1979), p. 64.

OVERVIEW 3.1

Key Periods in Educational History

Historical Group or Period	Educational Goals	Students
Preliterate societies 7000 BCE–5000 BCE	To teach group survival skills and group identity	Children in the group
China 3000 BCE–1900 CE	To prepare elite officials to govern the empire according to Confucian principles	Males of the gentry class
Egypt 3000 BCE–300 BCE	To prepare priest-scribes to administer the empire	Males of upper classes
Judaic 1200 BCE to present	To transmit Jewish religion and cultural identity	Children and adults in the group
Greek 1600 BCE–300 BCE	Athens: To cultivate civic responsibility and identification with the city-state and to develop well-rounded persons; Sparta: To train soldiers and military leaders	Male children of citizens; ages 7–20
Roman 750 BCE–450 CE	To develop civic responsibility and commitment for the republic and then empire; to train administrators and military leaders	Male children of citizens; ages 7–20
Arabic 700 CE–1350 CE	To construct commitment to Islamic beliefs; to develop expertise in mathematics, medicine, and science	Male children of upper classes; ages 7–20
Medieval 500 CE–1400 CE	To develop commitment to Christian beliefs and practices; to prepare individuals to assume roles in a hierarchical society	Male children of upper classes or those entering religious life; girls and young women entering religious communities; ages 7–20
Renaissance 1350 CE–1500 CE	To educate classical humanists in Greek and Latin literatures; to prepare courtiers to serve leaders	Male children of aristocracy and upper classes; ages 7–20
Reformation 1500 CE–1600 CE	To instill commitment to a particular religious denomination; to cultivate general literacy	Boys and girls ages 7–12 in vernacular schools; young men ages 7–12 of upper-class backgrounds in humanist schools

Instructional Methods	Curriculum	Agents	Influences on Modern Education
Informal instruction; children imitating adult skills and values	Survival skills of hunting, fishing, food gathering; stories, myths, songs, poems, dances	Parents, tribal elders, and priests	Emphasis on informal education and stories to transmit skills and values
Memorization and recitation of classic texts	Confucian classics	Government officials	Written examinations for civil service and professions
Memorizing and copying dictated texts	Religious or technical texts	Priests and scribes	Placing educational authority in a priestly elite; using education to prepare officials
Listening to, memorizing, reciting, analyzing, and debating sacred texts; reading and writing for literacy	The Torah, laws, rituals, and commentaries	Parents, priests, scribes, and rabbis	Concepts of monotheism and a covenant between God and humanity; religious observance and maintaining cultural identity.
Drill, memorization, recitation in primary schools; lecture, discussion, and dialogue in higher schools	Athens: reading, writing, arithmetic, drama, music, physical education, literature, poetry Sparta: drill, military songs, and tactics	Athens: private teachers and schools, Sophists, philosophers Sparta: military officers	Athens: the concept of the well-rounded, liberally educated person Sparta: the concept of serving the military state
Drill, memorization, and recitation in primary schools; declamation in rhetorical schools	Reading, writing, arithmetic, Laws of Twelve Tables, law, philosophy	Private schools and teachers; rhetorical schools	Using education to develop sense of civic commitment and to develop administrative skills
Drill, memorization, and recitation in lower schools; commentary and discussion in higher schools	Reading, writing, mathematics, religious literature, scientific studies	Mosques; court schools	Arabic numerals and computation; reentry of classical Greek texts to western educators
Drill, memorization, recitation, chanting in lower schools; textual analysis and disputation in universities and in higher schools	Reading, writing, arithmetic, liberal arts; philosophy, theology; crafts; military tactics, and chivalry	Parish, chantry, and cathedral schools; universities; apprenticeship; knighthood	Established structure, content, and organization of universities as major institutions of higher education; the transmission of liberal arts; institutionalization and preservation of knowledge
Memorization, translation, and analysis of Greek and Roman classics	Latin, Greek, classical literature, poetry, art	Classical humanist educators and schools such as the *lycée, gymnasium*, and Latin school	An emphasis on literary knowledge and style as expressed in classical literature; a two-track system of schools
Memorization, drill, indoctrination, catechetical instruction in vernacular schools; translation and analysis of classics in humanist schools	Reading, writing, arithmetic, catechism, religious beliefs and rituals; Latin and Greek; theology	Vernacular elementary schools for the masses; classical schools for the upper classes	A commitment to universal education to provide literacy to the masses; the origins of school systems with supervision to ensure doctrinal conformity; the dual-track school system based on socioeconomic class and career goals

education in situations of equality carries the ethical prescriptions that we should treat each person as an equal and should respect and even value their differences from us.

In contrast, Confucian ethics establishes well-known and observed patterns of behavior rather than flexible or fluid ones. People are accorded various levels of respect based on their age, position, status, and achievements. Character education means to learn one's place in the social network of relationships that form the community and follow the prescribed role behaviors that maintain social harmony.

■ Continuity & Change

Because change, novelty, and innovations can cause the unexpected and the uncertain, Confucius designed an approach to education that would maintain traditional knowledge and values. He tried to set educational patterns that would limit the unanticipated consequences caused by change. He sought to identify and replicate the behaviors that traditionally had maintained peace, security, and tranquility in the past. These behaviors were formed into rituals and ceremonies that students could learn and use to deal with situations in their lives. These rituals resembled the Patriotic program described in the From Preservice to Practice box. As you construct your educational philosophy and reflect on the purposes of education, compare and contrast Confucian and contemporary American ideals and values. How will you define civil behavior and values? Will these values reflect traditional standards or will they be open ended?

■ Respect for teachers

In China, teacher-student relationships were formal and followed hierarchical rules of approved behavior. In schools, teachers were to respect and obey the headmaster or principal; teachers were to respect their colleagues, especially older and more experienced teachers; students were to respect their teachers; and students were to respect each other, with younger students respecting older ones. Each of these levels of respect on the hierarchy of relationships carried with it duties and obligations. Students behaved properly when they held their teachers in high regard and respect. This respect for education, learning, and teachers is important in schools in China, South Korea, Singapore, and Japan where Confucianism is pervasive in the culture.[7] Confucianism's diffusion from China to other Asian countries illustrates how educational ideas and processes are transferred across cultures.

---

[7]T. R. Reid, *Confucius Lives Next Door: What Living in the East Teaches Us about Living in the West* (New York: Vintage Press, 2000); and see William Theodore de Bary, *Confucian Tradition and Global Education* (New York: Columbia University Press, 2007) for discussions of Confucianism's influence on the contemporary world, especially globalization.

TIME LINE
Ancient China

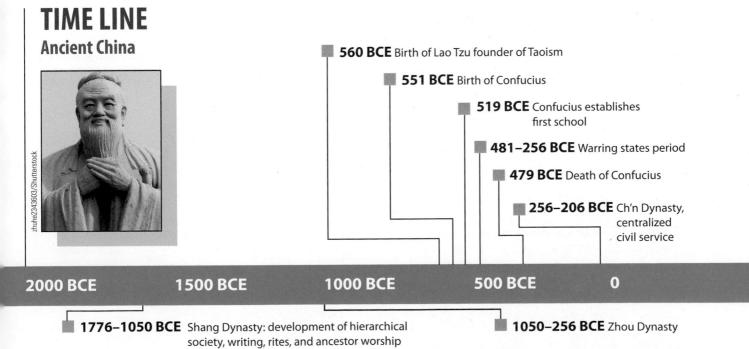

zhuhe2343603/Shutterstock

560 BCE Birth of Lao Tzu founder of Taoism

551 BCE Birth of Confucius

519 BCE Confucius establishes first school

481–256 BCE Warring states period

479 BCE Death of Confucius

256–206 BCE Ch'n Dynasty, centralized civil service

| 2000 BCE | 1500 BCE | 1000 BCE | 500 BCE | 0 |

1776–1050 BCE Shang Dynasty: development of hierarchical society, writing, rites, and ancestor worship

1050–256 BCE Zhou Dynasty

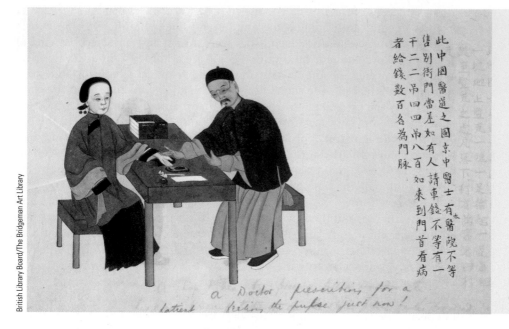

此中國醫道之圖京中醫士有醫院不等
售別術門當差如有人請車錢不等有一
千二吊四四吊八百如來到門首看病
者給錢數百各為門脉

a Doctor prescribing for a patient feeling the pulse just now!

Student and teacher preparing for examinations in 19th century imperial China.

China's Contribution to World and Western Education

Importance of examinations

☑ Standards & Assessment

☑ Standards & Assessment

An important educational legacy from China was its system of national examinations. Chinese educators designed comprehensive written essay examinations to test students' academic competence for positions in the imperial government. Students prepared for the examinations by studying ancient Chinese literature and Confucian texts with master teachers at imperial or temple schools. The examinations emphasized recalling memorized information rather than solving actual problems. The need to score high on the national examinations meant that teachers had to teach to the tests and not discuss or interpret them. Alternative thinking was seen as an unnecessary divergence from transmitting the heritage, and it was considered a waste of valuable classroom time.

The examination process, like the society, operated hierarchically and selectively. Students had to pass a series of rigorous examinations in ascending order; if they failed, they were dismissed from the process.[8]

---

[8]For a discussion of Confucianism and the examination system, access: **www.csupomona .edu/~plin/ls201/confucian2.thml**. Also, see Hilde De Weerdt, *Competitions Over Content: Negotiating Standards for the Civil Service Examinations in Imperial China* (Cambridge, MA: Harvard University Asia Center, 2007).

960–1279 CE Song Dynasty

1295 CE Publication of Marco Polo's *Tales of China*

206 BCE–220 CE Han Dynasty

1644–1911 CE Manchu Dynasty

500 CE　　　**1000 CE**　　　**1500 CE**　　　**2000 CE**

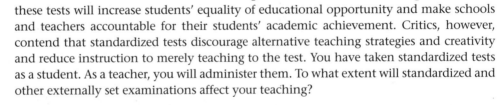

TECHNOLOGY @ SCHOOL

Connecting Ancient China to the History of Education

You can research the Internet to broaden your perspectives on ancient China as well as the other civilizations and historic periods discussed in this chapter. Access the following sites to build your perspectives on China: (1) the British Museum for the geography, chronology, and arts and crafts of ancient China at **www.ancientchina.co.uk**; (2) for the analects of Confucius and Taoism go to **http://eauc.evansville.edu/chpage.htm**.

REFOCUS   Think back to the focus questions at the beginning of this chapter. *Use these questions to construct your own history or autobiography of education.* For example, have family or group stories, like the oral tradition among prehistoric groups, shaped your ideas about education, schooling, teaching, and learning? Did you learn specifically defined standards of behavior and manners in a way that was similar to Confucian education? Or did you learn standards of behavior in a more permissive and flexible way? In other words, how did you learn what was appropriate or inappropriate for you to do? How did you learn the "should" and "should nots" of school and society?

Continuity & Change

In imperial days, only a few finalists were eligible for the empire's highest civil service positions. The educational and examination systems were reserved exclusively for upper-class males. Because women could not hold positions in the imperial government, the officials determined that it would waste time and resources to educate them in the classics.

Currently, national examinations, especially for university entrance, dominate education in modern China, Singapore, Japan, and South Korea. Other countries such as the United Kingdom and France also require national tests.

In the United States, the No Child Left Behind Act of 2001 mandates annual testing of students in grades 3–8 to measure academic achievement in reading and mathematics.[9] The act's premise is that these tests will increase students' equality of educational opportunity and make schools and teachers accountable for their students' academic achievement. Critics, however, contend that standardized tests discourage alternative teaching strategies and creativity and reduce instruction to merely teaching to the test. You have taken standardized tests as a student. As a teacher, you will administer them. To what extent will standardized and other externally set examinations affect your teaching?

Education in Ancient Egypt

Ancient Egypt, one of the world's oldest civilizations, originated as a river-valley culture. Because of the Nile River's life-sustaining water, agricultural groups established small village settlements on its banks and organized tribal kingdoms. About 3000 BCE, these kingdoms were consolidated into a large empire, which became a highly centralized political colossus.

While Confucius did not speculate about life after death, the ancient Egyptians were intensely concerned with the question of immortality. Their religious beliefs affirmed the divine origin of the pharaoh, or emperor. The concept of being ruled by a god-king gave supernatural sanctions to Egypt's ruling elites.

An unchanging cosmos

The concept of a king-priest gave high status and power to the priestly elite. Seeking to maintain the status, the priests, as guardians of the official state culture, represented knowledge and values as reflections of an orderly, unchanging, and eternal cosmos. As would be the case throughout much of history, a very close relationship developed between religion and education, with priests supervising schools.

---

[9]U.S. Department of Education, Office of the Secretary, *No Child Left Behind*, 2001 (Washington D.C.: U.S. Department of Education, 2001), pp. 3, 8.

Religious and Secular Concerns

Educationally, the Egyptians were both worldly and otherworldly. Although preoccupied with the supernatural, they developed technologies to irrigate the Nile Valley and to design and build Egypt's massive pyramids and temples. To administer and defend their vast empire, they studied civil administration and military tactics. Their obsession with mummification led them to study medicine, anatomy, and embalming. The Egyptians developed hieroglyphic script, a writing system that enabled them to record their religious beliefs and history.

In societies where most of the people were illiterate, literacy abilities (reading and writing) were the valuable skills of the educated ruling classes. Scribes—individuals who knew how to read and write—were highly important in largely illiterate societies and often were teachers. The teaching of writing and reading became a central feature of schooling that has persisted through the centuries and has become the language arts in contemporary schools.

Temple and court schools

Egypt, like China, needed a large civil service to collect revenues and to administer and defend its empire. By 2700 BCE, the Egyptians had established an extensive system of temple and court schools to train scribes, many of whom were priests, in reading and writing. As part of the temple complex, schools exemplified the close relationship between formal education and religion.[10] After a primary education, a small number of boys were selected to prepare for their future professions. Special advanced schools prepared priests, government officials, and physicians.

Educating scribes

In the scribal schools, students learned to write the hieroglyphic script by copying documents on papyrus, sheets made from reeds growing along the Nile. Teachers dictated to students, who copied what they heard. Centuries before the invention of the printing press, the students were reproducing the dictated copy of the text. It was highly important that students listened carefully to the teacher and recorded his words exactly as he said them. The goal was to reproduce a correct, exact copy of a text and definitely not to interpret it, nor to create a new version. Often students would chant a short passage until they had memorized it thoroughly. Advanced students studied mathematics, astronomy, religion, poetry, literature, medicine, and architecture.[11]

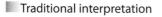 **Continuity & Change**

Egypt's rulers emphasized cultural continuity that maintained their privileged status and resisted change that might undermine it. The major purpose of Egyptian education was to transmit and reproduce the approved version of the cultural heritage that the religious and political elites had constructed. It also trained selected young Egyptian males in reading and writing, embalming, medicine, civil administration, and architecture.

Egypt's Historical Controversies

Traditional interpretation

Ancient Egypt's role in shaping Western civilization is controversial. In 332 BCE, Alexander the Great (336–323 BCE), the King of Macedon, conquered Persia, Mesopotamia, and Egypt.

 **Continuity & Change**

This conquest introduced Hellenistic civilization, which had incorporated Greek culture, to Egypt. Alexander's conquest brought Greek ideas to Egypt and Egyptian ideas to Greece. This cultural interface between Greece and Egypt caused change, which was exactly what the ancient Egyptians had sought to avoid.

How we interpret history is a source of power in the present. Here, we look at a controversy in interpreting Egypt's role in shaping Western civilization and education. According to conventional historical interpretation, ancient Egyptian civilization was a highly static despotism, and its major cultural legacy was its great architectural monuments. This interpretation identifies Greek culture, especially Athenian democracy, as

---

[10]For a thorough discussion of writing in Egyptian culture and education, see John Baines, *Visual and Written Culture in Ancient Egypt* (New York: Oxford University Press, 2007), pp. 117–140.
[11]For a discussion of science, medicine, and religion in ancient Egypt, see Moustafa Gadalla, *The Ancient Egyptian Culture Revealed* (Greensboro, NC: Tehuti Research Foundation, 2007).

the cradle of Western civilization, which includes American culture. (Greek culture and education are discussed later in the chapter.)

Bernal's theory

The historian Martin Bernal, challenging the traditional interpretation, argues that the ancient Greeks borrowed many of their concepts about government, philosophy, the arts, sciences, and medicine from ancient Egypt. Furthermore, the Egyptians, located in North Africa, were an African people, and the origins of Western culture were therefore African.[12] Though they recognize Egyptian and Greek interactions, Bernal's critics contend that he greatly overemphasizes Egypt's influence on ancient Greece.[13] While historians continue to debate the matter, tentative findings indicate that Egyptian–Greek contacts, particularly at Crete, introduced the Greeks to Egyptian knowledge and art.

This intriguing historical controversy has important educational significance. Whoever interprets the past gains the power of illuminating and shaping the present. In particular, the controversy relates to debates about Afrocentrism and an Afrocentric curriculum in schools. Did Western civilization originate in Africa or in Greece?

The Hebraic Educational Tradition

Monotheism

American education, like Western culture, is deeply rooted in the **Judeo-Christian tradition**. (The sections on the medieval and Reformation periods in this chapter discuss the Christian roots.) Here, we examine Hebraic or Judaic education, an ongoing religious and cultural tradition for the Jewish people and an important reference point for Christians and Muslims. All three religions—Judaism, Christianity, and Islam—are monotheistic in their belief in one God, a spiritual Creator, and in their reverence for a sacred book, the Torah, the Bible, or the Koran, whose contents were revealed by God to prophets.

---

[12]Martin Bernal, *Black Athena: The Afroasiatic Roots of Classical Civilization: The Fabrication of Ancient Greece 1785–1985* (New Brunswick, NJ: Rutgers University Press, 1987), pp. 2–3. The later Greek influence on Egyptian education is discussed in Raffaella Cribiore, *Gymnastics of the Mind: Greek Education in Hellenistic and Roman Egypt* (Princeton: Princeton University Press, 2005).
[13]For the ongoing controversy over ancient Egypt's possible influence on Greece, access: "Ancient Egypt-Mathematics and the Liberal Arts," at **http://math.truman.edu/~thammond/history/AncientEgypt.html.**

TIME LINE
Ancient Egypt

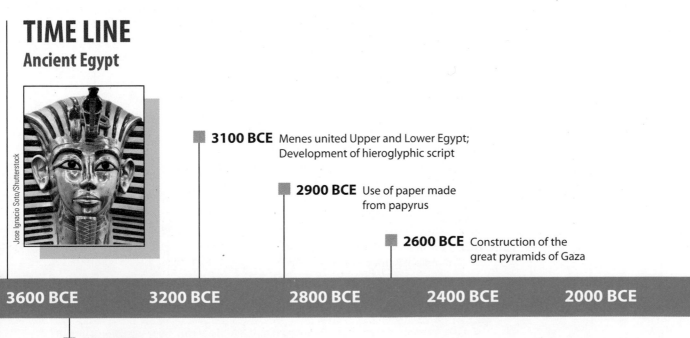

3100 BCE Menes united Upper and Lower Egypt; Development of hieroglyphic script

2900 BCE Use of paper made from papyrus

2600 BCE Construction of the great pyramids of Gaza

| 3600 BCE | 3200 BCE | 2800 BCE | 2400 BCE | 2000 BCE |

3500 BCE Settlements in Nile River Valley

Torah

Rabbinical schools

REFOCUS Think back to the Focus Questions at the beginning of this chapter. *Use these questions to construct your own history or autobiography of education.* Do you find emphasis on carefully listening to teachers, transmitting the cultural heritage, and instilling appropriate behavior among the purposes of contemporary American education? What is your opinion about religion's role in education? Why has the teaching of religion and religious observances been so controversial in American education? Refocus again on this question when you read Chapter 9, Legal Aspects of Education.

With their emphasis on reading and studying sacred scriptures, all three religions emphasize literacy to read the holy book, and education, to learn and apply its message to life.

In the Hebraic tradition, the Jewish people are specially chosen by God, who revealed the truth and the law to them. From these revelations came a holy covenant, a religiously based and sanctioned agreement, which bound the Jews to their Creator.[14] Moses, who led the Jewish people from bondage in Egypt to the Promised Land in Judea, received divine revelations on Mount Sinai. These revelations form an essential part of the **Torah**, the sacred scripture taught and studied by Jews from childhood on throughout their lives.[15] The written Torah includes the Five Books of Moses—Genesis, Exodus, Leviticus, Numbers, and Deuteronomy.

Judaic education aims at inculcating the young in their cultural tradition through a carefully designed process of transmitting religious beliefs and rituals from one generation to the next. It focuses on recitations and commentaries on the sacred texts and the study of laws and their moral and ethical prescriptions and proscriptions, which includes observing the commandments and properly following religious rituals and prayers.

Teaching and learning is seen as intrinsically valuable because it concerns God's covenant with the Jewish people and is also an instrument for shaping behavior according to religiously sanctioned group norms.[16] This covenantal learning is intergenerational and lifelong, beginning in childhood and continuing throughout adulthood.

For children, Judaism's basic educational purpose is to learn how to pray, to know and observe the commandments, and to identify with the Jewish people's special place in history. At first, as in most early societies, parents, responsible for their children's education, were the initial teachers. Parents, especially the father, taught the Torah and religious observances to their children. Children learned to honor their father and mother, as the commandments prescribed. As Jewish society became more settled and specialized, teachers (elders, priests, and scribes) who taught in more formal, school-like settings augmented, but did not replace, the parental role.

By the seventh century BCE, rabbis—men especially learned in scripture—emerged as teachers among the Jewish people in Israel and Babylonia.[17] In rabbinical schools, teaching methods emphasized careful listening to sacred readings by the rabbi and reading, memorization, and recitation. The purpose of learning to listen to the reading of a sacred text was to bring its message into the learner's mind. By listening, reading, and memorizing, students were expected to internalize and understand the lesson's meaning and message. To build group cohesion and identity, children listened to stories about important events in the history of the Hebrew people—such as their exodus from Egypt. Rituals were taught that commemorated these events.

---

[14]Hanan A. Alexander and Shmuel Glick, "The Judaic Tradition," in Randall Curren, ed., *A Companion to the Philosophy of Education* (Malden, MA: Blackwell Publishing, 2006), pp. 33–49.
[15]Ibid., p. 13.
[16]Ibid., p. 33.
[17]Ibid., pp. 34–35.

1650 BCE Scribes begin recording *Book of the Dead*

1300 BCE Construction of the temple at Karnak

332 BCE Alexander the Great conquers Egypt

| 1600 BCE | 1200 BCE | 800 BCE | 400 BCE | 0 |

The Jews, like the Egyptians, wanted to transmit religious beliefs to the young to perpetuate them. This kind of education sought to construct and perpetuate the ideal of being a special people of God in the young.

The Hebraic tradition brought the concept of monotheism into Arabic and Western cultures. Jesus Christ, whom Christians believe is the son of God, was raised in the Judaic culture. Jews who converted to Christianity, such as Saint Paul, carried Christianity throughout the Roman Empire. Muslims revere Mohammed, who was familiar with both Judaism and Christianity, as the prophet of Islam. As religions of the book, all three religious traditions invested in and influenced education.

Education in Ancient Greek and Roman Civilizations

The educational history of ancient Greece and Rome illuminates the origins of Western culture and education. Historically, Western culture is defined as that shaped by Europe and the European settlement of North and South America. A contemporary controversy is whether American education should transmit a Western cultural core or a multicultural one that includes Africa and Asia.

The Greeks and Romans sought to answer such persistent educational questions as: What is true, good, and beautiful? What models should education use in preparing good citizens? How should education respond to social, economic, and political change?

Homeric education

Generations have thrilled to the dramatic suspense of Homer's epic poems, the *Iliad* and the *Odyssey*. Appearing about 1200 BCE, Homer's epics helped Greeks define themselves and their culture. Like ritual ceremonies in preliterate societies, Homer's dramatic portrayal of the Greek warriors' battles against the Trojans served important educational purposes: (1) it preserved Greek culture by transmitting it from adults to the young; (2) it cultivated Greek cultural identity based on mythic and historical origins; and (3) it shaped the civic and ethical character of the young.[18] Agamemnon, Ulysses, Achilles,

---

[18]Louis Goldman, "Homer, Literacy, and Education," *Educational Theory* (Fall 1989), pp. 391–400. Also, see Lillian E. Doherty, ed., *Homer's Odyssey (Oxford Readings in Classical Studies)* (New York: Oxford University Press, 2009). For a thorough discussion of Greek culture, access Alexander Makedon, *In Search of Excellence: Historical Roots of Greek Culture* (Chicago State University) at **http://alexandermakedon.com/articles/articles.html**.

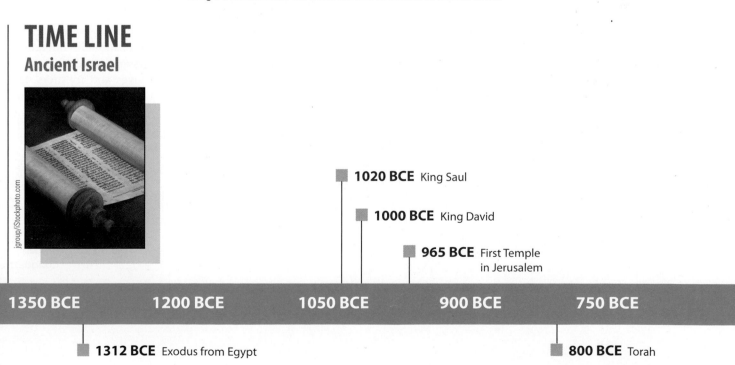

TIME LINE
Ancient Israel

jgroup/iStockphoto.com

1020 BCE King Saul

1000 BCE King David

965 BCE First Temple in Jerusalem

1350 BCE	1200 BCE	1050 BCE	900 BCE	750 BCE

1312 BCE Exodus from Egypt

800 BCE Torah

and other warriors dramatically personified life's heroic dimensions. Using these heroes as role models, young Greeks learned moral and ethical values, the behaviors expected of warrior-knights, and the character flaws that led to one's downfall.[19]

Citizenship education

Ancient Greece illuminates education's role in political socialization, preparing good citizens. Just as Americans, including some social-studies educators, often disagree on how to educate good citizens, the Greeks, too, debated the issue. Unlike the centralized Chinese and Egyptian empires, ancient Greece was divided into small and often competing city-states that, like Athens and Sparta, defined citizenship and civic responsibilities and rights differently. Athens, a democracy, emphasized its citizens' public responsibility in decision making. Sparta, Athens's chief rival, was an authoritarian military dictatorship whose citizens followed orders from their leaders.[20] While Athens had a variety of educational arrangements, Sparta had a state-controlled educational system whose purpose was to train all able-bodied males to be courageous soldiers and to prepare women to be the mothers and wives of soldiers.

Enculturation and formal education

The Greeks understood the importance of interrelating enculturation—immersion and participation in the city-state's total culture—with formal education. Through enculturation, Greek youths learned to identify with and to participate in their society and culture. Formal education, in turn, provided the skills and knowledge needed for personal development and citizenship. For example, the Athenians believed that a free man needed a liberal education to fulfill his potentialities as a person and citizen.[21]

The role of slaves

The Greek city-states used slave laborers to support their economies. The majority of slaves, including women and children, had been captured in war or were judicially sentenced to servitude. Although a few educated slaves tutored wealthy children in Athens, most slaves were domestic, agricultural, or commercial workers. While the Athenians developed the concept of a liberal education, they denied it to their slaves.

Education of women

In male-dominated Greek society, only a minority of exceptional women were formally educated. In Athens, where women had severely limited legal and economic rights, few attended schools. More fortunate young women were taught at home by tutors. Others, such as priestesses of cults, learned religious rituals at temple schools. In contrast to the sequestered Athenian women, Sparta's young women enjoyed a more open lifestyle and education. Sparta's state-controlled education system emphasized military and athletic training. Young Spartan women received the physical and gymnastic training that prepared them to be healthy mothers of future Spartan soldiers.

The life and career of the poet Sappho (630–572 BCE) sharply contrasted with the sequestered education of most Greek women. An early proponent of women's liberation, Sappho believed women should be educated for their own personal self-development rather than for their traditionally ascribed roles as future wives and mothers. She founded a women's school in Mytilene, on the island of Lesbos, where she taught

---

[19]Robert Holmes Beck, "The Iliad: Principles and Lessons," *Educational Theory* (Spring 1986), pp. 179–195. Also, see Douglas L. Cairns, ed., *Homer's Iliad (Oxford Readings in Philosophy)* (New York: Oxford University Press, 2002).
[20]Mogens Herman Hansen, *Polis: An Introduction to the Greek City State* (New York: Oxford University Press, 2006), pp. 33–37.
[21]Kevin Robb, *Literacy and Paideia in Ancient Greece* (New York: Oxford University Press, 1994).

586 BCE Babylonian Captivity

63 BCE Roman Conquest

| 600 BCE | 450 BCE | 300 BCE | 150 BCE | 0 |

young aristocratic women the cult rituals related to worship of Aphrodite, as well as cultural and decorative arts and skills, such as singing, dancing, playing the lyre, writing poetry, and etiquette.[22]

The Sophists

Continuity & Change

In the fifth century BCE, new wealth brought to Athens by colonial expansion generated social and educational change. Challenging the established aristocrats, the rising commercial class wanted a new kind of education that would prepare them to exercise political power. The **Sophists**, a traveling group of educators, designed a new method of teaching that responded to this socioeconomic change. Their method differed from the older Homeric education that relied on stories and models from the past and from the philosophical emphasis on the metaphysical search for truth.

The Sophists promised to create a popular public image for their students that would lead them to status and power. The way to power, the Sophists said, came from the ability to speak effectively and persuasively. Effective public speaking, or oratory, was important in Athens, where it could be used to persuade the assembly and courts in one's favor.[23]

Grammar, logic, and rhetoric

For the Sophists, the purpose of education was to develop their students' communication skills so they could become successful advocates and legislators. The Sophists' most important subjects were logic, grammar, and rhetoric, which developed into the liberal arts. Logic, the rules of correct argument, trained students to organize their presentations clearly, and grammar developed their powers of using language effectively. **Rhetoric**, the study of public speaking, was especially important for future orators.

Knowledge as power

The Sophists claimed they could educate their students to win public debates by teaching them how to (1) use crowd psychology to appeal emotionally to an audience; (2) organize a persuasive and convincing argument; and (3) be skillful public speakers who know what words, examples, and lines of reasoning to use to win a debate or legal trial.

If they were alive today, the Sophists would probably still argue that their educational method gives people what they want—the ability to organize ideas and to present them so forcefully that an audience is persuaded to accept their claims. Critics of the Sophists, such as Socrates and Plato, however, accused them of teaching students to argue for any side of an issue to win the case rather than being committed to the truth. The Sophists were like modern image makers who use the media to package political candidates and celebrities or to sell products to consumers. Although today's political debates take place on television rather than in the Athenian town center, the Sophists would argue that their techniques remain useful. It is still important to know one's audience, to appeal to their needs, and to use skilled persuasion to convince them. They would consider modern focus groups, public opinion polls, and negative political advertising to be useful and persuasive tools.

Protagoras's method

Protagoras (485–414 BCE), a prominent Sophist, devised a highly effective five-step teaching strategy.[24] He (1) delivered an outstanding speech so students knew their teacher could actually do what he taught and had a model to imitate. Then Protagoras had the students (2) analyze the speeches of famous orators to enlarge their repertoire of exemplary speaking styles; (3) study the key subjects of logic, grammar, and rhetoric; and (4) deliver practice orations, which he assessed to provide feedback to students. Finally, (5) the student orators delivered public speeches. Protagoras's method resembles present-day preservice teacher-education programs, in which prospective teachers

---

[22]For a biographical sketch of Sappho and a reading of "The Songs of Sappho," see Madonna M. Murphy, *The History and Philosophy of Education: Voices of Educational Pioneers* (Upper Saddle River, NJ: Pearson/Merrill/Prentice Hall, 2006), pp. 17–23. Also, see Jim Powell, *The Poetry of Sappho* (New York: Oxford University Press, 2007).
[23]For "The Sophists," access **www.pbs.org/empires/thegreeks/background/30_p1.html**.
[24]Edward Schiappa, *Protagoras and Logos: A Study in Greek Philosophy and Rhetoric* (Columbia: University of South Carolina Press, 2003).

▶ ‖   TEACHSOURCE VIDEO ACTIVITY

Digital Storytelling in the High School Classroom

Go to the Education CourseMate website to access the video entitled, "Digital Story telling in the High School Classroom," and then consider the connection to the Sophists. Although the video is about high school students using technology to organize a speech, it also deals with how a speech should be organized.

① If they were alive today, do you think the Sophists would make a similar use of technology to organize a presentation?

② Is content or method being emphasized in the case?

③ What advice would the Sophists give to the students to make their presentation more effective?

take courses in the liberal arts and professional education, practice a variety of teaching methods, and engage in clinical experience and student teaching supervised by an experienced cooperating teacher.

▌ **Enduring truth or relativism?**

The Sophists' approach to education raised serious controversies that are still with us today. The Sophists were ethical relativists, arguing that what we need to know depends on the circumstances in which we live. In many respects, the Sophists were the precursors of the cultural relativism found in pragmatism, postmodernism, and critical theory, discussed in Chapter 6, Philosophical Roots of Education. Socrates, Plato, and Aristotle all challenged the Sophists' relativism and insisted on the existence of enduring universal truths that all people must know. Isocrates, a teacher of oratory, tried to resolve the controversy by saying that students and citizens needed to know not only what is true but also how to apply it practically to the situations in which they live.

Socrates: Education by Self-Examination

Unlike the Sophists, who claimed that knowledge depends on the situations in which people use it, Socrates (469–399 BCE) believed knowledge is based on what is true universally—at all places and times.[25] Socrates is important in educational history because he firmly defended the academic freedom to think, question, and teach. He was also significant as the teacher of Plato, who later systematized many of Socrates' ideas into a coherent philosophy.[26]

▌ **Moral excellence**

Socrates stressed the ethical principles that a person should strive for moral excellence, live wisely, and act rationally. Moral excellence, Socrates believed, is far superior to the Sophists' technical training.

▌ **Role of the Socratic teacher**

Socrates' concept of the teacher differed from that of the Sophists. He did not believe that knowledge or wisdom could be transmitted from a teacher to a student because he believed the concepts of true knowledge were present, but buried, within the person's mind. A truly liberal education would stimulate learners to discover ideas by bringing to consciousness the truth that is latent in their minds.

▌ **Self-examination, dialogue, and the Socratic method**

Socrates encouraged students to use critical self-examination and reflection to find and bring to consciousness the universal truth present in each person's mind. As a teacher, Socrates asked leading questions that stimulated students to think deeply about and reflect on the meaning of life, truth, and justice. In answering these questions,

---

[25]For Socrates as philosopher and educator, see Hope May, *On Socrates* (Belmont, CA: Wadsworth/Thomson Learning, 2000).
[26]Gary Alan Scott, *Plato's Socrates as Educator* (Albany: State University of New York Press, 2000), pp. 1–12.

students engaged in rigorous discussion, or dialogue, in which they clarified, criticized, and reconstructed their basic concepts.

Plato illustrates how Socrates used the Socratic method in *Meno,* a dialogue between Socrates and Meno, a student of Gorgias and a leading Sophist. Guided by Socrates' questioning, Meno, in answering questions about virtue, identifies instances of particular kinds of virtue such as that displayed by the judicious legislator, the caring and nurturing mother, and the brave soldier. Through further questioning, Socrates leads Meno to recognize that these instances of particular virtue are really manifestations of a more general and unifying idea—that of universal form or idea of virtue. This rigorous dialogue approach, still known as the **Socratic method**, is challenging for both teachers and students.[27]

Frequenting the agora, Athens's central area, Socrates attracted a group of young men who joined him in critically examining all kinds of issues—religious, political, moral, and aesthetic. But as a social critic, Socrates made powerful enemies. Then, as now, some people, including those in high places, feared that critical thinking would challenge the status quo, and lead to unrest and their fall from power. In 399 BCE, Socrates was found guilty of charges of impiety to the gods and corrupting Athenian youth. Refusing to flee, he accepted his sentence of death.

Plato: Universal and Eternal Truths and Values

Reality as universal, eternal ideas

Socrates' pupil Plato (427–346 BCE) followed his mentor's educational path. Plato founded the Academy, a philosophical school, in 387 BCE. He wrote philosophical dialogues about truth, virtue, and justice, as well as the *Republic* and the *Laws,* treatises on politics, law, and education.[28] Plato's philosophy was an early form of idealism, which is discussed in Chapter 6, Philosophical Roots of Education.

Rejecting the Sophists' relativism, Plato argued that reality exists in an unchanging world of perfect ideas—universal concepts such as truth, goodness, justice, and beauty. Individual instances of these concepts, as they appear to our senses, are but imperfect representations of the universal and eternal concepts that reside in an absolute idea, the Form of the Good.

Truth as intellectual illumination

Plato's "Allegory of the Cave" illustrated his concept of finding, or being directed, to truth in the Form of the Good. Plato depicted prisoners in a dark cave who were chained so that they could see in only one direction. With a fire behind them, they saw only the shadows of objects that are carried by others before the flames. When one prisoner is freed, he makes his way to the mouth of the cave. Ascending from the dark world of shadows, he sees the real world illuminated by the sun. When he reenters the cave to tell the prisoners what he has seen, they scoff at him in disbelief. In the Allegory, the sun represents the Form of the Good, the source of all that is bright and beautiful and good and true. The difficult process of turning away from shadows to truth represents the process of self-examination and reflection found in the Socratic method.

Reminiscence

Plato's theory of knowledge is called **reminiscence**, a process by which individuals recall the ideas present but latent in their minds. Reminiscence implies that the human soul, before birth, existed in a spiritual world of pure ideas. At birth, these *innate* ideas are repressed within one's subconscious mind. For Plato, learning means that one rediscovers or recollects these perfect ideas.[29]

Universalism versus relativism

Proponents of universal truth and values such as Plato assert that genuine knowledge is universal, intellectual, changeless, and eternal, rather than relative and sensory. Because what is true is always true, education should also be universal and unchanging. The debate over this idea is presented in the Taking Issue box.

---

[27]Rene Saron and Barbara Neisser, eds., *Enquiring Minds: Socratic Dialogue in Education* (Oak Hill, Stratfordshire, UK: Trentham Book Publishers, 2004). Matt Copeland, *Socratic Circles: Fostering Critical and Creative Thinking in Middle and High School* (Portland, ME: Stenhouse Publishers, 2005).
[28]Devin Stauffer, *Plato's Introduction to the Question of Justice* (Albany: State University of New York Press, 2001).
[29]Gerald L. Gutek, *Historical and Philosophical Foundations of Education: A Biographical Introduction* (Columbus, OH: Merrill/Prentice Hall, 2011), pp. 37–42.

TAKING ISSUE

Read the brief introduction below, as well as the Question and the pros and cons list that follows. Then, answer the question using *your* own words and position.

Values in Education?

The ancient Greeks debated whether education should reflect universal values that were valid at all times and in all places or culturally relative values held by different peoples living at particular places and times. Socrates and Plato, who argued that truth was unchanging, debated this issue with the Sophists, who claimed that education was relative to time and circumstances. There are heated debates in the United States between those who want schools to instill universal moral values and by others who want students to clarify their values.

Question

Should we base moral education on universal values? (Think about this question as you read the PRO and CON arguments listed here. What is *your* take on this issue?)

Arguments PRO

1. Values, like truth, are universal and timeless. What is valuable is valid in all places and at all times. Public opinion polls do not make, nor change, what is good and beautiful.

2. Although we are members of different races and ethnic and language groups, we are all members of the same human family and have universal human rights.

3. Education should search for the answer to the enduring question, raised by Socrates and Plato: What is true, good, and beautiful?

4. Schools should emphasize the universal truths and values found in religion, philosophy, mathematics, literature, and science that transcend cultural differences and political boundaries.

Arguments CON

1. Values are tentative statements about what is right or wrong that are relative to various groups living in particular places at different times. What is valuable is determined by the culture or different groups in a particular society.

2. Because society is relative and changing, education needs to be flexible to adapt to social, economic, political, and technological change.

3. Education is a pragmatic means of personal and social adaptation. It should emphasize new ways of learning to prepare people to be efficient users of new technologies.

4. Schooling, based on people's needs, will differ from culture to culture and from time to time. That is why the constructivist approach and multicultural education is so useful in today's schools.

Question Reprise: What Is Your Stand?

Reflect again on the following question by explaining *your* stand about this issue. Should we base moral education on universal values?

The Republic

Plato's Ideal Society   **Plato's Republic** projected a plan for a perfect society ruled by an intellectual elite of philosopher-kings. Although Plato's utopian state was never implemented, his ideas are worth studying as an idealized version of a certain kind of society and education.[30]

The Republic's citizens were organized into three classes: (1) the philosopher-kings, or intellectual rulers; (2) the auxiliaries, or military defenders; and (3) the workers, who produced goods and provided services. An individual's placement in a particular class was determined by an assessment of her or his intellectual ability. Similar to those who argue, today, that test results ought to determine the kind of education that a person

---

[30]Plato, *Republic* (London: Folio Society, 2003); also see *Selected Dialogues of Plato:* The Benjamin Jowett Translation (New York: Modern Library, 2001).

should receive, the educators in Plato's Republic sorted people into groups based on their perceived intellectual ability and educated or trained them accordingly. In contrast, the Sophists argued that their methods made it possible to teach anyone who studied with them.

Education corresponding to social role

Once assigned to a class, individuals in the Republic would receive the education or training needed to perform their specific social, political, and economic functions. The philosopher-kings, as the most able intellectuals, identified academically gifted children and prepared them to be the Republic's future leaders. The second class, the warriors, considered more courageous than intellectual, would be trained in the military strategy and tactics needed to defend the Republic against its enemies. The third and largest class, the workers, who had greater physical than intellectual or military potentialities, would be trained vocationally as farmers, fishermen, and craftsmen. Plato believed that this system of educational tracking contributed to social justice in that the Republic's citizens were doing what was appropriate for them. Modern-day critics of tracking, or the homogenous grouping of students in schools, argue that screening devices, such as Plato's, reproduce the existing class situation rather than encouraging social mobility.

Women's education

Unlike most Athenian males, Plato did not believe than men were intellectually superior to women. Both men and women should receive the education that was appropriate to their intellectual abilities.[31] Women who possessed high-level cognitive powers could become philosopher-queens. Like men, women would receive the education or training appropriate to their abilities and their destined occupations.

State-run nurseries

Plato's Curriculum   In the Republic, Plato sought to design a society that would function like a perfect mechanism, without being disrupted by change. Like Confucius, he designed education for a hierarchical rather than an egalitarian society. Fearing that parents would pass on their ignorance and prejudices to their children, Plato wanted early childhood specialists to rear young children. Children, separated from their parents, would live in state nurseries to learn positive social and moral predispositions that inclined them to living and working in the Republic.

Plato's basic curriculum

From ages six to eighteen, children and adolescents attended state-supervised schools to study reading and writing, literature, arithmetic, choral singing, dancing, and gymnastics. After mastering reading and writing, students would read the approved classics. Plato, who believed in censorship, thought that young people should read only officially selected and approved poems and stories that epitomized truthfulness, obedience to authorities, courage, and control of emotions. After mastering basic mathematics, students studied geometry and astronomy, which cultivated higher-level abstract thinking. Gymnastics, useful for military training, included fencing, archery, javelin throwing, and horseback riding, which developed physical coordination and dexterity.

Higher education

From ages eighteen to twenty, students pursued intensive physical and military training. At twenty, the future philosopher-kings would be selected for ten years of additional higher education in more abstract and advanced mathematics, geometry, astronomy, music, and science. At age thirty, the less intellectually able in this group would become civil servants; the most intellectually gifted would continue their study of metaphysics, the philosophical search for truth. When their studies were completed, the philosopher-kings would rule the Republic. At age fifty, the philosopher-kings would become the Republic's elder statesmen.

Aristotle: Cultivation of Rationality

Plato's student Aristotle (384–322 BCE), the tutor of Alexander the Great, founded the Lyceum, an Athenian philosophical school. He wrote extensively on physics,

[31]Robert S. Brumbaugh, "Plato's Ideal Curriculum and Contemporary Philosophy of Education," *Educational Theory* (Spring 1987), pp. 169–177. Also, see Robbin Barrow, *Routledge Library Editions: Education Mini-Set K Philosophy of Education: Plato and Education* (New York and London: Routledge, 2012).

astronomy, zoology, botany, logic, ethics, and metaphysics. His *Nicomachean Ethics* and *Politics* examined education in relation to society and government.[32] Aristotle's *Ethics* emphasized leading an integrated and harmonious life that, avoiding extremes, took a moderate course.

An objective reality

Unlike his mentor, Plato, who believed that reality exists in the realm of pure ideas, Aristotle held that reality exists objectively, that is, outside of our minds. Whereas Plato founded philosophical idealism, Aristotle established realism. While Aristotle's realism sought to prepare the learner to deal with the actual problems of living, Plato's idealism encouraged the learner to aim for a better and higher world above the senses. (Both idealism and realism are discussed in Chapter 6, Philosophical Roots of Education.)

For Aristotle, objects exist outside of our minds but he believed that, by sensation and abstraction, we can acquire knowledge about them. Aristotle believed that humans possess intellect—the power to reason. As rational beings, they have the potential to know and follow the natural laws governing the universe.

Sensation as the root of knowledge

For Aristotle, knowing begins with one's sensation of objects in the environment. By abstracting an object's essentials from this sensory information, one forms a general concept about the object. The Aristotelian emphasis on sensory experience as the beginning of knowing and of instruction was later stressed by eighteenth- and nineteenth-century educators such as Pestalozzi.

Education as cultivation of rationality

Aristotle on Education   In his *Politics*, Aristotle argues that the good, or socially just, community depends on its citizens' rationality. Education's purpose is to cultivate liberally educated, rational people who can use their reason to make decisions to govern society. Aristotle was a proponent of liberal arts and science education. While he believed the liberal arts enlarged a person's knowledge and choices, Aristotle saw vocational training, though needed by some individuals, as limited to learning specific skills. Contemporary liberal arts and career educators often debate the same issues that concerned Aristotle and other Greek philosophers. As a teacher, you may encounter similar issues when students ask you why they should learn something they believe they will never use. What is your rationale for teaching certain skills and subjects but not others? How do we know what knowledge and skills we will use in the future?

Aristotle's curriculum

Aristotle was a proponent of compulsory schooling. Early childhood education included play, physical activities, music, and heroic and moral stories. Children from ages seven to fourteen learned reading, writing, arithmetic, and proper moral habits that would prepare them for the later study of the liberal arts and sciences. Their curriculum also included gymnastics and music to develop physical dexterity and emotional sensitivity. From age fifteen through twenty-one, youths were to study the liberal arts and sciences—mathematics, geometry, astronomy, grammar, literature, poetry, rhetoric, ethics, and politics. At age twenty-one, students would proceed to more advanced subjects, such as physics, cosmology, biology, psychology, logic, and metaphysics. Aristotle, like Plato, endorsed the doctrine of education as preparation in that each lower stage of schooling was to prepare students for the next higher stage. Later, Dewey and other progressives attacked the doctrine of education as preparation, arguing that students should pursue their interests and solve their immediate problems. Do you think the purpose of education is to prepare for future studies or to solve the problems in one's immediate life?

Limited roles for women

Believing women were intellectually inferior to men, Aristotle was concerned only with male education. Girls were to be trained to perform the gender-specific household and child-rearing duties appropriate for their future roles as wives and mothers.

Knowledge as concepts based on objects

Aristotle's Theory of Knowledge   Aristotle, a realist, differs from Plato, an idealist, in that knowledge arises from our knowing about objects rather than from ideas preexisting in the mind. Knowledge, in the school curriculum, focuses on classifying objects

---

[32]Alexander Moseley, *Aristotle (Continuum Library of Educational Thought)* (London: Continuum, 2010). Christopher Rowe and Sarah Brodie, *Aristotle: Nicomachean Ethics* (Oxford, UK: Oxford University Press, 2002).

into subjects. Early on, children were to learn that some things are like each other and other things are not like each other. Objects can be classified into minerals, plants, and animals. These three simple but basic categories lead to more specific subdivisions. For example, we can study minerals in the subjects of mineralogy and geology; plants in the subjects of botany and horticulture; animals in the subjects of zoology, ichthyology; and people in the subjects of anthropology, history, literature, and political science. Through the liberal arts and sciences, we can access and inform ourselves about these subjects. We can use this organized subject matter knowledge to make our decisions.

■ Aristotle's lasting influence

An Aristotelian school's primary purpose is to develop each student's rationality. As academic institutions, schools should offer a prescribed subject-matter curriculum based on academic scholarly and scientific disciplines. In their preservice preparations, teachers need to acquire expert knowledge of their subjects and learn the methods needed to motivate students and transmit this knowledge to them. Aristotle's philosophy has had great significance in Western education. Along with Christian doctrine, it became a foundation of medieval scholastic education, discussed later in this chapter, and of realism and perennialism, discussed in Chapter 6, Philosophical Roots of Education.

Isocrates: Oratory and Rhetoric

The Greek rhetorician Isocrates (436–388 BCE) is significant for his well-constructed educational theory, which, taking a middle course between the Sophists and Plato, emphasized both knowledge and rhetorical skills.[33]

■ Emphasis on rhetoric

Isocrates identified education's primary purpose as preparing clear-thinking, rational, truthful, and honest statesmen. He held that rhetoric, defined as the rational expression of thought, was crucial in educating leaders for the good of society. Rhetorical education should combine the arts and sciences with effective communication skills. Opposing the Sophists' emphasis on public relations skills and manipulating an audience, Isocrates saw the purpose of rhetoric as arguing for just policies that truly advanced society's welfare. Isocrates' students, who attended his school for four years, studied rhetoric, political philosophy, history, and ethics. They analyzed and imitated model orations and practiced

[33]Ekaterina V. Haskins, *Logos and Power in Isocrates and Aristotle* (Columbia: University of South Carolina Press, 2004). Also, see Gerald L. Gutek, *A History of the Western Educational Experience* (Prospect Heights, IL: Waveland Press, 1995), pp. 52–54.

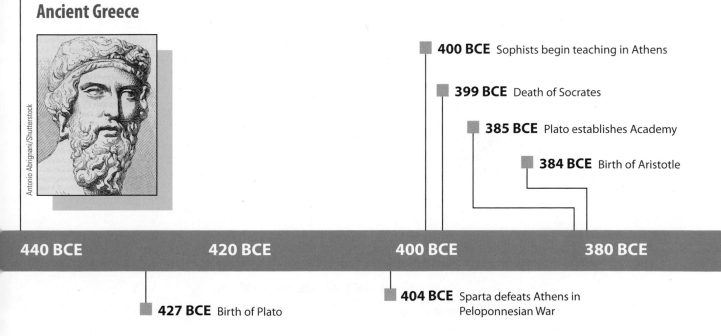

TIME LINE
Ancient Greece

Antonio Abrignani/Shutterstock

■ **400 BCE** Sophists begin teaching in Athens

■ **399 BCE** Death of Socrates

■ **385 BCE** Plato establishes Academy

■ **384 BCE** Birth of Aristotle

440 BCE   **420 BCE**   **400 BCE**   **380 BCE**

■ **427 BCE** Birth of Plato

■ **404 BCE** Sparta defeats Athens in Peloponnesian War

public speaking. Isocrates believed that he needed to serve as mentor to his students by demonstrating his command of knowledge, speaking skills, and ethical conduct.

Although Isocrates opposed the Sophists' opportunism, he also rejected Plato's emphasis on speculative theory. For Isocrates, education contributed to the development of public policy. Isocrates influenced the rhetorical tradition in Western education, especially the Roman educational theorist Quintilian.

The transmission of the philosophies of Plato, Aristotle, and Isocrates to Rome and then to Western culture illustrates how educational theories and practices are transferred from their place and time of origin to other places and historic periods.

Education in Ancient Rome

While Greek culture and education were developing in the eastern Mediterranean, the Romans were consolidating their political position on the Italian peninsula and then conquering the entire Mediterranean area. As Rome grew from a small republic to a great empire, Romans were preoccupied with war and politics. After they became an imperial power, they concentrated on the administration, law, and diplomacy needed to maintain their empire. Whereas the Greeks debated philosophical issues, the Romans concentrated on educating practical politicians, competent administrators, and skilled generals.

Roman law, originating with the Twelve Tables, developed into an extensive legal system designed to settle disputes over property rights and ownership, and it served as the foundation for later Western law. Highly skilled in architecture and engineering, the Romans constructed an extensive network of roads that facilitated trade and the rapid movement of their military legions throughout the empire. They built a system of aqueducts that carried fresh water from the mountains to Rome and the other cities. They developed architectural designs that used arches and columns to support massive temples and public buildings.

As in ancient Greece, only a minority of Romans were formally educated and literate. Schools were private and attended only by males who could pay tuition. Whereas upper-class girls often learned to read and write at home or were taught by tutors, boys from these families attended a *ludus*, a primary school, and then secondary schools taught by Latin and Greek grammar teachers.[34] Boys were escorted to these schools by educated Greek slaves, called *pedagogues*, from which the word *pedagogy*, meaning the art of instruction, is derived.

Rome's educational ideal was exemplified in the orator. The ideal Roman orator was the broadly and liberally educated man of public life—the senator, lawyer, teacher, civil servant, and politician. To examine the Roman ideal of oratory, we turn to Quintilian.

Quintilian: Master of Oratory   Marcus Fabius Quintilianus (35–95 CE), or Quintilian, was one of imperial Rome's most highly recognized rhetoricians.[35] The emperor appointed him to the first chair of Latin rhetoric.

Balancing Plato and the Sophists

Access to education

Ideal of the orator

Instruction based on stages of growth

[34]Robin Barrow, *Greek and Roman Education* (London: Duckworth Publishers, 2011). Also, see Iain Mcdougal, J. C. Yardley, and Mark Joyal, *Greek and Roman Education: A Sourcebook* (New York and London: Routledge, 2008).
[35]For a biographical sketch and an excerpt from Quintilian's *Institutio Oratoria*, see Madonna M. Murphy, *The History and Philosophy of Education: Voices of Educational Pioneers* (Upper Saddle River, NJ: Pearson/Merrill/Prentice Hall, 2006), pp. 59–66.

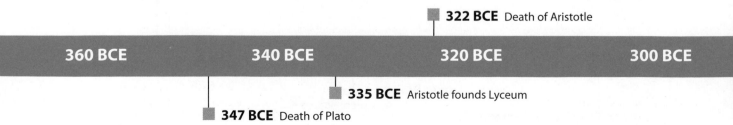

322 BCE Death of Aristotle

360 BCE   **340 BCE**   **320 BCE**   **300 BCE**

335 BCE Aristotle founds Lyceum

347 BCE Death of Plato

Quintilian's *Institutio Oratoria,* a systematic educational treatise, discussed (1) the education preparatory to studying rhetoric, (2) rhetorical and educational theory, and (3) the practice of public speaking or declamation. Quintilian emphasized the need to base instruction on the learner's readiness and stages of development. Anticipating the modern teacher's preservice preparation, he recognized the importance of students' individual differences, advised that instruction be appropriate to their readiness and abilities, and urged that teachers motivate students by making lessons interesting and engaging.

Quintilian developed an early version of stage-based learning that corresponded to the patterns of human development. He recognized the importance of early childhood in shaping the patterns of adult behavior. For the first stage, from birth until age seven, when children impulsively seek to satisfy their immediate needs and desires, he advised parents to select well-trained and well-spoken nurses, pedagogues, and companions for their children.

Reading and writing

In Quintilian's second stage of education, from seven to fourteen, the boy should learn from sense experiences, form clear ideas, and train his memory. He now learned to write the languages that he already spoke. The primary teacher, or *litterator,* who taught reading and writing in the ludus, must demonstrate teaching competence and ethical character. Instruction in reading and writing should be slow and thorough, with children learning the alphabet by tracing ivory letters. Like the twentieth-century educator, Maria Montessori, Quintilian advised that children learn to write by tracing the letters' outlines. Anticipating modern education, he urged that the school day include breaks for games and recreation so students could renew their energy.

Study of liberal arts

For the third stage of education, from fourteen to seventeen, Quintilian emphasized the liberal arts. He was a proponent of Greek and Latin bilingual and bicultural education. Students studied grammar, literature, history, and mythology in both the Greek and Latin languages. They also studied music, geometry, astronomy, and gymnastics.

Rhetorical studies

Prospective orators undertook rhetorical studies, the fourth stage, from ages seventeen to twenty-one. Rhetorical studies included drama, poetry, law, philosophy, public speaking, declamation, and debate.[36] Declamations—systematic speaking exercises—were especially

[36]For a hypertextual edition of Quintilian's *Institutes of Oratory,* visit **http://honeyl.public.iastate.edu/quintilian/index.html**.

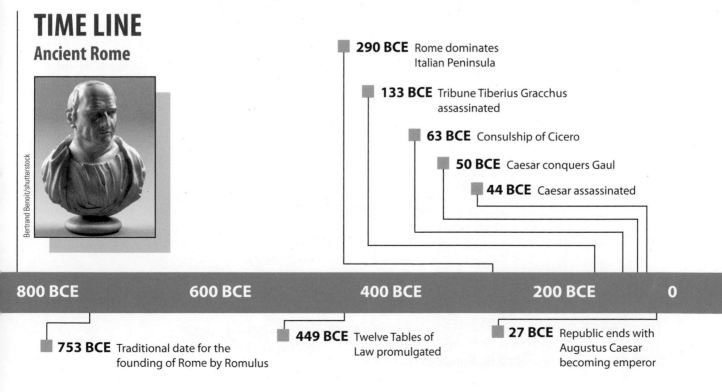

TIME LINE
Ancient Rome

290 BCE Rome dominates Italian Peninsula
133 BCE Tribune Tiberius Gracchus assassinated
63 BCE Consulship of Cicero
50 BCE Caesar conquers Gaul
44 BCE Caesar assassinated

800 BCE   600 BCE   400 BCE   200 BCE   0

753 BCE Traditional date for the founding of Rome by Romulus
449 BCE Twelve Tables of Law promulgated
27 BCE Republic ends with Augustus Caesar becoming emperor

important. When Quintilian assessed a student to be ready for public speaking, the novice orator spoke to an audience in the forum and then returned to the master rhetorician for expert criticism. The teacher corrected the student's mistakes with a sense of authority but also with patience, tact, and consideration. Quintilian's program of rhetorical studies resembled contemporary preservice teacher education. The practice oration was like supervised student teaching. The supervisor's critique of the beginning teacher's classroom skills resembles the master rhetorician's critique of the novice orator's speaking abilities.

Greek and Roman Contributions to Western Education

 Liberal arts

REFOCUS Think back to the Focus Questions at the beginning of this chapter. *Use these questions to construct your own history or autobiography of education.* For example, has your educational experience been speculative and abstract like the Greeks, or has it been practical and applied in the Roman sense? Has your education's purpose been to prepare you for the next phase of schooling, or did it help you deal with the problems you face in daily life?

Western culture inherited a rich educational legacy from ancient Greece and Rome. Believing it possible to cultivate human excellence, the Greeks and Romans gave education an important role in promoting a society's political well-being. Some Greco-Roman educational practices, however, including the distinction between liberal education and vocational training, have led to curricular controversies lasting throughout Western educational history.

Many ideas originated by the Greeks and Romans influenced Arab scholars, who preserved and interpreted them. As Europeans encountered Arabic scholarship, these ideas were transmitted back to European culture and later to American culture.

Islam, Arabic Learning, and Education

Mohammed

The Koran

Islamic civilization, originating with the Arabs, became a global cultural and educational force through its ability to absorb, reinterpret, and transmit knowledge from one world region to another.[37] Islamic culture originated with Mohammed (569–632), an Arab religious reformer and proselytizer, who is revered by his followers as the last and most important of God's prophets. Mohammed began his religious mission in Arabia, in Mecca, in 610, where he preached the need for faith, prayer, repentance, and morality. He incorporated his beliefs into **Islam**, a new religion, with a sacred book, the **Koran**, or Qur'an. Like Judaism and Christianity, Islam, a monotheistic religion, affirms the existence of one God, the Creator of the universe.

[37]Adam J. Silverstein, *Islamic History: A Very Short Introduction* (New York: Oxford University Press, 2010).

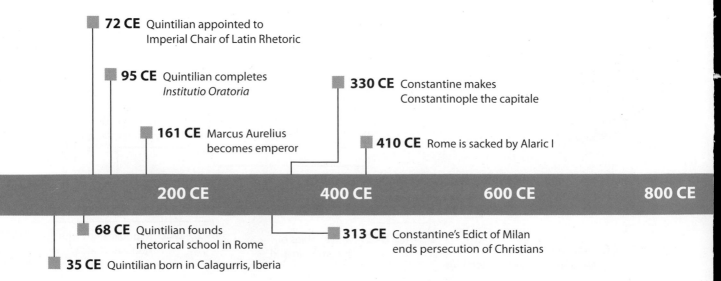

72 CE Quintilian appointed to Imperial Chair of Latin Rhetoric

95 CE Quintilian completes *Institutio Oratoria*

330 CE Constantine makes Constantinople the capitale

161 CE Marcus Aurelius becomes emperor

410 CE Rome is sacked by Alaric I

200 CE **400 CE** **600 CE** **800 CE**

68 CE Quintilian founds rhetorical school in Rome

313 CE Constantine's Edict of Milan ends persecution of Christians

35 CE Quintilian born in Calagurris, Iberia

Islamic religion and culture are widespread, and in the twenty-first century interactions are increasing between Muslims and others throughout the world. This photograph is of students at an Islamic school in Asia.

Paul Chesley/Stone/Getty Images

Written in Arabic, the Koran prescribes the pillars of faith and religious observance. Prayers are to be said five times each day at dawn, noon, midafternoon, sunset, and nightfall. The Koran enjoins Muslims to give to the poor. Annually, in the month of Ramadan, fasting from food, drink, and sexual relations is prescribed from dawn until sundown. The pilgrimage to Mecca—the Hajj—is an obligation for those who are physically and financially able to perform it.[38]

Today, Islam is the religious faith of one-eighth of the world's population. It is the dominant religion in the Arab countries of the Middle East and North Africa, and its influence extends to Indonesia, Malaysia, and Pakistan in Asia. In addition, Muslims, followers of Islam, live in countries throughout the world.

---

[38]For Islam, access **www.encyclopedia.com/topic/Islam.aspx**.

TIME LINE
Islam

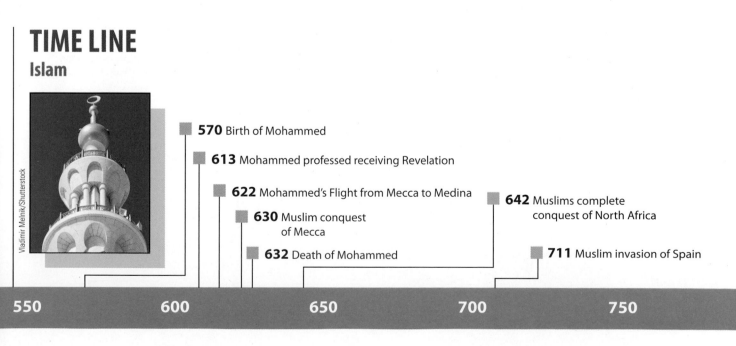

Vladimir Melnik/Shutterstock

570 Birth of Mohammed

613 Mohammed professed receiving Revelation

622 Mohammed's Flight from Mecca to Medina

630 Muslim conquest of Mecca

632 Death of Mohammed

642 Muslims complete conquest of North Africa

711 Muslim invasion of Spain

| 550 | 600 | 650 | 700 | 750 |

By 661, Arabian forces had established Islam as the official religion in Palestine, Syria, Persia, and Egypt. The cities of Baghdad, Cairo, Damascus, and Cordoba became renowned centers of Islamic culture and education. Baghdad, in particular, a prominent educational center, attracted Arab, Greek, Persian, and Jewish scholars.

Mohammed's followers extended Islamic influence through conquest and conversion. After their conquest of North Africa, the Arabs gained control of much of Spain. Here, Islamic Arabs and Western Christians not only struggled for power and territory but also borrowed ideas from each other.[39] During the Moorish period, Cordoba, with a population of 500,000 people, 700 mosques, and 70 libraries, was a leading Arab cultural and educational center.[40] The Islamic, or Moorish, kingdoms of Spain persisted until 1492, when they were conquered by the armies of Christian Spain.[41]

Islamic scholars translated the texts of ancient Greek authors such as Aristotle, Euclid, Archimedes, and Hippocrates into Arabic. The translated works became important in Islamic education and, through contacts between Arabs and Europeans, were reintroduced into Western education. In some cases, these ancient texts had been lost in the early Middle Ages. (The medieval period of Western history is discussed later in the chapter.) In particular, Ibn-Rushd, or Averroës (1126–1198) wrote important commentaries on Aristotle that influenced medieval European Scholastic educators.

Islamic scholars contributed to astronomy, mathematics, and medicine. In mathematics, Arab scholars adopted the number system from the Indians but made the crucial addition of zero. This innovation made it possible to replace the cumbersome Latin system.

In the twenty-first century's global economy, there is increasing interaction between the Arabic and Islamic and European and American societies. The numbers of Arab and Islamic people have increased in many European countries such as France, the United Kingdom, and Italy, as well as in the United States. Some of these interactions have been clouded by suspicion and hostility because of terrorist attacks, such as that of 9/11, and the persistent tensions in the Middle East. However, abroad and in the United States, there have been positive efforts at dialogue and mutual understanding, especially through programs of multicultural education. Today, more Americans are learning more about Arabic civilization and Islam. Many American schools and colleges now include units and courses on the Arabic language and culture.

REFOCUS   Think back to the FOCUS QUESTIONS at the beginning of this chapter. *Use these questions to construct your own history or autobiography of education.* Have events such as the "war on terrorism," the wars in Iraq and Afghanistan, and the "Arab Spring" caused you to rethink your world view? For example, what do you know about Arabic culture and Islam?

---

[39]See **www.islamicity.com/mosque/ihame/Sec5.htm** (September 25, 2003), pp. 1–2.
[40]Ibid.
[41]Richard Fletcher, *A Vanished World: Muslims, Christians, and Jews in Medieval Spain* (New York: Oxford University Press, 2006). Also, see Richard Fletcher, *Moorish Spain* (Berkeley, CA: University of California Press, 2006).

978 Muslims consolidate control of Spain

800   850   900   950   1000

Medieval Culture and Education

Decline and revival in learning

Historians designate the period between the fall of Rome and the Renaissance (c. 500–1400) as the Middle Ages, or medieval period, in that it spanned the time between the end of the Greco-Roman classical era and the beginning of the modern period. The medieval period was characterized first by a decline in learning and then by its revival by Scholastic educators.

Institutions of learning

After the Roman Empire in the west collapsed, the Roman Catholic Church, headed by the pope in Rome, partially filled the resulting political, cultural, and educational vacuum. The Church conducted primary education in parish, chantry (liturgical music), and monastic schools. At the secondary level, both monastic and cathedral schools (conducted by the bishop) offered religious and liberal arts curricula. Universities such as Paris, Bologna, Salerno, Oxford, and Cambridge provided higher education and professional education in theology, law, and medicine.[42] Merchant and craft guilds supported vocational schools to train their apprentices in specific trades. Knights, who were the feudal aristocrats, learned military tactics and the chivalric code.

Access to schooling

As in the earlier Greek and Roman eras, class and gender restrictions limited schooling to only a small minority. The majority of students were men studying for religious careers as priests or monks. Most people were serfs, usually illiterate, working as farm laborers on the estates of feudal lords. The feudal system, in which a few lords owned most of the land, had replaced the centralized Roman empire.

Education of medieval women

Women's education in medieval society varied according to their socioeconomic class. Although medieval Christianity stressed women's spiritual equality and the sacramental nature of marriage, women were still consigned to traditional gender-prescribed roles. Girls of the serf and peasant classes learned household and child-rearing chores by imitating their mothers. Women of the noble classes learned their roles ascribed by the code of chivalry, which often meant managing the domestic life of castle or manor.[43] The Church's religious communities provided an educational opportunity for some women. Convents, like monasteries, had libraries and schools to prepare nuns to follow the religious rules of their communities. With these limited possibilities for women's education, medieval schools and universities were reserved for men, guaranteeing male social dominance.

Hildegard of Bingen

Hildegard of Bingen (1098–1179), a noted scholar, was educated as a Benedictine nun or sister.[44] (In the Catholic Church, religious orders were named after their founders; for example, the Benedictines followed the rules established by St. Benedict.) Hildegard was the abbess, or the superior, of a Benedictine convent in Germany, where she directed the nuns' religious and educational formation. A scholar, teacher, writer, and composer, Hildegard, like most medieval educators, worked within a Christian religious frame of reference. She wrote *The Ways of God* and *The Book of Divine Works* to guide women's spiritual development. A versatile educator, Hildegard composed religious hymns and wrote medical tracts about the causes, symptoms, and cures of illnesses.

[42]C. Stephen Jaeger, *The Envy of Angels: Cathedral Schools and Social Ideals in Medieval Europe, 950–1200* (Philadelphia: University of Pennsylvania Press, 2000), p. 153. Olaf Pedersen, *The First Universities: Studium Generale and the Origins of University Education in Europe* (Cambridge: Cambridge University Press, 2009).

[43]Judith M. Bennett, *Medieval Women in Modern Perspective* (Washington, D.C.: American Historical Association, 2000).

[44]For a biographical sketch and an excerpt from Hildegard's writings, see Madonna M. Murphy, *The History and Philosophy of Education*, pp. 104–112. For a biography, see Fiona Maddocks, *Hildegard of Bingen: The Woman of Her Age* (New York: Doubleday/Random House, 2001). Also, see Hildegard of Bingen and Mark Atherton, *Selected Writings: Hildegard of Bingen* (New York: Penguin Books, 2001).

Aquinas: Scholastic Education

Faith and reason combined

By the eleventh century, medieval educators had developed **Scholasticism**—a method of theological and philosophical scholarship and teaching. The Scholastics adhered to the scriptures and doctrines of the Christian faith and human reasoning, especially Aristotle's philosophy, as complementary sources of truth. The Scholastics believed that the Bible and the Church's doctrines conveyed supernatural truths. The human mind could deduce natural principles that, when illuminated by faith, led to the truth.

Reconciling scriptures with Greek reasoning

Scholastic philosophy and education reached its zenith in the *Summa Theologiae* of Saint Thomas Aquinas (1225–1274), a Dominican theologian at the University of Paris. Aquinas sought to reconcile authorities—that is, to link Christian doctrine with Aristotle's Greek philosophy. Aquinas used both faith and reason to answer basic questions about the Christian concept of God, the nature of humankind and the universe, and the relationship between God and humans.[45] For Aquinas, humans possess *both* a physical body and a spiritual soul. Although they live temporarily on Earth, their ultimate purpose is to experience eternity with God in heaven. Aquinas agreed with Aristotle that human knowledge begins in sensation and is completed by conceptualization. (See Overview 3.2 for the ideas of Aquinas and other educators discussed in this chapter.)

In *de Magistro* (*Concerning the Teacher*), Aquinas portrayed the teacher's vocation as combining faith, love, and learning. Teachers need to be contemplative and reflective scholars, expert in their subjects, active and skilled instructors, and lovers of humanity. Aquinas's ideas suggest that preservice teachers, as well as all teachers, should have a vocation, or a calling to teach, and possess an in-depth knowledge of their subject matter. Aquinas called upon teachers to reflect on their teaching to find the deeper meaning of what they are doing in the classroom.

Subject-matter disciplines

Scholastic teachers were clerics, or members of religious communities, who taught in schools governed and protected by the Church. Following the Greco-Roman liberal arts tradition, the curriculum was organized into formal subjects. For example, in higher education, the subject disciplines were logic, mathematics, natural and moral philosophy, metaphysics, and theology. In their teaching, Scholastics used the syllogism—deductive reasoning—to create organized bodies of knowledge. They emphasized basic principles and their application to life.[46]

Aquinas's philosophy, called Thomism, has influenced education in Catholic schools, especially colleges and universities. In the United States, Catholic schools are the largest nonpublic school system, enrolling 2,009,640 students, or 42.8 percent of all private school enrollments in 7,115 schools.[47] Thomism also influenced perennialist educators such as Robert Hutchins, Jacques Maritain, and Mortimer Adler, who are all discussed in Chapter 6, Philosophical Roots of Education.

> **REFOCUS** Think back to the Focus Questions at the beginning of this chapter. *Use these questions to construct your own history or autobiography of education.* For example, medieval educators sought to reconcile faith and reason as complementary sources of truth. In your own educational experience, reflect on science and religion. Have you encountered conflicts, or have these areas been complementary? Is there a conflict between religion and separation of church and state in education?

The Medieval Contribution to Western Education

Preserving and institutionalizing knowledge

The medieval educators recorded, preserved, and transmitted knowledge by presenting it in a scholastic framework based on the Christian religion and Aristotle's philosophy. Parish, monastic, and cathedral schools and universities, under Church sponsorship and supervision, transmitted knowledge as organized subjects. The medieval period formed a cultural bridge between Greco-Roman classical education and modern education.

---

[45]G. K. Chesterton, *St. Thomas Aquinas: "The Dumb Ox"* (Nashville, TN: Sam Torade Book Arts, 2010). Fergus Kerr, *Thomas Aquinas: A Very Short Introduction* (New York: Oxford University Press, 2009). Francis Selman, *Aquinas 101: A Basic Introduction to the Thought of Saint Thomas Aquinas* (Notre Dame, IN: Christian Classics/Ave Maria Press, 2007).

[46]John W. Donohue, *St. Thomas Aquinas and Education* (New York: Random House, 1968), pp. 76–89. Also, see Vivian Boland, *St. Thomas Aquinas* (*Continuum Library of Educational Thought*) (London: Continuum, 2008).

[47]See **www2.ed.gov**. Also access the National Catholic Education Association at **www.ncea .org/news/AnnualDataReport.asp#enrollment**.

OVERVIEW 3.2

Major Educational Theorists to 1600 CE

Theorist	Philosophical Orientation	View of Human Nature
Confucius 551–478 BCE (Chinese)	Developed an ethical system of hierarchical human relationships and roles; emphasized order and civility through subordination.	Human beings need a highly stable society in which they accept the duties of their station in life.
Socrates 469–399 BCE (Greek)	Social and educational iconoclast who asked basic philosophical questions with a tendency to idealism.	Human beings can find the truth within themselves by dialectical self-examination.
Plato 427–346 BCE (Greek)	An idealist who established the contours of Western philosophy; sociopolitical conservative.	Human beings can be classified on the basis of their intellectual capabilities.
Aristotle 384–322 BCE (Greek)	Philosophical realist; views of society, politics, and education based on observation of natural and social phenomena.	Human beings have the power of reason to guide their decisions.
Isocrates 436–388 BCE (Greek)	Rhetorician; oratorical education in service of self and society.	Human beings have the power to use speech (discourse) to influence social and political decisions.
Quintilian 35–95 CE (Roman)	Rhetorician; oratory for personal advancement and public service.	Certain individuals with the right dispositions can be prepared as leaders through liberal and oratorical education.
Hildegard of Bingen 1098–1179 CE (German)	Medieval abbess; Christian spirituality and natural medical science.	Human beings need spiritual development and natural knowledge.
Aquinas 1225–1274 CE (Italian medieval theologian)	Christian theology and Aristotelian (realist) philosophy.	Human beings possess both a spiritual nature (soul) and a physical nature (body).
Erasmus 1465–1536 CE (Dutch Renaissance humanist)	Christian orientation; the educator as social and intellectual critic.	Human beings are capable of profound insights but also of great stupidity.
Luther 1483–1546 CE (German Protestant)	Protestant theological orientation; salvation by faith.	Human beings are saved by faith; individual conscience shaped by scripture and Reformed theology.

Renaissance Classical Humanism

Reviving humanistic aspects of the classics

The Renaissance, a transitional period between the medieval and modern ages, began in the fourteenth century and reached its zenith in the fifteenth century. It signaled a revival of the humanistic aspects of the Greek and Latin classics. Like the medieval Scholastics, Renaissance educators, called **classical humanists**, looked to the past rather than the future. Unlike the Scholastics, however, classical humanists emphasized literature rather than theology.[48]

---

[48]Charles G. Nauert, *Humanism and the Culture of Renaissance Europe* (Cambridge: Cambridge University Press, 2006).

Views on Education and Curriculum

Education prepares people for their sociopolitical roles by cultivating reverence for ancestors and traditions; curriculum of ancient Chinese classics and Confucius's *Analects*; (proverbial wisdom) highly selective examinations.

Use of probing intellectual dialogue to answer enduring questions about truth, goodness, and beauty; education should cultivate moral excellence.

Reminiscence of latent ideas; music, gymnastics, geometry, astronomy, basic literary skills; philosophy for philosopher-kings.

Objective and scientific emphasis; basic literary skills, mathematics, natural and physical sciences, philosophy.

Rhetorical studies; basic literary skills; politics, history, rhetoric, declamation, public speaking.

Basic literary skills; grammar, history, literature, drama, philosophy, public speaking, law.

Women should have a multidimensional education in religion, nature studies, and music.

Education should be based on human nature, with appropriate studies for both spiritual and physical dimensions.

Education for literary elite that stressed criticism and analysis.

Elementary schools to teach reading, writing, arithmetic, religion; secondary schools to prepare leaders by offering classics, Latin, Greek, and religion; vocational training.

Contribution and Influence

Confucian ethics shaped Chinese culture for centuries, creating a value system of enduring importance.

Socratic dialogue as a teaching method; teacher as a role model.

Use of schools for sorting students according to intellectual abilities; education for universal truth and values.

Emphasis on liberally educated, well-rounded person; importance of reason.

Use of knowledge in public affairs and in political leadership; teacher education has both content and practice dimensions.

Role of motivation in learning; recognition of individual differences.

Teacher as mentor and guide to the individual's spiritual, natural, and moral development.

Teacher as moral agent; education related to universal theological goals; synthesis of theology and philosophy; dominant philosophy in Roman Catholic schools.

Role of secondary and higher education in literary and social criticism; emphasis on critical thinking.

Emphasis on universal literacy; schools to stress religious values, vocational skills, knowledge; close relationship of religion, schooling, and the state.

Classical humanism in Italy

In Italy, an artistic and literary center of the southern Renaissance, humanists saw themselves as critics and custodians of culture, especially in literature, art, music, and architecture. Dante, Petrarch, and Boccaccio, the great writers of their age, wrote in Italian rather than in Latin. Italian nobles established humanist schools to educate their children in revived classical learning.[49]

The courtier as a model

From their study of the Greek and Latin classics, humanist educators discovered models of literary excellence and style and portrayed the courtier as the ideal of the

---

[49]Robert Black, *Humanism and Education in Medieval and Renaissance Italy: Tradition and Innovation in Latin Schools from the Twelfth to the Fifteenth Century* (Cambridge: Cambridge University Press, 2007).

educated person. Courtiers were often employed by wealthy nobles as counselors, secretaries, and tutors. Baldesar Castiglione (1478–1529) in *The Book of the Courtier* presented a prospectus on how to educate the courtier in the liberal arts and the classical literature.[50] The courtier was to be a culturally sophisticated, tactful, and diplomatic person.[51]

Critical thinking

The Renaissance humanist educators were literary critics—writers, poets, translators, and editors. As artist-teachers and cultural critics, they brought wit, charm, and satire as well as erudition to their work. They sought to educate a critically minded elite who could challenge conventional thinking and expose and correct mediocrity in literature and life. In northern Europe, classical humanist scholars, by critically examining medieval theological texts, prepared the path for the Protestant Reformation.

Although Renaissance humanists were critics, they were rarely social activists. Neither did they seek to influence popular opinion. They often kept a distance between themselves and the mass of people, distilling their conception of human nature from a carefully aged literature. As a vintage wine is used to grace an elegant dinner, humanist education was for the connoisseur rather than for the masses.

Limited access to schools

The Renaissance did not dramatically increase school attendance. Humanist preparatory and secondary schools educated children of the nobility and upper classes. Elementary schools served the commercial middle classes. Children in lower socioeconomic classes received little, if any, formal schooling.

---

[50]A commentary is Baldesar Castiglione, *The Book of the Courtier* (New York: Barnes and Noble Books, 2005).
[51]Peter Burke, *The Fortunes of the Courtier: The European Reception of Castiglione's Cortegiano* (University Park: Pennsylvania State University Press, 1996).

TIME LINE
Middle Ages
(Medieval Period)

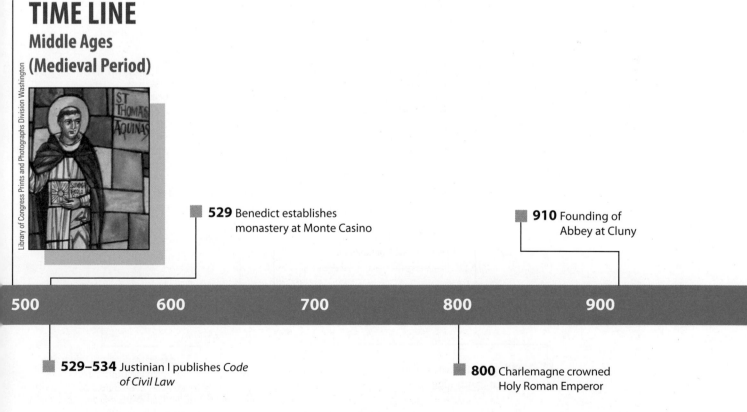

529 Benedict establishes monastery at Monte Casino

910 Founding of Abbey at Cluny

500   600   700   800   900

529–534 Justinian I publishes *Code of Civil Law*

800 Charlemagne crowned Holy Roman Emperor

Erasmus: Critic and Humanist

Erasmus on education

Desiderius Erasmus (1465–1536), a leading scholar, portrayed the model teacher as a cosmopolitan Christian humanist.[52] Ecumenical and cosmopolitan in his worldview, Erasmus emphasized the unifying features of Christianity shared by all believers rather than the doctrines that separated them. Although he could be a sarcastic critic, Erasmus had a gentle disposition when it came to children's education. Advising parents and teachers to be worthy cultural and ethical models for their children, Erasmus understood the importance of shaping predispositions that were favorable to education early in a child's life.

Erasmus believed that a teacher's worldview and academic preparation were highly important for success as a humanist educator. Teachers needed to be open to alternative ideas and not limited by narrow local interests. As part of their preservice preparation, teachers needed to be well educated in the liberal arts, especially in the classical Greek and Latin languages and literature, as well as in history and religion. They needed to have a global outlook.

Promoting books and literature

As a humanist educator, Erasmus specialized in literary criticism and interpretation. He suggested that teachers could motivate students to read good books by having them relate their meaning to their own lives. He encouraged teachers to use conversations, games, and activities to describe a book's content and explore its meaning. Erasmus developed the following method for teaching literature: (1) present the author's biography; (2) identify the work's type, or genre; (3) discuss the plot; (4) reflect on the book's moral and philosophical implications; (5) analyze the author's writing style.[53]

Opposition to violence

Erasmus's *The Education of the Christian Prince* (1516) stated his opposition to war and violence.[54] He advised the prince's tutor to make sure that the prince learned about the people of his kingdom—about their traditions, customs, work, and problems. Unlike Niccolo di Bernardo Machiavelli (1469–1527), an Italian humanist, who urged that the king should rule by fear and manipulation, Erasmus advised the prince to gain his people's love and respect by studying the arts of peace, especially diplomacy, to avoid war.

---

[52]For biographies of Erasmus, visit **www.newadvent.org/cathen/05510b.htm**; Maurice Wilkinson, *Erasmus of Rotterdam* (Charleston, SC: BiblioBazaar, 2008).
[53]For Erasmus and his texts, access **www.archive.org/details/erasmuse00caperich**; also see **www.kjvonly.org/doug/kutilek_erasmus.htm**.
[54]Robert D. Sider and John B. Payne, eds., *Collected Works of Erasmus* (Toronto: University of Toronto Press, 1994).

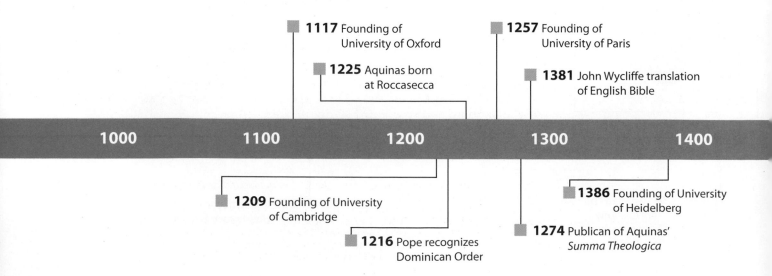

1117 Founding of University of Oxford

1257 Founding of University of Paris

1225 Aquinas born at Roccasecca

1381 John Wycliffe translation of English Bible

1000   1100   1200   1300   1400

1209 Founding of University of Cambridge

1386 Founding of University of Heidelberg

1216 Pope recognizes Dominican Order

1274 Publican of Aquinas' *Summa Theologica*

The Renaissance Contribution to Western Education

Emphasis on classical languages and literature

Renaissance humanists emphasized knowledge of Latin and Greek as hallmarks of the educated person. For centuries, this classical humanist preference shaped Western secondary and higher education. In Europe and the United States, many colleges and universities required students to demonstrate their knowledge of Latin for admission until the late nineteenth century.

Humanist (not scientific) knowledge

It is important to note that Erasmus and other Renaissance educators were moving to a humanist, or human-centered, rather than a theocentric conception of knowledge. However, they explored their concerns through literature, not science. The humanists' literary approach to education was later challenged by Rousseau, Pestalozzi, Spencer, and Dewey (discussed in Chapter 4, Pioneers of Teaching and Learning), who all argued against instruction that emphasized literature over experience.

The printing press

In Europe, the invention of the printing press in 1423 advanced literacy and schooling dramatically. Before the printing press, students painstakingly created their own copy of a text by taking dictation from teachers. The university lecture was and still is an exercise in which students record their professor's words.

By the mid-fifteenth century, European printers were experimenting with movable metal type. Johannes Gutenberg, a German jeweler, invented a durable metal alloy to form letters for the printing press. His Bible, in 1455, was the first major book printed. Printing spread throughout Europe, multiplying the output and cutting the costs of books. It made information accessible to a growing population of readers.[55] It brought more textbooks into the schools and made the text part of the teacher's method of instruction. The printing press inaugurated the *information revolution*, a momentous technological innovation, whose consequences were similar to the advent of data storage, retrieval, and dissemination by electronic computers. (See Overview 3.3 for the invention of the printing press and other significant events in the history of education.)

> **REFOCUS**   Think back to the Focus Questions at the beginning of this chapter. *Use these questions to construct your own history or autobiography of education.* For example, the Renaissance humanist educators regarded themselves as well-educated models and critics of learning. In your own educational experience, have you encountered teachers who acted as models and critics of learning? Do you plan to be such a model and critic?

The Religious Reformation and Education

Social and religious change

A growing climate of social, political, and economic change in Europe provided the backdrop for the Protestant Reformation of the sixteenth and seventeenth centuries. Humanist criticism of the medieval Scholastics' theological interpretations generated religious questions about the Catholic Church's authority to enforce doctrinal conformity. The new economic power of the middle classes caused them to question the political status quo. The emergence of centralized national states shifted people's loyalty to their own monarchs and away from the pope. Protestant religious reformers—such as John Calvin, Martin Luther, Philipp Melanchthon, and Ulrich Zwingli—sought to free themselves and their followers from papal authority and to redefine Christian religious doctrines and practices.[56] While doing so, Protestant reformers formulated their own educational theories, established their own schools, structured their own curricula, and reared their children in the reformed creeds.

Extension of popular literacy

Luther, Melanchthon, Calvin, and other Reformation leaders were concerned with knowledge, education, and schooling because they wanted to enlist these powerful cultural weapons to promote the Protestant cause. They asserted that every person had not only the right but also the religious obligation to read the Bible as the primary

---

[55]Elizabeth L. Eisenstein, *The Printing Revolution in Early Modern Europe* (Cambridge, UK: Cambridge University Press, 2005).

[56]W. Robert Godfrey, *Reformation Sketches: Insights into Luther, Calvin, and the Confessions* (Phillipsburg, NJ: P&R Publishers, 2003); Patrick Collinson, *The Reformation: A History* (New York: Modern Library, 2004); Diarmaid MacCulloch, *The Reformation* (New York: Penguin, 2005); John Calvin, *Institutes of the Christian Religion* (Peabody, MA: Hendrickson Publishers, 2008); F. Bruce Gordon, *Calvin* (New Haven: Yale University Press, 2011).

OVERVIEW 3.3

Significant Events in the History of Western Education to 1650 CE

Period	Political and Social Events		Significant Educational Events	
Greek	1200 BCE	Trojan War	c. 1200 BCE	Homer's *Iliad* and *Odyssey*
	594 BCE	Athenian constitutional reforms	399 BCE	Trial of Socrates
	479–338 BCE	Golden Age of Greek (Athenian) culture	395 BCE	Plato's *Republic*
	445–431 BCE	Age of Pericles	392 BCE	Isocrates established rhetorical school in Athens s
	431–404 BCE	Peloponnesian War between Athens and Sparta	387 BCE	Plato founds Academy
	336–323 BCE	Alexander the Great	330 BCE	Aristotle's *Politics*
Roman	753 BCE	Traditional date of Rome's founding	449 BCE	Latin primary schools, or *ludi*, appear
	510 BCE	Roman republic established	167 BCE	Greek grammar school opened in Rome
	272 BCE	Rome dominates Italian peninsula		
	146 BCE	Greece becomes Roman province	96 CE	Quintilian's *Institutio Oratoria*
	49–44 BCE	Dictatorship of Julius Caesar		
	31 BCE	Roman empire begins		
	476 CE	Fall of Rome in the West		
Medieval	713	Arab conquest of Spain	1079–1142	Abelard, author of *Sic et Non*
	800	Charlemagne crowned Holy Roman Emperor	1180	University of Paris granted papal charter and recognition
	1096–1291	Crusades to the Holy Land	1209	University of Cambridge founded
	1182–1226	St. Francis of Assisi	1225–1274	Thomas Aquinas, author of *Summa Theologiae*
Renaissance	1295	Explorations of Marco Polo	1428	Da Feltre, classical humanist educator, established court school at Mantua
	1304–1374	Petrarch, author of odes and sonnets	1509	Erasmus's *The Praise of Folly*
	1313–1375	Boccaccio, founder of Italian vernacular literature		
	1384	Founding of Brethren of the Common Life		
	1393–1464	Cosimo de'Medici encourages revival of art and learning in Florence		
	1423	Invention of printing press		
Reformation	1455	Gutenberg Bible printed	1524	Luther's "Letter … in Behalf of Christian Schools"
	1492	Columbus arrives in America		
	1517	Luther posts "Ninety-Five Theses" calling for church reform	1524	Melanchthon, an associate of Luther, writes school codes in German states
	1509–1564	John Calvin, Protestant reformer, founder of Calvinism	1630–1650	John Knox organizes Calvinist schools in Scotland
	1509–1547	King Henry VIII of England, founder of the Church of England		
	1540	Jesuit order founded by Loyola		
	1545	Council of Trent launches Roman Catholic Counter Reformation		

Private Collection/Archives Charmet/The Bridgeman Art Library

Illustration from a catechism illustrates the death of a religiously righteous man.

authority of truth. Regarding Bible reading as essential to salvation, the Protestant reformers promoted universal primary schooling to advance literacy.

Protestants established **vernacular schools** to instruct children in the spoken languages used in their religious services—for example, German, Swedish, or English—rather than Latin. These primary schools, under denominational control, offered a basic curriculum of reading, writing, arithmetic, and religion. Catholic liturgies remained in Latin rather than vernacular languages, although, to compete with Protestants, Catholic schools also began to teach vernacular languages along with Latin.

TIME LINE
The Renaissance

Georgios Kollidas/Shutterstock.com

| 1300 | 1340 | 1380 | 1420 |

1310 Dante's *Divine Comedy* published

The catechism

Both Protestants and Catholics used schools to instill officially sanctioned religious beliefs and practices approved by the particular denominations. Only members of the particular officially sanctioned church were hired as teachers. Religious authorities closely supervised teachers to make certain they were teaching approved doctrines. In fact, teacher supervision and licensing developed during the Reformation.

Religious educators developed the catechistic method of instruction. Catechisms were organized into questions and answers that summarized the particular denomination's doctrines and practices. Students were expected to memorize the set answers and to recite them as the teacher read the particular questions. Although memorization had always been a feature of schooling, the catechistic method reinforced it. The belief was that if children memorized the catechism, they would internalize the doctrines of their church. The question-and-answer format gained such a powerful hold on teaching methods that it was also used to teach secular subjects such as history and geography.

For example, Calvin's *Catechism of the Church of Geneva* used the question and answer method:

Master: What is the chief end of human life?
Scholar: To know God by whom men were created.

In the nineteenth century, the same method appeared in Davenport's *History of the United States:*

Q. When did the battle of Lexington take place?
A. On the 19th of April, 1775; here was shed the first blood in the American Revolution.[57]

Rising literacy

Continuity & Change

Religious and economic change worked to increase primary (elementary) school attendance and literacy rates. The Protestant emphasis on reading the Bible caused more children to attend school. The middle classes (the commercial and merchant sectors) sent their children to school to learn the practical skills of reading, writing, and arithmetic. For example, only 10 percent of men and 2 percent of women in England were literate in 1500. By 1600, literacy rates had increased to 28 percent for men and 9 percent for women; by 1700, nearly 40 percent of English men and about 32 percent of English women were literate. Literacy rates tended to be higher in northern than in southern and eastern Europe and in urban rather than rural areas.[58]

---

[57]John Calvin, *Tracts and Treatises on the Doctrine and Worship of the Church,* II, trans. Henry Beveride (Grand Rapids, MI: Wm. B. Eerdmans Publishing Co., 1958), p. 37; and Bishop Davenport, *History of the United States* (Philadelphia: William Marchall and Co., 1833), p. 31.
[58]Mary Jo Maynes, *Schooling in Western Europe: A Social History* (Albany: State University of New York Press, 1985).

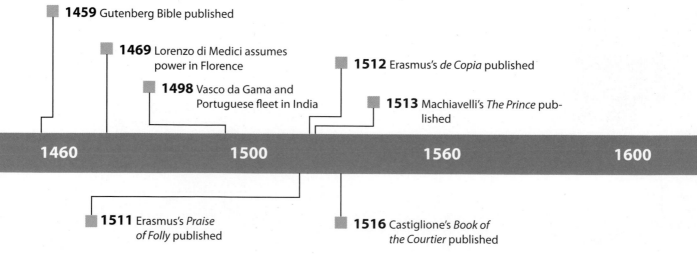

1459 Gutenberg Bible published

1469 Lorenzo di Medici assumes power in Florence

1512 Erasmus's *de Copia* published

1498 Vasco da Gama and Portuguese fleet in India

1513 Machiavelli's *The Prince* published

| 1460 | 1500 | 1560 | 1600 |

1511 Erasmus's *Praise of Folly* published

1516 Castiglione's *Book of the Courtier* published

Gender, class, and school attendance

The Protestant reformers wanted both girls and boys to attend primary vernacular schools, and their efforts increased school attendance for both sexes. Nevertheless, Protestant leaders continued to reserve the prestigious classical humanist preparatory and secondary schools for upper-class boys. Preparatory and secondary schools such as the German *gymnasium*, the English Latin grammar school, and the French *lycée* prepared upper-class boys in Latin and Greek, the classical languages needed for university entry. This male elite was prepared for leadership roles in the church and state.

Many strong personalities such as Calvin, Zwingli, Ignatius Loyola, and Henry VIII were leaders of the Protestant Reformation and the Roman Catholic Counter Reformation. Martin Luther was a leading German Protestant reformer, whose influence extended throughout northern Europe.

Luther: Protestant Reformer

Luther challenges Papal Authority

Martin Luther (1483–1546) stands out as one of the most important religious reformers in shaping Western history and education.[59] Luther, an Augustinian monk, posted his famous *Ninety-Five Theses* on the door of the castle church at Wittenberg in 1517. He challenged the authority of the pope and the Roman Catholic Church. Luther's challenges were a catalyst for the Protestant Reformation, which spread throughout Western Europe.

Education as part of religious reform

Luther believed that education was a potent ally of religious reformation. He saw church, state, family, and school as interrelated agencies of education. Believing that the family had a key role in forming children's characters and behaviors, Luther encouraged family Bible reading and prayer. He also wanted parents to provide their children with vocational training so they could support themselves as adults and become productive citizens.

Luther on schooling

Luther's "Letter to the Mayors and Aldermen of All the Cities of Germany in Behalf of Christian Schools" stated that public officials were responsible for providing and

---

[59]Biographies of Luther are James A. Nestigen, *Martin Luther: A Life* (Minneapolis, MN: Augsburg, 2003); Fredrick Nohl, *Luther: Biography of a Reformer* (St. Louis, MO: Concordia Publishing House, 2003); James M. Kittelson, *Luther: The Reformer* (Philadelphia: Fortress, 2003); Stephen T. Nichols, *The Reformation: How a Monk and a Mallet Changed the World* (Wheaton, IL: Crossway Books, 2007); Heiko A. Oberman, *Luther: Man Between God and the Devil* (New Haven: Yale University Press, 2006).

TIME LINE
The Reformation

Steven Wynn/iStockphoto.com

1517 Luther posts "95 Theses" in Wittenberg

1519 Zwingli begins preaching religious reform in Geneva

1520 Luther's *Treatises to Christian Nobility* published

1521 Catholic Church excommunicates Luther

1534 Henry VIII declared head of Church of England

| 1500 | 1510 | 1520 | 1530 |

supervising schools. Government should support schools because they promoted civil order, economic growth, and religious values.[60] State officials should inspect schools to ensure that teachers were educating children in correct religious doctrines and preparing them to become literate, orderly, and productive citizens. Higher education in the *gymnasien* (German secondary schools) and universities would prepare well-educated ministers for the Lutheran Church.

Luther's views on women's education blended traditional gender roles with some more open ideas. Influenced by Saint Paul, he believed that the husband, as the head of the household, had authority over his wife. Domestic duties and child-rearing remained women's appropriate roles. However, Luther's emphasis that everyone should read the Bible in one's own language meant that girls as well as boys should attend primary vernacular schools to learn to read. Schooling thus gave women a shared, if subordinate, role in educating their own children.

To implement educational reforms, Luther relied heavily on the humanist educator, Philipp Melanchthon (1497–1560). In 1559, Melanchthon drafted the *School Code of Württemberg*, which became a model for other German states. The code specified that primary vernacular schools be established in every village to teach religion, reading, writing, arithmetic, and music. Classical secondary schools, *gymnasien*, were to provide Latin and Greek instruction for those select young men expected to attend universities.

Luther on women's education

School codes

The Reformation's Contribution to Western Education

The Protestant Reformation reconfirmed some educational developments from the Renaissance, especially the **dual-track system of schools.** While vernacular schools provided primary instruction for the lower socioeconomic classes, classical humanist grammar schools prepared upper-class males for higher education. European colonists brought this two-track school structure to North and South America.

From ancient times through the twenty-first century, religion has influenced education and schooling. Many schools were and are sponsored by churches, temples, synagogues, and mosques. In the United States, too, early schools and colleges were affiliated with religious denominations. Currently, 3,756,000 U.S. elementary and secondary students attend religiously affiliated schools in the United States.[61]

In the eighteenth century, the naturalism and rationalism of the Enlightenment, in Europe and the Americas, generated new ideas about education, schools, and teaching.

REFOCUS Think back to the Focus Questions at the beginning of this chapter. *Use these questions to construct your own history or autobiography of education.* For example, the question-and-answer response to previously memorized lessons was used during the Reformation. Did you encounter this method in your own schooling? What is your opinion of this method? What are its strengths and weaknesses? Has religion influenced your views of education and its purposes?

---

[60]For a biographical sketch, a commentary on Luther's educational ideas, and an excerpt from his "Letter to the Mayors and Aldermen of All the Cities of Germany in Behalf of Christian Schools," see Madonna M. Murphy, *The History and Philosophy of Education: Voices of Educational Pioneers* (Upper Saddle River, NJ: Pearson/Merrill/Prentice Hall, 2006), pp. 143–149.
[61]See **www.ed.gov/**; enrollments for religiously affiliated schools for 2009–2010; **www.ncea .org/news/AnnualDataReport.asp#enrollment/nces.ed.gov/pubs/ps/97459ch3.asp.**

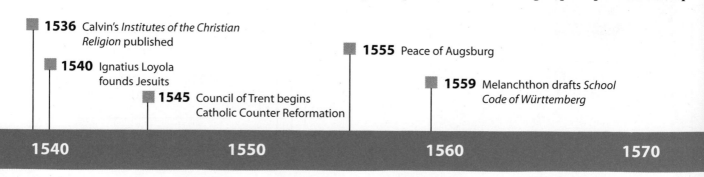

1536 Calvin's *Institutes of the Christian Religion* published

1540 Ignatius Loyola founds Jesuits

1545 Council of Trent begins Catholic Counter Reformation

1555 Peace of Augsburg

1559 Melanchthon drafts *School Code of Württemberg*

1540   1550   1560   1570

The Enlightenment's Influence on Education

■ Reason and the scientific method

■ **REFOCUS**   Think back to the Focus Questions at the beginning of this chapter. *Use these questions to construct your own history or autobiography of education.* Did you encounter the Enlightenment principles emphasizing reason, the scientific method, and separation of church and state in your own education?

■ **REFOCUS**   **Constructing Your Own History or Auto-biography of Education**   Throughout this chapter, we have suggested ways in which you might write your own history or autobiography of education. You may want to reflect on and revise your autobiography and your history of education as you read the next two chapters. Chapter 4, Pioneers of Teaching and Learning, considers how mentors influence a person's education. As you read this chapter, you can identify your mentors and add this commentary to your history and autobiography. Then Chapter 5, Historical Development of American Education, provides an opportunity to situate your own educational narrative in this historical context. Chapter 6, Philosophical Roots of Education, encourages you to develop your own philosophy of education in relationship to your own educational history and autobiography.

Unlike the medieval Scholastics and Renaissance humanists who based their philosophies of education on the past, the Enlightenment philosophers, scientists, and educators used reason and science to study the present to improve the future. They used the scientific method of empirical observation to discover how the natural world functioned. They observed children—especially their activities and play—to construct a natural method of instruction based on stages of human development. The Enlightenment worldview that children were naturally good and that teachers should base instruction on children's interests and needs influenced the educational reformers—Rousseau, Pestalozzi, and the progressive educators, discussed in Chapter 4, Pioneers of Teaching and Learning, and Chapter 6, Philosophical Roots of Education.

Leaders of the American Revolution, such as Benjamin Franklin and Thomas Jefferson, whose ideas are discussed in Chapter 5, Historical Development of American Education, were especially influenced by Enlightenment political philosophy. The Declaration of Independence and the Constitution embodied such Enlightenment principles as the natural rights of life, liberty, and pursuit of happiness, and republican government free from absolutism.

Enlightenment ideas took root in the United States, where they nourished an optimistic faith in political democracy and universal education. They influenced Franklin's emphasis on utilitarian and scientific education and Jefferson's arguments for separation of church and state and education in state-supported schools. Convinced of their ability to direct their own future, Americans saw education as the key to progress.

The discussion of the influence of the Enlightenment on education is continued in Chapter 4, Pioneers of Teaching and Learning, and Chapter 5, Historical Development of American Education.

TIME LINE
The Enlightenment

The Library of Congress

■ **1690** Locke's *Two Treatises on Government* published

| 1690 | 1700 | 1710 | 1720 | 1730 |

Summing Up

1 We examined major historical periods to reflect on the following questions: What is knowledge? What is education? What are the purposes of education? What is schooling? Who should attend school? How should teaching and learning be implemented? Contemporary educators continue to reflect on these highly important questions. Some emphasize traditional knowledge and values, as did Confucius in ancient China, or the preservation of the culture, as in ancient Egypt. Some answer in universal terms, as did Plato; others, like the Sophists, base their responses on specific cultural conditions and situations.

2 We examined the purpose of education as contributing to cultural continuity or change. Throughout the ancient and medieval periods, education was used to preserve and transmit the culture from one generation to the next.

3 Ever increasing connections in the world's economic and information systems make it imperative to understand the global origins and interconnections of education. By examining education in such culturally different societies as ancient China, Egypt, Israel, Greece, and Rome, we explored how cultural interactions changed ideas about knowledge, the purpose of education, and schooling.

4 Many American ideas about education, especially the liberal arts and sciences, originated in ancient Greece and Rome. Socrates, Plato, Aristotle, and Isocrates developed concepts of the educated person, rational inquiry, freedom of thought, and the ideal of liberal education. The concept and methods of rhetorical education were devised by the Sophists, refined by Isocrates, and further developed by the Roman rhetorician Quintilian.

5 During the medieval period, the foundations of the university were established. Medieval education incorporated the mathematical and scientific contributions, especially of the ancient Greeks, that entered the Western world by way of the Arabs. Renaissance classical humanist educators elaborated on the concept of the well-rounded, liberally educated person. The Protestant Reformation's emphasis on literacy and vernacular education, as well as religion, directly influenced colonial American schools. The Enlightenment was especially influential in shaping American political and educational institutions.

6 From the classical period of ancient Greece and Rome to the Protestant Reformation in the fifteenth century, only a minority of children attended schools. Males of wealthy families had the greatest opportunity to attend school. School attendance for both boys and girls began to increase during the Reformation as a result of the Protestant emphasis on literacy to read the Bible and the invention of the printing press.

7 Schools in Western Europe developed into a two-track set of institutions based on socioeconomic class differences. Common people attended primary schools, and upper-class males attended preparatory schools that prepared them for admission to colleges and universities. Girls attended primary schools but were generally excluded from secondary and higher education.

8 Slowly over time, the profession of teaching emerged. Teachers in ancient China were respected as sages; in Egyptian, Hebraic, Islamic, and Christian societies, teachers were identified with religion.

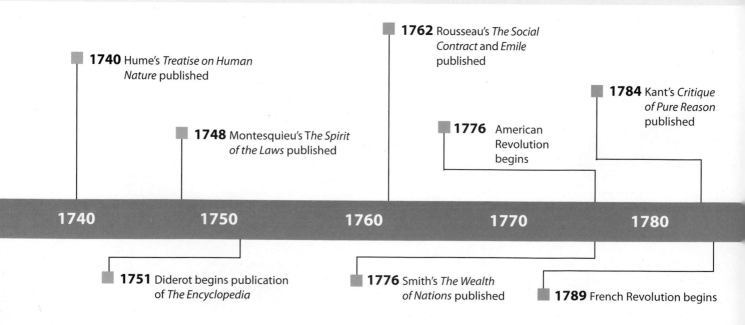

1740 Hume's *Treatise on Human Nature* published

1748 Montesquieu's *The Spirit of the Laws* published

1751 Diderot begins publication of *The Encyclopedia*

1762 Rousseau's *The Social Contract* and *Emile* published

1776 American Revolution begins

1776 Smith's *The Wealth of Nations* published

1784 Kant's *Critique of Pure Reason* published

1789 French Revolution begins

| 1740 | 1750 | 1760 | 1770 | 1780 |

Key Terms

The numbers indicate the pages where explanations of the key terms can be found.

enculturation 53	rhetoric 68	Koran 77
Confucius 56	Socratic method 70	Scholasticism 81
Judeo-Christian Tradition 64	reminiscence 70	classical humanists 82
Torah 65	Plato's Republic 71	vernacular schools 88
Sophists 68	Islam 77	dual-track system of schools 91

Certification Connection Activity

This chapter examines how the supervision of teachers originated in the Protestant Reformation. Supervisors, often ministers, inspected schools to make certain that teachers were teaching the religious doctrines approved by the particular church. Reflect on the supervision of teachers today, especially the role played by cooperating teachers and supervisors during student teaching or other clinical experiences. Why are teachers supervised today? How has the process of supervision changed over time?

Discussion Questions

1. Observe classes in kindergartens and primary grades, and note how holiday observances, stories, and art are used to introduce children to their culture. Are these observances and activities similar to or unlike the oral tradition of education in preliterate societies and the religious observances in Hebraic education?

2. Reflect on Confucius's emphasis on appropriate and proper relationships. Today, it is common to talk about "having a relationship" or "being in a relationship." How does the modern sense of relationship compare and contrast with that of Confucius? Also, examine the Confucian ethical principle of behaving according to one's rank in society. Compare and contrast the concept of Confucian ethical behavior with that of modern American society. What are the educational implications of these historically generated concepts of relationships, especially between teachers and students?

3. Throughout most of history, the teacher's role was to maintain cultural continuity by transmitting the heritage, especially a particular group's language, knowledge, beliefs, and values. What is your reaction to the teacher as an agent of cultural continuity and transmitter of culture? Have you encountered teachers as transmitters of knowledge in your own educational experience? Reconsider this question after you have read the section on Paulo Freire in Chapter 4, Pioneers of Teaching and Learning, and the sections on Postmodernism and Critical Theory in Chapter 6, Philosophical Roots of Education.

4. Whereas the Arabic scholars deliberately borrowed knowledge from other cultures, the ancient Chinese resisted cultural borrowing. Can you identify contemporary examples of borrowing educational ideas and methods from other countries? Do you favor or oppose such borrowing in American education?

5. What do you suppose the Sophists would think about such trends as focus groups, public opinion polls, sound-bite commercials, and the negative advertising used in modern political campaigns? What are the educational implications of the use of television, the Internet, and social networking to generate public opinion? How do these sources of information affect teaching and learning in schools?

6. How did gender, socioeconomic class, and religion affect education and schooling in the past? How do these factors affect education today?

Suggested Projects for Professional Development

1. Research websites on Confucius and Confucian education. Identify the most informative sites, and prepare an annotated list of sites about Confucius and his ideas on education. When you have completed your list, share it with members of the class.

2. Research and prepare an annotated list of websites about Islamic education in which you discuss how this information might be useful for teachers. When you have completed your list, share it with members of the class.

❸ If you are located near a museum that has exhibits on ancient civilizations such as the Chinese, Egyptian, Greek, and Roman, visit them and design a field trip for students at the grade level that you are preparing to teach. In your design, include some questions that will guide the students in understanding these civilizations. It may also be possible for you to access exhibits at museums online if one is not located in your area.

❹ Find and access a hypertextual edition of Quintilian's *Institutio Oratoria* or *Institutes of Oratory*. Read a chapter of the *Institutes*, and discuss it with the students in your class. If time permits, organize a panel discussion in which several students read and report on selected chapters as a class project.

❺ To gain a global perspective on professional development, arrange a panel in which international students discuss the status of the teacher and teacher-student relationships in their countries. Compare and contrast their opinions with how these topics are viewed in the United States

❻ Enter the debate—Is ancient Egypt or Greece the major shaping influence in Western civilization?—by finding and watching videos on Bernal and Egypt and by finding and reading Bernal's thesis on "The Blackening of Egypt and the Formation of the Classics." Consider the following questions: How is the interpretation of history a source of power? Why did Bernal's thesis generate debate? What is the contemporary significance of the debate?

Suggested Resources

Internet Resources

 For education in preliterate societies, access PROJECT-History of Education-Education in Preliterate Societies at **www.referatele.com**.

For an essay on children of youth in ancient China, access Children and Youth in History at **www.chnm.gmu.edu**.

For the Chinese imperial examination system, access the Society for Anglo-Chinese Understanding at **www.sacu.org**.

For a discussion of "Greek Thought: Socrates, Plato, and Aristotle," access The History Guide at **www.historyguide.org**.

For a discussion of ancient Greek philosophy, access the Internet Encyclopedia of Philosophy at **www.iep.utm.edu**.

For a discussion of Islam, access the Foundation for Islamic Education at **www.Fiesite.org**; for Islamic history, visit **www.islamicity.com**.

For a discussion and sources of Aquinas and Thomist philosophy, visit **www.aquinasonline.com**.

For life in ancient Egypt, especially hieroglyphics, access **www.Watson.org**.

For a list of extensive topics on ancient Jewish history, access **www.jewishvirtuallibrary.org**.

For Confucius's life, philosophy, and educational ideas, access the Stanford Encyclopedia of philosophy at **http://plato.stanford.edu**. For Confucius on the analects, morality, and self-cultivation, access the Internet Encyclopedia of Philosophy at **www.iep.utm.edu**.

For a hypertextual edition of Quintilian's *Institutio Oratoria* or *Institutes of Oratory*, access **http://honeyl.public.iastate.edu/quintilian**.

To read Bernal's thesis on "The Blackening of Egypt and the Formation of the Classics," access **www.inst.at/trans/15Nr/plenum/bernal15EN.htm**.

Publications

Baines, John. *Visual and Written Culture in Ancient Egypt*. New York: Oxford University Press, 2007. *An examination of the visual and written aspects of Egyptian culture, with a discussion of writing and scribal culture.*

Black, Robert. *Humanism and Education in Medieval and Renaissance Italy: Tradition and Innovation in Latin Schools from the Twelfth to the Fifteenth Century*. Cambridge, UK: Cambridge University Press, 2007. *Discusses the history of the Italian Renaissance in its intellectual, philosophical, and political context.*

Cribiore, Rafaella. *Gymnastics of the Mind: Greek Education in Hellenistic and Roman Egypt*. Princeton: Princeton University Press, 2005. *Provides an analysis of the transference of Greek education to Egypt.*

De Bary, William Theodore. *Confucian Tradition and Global Education*. New York: Columbia University Press, 2007. *Considers the relevance of Confucianism in the contemporary world, especially to globalization.*

Fergus, Kerr. Thomas Aquinas: *A Very Short Introduction*. New York: Oxford University Press, 2009. *Provides the reader with a readable entry into the ideas of the medieval thinker.*

Gadalla, Moustafa. *The Ancient Egyptian Culture Revealed*. Greensboro, NC: Tehuti Research Foundation, 2007. *Provides a discussion of the religious and cultural aspects of ancient Egyptian culture, especially the sciences and medicine.*

Gardner, Daniel K. *The Four Books: The Basic Teachings of the Later Confucian Tradition*. Indianapolis, IN: Hackett Publishing Co., 2007. *Provides an introduction to the basic Confucian texts.*

Gutek, Gerald. *Historical and Philosophical Foundations of Education: A Biographical Introduction*. Columbus, OH: Merrill/Prentice Hall, 2011. *Contains essays that provide biographies and discussions of the educational ideas of Confucius, Plato, Aristotle, Aquinas, Erasmus, Calvin, and others in their historical contexts.*

____. *Historical and Philosophical Foundations of Education: Selected Readings.* Columbus, OH: Merrill/Prentice Hall, 2001. *Primary source documents highlight the educational philosophies of Plato, Aristotle, Aquinas, Erasmus, Calvin, and other educational thinkers.*

MacCulloch, Diarmaid. *The Reformation.* New York: Penguin, 2005. *Examines the major actors and social and intellectual trends of the Reformation.*

Mcdougall, Iain, J. C. Yardley, and Mark Joyal. *Greek and Roman Education: A Source Book.* London: Routledge, 2008. *A comprehensive and careful edition of the major sources of ancient Greek and Roman education.*

Murphy, Madonna M. *The History and Philosophy of Education: Voices of Educational Pioneers.* Upper Saddle River, NJ: Pearson/Merrill/Prentice Hall, 2006. *Provides a well-organized and comprehensive treatment of the world's leading educators from antiquity to the present, with biographical sketches, time lines, commentaries, and primary source readings.*

Nichols, Aidan. *Discovering Aquinas: An Introduction to His Life, Work and Influence.* Grand Rapids, MI: William B. Eerdmans Publishing, 2002. *Provides a biography and commentary on Thomas Aquinas and his theology and philosophy.*

Nichols, Stephen J. *The Reformation: How a Monk and a Mallet Changed the World.* Wheaton, IL: Crossway Books, 2007. *An engaging account of leading Protestant reformers such as Luther, Zwingli, and Calvin.*

Oldstone-Moore, Jennifer. *Confucianism.* Oxford and New York: Oxford University Press, 2002. *A highly readable account of Confucius and his ethical system.*

Pedersen, Olaf. *The First Universities: Studium Generale and the Origins of University Education in Europe:* Cambridge: Cambridge University Press, 2009. *Provides a well-researched discussion of how the entry of the liberal arts through the general studies curriculum contributed to the founding of the medieval universities.*

Poulakos, Takis, and David DePew. *Isocrates and Civic Education.* Austin: University of Texas Press, 2009. *A well-done edition of Isocrates's ideas on education.*

Silverstein, Adam J. *Islamic History: A Very Short Introduction.* Oxford: Oxford University Press, 2010. *Provides a useful entry to the study of Islamic history and its sources.*

Additional resources for this chapter, including the TeachSource Videos, can be found on the Education CourseMate website. Go to **CengageBrain.com** to access the site.

Pioneers of Teaching and Learning

This chapter examines how leading educational pioneers developed new ideas about education and designed innovative teaching and learning strategies. These innovators developed new ideas about schools, curriculum, and methods of instruction that shaped teachers' preservice preparation and classroom practices.

Pioneers such as Johann Amos Comenius, Jean-Jacques Rousseau, and Johann Heinrich Pestalozzi challenged traditional concepts of child depravity and passive learning that had long dominated schooling. The **child depravity theory**, which asserted that children are born with a tendency to evil, led to authoritarian teaching methods in which teachers used psychological and physical coercion to exorcise the child's inclination to disorder and laziness. In contrast, the educational pioneers asserted the **naturalist theory** that children are naturally good and that teachers should base instruction on children's natural development.

Educators such as Friedrich Froebel, Maria Montessori, Herbert Spencer, John Dewey, Jean Piaget, and Paulo Freire argued that (1) education should be aligned with the natural stages of human growth and development, and (2) children learn by interacting with the objects and situations in their everyday environments. Froebel's kindergarten and Montessori's prepared environment proposed bold new vistas for early childhood education. Both Dewey and Piaget emphasized children's explorations and interactions with their environments as the most intelligent and effective way to learn. Herbert Spencer proposed a utilitarian and scientific curriculum to prepare individuals to adapt successfully to their environments. Freire wanted education to raise the consciousness of marginalized people so they could liberate themselves from oppressive social, economic, political, and educational conditions. Johann Herbart devised a method to systematize and to structure instruction.

As you read this chapter, consider the following questions:

FOCUS QUESTIONS

- Who qualifies as an educational pioneer? How did the pioneers develop their ideas about education? Can these pioneers contribute to my ideas about teaching and learning and to the construction of my history or autobiography of education?
- How did the educational pioneers respond to issues of socioeconomic and cultural diversity and privilege?
- Did the pioneers want education to contribute to cultural continuity or generate change?
- How did the educational pioneers contribute to the development of the teaching profession?
- Did the educational pioneers set standards in education, especially for curriculum and instruction?
- How did the educational pioneers respond to technology?

Constructing Your Own History or Autobiography of Education

You might think about these pioneers in education as educational mentors from the past who can illuminate your ideas about teaching and learning in the present. A mentor is a significant person whose life, ideas, and behavior serve as a model, or an exemplar, for another person. For example, in Chapter 3, Global Origins of American Education, we saw that Socrates was a mentor for Plato, who, in turn, was Aristotle's mentor. You can relate these pioneers to your contemporary mentors, especially teachers, who shaped your ideas on education and, perhaps, your decision to become a teacher. Then, you can reflect on how the pioneers in this chapter contributed to your ideas about teaching and learning.

---

*This chapter was revised by Gerald L. Gutek.

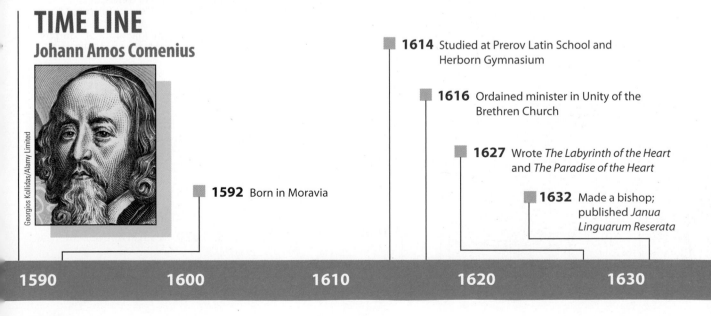

TIME LINE
Johann Amos Comenius

Georgios Kollidas/Alamy Limited

1614 Studied at Prerov Latin School and Herborn Gymnasium

1616 Ordained minister in Unity of the Brethren Church

1627 Wrote *The Labyrinth of the Heart* and *The Paradise of the Heart*

1592 Born in Moravia

1632 Made a bishop; published *Janua Linguarum Reserata*

| 1590 | 1600 | 1610 | 1620 | 1630 |

Comenius: Pansophism as a New Method

Jan Komensky (1592–1670), or Johann Comenius, was born in the Moravian town of Nivnitz, which is now in the Czech Republic.[1] He lived during Europe's post-Reformation religious wars between Catholics and Protestants—a time of intense sectarian violence. He was a bishop and educator of the Moravian Brethren, a small, often persecuted, Protestant church. Religious persecution forced Comenius to flee his homeland and live as a refugee in other countries. Working to end religious intolerance, he constructed a new educational philosophy, *pansophism,* to cultivate universal understanding. A pioneering peace educator, Comenius believed that universally shared knowledge would convince people to renounce their ethnic and religious hatreds and live harmoniously in a peaceful world order.[2]

Comenius was a transitional figure between the Renaissance humanist educators discussed in Chapter 3 and the naturalist reformers examined in this chapter. Comenius's sensory method of teaching, rather than passive memorization, inspired later educators such as Rousseau, Pestalozzi, Montessori, and Dewey. Because Latin was still an important language in education, he wrote *Gate of Tongues Unlocked,* which related teaching Latin to the students' own spoken vernacular language. Lessons began with short, simple phrases and gradually moved to longer, more complex sentences. The innovative Comenius wrote and illustrated the early picture book, *The Visible World in Pictures,* as a teaching aid.[3]

Principles of Teaching and Learning

Comenius rejected the child depravity doctrine that children were inherently bad and that teachers needed to use corporal punishment to discipline them. Instead, he wanted teachers to be caring persons who respected children's dignity and created engaging

> Pansophism

> Learning language by natural means

> Respecting children's needs and development

---

[1]For biographies of Comenius, see Daniel Murphy, *Comenius: A Critical Reassessment of His Life and Work* (Dublin, Ireland: Irish Academic Press, 1995) and M. W. Keatinge, *The Historical Life of John Amos Comenius* (Whitefish, MT: Kessinger Publishers, 2007).
[2]Johann Comenius, *The Labyrinth of the World and the Paradise of the Heart,* translated and introduced by Howard Louthan and Andrea Sterk (New York: Paulist Press, 1998), pp. 17–26. Also, access *The Labyrinth of the World and the Paradise of the Heart* at The Online Books Page at **http://onlinebooks.library.upenn.edu**.
Reprints of Comenius's works are M. W. Keatinge, *The Great Didactic of John Amos Comenius* (Whitefish, MT: Kessinger Publishers, 2005); Comenius, *Orbis Pictus* (Whitefish, MT: Kessinger Publishers, 2007); Comenius, *School of Infancy* (Whitefish, MT: Kessinger Publishers, 2003); Comenius, *Why God Gives Children and In What Parents Ought to Educate Them* (Whitefish, MT: Kessinger Publishers, 2010).
[3]For a brief biography and excerpt from Comenius's *Great Didactic,* see Madonna M. Murphy, *The History and Philosophy of Education: Voices of Educational Pioneers* (Upper Saddle River, NJ: Pearson/Merrill/Prentice Hall, 2006), pp. 150–156.

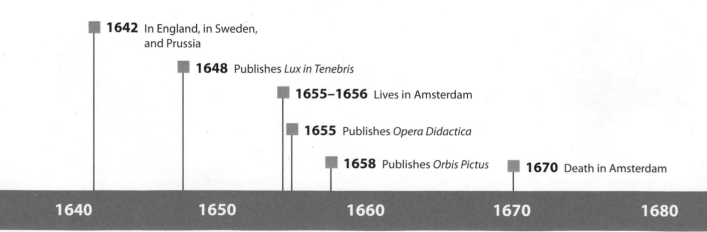

1642 In England, in Sweden, and Prussia

1648 Publishes *Lux in Tenebris*

1655–1656 Lives in Amsterdam

1655 Publishes *Opera Didactica*

1658 Publishes *Orbis Pictus*

1670 Death in Amsterdam

1640 1650 1660 1670 1680

Illustrations of panels in Comenius Orbis Pictus depicting the work of the scientist, theologian, and educator.

Interfoto/Personalities/Alamy Limited

Principles of teaching

and pleasant classrooms. An early advocate of learning readiness, Comenius warned against hurrying or pressuring children. He believed children learn most efficiently when they are developmentally ready to learn a particular skill or subject. Teachers should calibrate lessons to children's natural stages of development. He advised teachers to organize their lessons into easily assimilated small steps that made learning gradual, cumulative, and pleasant.

The following Comenian principles apply to the preservice preparation of teachers and to classroom practice: (1) use objects or pictures to illustrate concepts; (2) organize lessons around students' everyday experience (3) be clear and direct in presenting material; (4) emphasize the general aspect rather than the details in a lesson; (5) extend children's horizons by emphasizing that we live in an environment shared with plants, animals, and other people; (6) present lessons in sequence, stressing one thing at a time; (7) do not leave a specific skill or subject until students thoroughly

TIME LINE
Jean-Jacques Rousseau

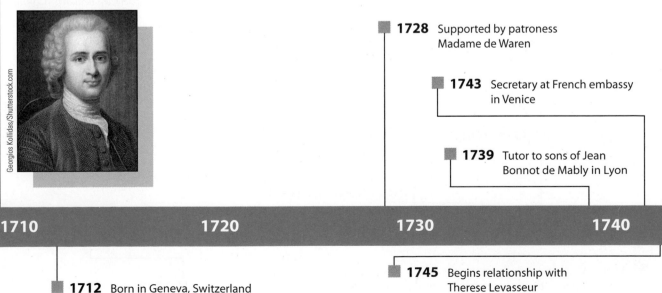

Georgios Kollidas/Shutterstock.com

1728 Supported by patroness Madame de Waren

1743 Secretary at French embassy in Venice

1739 Tutor to sons of Jean Bonnot de Mably in Lyon

| 1710 | 1720 | 1730 | 1740 |

1712 Born in Geneva, Switzerland

1745 Begins relationship with Therese Levasseur

understand it.[4] Comenius's emphasis on children's readiness, using concrete objects, and proceeding gradually in instruction became an integral part of preservice teacher-education programs.

Education and Schooling

 Universal knowledge, a force for peace

Comenius, a pioneer in multicultural and peace education, respected religious and cultural diversity but also believed all persons were members of a common human family. He believed that schooling, by cultivating universal knowledge and values, could promote international understanding and peace and create a nonviolent world.

An innovator, Comenius used the technological inventions of his time, such as the printing press, to diffuse his ideas. He also wrote textbooks that included illustrations.

Influence on Educational Practices Today

As a forward-looking educator, Comenius can serve as a historical mentor for today's teachers. He advised teachers against rushing or pressuring children to learn things they weren't ready for and to create pleasant and caring classroom climates.

He wanted teachers to do the following:

- Respect universal human rights and children's dignity as persons.
- Recognize children's stages of development and learning readiness.
- Use objects and pictures to encourage children to use their senses in learning.

REFOCUS   After reading about Comenius, think back to the questions at the beginning of the chapter. *Use these questions to construct your own history or autobiography of education.* Can Comenius serve as a historical mentor, or model, for you as a teacher? In your educational experience, were there teachers who used Comenius's principles? For Comenius, what were the most important purposes of education? Do you plan to include Comenius's ideas in your history or autobiography of education?

Rousseau: Educating the Natural Child

 Noble savages in the state of nature

Jean-Jacques Rousseau (1712–1778), a Swiss-born French theorist, lived during the eighteenth-century Age of Reason, which influenced the American and French Revolutions.[5] He was among the Parisian intellectuals who questioned the authority of the established church and absolute monarchy.

---

[4]Gerald L. Gutek, *Historical and Philosophical Foundations of Education: Selected Readings* (Columbus, OH: Merrill, 2001), pp. 50–57.
[5]For Rousseau's life and ideas, see Jean-Jacques Rousseau, *Confessions*, Patrick Coleman, ed., and Angela Scholar, trans. (New York: Oxford University Press, 2000); Rousseau and Russell Gaulbourne, *Reveries of the Solitary Walker* (New York: Oxford University Press, 2011); David Gauthier, *Rousseau: the Sentiment of Existence* (Cambridge: Cambridge University Press, 2006); Robert Walker, *Rousseau: The Age of the Enlightenment* (Princeton: Princeton University Press, 2012); Leo Damrosch, *Jean-Jacques Rousseau: Restless Genius* (New York: Houghton Mifflin, 2007).

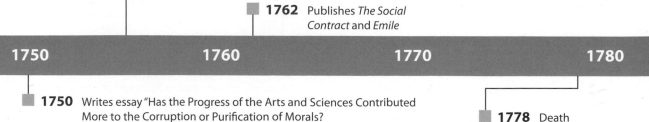

1755 Publishes *Discourse on the Origin and Foundations of Inequality among Men*

1762 Publishes *The Social Contract* and *Emile*

| 1750 | 1760 | 1770 | 1780 |

1750 Writes essay "Has the Progress of the Arts and Sciences Contributed More to the Corruption or Purification of Morals?"

1778 Death

OVERVIEW 4.1

Educational Pioneers

Pioneer	Historical Context	Purpose of Education	Curriculum
Comenius 1592–1670 (Czech)	Seventeenth-century religious war following Protestant Reformation	Relate instruction to children's natural growth and development; contribute to peace and social justice	Vernacular language, reading, writing, mathematics, religion, history, Latin; universal knowledge
Rousseau 1712–1778 (Swiss-French)	Eighteenth-century French Enlightenment	Create learning environments in which children's natural goodness can grow	Nature; the environment
Pestalozzi 1747–1827 (Swiss)	Early nineteenth century, post-Napoleonic period and early industrialism	Develop the human being's moral, mental, and physical powers harmoniously; use sense perception in forming clear ideas	Object lessons; form, number, sound
Herbart 1776–1841 (German)	Mid-nineteenth-century developments in European philosophy and psychology	Develop multiple interests and moral character	Academic and humanistic studies, especially history and literature
Froebel 1782–1852 (German)	Nineteenth-century resurgence of philosophical idealism and nationalism	Develop the latent spiritual essence of the child in a prepared environment	Songs, stories, games, gifts, occupations
Spencer 1820-1903 (English)	Darwin's theory of evolution in 1859 and rise of nineteenth-century industrial corporations	Enable human beings to live effectively, economically, and scientifically	Practical, utilitarian, and scientific subjects
Dewey 1859–1952 (American)	Early twentieth-century American progressive movement, growth of science, and rise of pragmatic philosophy	Contribute to the individual's personal, social, and intellectual growth	Making and doing; history and geography; science; problems
Addams 1860–1935 (American)	First half of twentieth century, period of massive immigration and urban change	Assimilate immigrants into American society while preserving their ethnic cultural heritages	Wide range of practical skills for life in urban centers, along with arts and sciences, and problem solving
Montessori 1870–1952 (Italian)	Late nineteenth- and early twentieth-century assertion of feminism; greater attention to early childhood education	Assist children's sensory, physical, and intellectual development in a prepared environment	Motor and sensory skills; preplanned materials
Piaget 1896–1980 (Swiss)	Twentieth-century developments in psychology by Freud, Hall, Jung, and others	Structure instruction on children's patterns of growth and stages of development	Concrete and formal operations
Freire 1921–1997 (Brazilian)	Late twentieth-century critique of neocolonialism and globalism	Raise consciousness about exploitative conditions	Literary circles and critical dialogues

Methods of Instruction	Role of the Teacher	Significance	Influence on Today's Schools
Based on readiness and stages of human growth; gradual, cumulative, orderly; use of objects	A permissive facilitator of learning; calibrates instruction to child's stages of development	Developed a more humane view of the child; educational method incorporating sensation	Schools organized according to children's stages of development
Reliance on sensation; experience with nature	Assists nature, rather than imposing social conventions on the child	Led a Romantic revolt against the doctrine of child depravity; a forerunner of child-centered progressivism	Permissive teaching based on child freedom
Reliance on sensation; object lessons; simple to complex; near to far; concrete to abstract	Acts as a caring facilitator of learning by creating a home-like school environment; skilled in using the special method	Devised an educational method that changed instruction in elementary schools	Schooling based on emotional security and object learning
Systematic organization of instruction: preparation, presentation, association, generalization, application	A well-prepared professional who follows the prescribed sequence in teaching	Devised an education method that stressed sequential organization of instruction and moral character development	Teacher preparation based on a prescribed method and entry of history and literature into curriculum as a moral core
Self-activity; play; imitation	Facilitates children's growth	Created the kindergarten, a special early childhood learning environment	Preschools designed to liberate the child's creativity
Reliance on sensation and the scientific method; activities	Organizes instruction in basic activities	A leading curriculum theorist who stressed scientific knowledge	Schooling that stresses scientific knowledge and competitive values
Problem solving according to the scientific method	Creates a learning environment based on learners' shared experiences	Developed the pragmatic experimentalist philosophy of education	Schooling that emphasizes problem solving and activities in a context of community
Begin with learner's neighborhood, culture, and needs; lead to broader social realities and connections	Engages in a reciprocal or mutual learning experience with students	Developed a progressive theory of urban and multicultural education	Respect for multicultural pluralism in a shared American cultural context
Spontaneous learning; activities; practical, sensory, and formal skills; exercises for practical life	Acts as a director of learning by using didactic materials in a prepared environment	Developed a widely used method and philosophy of early childhood education	Early childhood schooling that is intellectually and developmentally stimulating
Individualized programs; exploration and experimentation with concrete materials	Organizes instruction according to stages of cognitive development	Formulated a theory of cognitive development	Schooling organized around cognitive developmental stages
Use of personal and group autobiographies	Stimulates awareness of real conditions of life	Formulated a theory and praxis of critical consciousness	Influenced critical theory and liberation pedagogy

Rousseau's books *On the Origin of the Inequality of Mankind* and *The Social Contract* condemned social inequalities based on birth, wealth, and property.[6] In the original state of nature, according to Rousseau, people were "noble savages," who were innocent, free, and uncorrupted by socioeconomic artificialities. Rousseau is often criticized for his personal inconsistency regarding children. Although he championed children's rights in his books, he abandoned his own children in orphanages instead of rearing and educating them himself.

Emile: A novel of education

Rousseau conveyed his educational philosophy in 1762 through his novel *Emile,* the story of a boy's education from infancy to adulthood.[7] Rousseau's highly controversial novel rejected the principle that education should socialize the child. Attacking the child-depravity doctrine and book-dominated education, he argued that children's instincts and needs are naturally good and should be satisfied rather than repressed by authoritarian schools and coercive teachers. He wanted to liberate people from society's imprisoning institutions, of which the school was one of the most coercive, in that it prepared people to accept the restrictions imposed by other institutions.

Principles of Teaching and Learning

Stages of development

Like Comenius, Rousseau emphasized the crucial importance of stages of human development. In *Emile,* he identified five developmental stages: infancy, childhood, boyhood, adolescence, and youth. Each stage is sequential, exhibiting its own conditions for readiness to learn and leading to the next stage.[8] To preserve the child's natural goodness, a tutor homeschools Emile on a country estate away from the conformity and role-playing of artificial and corrupt society and schools. Homeschooling is preferred to schools that miseducate children to follow social conventions rather than their own natural instincts.

Infancy: first contacts with environment

In Rousseau's first stage, infancy (birth to age five), his fictional character Emile begins to construct his initial impressions of reality; he learns directly by using his senses to examine the objects in his environment.

Childhood: exploring the world through senses

During childhood (from age five to twelve), Emile constructs his own personal self-identity as he learns that his actions cause either painful or pleasurable consequences. Naturally curious, Emile continues to use his senses to learn more about the world. Calling the eyes, ears, hands, and feet the first teachers, Rousseau judged learning through sensation to be much more effective than teaching children words they do not understand. The tutor deliberately refrains from introducing books at this stage so Emile will not substitute reading for direct experience with nature.

Boyhood: natural science

During boyhood (from age twelve to fifteen), Emile learns natural science by observing plant and animal growth cycles. Exploring his surroundings, he learns geography directly rather than from studying maps. Emile also learns a manual trade, carpentry, to connect mental and physical work.

Adolescence: entering society

When he reaches adolescence (from age fifteen to eighteen), Emile is ready to learn about the broader world of society, politics, art, and commerce. Visits to museums, theaters, art galleries, and libraries cultivate his aesthetic tastes. During the last stage

[6]Jean-Jacques Rousseau, *Discourse on Political Economy and the Social Contract* (trans. Christopher Betts) (New York: Oxford University Press, 2009); Joshua Cohen, *Rousseau: A Free Community of Equals* (New York: Oxford University Press, 2010); Ethan Putterman, *Rousseau, Law, and the Sovereignty of the People* (Cambridge: Cambridge University Press, 2010); Christie McDonald and Stanley Hoffman, *Rousseau and Freedom* (Cambridge: Cambridge University Press, 2010).
[7]Jean-Jacques Rousseau, *Emile, or on Education* (includes Emile and Sophie; or the Solitaries). Christoper Kelly ed., Allan Bloom, trans. (Lebanon, NH: Dartmouth College Press, 2009); Jean-Jacques Rousseau, *Emile,* with an introduction by Gerald L. Gutek (New York: Barnes and Noble, 2005). For a critique of *Emile* by a contemporary of Rousseau, see H.S. Gerdil, *The Anti-Emile: Reflections on the Theory and Practice of Education against the Principles of Rousseau* (South Bend, IN: St. Augustine Press, 2011).
[8]Christopher Winch, "Rousseau on Learning: A Re-Evaluation," *Educational Theory* (Fall 1996), pp. 424–425. For a commentary on the role of parents and the state in education, see Laurence B. Reardon, *The State as Parent: Locke, Rousseau, and the Transformation of the Family* (Scranton, PA: University of Scranton Press, 2011).

of education (from age eighteen to twenty), Emile visits Paris and the major European cities to broaden his cultural awareness. After he meets his future wife, Sophie, Emile tells his tutor at the book's end that he plans to educate his children in the same way he was educated, according to nature.

Education and Schooling

Education versus schooling

Rousseau was suspicious of schools, which he believed taught children to conform to society's artificial rules rather than live spontaneously according to nature. School-induced socialization forced children into the routines and the roles adults preferred instead of letting them follow their own natural instincts, interests, and needs.[9] By forcing children to memorize books, traditional teachers thwarted the child's own power to learn from direct experience. Emile, a child of nature, expresses rather than represses his natural instincts and impulses. If pleasure is enjoyed, Emile earned his reward. If his actions cause pain, Emile brought these consequences upon himself. Either way, he learned from the experience. Rousseau highlighted the following principles in his philosophy of education: (1) childhood is the natural foundation for future human growth and development; (2) children's natural interests and instincts will lead to a thorough exploration of the environment; (3) human beings, in their life cycles, go through necessary stages of development; and (4) adult coercion negatively impacts children's development.

Influence on Educational Practices Today

Impact on progressive educators

Although his critics disparage the story of Emile's education as a fictitious and impractical account of a one-to-one relationship between the student and teacher, Rousseau has influenced modern education. Rousseau's argument that the curriculum should arise from children's interests and needs profoundly affected child-centered progressive educators. (See Chapter 6, Philosophical Roots of Education, for more on progressive education.) Rousseau's ideas also anticipated constructivism, in which children interpret their own reality rather than learn information from indirect sources. Despite his distrust of schools, Rousseau's insights that teachers should follow children's interests and that children should learn from their direct interaction with the environment have shaped preservice preparation and classroom practice.

REFOCUS After reading about Rousseau, think back to the questions at the beginning of the chapter. *Use these questions to construct your own history or autobiography of education.* How did Rousseau's ideas about nature and society shape his philosophy of education? Can Rousseau serve as a historical mentor, or model, for you as a teacher? In your educational experience, were there teachers who used Rousseau's principles? Do you plan to incorporate Rousseau's ideas into your history or autobiography of education?

Pestalozzi: Educating the Whole Child's Mind, Body, and Emotions

Continuity & Change

The life of the Swiss educator Johann Heinrich Pestalozzi (1747–1827) took place during the early industrial revolution in Europe and America when factory-made products were replacing home handicrafts. Early industrialization changed family life as women and children worked outside of the home.[10] Concerned about the impact of this economic change on families and children, Pestalozzi sought to develop schools that, like loving families, would nurture children's holistic development. His ideas about

[9]Eugene Iheoma, "Rousseau's Views on Teaching," *Journal of Educational Thought* 31 (April 1997), pp. 69–81.
[10]For Pestalozzi's educational novel, see Johann Heinrich Pestalozzi, *Leonard and Gertrude* (Toronto: University of Toronto Libraries, 2011); for a biography, see Hermann Krusi, *His Life, Work and Influence* (Whitefish, MT: Kessinger Publishing, 2005); for a brief biography, and excerpts from Pestalozzi's *Diary* and *Methods,* see Madonna M. Murphy, *The History and Philosophy of Education: Voices of Educational Pioneers* (Upper Saddle River, NJ: Pearson/Merrill/Prentice Hall, 2006), pp. 179–186.

the relationship of families and schools are useful in today's rapidly changing global society. An attentive reader of *Emile*, Pestalozzi agreed with Rousseau that humans are naturally good but were spoiled by a corrupt society, that traditional schools followed dull routines of memorization and recitation, and that educational reform could improve society.[11] Although Rousseau was a historical mentor for him, Pestalozzi significantly revised Rousseau's method. While Rousseau rejected schools, Pestalozzi believed that schools, if properly organized, could become centers of effective learning. He reconstituted Rousseau's homeschool approach into simultaneous group instruction in schools.

Simultaneous group instruction

In his schools at Burgdorf and Yverdon, Pestalozzi developed a preservice teacher-education program where he served as a mentor to the future teachers being trained in his method. Like Comenius, Pestalozzi emphasized the right of children to be taught by caring teachers in a safe environment.[12]

Philosophically, Pestalozzi, a realist like Aristotle, believed that the mind formed concepts by abstracting data conveyed to it by the senses. His method of object-centered instruction influenced Froebel and Montessori, discussed later in this chapter, as well as later progressive educators. (See Chapter 6, Philosophical Roots of Education, for more on realism and progressivism.)

Principles of Teaching and Learning

A safe school with caring teachers

Pestalozzi organized his approach to teaching into "general" and "special" methods. The general method, which had to be in place before more specific instruction occurred, sought to create a caring and emotionally healthy homelike school environment. This required teachers who, emotionally secure themselves, could win students' trust and affection and nurture their self-esteem.

Sensory learning

After the general method was in place, Pestalozzi implemented his special method, which stressed direct sensory learning. Guided by Rousseau's warnings against highly abstract lessons that were remote from children's everyday life, Pestalozzi began instruction with children's direct experiences in their environment.

---

[11]Gerald L. Gutek, *Pestalozzi and Education* (Prospect Heights, IL: Waveland Press, 1999), pp. 21–51.
[12]Johann Heinrich Pestalozzi, *How Gertrude Teaches Her Children* (Ann Arbor, MI: University of Michigan Library, 2009).

TIME LINE
Johann Heinrich Pestalozzi

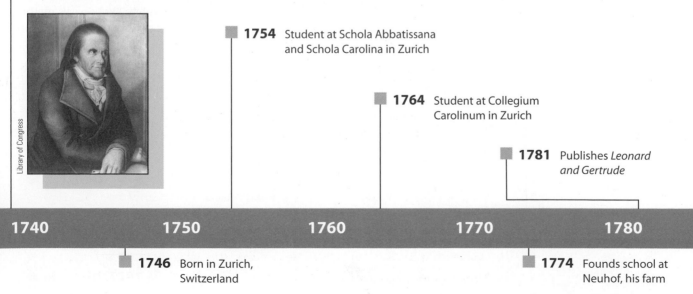

Library of Congress

1754 Student at Schola Abbatissana and Schola Carolina in Zurich

1764 Student at Collegium Carolinum in Zurich

1781 Publishes *Leonard and Gertrude*

1740	1750	1760	1770	1780

1746 Born in Zurich, Switzerland

1774 Founds school at Neuhof, his farm

Pestalozzi teaching students at his institute at Burgdorf, Switzerland; note the large wall charts used in teaching counting and arithmetic.

Library of Congress

In this approach, children studied the objects—plants, rocks, animals, and man-made items—that they found in their daily experience in the social and natural environments.

In the **object lessons**, children were to learn the form, number, and names of objects. To learn an object's form, they traced and outlined its shape and made sketches of it. To learn numbers, they counted the objects and then learned their names. The students moved gradually from drawing exercises to writing and reading. The first writing exercises consisted of drawing lessons in which the children drew a series of rising and falling strokes and open and closed curves. Developing children's motor coordination and hand muscles, these drawing and tracing exercises prepared them for writing. From counting exercises, they moved to adding, subtracting, multiplying, and dividing objects.

▌ Methods for teaching and learning

Pestalozzi incorporated the following strategies in his preservice teacher-preparation program. Teachers should (1) begin with concrete objects before moving to more abstract concepts; (2) begin with the learner's immediate environment before moving to what is distant and remote; (3) begin with easy and simple exercises before moving to complex ones; and (4) always proceed gradually and cumulatively. Pestalozzi's method was incorporated into elementary-schools and teacher education programs in Europe and the United States.

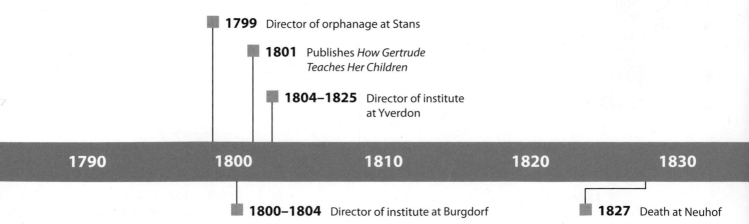

1799 Director of orphanage at Stans

1801 Publishes *How Gertrude Teaches Her Children*

1804–1825 Director of institute at Yverdon

| 1790 | 1800 | 1810 | 1820 | 1830 |

1800–1804 Director of institute at Burgdorf

1827 Death at Neuhof

Natural, learning in a caring environment

Education and Schooling

Both Rousseau and Pestalozzi defined "knowing" as understanding nature, its patterns, and its laws. Pestalozzi stressed empirical, or sensory, learning, through which children learn about their environment by carefully observing natural phenomena. Like Comenius, Pestalozzi believed children should learn gradually, not be hurried, and should understand what they are studying before moving on to the next lesson.

Educating Children with Special Needs Pestalozzi was dedicated to teaching children with special needs. He opened his schools to children who were poor and hungry victims of poverty and to those who had social, emotional, and psychological problems. If children came to school without breakfast, he fed them before he attempted to teach them. If they were frightened, he comforted them. For him, a teacher needed to be a caring person as well as an expert in teaching methods. Pestalozzi's principles are applicable to teaching children with special needs as well as children generally.

Pestalozzianism brought to United States

REFOCUS After reading about Pestalozzi, think back to the questions at the beginning of the chapter. *Use these questions to construct your own history or autobiography of education.* Note that both Comenius and Rousseau served as historical mentors or models for Pestalozzi. How did Pestalozzi define the purposes of education? How might Pestalozzi serve as a historical mentor, or model, for you as a teacher? In your educational experience, were there teachers who used Pestalozzi's principles? Do you plan on incorporating Pestalozzian principles into your history or autobiography of education?

Influence on Educational Practices Today

Pestalozzi's object lessons were introduced into the American elementary-school curriculum in the nineteenth century. His emphasis on having students manipulate the objects in their environment was a forerunner of process-based learning. His belief in holistic education stimulated educators to encourage both cognitive and affective learning. Pestalozzi's general method remains highly meaningful for American teachers who are concerned with educating

TIME LINE
Johann Friedrich Herbart

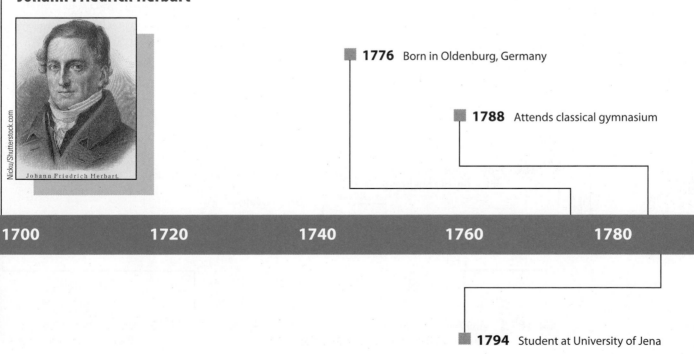

Nicku/Shutterstock.com

Johann Friedrich Herbart

1776 Born in Oldenburg, Germany

1788 Attends classical gymnasium

| 1700 | 1720 | 1740 | 1760 | 1780 |

1794 Student at University of Jena

at-risk children.[13] His assertion that emotional security is a necessary precondition for skill and subject learning strongly anticipated the contemporary emphasis on safe and secure schools that are free of bullying and violence.

Herbart: Systematizing Teaching

Johann Friedrich Herbart (1776–1841), a German professor of philosophy and psychology, devised an educational method that systematized instruction and encouraged students' moral development. In particular, he used history and literature to construct networks of ideas in students' minds.[14]

Principles of Teaching and Learning

Apperceptive mass

Herbart defined *interest* as a person's ability to focus on and retain an idea in consciousness. He reasoned that a large mass or network of ideas would generate a great number of interests. Ideas related to each other formed a network, or what he termed an "apperceptive mass," in the mind. Informed by Herbart's psychology, teachers were advised to introduce students to an increasing number of ideas and to help them construct relationships between ideas.

Moral development

Concerned with students' moral development, Herbart emphasized the humanities, especially history and literature as rich sources of moral values. By studying the lives of great men and women, students could discover how people made their moral decisions. Literature provided a framework for placing values into a humanistic perspective. Herbart was influential in bringing history and literature into the curriculum at a time when it was dominated by the classical Greek and Latin languages.

---

[13]Rebecca Wild, *Raising Curious, Creative, Confident Kids: The Pestalozzi Experiment in Child-Based Education* (Boston: Shambhala, 2000). For the introduction of Pestalozzianism in the United States, see Henry Barnard, ed., *Pestalozzi and Pestalozzianism: Life, Education Principles and Methods of John Henry Pestalozzi* (Ann Arbor: University of Michigan University Library/Michigan Historical Reprint Series, 2005).

[14]For a biography and excerpts from Herbart's *Outlines of Educational Doctrine*, see Madonna M. Murphy, *The History and Philosophy of Education: Voices of Educational Pioneers* (Upper Saddle River, NJ: Pearson/Merrill/Prentice Hall, 2006), pp. 194–201. For Herbart's text on the "Meaning of Education," see **www.archive.org**.

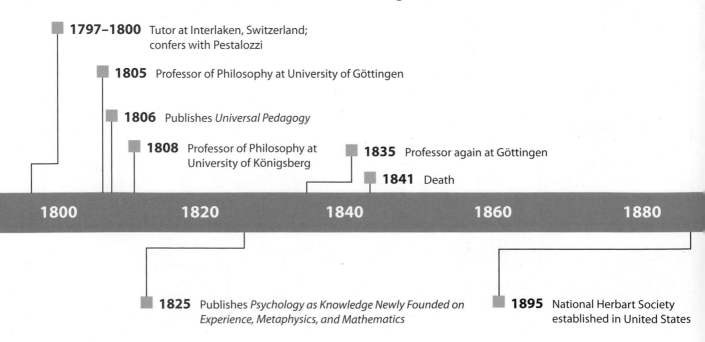

1797–1800 Tutor at Interlaken, Switzerland; confers with Pestalozzi

1805 Professor of Philosophy at University of Göttingen

1806 Publishes *Universal Pedagogy*

1808 Professor of Philosophy at University of Königsberg

1835 Professor again at Göttingen

1841 Death

| 1800 | 1820 | 1840 | 1860 | 1880 |

1825 Publishes *Psychology as Knowledge Newly Founded on Experience, Metaphysics, and Mathematics*

1895 National Herbart Society established in United States

Education and Schooling

Instruction as a sequence of steps

Seeking to systematize teaching, Herbart structured instruction into a precise sequence of five steps:

1. Preparation, in which teachers encourage readiness in students to receive the new concept or material they are planning to introduce

2. Presentation, in which teachers clearly identify and present the new concept

3. Association, in which the new concept is compared and contrasted with ideas that students already know

4. Generalization, in which a principle is formed that combines the new and previous learning

5. Application, in which appropriate examinations and exercises assess whether students have mastered and learned the new principle[15]

History and literature

Influence on Educational Practices Today

Herbart's method gained wide acceptance in teacher-education programs in the United States and in other countries, especially Japan. Teachers were trained to use Herbart's steps to systematically organize instruction. Herbart's view of moral education brought history and literature into the curriculum. Despite its popularity, John Dewey and progressive educators criticized Herbart's method, claiming that it reduced students to passive receivers of information rather than active learners.

In the late nineteenth and early twentieth centuries, preservice teacher-preparation programs featured Herbart's methodological emphasis on systematic and sequential instruction. Herbart's method is especially relevant to the No Child Left Behind (NCLB) guidelines that time spent on instruction should be efficient and effective and that students should be tested to assess the degree to which they have mastered skills and subjects. The implications of Herbart's method for teachers today are to (1) clearly identify the skills and

REFOCUS After reading about Herbart, think back to the questions at the beginning of the chapter. *Use these questions to construct your own history or autobiography of education.* How did Herbart define the purposes of education? How might Herbart serve as a historical mentor, or model, for you as a teacher? In your educational experience, were there teachers who used Herbart's principles? Do you plan to incorporate Herbart's principles into your history or autobiography of education?

---

[15]Herbart's original four-step method was restructured by the American Herbartian educators into the five steps generally used in the United States. For more information about the American Herbartians, access "Herbart and the Herbartians" at **www.archive.org**.

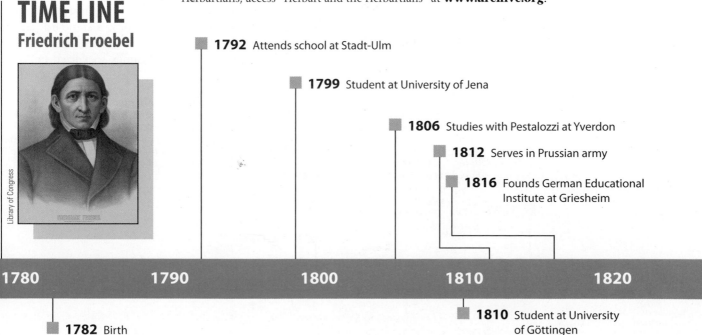

TIME LINE
Friedrich Froebel

Library of Congress

1792 Attends school at Stadt-Ulm

1799 Student at University of Jena

1806 Studies with Pestalozzi at Yverdon

1812 Serves in Prussian army

1816 Founds German Educational Institute at Griesheim

1780   **1790**   **1800**   **1810**   **1820**

1810 Student at University of Göttingen

1782 Birth

concepts they plan to introduce to students; (2) develop well-organized and clearly presented lessons; and (3) test students to verify their comprehension and application of the skills and subjects presented to them.

Froebel: The Kindergarten Movement

Idealism and nationalism

The German educator Friedrich Froebel (1782–1852) created the *kindergarten*—literally, "children's garden"—a school for early childhood education.[16] Philosophically an idealist, like Plato, Froebel believed an inherent spirituality was at the core of human nature. (For more on idealism, see Chapter 6, Philosophical Roots of Education.) Every child, he believed, possesses an innate interior spiritual essence, a power, striving to be externalized. Froebel designed his kindergarten as an educational environment in which children's inherent but latent spirituality could be actualized through activity. A nationalist, he believed that the people of each country, including his native Germany, shared a common folk spirit which was manifested in the nation's stories, songs, and fables. Thus, storytelling and singing were important in the kindergarten.

Student of Pestalozzi

Froebel's desire to become a teacher took him to Pestalozzi's institute at Yverdon, where from 1808 to 1810, he interned in the teacher-training program. Pestalozzi served as a mentor for Froebel. Just as Pestalozzi had revised Rousseau's ideas, Froebel restructured Pestalozzi's method. Froebel endorsed certain aspects of Pestalozzi's method, such as using sensation and objects in a caring school atmosphere, but he believed that Pestalozzi's process needed a more philosophical foundation. Froebel gave Pestalozzi's object lesson a more symbolic meaning by asserting that the concrete object would stimulate recall of a corresponding concept in the child's mind. He eagerly accepted Pestalozzi's vision of schools as emotionally secure places for children but redefined the child's growth in spiritual terms. Like Comenius, Rousseau, and Pestalozzi, Froebel wanted teachers to be sensitive to children's readiness and needs rather than taskmasters who heard preset recitations and forced children to memorize words they did not understand.

Principles of Teaching and Learning

Kindergarten: a prepared, permissive environment

Froebel designed the kindergarten as a prepared environment in which children externalized their inner spirituality through activity. His first kindergarten, founded in 1837 at Blankenburg, was a permissive learning environment that featured games, play, songs, stories, and crafts.[17] The kindergarten's activities, now a standard part of early childhood education, stimulated children's imaginations and introduced them to the culture's folk heroes and heroines and values. The games socialized children

---

[16]Norman Brosterman, *Inventing Kindergarten* (New York: Harry N. Abrams, 1997), pp. 14–18, 22–29. For Froebel's life, see Friedrich Froebel, *Autobiography of Friedrich Froebel,* translated and annotated by Emilie Michaelis and H. Keatley Moore (General Books, 2010).

[17]For a brief biography, time line, and excerpt from Froebel's *The Education of Man,* see Madonna M. Murphy, *The History and Philosophy of Education: Voices of Educational Pioneers* (Upper Saddle River, NJ: Pearson/Merrill/Prentice Hall, 2006), pp. 201–209. For an online text of Froebel's *Education of Man,* access **www.archive.org**.

1837 Establishes Kindergarten at Blankenburg

1852 Death

1830   1840   1850   1860   1870

FROM PRESERVICE TO PRACTICE

Using a Story to Connect the Past and Present

The chapter's author shares a children's book he had written, *My Grandfather Owns a Grocery Store,* with a kindergarten class.

My grandson, Luke, invited me to read my book, *My Grandfather Owns a Grocery Store,* to his kindergarten class. The book was a self-published family project—I wrote the text about my grandparents' neighborhood grocery store where I helped out as a child. My daughters, their husbands, and my grandchildren illustrated the book with drawings and sketches.

The kindergarten class sat in a circle in front of me; I was seated on a stool. I told the children about the book—how I wrote it from childhood memories of my grandparents, their neighborhood grocery store, and how I helped to stock the shelves and arrange the fruit. I would read a page or two, then show them the illustrations and ask them if they had any questions.

I read about how my grandparents opened their store early in the morning so that the women in the neighborhood could buy fresh bread and lunch meat to pack their husbands' and their children's lunches. I explained that when I was a child, many people did not have refrigerators and used iceboxes instead. The children did not know what an icebox was. So, I explained that it was a large wooden chest that contained a large block of ice. I told them that an iceman came on a truck and delivered big blocks of ice to use to keep the food cold

so it wouldn't spoil. I asked them what happens to ice—they said it melts. Then, I asked them if they had refrigerators. They all raised their hands. Some volunteered that they had two refrigerators.

Then I read on and told them how my grandfather showed me how to arrange the cans of beans and peas so that people could see the labels. I told them how I arranged the oranges and apples in pyramids. I asked them what a pyramid is. One child raised his hand and showed the class the shape of a pyramid. I said it was difficult to arrange a pyramid with apples and oranges because they are shaped like balls and will roll away. Then I explained how I made a pyramid.

After the class, my daughter, Laura—who is Luke's mother and an elementary teacher—and I discussed my visit to the kindergarten. She believed that the lesson was positive in that it made a connection with the children's own experiences—all the children had been in large grocery stores somewhat like the smaller neighborhood grocery stores of the past. As a historian of education, I also thought about how Friedrich Froebel would critique my teaching. I think he would approve of the use of a story to build a cultural connection to the children's heritage. I think he would have also approved of my use of the geometric shape, the pyramid, to illustrate how I arranged oranges and apples.

Case Questions

1. What aspects of Froebel's kindergarten philosophy did the author use?
2. Would you use Froebel's method if you were teaching the class?
3. Have you had an educational experience like the one in the excerpt?

Gifts and occupations

and developed their physical and motor skills. As the boys and girls played with other children, they became part of the group and were prepared for further socialized learning activities.[18] The curriculum also included what Froebel called *gifts,* or objects with fixed form, such as spheres, cubes, and cylinders, intended to bring to consciousness the underlying concept represented by the object. In addition, Froebel's kindergarten featured what he designated as *occupations,* materials that children could shape and use in design and construction activities. For example, clay, sand, cardboard, and sticks could be manipulated and shaped into castles, cities, and mountains.[19]

[18]Evelyn Lawrence, ed., *Routledge Library Editions: Education Mini-Set K Philosophy of Education: Friedrich Froebel and English Education,* Vol. 18 (New York and London: Routledge, 2012). For Froebel's *Education of Man, Mother Songs,* and reminiscences, access the Froebel Web at **www.froebelweb.org**.
[19]Scott Bultman, *The Froebel Gifts: The Building Gifts 2–6, Ages 3 & Up* (Grand Rapids, MI: Kindergarten Messenger, 2000). For applying Froebel's kindergarten philosophy to contemporary education, see Helen Tovey, *Bringing the Froebel Approach to Your Early Years Practice* (New York and London: Routledge, 2011).

Education and Schooling

Importance of teacher's personality

Continuity & Change

Spread of the kindergarten movement

We often form our first impressions of schools and teachers when we are in kindergarten, and we carry these impressions with us throughout our lives. Froebel believed the kindergarten teacher's personality to be of paramount importance. Did the teacher really understand the child's nature and respect the dignity of the child's personality? Did the teacher personify the highest cultural values so that children had a model they could emulate? Preservice experiences should help teachers become sensitive to children's needs and give them the knowledge and skills to create caring and wholesome learning environments. Froebel would encourage kindergarten teachers to resist contemporary pressures to introduce academic subjects into kindergartens as a premature pressure that comes from adults, often parents, rather than children's needs and readiness.[20]

REFOCUS After reading about Froebel, think back to the questions at the beginning of the chapter. *Use these questions to construct your own history or autobiography of education.* For Froebel, what are the purposes of education? Note how Froebel reconceptualized the ideas of Pestalozzi, his mentor. How might Froebel serve as a historical mentor, or model, for you as a teacher? In your educational experience, were there teachers who used Froebel's principles? Do you plan to incorporate Froebel's ideas into your history or autobiography of education?

Influence on Educational Practices Today

Kindergarten education grew into an international movement. German immigrants imported the kindergarten to the United States, where it became part of the American school system. Elizabeth Peabody, who founded an English-language kindergarten, worked to make the kindergarten part of the American school system.[21]

Spencer: Social Darwinist and Utilitarian Educator

Theory of evolution

Continuity & Change

A social theory based on Darwin

Herbert Spencer (1820–1903) was an English social theorist whose ideas were very popular and influential in the United States in the late nineteenth and early twentieth centuries. Spencer based his social and educational philosophy on his interpretation of Charles Darwin's theory of evolution.[22] According to Darwin, species evolved naturally and gradually over long periods of time. Members of certain species survived and reproduced themselves by successfully adapting to changes in the environment. As their offspring inherited these favorable adaptive characteristics, they too survived and continued the life of the species. Those unable to adapt—the unfit—perished.[23]

Spencer, a key proponent of **social Darwinism,** applied Darwin's biological theory to society and believed that the fittest individuals of each generation would survive because of their skills, intelligence, and adaptability.[24] For Spencer, competition, a natural ethical force, motivated the best-equipped members of the human species to climb to the top of the socioeconomic ladder. Winning the competitive race

[20]For a discussion of academic pressures on children, see Shama Olfman, *All Work and No Play: How Educational Reforms Are Harming Our Preschoolers* (Westport, CT: Praeger, 2003).

[21]Bertha von Marenholtz-Bulow, *How Kindergarten Came to America: Friedrich Froebel's Radical Vision of Early Childhood Education* (New York and London: The New Press, 2007).

[22]For a succinct and clearly written exposition on Darwin, see Mark Ridley, *How to Read Darwin* (New York: W. W. Norton, 2006).

[23]For Darwin, see Charles Darwin, *The Autobiography of Charles Darwin, 1809–1883,* Nora Barlow, ed. (New York: Norton, 1993); Charles Darwin, *Origin of Species* (New York: Gramercy Press, 1995); Darwin, *The Descent of Man* (New York: Prometheus Books, 1997).

[24]Reprints of Spencer's works are Herbert Spencer, *Essays: Scientific, Political, and Speculative* (London: Routledge/Thoemmes Press, 1996); Spencer, *Collected Writings* (London: Routledge/Thoemmes Press, 1996); Spencer, *The Principles of Psychology* (London: Routledge/ Thoemmes Press, 1996).

over slower and duller individuals, the fittest would inherit the earth and populate it with their intelligent and productive children. The unfit—lazy, stupid, or weak individuals—would slowly disappear. Competition would improve the human race and result in gradual but inevitable progress.[25] Many American educators applied Spencer's ideas of competition to students in their classrooms. Later, Dewey and the progressives fought to replace competition in schools with cooperation.

Opposition to public schools

Spencer believed that schools should compete against each other so that the strong academic schools prevailed against the inferior ones. He opposed state-funded public schools, which he argued would create a monopoly for mediocrity by catering to the average rather than the gifted students in the school-age population. Private schools, in contrast, as they competed for the most able students, would become centers of educational innovation. Like contemporary proponents of vouchers, Spencer believed the best schools would attract the brightest students and the most capable teachers.

Principles of Teaching and Learning

Education for utilitarian purposes

Though a naturalist in education, Spencer defined nature differently than Rousseau and Pestalozzi. For him, nature meant the law of the jungle and survival of the fittest.[26] He believed that people in an industrialized society needed a **utilitarian education** to learn useful scientific and technological skills and subjects. Spencer emphasized science and technology in the curriculum as the best way to prepare individuals to be efficient producers in a competitive industrial society.[27]

Education and Schooling

Spencer was highly critical of traditional schools because they resisted change and continued to transmit what he considered to be an obsolete curriculum of Latin and Greek languages, literature, and history. In contrast, he wanted teachers to be curriculum and

---

[25]Mark Francis, *Herbert Spencer and the Invention of Modern Life* (Ithaca, NY: Cornell University Press, 2007).
[26]For a critique of Spencer, see Kieran Egan, *Getting It Wrong from the Beginning: Our Progressivist Inheritance from Herbert Spencer, John Dewey, and Jean Piaget* (New York: Yale University Press, 2002).
[27]Alberto Mingardi and John Meadowcraft, *Herbert Spencer (Major Conservative and Libertarian Thinker)* (New York: Continuum, 2011).

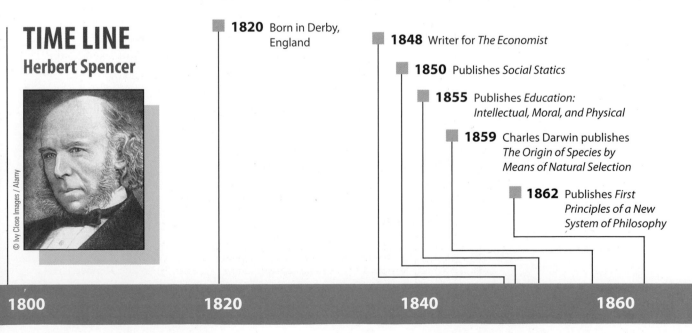

TIME LINE
Herbert Spencer

© Ivy Close Images / Alamy

1820 Born in Derby, England

1848 Writer for *The Economist*

1850 Publishes *Social Statics*

1855 Publishes *Education: Intellectual, Moral, and Physical*

1859 Charles Darwin publishes *The Origin of Species by Means of Natural Selection*

1862 Publishes *First Principles of a New System of Philosophy*

| 1800 | 1820 | 1840 | 1860 |

Continuity & Change

■ Science emphasis

instructional innovators who promoted science and technology in their classrooms. He wanted to modernize the curriculum so that it focused on the physical, biological, and social sciences as well as applied technology and engineering. Today, he would probably include computer literacy, genetics, and bioengineering in his list of useful subjects.

Introducing a rationale still used in modern curriculum making, Spencer ranked activities according to the degree that they promoted health, positive social relationships, and economic productivity. He gave science a high priority because it related to the effective performance of all life activities.[28] For example, scientific fields such as anatomy and physiology explain human growth, especially physical development. Scientific information about nutrition can be applied to a healthy diet. Spencer identified five types of activities to be used in constructing the curriculum: (1) self-preservation activities needed to perform all other activities; (2) occupational or professional activities that enable a person to earn a living; (3) child-rearing activities; (4) social and political participation activities; and (5) leisure and recreation activities.

Influence on Educational Practices Today

■ Impact on curriculum design

✓ Standards & Assessment

American educators were highly receptive to Spencer's ideas. In 1918, a National Education Association committee, in its landmark *Cardinal Principles of Secondary Education,* reiterated Spencer's list of basic life activities. Contemporary curriculum designers continue to use Spencer's rationale when they organize the curriculum on human needs and activities.

Although social Darwinism dominated American social science and education in the late nineteenth century, John Dewey's experimentalism and progressive reform eclipsed it in the early twentieth century. Key social Darwinist ideas reemerged in the contemporary neoconservative educational agenda, however, which includes providing vouchers to attend private schools, reducing government's regulatory powers, and emphasizing teaching market-driven basic skills to increase economic productivity. The standardized testing required in the NCLB introduces competition between schools, as it identifies achieving and nonachieving schools and teachers.

Spencer would raise entry standards for students to preservice teacher-education programs to make them more competitive. Only the brightest applicants would be accepted. The program would stress science and technology. Ending teacher tenure, teaching would be competitive, with competent teachers replacing incompetent ones, and merit pay would be used in teacher compensation.

■ **REFOCUS** After reading about Spencer, think back to the questions at the beginning of the chapter. *Use these questions to construct your own history or autobiography of education.* For Spencer, what are the purposes of education? Note how Spencer reconceptualized Charles Darwin's evolutionary theory. How might Spencer serve as a historical mentor, or model, for you as a teacher? In your educational experience, were there teachers who used Spencer's principles? Do you plan to include Spencer's ideas in your history or autobiography of education?

---

[28]Michael Taylor, *Philosophy of Herbert Spencer* (New York: Continuum, 2007).

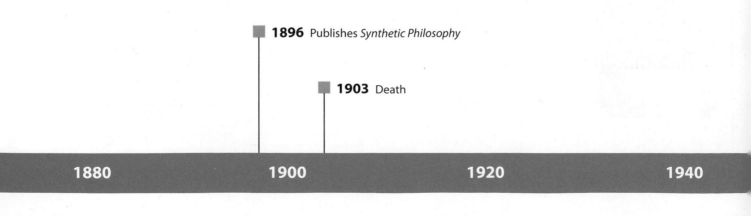

■ **1896** Publishes *Synthetic Philosophy*

■ **1903** Death

1880   **1900**   **1920**   **1940**

Dewey: Learning Through Experience

School and society

Laboratory school

John Dewey (1859–1952) developed his pioneering experimentalist philosophy of education in the context of the social, political, scientific, and technological changes taking place in the United States in the first half of the twentieth century.[29] Dewey's pragmatic philosophy, which encouraged progressive social reforms, incorporated elements of the theories of evolution and relativity. Believing that cooperative group activity enhanced social intelligence, Dewey rejected Spencer's social Darwinist emphasis on individual competition.[30] (For a discussion of pragmatism, see Chapter 6, Philosophical Roots of Education.)

In 1896, Dewey established his Laboratory School at the University of Chicago. Dewey saw the school as an experimental setting in which educational ideas were tested in classroom practice. He called the school a "miniature society" and an "embryonic community," in which children learned collaboratively by working together to solve problems. Dewey organized the curriculum into constructive, experimental, and creative activities that accomplished the following:

- Developed children's sensory and physical coordination
- Provided opportunities for children to make and do things based on their interests
- Stimulated children to formulate, examine, and test their ideas by acting on them

In Dewey's experimentalist philosophy, using the scientific method to solve problems is the key to both thinking and learning. The problem-solving mode of instruction became the central method of learning at the Laboratory School.[31]

---

[29]For a biography of Dewey, see Jay Martin, *The Education of John Dewey: A Biography* (New York: Columbia University Press, 2002).

[30]For Dewey's relationship to the development of pragmatism, see Louis Menard, *The Metaphysical Club: The Story of Ideas in America* (New York: Farrar, Straus and Giroux, 2001). For Dewey as an American pragmatist, access **www.dewey.pragmatism.org**.

[31]John Dewey, *The Child and the Curriculum* (Toronto: University of Toronto Libraries, 2011). A commentary is Laurel N. Tanner, *Dewey's Laboratory School: Lessons for Today* (New York: Teachers College Press, 1997).

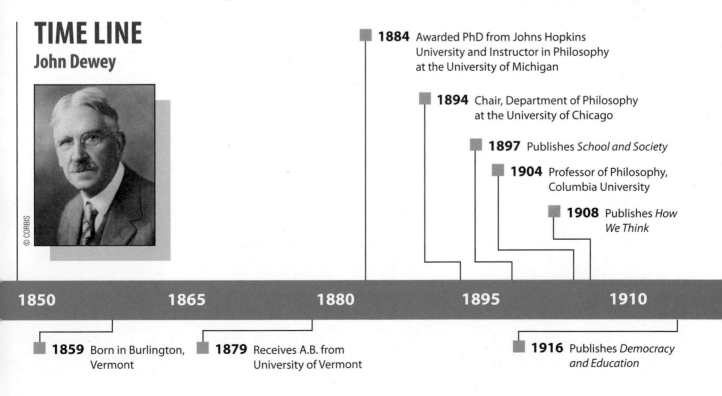

TIME LINE
John Dewey

1884 Awarded PhD from Johns Hopkins University and Instructor in Philosophy at the University of Michigan

1894 Chair, Department of Philosophy at the University of Chicago

1897 Publishes *School and Society*

1904 Professor of Philosophy, Columbia University

1908 Publishes *How We Think*

| 1850 | 1865 | 1880 | 1895 | 1910 |

1859 Born in Burlington, Vermont

1879 Receives A.B. from University of Vermont

1916 Publishes *Democracy and Education*

Principles of Teaching and Learning

Confronting problems

Dewey's *The Child and the Curriculum* emphasized his experimentalist philosophy of education. According to Dewey: (1) children as socially active human beings are eager to explore their environment; (2) learners encounter personal and social problems as they interact with their environment; (3) these problems stimulate children to use their intelligence to solve the problem and expand their experience in an active, instrumental manner.[32]

For Dewey, the **scientific method** is the most effective process we have to solve problems. By using the scientific method, children learn how to think reflectively and to direct their experiences in ways that lead to personal and social growth. Dewey designed a method, "The Complete Act of Thought," which he believed facilitated using the scientific method to solve all kinds of life problems. Dewey's method involved a sequence of five steps:

1. Encountering a "problematic situation" that contains something new or different from past experience and that blocks ongoing activity

2. Locating and defining the specific new or different feature that caused the problem

3. Reflecting on past experience and researching the problem to find information to use in solving it

4. Reflecting on the problem and constructing possible solutions to solve it

5. Testing the possible solution that is most likely to solve the problem to determine if it worked[33]

Reconstructing knowledge to solve problems

For Dewey, genuine knowledge is not inert information that teachers transmit to students; it is an instrument to solve problems. We use our fund of human knowledge—past ideas, discoveries, and inventions—to frame hypothetical solutions to current problems and then test and reconstruct this knowledge in light of present needs. Because people and their environments constantly change, knowledge, too, is continually reconfigured or reconstructed. After a problem has been solved, its solution enters into past experience and can be used to solve future problems.

Education and Schooling

Education for personal and social growth

For Dewey, education is a social process in which the group's immature members, especially children, learn to share and participate in group life. Through education, children access their cultural heritage and learn to use it in problem solving. Seeing

---

[32]Gregory Pappas, *John Dewey's Ethics: Democracy as Experience* (Bloomington, IN: Indiana University Press, 2008).
[33]John Dewey, *Democracy and Education,* with an introduction by Gerald L. Gutek (New York: Barnes and Noble, 2005), pp. 164–65. (Originally published in 1916.)

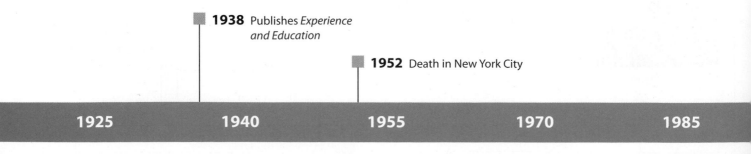

1938 Publishes *Experience and Education*

1952 Death in New York City

| 1925 | 1940 | 1955 | 1970 | 1985 |

education's sole purpose as social growth, Dewey said "(i) the educational process has no end beyond itself; it is its own end; and that (ii) the educational process is one of continual reorganizing, reconstructing, transforming."[34]

Three levels of curriculum

Dewey's curriculum consists of three levels of learning activities and processes. The first level, "making and doing," engages children in projects in which they explore their environment and act on their ideas. These activities develop sensory and motor skills and encourage socialization through collaborative group projects. The second level broadens students' concepts of space and time through projects in history and geography. The third level, "science," brings students into contact with various subjects such as biology, chemistry, and social studies that they can use as resources in problem solving. These three curricular levels move learning from simple impulses to careful observation of the environment, to planning actions, and finally to reflecting on and testing the consequences of action.

Schools are liberating and democratic

Dewey saw democratic education and schooling as open-ended processes in which students and teachers can test all ideas, beliefs, and values. Opposing the separation of people from each other because of ethnicity, race, gender, or economic class, Dewey believed that democratic communities encourage people to share their experiences to solve common problems.

Continuity & Change

Impact on progressivism

REFOCUS After reading about Dewey, think back to the questions at the beginning of the chapter. *Use these questions to construct your own history or autobiography of education.* How did Dewey define the purposes of education? Note how Dewey included science, social reform, and relativism in his philosophy. How might Dewey serve as a historical mentor, or model, for you as a teacher? In your educational experience, were there teachers who used Dewey's problem-solving methods? Do you plan to include Dewey's experimentalism in your history or autobiography of education?

Influence on Educational Practices Today

By applying pragmatism to education, Dewey worked to open schools to social reform and change. Dewey's ideas about socially expanding children's experience stimulated progressive education, which emphasized children's interests and needs. Today, educators who relate schooling to social change and reform are often following Dewey's pioneering educational concepts.[35]

Dewey's influence can be seen in "hands-on" or process-oriented teaching and learning. Dewey would construct the preservice education of teachers on the principles of (1) seeing education in

---

[34]Ibid., p. 54.

[35]For analyses of Dewey's work in educational philosophy, see Matt Parmental, "The Structure of Dewey's Scientific Ethics," and Eric Bredo, "Understanding Dewey's Ethics," in *Philosophy of Education* (Urbana: Philosophy of Education Society/University of Illinois at Urbana-Champaign, 2000), pp. 143–154. Also, see Douglas J. Simpson, ed., and Sam F Stuck, Jr., ed., *Teachers, Leaders, and Schools: Essays by John Dewey* (Carbondale: Southern Illinois University Press, 2010).

TIME LINE
Jane Addams

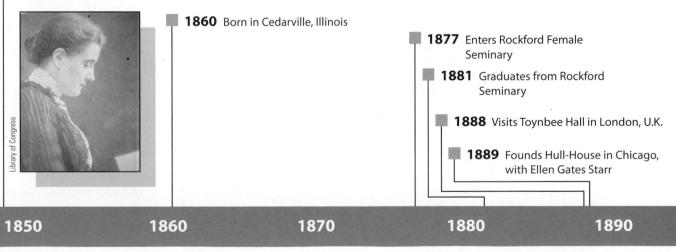

Library of Congress

1860 Born in Cedarville, Illinois

1877 Enters Rockford Female Seminary

1881 Graduates from Rockford Seminary

1888 Visits Toynbee Hall in London, U.K.

1889 Founds Hull-House in Chicago, with Ellen Gates Starr

| 1850 | 1860 | 1870 | 1880 | 1890 |

broad social terms, and (2) developing competencies in using the scientific method to solve problems. Practicing teachers would use group activities, collaborative learning, and process-centered strategies in their classrooms.

Hull-House

Addams: Socialized Education

Jane Addams (1860–1935)—the founder of Hull-House and a pioneering leader in social work, the peace movement, and women's rights—developed an educational philosophy called **socialized education.** She arrived at her educational ideas from her efforts to improve the living and working conditions of immigrants in Chicago and to mobilize women to work for social and educational reforms. Addams was a pioneer of multicultural, international, and women's education.

Rebelling against the Victorian era's gender restrictions on women, Addams rejected the traditional curriculum that limited women's educational choices and opportunities.[36] She wanted women to define their own lives, to choose their own careers, and to participate fully in politics, society, and education.[37]

In 1889, Jane Addams established Hull-House on Chicago's Near West Side in a culturally diverse but impoverished neighborhood of immigrants from southern and eastern Europe. Addams and her coworkers, a cadre of young middle-class women, educated the immigrants and, in turn, were educated by them. Addams and her coworkers learned how the immigrants used their own initiative to survive in a new country. In turn, Hull-House provided a settlement house where immigrants learned how to obtain jobs, pay rent, find health care, and educate their children.[38]

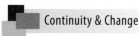

Continuity & Change

Proponent of multiculturalism

Principles of Teaching and Learning

Because of her work with immigrants in Chicago, Addams saw how urbanization, industrialization, and technology were changing society. She argued that education needed to take on new and broadened social purposes. Teachers needed to understand

---

[36]Victoria Bissell Brown, *The Education of Jane Addams* (Philadelphia: University of Pennsylvania Press, 2004), pp. 72–91.

[37]*Jane Addams, Peace and Bread in Time of War* (Urbana and Chicago: University of Illinois Press, 2002); and Jane Addams, Emily G. Balch, and Alice Hamilton, *Women at the Hague: The International Congress of Women and Its Results* (Urbana and Chicago: University of Illinois Press, 2003).

[38]Biographies of Addams are Allen F. Davis, *American Heroine: The Life and Legend of Jane Addams* (Chicago: Ivan R. Dee, 2000); James W. Linn, *Jane Addams: A Biography* (Urbana and Chicago: University of Illinois Press, 2000); Louise W. Knight, *Jane Addams: Spirit in Action* (New York: W. W. Norton, 2010). For Addams as a writer, see Katherine Joslin, *Jane Addams, a Writer's Life* (Urbana and Chicago: University of Illinois Press, 2004).

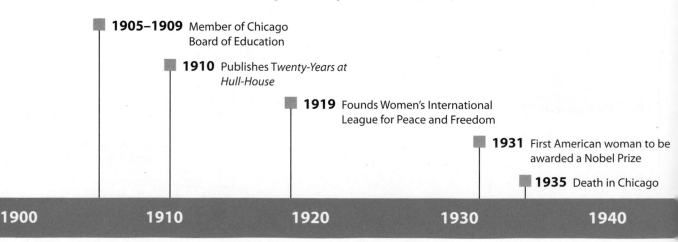

1905–1909 Member of Chicago Board of Education

1910 Publishes *Twenty-Years at Hull-House*

1919 Founds Women's International League for Peace and Freedom

1931 First American woman to be awarded a Nobel Prize

1935 Death in Chicago

| 1900 | 1910 | 1920 | 1930 | 1940 |

the economic, demographic, and technological trends that were reshaping American society from a rural to an urban society and prepare their students to deal with them in intelligent, socially responsible, and democratic ways.[39]

Believing that cultural diversity could contribute to America's broad common culture, Addams sought to build connections between immigrants and the larger American society. Based on what she had learned from the immigrants at Hull-House, Addams wanted public schools to feature a multicultural curriculum that included the history, customs, songs, crafts, and stories of ethnic and racial groups.[40]

Education and Schooling

Addams's socialized education, which was influenced by progressivism and pragmatism, defined education in very broad social, economic, and political terms. She saw schools as agencies, much like settlement houses, that had the mission of restoring a sense of community in a country undergoing a profound transition from a rural to an urban industrialized and technological society. She envisioned schools as multifunctional agencies that socialized as well as taught children academic skills and subjects. Teachers, like social workers, had many-faceted responsibilities for their students' social well-being. The curriculum should be reconstituted to provide broadened experiences that explored children's immediate environment and highlighted connections with a technological society.

Addams's enlarged concept of teaching with a social-justice mission has important implications for preservice teacher education. It means that prospective teachers need to examine issues of social change and social justice in relationship to education and schooling. For practicing teachers, it means that the classroom needs to be connected to the people in the community it serves.

■ Multifunctional education

---

[39]Jane Addams, *Democracy and Social Ethics* (Urbana and Chicago: University of Illinois Press, 2002, 1905), pp. 80–97. Also, see Sandra Opdycke, *Jane Addams and Her Vision for America* (New York: Prentice-Hall, 2011).
[40]Jane Addams, *The Spirit of Youth and the City Streets* (New York: Macmillan, 1909), pp. 98–103. Also, see Maurice Harringon, *The Social Philosophy of Jane Addams* (Urbana, IL: University of Illinois Press, 2009).

TIME LINE
Maria Montessori

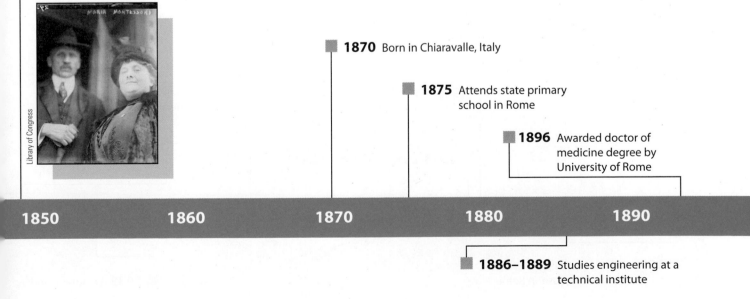

Library of Congress

1870 Born in Chiaravalle, Italy

1875 Attends state primary school in Rome

1896 Awarded doctor of medicine degree by University of Rome

| 1850 | 1860 | 1870 | 1880 | 1890 |

1886–1889 Studies engineering at a technical institute

Influence on Educational Practices Today

Addams's belief that education must be free from gender biases corresponds with the goals of contemporary women's education, especially equal rights for women and their freedom to define their lives and choose their careers.

Her belief that industrialism should be infused with broad social purposes applies to the argument that technology should advance greater communication and sharing rather than generate consumer-oriented materialism. Her crusade for a world without war provides a needed message for a world wracked by violence and terrorism.

 REFOCUS After reading about Addams, think back to the questions at the beginning of the chapter. *Use these questions to construct your own history or autobiography of education.* How did Addams define the purposes of education? Note how Addams's experience in working with immigrants in an urban setting shaped her philosophy of socialized education. How might Addams serve as a historical mentor, or model, for you as a teacher? In your educational experience, were there teachers who used Addams's principles? Do you plan to include elements of Addams's socialized education in your history or autobiography of education?

Montessori: The Prepared Environment

Early childhood and feminism

The Italian educator Maria Montessori (1870–1952) devised an internationally popular method of early childhood education.[41] Like Pestalozzi and Froebel, Montessori recognized that children's early experiences have an important formative and continuing influence on their later lives.

As a pioneering women's educator, Montessori vigorously challenged those who, because of sexist stereotyping, argued that women should be excluded from higher and professional education. Defying the traditional barriers to women's education, Montessori, after an initial rejection, was admitted to the University of Rome and became the first woman in Italy to earn a degree of doctor of medicine.[42]

As a physician, Montessori worked with children categorized as mentally handicapped and psychologically impaired. Her methods with these children proved to be so effective that she concluded they were applicable to all children.

---

[41]Biographies of Montessori are Rita Kramer, *Maria Montessori: A Biography* (Reading, MA: Perseus Books, 1988); and E. M. Standing, *Maria Montessori: Her Life and Work,* introduction by Lee Havis (New York: Plume/Penguin Books, 1998).

[42]For a brief biography and an excerpt from Montessori's *My System of Education,* see Madonna M. Murphy, *The History and Philosophy of Education: Voices of Educational Pioneers* (Upper Saddle River, NJ: Pearson/Merrill/Prentice Hall, 2006), pp. 368–375. For Montessori's educational theory, see Marion O'Donnell, *Maria Montessori* (*Continuum Library of Educational Thought*) (New York: Continuum, 2007), and Angeline S. Lillard, *Montessori: The Science Behind the Genius* (New York: Oxford University Press, 2008).

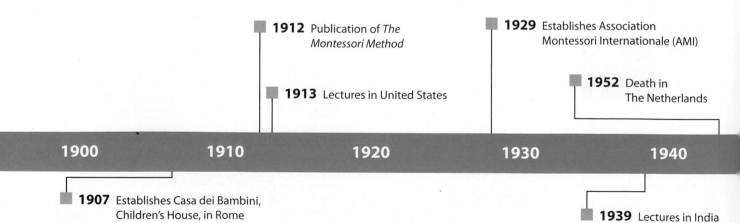

1912 Publication of *The Montessori Method*

1929 Establishes Association Montessori Internationale (AMI)

1913 Lectures in United States

1952 Death in The Netherlands

1900   **1910**   **1920**   **1930**   **1940**

1907 Establishes Casa dei Bambini, Children's House, in Rome

1939 Lectures in India

Principles of Teaching and Learning

Emphasis on structured work

In 1908, Maria Montessori established a children's school, the *Casa dei Bambini,* for impoverished children in the slums of Rome. In this school, Montessori designed a specially prepared environment that featured methods, materials, and activities based on her observations of children.[43] She had refined her theory by conducting extensive research on the work of Itard and Seguin, two early pioneers in special education. Contrary to the opinions of many conventional educators, Montessori believed that children possess an inner need to work at what interests them without the prodding of teachers and without being motivated by external rewards and punishments. Children, she found, are capable of sustained concentration and work. Enjoying structure and preferring work to play, they like to repeat actions until they master a given skill. In fact, children's capacity for spontaneous learning leads them to begin reading and writing on their own initiative.

Education and Schooling

Types of activity

Montessori's curriculum included three major types of activities and experiences: practical, sensory, and formal skills and studies. Children learned to perform such practical activities as setting the table, serving a meal, washing dishes, tying and buttoning clothing, and practicing basic manners and social etiquette. Special exercises were used to develop sensory acuity and muscular and physical coordination. Children learned the alphabet by tracing movable sandpaper letters. They learned to write and then learned to read. They used colored rods of various sizes and cups to learn counting and measuring.

Didactic materials

Montessori designed preplanned teaching (*didactic*) devices and materials to develop children's practical, sensory, and formal skills. Examples included lacing and buttoning frames and packets to be identified by their smell. Because they direct learning in the prepared environment, Montessori educators are called "directresses"

---

[43]Gerald Lee Gutek, ed., *The Montessori Method: The Origins of an Educational Innovation: Including an Abridged and Annotated Edition of Maria Montessori's* The Montessori Method (Lanham, MD: Rowman and Littlefield Publishers, 2004). For a digital copy of the *Montessori Method,* access **www.digital.library.upenn.edu**.

TIME LINE
Jean Piaget

Horst Tappe/Lebrecht Music & Arts

1924 Publishes *Judgment and Reasoning in the Child*

1925–1929 Professor Psychology, Sociology, and Philosophy of Science, University of Neuchatel

1929–1939 Professor History of Scientific Thought, University of Geneva

1932–1971 Director, Institute of Educational Sciences, Geneva

1896 Born in Neuchatel, Switzerland

1870	1885	1900	1915	1930

1921–1925 Research Director, Institut Jean-Jacques Rousseau, Geneva

1936 Publishes *Origins of Intelligence in the Child*

Elizabeth Crews/The Image Works

Children in today's Montessori schools use specially designed didactic materials in an environment prepared to encourage learning.

rather than "teachers." Guided by the directress, children use the Montessori apparatus in a prescribed way to acquire the desired skill, sensory, or intellectual outcome.

Influence on Educational Practices Today

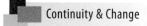
Key contributions

Montessori made a pioneering contribution to education when she emphasized that early childhood education has a highly formative power over a person's adult development. Her significant educational contributions include her (1) concept of sensitive periods, or phases of development, when children are ready to work with materials that are especially useful in sensory, motor, and cognitive learning; (2) belief that children are capable of sustained self-directed work in learning a particular skill; and (3) emphasis on the school as part of the community and the need for parent participation and support. She anticipated the current movement to provide earlier enrichment opportunities for young children.[44]

Continuity & Change

[44]Gerald L. Gutek, "Maria Montessori: Contributions to Educational Psychology," in Barry J. Zimmerman and Dale H. Schunk, *Educational Psychology: A Century of Contributions* (Mahwah, NJ: Lawrence Erlbaum, 2003), pp. 171–186.

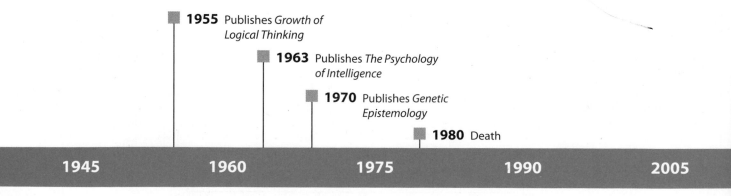

1955 Publishes *Growth of Logical Thinking*

1963 Publishes *The Psychology of Intelligence*

1970 Publishes *Genetic Epistemology*

1980 Death

1945   1960   1975   1990   2005

Montessori movement in
United States

REFOCUS   After reading about Montessori, think back to the questions at the beginning of the chapter. *Use these questions to construct your own history or autobiography of education.* For Montessori, what are the purposes of education? How might Montessori serve as a historical mentor, or model, for you as a teacher? In your educational experience, were there teachers who used the Montessori method? Do you plan to include elements of the Montessori method in your history or autobiography of education?

About 6,000 of the world's 20,000 **Montessori schools** worldwide are in the United States. Most of these are private schools, enrolling children between the ages of two and six. Some public-school systems have established Montessori units, especially as magnet or charter schools.[45]

Although some universities have Montessori training programs, most Montessori training programs are private, associated with either the American Montessori Association or the Montessori International Society. These organizations subscribe to Montessori's admonition that preservice training should closely follow the method she designed. Prospective directresses study the Montessori method and are trained in using the didactic materials in the prepared environment.

Piaget: Developmental Growth

The Swiss psychologist Jean Piaget (1896–1980) developed significant pioneering insights into children's cognitive, moral, and language development.[46] Like Montessori, Piaget used clinical observation to discover how children construct and act on their ideas.[47]

Principles of Teaching and Learning

Cognitive development

Piaget discovered that children construct their concepts about reality by actively exploring their environment. According to Piaget, intelligence develops through a series of stages, characterized by the child's set of mental structures and operations at a particular age. With each new stage, children develop new mental abilities that enable them to reconstruct the concepts they constructed at an earlier stage into a more complex cognitive map of the world.[48] Based on his stage-learning theory of development, Piaget identified four qualitatively distinct but interrelated periods of cognitive growth:

Sensorimotor stage

1. The **sensorimotor stage**, from birth to two years, occurs when children learn by actively exploring their immediate environment. Children begin their earliest environmental explorations using their senses—their mouths, eyes, noses, and hands. Displaying a largely nonverbal intelligence, they learn to coordinate their senses and to construct simple concepts of space, time, and causality at the visual, auditory, tactile, and motor levels. These rudimentary concepts, however, are limited to children's immediate situations.[49]

Preoperational stage

2. The **preoperational stage**, from two to seven years, occurs when intuition combines with speech to lead to operational thinking involving concepts of space, time, and cause-and-effect relationships that extend beyond the immediate situation. Children now reconstruct their concepts by grouping and naming objects. They use signs and symbols to represent their ideas and experiences as they reorganize the mental structures and networks constructed in the first stage into a more complex, higher-order, view of reality.[50]

Concrete-operational
period

3. The **concrete-operational period**, from seven to eleven years, occurs when children begin thinking in a mathematical and logical way. They become adept at

[45]Timothy D. Seldin, "Montessori," in James W. Guthrie, ed., *Encyclopedia of Education,* 2nd ed., Vol. 5 (New York: Macmillan Reference USA/Thomson Gale, 2003), p. 1697.

[46]For a brief biography, time line, and an excerpt from Piaget on children's intellectual development, see Madonna M. Murphy, *The History and Philosophy of Education: Voices of Educational Pioneers* (Upper Saddle River, NJ: Pearson/Merrill/Prentice Hall, 2006), pp. 375–383.

[47]David Elkind, "Piaget, Jean (1896–1980)," in Guthrie, *Encyclopedia of Education,* 2nd ed., vol. 5 (New York: Macmillan Reference USA/Thomson Gale, 2003), p. 1895.

[48]Ibid., p. 1897.

[49]Ibid.

[50]Ibid.

▶ ❙❙ TeachSource Video Activity

Piaget's Stages of Development

Go to the Education CourseMate website to access the following BBC Motion Gallery videos on Piaget's Stages of Development: 0-2 years, Piaget's Sensorimotor Stage; 2-5 years, Piaget's Preoperational Stage; 5-11 years, Piaget's Concrete Operational Stage; 12-18 years, Piaget's Formal Operational Stage. Then answer the following questions:

❶ How do these videos illustrate that Piaget was a pioneer educational thinker?

❷ How did Piaget's theory of children's cognitive development bring changes to classroom instruction?

❸ Which of the theories of the pioneers in this chapter are most like and most unlike Piaget's theory?

** This video reinforces key concepts found in Section II: Instruction and Assessment of the Praxis II Exam.**

recognizing such general characteristics as size, length, and weight, and in using them to perform more complex mental operations. As before, they reconstruct the concepts developed in earlier stages into more abstract and complex levels. Coinciding with the years of elementary school, children in the concrete-operational stage exercise their reasoning skills and deal with clock and calendar time, map and geographical space, and experimental cause and effect.[51]

Formal-operational period

4. At the **formal-operational period,** from age eleven through early adulthood, individuals construct logical propositions and interpret space, historical time, and multiple cause-and-effect relationships. They use such multivariate thinking to construct possible plans of action.[52] Now that adolescents understand cause-and-effect relationships, they can use the scientific method and can learn complex mathematical, linguistic, and mechanical processes.[53]

Piaget's stage-learning theory of development has many important applications to education. Viewing the world differently than adults, children are constantly reconstructing and repatterning their view of reality as they proceed through the stages of development. Thus, children's conceptions of reality often differ from the kinds of curriculum and instruction adults frequently impose on them.

Early-childhood and elementary education should be based on how children develop and act on their own thinking and learning processes. As they move through the stages of development, children have their own readiness for new learning based on the cognitive level they have reached. This, in turn, determines their readiness for new and higher-order learning experiences.[54] Although a rich environment can stimulate readiness, we cannot force learning on children.

---

[51]Ibid.
[52]C. J. Brainerd, "Jean Piaget, Learning Research, and American Education," in Barry J. Zimmerman and Dale H. Schunk, ed., *Educational Psychology: A Century of Contributions* (Mahwah, NJ: Lawrence Erlbaum, 2003), p. 257; and Elkind, p. 1897.
[53]Jean Piaget, *The Origins of Intelligence in Children,* trans. Margaret Cook (New York: Norton, 1952), pp. 24–40; also see Ulrich Muller, Jeremy I. M. Carpendale, and Leslie Smith, eds., *The Cambridge Companion to Piaget* (Cambridge: Cambridge University Press, 2009); and Richard Kohler, *Jean Piaget (Continuum Library of Educational Thought)* (New York: Continuum, 2008).
[54]Brainerd, p. 260.

Education and Schooling

Piaget accentuated children's environment as their setting for learning. Outside of school, children learn directly and informally from their environment. The most effective classroom teaching strategies replicate the informal learning children use in their everyday out-of-school lives.[55]

Constructivism

As they interact with their environment, children build knowledge of their world through a creative process known as **constructivism**.[56] As they discover gaps between their existing concepts and the new situations they encounter when exploring their environment, children reconceptualize their existing knowledge with their new information to construct more complete higher-order concepts.[57] To stimulate children's explorations, teachers can design their classrooms as learning centers stocked with materials that engage children's curiosity.[58] The following principles from Piaget can guide teachers' preservice preparation and classroom practice:

1. Encourage children to explore and experiment.

2. Individualize instruction so children can learn at their own level of readiness.

Informal learning and constructivism

3. Design the classroom as a learning center stocked with concrete materials that children can touch, manipulate, and use.

REFOCUS After reading about Piaget, think back to the questions at the beginning of the chapter. *Use these questions to construct your own history or autobiography of education.* For Piaget, what are the purposes of education? Note how Piaget incorporated ideas such as learning through the senses, exploring the environment, and using objects from other pioneers such as Rousseau, Pestalozzi, Dewey, and Montessori. How might Piaget serve as a historical mentor, or model, for you as a teacher? In your educational experience, were there teachers who used Piaget's principles? Do you plan on incorporating Piaget's ideas into your history or autobiography of education?

Influence on Educational Practices Today

Piaget's cognitive psychology connected how children learn to think and reason with teaching and learning in schools. His theory generated significant changes in early childhood and elementary education, not only in the United States, but throughout the world. His ideas stimulated a movement to make classroom settings more informal and more related to how children learn. Piaget's assertion that children construct rather than copy their versions of reality influenced contemporary constructivist instruction.[59]

[55]Ibid., p. 284.
[56]Susan Puss, *Parallel Paths to Constructionism: Jean Piaget and Lev Vygotsky* (Greenwich CT: Information Age Publishing, 2004).
[57]Ibid., p. 271.
[58]Piaget, *Origins of Intelligence*, pp. 23–42.
[59]Elkind, p. 1894.

TIME LINE
Paulo Freire

Globo via Getty Images

1921 Born in Recife, Brazil

1946 Director Department of Education and Culture of Social Services in Permambuco, Brazil

| 1910 | 1920 | 1930 | 1940 | 1950 |

Freire: Liberation Pedagogy

Liberation pedagogy

Paulo Freire (1921–1997) constructed his philosophy of **liberation pedagogy** while conducting a literacy campaign among the impoverished illiterate peasants and urban poor in his native Brazil.[60] For Freire, literacy meant more than learning to read and write; it raised people's consciousness about the conditions of their lives, especially those that exploited and marginalized them.[61] Freire's *Pedagogy of the Oppressed* expressed his commitment to an education that empowered people to resist and overcome the forces that oppressed and marginalized them.[62]

Principles of Teaching and Learning

An important goal of Freire's philosophy is *conscientizaçao,* a Portuguese word meaning to be conscious and critically aware of the social, political, and economic conditions and contradictions that affect a person's life. To raise their consciousness, students, in dialogue with their teachers, need to reflect on their own lives and write their personal and collective histories of their racial, ethnic, language, economic, and social groups. They must consciously examine the real situations in which they live, identifying those individuals, groups, and conditions that deny them the freedom to define and express themselves.[63]

Education and Schooling

Freire asserted that the school's curriculum and instruction can either indoctrinate students to conform to an official version of knowledge, or it can challenge them to develop a critical consciousness that empowers them to engage in self-liberation. For example, an official version of history that celebrates the achievements of white

---

[60]For a brief biography and an excerpt from Freire's *Pedagogy of the Oppressed,* see Madonna M. Murphy, *The History and Philosophy of Education: Voices of Educational Pioneers* (Upper Saddle River, NJ: Pearson/Merrill/Prentice Hall, 2006), pp. 383–391. Also, access the Paulo Freire Institute, UCLA at **www.paulofreireinstitute.org**.
[61]Richard Shaull, preface to Paulo Freire, *Pedagogy of the Oppressed* (New York: Continuum, 1984), pp. 9–11. Also, see John Dale and Emory J. Hyslop-Margison, *Paulo Freire: Teaching for Freedom and Transformation: The Philosophical Influences on the Work of Paulo Freire* (London and New York: Springer, 2010).
[62]Among several editions is Paulo Freire, *Pedagogy of the Oppressed,* Myra Bergman Ramos, trans., and introduction by Donaldo Macedo (New York: Continuum, 2000). Also, see Freire, *Pedagogy of Hope: Reliving Pedagogy of the Oppressed* (New York: Continuum, 2004); and Freire, *Education for Critical Consciousness* (Continuum, 2005).
[63]Paulo Freire, *Pedagogy of Freedom: Ethics, Democracy, and Civic Courage* (Lanham, MD: Rowman and Littlefield, 1998), p. 51.

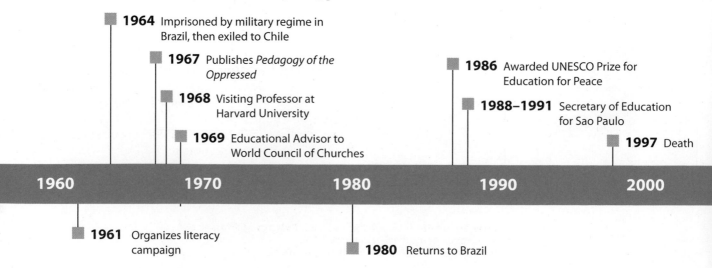

1964 Imprisoned by military regime in Brazil, then exiled to Chile

1967 Publishes *Pedagogy of the Oppressed*

1968 Visiting Professor at Harvard University

1969 Educational Advisor to World Council of Churches

1986 Awarded UNESCO Prize for Education for Peace

1988–1991 Secretary of Education for Sao Paulo

1997 Death

| 1960 | 1970 | 1980 | 1990 | 2000 |

1961 Organizes literacy campaign

1980 Returns to Brazil

TECHNOLOGY @ SCHOOL

Paulo Freire's Liberation Pedagogy

You can research the Internet to broaden your perspectives on Paulo Freire's liberation pedagogy. For sites committed to Freire's pedagogy, access the Paulo Freire Institute, UCLA at **www.paulofreireinstitute.org** and the Freire Project at **www.freireproject.org.** You might relate the discussion of Freire's educational ideas on these sites to the commentary about him in this chapter.

Euro American males and minimizes the contributions of women, African Americans, Latinos, and other minority groups creates a false consciousness. An education that defines a person's worth in terms of wealth and power and sees schooling as a ticket to success in an exploitative economic system cannot be truly humanizing.[64]

Reality of school situations

For Freire, teachers should be neither impartial nor uncommitted on social, political, and economic issues.[65] Rather, he wants teachers to develop a critical consciousness about the real power relationships in the schools and of the conditions that affect their students. For example, teachers in schools in economically depressed areas need to know that their students' lives are being blighted by poverty, poor access to health care and recreational services, drug abuse, and gang violence. When they understand the true reality of their school situations, teachers can resist these oppressive conditions and work to empower their students.

Standards & Assessment

For Freire, real learning takes place as teachers and students engage in open and ongoing dialogue. He attacks instruction that leads to false, rather than critical, consciousness in students' perceptions of reality.

Opposes teacher talk

An example is "teacher talk." Teacher talk implies that teachers can transmit knowledge to students by telling them what is true: students memorize what the teacher says and passively deposit it in their minds for later recall on tests. Freire calls the teacher-talking–student-listening method educational "banking," in which each bit of information is deposited to be cashed in the future, usually for an examination.[66]

Continuity & Change

Standards & Assessment

For educators inspired by Freire, the standardized tests used in the contemporary standards movement, such as in NCLB, are an example of the banking model. The tests, constructed from officially transmitted knowledge, sort students into groups, often isolating marginalized students and thereby reproducing the inequalities of the existing system.

Influence on Educational Practices Today

REFOCUS   After reading about Freire, think back to the questions at the beginning of the chapter. *Use these questions to construct your own history or autobiography of education.* For Freire, what are the purposes of education? Note how Freire constructed a revolutionary approach to education that differed from many of the other pioneers. How might Freire serve as a historical mentor, or model, for you as a teacher? In your educational experience, were there teachers who used Freire's principles? Are there elements of Freire's liberation pedagogy that you plan to incorporate into your history or autobiography of education?

Freire is esteemed as a genuine educational pioneer by contemporary critical theorists. (See Chapter 6, Philosophical Roots of Education, for more on critical theory.) Freire worked to transform teaching and learning from the limited concept of transmitting information to engaging in the project of completing one's identity and meaning in a world that needs to be made more equitable, humane, and just. According to Freire, preservice preparation should involve future teachers in dialogues in which they critically assess the social, economic, and political conditions that have an impact on schools. In their classroom practice, teachers should help students work for social justice by creating a true consciousness that exposes the conditions that marginalize them and their communities.

---

[64]Stanley Aronowitz, introduction to Freire, *Pedagogy of Freedom,* p. 4.
[65] Paolo Freire, *Pedagogy of Freedom,* p. 22.
[66]Paolo Freire, *Pedagogy of the Oppressed,* pp. 57–59.

◼ TAKING ISSUE

Read the brief introduction below, as well as the Question and the pros and cons list that follows. Then, answer the question using your own words and position.

Commitment to Social Justice in Education?

You have just read about Paulo Freire who said that teachers cannot remain neutral on issues of social justice. Freire argued that teachers should be committed to empowering dispossessed and marginalized individuals and groups. Return to the earlier section on Herbert Spencer in this chapter. Spencer, a social Darwinist, argued that teachers who tried to promote social equality were making a serious mistake that attempted to interfere with the natural law of competition.

Question

Should teachers be committed to social justice education that seeks to empower marginalized groups? (Think about this question as you read the PRO and CON arguments listed here. What is *your* take on this issue?)

Arguments PRO	Arguments CON
1. If teachers do not take a stand on social issues, they are merely reinforcing the discriminatory status quo.	1. The teacher's function is to educate students in the skills and subjects needed to earn a living; it is not to indoctrinate students in a political ideology.
2. Education can be a positive agency of social change that promotes equality among individuals and groups.	2. Trying to change society is a utopian dream that disrupts the natural flow of events.
3. Teachers need to raise students' consciousness about the agents and conditions that exploit them.	3. Teachers should encourage competition that brings out the best in people.
4. Teachers should join forces with progressive groups and organizations that are working for social justice.	4. Society is improved through individual efforts and hard work, not by "raising consciousness."

Question Reprise: What Is Your Stand?

Reflect again on the following question by explaining *your* stand about this issue. Should teachers be committed to social justice education that seeks to empower marginalized groups?

Thinking about Pioneers in Education as Historical Mentors

◼ REFOCUS   Constructing Your Own History or Autobiography of Education

This chapter examined the contributions of pioneering educators and encouraged you to consider them as historical mentors in developing your own history or autobiography of education.

As a teacher, you will encounter potential pioneers—scholars, authors, professors, and teaching colleagues—who develop new ideas and methods of education. As you appraise these present-day educators, identify those you think will become a pioneer in education, especially those whose ideas will aid teachers in becoming more effective in their classrooms.

As you construct your own history or autobiography of education, think back to the contributions made by the pioneers in this chapter. Which of them would you like to emulate, and which of them do you reject? Do you want to incorporate their educational ideas and methods in your own teaching?

Summing Up

1 Rejecting the child depravity doctrine, Comenius, Rousseau, Pestalozzi, and Froebel believed that education should be calibrated with children's natural growth and goodness.

2 Pestalozzi designed simultaneous group teaching methods that used objects in children's immediate environments. Herbart systematized teaching methods. Froebel used the philosophy of idealism to construct the kindergarten concept. Both Pestalozzi and Froebel encouraged teachers to be sensitive to children's interests and needs.

3 Relating education to the society and economy, Spencer designed a curriculum based on human activities. Dewey's pioneering work at the University of Chicago Laboratory School stimulated progressive educational reform. Montessori's prepared environment enjoys global popularity in early childhood education.

4 Addams's philosophy of socialized education contributed to multicultural education, to an examination of technology's impact on society, and to the movement for women's rights and education.

5 Piaget's developmental psychology provided insights into children's cognitive operations and generated change in curriculum and teaching methods, such as constructivism.

6 Freire's liberation theory calls for radically transforming education and schooling into forces for human liberation.

Key Terms

The numbers indicate the pages where explanations of the key terms can be found.

child depravity theory 97
naturalist theory 97
object lesson 107
social Darwinism 113
utilitarian education 114

scientific method 117
socialized education 119
Montessori schools 124
sensorimotor stage 124
preoperational stage 124

concrete-operational period 124
formal-operational period 125
constructivism 126
liberation pedagogy 127

Certification Connection Activity

This chapter discusses the significant educational contributions of pioneers of education. As you read the chapter, give special attention to how the ideas and methods of these pioneers contributed to changing perspectives on child development and innovations in instruction. Be able to trace developments in learning theory that influence teaching and learning, a significant topic in Praxis II, Principles of Learning and Teaching. Describe in your journal how the transition to theories that focused on the child as the critical factor in the learning process impacts the selection of appropriate teaching strategies for the modern classroom.

Discussion Questions

1 How would you define an educational mentor? Who were the mentors that contributed to your ideas about education, schools, and teaching? Which of the pioneers in the chapter most and least appeals to you as a historical mentor?

2 Rousseau's *Emile* has had a polarizing effect on its readers. Some see it as liberating children from oppressive adult influences while critics contend it portrays an overly romantic and unrealistic view of children and their education. What is your opinion? Can you resolve this issue?

3 Proponents of Jane Addams's philosophy of socialized education argue that it relates schools to social and technological change while critics contend it diverts schools from teaching academic skills and subjects. What is your opinion? Can you resolve this issue?

4 Reflect on trends such as whole-language learning, collaborative learning, constructivism, portfolio assessment, use of technology, and the standards movement. How might the pioneers discussed in this chapter react to these trends?

5 Proponents of Freire's educational theory argue it can empower dispossessed and marginalized people, while critics contend that it politicizes schools and generates class conflict. What is your opinion? Can you resolve this issue?

6 Do you support Spencer's argument that education should stimulate competition or Dewey's view that it should encourage cooperation? If these views on competition and cooperation were implemented in your teacher-education program, what do you think would happen?

Suggested Projects for Professional Development

❶ Explore Jane Addams's Hull-House, giving special attention to "Re-Defining Democracy: Jane Addams and the Hull-House Settlement," by accessing the Hull-House Museum at the University of Illinois at Chicago website. Then react to Addams's argument that there should be close relationships between schools and social agencies.

❷ Do some primary source reading on Comenius. Access online copies of Comenius's *School of Infancy* and his *The Great Didactic* from the Online Books Page website.

❸ Go to the Education CourseMate website to view the BBC Motion Gallery video entitled "Montessori Education." Based on Lesley Britton's description of the Montessori approach, consider the question, "What is the difference between Montessori and traditional teaching methods?"

❹ Visit a kindergarten, and observe the main features of the educational environment. Do you find an emphasis on play, developmental activities, socialization, the introduction to academic skills, and the use of technology? How might Froebel react to your findings?

❺ Visit a Montessori school, and observe the main features of the educational environment. Do you find an emphasis on play, developmental activities, individualized learning, socialization, the use of didactic learning materials, the introduction to academic skills, and the use of technology? How might Maria Montessori react to your findings?

❻ Read the article "Locke: Empiricist Educator" at the CourseMate website. Analyze John Locke's ideas about how we form our simple ideas from sensation and how we construct higher order compound and complex ideas. How does Locke's theory of knowledge agree or disagree with the other pioneers in this chapter?

❼ Examine the programs of the following organizations (see their websites) to promote Froebel's educational philosophy: the International Froebel Society and the Froebel Foundation USA.

❽ Did Herbert Spencer attempt to limit social innovations by applying social Darwinism to modern society, or did he try to remove restrictions on individual freedom? To answer the questions go to Peter Richards, "Was Herbert Spencer a Social Darwinist or Libertarian Prophet?" at the Ludwig von Mises Institute website. Compare and contrast with the discussion of Spencer in this chapter.

❾ Do a survey of Dewey that includes videos, photographs, and publications at the Center for Dewey Studies, which you can find at the Southern Illinois University website.

❿ Go to the Education CourseMate website to watch the video entitled, "Educational Technology: Issues of Equity and Access." Then review the sections on Dewey and Addams in the chapter. Would Dewey and Addams consider inequality in access to educational technology as an obstacle to participation in a democratic society?

Suggested Resources

Internet Resources

For Comenius's methods on language instruction, access **www.comeniusfoundation.org**.

Short biographical sketches and information about Jean-Jacques Rousseau, Johann Heinrich Pestalozzi, Friedrich Froebel, and other educational pioneers can be found at **www.infed.org/thinkers**.

For an extensive collection of books and articles by and about Comenius, access The Online Books Page at **http://onlinebooks.library.upenn.edu**.

To view Comenius's *Orbis Pictus,* access the Hathitrust Digital Library at **www.hathitrust.org**.

For Rousseau's *Emile,* access the Emile Project at the Institute for Learning Technologies at **www.ilt.columbia.edu/publications/emile.html**.

For the lives and philosophies of Rousseau, Dewey, and Addams, access Internet Encyclopedia of Philosophy at **www.iep.utm.edu**.

For biographies and a slide show on Pestalozzi, access PestalozziWorld at **www.pestalozziworld.com**.

For biographies of Comenius, Rousseau, Pestalozzi, and Froebel, access Encyclopedia.com at **www.encyclopedia.com**.

For links to Pestalozzi sites, access **www.jhpestalozzi.org**.

For archives, links, and other resources about Froebel, access the International Froebel Society at **www.intFroebelsoc.org**.

For the philosophy, history, and projects related to Froebel, access the Froebel Foundation USA at **www.FroebelFoundation.org**.

For Dewey's publications and for books and articles about him, especially as a pragmatist, access **www.dewey.pragmatism.org**.

For a biography of Dewey, access **www.biography.com**.

For Jane Addams's life and philosophy, access the Stanford Encyclopedia of Philosophy at **http://plato.stanford.edu**.

For a chronology and images of Jane Addams and her papers, access the Jane Addams Paper Project at **www.janeaddamsproject.org**.

For information on Maria Montessori, consult the "International Montessori Index" at **www.montessori.edu** and Montessori Online at **www.montessori.org**. Also, access the

American Montessori Association at **www.amshq .org**, and the North American Teachers' Association at **www.Montessori-namta.org**.

For a biography and bibliography of Piaget, access the Jean Piaget Society at **www.piaget.org**.

For human intelligence and Piaget, access **www.indiana.edu/~intell/piaget.shtml**.

For a biography of Freire, access **www.columbia.edu/itc/tc /parker/adlearnville/transformativelearning/freire.html**.

For forums, resources, and videos about Freire and Critical Theory, access the Freire Project at **www.freireproject.org**.

For an interpretation of Herbert Spencer's influence on economics, society, and education in late nineteenth-century America, access "The Richest Man in the World" at WGBH American Experience at **www.pbs.org**. The site provides a transcript, time line, and teacher's guide.

Publications

Brown, Victoria Bissell. *The Education of Jane Addams.* Philadelphia: University of Pennsylvania Press, 2004. *A biography of Jane Addams that explores the origin and sources of her concepts of social reform, education, women's rights, and world peace.*

Cochran, Molly, ed. *The Cambridge Companion to Dewey.* Cambridge: Cambridge University Press, 2010. *Contains essays by scholars on Dewey's life, work, and philosophy.*

Damrosch, Leo. *Jean-Jacques Rousseau: Restless Genius.* Boston: Houghton Mifflin, 2005. *Damrosch's highly acclaimed biography provides a definitive account of the French philosopher's life and works.*

Dewey, John. *Democracy and Education,* introduction by Gerald L. Gutek. New York: Barnes and Noble, 2005. *An edition of Dewey's important book on philosophy of education, published originally in 1916, with an introductory essay that places the book in its historical and educational contexts.*

Dewey, John. *How We Think,* introduction by Gerald L. Gutek. New York: Barnes and Noble, 2005. *An edition of Dewey's important work on thinking as inquiry, published originally in 1910, with an introductory essay that places the book in its historical and educational contexts.*

Francis, Mark. *Herbert Spencer and the Invention of Modern Life.* Ithaca, NY: Cornell University Press, 2007. *Provides an interpretation of Spencer's relevance to contemporary society.*

Freire, Paulo. *Pedagogy of the Oppressed.* Translated by Myra Bergman Ramos. New York: Continuum, 2000. *Freire establishes the educational and ideological rationale for his liberation pedagogy.*

Gutek, Gerald L. *Historical and Philosophical Foundations of Education: A Biographical Introduction.* Columbus, OH: Merrill, 2011. *Placing each educator in historical and cultural context, Gutek examines the educational ideas of*

Plato, Quintilian, Aquinas, Calvin, Rousseau, Pestalozzi, Froebel, Spencer, Montessori, Addams, Dewey, Du Bois, Gandhi, and Mao.

Gutek, Gerald L. *The Montessori Method: The Origins of an Educational Innovation: Including an Abridged and Annotated Edition of Maria Montessori's* The Montessori Method. Lanham, MD: Rowman and Littlefield Publishers, 2004. *Provides an introductory biography of Maria Montessori and analysis of her educational method.*

Johnston, James S. *Inquiry and Education: John Dewey and the Quest for Democracy.* Albany: State University of New York Press, 2006. *Examines Dewey's method of thought in relationship to education.*

Knight, Louise W. *Citizen: Jane Addams and the Struggle for Democracy.* Chicago: University of Chicago Press, 2006. *Provides an engaging narrative of Jane Addams's intellectual journal to become an international social, educational, and political theorist and activist.*

Lilley, Irene M. *Friedrich Froebel: A Selection from His Writings.* New York and London: Cambridge University Press, 2010. *This reissuing of Lilley's book provides an excellent introduction and selections to Froebel's educational philosophy and method.*

Martin, Jay. *The Education of John Dewey.* New York: Columbia University Press, 2002. *A thorough discussion of John Dewey's life and education, with emphasis on how Dewey's emotional life influenced his philosophy.*

Morrow, Raymond A., and Carlos Alberto Torres. *Reading Freire and Habermas: Critical Pedagogy and Transformative Social Change.* New York: Teachers College Press, Columbia University, 2002. *Relates Freire to the construction of critical pedagogy.*

Murphy, Madonna M. *The History and Philosophy of Education: Voices of Educational Pioneers.* Upper Saddle River, NJ: Pearson/Merrill/Prentice Hall, 2006. *Places leading educational pioneers in their historical and philosophical contexts and provides primary source listings, time lines, websites, and other useful resources.*

Piaget, Jean. *The Child's Conception of the World: A 20th-Century Classic of Child Psychology.* Translated by Joan and Andrew Tomlinson. Lanham, MD: Rowman and Littlefield Publishers, 2007. *Piaget's analysis of how children develop their reasoning powers.*

Povell, Phyllis. *Montessori Comes to America: The Leadership of Maria Montessori and Nancy McCormick Rambusch.* New York: University Press of America, 2009. *Povell's insightful narrative provides the history of Montessori education in the United States and analyzes the leadership styles of Montessori and Rambush.*

Rossatto, Cesar Augusto. *Engaging Paulo Freire's Pedagogy of Possibility: From Blind to Transformative Optimism.* Lanham, MD: Rowman and Littlefield Publishers, 2005. *A teacher-educator provides a cross-cultural analysis of Freire's theory in light of contemporary trends and issues such as globalization.*

Rousseau, Jean-Jacques. *Emile*, introduction by Gerald L. Gutek. New York: Barnes and Noble, 2005. *An edition of Rousseau's classic work,* Emile, *published originally in 1762, with an introduction that identifies and examines the book's key concepts.*

Tovey, Helen. *Bringing the Froebel Approach to Your Early Years Practice.* New York and London: Routledge, 2011. *Tovey considers Froebel's principle and applies them to contemporary early childhood education.*

Zimmerman, Barry J., and Dale H. Schunk, eds. *Educational Psychology: A Century of Contributions.* Mahwah, NJ: Lawrence Erlbaum, 2003. *This book, a project of the Educational Psychology division of the American Psychological Association, contains essays on Piaget and other leading educational psychologists of the twentieth century.*

Additional resources for this chapter, including the TeachSource Videos, can be found on the Education CourseMate website. Go to **CengageBrain.com** to access the site.

CHAPTER

5

Historical Development of American Education

This chapter on the history of American education analyzes how individuals and groups built schools and developed educational processes in the United States. It examines (1) the introduction of European educational ideas and institutions to North America during the colonial period; (2) the efforts to create a uniquely American educational system during the revolutionary and early national eras; (3) the establishment of public education during the common school movement; (4) the development of secondary education from the Latin grammar school, through the academy, to today's comprehensive high school; (5) the development of colleges and universities; and (6) the immigration and the education of culturally diverse populations.

As you read this chapter, consider the following questions:

FOCUS QUESTIONS

- How did Americans adapt European educational ideas and institutions to life in the new world?

- How were elementary, secondary, and higher-education institutions established in the United States?

- How did social, economic, and political change affect public education in the United States?

- How did the American educational ladder develop and does it still function effectively today?

- How did immigration contribute to making the United States into a culturally diverse society, and what are the implications of cultural pluralism on contemporary schools?

---

*This chapter was revised by Gerald L. Gutek.

Constructing Your Own History or Autobiography of Education

In Chapter 3, Global Origins of American Education, and Chapter 4, Pioneers of Teaching and Learning, you were encouraged to reflect on your educational experience and construct your own educational history and autobiography. This chapter provides an engagement with America's educational past. To situate yourself in the history of American education, reflect on your educational experience and that of your family members—grandparents, parents, and other people who are significant in your life. Consider how immigration, ethnicity, race, and language shaped your educational experience and that of your family. What schools, colleges, or other institutions played a role in your education and that of members of your family?

The Colonial Period

Effect on Native Americans

North America's colonization in the seventeenth and eighteenth centuries caused complex cultural encounters and often violent conflicts between Europeans and the indigenous Native Americans. The Europeans, who carried contagious diseases such as measles and smallpox, infected the Native Americans who lacked immunity to these illnesses. Epidemics of these contagious illnesses ravaged the tribes living along the Atlantic coast. For example, a smallpox epidemic in 1618–1619 killed 90 percent of the Native Americans in the Massachusetts Bay colony.[1]

The Native Americans and the European colonists held different concepts about nature, property, and the uses of the environment. For the American Indians, nature—the natural environment and resources—was to be respected and used as necessary for

▶ ‖ TEACHSOURCE VIDEO ACTIVITY

Freedom Writers: Teachers Can Inspire Students to Learn and Achieve

Go to the Education CourseMate website to access the ABC News video entitled, "Freedom Writers: Teachers Can Inspire Students to Learn and Achieve." Consider the video's connections to writing your own educational autobiography. The high school students in Ms. Gruen's class constructed their own self-identities through autobiographical writing. The author encourages you to develop your identity by reflecting and writing your own educational autobiography, history, and philosophy.

❶ Why did Ms. Gruen encourage her students to engage in autobiographical writing?

❷ How can you apply the methods used by the Freedom Writers to your own autobiographical writing?

---

[1]For European and Native Americans relationships, see Peter C. Mancell and James H. Merrell, *American Encounters: Natives and Newcomers From European Contact to Indian Removal, 1500–1850* (New York: Routledge, 2006). Margaret Szasz, *Indian Education in the American Colonies, 1607–1783* (Lincoln: University of Nebraska Press, 2007).

food and shelter. For the Europeans, the environment's resources were to be developed, or exploited, for sustenance but also for wealth and profit.

Many Europeans regarded the indigenous peoples as culturally inferior, lesser humans who needed to be saved, civilized, or eliminated. What was common to most Europeans in North America was their belief that European culture and language—English, French, or Spanish—were superior to that of the Native Americans.

Many ethnic groups among colonists

The European colonists came from many ethnic and language backgrounds. The French established settlements in Canada and the Mississippi Valley; the Spanish in Mexico, Florida, and the Southwest; the Dutch in New Netherlands, now New York State; and the English in the original thirteen colonies that became the United States after the Revolutionary War. The English, who defeated the Dutch and the French, had the most pervasive impact on colonial American politics, society, and education.

Continuity & Change

The colonists at first recreated the socioeconomic-class–based **dual-track school system** that they had known in Europe. Most boys and girls attended primary schools where they learned reading, writing, arithmetic, and religion. Boys from the more privileged classes attended **Latin grammar schools**, that is, preparatory schools that taught the Latin and Greek languages and literatures needed for admission to colonial colleges. (For the origins of the dual-track school system, see Chapter 3, Global Origins of American Education.)

New England Colonies

The New England colonies of Massachusetts, Connecticut, and New Hampshire were a crucible for the development of American educational ideas and institutions. Massachusetts enacted the first formal education laws in British North America. (See Overview 5.1 for significant events in American education.)

Puritan schools

The English settlers in Massachusetts believed that a literate people who knew God's commandments as preached by their Puritan ministers could resist the devil's temptations. Following their Protestant injunction to read the Bible, the church-controlled schools emphasized reading, writing, arithmetic, and religion.

Schools for religious conformity and social and economic utility

Following John Calvin's theology, Puritan schools were guided by interpenetrating economic and religious purposes. According to the Calvinist work ethic, good Puritans were to be responsible citizens and productive businessmen and farmers who attended church, read the Bible, and worked diligently. Puritan teachers stressed values of punctuality, honesty, obedience to authority, and hard work. American education continues to emphasize the relationship between education and economic productivity.

Child seen as sinful

Child Depravity   The concept of child depravity shaped the Puritan child-rearing and educational practices. Children were regarded as depraved, or at least inclined to evil. Children's play was seen as idleness and children's talk as gibberish. Following the adage "Spare the rod and spoil the child," Puritan teachers relied on firm discipline and corporal punishment to manage their classes. At home, children were to help with household and farm chores. Revisit Chapter 4, Pioneers of Teaching and Learning, to see how Comenius, Rousseau, Pestalozzi, and Froebel opposed the doctrine of child depravity.

A teacher for every town

"Old Deluder Satan"   Believing that a Godly people were a literate people, the Puritan settlers began to establish schools soon after their arrival in Massachusetts. In 1642, the Massachusetts General Court, the colony's legislative body, enacted a law requiring parents and guardians to ensure that children in their care learned to read and understand the principles of religion and the commonwealth's laws. In 1647, the General Court enacted the "Old Deluder Satan" Act, a law intended to outwit Satan, whom, the Puritans believed, deceived ignorant people into sinning. The law required every town of fifty or more families to appoint a reading and writing teacher. Towns of one hundred or more families were to employ a Latin teacher to prepare young men to enter Harvard College.

The three R's, plus religion

The Town School   The New England colonists recreated the European dual-track system, establishing primary town schools for the majority of students and Latin grammar schools for upper-class boys. The New England **town school**, a locally controlled institution, educated both boys and girls from ages six to thirteen or fourteen. Attendance could be irregular, depending on weather conditions and the need for children to work on family farms. The school's curriculum included reading, writing, arithmetic, catechism, and religious hymns. Children learned the alphabet, syllables, words, and sentences by memorizing the **hornbook**, a sheet of parchment covered by transparent material made by flattening cattle horns. The older children read the *New England Primer*, which included religious materials such as the Westminster catechism, the Ten Commandments, the Lord's Prayer, and the Apostle's Creed.[2] Arithmetic was primarily counting, adding, and subtracting.

Atmosphere of the town school

The New England town school, often a crude log structure, was dominated by the teacher's pulpit-like desk at the front of the single room. Seated on wooden benches, pupils memorized their assignments until called before the schoolmaster to recite. Most teachers were men, some of whom temporarily taught school while preparing for the ministry. Others took the job to repay debts owed for their voyage to North America. Very few elementary teachers were trained in educational methods, and they often relied on corporal punishment to maintain discipline.

Classics for upper-class boys

The Latin Grammar School   Upper-class boys attended Latin grammar schools, which prepared them for college entry. These boys generally had learned to read and write English from private tutors. Entering the Latin grammar school at age eight, the student would complete his studies at fifteen or sixteen. He studied such Latin authors as Cicero, Terence, Caesar, Livy, Vergil, and Horace. More advanced students studied such Greek authors as Isocrates, Hesiod, and Homer. Little attention was given to mathematics, science, or modern languages. Usually college graduates, the Latin masters who taught in these schools were better paid and accorded higher social status than elementary teachers.

Harvard College

Established in 1636, Harvard was founded on the Puritan belief that future ministers and other leaders needed a thorough classical and theological education. The applicants were typically young men from the wealthier and more favored families. To be admitted to the College, the applicants had to demonstrate their competency in Latin and Greek. The four-year curriculum reflected the Puritan belief that ministers and other leaders needed a liberal arts education, with an emphasis on the classics. Harvard taught grammar, logic, rhetoric, mathematics, geometry, astronomy, ethics, philosophy, and natural science. Especially important for future ministers were Calvin's theology, Hebrew, Greek, and ancient history.

Diverse cultures

Middle Atlantic Colonies

Although the other colonial regions—the Middle Atlantic and southern colonies—shared a common European culture with New England, they exhibited significant differences in the provision and maintenance of schools. The settlers in the Middle Atlantic colonies—New York, New Jersey, Delaware, and Pennsylvania—were more culturally pluralistic than the homogenous Puritans of Massachusetts and Connecticut. The Dutch had settled New Netherlands, which later became New York; Swedes had settled Delaware, and some Germans located in Pennsylvania. The Middle Atlantic colonies' ethnic, language, and religious diversity influenced education. While Puritan New England created uniform town schools, the different churches in the Middle Atlantic colonies established parochial schools to educate children in their own religious beliefs and practices.

---

[2]Melissa Freeman and Sandra Mathison, *Researching Children's Experiences* (New York: Guilford Publications, 2009), pp. 1–17. Also, see Jennifer E. Monaghan, *Learning to Read and Write in Colonial America* (Amherst: University of Massachusetts Press, 2007).

OVERVIEW 5.1

Significant Events in the History of American Education

Major Political Events		Significant Educational Events	
1630	Massachusetts Bay Colony settled	1636	Harvard College, first English-speaking college in western hemisphere, founded
		1642	First education law enacted in Massachusetts
		1647	Massachusetts enacted Old Deluder Satan Act, requiring establishment of schools
		1751	Benjamin Franklin's Academy established in Philadelphia
1775–1783	American Revolution	1783	Noah Webster's *American Spelling Book* published
1788	U.S. Constitution ratified	1785	Northwest Ordinance, first national education law, enacted
		1821	First public high school in the United States opened in Boston
			Emma Willard's Female Seminary, a school of higher education for women, established in Troy, New York
		1823	First private normal school in the United States opened in Concord, Vermont
1824	Bureau of Indian Affairs established	1825	Webster's *American Dictionary* completed
		1827	Massachusetts law requiring public high schools passed
1830	Indian Removal Act	1837	Horace Mann appointed secretary of Massachusetts board of education
1846–1848	Mexican-American War; U.S. acquisition of southwestern territories	1839	First public normal school opened in Lexington, Massachusetts
1849	Gold rush to California	1855	First German-language kindergarten in the United States established
		1860	First English-language kindergarten in the United States established
1861–1865	Civil War	1862	Morrill Land Grant College Act passed, establishing in each state a college for agricultural and mechanical instruction
		1865	Freedmen's Bureau established
		1872	Kalamazoo decision upheld taxation for public high schools
1887	Dawes Act divides tribal lands	1881	Booker T. Washington established Tuskegee Institute
		1892	NEA established Committee of Ten
1898	Spanish-American War; U.S. acquisition of Puerto Rico and the Philippines	1896	*Plessy v. Ferguson* decision upheld constitutionality of "separate but equal" doctrine
		1909	First junior high school established in Berkeley, California

Major Political Events		Significant Educational Events	
1914–1918	World War I	1917	Smith-Hughes Act passed, providing funds for vocational education, home economics, and agricultural subjects
		1918	*Cardinal Principles of Secondary Education* published
		1919	Progressive Education Association organized
1929	Beginning of the Great Depression	1930s	New Deal programs provided federal funds for conservation projects and school construction
1939–1945	World War II	1944	G.I. Bill provided federal funds for continuing education of veterans
1950–1953	Korean War	1954	*Brown v. Board of Education of Topeka* ended *de jure,* or legally enforced, racial segregation of public schools
		1957	Soviet Union launched Sputnik, leading to a reevaluation of American education
		1958	National Defense Education Act passed, providing federal funds to improve science, math, and modern foreign-language instruction and guidance services
		1964	Civil Rights Act authorizes federal lawsuits for school desegregation
1965–1973	Vietnam War	1965	Elementary and Secondary Education Act passed, providing federal funds to public schools, especially for compensatory education
		1968	Bilingual Education Act enacted
		1972	Title IX Education Amendment passed, outlawing sex discrimination in schools receiving federal financial assistance
		1975	Education for All Handicapped Children (Public Law 94-142) passed
		1980	Department of Education established in federal government with cabinet status
		1983	Publication of *A Nation at Risk* stimulated national movement to reform education
1990	End of Cold War	1994	Goals 2000: The Educate America Act outlines national education goals
1991	Gulf War	1996	The nation's first educational technology plan: Getting Students Ready for the Twenty-First Century: Meeting the Technology Literacy Challenge
2001	Terrorist attacks on New York City and Washington, D.C.	2001	No Child Left Behind Act enacted
2003	Iraq War		
2009	Inauguration of first African American U.S. president		
2009	Global economic recession	2010	21st Century Skills and Common Core Standards Movements

Private schools

New York The Dutch originally settled in New Amsterdam, which was renamed "New York" after its conquest by the English. Members of the Reformed Church, the Dutch colonists established Dutch-language parochial schools to teach reading, writing, and religion. These Dutch parochial schools continued to operate after the colony came under England's domination.[3] When New York City grew into a thriving commercial port, private for-profit schools, called private-venture schools, offered navigation, surveying, bookkeeping, Spanish, French, and geography.

Quaker schools

Pennsylvania As a proprietary colony founded by William Penn, Pennsylvania became a refuge for the Society of Friends, or Quakers, a religious denomination persecuted in England. As pacifist conscientious objectors, Quakers refused to support war efforts or serve in the military. Because of their tolerance, the Quakers welcomed members of other small churches, such as the German pietists, to Pennsylvania. Quaker schools were open to all children, including blacks and Native Americans. (Philadelphia had a small African American community, and some Native Americans remained in the colony.) While Quaker schools taught the standard reading, writing, arithmetic, and religion found in other colonial primary schools, they were unique in offering vocational training, crafts, and agriculture. Rejecting the doctrine of child depravity and corporal punishment, Quaker teachers used gentle persuasion to motivate their pupils.

Private tutors

Southern Colonies The southern colonies—Maryland, Virginia, the Carolinas, and Georgia—presented still another economic and educational pattern. Except for flourishing tidewater cities such as Charleston and Williamsburg, the southern population was more dispersed than in New England or the Middle Atlantic colonies. This made it difficult for rural families to establish centrally located schools. The economically advantaged children of wealthy white plantation owners often studied with private tutors. Some families sent their children to private schools sponsored by the Church of England in towns such as Williamsburg or Charleston.

The slave system, which used the forced labor of captive Africans on plantations, profoundly shaped culture, economics, and politics in the South. Although slavery existed throughout the colonies, the largest population of enslaved Africans was in the southern colonies. Africans were seized by force and brutally transported in slave ships to North America to work on southern plantations. The enslaved Africans were trained as agricultural field hands, craftspeople, or domestic servants, but they were generally forbidden to learn to read or write. Some notable exceptions learned to read secretly. Over time, the African heritage became the foundation of African American religion and culture.[4]

Class bias in schooling

The slave system also affected economically disadvantaged, nonslaveholding whites. While wealthy plantation owners occupied the most productive land, the poorer farmers settled in less fertile backcountry or mountainous areas. The wealthy and politically powerful plantation elite focused on the education of their own children but provided few schools for the rest of the population.

Colonial Education: A Summary View

Parallels among regions

Despite regional religious and language differences, the New England, Middle Atlantic, and southern colonies were British colonies that followed Western European educational patterns.[5] The schools operated by different churches in the Middle Atlantic colonies

---

[3]For the Dutch in North America, see Jaap Jacobs, *New Netherlands: A Dutch Colony in Seventeenth Century America* (Leiden, The Netherlands: Brill, 2005); and Russell Shorto, *The Island at the Center of the World: The Epic Story of Dutch Manhattan and the Forgotten Colony that Shaped America* (New York: Random House, 2004).

[4]Ira Berlin, *Many Thousands Gone: The First Two Centuries of Slavery in North America* (Cambridge, MA: Belknap Press, 1998).

[5]Lawrence A. Cremin, *American Education: The Colonial Experience, 1607–1783* (New York: Harper and Row, 1970).

Gender discrimination

were forerunners of faith-based private schools. Educational opportunities were gender based in all three regions. Both girls and boys attended primary schools, but Latin grammar schools and colleges were reserved for males. Women's education was limited to primary schooling, where they learned the basics (reading and writing) to fulfill their family and religious responsibilities. Many, especially men who controlled educational institutions, believed that women were intellectually incapable of higher studies.

Tracking by social class

> **REFOCUS** After reading about colonial education, think back to the questions at the beginning of the chapter. *Use these questions to construct your own history or autobiography of education.* How were European educational ideas, institutions, and processes transported to North America during the colonial period? How were these ideas, institutions, and processes continued or changed over time? Have educational ideas from the colonial era shaped your educational experience? If so, consider including them in your educational history or autobiography.

The colonial school system reflected a European class orientation. Primary schools provided basic literacy but discouraged upward social mobility. Only a few pupils who completed primary schools advanced to Latin grammar schools and colonial colleges. The sons of the upper classes attended the preparatory Latin grammar schools and, if successful, entered college. During the nineteenth century, frontier egalitarianism, political democratization, and economic change would erode these European-based educational structures to create the American system of universal public education.

In the late colonial period, the 1760s and 1770s, Britain's American colonies experienced population and economic growth. Businessmen in the commercial cities of New York, Boston, Philadelphia, and Charleston, as well as settlers on the frontier, especially the Scotch-Irish Presbyterians, began to resist taxation by the British government. Their resistance to taxation without their consent grew into a revolutionary movement for independence.

The Early National Period

Northwest Ordinance

The American Revolution, which began in 1776, ended British rule in the thirteen colonies. The victorious rebels created a republic with an elected representative government. Although the inherited vernacular and denominational primary schools and Latin grammar schools continued into the early national period, several of the new republic's leaders wanted to create schools that emphasized American cultural identity and democratic political processes.

Operating under the Articles of Confederation, Congress enacted the earliest federal educational legislation with the Northwest Ordinance of 1785. The Northwest Ordinance reserved a section of each thirty-six-square-mile township for education. The Northwest Ordinance set the precedent for using federal **land grants** for education in the nineteenth century.

Tradition of local control

The U.S. Constitution, which was ratified in 1788 and became the law of the land, did not specifically address education. The Tenth Amendment's "reserved powers" clause (which reserves to the states all powers not specifically delegated to the federal government or prohibited to the states by the Constitution) left responsibility for education with the individual states. The New England tradition of local school control also contributed to a state and local rather than a national school system in the United States.

New educational ideas for the new nation

During the early national period, several leaders, including Benjamin Franklin, Thomas Jefferson, Benjamin Rush, and Noah Webster, developed proposals for schools in the new republic. Their proposals suggested a new approach to American education in which schools would (1) prepare people for republican citizenship; (2) include utilitarian and scientific skills and subjects to aid in developing the nation's vast expanses of frontier land and abundant natural resources; and (3) eliminate European attitudes to construct a uniquely American culture.[6]

---

[6]Jacqueline S. Reinier, *From Virtue to Character: American Childhood, 1775–1850* (New York: Twayne of Macmillan, 1996), p. xi.

Franklin: The Academy

Franklin's academy

Benjamin Franklin (1706–1790), a leading statesman, scientist, and publicist, founded an **academy**, that is, a private secondary school, and described its curriculum in his "Proposals Relating to the Education of Youth in Pennsylvania."[7] Franklin's emphasis on useful knowledge and science differed notably from the traditional Latin grammar school. English grammar, composition, rhetoric, and public speaking replaced Latin and Greek as the principal language studies. Students could also elect a second language related to their future careers. For example, prospective clergy could choose Latin and Greek, and those planning on commercial careers could elect French, Spanish, or German. Mathematics was taught for its practical application to bookkeeping, surveying, and engineering rather than as an abstract subject. History and biography provided moral models for students to learn how famous people made their political and ethical decisions.

Emphasis on science and practical skills

Prophetically, Franklin recognized how important science, invention, and technology would be in America's future. His curriculum featured the useful skills that schools had traditionally ignored, such as carpentry, shipbuilding, engraving, printing, and farming. By the mid-nineteenth century, the United States had many academies that resembled Franklin's plan.

---

[7]Walter Isaacson, *Benjamin Franklin: An American Life* (New York: Simon and Schuster, 2003), pp. 146–147. Other biographies of Franklin are: H. W. Brands, *The First American: The Life and Times of Benjamin Franklin* (New York: Anchor Books/Random House, 2000); James Srodes, *Franklin: The Essential Founding Father* (Washington, D.C.: Regnery, 2002); Walter Isaacson, *Benjamin Franklin: An American Life* (New York: Simon and Schuster, 2003); Edmund S. Morgan, *Benjamin Franklin* (New Haven, CT: Yale University Press, 2002). For a brief biography and excerpts from Franklin's *Autobiography* and "Proposals Relating to the Education of Youth in Pennsylvania," see Madonna M. Murphy, *The History and Philosophy of Education: Voices of Educational Pioneers* (Upper Saddle River, NJ: Pearson/Merrill/Prentice Hall, 2006), pp. 227–234.

TIME LINE
Benjamin Franklin

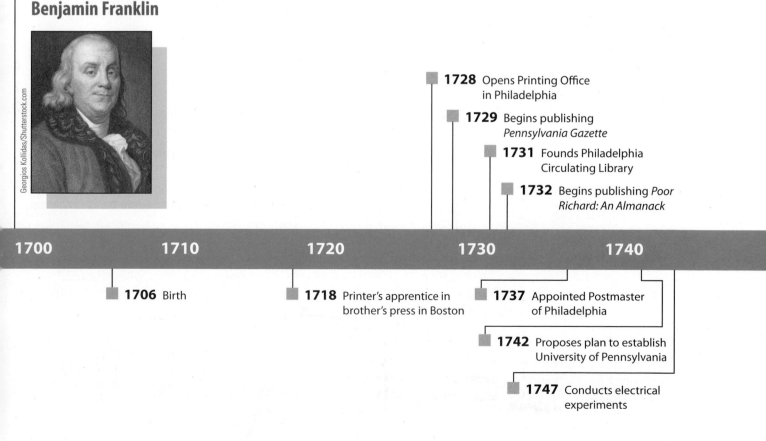

1728 Opens Printing Office in Philadelphia

1729 Begins publishing *Pennsylvania Gazette*

1731 Founds Philadelphia Circulating Library

1732 Begins publishing *Poor Richard: An Almanack*

1700 — 1710 — 1720 — 1730 — 1740

1706 Birth

1718 Printer's apprentice in brother's press in Boston

1737 Appointed Postmaster of Philadelphia

1742 Proposes plan to establish University of Pennsylvania

1747 Conducts electrical experiments

Georgios Kollidas/Shutterstock.com

Jefferson: Education for Citizenship

Education for citizenship

Thomas Jefferson (1743–1826), author of the Declaration of Independence and the third president of the United States, expressed his educational philosophy in his "Bill for the More General Diffusion of Knowledge," introduced in the Virginia legislature in 1779. Jefferson was also the principal founder of the University of Virginia.[8] Education's major purpose, Jefferson stated, was to promote a republican society of literate and well-informed citizens. Committed to separation of church and state, he believed that the state, not the churches, had the primary educational role. State-sponsored schools, not private ones, would be funded by public taxes.[9]

Jefferson's plan

Jefferson's bill, though not passed, raised important issues for the new nation. For example, it promoted state-established public schools and sought to provide both equity and excellence in education. It would have subdivided Virginia's counties into districts. The bill stipulated that free children, both girls and boys, could attend an elementary school in each district, where they would study reading, writing, arithmetic, and history. The state would pay for the first three years of a student's attendance. Jefferson's proposal also would have established twenty grammar schools throughout the state to provide secondary education to boys. In these grammar schools, students would study Latin, Greek, English, geography, and higher mathematics.

Scholarships based on merit

Jefferson's bill anticipated the idea of academic merit scholarships. In each district school, the most academically able male student who could not afford to pay tuition would receive a scholarship to continue his education at a grammar school. The ten scholarship students of highest academic achievement would receive additional state aid to attend the College of William and Mary.

Jefferson's plan represented an early compromise over issues of equity and excellence in American education. Although its provision of primary school for most children was a step toward equity, the concept of academic selectivity tilted toward the

---

[8]For a biography and excerpts from Jefferson's "Bill for the More General Diffusion of Knowledge", see Murphy, *The History and Philosophy of Education: Voices of Educational Pioneers,* pp. 235–241. Also, see R. B. Bernstein, *Thomas Jefferson* (New York: Oxford University Press, 2003).
[9]Julius P. Boyd, ed., *The Papers of Thomas Jefferson,* Vol. II (Princeton, NJ: Princeton University Press, 1950), pp. 526–533.

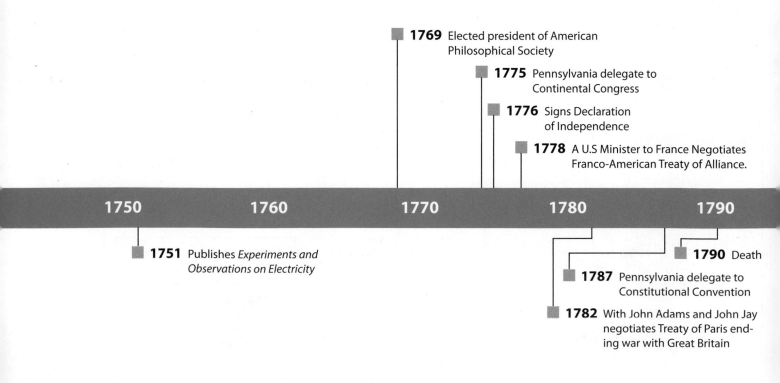

1769 Elected president of American Philosophical Society

1775 Pennsylvania delegate to Continental Congress

1776 Signs Declaration of Independence

1778 A U.S Minister to France Negotiates Franco-American Treaty of Alliance.

1750   1760   1770   1780   1790

1751 Publishes *Experiments and Observations on Electricity*

1790 Death

1787 Pennsylvania delegate to Constitutional Convention

1782 With John Adams and John Jay negotiates Treaty of Paris ending war with Great Britain

idea of secondary schools as "sorting machines" that identified and educated the most academically able students.

Benjamin Rush: Church-Related Schools

Religion and science

Benjamin Rush (1745–1813), a leading physician and medical educator of the early republic, did not subscribe to Jefferson's principle of separation of church and state. Seeing no conflict between science, republican government, and religion, Rush wanted the Bible and Christian principles taught in schools and in colleges. Anticipating the contemporary theory of "intelligent design," Rush believed that science revealed God's perfect design in creating the natural order.[10] Unlike Jefferson, Rush did not believe that government support of church-related schools threatened freedom of religion and scientific inquiry.

Rush's plan for a comprehensive system of state schools and colleges combined private and public interests. Private citizens' groups, especially members of churches, would raise money for a school and then would receive a charter from the state to be eligible for public funds. Emphasizing the nation's Christian roots, Rush wanted schools to be denominationally affiliated and offer a faith-based education.

A determined advocate of women's education, Rush rejected the sexist bias that women were intellectually inferior to men and needed only a limited education. Arguing that women's intellectual powers were equal to men's, he proposed a system of academies and colleges for women.

> **REFOCUS**   Think back to the questions at the beginning of the chapter. *Use these questions to construct your own history or autobiography of education.* In situating yourself in the history of American education, consider the efforts of Franklin, Jefferson, Rush, and Webster to use education to construct a distinctive American cultural identity. Did they succeed? How did political and social change in the early national period change the educational institutions and processes inherited from the colonial era?
>
> Has the emphasis on a distinctive American cultural identity that was generated in the early national period shaped your education? As you write your own educational history or autobiography, consider whether particular school subjects, ceremonies, or events shaped your cultural identity as an American.

[10]Hyman Kuritz, "Benjamin Rush: His Theory of Republican Education," *History of Education Quarterly* (Winter 1967), pp. 435–36. For a biography of Rush, see Alyn Brodsky, *Benjamin Rush: Patriot and Physician* (New York: St. Martin's Press, 2004).

TIMELINE
Thomas Jefferson

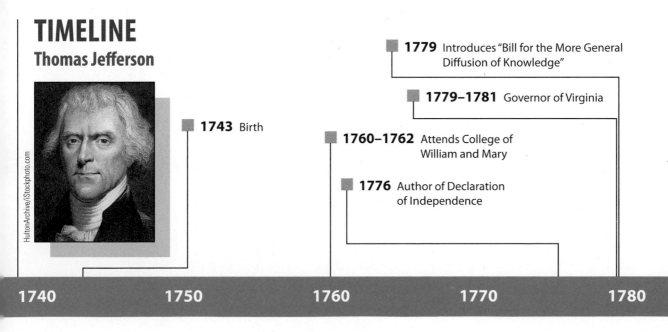

HultonArchive/iStockphoto.com

1743 Birth

1760–1762 Attends College of William and Mary

1776 Author of Declaration of Independence

1779 Introduces "Bill for the More General Diffusion of Knowledge"

1779–1781 Governor of Virginia

| 1740 | 1750 | 1760 | 1770 | 1780 |

▶ ‖ **TEACHSOURCE VIDEO ACTIVITY**

Benefits of a Multicultural History Curriculum

Go to the Education CourseMate website to access the following ABC News video entitled, "Benefits of a Multicultural History Curriculum," and then answer the following questions:

1 Identify and examine the major issues between multiculturalists and traditionalists on the writing and teaching of history.

2 Do you think some groups are underrepresented in historical writing and teaching?

Webster: Schoolmaster of the Republic

▨ Learning American culture through language

Noah Webster (1758–1843), a prominent educator and lexicographer, was one of the early republic's leading cultural nationalists.[11] Webster wanted the United States to be culturally independent with its own "language as well as government." Believing that a common language and literature would build a sense of national identity, Webster worked to construct a distinctive American version of the English language with its own idiom, pronunciation, and style.

▨ Webster's influence on "Americanization"

Believing that textbooks had a powerful influence on teaching and learning, Webster wrote spelling and reading books that emphasized American identity and achievements.[12] His *American Dictionary* was published in 1828 after years of intensive research.

▨ Continuity & Change

Esteemed as the "schoolmaster of the republic," Noah Webster promoted a monocultural American identity with its own distinctive American version of English as the national language. For many years, public schools had "Americanized" immigrant children by imposing this monolithic cultural version on them. Today, multicultural and bilingual education programs, recognizing America's diversity, seek to broaden the contours of American cultural identity.

---

[11]Joshua Kendall, *The Forgotten Founding Father: Noah Webster's Obsession and the Creation of an American Culture* (New York: G.P. Putnam's Sons, 2010), pp. 69–75.
[12]For a brief biography and excerpts from Webster's *On Being an American,* see Murphy, *The History and Philosophy of Education: Voices of Educational Pioneers,* pp. 242–248.

1825 Opening of University of Virginia

1801–1809 U.S. President

1826 Death

| 1790 | 1800 | 1810 | 1820 | 1830 |

The Movement toward Public Schooling

Sunday schools

In the early nineteenth century, there were efforts to use private voluntary arrangements such as Sunday and monitorial schools as alternatives to public tax-supported schools. During that time, some children worked in the factories of the industrializing Northeast. Philanthropic individuals and organizations established Sunday schools in the larger cities such as New York and Philadelphia. Functioning on Sundays when factories were closed, Sunday schools provided a minimal basic education of writing, reading, arithmetic, and religion.

Students as assistant teachers

The **monitorial method** used monitors—older and more experienced pupils trained by a master teacher—as aides in teaching classes, taking attendance, and maintaining order. For example, the master teacher would train monitors in a particular skill, such as adding single-digit numbers. These monitors would then teach that skill to classes of younger, less experienced pupils. Designed to teach basic skills to masses of students, private philanthropists who wanted a large but inexpensive school system funded monitorial schools. Like Sunday schools, monitorial schools were popular in large eastern cities. For example, more than 600,000 children attended the New York Free School Society's monitorial schools.[13] In the 1840s, common schools replaced monitorial schools when their educational limitations become increasingly apparent.

Rise and fall of monitorial schools

The Common School

Growth of the common school

The common school movement of the first half of the nineteenth century is highly significant in American education because it created publicly controlled and funded elementary education. The **common school**, the forerunner of today's elementary public school, offered a basic curriculum of reading, writing, spelling, and arithmetic. Over time, history, geography, hygiene, and singing were added. It was called a "common" school because it was open to children of all social and economic classes. Historically, however, enslaved African children in the South were excluded from common

---

[13]William R. Johnson, "'Chanting Choristes': Simultaneous Recitation in Baltimore's Nineteenth-Century Primary Schools," *History of Education Quarterly* (Spring 1994), pp. 1–12.

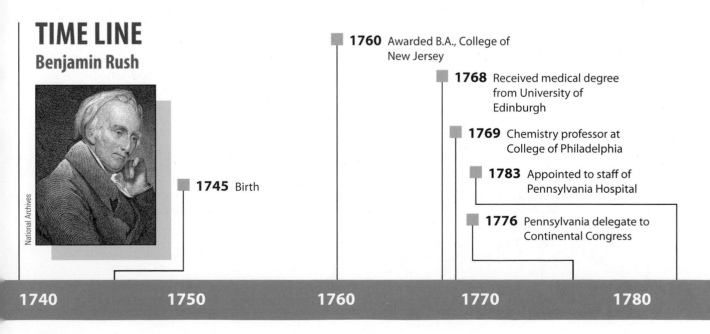

TIME LINE
Benjamin Rush

National Archives

1745 Birth

1760 Awarded B.A., College of New Jersey

1768 Received medical degree from University of Edinburgh

1769 Chemistry professor at College of Philadelphia

1783 Appointed to staff of Pennsylvania Hospital

1776 Pennsylvania delegate to Continental Congress

1740   **1750**   **1760**   **1770**   **1780**

schools until the Civil War and the Thirteenth Amendment ended slavery, and more public schools were established during the Reconstruction period.

In 2010, the Council of Chief State School Officers (CCSSO) and the National Governors Association Center for Best Practices (NGA Center) approved Kindergarten–12 Common Core State Standards for English language arts and mathematics. The Partnership for 21st Century Skills also identified core subjects. In historical retrospect, these subjects and standards use the word "common" as did the nineteenth-century advocates of common schools. The term means that the core subjects and standards apply to all schools and students. Although the list of 21st Century Skills subjects has been expanded to include world languages and economics, it still emphasizes the common school subjects of English language skills, art, mathematics, science, geography, history, and government and civics. The twenty-first century themes of civic and health literacy were also emphasized in nineteenth-century common schools.

Because of the historic tradition of local control and the Tenth Amendment of the U.S. Constitution's reservation of education to the states, the United States, unlike France and Japan, did not establish a national school system. The patterns by which common schools were established differed from state to state and even within a given state. Especially on the western frontier, where there were many small school districts, resources and support for schooling varied significantly from one district to another. Because of this history, public-education funding is still seriously uneven in the school districts and states.

The common-school movement gained momentum between 1820 and 1850. The New England states of Massachusetts and Connecticut, with a tradition of town and district schools, were the earliest to establish common schools. In 1826, Massachusetts required every town to elect a school committee responsible for all the schools in its area of jurisdiction. Ten years later, in 1836, Massachusetts established the first state board of education. Connecticut then followed its neighbor's example. Other northern states generally adopted New England's common school model. As the frontier moved westward and new states were admitted to the Union, they, too, established common or public elementary-school systems. In the South, however, with some exceptions such as North Carolina, common schools were not generally established until the Reconstruction period, 1865–1876, after the Civil War.

State legislatures typically established common schools in the following sequence:

- First, they permitted residents to organize local school districts with the approval of local voters.
- Second, they deliberately encouraged, but did not mandate, establishing school districts, electing school boards, and levying taxes to fund schools.
- Third, they made common schools compulsory by mandating the establishment of districts, election of boards, and collecting taxes to support schools.

 Continuity & Change

A Common Education

Differences among regions

Three stages of legislation

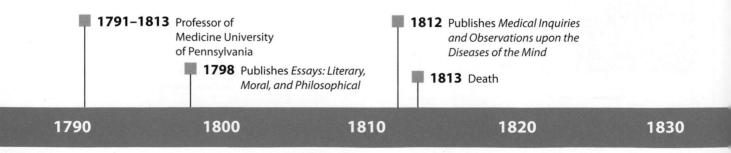

1791–1813 Professor of Medicine University of Pennsylvania

1798 Publishes *Essays: Literary, Moral, and Philosophical*

1812 Publishes *Medical Inquiries and Observations upon the Diseases of the Mind*

1813 Death

1790   1800   1810   1820   1830

Common schools laid the foundation of the American public-school system. Later in the nineteenth century, the American **educational ladder** was completed as high schools connected elementary schools to state colleges and universities. Horace Mann was one of the most prominent common school leaders.

Mann: The Struggle for Public Schools

When the Massachusetts legislature established a state board of education in 1837, it appointed Horace Mann (1796–1859), a prominent Whig political leader and a steadfast proponent of common schools, as its secretary.[14] His *Annual Reports* expressed his philosophy of education and opinions on educational issues. As editor of the *Common School Journal*, Mann also sought to win national support for public schools.[15] (For Mann's appointment and other events in American education, see Overview 5.1.)

Building support for common schools

Mann used his political acumen to mobilize support and build a coalition for public education. He convinced taxpayers that it was in their self-interest to support public schools. Applying the Calvinist *stewardship theory* to his common-school campaign, Mann argued that wealthy people, as stewards of society, had a special responsibility to provide public education. He told businessmen that tax-supported public education was an investment in Massachusetts's economic growth. Common schools would train productive workers to be responsible citizens who obeyed the law and worked hard and diligently. Mann convinced workers and farmers that common schools would be the great social equalizer, providing their children with the skills and knowledge needed to climb the economic ladder.

Public schools and democratic society

Building on Jefferson's case for civic education, Mann argued that public education was necessary for a democratic society. Citizens needed to be literate to make intelligent and responsible decisions as voters, members of juries, elected public officials, and civil servants.

---

[14]The definitive biography remains Jonathan Messerli, *Horace Mann: A Biography* (New York: Knopf, 1972). Reprints of books on Horace Mann are B. A. Hinsdale, *Horace Mann and the Common School Revival in the United States* (Whitefish, MT: Kessinger Publishing, 2007); Matthew Hale Smith, William B. Fowle, and Horace Mann, *The Bible, The Rod, and Religion in Common Schools* (Whitefish, MT: Kessinger Publishing, 2008); Joy Elmer Morgan, *Horace Mann: His Ideas and Ideals* (Whitefish, MT: Kessinger Publishing, 2008).
[15]For a brief biography and excerpts from Mann's Report No. 12, see Madonna Murphy, *The History and Philosophy of Education: Voices of Educational Pioneers*, pp. 259–265.

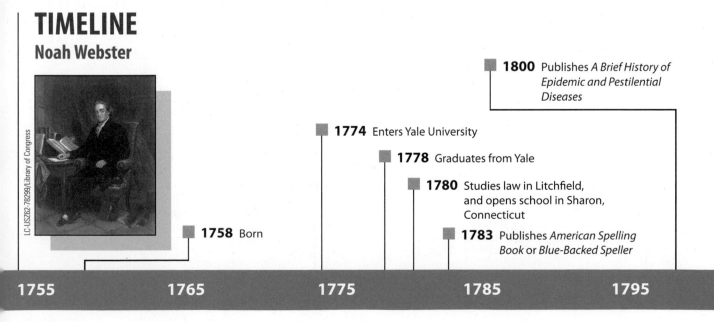

TIMELINE
Noah Webster

LC-USZ62-78299/Library of Congress

1800 Publishes *A Brief History of Epidemic and Pestilential Diseases*

1774 Enters Yale University

1778 Graduates from Yale

1780 Studies law in Litchfield, and opens school in Sharon, Connecticut

1758 Born

1783 Publishes *American Spelling Book* or *Blue-Backed Speller*

| 1755 | 1765 | 1775 | 1785 | 1795 |

Whereas Jefferson sought to improve educational opportunity for academically talented young men, Mann wanted to provide greater equality of access to schools. Although common schools would minimize class differences, Mann, like a true Whig, believed the upper social classes should still control the economic and political system. Like Noah Webster, Mann supported an "Americanization" policy, arguing that a common-school system would provide the United States, as a nation of immigrants, with a unifying common culture.

School taxes

Mann constructed the general public-school philosophy in that public schools would be (1) organized as a statewide system, funded by local and state taxes; (2) governed by elected school boards who carried out state mandates; (3) staffed by professionally educated teachers; and (4) free of church control.

Normal Schools and Women's Education

In addition to providing publicly supported elementary education for the majority of American children, the common-school movement had two important complementary consequences: (1) it led to the establishing of **normal schools**, which provided early preservice teacher preparation; and (2) it opened elementary-school teaching as an important career path for women.

Rise of normal schools

Named after the French *école normale* on which they were modeled, normal schools were the dominant institution for preparing elementary-school teachers from the 1860s to 1920. While most normal schools were state institutions, others were part of public-school systems in large cities or were private or religious institutions. Normal-school enrollments increased from 29,100 in 1875 to 116,600 in 1899 and reached 119,000 students in 1915.

Although there were exceptions, most normal schools offered two-year teacher education programs that were organized into three components: academic courses, pedagogical courses, and clinical experiences. Academic courses, often in the liberal arts and sciences, were related to the skills and subjects taught in elementary schools. For example, English language and literature courses that related to teaching reading, writing, grammar, spelling, and literature; mathematics, algebra, and geometry that related to arithmetic; American and European history and geography that related to civics and social studies; and physics, chemistry, botany, and biology that related to general science and nature studies. More directly related to education, pedagogical courses included the history, philosophy, and psychology of education; methods of instruction; and classroom management. Clinical experiences involved observation of experienced teachers in school classrooms and supervised practice teaching. In the twentieth century, many normal schools were reorganized as four-year teacher-education colleges.[16]

---

[16]James W. Fraser, *Preparing America's Teachers: A History* (New York: Teachers College Press, 2007), pp. 27–40, 43–58. For the history of the normal school, see Christine A. Ogren, *The American State Normal School: "An Instrument of Great Good."* (New York: Palgrave Macmillan, 2005).

1806 Publishes *A Compendious Dictionary of the English Language*

1828 Publishes *An American Dictionary of the English Language*

1843 Death

| 1805 | 1815 | 1825 | 1835 | 1845 |

Expanding opportunities for women

The establishment of common schools created a demand for professionally prepared teachers, and many women entered teaching careers in the expanding elementary-school system. The normal schools prepared women for these careers and also opened opportunities for higher education previously denied them. Although salaries were low and conditions demanding, teaching gave middle-class women an opportunity for careers outside the home. Until the Civil War, most rural schoolteachers were men. By 1900, however, 71 percent of rural teachers were women.

Catharine Beecher: Preparing Women as Teachers

Reform and women's rights

In the nineteenth century, feminist leaders such as Elizabeth Cady Stanton, Emma Willard, and Susan B. Anthony spoke out for women's educational and political equality. Prominent among these women was Catharine Beecher (1800–1878), a teacher educator, who connected the common school to women's education.[17] Beecher founded and operated the Hartford Female Seminary, in Hartford, Connecticut, from 1823 until 1831. She then created the Western Female Institute as a model for a proposed network of teacher-education institutions.

A key role for women

Teaching, Beecher reasoned, gave educated women a socially useful career path at a time when their opportunities for higher education and professional positions were severely limited. Importantly, it made women financially independent and gave them the opportunity to shape future generations morally.

Envisioning elementary-school teaching as a woman's profession, Beecher contributed to the feminization of elementary teaching. Women's colleges would open higher education to women and prepare them to staff the growing public-school system.[18] She argued that ninety thousand teachers were needed to bring civilization to the untamed western frontier.[19] Beecher was part of a network of women educators such as Emma Willard, Zilpah Grant, and Mary Lyon who prepared women for teaching careers.

---

[17]Kathryn Kish Sklar, *Catharine Beecher: A Study in American Domesticity* (New York: W. W. Norton & Co., 1976), p. xiv. Also see Barbara A. White, *The Beecher Sisters* (New Haven, CT, and London: Yale University Press, 2003).

[18]Catharine Beecher, *An Essay on the Education of Female Teachers* (New York: Van Nostrand & Dwight, 1835), pp. 14–18.

[19]Ibid., p. 19.

TIME LINE
Horace Mann

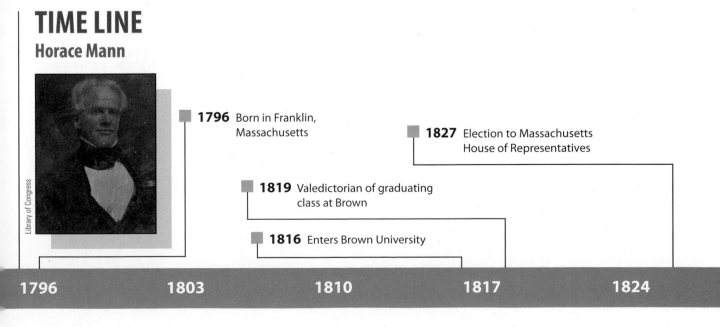

1796 Born in Franklin, Massachusetts

1827 Election to Massachusetts House of Representatives

1819 Valedictorian of graduating class at Brown

1816 Enters Brown University

| 1796 | 1803 | 1810 | 1817 | 1824 |

The one-room school represented a form of direct democracy in school government: the elected school board set the tax rate and hired and supervised the teacher. The small rural school also served as a cultural center for the community.

The Granger Collection, NYC

As a teacher educator, Beecher had clear ideas about preservice preparation and classroom practice. In their preservice work, students would study evangelical Christian morality, discuss the civilizing mission of women as teachers, and observe experienced teachers.[20] In practice, women teachers needed to use their "sensibility," their intuitive insights, about children to manage their classrooms, teach a common curriculum that encouraged literacy and civility, and serve as moral mentors.

▎Direct democracy in small districts

The One-Room School The local school district, often having only a single one-room school, was almost a direct democracy in which an elected school board set the tax rate and hired and supervised the teacher.[21] Many small districts were consolidated into larger ones in the early twentieth century, as described in Chapter 7, Governing and Administering Public Education.

[20]Ellen C. DuBois and Lynn Dumenil, *Through Women's Eyes: An American History with Documents* (Boston: Bedford/St. Martins, 2005), pp. 139–141.
[21]A Web presentation on the one-room school is "One Room Schools: Michigan's Educational Legacy," Clarke Historical Library, Central Michigan University: **http://clarke.cmich.edu /resource_tab/information_and_exhibits/one_room_schools/one_room_schools_index. html.**

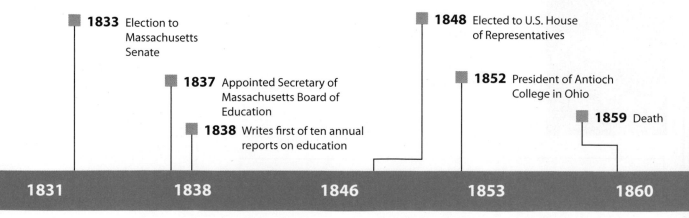

1833 Election to Massachusetts Senate

1837 Appointed Secretary of Massachusetts Board of Education

1838 Writes first of ten annual reports on education

1848 Elected to U.S. House of Representatives

1852 President of Antioch College in Ohio

1859 Death

| 1831 | 1838 | 1846 | 1853 | 1860 |

Teacher certification was simple but chaotic in that each board issued its own certificates to its teachers, which other districts often refused to recognize. Today's more uniform state certification and accreditation by the National Council for Accreditation of Teacher Education (NCATE) is a step toward greater professionalization for teachers.

The typical schoolhouse

On the western frontier, the one-room log school was often the first community building constructed. By the 1870s, wood-frame schoolhouses, painted white or red, replaced the crude log structures. These improved buildings, heated by wood-burning stoves, included slate blackboards and cloakrooms. The teacher's desk stood on a raised platform at the front of the room. Many classrooms had large double desks that seated two pupils. Later, these often were replaced with single desks, each with a desktop attached to the back of the chair in front of it. Thus, all the desks were immovable and arranged in straight rows, one behind the other.[22]

Basic curriculum

The pupils, ranging in age from five to seventeen, studied a basic curriculum of reading, writing (penmanship), grammar, spelling, arithmetic, history, geography, music, drawing, and hygiene. Many teachers used the recitation method, in which each pupil stood and recited a previously assigned lesson they had memorized. Later in the nineteenth century, teachers who attended normal schools used the methods of Pestalozzi and Herbart, especially simultaneous group instruction, to improve their teaching. Schools emphasized the values of punctuality, honesty, and hard work. The rural one-room schoolteachers, expected to be disciplinarians as well as instructors, had "to be their own janitors, record keepers, and school administrators."[23] For more about one-room schools, see the Technology @ School box.

REFOCUS Think back to the questions at the beginning of the chapter. *Use these questions to construct your own history or autobiography of education.* Reflect on Mann's and Beecher's efforts to create public schools and establish teacher-education programs. Did they accomplish their mission? How did the establishment of common schools relate to the growth and development of teacher education? As you write your own history or autobiography of education, consider how the American system of public education has shaped your educational experience. Do some research to see if any members of your extended family attended one-room schools.

[22]Wayne E. Fuller, *One-Room Schools of the Middle West: An Illustrated History* (Lawrence: University of Kansas Press, 1994), pp. 7–19, 18–27, 30–40.
[23]Ibid., p. 61.

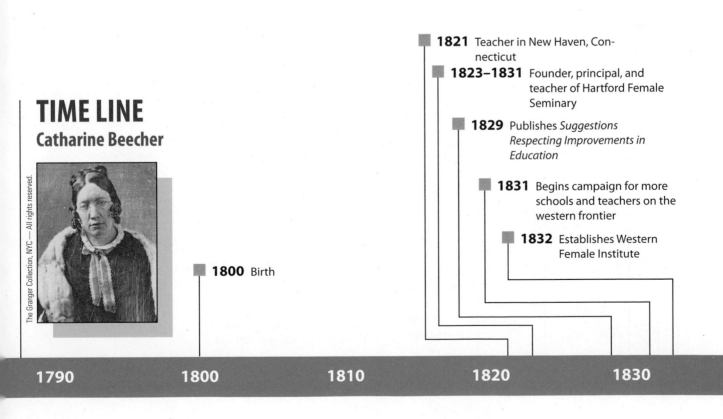

TIME LINE
Catharine Beecher

1821 Teacher in New Haven, Connecticut

1823–1831 Founder, principal, and teacher of Hartford Female Seminary

1829 Publishes *Suggestions Respecting Improvements in Education*

1831 Begins campaign for more schools and teachers on the western frontier

1832 Establishes Western Female Institute

1800 Birth

1790   1800   1810   1820   1830

TECHNOLOGY@SCHOOL

Researching the One-Room School

Y ou can research the one-room school to make a personal connection to the careers of America's pioneer teachers. Consult these websites for more on one-room schools:

■ For one-room schoolhouse historical information, at the Northern Illinois University Blackwell Museum, access **www .cedu.niu.edu/blackwell/oneroom/information.shtml**.

■ For information on one-room schools, McGuffey readers, and penmanship, access Country School Association of America at **www.countryschoolassociation.org/research.php**.

■ For an introduction to the Kansas One Room School House Project, access **www.kansasheritage.US/orsh/about.htm**.

■ For a state listing of sites, stories, photos, lessons, and a bibliography, access the One-Room Schoolhouse Center at **http://oneroomschoolhousecenter.weebly.com**.

These sites provide information about teachers, students, architecture, textbooks, and curriculum in one-room schools. You can continue your research at your local or school library to identify articles and books on this subject.

Contact local museums and history societies in your area to see if they have materials on one-room schools. You can also locate and interview individuals who attended one-room schools. Share your research with colleagues in the course.

McGuffey Readers

120 million copies

Patriotism and moral values

The development of public elementary schools and teacher-education programs generated a demand for textbooks. William Holmes McGuffey (1800–1873), clergyman, professor, and college president, wrote the widely used and highly popular McGuffey readers. Reaffirming the values of white, middle-class, Protestant Americans, McGuffey readers emphasized literacy, hard work, diligence, punctuality, patriotism, and civility. Stressing patriotism and heroism, reading selections included the orations of

1837 Founds Ladies' Society for Promoting Education in the West

1839 Publishes *The Moral Instructor for Schools and Families: Containing Lessons on the Duties of Life*

1841 Publishes *A Treatise on Domestic Economy for the Use of Young Ladies at Home and at School*

1847 Co-founder with William Slade of Board of National Popular Education

1852 Founds American Women's Educational Association

1856 Publishes *Physiology and Calisthenics for Schools and Families*

1878 Death

| 1840 | 1850 | 1860 | 1870 | 1880 |

Patrick Henry, Daniel Webster, and George Washington. More than 120 million copies of McGuffey's readers were sold between 1836 and 1920.[24]

The Development of American Secondary Schools

Completing the educational ladder

With the establishment of public elementary schools, the first rung of the American educational ladder was now in place. The highest rung was filled by the state colleges. However, these upper and lower steps remained disconnected in the middle. The next section examines how the establishment of public high schools completed the ladder.

The Academy: Forerunner of the High School

Academy replaces grammar school

Anticipated by Benjamin Franklin's plan, the academy replaced the colonial Latin grammar school as the major American secondary school in the first half of the nineteenth century. By 1855, more than 6,000 academies enrolled 263,000 students. Unlike the Latin grammar schools, which were exclusively attended by males preparing for college entry, academies were both single-sex and coeducational. They offered college-preparatory programs as well as a range of other programs.

Broader curriculum and student body

Academy programs followed three patterns: (1) the traditional college-preparatory curriculum, which emphasized Latin and Greek; (2) the English-language curriculum, a general program for students who would end their formal education upon completing secondary school; and (3) the normal curriculum, which prepared elementary-school teachers. Some males also attended military academies such as the Citadel in South Carolina.

Academies for women

Some academies were founded to educate young women. For example, in 1821, Emma Willard, a leader in the women's rights movement, established New York's Troy Female Seminary. Along with domestic science programs, women's academies offered classical and modern languages, science, mathematics, art, music, and the teacher-preparation, or normal, curriculum. Although most academies were private, some were semipublic institutions partially funded by cities and states. Academies were popular secondary schools until the 1870s, when public high schools began to replace them. Today, private academies still provide secondary education for a small percentage of the school-age population.

The High School

Taxes for public high schools

Although a few **high schools**, such as the Boston English Classical School, were operating in the early nineteenth century, the high school became the country's dominant secondary school after 1860. In the 1870s, the courts ruled in a series of cases (especially the Kalamazoo, Michigan, case in 1874) that school districts could levy taxes to establish and support public high schools.[25] By 1890, public high schools enrolled more than twice as many students as private academies.[26]

Compulsory attendance

In the late nineteenth and early twentieth centuries, the states passed compulsory attendance laws that established the age range that students had to attend school. While students could attend approved nonpublic schools, the states set minimum standards for all schools.

[24]James M. Lower, "William Holmes McGuffey: A Book or a Man? Or More?" *Vitae Scholasticae* (Fall 1984), pp. 311–320; Harvey C. Minnich, *William Holmes McGuffey and His Readers* (Whitefish, MT: Kessinger Publishing, 2008); for a reprint of a McGuffey reader, see Williams Holmes McGuffey, *McGuffey's Fifth Eclectic Reader* (Charleston, SC: Bibliolife, 2008).
[25]See *Stuart v. School District No. 1 of Village of Kalamazoo,* 30 Mich. 69 (1874).
[26]L. Dean Webb, *The History of American Education: A Great American Experiment* (Upper Saddle River, NJ: Pearson/Merrill/Prentice Hall, 2006), pp. 173–183.

The progressives supported compulsory attendance legislation. They worked for the enactment of child labor laws, such as the Keating-Owen Child Labor Act of 1916, which restricted employment of children and adolescents so that they would attend school rather than enter the workforce. Compulsory attendance was sometimes opposed by immigrant parents, who feared it was a strategy to erode their children's ethnic heritage, and among farmers, who needed their children to work on the farm.[27]

Urbanization and the High School   In the late nineteenth and early twentieth centuries, the convergence of several significant socioeconomic and educational trends created a favorable climate for the establishment of high schools. The United States was changing from an agricultural and rural society to an industrial and urban nation. For example, New York City's population quadrupled between 1860 and 1910. By 1930, more than 25 percent of all Americans lived in seven great urban areas: New York, Chicago, Philadelphia, Boston, Detroit, Los Angeles, and Cleveland. The high school was an educational response to an urban and industrial society's need for more specialized occupations, professions, and services.[28] This socioeconomic change was concurrent with important developments in adolescent psychology. G. Stanley Hall, for example, argued that adolescents, at a crucial stage in their development, were best educated in high schools.

Reshaping the High-School Curriculum   Since its establishment, there has been debate about the purposes of high schools. Whereas liberal arts and science college professors saw them as college-preparatory institutions, vocational educators wanted high schools to prepare adolescents to enter the workforce. In some large cities, high schools, called "people's colleges," offered liberal arts and science courses as well as work-related programs.[29] In 1892, the National Education Association (NEA) established the **Committee of Ten**, chaired by Harvard University President Charles Eliot, to define the high school's mission and purposes. The committee made two important recommendations: (1) subjects should be taught uniformly for both college-preparatory students and those who completed their formal education upon graduation; and (2) an endorsement of the pattern of eight years of elementary and four years of secondary education.[30] It identified four curricula as appropriate for the high school: classical, Latin-scientific, modern language, and English. These recommendations reflected a general college-preparatory orientation because each curriculum included foreign languages, mathematics, science, English, and history.

By 1918, all states had enacted compulsory attendance laws, with thirty states mandating full-time attendance until age sixteen.[31] Increasing enrollments made high-school students more representative of the general adolescent population and more culturally diverse than in the past when students came primarily from the upper- and upper-middle classes.

The NEA's **Commission on the Reorganization of Secondary Education** in the *Cardinal Principles of Secondary Education* (1918) responded to the socioeconomic changes in the high-school student population. The Commission redefined the high school as a comprehensive institution serving the country's pluralistic social, cultural, and economic populations. It recommended the following: (1) establishing differentiated curricula to meet agricultural, commercial, industrial, and domestic as well as

Effort to standardize curriculum

Rising diversity

---

[27]Michael McGeer, *A Fierce Discontent: The Rise and Fall of the Progressive Movement in America, 1870–1920* (New York: Free Press, 2003), pp. 190–111.

[28]William J. Reese, *The Origins of the American High School* (New Haven, CT: Yale University Press, 1995); Jurgen Herbst, *The Once and Future School: Three Hundred Years of American Secondary Education* (New York: Routledge, 1996); David F. Labaree, *The Making of an American High School: The Credentials Market and the Central High School of Philadelphia, 1839–1939* (New Haven, CT: Yale University Press, 2009).

[29]Herbst, *The Once and Future School*, pp. 95–106.

[30]National Education Association, *Report of the Committee on Secondary School Studies* (Washington, D.C.: U.S. Government Printing Office, 1893).

[31]L. Dean Webb, *The History of American Education: A Great American Experiment*, p. 176.

college-preparatory needs; and (2) maintaining the high school's integrative and comprehensive social character.[32] The Commission's recommendations paralleled Herbert Spencer's curriculum theory based on needs as discussed in Chapter 4, Pioneers of Teaching and Learning.

Secondary-School Organization

Differentiated programs for varied students

By the 1920s, four curricular patterns were used in high schools: (1) the college-preparatory program, which included English language and literature, foreign languages, mathematics, natural and physical sciences, and history and social studies; (2) the commercial or business program with courses in bookkeeping, shorthand, and typing; (3) the industrial, vocational, home economics, and agricultural programs; and (4) the general academic program for students planning to complete their formal education upon graduation.

A four-year sequence

Despite variations, the typical high-school pattern followed a four-year sequence encompassing grades 9–12 and generally including ages fourteen to eighteen. Variations included reorganized six-year schools, where students attended a combined junior-senior high school after completing a six-year elementary school; three-year junior high schools, comprising grades 7–9; and three-year senior high schools for grades 10–12.

Junior high schools

In the 1920s and 1930s, educators designed the **junior high school** as a transitional institution between elementary and high school that was oriented to early adolescents' developmental needs. Junior high schools were either two-year institutions that encompassed grades 7 and 8, or three-year institutions that also included ninth grade. The junior high school curriculum extended beyond that of elementary schools by including some vocational and commercial courses. By 1920, there were 883 junior high schools in the United States. By the 1940s, more than 50 percent of young adolescents were attending junior high schools.[33]

Middle schools

In the 1960s, **middle schools** became another type of transitional institution between elementary and high school.[34] They generally include grades 6–8 (ages eleven through thirteen) and facilitate a gradual transition from childhood to adolescence by emphasizing programs oriented to preadolescent development and needs. Often using new architectural designs, middle schools featured learning centers, language laboratories, and arts centers. Their numbers grew rapidly from 1,434 in 1971 to 9,750 in 2000.[35] Although most school districts today use the middle-school model, some retain the junior-high-school approach.[36]

The Development of Educational Technology

Early technologies

In the twentieth century, America's schools began to integrate educational technology into their classrooms. Using technology in classroom instruction is an important component of preservice teacher-education programs. Competency in educational technology is mandated by many state certification programs and is a standard in professional teacher accreditation.

Educational technology entered the schools in the late 1920s when radio and motion pictures were introduced in schools. The National Association of Educational

---

[32]Commission on the Reorganization of Secondary Education, Cardinal Principles of American Secondary Education, Bulletin no. 35 (Washington, D.C.: U.S. Government Printing Office, 1918).
[33]Douglas MacIver and Allen Ruby, "Middle Schools," in James W. Guthrie, ed., Encyclopedia of Education, 2nd ed., Vol. 5 (New York: Macmillan/Thomson Gale, 2003), p. 1630.
[34]For middle-school education, see Thomas Dickinson, ed., Reinventing the Middle School (New York: Routledge Farmer, 2001).
[35]MacIver and Ruby, "Middle Schools," p. 1630.
[36]For developments in middle-school education, see Anthony W. Jackson and Gayle A. Davis, Turning Points 2000: Educating Adolescents in the 21st Century (New York: Teachers College Press, 2000).

Broadcasting was organized to encourage the development of radio instruction and the exchange of educational scripts. "Schools of the Air" on commercial frequencies brought cultural and music-appreciation programs into classrooms in the late 1930s and 1940s.

Alexander J. Stoddard initiated the National Program in the Use of Television in the Schools in 1957, and the Midwest Program on Airborne Television Instruction began telecasting lessons to schools in 1961.[37] Along with educational television, other instructional technologies such as programmed learning, computer-assisted instruction, and educational videos were being used in the schools by the early 1970s. Today, many high schools have their own television studio and channel. Closed-circuit television frequently augments preservice teacher education, providing student teachers with an instant videotaped critique of their teaching.

Computers

The 1990s saw large-scale development and implementation of computer-based educational technology. Electronic data retrieval, the Internet, and computer-assisted instruction brought significant change to instruction.[38] Tim Berners-Lee, with Robert Cilia, developed the prototype for the World Wide Web in 1990, creating an electronic means of quickly disseminating and accessing information. An important development occurred in 1993, when Marc Andresen and Eric Bina developed Mosaic, a software program capable of electronically displaying graphics with accompanying texts.[39] States and local school districts rushed to increase the number of computers in classrooms, improve Internet access, and provide increased technical support for schools. Recognizing that the country was in the midst of a technological transformation, the U.S. Department of Education issued a national plan, "Getting America's Students Ready for the Twenty-First Century: Meeting the Technology Literacy Challenge," in 1996, with the following goals:

Standards & Assessment

- Providing access to information technology for all students and teachers
- Helping teachers to use technology effectively in instruction
- Developing technology and information literacy skills for all students
- Conducting more research and evaluation to improve technology instruction
- Transforming teaching and learning through digital content and networked applications[40]

Today, teacher-education programs include preservice and in-service training in using educational technology in professional-development experiences.

The American College and University

Colleges of the colonial period

Colleges were established in North America as early as the colonial period of the seventeenth century, when Protestant denominations established church-affiliated and church-controlled institutions. Believing that well-educated ministers were needed to establish Christianity in the New World, the Massachusetts General Court chartered Harvard College in 1636. By 1754, Yale, William and Mary, Princeton, and King's College (later Columbia University) had also been established as church-affiliated institutions

---

[37]Gerald L. Gutek, *An Historical Introduction to American Education* (Prospect Heights, IL: Waveland Press, 1991), pp. 206–207.
[38]Allan Collins and Richard Halverson, *Rethinking Education in the Age of Technology: The Digital Revolution and Schooling in America* (New York: Teachers College Press, 2009), pp. 66–90.
[39]For the history of the Web, see Robert Cailliau and James Gilles, *How the Web Was Born: The Story of the World Wide Web* (New York: Oxford University Press, 2000). For networking among teachers, see Kira J. Baker-Doyle, *The Networked Teacher: How New Teachers Build Social Networks* (New York: Teachers College Press, 2011).
[40]See Office of Educational Technology, U.S. Department of Education at **www2.ed.gov /about/offices/list/os/technology/index.html.**

of higher learning. Other colonial colleges were the University of Pennsylvania, Dartmouth, Brown, and Rutgers. The general colonial college curriculum included the following:

Colonial curriculum

- First year: Latin, Greek, Hebrew, rhetoric, and logic
- Second year: Greek, Hebrew, logic, and natural philosophy
- Third year: natural philosophy, metaphysics, and ethics
- Fourth year: mathematics and a review of Greek, Latin, logic, and natural philosophy[41]

The University of Virginia, designed by Thomas Jefferson, was the model for the modern state university. Jefferson saw the University's purpose as encouraging the "illimitable freedom of the human mind … to follow truth wherever it may lead."[42] Since the University of Virginia opened in 1825, states have been establishing colleges and universities. Along with the state colleges and universities, churches continued to establish liberal arts colleges, especially in the new states that entered the Union. Thus, the pattern of both state and private institutions of higher learning was established in the United States.

Morrill Act and land-grant colleges

In the 1850s, critics of traditional liberal arts colleges argued that the federal government should provide land grants to the states to establish more practical agricultural and engineering institutions. In response, the Morrill Act of 1862 granted each state 30,000 acres of public land for each senator and representative in Congress. The income from this land grant was to support state colleges for agricultural and mechanical (engineering) education.[43] **Land-grant colleges** and universities today are typically large institutions that include agriculture, teacher education, engineering, and other applied sciences and technologies as well as liberal arts and professional education. Still another important development in higher education came when Johns Hopkins University was founded in 1876 as a graduate research institution based on the German university seminar model.

Community colleges

Today, one of the most available and popular higher-education institutions is the two-year community college. Some two-year institutions originated as junior colleges in the late nineteenth and early twentieth centuries, when several university presidents recommended that the first two years of undergraduate education take place at another institution rather than at a four-year college. After World War II, many junior colleges were reorganized into community colleges, and numerous new community colleges were established with the broader function of serving their communities' educational needs. As important constituents in statewide higher-education systems, community colleges are exceptionally responsive in providing training for technological change, especially those related to the communications and electronic data revolutions.

REFOCUS Think back to the questions at the beginning of the chapter. *Use these questions to construct your own history or autobiography of education.* Consider how the high school completes the education ladder as a transitional bridge between elementary and higher education. Continue to write your own history or autobiography of education by reflecting on your experience as a student in high school. What did you think were the purposes of secondary education? Were these purposes clear to you, and did you agree with them? Also, consider how educational technology, especially computers and electronic information, have changed American education and preservice teacher preparation. Are these innovations present in your teacher-preparation program, and, if so, how have they changed your perception of teaching and learning?

G.I. Bill

Rising enrollments

A large-scale increase in college and university attendance occurred after Congress enacted the Servicemen's Readjustment Act, known as the G.I. Bill, in 1944, as World War II was ending. To help readjust society to peacetime and reintegrate returning military personnel into the economy, the G.I. Bill provided federal funds to subsidize veterans' tuition, fees, books, and living expenses. College and university enrollments expanded between 1944 and

---

[41]John R. Thelin, *A History of American Higher Education* (Baltimore, MD: Johns Hopkins University Press, 2004), pp. 2–38; also see Christopher J. Lucas, *American Higher Education: A History* (New York: St Martin's Press, 2006); and David J. Hoeveler, *Creating the American Mind: Intellect and Politics in the Colonial Colleges* (Lanham, MD: Rowman and Littlefield Publishers, 2007).
[42]Noble E. Cunningham, Jr., *In Pursuit of Reason: the Life of Thomas Jefferson* (New York: Ballantine Books, 1987), pp. 344–345.
[43]Benjamin E. Andrews, *The Land Grant of 1862 and the Land-Grant College* (Washington, D.C.: U.S. Government Printing Office, 1918).

1951, when 7,800,000 veterans used the Bill's assistance to attend technical schools, colleges, and universities.[44]

Immigration and Education in a Culturally Diverse Society

The next section examines the origins of ethnic, racial, language, and cultural diversity and pluralism in American society and education. It presents a topical rather than a strictly chronological discussion of the United States as a nation of immigrants and examines the educational history of African-, Native-, Latino-, Asian-, and Arab Americans.

Historically, the United States has been, as it is today, a racially, ethnically, and culturally diverse nation. With the exception of Native Americans, Americans trace their roots to other continents, especially to Europe, Africa, and Asia.

European Immigration

Before the Civil War, European immigrants to the United States came mainly from northern Europe—from England, Scotland, Ireland, Norway, Sweden, Denmark, and Germany. Most of these immigrants were Protestants—Anglicans, Presbyterians, Quakers, Baptists, Methodists, and Lutherans.

Irish and German immigration

Irish and German Immigration   In the 1840s, more Irish and Germans immigrated to the United States because of economic and political pressures in their native countries. For example, the potato famine had devastated Ireland's economy. The Irish were predominately Roman Catholics, and the Germans were primarily Lutherans and Catholics. Until the arrival of the Catholic Irish and Germans, the population of the United States, though divided into a denominational array of churches, was generally Protestant. Despite separation of church and state, many public schools, at that time, began the school day with a reading from the King James version of the Bible and emphasized a generalized Protestant value orientation. Led by their bishops, the Catholics resisted what they believed was a Protestant orientation in public schooling and created their own system of parochial schools.

Southern and Eastern European immigration

Changing Immigration Patterns   After the Civil War, immigration patterns shifted from northern to central, southern, and eastern Europe. The new immigrants were now Italians and Greeks; Slavic ethnic groups such as Poles, Russians, Czechs, Slovaks, Croats, Slovenes, Serbs; Arabs from Syria and Lebanon; and Jews from eastern Europe, seeking to escape the pogroms in Russia. In the 1890s, 1,914,000 immigrants came from southern and eastern Europe, In the twentieth century's first decade, from 1900 to 1910, the number of European immigrants reached 6,224,000, swelling the total number of immigrants to 13,500,000. After 1910, the number of European immigrants declined.[45]

Restrictions on immigration

Immigration Policy Controversies   The twenty-first century debates over immigration policy are not new. Although it is a country of immigrants, periodic efforts have been made to restrict immigration to the United States. In 1924, Congress established a quota system designed to restrict immigration from southern and eastern Europe. The law set more generous quotas for immigrants from the United Kingdom,

---

[44]Gerald L. Gutek, *American Education 1945–2000: A History and Commentary* (Prospect Heights, IL: Waveland Press, 2000), pp. 9–14.
[45]Oscar Handlin, "The Immigration Contribution," in Richard Leopold and Arthur Link, eds., *Problems in American History* (New York: Prentice-Hall, 1952), pp. 643–690; and *Population Abstract of the United States* (Washington D.C: Government Printing Office, 1980), p. 199.

Ireland, and the countries of northern and western Europe than it did for those from southern and eastern Europe. The ideological rationale behind the quota system was that immigrants from the British Isles, Germany, and the Scandinavian countries could assimilate into American society more readily than immigrant from other countries.

Ethnic enclaves

Ethnicity   The first generation of immigrants, especially in large northern cities such as New York, Chicago, and Cleveland, generally lived in homogenous communities with members of their own ethnic, language, and religious group. Except for some work situations, they generally spoke the language of their country of origin, attended church services in that language, and read the same foreign-language newspaper. They were members of the same ethnic, social, and athletic societies.

Through much of the twentieth century, public-school students attended schools in specifically designated attendance areas. The public schools educated children who lived in these designated neighborhood attendance areas. When these attendance areas were coterminous with an ethnic community, the majority of a particular school's students were often from the same ethnic and language group. When the schools overlapped ethnic neighborhoods, their student populations were somewhat more ethnically and culturally diverse. Because immigrant adolescents in the late nineteenth and early twentieth centuries had very low rates of participation in secondary education, their enrollments in comprehensive high schools were also low.

Assimilation and Americanization

The Assimilationist Ideology   The ethnic community sometimes ran into conflict with the dominant public-school ideology of Americanization that immigrant children should be assimilated as quickly as possible into American society. **Assimilation** meant that immigrant children should learn to speak and read the English language, learn the values of hard work and punctuality inscribed in the Protestant ethic, and obey the laws of the United States. The assimilationist ideology grew out of the common school philosophy that public schools should be agencies of constructing shared knowledge and values. When seen through the lenses of the assimilationist ideology, the ethnic neighborhoods were viewed as obstacles to bringing immigrants into American society. Public schools were identified as agencies that could teach immigrant children to become Americans. The prominent educator, Ellwood P. Cubberley, whose books were widely used in teacher-education programs, clearly articulated the

Cubberley on assimilation in public education

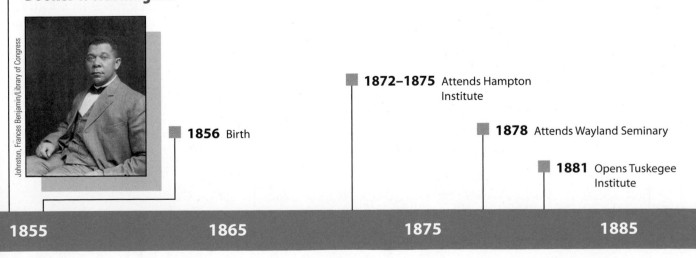

TIMELINE
Booker T. Washington

Johnston, Frances Benjamin/Library of Congress

1856 Birth

1872–1875 Attends Hampton Institute

1878 Attends Wayland Seminary

1881 Opens Tuskegee Institute

1855   **1865**   **1875**   **1885**

assimilationist ideology. In describing the challenge to assimilate the new immigrants, Cubberley stated:

> Everywhere these people tend to settle in groups or settlements, and to set up here their national manners, customs, and observances. Our task is to break up these groups of people as a part of our American race, and to implant in their children, so far as it can be done, the Anglo-Saxon conception of righteousness, law and order, and popular government, and to awaken in them a reverence for our democratic institutions and for those things in our national life which we as a people hold to be of abiding worth.[46]

The strategy of assimilation that was applied to European immigrants was also used in the education of other racial and language groups such as African-, Latino-, Asian-, and Arab Americans.

African Americans

The Civil War, the Emancipation Proclamation, and the Thirteenth Amendment ended slavery in the United States. Emancipation brought with it the challenge of educating the freed men, women, and their children, especially in the South.

Freedmen's Bureau

In 1865, Congress established the Freedmen's Bureau to provide economic and educational assistance to African Americans in the South during the Reconstruction period. Under the leadership of General O. O. Howard, the Bureau established schools that by 1869 had enrolled 114,000 African American students. Bureau schools followed a New England common-school curriculum of reading, writing, grammar, geography, arithmetic, and music, especially singing. Many schools functioned until 1872, when Bureau operations ended.[47]

Stereotypes limited teaching

Although it had prepared some African American teachers, many Freedmen's Bureau schools were staffed by northern white schoolteachers, who carried their educational philosophies and teaching methods to the South. Though well intentioned, many of these teachers believed that African American students needed only a limited basic education. Rather than encouraging educational self-determination, educators such as Samuel C. Armstrong, the mentor of Booker T. Washington, emphasized industrial training and social control that kept African Americans in a subordinate economic and social position.[48]

---

[46]Ellwood P. Cubberley, *Changing Conceptions of Education* (Boston: Houghton-Mifflin, 1909), pp. 13–15.
[47]Paul A. Cimbala and Hans L. Trefousee, *The Freedmen's Bureau: Reconstructing the American South after the Civil War* (Malabar, FL: Krieger Publishing Co., 2005).
[48]Robert Francis Engs, *Educating the Disenfranchised and Disinherited: Samuel Chapman Armstrong and Hampton Institute, 1839–1893* (Knoxville: University of Tennessee Press, 1999).

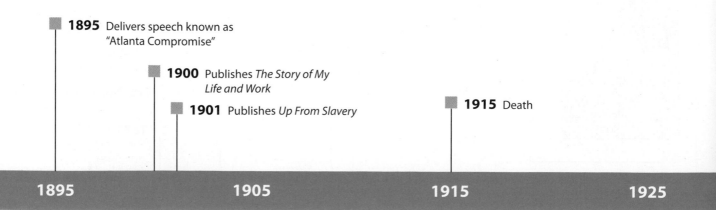

1895 Delivers speech known as "Atlanta Compromise"

1900 Publishes *The Story of My Life and Work*

1901 Publishes *Up From Slavery*

1915 Death

1895   1905   1915   1925

FROM PRESERVICE TO PRACTICE

Connecting the Past and the Present: Constructing an Educational Autobiography

Irene Stopek, a college sophomore, had enrolled in a course in the history of education that examined education from the earliest times to the present. Professor Grace Standish, the course instructor, told the students during the first class meeting that they would be examining the most important ideas that had influenced our thinking about schools and teachers. She said that a study of such magnitude need not be overwhelming or remote; it could be very personal if the students began their journey into the history of education by reflecting on how they had developed their own ideas about schools and teaching. She advised them that they could construct their own educational autobiography as part of the course requirements. Several students, including Irene, who appeared to be overwhelmed by the challenge, asked how they might research on and complete this assignment.

Reassuring them, Professor Standish told them her own story about how she decided to become a professor of education. She told them about the importance her parents gave to education, about teachers who encouraged her, and how her experiences as a high-school social studies teacher led her to pursue graduate study in education. She then described how a professor acted as her mentor and guided her through her graduate work and doctoral dissertation.

Irene now began to reflect on her decision to enter teacher education and how she envisioned herself as an elementary-school teacher. She searched her memories to discover how and why she formed that mental portrait of herself as a teacher. She remembered her mother telling the family story of how her own parents had emigrated from Czechoslovakia as refugees after World War II and how they struggled to learn English, find jobs, and send their own children to school. Irene planned to begin her research by asking her mother to narrate her own family's story—its history— about American education.

Case Questions

1. What questions would you ask family members about their educational experiences?
2. Did your family's experience with education influence your decision to become a teacher?
3. How did your own educational experiences shape your ideas about schools and teachers?

Washington: From Slavery to Freedom   Booker T. Washington (1856–1915) was the leading African American educational spokesperson after the Civil War. As illustrated in his autobiography, *Up from Slavery*, Washington was a transitional figure. Born

TIMELINE
W.E.B. Du Bois

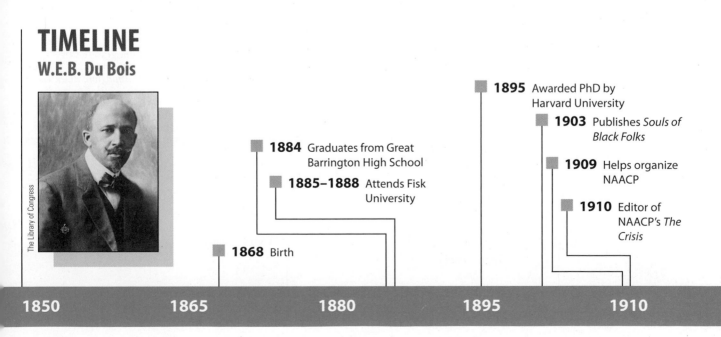

The Library of Congress

1895 Awarded PhD by Harvard University

1903 Publishes *Souls of Black Folks*

1884 Graduates from Great Barrington High School

1885–1888 Attends Fisk University

1909 Helps organize NAACP

1910 Editor of NAACP's *The Crisis*

1868 Birth

| 1850 | 1865 | 1880 | 1895 | 1910 |

a slave, he experienced the hectic years of Reconstruction and cautiously developed a compromise with the white power establishment.[49]

"Uplift" through work

As a student at Hampton Institute, Washington endorsed industrial education, the educational philosophy of Armstrong, his mentor. Armstrong believed that African American youth should be trained as skilled domestic servants, farmers, and vocational workers in trades rather than educated for the professions. Washington subscribed to Armstrong's philosophy of moral and economic "uplift" through work.

Washington's influence at Tuskegee

In 1881, Washington was appointed principal of the educational institute that the Alabama legislature had established for African Americans at Tuskegee. Washington shaped the Tuskegee curriculum according to his belief that southern African Americans were a landless agricultural class. He wanted to create an economic base—primarily in farming but also in vocational trades—that would provide jobs. Even if they were low-level jobs, Washington believed they would build an economic foundation that African Americans could use to climb slowly upward. Thus, Tuskegee's curriculum emphasized basic academic, agricultural, and occupational skills; the values of hard work; and the dignity of labor. It encouraged students to become elementary-school teachers, farmers, and artisans, but discouraged entry to higher education and participation in law and politics. Entry into professional education and political action, Washington believed, were premature and would conflict with the South's dominant white power structure.

Theory of social separation

Washington, a dynamic and popular platform speaker, developed a symbiotic racial theory that blacks and whites were mutually dependent economically but could remain separate socially. In 1885, Washington voiced his philosophy to an approving white audience in an address at the Cotton Exposition in Atlanta, Georgia, when he said, "In all things that are purely social, we can be as separate as the fingers, yet one as the hand in all things essential to mutual progress."[50]

Controversy about Washington

Today, Washington is a controversial figure in history. Defenders say he made the best of a bad situation and that, although he compromised on racial issues, he preserved and slowly advanced African Americans' educational opportunities. Critics see Washington as the head of a large educational machine that he ruthlessly controlled to promote his own power rather than to improve the situation of African Americans. One of Washington's outspoken critics was W. E. B. Du Bois.[51]

Du Bois: Challenger to the System   A sociologist, historian, and civil rights activist, W. E. B. Du Bois (1868–1963) attacked the rigid system of racial segregation that had been established in the South in the late nineteenth and early twentieth centuries

---

[49]Booker T. Washington, *Up from Slavery* (New York: Doubleday, 1938). For biographies of Washington, see Robert J. Norrell, *Up From History: The Life of Booker T. Washington* (Cambridge, MA: Harvard University Press, 2011); and Raymond W. Smock, *Booker T. Washington: Black Leadership in the Age of Jim Crow* (Chicago: Ivan R. Dee Publisher, 2009).

[50]Booker T. Washington, *Selected Speeches of Booker T. Washington* (New York: Doubleday, 1932); and Washington, *Character Building* (Radford, VA: Wilder Publications, 2008).

[51]For the controversy between Washington and Du Bois, see Jacqueline M. Moore, *Booker T. Washington, W. E. B. Du Bois, and the Struggle for Racial Uplift* (Wilmington, DE: Scholar Resources, 2003), pp. 61–87.

1935 Publishes *Black Reconstruction*

1963 Death

| 1925 | 1940 | 1955 | 1970 | 1985 |

Bettmann/Corbis

Students at the Tuskegee Institution in Alabama, where Booker T. Washington emphasized industrial education.

after Reconstruction ended in 1876.[52] Becoming an activist for civil rights, he challenged Washington's accommodationist philosophy.

Du Bois as a scholar

Unlike Washington, whose roots were in southern agriculture, Du Bois's career spanned both sides of the Mason-Dixon Line. Born in Massachusetts, he attended Fisk University in Nashville, did graduate work in Germany, earned his doctorate at Harvard University, and directed the Atlanta University Studies of Black American Life.[53] His important book, *The Philadelphia Negro: A Social Study*, examined the social, economic, and educational problems of an urban African American community.[54] His *Souls of Black Folk* told how African Americans had developed a dual consciousness—one side of which expressed their African roots and the other that presented the submissiveness demanded by many white Americans.[55]

Du Bois as a civil rights leader

In 1909, Du Bois helped organize the National Association for the Advancement of Colored People (NAACP). His editorials in *The Crisis,* the NAACP's major publication, argued that all American children and youth, including African Americans, should have genuine equality of educational opportunity. Du Bois and the NAACP were persistent adversaries of racially segregated schools, and his dedicated activism helped overturn racial segregation in public schools.

Promoting social and educational change

Unlike Booker T. Washington, Du Bois urged African Americans to organize and actively seek their civil rights. Believing that African Americans needed well-educated leaders, especially in the professions, Du Bois developed the concept of the "talented tenth," according to which at least 10 percent of the African American population should receive a higher education. Du Bois was adamant that a person's career should

[52]For the definitive biography of Du Bois, see David Levering Lewis, *W. E. B. Du Bois: Biography of a Race, 1868–1919* (New York: Henry Holt, 1973); and David Levering Lewis, *W. E. B. Du Bois: The Fight for Equality and the American Century, 1919–1963* (New York: Henry Holt, 2000).
[53]For a highly useful edition of Du Bois's works, see Eugene F. Provenzo, Jr., ed., *Du Bois on Education* (Lanham, MD: Rowman & Littlefield, 2002).
[54]W. E. B. Du Bois, *The Philadelphia Negro: A Social Study* (Philadelphia: University of Pennsylvania Press, 1998). See also Michael B. Katz and Thomas J. Segrue, eds., *W. E. B. Du Bois, Race, and the City: The Philadelphia Negro and Its Legacy* (Philadelphia: University of Pennsylvania Press, 1998).
[55]W. E. B. Du Bois, *The Souls of Black Folk* (New York: Simon and Schuster, 2005).

be determined by ability and choice, not by racial stereotyping. A prophetic leader, Du Bois set the stage for the significant changes in American race relations that came after the 1960s.

African American Demographic and Social Change   While Washington and Du Bois engaged in debates over social and educational policy, important changes were taking place in the African American population. No longer concentrated in the rural South, African Americans were moving to the large northern cities. World War I (1917–19) and World War II (1941–45) generated manpower needs in the war industries. An estimated 1,600,000 African Americans migrated from the rural South to large northern cities to take jobs and improve their economic condition. The African American population in the North increased by an estimated 40 percent as large black communities developed in New York, Philadelphia, Boston, Chicago, Detroit, and Cleveland. Blacks joined labor unions, and a new spirit of activism was born. The African American situation was much more complex than it was in the post-Reconstruction era when Booker T. Washington constructed his philosophy of industrial education. An urban black community now existed along with the Southern rural and agricultural community. (Racial integration and social change is discussed in Chapter 11, Social Class, Race, and School Achievement, and elsewhere in this book.)

Native Americans

■ Traditional tribal education

Education among pre-Columbian Native Americans was largely informal. Children learned skills, social roles, and cultural patterns from their group's oral tradition, from parents and elders, and from direct experience with tribal life. (See Chapter 3, Global Origins of American Education, for information about education in preliterate societies.)

Marked by suspicion and violence, encounters among Native Americans and European colonists affected both cultures. As colonists attempted to recreate European culture in North America, and Native Americans sought to preserve their culture, both groups changed.[56]

European colonists' efforts to "civilize" North American indigenous peoples rested on the Europeans' belief in their own cultural superiority. In the Mississippi Valley, French missionaries, especially the Jesuits, sought to convert Native Americans to Catholicism and to educate French colonists' children in the language and culture of France.

■ Missionary educational efforts

In the Spanish-controlled Southwest, Jesuit and Franciscan priests sought to alleviate exploitation of Native Americans by Spanish landlords by establishing missions to protect, control, and convert the tribes to Catholicism. Mission schools taught religion, reading, writing, and craft skills.[57] The Moravians—religious followers of John Amos Comenius, in Pennsylvania, Ohio, and North Carolina—taught the Native American tribes and translated the Bible and religious tracts into Indian languages.

Among the early Native American educators, Sequoyah (1770–1831), a Cherokee, devised an alphabet in his native language that developed into Cherokee as a written language.

■ Assimilationist education

In the nineteenth century, the U.S. government forcibly relocated the majority of Native Americans to reservations west of the Mississippi River in remote areas of the Great Plains and the Southwest. After 1870, the federal Bureau of Indian Affairs (BIA), encouraged by well-intentioned but misguided reformers, again attempted to "civilize" Native Americans by assimilating them into white society. These so-called reformers

---

[56]Colin G. Calloway, *New Worlds for All: Indians, Europeans, and the Remaking of Early America* (Baltimore, MD: Johns Hopkins University Press, 1997), p. 42.
[57]Christopher Vecsey, *On the Padres' Trail* (Notre Dame, IN: University of Notre Dame Press, 1996).

sought to eradicate tribal cultures and instill what they saw as white values through industrial training.[58]

Boarding schools

From 1890 to the 1930s, the BIA used **boarding schools** to implement the assimilationist educational policy. Boarding schools emphasized a basic curriculum of reading, writing, arithmetic, and vocational training. Ruled by military discipline, Native American youngsters in these schools, forbidden to speak their own native languages, were forced to use English.

Students' reactions

Native American youngsters variously resisted, passively accepted, or accommodated to the boarding schools' regimens. Active resisters repeatedly ran away from the boarding schools. Accommodationists tried to gain skill in using English without losing their tribal identities.[59] Some passively accepted the boarding schools' programs as a way to learn a trade useful for earning a living.[60] Many students suffered a loss of cultural identity, feeling trapped in a never-never land between two different cultures.

Contemporary schooling

After the boarding-school policy was discontinued in the 1930s, Native American education experienced significant changes. Many Native Americans left reservations to live in large cities where their children generally attended public schools. Children on tribal reservations attended BIA schools, public schools, or nonpublic schools.

Ending the assimilationist policies, the Indian Self-Determination and Education Assistance Act of 1975 encouraged Native Americans "to control their own education activities."[61]

Alienation from the system

Although assimilation is no longer an official government policy, many Native Americans remain alienated from the educational system. Compared to the national population, a greater percentage of Native Americans are under twenty years of age, but their participation in schooling is far lower than the national average. An extremely high dropout rate places Native American high-school completion far below that of the U.S. population at large.

Latino Americans

Latino peoples and cultures

Latino Americans comprise the fastest-growing ethnic group in the United States. Latino, a collective term, identifies Spanish-speaking people whose ethnic groups originated in Mexico, Puerto Rico, Cuba, or other Latin American countries. Although Latino Americans may speak Spanish as a common language and share many Spanish traditions, each group has its own distinctive culture.[62]

Assimilation in the Southwest

Mexican Americans are the largest Latino group in the United States.[63] The 1848 Treaty of Guadeloupe Hidalgo, which ended the Mexican War, forced Mexico to cede to the United States the vast territories that now comprise Arizona, California, Colorado, Nevada, New Mexico, and Utah. This territory, along with Texas, was home to a large Mexican population.[64] In these states, public schools followed the

---

[58]David W. Adams, *Education for Extinction: American Indians and the Boarding School Experience, 1875–1928* (Lawrence: University Press of Kansas, 1995), pp. 12–24. Also see Ruth Spack, *America's Second Tongue: American Indian Education and the Ownership of English, 1860–1900* (Lincoln: University of Nebraska Press, 2002), p. 75.
[59]Spack, *America's Second Tongue*, p. 131.
[60]David W. Adams, "From Bullets to Boarding Schools: The Educational Assault on Native American Identity, 1878–1928," in Philip Weeks, ed., *The American Indian Experience* (Arlington Heights, IL: Forum Press, 1988), pp. 218–239. For a history of a boarding school based on reflections of its students, see K. Tsianina Lomawaima, *They Called It Prairie Light: The Story of Chilocco Indian School* (Lincoln: University of Nebraska Press, 1994).
[61]George Pierre Castile, *To Show Heart: Native American Self-Determination and Federal Indian Policy, 1960–1975* (Tucson: University of Arizona Press, 1998).
[62]Joseph A. Rodriguez and Vicki L. Ruiz, "At Loose Ends: Twentieth-Century Latinos in Current United States History Textbooks," *Journal of American History* 86 (March 2000), pp. 1689–1699.
[63]Victoria-Marie MacDonald, "Hispanic, Latino, Chicano, or 'Other'? Deconstructing the Relationship between Historians and Hispanic-American Educational History," *History of Education Quarterly* 41 (Fall 2001), pp. 368–369.
[64]Manuel G. Gonzales, *Mexicanos: A History of Mexicans in the United States* (Bloomington: Indiana University Press, 2009). Also, see Victor Zuniga and Ruben Hernandez-Leon, eds., *New Destinations: Mexican Immigration in the United States* (New York: Russell Sage Foundation, 2006).

Americanization assimilationist policy then used throughout the United States. Mexican American children were taught in English, rather than their vernacular Spanish, and their Chicano cultural heritage was ignored. Consequently, schooling imposed a negative self-image, often portraying Mexican Americans as conquered people of an inferior culture.[65] Bilingual and multicultural education, replacing "Americanization," contributes to maintaining a Mexican American historical consciousness. (For more on bilingual and multicultural education, see Chapter 12, Providing Equal Educational Opportunity.)

■ Few educational opportunities

The Mexican American population increased as migrant workers crossed the U.S.-Mexican border to work in the United States. Because Mexicans provided cheap labor as ranch workers, railroad crews, and especially farm workers, employers encouraged their entry. Wages were low, housing was frequently squalid, and working conditions were harsh. Children of the migrant workers, even if not working in the fields with their parents, had few or no educational opportunities. Although many migrant workers returned to Mexico, others remained in the United States, either legally or illegally. Since World War II, many Mexican Americans have relocated from the Southwest to other states, often to the large Northeastern and Midwestern cities. Today, approximately 90 percent of Mexican Americans live in urban areas.

■ Chicano movement

In the late 1960s, the *Chicano movimiento*, or movement, similar to the African American civil rights movement, pursued two goals: (1) organizing Mexican Americans to work for improved social, economic, and educational conditions; (2) preserving the Mexican American cultural heritage as a source of group identity.[66] The League of United Latin American Citizens (LULAC), organized in 1929 to promote Latino civil rights, attracted middle-class professionals. Cesar Chavez organized the United Farm Workers to secure improved working conditions and higher wages for agricultural workers.[67] The Chicano movement encouraged Mexican American political activity, economic development, and educational participation. Despite increased Mexican American attendance in elementary and secondary education, higher-education enrollments fall below the national average.[68]

■ "Americanization" of Puerto Ricans

The history of Puerto Rican Americans, another large Latino group, begins with the Spanish-American War of 1898, when defeated Spain ceded Puerto Rico to the United States. Puerto Rico, a U.S. possession, attained Commonwealth status in 1952.[69]

Believing that Puerto Rico needed American-style social and economic development, U.S. officials overhauled the old Spanish school system.[70] They made school attendance compulsory, established American-style public schools, and employed English-speaking teachers trained in U.S. teaching methods. Although some classes continued to be taught in Spanish, English was made compulsory to promote "Americanization." Students were often caught between two cultural identities—their island's indigenous Hispanic culture and the imposed English-speaking American culture.

■ Dropout rates

Puerto Rican immigration to the U.S. mainland has been continuous since the early twentieth century. Today, more than two million Puerto Rican Americans live in large urban centers such as New York, Chicago, and Philadelphia. Historically, their high-school dropout rates have been high and college attendance rates low. In recent years, however, Puerto Rican Americans have become more politically active,

---

[65]For the educational experience of Mexican American children, see Marcos Pizarro, *Chicanas and Chicanos in School: Racial Profiling, Identity, Battles, and Empowerment* (Austin: University of Texas Press, 2005); and Patricia Gandora and Frances Contreras, *The Latino Education Crisis: The Consequences of Failed Social Policies* (Cambridge, MA: Harvard University Press, 2010).

[66]Richard Valencia, *Chicano Students and the Courts: The Mexican American Legal Struggle for Educational Equality* (New York: New York University Press, 2008).

[67]Frederick J. Dalton, *The Moral Vision of Cesar Chavez* (Maryknoll, NY: Orbis Books, 2003).

[68]Vicki L. Ruiz and John R. Chavez, eds., *Memories and Migrations: Mapping Boricua and Chicana Histories* (Urbana and Chicago: University of Illinois Press, 2008).

[69]For the history of Puerto Rico as a U.S. possession, see Jose Trias Monge, *Puerto Rico: The Trials of the Oldest Colony in the World* (New Haven, CT: Yale University Press, 1997).

[70]Gervasio Luis Garcia, "I Am the Other: Puerto Rico in the Eyes of North Americans, 1898," *Journal of American History* 38 (June 2000), p. 41.

especially in New York and Chicago, and have improved their economic and educational position.

The Cuban American experience in the United States represents a different pattern from other Latino groups in that it originated as a community in political exile from its native land.[71] Several waves of immigration from Cuba combined to form the Cuban American community. The first exiles, from 1959 to 1973, fled Fidel Castro's repressive Communist regime. Many were upper- and middle-class Cubans who brought with them the political, economic, and educational background and organizations needed to create a distinctive Cuban American cultural community. The Mariel immigrants of the 1980s came from Cuba's disadvantaged underclass. The Cuban American community, mirroring some aspects of the Cuba they left, has created a unique but also a *permeable* culture.[72]

In the twenty-first century, Latino Americans are playing a larger role in American social, political, and economic life, as evidenced by the growing and influential Latino professional and business middle classes. The concept of "permeable cultures" is useful in interpreting Latino American cultures. The term *permeable* refers to the tendency to move back and forth from Latino to Anglo cultures. Latinos selectively create their own Hispanic-American cultural patterns.[73]

Public schools, with the Bilingual Education Act (1968) and the Supreme Court decision in *Lau v. Nichols* (1974), replaced the assimilationist "Americanization" policies with bilingual and multicultural educational programs. (See Chapter 12, Providing Equal Educational Opportunity.) Recently, however, bilingual education has become politically controversial, with some states making English the official language. Led by California in 1998, several states have reduced or ended their bilingual education programs.[74]

Asian Americans

Asian immigrants arrived in the United States through the Pacific Coast cities of Seattle, Los Angeles, and San Francisco. The earliest Asian immigrants, from China and Japan, tended to settle in California, Oregon, and Washington.[75] More recent Asian immigrants include Filipinos, Indians, Thais, Koreans, Vietnamese, Laotians, and Cambodians.

Chinese Americans   From 1848 to 1882, 228,945 Chinese immigrated to the United States. They were often single, male contract laborers who worked in mining, farming, and railroad construction. Later, the immigrants, who did not return to China, were joined by their wives and family members. The Chinese settled in communities in larger West Coast cities such as Seattle, San Francisco, and Los Angeles with their own social, religious, cultural, fraternal, and educational societies.

As of 1880, 105,465 Chinese were living in the United States. In 1882, the U.S. Congress enacted the Chinese Exclusion Act that prohibited further Chinese immigration and denied citizenship to Chinese already in the country. Chinese immigrants encountered serious racial discrimination. For example, California's Alien Land Law that prohibited aliens ineligible for citizenship from owning land was directed against Chinese immigrants. The San Francisco Board of Education required Chinese students to attend segregated schools. The Magnuson Act in 1943 repealed the Exclusion Act

Margin notes:

Varied educational backgrounds

Bilingual education

Early Chinese immigrants

Excluding Asian immigrants

---

[71]Alex Anton and Roger E. Hernandez, *Cubans in America: A Vibrant History of a People in Exile* (New York: Kinsington Books, 2003).

[72]Maria Cristina Garcia, *Havana USA: Cuban Exiles and Cuban Americans in South Florida, 1959–1994* (Berkeley and Los Angeles: University of California Press, 1996), pp. 111–118. Also see Alex Stepick, *This Land Is Our Land: Immigrants and Power in Miami* (Berkeley: University of California Press, 2003).

[73]Rodriguez and Ruiz, "At Loose Ends," p. 1696.

[74]Guadalupe San Miguel, *Contested Policy: The Rise and Fall of Federal Bilingual Policy in the United States, 1960–2001* (Denton: University of North Texas Press, 2004).

[75]*Angel Island Immigrant Journeys: A Curriculum Guide for Grades 3–12* (San Francisco, CA: Angel Island Immigration Station Foundations, 2004). Also, see Xiaojian Zhao, *Remaking Chinese American Immigration, Family, and Community* (New Brunswick, NJ: Rutgers University Press, 2002).

and permitted Chinese residing in the United States to become citizens. Currently, the Chinese American population stands at 3,353,486.[76]

Lau v. Nichols

In 1973, the U.S. Supreme Court heard the *Lau v. Nichols* case, which had been appealed from lower district and appeals courts. Parents of non-English-speaking Chinese students had sued the San Francisco Unified School District. The plaintiffs charged that the District had failed to provide supplemental English language instruction to 1,800 students of Chinese ancestry who did not speak English. They alleged that the District's policy caused unequal educational opportunities in violation of the Fourteenth Amendment. Upholding the plaintiffs, the Supreme Court ruled that:

> Basic English skills are necessary to children to participate in the public school educational program; children who do not understand English will find their classroom experiences wholly incomprehensible and in no way meaningful....The failure of the San Francisco school system to provide English language instruction to approximately 1,800 students of Chinese ancestry who do not speak English, or to provide them with other adequate instructional procedures, denies them a meaningful opportunity to participate in the public educational program and thus violates...the Civil Rights Act of 1964....[77]

The enactment of the Bilingual Education Act (1968) and the Supreme Court decision in *Lau v. Nichols* (1974) dismantled the assimilationist ideology that had shaped public-school policies on the education of immigrant and non-English-speaking children. Public schools and teacher-education programs began to emphasize bilingual-bicultural and multicultural education. However, these programs remain controversial. Some states have reduced or eliminated bilingual education programs.[78]

Japanese immigrants

Japanese Americans   Japanese immigration began in the 1860s when American labor contractors recruited Japanese men to work on sugar and pineapple plantations in Hawaii. Later, Japanese workers also immigrated to California. The largest Japanese immigrant communities were in Hawaii, Washington, Oregon, and California.[79] Japanese immigration continued until 1910, when it declined because of economic and political issues between Japan and the United States.[80] Of the 27,000,000 immigrants who came to the United States between 1881 and 1930, only 275,308 were Japanese.[81] The Japanese called the immigrants, *Issei,* and their children, *Nisei.*

In Los Angeles and Seattle, Japanese American communities developed as Japanese entrepreneurs operated hotels, restaurants, and grocery stores. Like the European and Chinese immigrants, the Japanese Americans established Japanese-language newspapers, religious and benevolent societies, and recreational organizations. Seeking to maintain their language and culture, Japanese Americans established private Japanese-language schools that taught Japanese language, history, and geography.[82]

Issei and Nisei

As with other immigrant children, state compulsory school-attendance laws required Japanese American children to attend school. The Issei, the first generation immigrants, were familiar with the schools that the Japanese government had established.

---

[76]Chinese Population in the United States (2000). U.S. Census. For an autobiographical perspective, see Jean Lau Chin, *Learning from My Mother's Voice: Family Legend and the Chinese American Experience* (New York: Teachers College Press, 2005).
[77]*Lau v. Nichols*, 414 US 563 (1974).
[78]Guadalupe San Miguel, *Contested Policy: The Rise and Fall of Federal Bilingual Policy in the United States, 1960–2001* (Denton: University of North Texas Press, 2004).
[79]Paul Spickard, *Japanese Americans: The Formation and Transformation of an Ethnic Group* (New Brunswick, NJ: Rutgers University Press, 2009), p. 11.
[80]David J. O'Brien and Stephen S. Fugita, *The Japanese American Experience* (Bloomington: Indiana University Press, 1991), pp. 4–17.
[81]Spickard, *Japanese Americans*, p. 22.
[82]Spickard, *Japanese Americans*, p. 79. For Japanese language schools, see Toyotomi Morimot, *Japanese Americans and Cultural Continuity: Maintaining Language and Heritage* (New York: Garland, 1997); and Agato Noriko, *Teaching Mikadoism: The Attack on Japanese Language Schools in Hawaii, California, and Washington* (Honolulu: University of Hawaii Press, 2006).

Unlike some immigrants from southern and eastern European, Mexico, and China, who had limited experience with compulsory schooling, the Japanese were more receptive to it. Japanese Americans of the second generation, the Nisei, had higher public-school attendance rates than other groups. However, Japanese American children encountered racial segregation and the assimilationist ideology in the public schools. In 1906, the San Francisco Board of Education required Asian children to attend segregated schools. When the Japanese government protested, the Board rescinded its segregationist policy.

Japanese American internment

Japanese Americans faced strong anti-Japanese hostility after Japan attacked the U.S. naval base at Pearl Harbor on Oahu in Hawaii on December 7, 1941. Suspicious that the Japanese on the West Coast might commit acts of sabotage, the U.S. Government interned 110,000 people of Japanese ancestry, many of whom were American citizens, in relocation camps. Located in remote areas in California, Arizona, Idaho, Wyoming, Colorado, and Arkansas, the internment camps, called relocation centers, lacked adequate housing and other basic services. Over time, the internees established social and recreational activities. Japanese American teachers organized schools for the children and adult-education classes for the adults.

The suspicions that led the U.S. government to intern the Japanese Americans proved to be groundless. Not a single act of sabotage was committed by a Japanese American during World War II. Despite resentment over the government's repressive action, 20,000 Japanese Americans, the majority from Hawaii but 6,000 recruits from the camps, served in the U.S. armed forces during World War II.

By 1945, most of the camps were closed. In the 1980s, the U.S. government admitted its wartime action had violated the internees' civil liberties and compensated the internees. The Civil Liberties Act of 1988 provided a presidential letter of apology and monetary reparations for more than 82,000 persons of Japanese ancestry who had been interned without due process of law during World War II.[83]

Japanese Americans reconstituted their communities within the larger American society in the 1950s. Participation in postsecondary and professional education increased as nearly 90 percent of Japanese Americans were attending institutions of higher education.[84]

New Asian immigrants

Other Asian Americans   After the 1960s, immigration increased among other Asian groups, especially Koreans and Indians. Following the collapse of American-supported governments in South Vietnam in the 1970s, Vietnamese, Cambodians, Laotians, and Hmong arrived with differing educational backgrounds. For example, among the South Vietnamese were former military officers, government officials, businesspersons, and professionals. The Hmong, by contrast, came from a rural culture without a written language. Along with the more recent Asian American immigrants, there is also an older, well-established Filipino American population.

Arab Americans

Arab Americans

The designation "Arab," a cultural and linguistic rather than a racial term, refers to those who speak Arabic as their first language. An Arab American is an American of Arabic descent. The majority of Arab Americans are descendants of immigrants from Lebanon, Syria, Palestine, Iraq, Jordan, and Egypt. The majority of Arabs are Muslims, followers of Islam, but millions are Christians.

The early Arab immigrants came to the United States from the Turkish Ottoman Empire in the late nineteenth century, especially between 1875 and 1915.[85] Many early

---

[83]Spickard, *Japanese Americans,* pp. 132–133. Also, see Minoru Kiyota and Ronald S. Green, *The Case of Japanese Americans during World War II: Suppression of Civil Liberty* (Lewiston, NY: E. Mellen Press, 2004); and Kenneth K. Takemoto, *Nisei Memories: My Parents' Talk about the War Years* (Seattle: University of Washington Press, 2006).
[84]Allan W. Austin, *From Concentration Camps to Campus: Japanese American Students and World War II* (Urbana: University of Illinois Press, 2004).
[85]Gregory Orfalea, *The Arab Americans: A History* (New York: Olive Branch Press, 2006).

immigrants from Lebanon and Syria were Orthodox or Catholic Christians who settled in ethnic neighborhoods in the northeastern states. Some became small business owners, merchants, and restaurateurs. Like other immigrant groups, they established fraternal organizations and recreational societies such as the Syrian Brotherhood Orthodox Society, often sponsored by a church or mosque.[86] One of the earliest Arabic newspapers, *Kawkab America, The Star of America*, was founded in 1892.[87]

A more recent wave of Arab immigration, especially from Palestine, Egypt, and Jordan, which began after World War II, still continues.[88] More recent immigrants are predominately Islamic and generally have more formal education than earlier immigrants.

Arab Americans have much in common with other immigrant groups. Many older Arab Americans became assimilated by attending public schools, through membership in community and political organizations, and through business and work. While assimilating into the larger American society, many maintained their Arabic culture through language, customs, religion, music, literature, and storytelling.[89] Many immigrants were bilingual and often established Arabic language, culture, and religion classes in churches or mosques.

The proportion of Arab Americans who attend college is higher than the national average, with many earning advanced degrees. Many Arab Americans are self-employed in family-owned businesses. About 60 percent of Arab Americans in the workforce are executives, professionals, and office and sales staff.

After the terrorist attacks on September 11, 2001, concerns arose that Arab Americans might be victims of stereotyping and discrimination. Isolated instances of discriminatory acts occurred, but the Arab American community took a proactive stance to educate the general population about its history and culture. Educators, too, have worked to include Arab Americans within the context of multicultural education.[90]

The Immigration Controversy

Immigration issues

Today, immigration is a hotly debated political issue. Some policy makers want to liberalize immigration law to allow some of the illegal or undocumented aliens in the United States to become legal immigrants.[91] Others argue that it is necessary, given economic and security concerns, to limit the numbers of immigrants entering the country and to identify and deport illegal immigrants.

The debate focuses on immigrants' impact on the economy, national security, and American cultural identity. Although some people believe that immigrants make a needed contribution to the viability of the economy, others contend that they are taking jobs away from American citizens. Contending that immigrants, especially illegal immigrants, are an expensive burden on the country's educational, health care, and social services, critics of the current policy want laws to restrict immigration and stop illegal immigration. Critics fear that the movement of illegal immigrants across U.S. borders threatens national security, especially in the war on terrorism. For the immigration controversy, see the Taking Issue Box that follows.[92]

---

[86]For the Arab American experience, see Amir B. Maruasti and Karen D. McKinney, *Middle Eastern Lives in America* (Lanham, MD: Rowman & Littlefield, 2004); and Randa A. Kayyali, *The Arab American* (Westport, CT: Greenwood Press, 2006).
[87]Elizabeth Boosahda, *Arab-American Faces and Voices: The Origins of an Immigrant Community* (Austin: University of Texas Press, 2003), pp. 84–86.
[88]For the Palestinian experience and the forming of Arab American identity, see Edward Said, *Out of Place* (New York: Knopf, 1999).
[89]Boosahda, *Arab-American Faces and Voices*, p. 9.
[90]For example, see Patty Adeed and G. Pritchy Smith, "Arab Americans: Concepts and Materials," in James Banks, ed., *Teaching Strategies for Ethnic Studies* (Boston: Allyn and Bacon, 1997).
[91]For the history and issues related to immigration, access the Immigration Policy Center at **www.immigrationpolicy.org/issues.**
[92]For issues related to immigrant students, see Carola Suarez-Orozco, Marcelo M. Suarez-Orozco, and Inna Todorova, *Learning a New Land: Immigrant Students in American Society* (Cambridge, MD: Harvard University Press, 2010).

TAKING ISSUE

Read the brief introduction below, as well as the Question and the pros and cons list that follows. Then answer the question using your own words and position.

Immigration, Language, and Education

Immigration controversies have generated important policy issues about the liberalization or restriction of immigration and the provision of health care and educational services received by illegal aliens and their children. In schools, immigration issues have had educational implications about the language used in instruction.

Question

Should English be the exclusively used language of instruction in American public schools? (Think about this question as you read the PRO and CON arguments listed here. What is *your* take on this issue?)

Arguments PRO	Arguments CON
1 Historically, immigrants have advanced economically, socially, and politically by learning the English language.	1 As a nation of immigrants, American society and education are unfinished open-ended projects in which the contributions of all racial, ethnic, and gender groups need to be recognized.
2 As Noah Webster argued, the United States, as a nation of immigrants, needs to have English as its unifying national language.	2 When English is a child's second language, bilingual education makes the transition to English a more effective and less anxiety-generating process.
3 Non-English-speaking children learn more effectively by immersion in classes conducted in English rather than in bilingual programs.	3 Bilingual and bicultural instruction promotes a fuller and more authentic identity for immigrant children.
4 Bilingual programs duplicate educational services and use sources that could be better directed to improving English language literacy and competency.	4 Knowing and using several languages is an asset in today's global and interconnected world.

Question Reprise: What is Your Stand?

Reflect again on the following question by explaining *your* stand about this issue: Should English be the exclusively used language of instruction in American public schools?

Connecting with the History of Education throughout this Book

This chapter helps to establish the general historical context of American education for the other chapters in this book. For example: Chapter 7, Governing and Administering Public Education, discusses the history of the federal government's educational role and the establishment of the U.S. Department of Education; Chapter 12, Providing Equal Educational Opportunity, includes historical introductions to discussions of segregation in American education, compensatory education, bilingual education, education for children with disabilities, the Education for All Handicapped Children Act of 1975, and No Child Left Behind. Chapter 13, The Changing Purposes of American Education, includes a historical overview of major policy reports such as *High School* and a *Nation at Risk*.

REFOCUS CONSTRUCTING YOUR OWN HISTORY OR AUTOBIOGRAPHY OF EDUCATION

Think back to the questions at the beginning of the chapter. *Use these questions to construct your own history or autobiography of education.* How did the United States become a culturally diverse society? Reflect on the roles of African-, Latino-, Asian-, and Arab Americans in American culture and their contributions. As you write your own educational history or autobiography, reflect on the contributions and the problems of your own racial, ethnic, or language group. You may wish to consult parents, family members, and others of your group about their educational experiences.

Summing Up

① The European colonists transported and established religious and socioeconomic-class-based educational institutions in North America. Primary vernacular schools provided a basic curriculum of reading, writing, arithmetic, and religion. The Latin grammar school and the colonial college, reserved for upper-class boys and men, provided a classical curriculum to prepare them for leadership roles in church, state, and society.

② After the United States won its independence, the common-school movement led to the establishment of public elementary schools, first in northern states and then throughout the country.

③ The public high school in the late nineteenth century completed the American educational ladder that connected public elementary schools to state colleges and universities.

④ Since the mid-twentieth century, the infusion of technology, especially computers, has been transforming education and creating global economic and communications systems.

⑤ By the mid-twentieth century, concerted efforts were being made to provide equal educational opportunities to children with disabilities and to the children of minority groups, especially African Americans, Native Americans, and Latino Americans. Recent trends in American education have included more groups in the mainstream of American education.

⑥ The United States is a country of immigrants. Immigrants came from Europe, Mexico, Central and South America, Asia, and Africa. Public-school policy for the education of immigrants changed from assimilation to multiculturalism.

Key Terms

The numbers indicate the pages where explanations of the key terms can be found.

dual-track school system 136
Latin grammar school 136
town school 137
hornbook 137
land grant 141
academy 142
monitorial method 146
common school 146

educational ladder 148
normal school 149
high school 154
Committee of Ten 155
Commission on the Reorganization of
    Secondary Education 155
junior high school 156

middle school 156
land-grant college 158
assimilation 160
boarding schools 166
Americanization 167

Certification Connection Activity

This chapter discussed the history of teaching certification, which began as local districts issued their own certificates and licenses to teachers. These certificates were often only valid in the district that issued them. Later, the states began to standardize teacher certification throughout the state. Today, teacher certification is controlled by each state, usually through the state certification board or a similar agency. Because of this history, there is no national uniform teacher certification in the United States. Ascertain how teachers are certificated in your state. How do NCATE and similar accrediting agencies work to bring about some uniformity in teacher programs and certification? What problems do you expect to encounter in certification, especially if you move to a state other than the one of your initial certification?

Discussion Questions

① Reflect on the Puritan beliefs about children, work, play, and social and religious conformity. How have these beliefs shaped American culture and education?

② Reflect on the policies of assimilation and Americanization that once dominated American public education. Consider these policies in terms of contemporary immigrant education, bilingual and bicultural education, and multiculturalism.

③ How do you think Jefferson and Rush would react to the teaching of Intelligent Design in the school curriculum generally and in science courses specifically?

4 How did the Reconstruction period shape education in the southern states?

5 Horace Mann and other common-school leaders believed that public education should construct a commonly shared general culture. Do you favor or oppose this policy for contemporary education?

6 Occupying the rung between elementary and higher education, the purposes of secondary schools have often been controversial. Are they still controversial? How would you define the purposes of American secondary education?

7 Consider the educational experiences of the racial and ethnic groups discussed in this chapter. Has this history been similar or different for the various groups?

8 Identify the historical trends that had the most powerful shaping influence on teacher education.

Projects for Professional Development

1 For resources on African American, Native American, and immigration history, visit the Library of Congress's American Memories Collection. Review the sources in the collection, and identify those that supplement this chapter's sections.

2 Booker T. Washington is a controversial historical figure. Visit the website of the Booker T. Washington National Monument and also the website for the Washington papers. How is Washington depicted? Do you agree or disagree with the presentation of Washington as a leader?

3 Invite representatives of African American, Latino American, Native American, Asian American, and Arab American organizations to speak to your class about the educational issues facing these groups. Try to identify both common and distinctive issues.

4 What is your opinion of the U.S. attempt to use schooling to assimilate Native American children? Research this question by accessing the articles on "Indian Boarding Schools in the Pacific Northwest" at University Libraries, University of Washington; and PBS's "Indian Country Diaries–Indian Boarding Schools." Listen to the story and read the script of NPR's "American Indian Boarding Schools Haunt Many."

5 Reflect on the major historical developments treated in this chapter. Then develop a class project using oral interviews with experienced K–12 school administrators and classroom teachers that focus on major changes in their professional work. You might ask: What was school like when you began your work as an administrator or teacher? How has the curriculum remained the same or changed? What changes have you observed in students' academic readiness, interests, and behavior? How has technology, especially computers, changed instruction?

6 Research images and resources on Chinese American and Asian American immigration history. Using these resources to supplement the discussion in this chapter, compare and contrast the immigration of Chinese Americans and other Asian Americans with that of European Americans, African Americans, and Latino Americans.

Suggested Resources

Internet Resources

For primary sources, access "Benjamin Franklin's Autobiography," at **http://earlyamerica.com/lives/franklin**.

For a biography and chronology on Jefferson, access "Monticello Resources" at **www.monticello.org/site/jefferson**.

For Rush's essay on education, access "Benjamin Rush on Public Schooling" at **www.schoolchoices.org/roo/rush .htm**. For a tour, history, research, and activities about Colonial Williamsburg, access **www.cwf.org**. This site includes materials for teachers about the colonial period.

For Jefferson documents, access the Thomas Jefferson Digital Archive at the University of Virginia: **http://guides.lib.virginia .edu/TJ**.

For biographies of Mary Lyon, Jane Addams, Catharine Beecher, and other leaders in women's rights and education, access the resource center at **www.nwhp.org**.

For a biography and resources on W. E. B. Du Bois, access **www.webdubois.org**.

For images and discussion of the Chinese in California and the relocation of Japanese Americans during World War II, go to "Collections" at **http://bancroft.berkeley.edu**.

For resources on one-room schools, access One-Room Schools at Iowa Pathways at **www.iptv.org/IowaPathways**, and click "My Path."

For a "Day at School" at the Clarke Historical Library, access at **http://clarke.cmich.edu/resource_tab/information_and _exhibits/one_room_schools/a_day_at_school.html**.

For resources on African American, Native American, and immigration history, access the Library of Congress's American Memories Collection at **http://memory.loc.gov/ammem /index.html**.

For information on Booker T. Washington, access the Booker T. Washington National Monument at **www.nps.gov/bowa /index.htm** and the Washington papers at **www.historycooperative.org/btw**.

To read more about Indian Boarding Schools, access "Indian Boarding Schools in the Pacific Northwest," University Libraries, University of Washington, at **http://content.lib.washington .edu/aipnw/marr.html**; PBS's "Indian Country Diaries–Indian Boarding Schools" at **www.pbs.org/indiancountry/ history/boarding.html**; and NPR's "American Indian Boarding Schools Haunt Many" at **www.npr.org/templates/story/story .php?storyId=16516865.**

For images and resources on Chinese American, African American, and immigration history, access the home page at **www.immigrants.harpweek.com** and at **http://newton .uor.edu/Departments&Programs/AsianStudiesDept /index.html**.

Publications

Austin, Allan W. *From Concentration Camps to Campus: Japanese American Students and World War II.* Urbana: University of Illinois Press, 2004. *Provides a discussion of how Japanese Americans overcame the trauma of internment during World War II to have the highest enrollments in higher education of any minority group in the United States.*

Chan, Sucheng, and Madeline Y. Hsu, eds. *Chinese Americans and the Politics of Race and Culture.* Philadelphia: Temple University Press, 2008. *An anthology of essays on Chinese-American history, culture, and identity.*

Collins, Allan, and Richard Halverson. *Rethinking Education in the Age of Technology: The Digital Revolution and Schooling in America.* New York: Teachers College Press, 2009. *Provides a discussion of how technology is transforming and reshaping American education.*

DuBois, Ellen C., and Lynn Dumenil. *Through Women's Eyes: An American History with Documents.* Boston: Bedford/St. Martin's, 2005. *Examines the contributions of women in American history, with reference to issues, persons, and developments.*

Fontenot, Chester J., Jr., and Mary Alice, Morgan, eds. *W. E. B. Du Bois and Race: Essays Celebrating the Centennial Publication of* The Souls of Black Folk. Macon, GA: Mercer University Press, 2001. *Provides essays commenting on the significance of Du Bois's* Souls of Black Folk *to African American history and to general American history and education.*

Gandara, Patricia, and Frances Contreras. *The Latino Education Crisis: The Consequences of Failed Social Policies.* Cambridge: Harvard University Press, 2010. *Provides a policy analysis on the perspective of the impact of social and educational policies on Latino education.*

Kloosterman, Valentina. *Latino Students in American Schools: Historical and Contemporary Views.* New York: Praeger, 2003. *Provides a discussion of the education of Latino students in a historical perspective.*

Lassone, Cynthia A, Robert J. Michael, and Jerusalem Rivera-Wilson. *Current Issues in Teacher Education: History, Perspectives, and Implications.* Springfield, IL: Charles C. Thomas, 2008. *Provides a historical background on selected contemporary issues in teacher education.*

Lewis, David Levering. *W. E. B. Du Bois: The Fight for Equality and the American Century 1919–1963.* New York: Holt, 2000. *In this second volume of his biographical study of Du Bois, Lewis examines the contributions of the great African American scholar and activist.*

Mitchell, Mary Niall. *Raising Freedom's Child: Black Children and Visions of the Future after Slavery.* New York: New York University Press, 2008. *Contains a discussion of African American schooling in the general cultural context of African American emancipation.*

Moore, Jacqueline M. *Booker T. Washington, W. E. B. Du Bois, and the Struggle for Racial Uplift.* Wilmington, DE: Scholarly Resources, 2003. *Presents a well-balanced examination of the differences between Washington and Du Bois as well as alternatives to their positions.*

Ogren, Christine A. *The American State Normal School: "An Instrument of Great Good."* New York: Palgrave Macmillan, 2005. *Develops a historical appraisal of the importance of normal schools in the history of American teacher education.*

Patterson, James T. *Brown v. Board of Education: A Civil Rights Milestone and Its Troubled Legacy.* New York: Oxford University Press, 2001. *Patterson examines the highly significant case that ended legally sanctioned racial segregation in the United States.*

Provenzo, Eugene F., Jr. *Du Bois on Education.* Lanham, MD: Rowman and Littlefield, 2002. *Provides a well-edited and comprehensive collection of Du Bois's major works on education and an extensive bibliography.*

Reyhner, Jon A., and Jeanne M. Oyawin Eder. *American Indian Education: A History.* Norman: University of Oklahoma Press, 2006. *Provides a comprehensive history of American Indian education, including discussions of missionary, government, and boarding schools.*

Spack, Ruth. *America's Second Tongue: American Indian Education and the Ownership of English, 1860–1900.* Lincoln: University of Nebraska Press, 2002. *Examines English-language instruction in terms of federal policy and Indian schools.*

Urban, Wayne J., and Jennings L, Wagoner., Jr. *American Education: A History.* New York: Routledge, 2008. *Provides a comprehensive analysis of the major periods of American history of education in the broad context of national and international events.*

Valencia, Richard. *Chicano Students and the Courts: The Mexican American Legal Struggle for Educational Equality.* New York: New York University Press, 2008. *An in-depth treatment of issues in the legal rights of Chicano students such as school organization, financing, bilingual and bicultural education, and undocumented students.*

Watras, Joseph. *A History of American Education.* Boston: Allyn and Bacon, 2007. *This well-written and carefully organized history of American education examines the implications of the ideas of leading educators and reform movements for teachers and schools in a historical perspective.*

Webb, L. Dean. *The History of American Education: A Great American Experiment.* Upper Saddle River, NJ: Pearson/Merrill/Prentice Hall, 2006. *Provides a comprehensive treatment of the history of American education, with relevant documents.*

 Additional resources for this chapter, including the TeachSource Videos, can be found on the Education CourseMate website. Go to **CengageBrain.com** to access the site.

Philosophical Roots of Education

Teachers must meet such immediate daily demands as preparing lessons, assessing student performance, and creating and managing a fair and equitable classroom environment. Because of their urgency, these challenges sometimes preoccupy teachers in their early professional careers from constructing what the National Council for Accreditation of Teacher Education (NCATE) standards call a "conceptual framework," an intellectual philosophy of education that gives meaning to teaching by connecting its daily demands with long-term professional commitment and direction.[1] A conceptual framework contributes to a sense of professional coherence that helps teachers place immediate short-term objectives into relationship with long-term goals.

In encouraging teachers to become reflective practitioners, the Interstate New Teacher Assessment and Support Consortium (INTASC) has established standards to improve teachers' preservice preparation and professional development. INTASC describes teaching as a dynamic process in which teachers transform their preservice expectations into meaningful practice that places knowledge, dispositions, and performance into a coherent whole. To become a reflective practitioner means that teachers need to think philosophically about education's broad cultural and ethical implications.

We can define a philosophy as the most general way of thinking about the meaning of our lives in the world and reflecting deeply on

---

*This chapter was revised by Gerald L. Gutek.
[1] **www.ncate.org/Standards/NCATEUnitStandards/UnitStandardsinEffect2008 /tabid/476/Default.aspx.**

what is true or false, good or evil, right or wrong, and beautiful or ugly.[2] This chapter provides you with a conceptual framework, a theoretical map, upon which you can reflect on your ideas about education and construct your own philosophy of education. The following focusing questions can guide you as you read the chapter and in building your own philosophy of education:

FOCUS QUESTIONS

■ What are the major philosophies and theories of education? How have these philosophies and theories shaped our ideas about the purpose and meaning of education and schooling?

■ How do philosophies and theories of education influence curriculum, teaching, and learning in schools, including what is taught, how it is taught, teachers' professional and ethical behavior with students and with their colleagues, and their attitudes about cultural diversity and social justice?

■ What are the subdivisions of philosophy, how are they defined, and how do they reflect your beliefs and your teaching about truth, knowledge, and values?

■ How are contemporary trends in education such as multiculturalism, the standards movement, and educational technology rooted in underlying philosophies and theories?

■ What does it mean to have a philosophy of education?

As you progress from preservice professional education courses to classroom practice, you will often reflect on what you are teaching, why you are teaching it, and how you teach it. You will often ask yourself whether your teaching makes a difference in your students' lives and in your own life. This self-reflection is a way to develop a coherent conceptual framework that leads to reflective classroom practice.

These focusing questions require deep thinking and searching discussion to answer. As you progress from preservice to practice, you will rethink and redefine your answers to these questions as your teaching experience grows more complete and complex. Just as students maintain portfolios to record their own progress, teachers can keep journals with daily entries about their classroom, successes, and problems to guide their process of constructing a conceptual framework that explains what they are doing and why they are doing it.

Constructing Your Philosophy of Education

In Chapter 3, Global Origins of American Education, Chapter 4, Pioneers of Teaching and Learning, and Chapter 5, Historical Development of American Education, you were encouraged to write your own history of education and

---

[2]For introductions to philosophy of education, see Nell Noddings, *Philosophy of Education* (Denver, CO: Westview, 2011); Richard Bailey, *Philosophy of Education: An Introduction* (New York: Continuum, 2010); Sheila G. Dunn, *Philosophical Foundations of Education: Connecting Philosophy to Theory and Practice* (Upper Saddle River, NJ: Pearson/Merrill/Prentice Hall, 2005); Robin Barrow and Ronald Woods, *An Introduction to the Philosophy of Education* (New York: Routledge, 2006); David T. Hansen, *Ethical Visions of Education: Philosophy in Practice* (New York: Teachers College Press, 2007).

educational autobiography. You can now revisit and extend your historical and autobiographical reflections about the people and events that shaped your ideas about education, schooling, teaching, and learning as the background for constructing your own philosophy of education. Begin by asking yourself what you believe is true and valuable and how your educational experiences have shaped these beliefs. You can think about the relationship between knowledge and knowing and between teaching and learning. You can determine if the philosophies and theories in this chapter are similar to or different from your own educational experiences. You can determine if your encounters with these philosophies and theories confirm or cause you to revise your beliefs about what is true and valuable, about knowledge and knowing, and about teaching and learning. Finally, you can make some judgments about how they influence what, why, and how you teach.

Figure 6.1	Differences Between "Philosophies" and "Theories" of Education

GENERAL	SPECIFIC
←	→
Philosophies	**Theories**
Wide-ranging, systematic, complete, global	Focused on education; no complete philosophical system offered
Components related to metaphysics, epistemology, axiology, and logic	Components related to specifics of education, such as curriculum, teaching, and learning
Insights derived from the general philosophical system	Insights derived from more general philosophies or from school contexts

▌ Philosophies and theories

This chapter examines five philosophies and four theories of education. Comprehensive **philosophies**, such as idealism and realism, present a general worldview that includes education. Educational **theories**, often derived from philosophies or arising from practice, focus more specifically on education, schools, curriculum, and teaching and learning (see Figure 6.1). The general philosophies examined in this chapter link to the more specific theories of education. For example, the philosophy of realism closely relates to the theories of perennialism and essentialism. Similarly, aspects of progressivism derive from pragmatism.

To construct your own philosophy of education, you need to think like a philosopher and use philosophy's terminology.

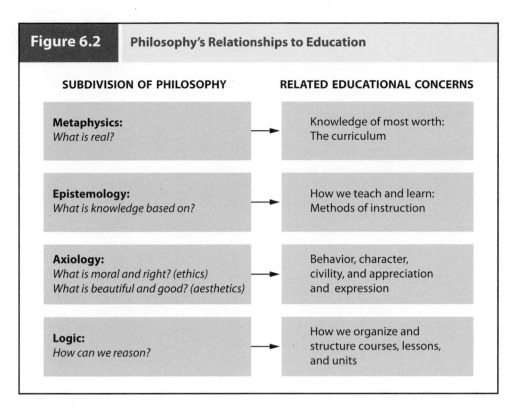

Figure 6.2 **Philosophy's Relationships to Education**

SUBDIVISION OF PHILOSOPHY	RELATED EDUCATIONAL CONCERNS
Metaphysics: *What is real?*	Knowledge of most worth: The curriculum
Epistemology: *What is knowledge based on?*	How we teach and learn: Methods of instruction
Axiology: *What is moral and right? (ethics)* *What is beautiful and good? (aesthetics)*	Behavior, character, civility, and appreciation and expression
Logic: *How can we reason?*	How we organize and structure courses, lessons, and units

Special Terminology

Philosophy of education uses the terms *metaphysics, epistemology, axiology,* and *logic.*[3] Figure 6.2 summarizes the relationship between these terms and education.

◼ Reality and existence

Metaphysics considers questions about ultimate reality. What is ultimately real or not real? Is there a spiritual realm of existence separate from the material world? Idealists, for example, see reality primarily in nonmaterial intellectual, conceptual, or spiritual terms. Realists see it as an objective order that exists independently of humankind. The subjects taught in schools represent how curriculum designers, teachers, and textbook authors describe their beliefs about "reality" to students.

◼ Knowledge and knowing

Epistemology, which deals with knowledge and knowing, influences methods of teaching and learning. It asks, "On what do we base our knowledge of the world and our understanding of truth? Does our knowledge derive from divine revelation, from ideas latent in our own minds, from empirical evidence, or from something else?" Teachers who believe that the universe exists as an orderly structure will emphasize the systematic and sequential teaching of subjects to reproduce this order in students' minds. They will use subject matter to transmit this conception of reality to students. In contrast, teachers who believe the process of how we know is most important will involve students in problem solving to construct their own view of reality. There is an important difference between transmitting knowledge about an antecedent reality that exists prior to the students' experience and encouraging students to make or construct their own version of reality. Which of these approaches to reality will you emphasize in your philosophy of education?

◼ What is of value?

Axiology, which prescribes and proscribes values—what we should or should not do—is subdivided into *ethics* and *aesthetics.* Teachers often call these prescriptions and proscriptions, that is, appropriate or inappropriate behavior. **Ethics** examines moral values and prescribes the standards of ethical behavior; **aesthetics** addresses values

---

[3]For a discussion of philosophical terminology, see Gerald L. Gutek, *New Perspectives on Philosophy and Education* (Columbus, OH: Pearson, 2009), pp. 3–7.

OVERVIEW 6.1

Philosophies of Education

Philosophy	Metaphysics	Epistemology	Axiology	Educational Implications	Proponents
Idealism	Reality is spiritual or mental and unchanging.	Knowing is the intuitive recall of ideas present in the mind.	Values are universal, absolute, and eternal.	A subject-matter curriculum emphasizes the culture's great and enduring ideas.	Emerson Froebel Hegel Plato
Realism	Reality is objective and exists independently of us, but we can know it.	Knowing consists of conceptualization based on sensation and abstraction.	Values are absolute and eternal, based on universal natural laws.	A subject-matter curriculum emphasizes the arts, humanities, and sciences.	Aquinas Aristotle Broudy Maritain Pestalozzi
Pragmatism (experimentalism)	Rejects metaphysics, asserting that hypotheses about reality are based on experience, the individual's interaction with a changing environment.	Knowing results from experiencing, testing ideas by acting on them, and using the scientific method.	Values are situational and culturally relative.	Instruction that uses the scientific method to solve problems.	Childs Dewey James Peirce
Existentialism	Discounts metaphysics, arguing that our beliefs about reality are subjective, with existence preceding essence.	Our knowing comes from making personal choices.	Values are to be freely chosen by the person.	Classroom dialogues to stimulate awareness that each person creates a self-concept through significant choices.	Kierkegaard Sartre Marcel Morris
Postmodernism	Rejects metaphysics as a historical construction used for socioeconomic domination.	Deconstructs texts (canons) to find their origin and use by dominant groups and classes.	Emphasizes the values of marginalized persons and groups.	Schools are sites of democratic criticism and social change to empower dominated groups.	Derrida Foucault

in beauty and art. Teachers—like parents and society in general—convey their values to the young by rewarding and reinforcing behavior that corresponds to teachers' conceptions of what is true, good, and beautiful, and also what is right and wrong. Moreover, the environment teachers create in their classrooms immerses students in a moral climate that reflects the teacher's ethical and aesthetic sensibilities. For example, sharing and respecting the rights of others are prescribed values. In contrast, cheating and bullying are proscribed as unethical behaviors.

Deductive and inductive thinking

Concerned with correct and valid thinking, logic examines the rules of inference we use to frame our propositions and arguments. **Deductive logic** moves from general principles and statements to particular instances and applications. For example, we begin with the premise—all deciduous trees seasonally drop their leaves; state the sub-premise—the maple tree drops its leaves in the fall, and then reach a conclusion—the maple is a deciduous tree. In terms of deductive inference, if the premises are true, then the conclusion must be true. **Inductive logic** moves from the particular instance to tentative generalizations that are subject to further verification and possible revision.

It moves from limited data to a more general conclusion. For example, (a) the earth's temperature has been increasing over the past fifty years; (b) this global warming is due to the greenhouse effect caused by emissions from the burning of fossil fuels; (c) if we continue to generate emissions from fossil fuels, the earth's temperature will continue to rise. Curriculum and instruction are organized on conceptions of logic. Think about the differences in teaching a science course from the two examples used.[4] Does something in the subject itself logically dictate how lessons should be organized and presented to students (the deductive approach)? Or should teachers take their cues from students' interest, readiness, and experience in organizing instruction (an inductive approach)?

Using this terminology, we now examine the philosophies of idealism, realism, pragmatism, existentialism, and postmodernism. After discussing the key concepts of each philosophy, we will see how it answers the focus questions asked at the beginning of the chapter and aids teachers in constructing their own philosophies of education. (See Overview 6.1 for the philosophies discussed in this chapter.)

Idealism

Notable idealist thinkers

Idealism, one of the oldest Western philosophies, begins with Plato (428–347 BCE), who taught his philosophy in the ancient Greek city-state of Athens. Much later, in nineteenth-century Germany, Georg W. F. Hegel (1770–1831), a university professor, lectured to his students about a philosophy of history in which the major periods in human history represented the unfolding of the ideas in the mind of the Absolute, or God.[5] In the United States, Ralph Waldo Emerson (1803–1882) and Henry David Thoreau (1817–1862) developed an American version of idealism, called transcendentalism, that emphasized finding truth in nature. Friedrich Froebel (discussed in Chapter 4, Pioneers of Teaching and Learning) developed his kindergarten on idealist principles that emphasized the unfolding of children's spiritual nature. Asian religions such as Hinduism and Buddhism also rest on an idealist spiritual worldview.

Key Concepts

Universal, eternal truth

Metaphysics   Idealists believe that the spiritual, conceptual, nonmaterial world is ultimately real. They see the world as the creation of a great universal mind, the mind of the Absolute or God. For idealists, the person's spiritual essence, or soul, is the permanent element of human nature that gives individuals the power to think and feel. This intellectual or spiritual world of ideas is universal and eternal. Because it is perfect like its Creator, it does not need to change. Like the Universal Spirit itself, goodness, truth, and beauty are the same everywhere in the world throughout time.

Macrocosm and microcosm

Idealists, such as the American transcendentalists, use the concepts of macrocosm and microcosm to explain how they perceive reality. **Macrocosm** refers to the universal mind, the first cause, creator, or God. Regardless of what it is called, the macrocosmic mind is the whole of existence. It is the one, all-inclusive, and complete self of which all lesser selves are part. The universal, macrocosmic mind is continually thinking and valuing. The **microcosm**, the personal mind or spirit, is a limited and lesser self but nevertheless spiritual and intellectual like the great being of which it is a part.

[4]Samir Okasha, *Philosophy of Science: A Very Short Introduction* (Oxford, UK: Oxford University Press, 2002), pp. 18–24.
[5]For biographies and the ideas of Plato and Hegel, see David Bostock, "Plato," in Ted Honderich, ed., *The Philosophers: Introducing Great Western Thinkers* (Oxford, UK: Oxford University Press, 1999), pp. 15–21; and Peter Singer, "Georg Wilhelm Friedrich Hegel," in Honderich, *The Philosophers,* pp. 131–137.

Latent knowledge

Epistemology   Idealists believe that the ideas that make up reality have always existed in the mind of the Absolute, or God. When we know something, it means that we have reached a conscious understanding of one or more of these ideas. Plato developed the epistemology of reminiscence, by which we remember **a priori ideas** that already are lodged deep in our minds but of which we are not conscious. The individual, through deep thought and introspection, searches his or her own mind and discovers in it the ideas that are copies of those in the macrocosmic mind. The teacher asks the probing questions that challenge students to become conscious of this interior but latent knowledge. The educational process of searching within for the truth is intended to stimulate students to arrive at a broad, general, and unifying perspective of the universe.[6]

Hierarchy of subjects

Idealist teachers believe that the Absolute or God has been revealed, over time, to those who have sought the truth. These truth-seekers have recorded their discoveries and revelations in bodies of knowledge, or "subjects," especially the liberal arts. Schools, as repositories of this universal and eternal truth, have organized teaching and learning into a hierarchical curriculum of academic subjects, in which some subjects are more important than others. At the top of the hierarchy are the most general disciplines, philosophy, and theology. These highly abstract subjects transcend the limitations of time, place, and circumstance and transfer to a wide range of situations. Mathematics is valuable, too, because it cultivates abstract thinking. History and literature rank high as sources of moral and cultural models. Somewhat lower in the curriculum, the natural and physical sciences address particular cause-and-effect relationships. Language is important as an essential tool of communication and expression at all stages of learning. In leading students through the learning process, the teacher's overarching purpose is to create a transdisciplinary integration of knowledge that relates these subjects to each other as a form of higher-order thinking.

Enduring values

Axiology   Because they believe that truth, goodness, and beauty exist in a universal and eternal order, idealists prescribe values that are unchanging and applicable to all people everywhere. Thus, ethical behavior reflects the enduring knowledge and values of human culture. Philosophy, theology, history, literature, and art are rich sources for transmitting values because they provide the contents and the contexts through which students can encounter worthy models, especially in the classics—the great transgenerational works that have been enjoyed through the centuries.

Logical consistency

Logic   For idealists, logic, too, follows the whole-to-part relationship between the Absolute and individual minds. The part, a specific idea or principle, is derived from and agrees with the whole, which is more general. Idealist teachers would use deductive logic to organize lessons that begin with general principles or rules and use specific cases or examples to illustrate them. For example, an idealist teacher of literature might introduce the general concept of respect for others who are different from us by referring to Henry David Thoreau, who took his own path to civil disobedience at Walden Pond.

The Basic Questions

Knowledge of universal ideas

If you were to ask an idealist teacher, "What is knowledge?" she or he would reply that knowledge is about the universal spiritual truths that underlie reality and about the ideas that reflect that truth. Because knowledge is about universal ideas, then education is the intellectual process of bringing these ideas to the learner's consciousness.

Schooling: an intellectual pursuit of truth

If you ask an idealist teacher, "What is the school?" she or he would answer that it is an intellectual institution where teachers and students pursue the questions Socrates and Plato asked: "What is truth? What is beauty? What is the good life?" To answer these questions, we need to think deeply and bring to consciousness the answers that are present in our minds. We need to read the great books and study the great works of art in which writers and artists have captured insights into this truth.

---

[6]Gutek, *New Perspectives on Philosophy and Education*, pp. 28–29.

The students, in the Pragmatist mode, are engaged in interdisciplinary collaborative group interaction.

Birgit Koch/Fotosonline/Alamy Limited

Who should attend school? The idealist would say everyone. Although students have varying intellectual abilities, all should have the opportunity to cultivate their minds as far as possible. Gifted students need the greatest intellectual challenges that the teacher can provide. However, all students have the right and opportunity to pursue the same intellectual curriculum.

How should we teach? The idealist would say that thinking and learning are the processes of bringing latent ideas to conscious reflection. An effective means of doing this is the **Socratic method**, in which the teacher stimulates the learner's awareness of ideas by asking leading questions.[7] Another important aspect of idealist methodology is modeling. Teachers should be models worthy of student imitation—they should have wide knowledge of the cultural heritage and lead exemplary lives.

Idealists want to safeguard the academic quality of education by maintaining high intellectual standards and resisting any tendency toward mediocrity. In Plato's *Republic,* for example, intellectual standards were so high that only a gifted minority became philosopher-kings. Today's idealists would insist that individuals should have an education that will take them as far as their intellectual ability enables them to go.

Idealists would endorse standards that require teachers to have high intellectual expectations of students and require students to strive to achieve intellectual excellence. Standards, moreover, would not be geared to the statistical average but should raise expectations as high as possible. Standardization, however, should not substitute for individual intellectual and moral excellence.

Implications for Today's Classroom Teacher

Rejecting the consumerism and vocationalism that often shape values in contemporary society and education, idealism seeks to create schools that are intellectual centers of teaching and learning. It sees teachers as vital agents in guiding students to realize their fullest intellectual potential, and it encourages teachers and their students to encounter and appreciate the finest and most enduring achievements of the culture.

Socratic method

✓ Standards & Assessment

High standards

✓ Standards & Assessment

 Intellectual development, not vocational training

---

[7]For Socrates, Plato, and Aristotle, see C. D. C. Reeve, "The Socratic Movement," in Randall Curren, ed., *A Companion to the Philosophy of Education* (Malden, MA: Blackwell Publishing, 2006), pp. 7–24.

Teachers introduce students to the classics—great and enduring works of art, literature, and music—so that they can experience and share in the time-tested cultural values these works convey.

Internet Use

In using technology or any innovation, idealists want educators to be guided by the paramount purpose of education—to find the truth by ensuring that schools are intellectual centers. They recognize that the Internet can make the great books accessible to more students. However, idealists insist that technology should be a means, an instrument, of education rather than an end. The content matters most, not the technical apparatus that transmits it.[8]

How might a teacher use idealism in developing a lesson? A fifth-grade social studies teacher might illustrate the power of ideas and higher ethical law by a unit on the life and moral impact of Mohandas Gandhi, the father of India's independence. Students would study Gandhi's biography and reflect on his principle of nonviolent protest against injustice that guided his movement against racism in South Africa and against British colonialism in India. An important outcome of the lesson would be the realization that Gandhi considered social justice to be based on principles of universal human rights.

REFOCUS *Use these questions to construct your own philosophy of education. What elements of idealism appeal to you as a teacher? Which appeal least? Why? Are there elements of idealism that you would like to incorporate into your philosophy of education?*

Realism

A real world of objects

The Greek philosopher Aristotle (384–322 BCE), a student of Plato, developed **realism**, which asserts that reality exists outside of our minds or is objective, not latent or internal to our minds as Plato claimed. As described in Chapter 3, Global Origins of American Education, during the Middle Ages, Thomas Aquinas (1224–1274) constructed a synthesis of Aristotle's natural realism and Christian doctrine known as Thomism.[9] Scientific realism brings realism into the twenty-first century. Scientific realists assert that reality exists independently of our knowing it and that the scientific method is the best way to get an accurate description of what the world is and how it works.[10] To explain and use our scientific findings, we have to construct theories. As scientific investigation provides more accurate and verified information about the world, we can revise and refine our theories so that they correspond more accurately to reality.

Realists assert that (1) there is a world of real existence, of objects, not made by human beings; (2) the human mind can know about the real world; and (3) such knowledge is the most reliable guide to individual and social action and behavior. Beginning with these principles, we can examine realism's educational implications.

Key Concepts

Knowing as sensation, then abstraction

Metaphysics and Epistemology   Realists believe in a material world that is independent of and external to the knower's mind.[11] All objects are composed of matter. Matter, in turn, is organized as it takes on the form or structure of an object.

Knowing (epistemology) involves two necessary and related stages: sensation and abstraction. First, the knower perceives an object and records sensory data about it in

[8]For education, philosophy, and technology, see Christina E. Erneling, *Towards Discursive Education: Philosophy, Technology, and Modern Education* (New York: Cambridge University Press, 2010). Marc de Vries, *Teaching about Technology: An Introduction to the Philosophy of Technology for Non-Philosophers* (Dordrecht: Springen, 2005).

[9]For biographies and the ideas of Aristotle and Aquinas, see David Charles, "Aristotle," in Honderich, *The Philosophers*, pp. 23–31; and Alexander Brodie, "St. Thomas Aquinas," in Honderich, *The Philosophers*, pp. 39–47. Also, see Jonathan Barnes, *Aristotle: A Very Short Introduction* (Oxford, UK: Oxford University Press, 2000), p. 30.

[10]Okasha, *Philosophy of Science*, pp. 58–62.

[11] For the application of the principles of scientific realism to the social sciences, see Peter T. Manicas, *A Realist Philosophy of Social Science: Explanation and Understanding* (Cambridge, UK: Cambridge University Press, 2006).

Bananastock/Jupiter Images

Realist philosophy empha-sizes sensory learning and organizing objects into categories such as chem-istry, as these students are doing in a science class.

her or his mind, such as color, size, weight, smell, or sound. The mind sorts these data into qualities that are always present in the object and those that are sometimes pres-ent. By identifying the necessary qualities (those always present), the learner abstracts a concept of the object and recognizes it as belonging to a certain class. This classifica-tion affirms that the object shares certain qualities with other members of the same class but not with objects of a different class.

Curriculum of organized subjects

Like idealists, realists believe that a curriculum of organized, separate subjects pro-vides the most accurate and efficient way for students to learn about reality. Organiz-ing subject matter into categories, as scientists and scholars do, is an orderly method of classifying objects. For example, past human experiences can be organized into his-tory. Botany studies plants systematically according to their classifications. Political organizations such as nations, governments, legislatures, and judicial systems can be grouped under political science. The realist acquires knowledge about reality through systematic inquiry into subjects like these.

Rational behavior, based on reality

Axiology   For realists, certain rules should govern intelligent rational behavior. Aristotle defined humans as rational animals. Therefore, people are most human when they act in a rational way, which means to make decisions based on knowledge. From their observations of natural and social realities, people can develop theories about how nature and society function. When they make their decisions and act according to these theories, they are behaving rationally.

Deductive and inductive logic

Logic   Realist teachers may use logic both deductively and inductively. For example, students in a botany class might examine roses that differ in color, scent, and size but conclude, through induction, that all are members of the same genus. However, when the class plants a rose garden on the school grounds as a project, the students can find information about roses in the library and on the Web and deduce the correct loca-tions and amounts of fertilizer and water for each rose they plant.

The Basic Questions

Knowledge concerns objects

To begin our philosophical cross-examination, we again ask, "What is knowledge?" Realists would reply that knowledge is about the world in which we live. When we know something, our knowledge is always about an object. Our concepts are valid when they correspond to those objects as they really exist.[12] Scientific realists would add that our concepts, to be accurate, should be based on a scientific description and verification of this correspondence.

Education via subject-matter disciplines

Formal education, the realists would say, is the study of knowledge organized and classified into subject-matter disciplines. History, languages, science, and mathematics

[12]Andrew Newman, *The Correspondence Theory of Truth: An Essay on the Metaphysics of Prediction* (New York: Cambridge University Press, 2002).

are some of these organized bodies of knowledge. Knowledge of these subjects informs us about the world in which we live; this knowledge is our best guide in conducting our daily affairs.

For realists, society establishes schools as academic institutions to provide students with knowledge about the objective world in which they live. Because all persons have a rational potentiality, schooling should be available to all. Realists would oppose sorting students into separate academic and vocational tracks. All students should pursue the same academic curriculum, which will prepare them to make rational decisions, informed by knowledge.

Implications for Today's Classroom Teacher

Classrooms for learning, not therapy

In realist classrooms, the teacher's primary responsibility is to bring students' ideas about the world into correspondence with reality by teaching skills (such as reading, writing, or computation) and subjects (such as history, mathematics, or science) that are based on authoritative and expert knowledge. Although they appreciate that their students are emotional as well as rational persons, realists focus on cognitive learning and subject-matter mastery. Realist teachers oppose the intrusion of nonacademic activities that interfere with the school's primary purpose as a center of disciplined academic inquiry.

> **REFOCUS** *Use these questions to construct your own philosophy of education. What elements of realism appeal to you as a teacher? Which appeal least? Why? Are there elements of realism that you would like to incorporate into your philosophy of education?*

In the preservice preparation of teachers, subject-matter knowledge and competency is given high priority. For example, the history teacher should be a historian with an academic major in history. In addition, realist teachers should have a general education in the liberal arts and sciences so that they understand and can demonstrate relationships between their special area of expertise and other subjects. Realist teachers use a wide repertoire of methods, such as lecture, discussion, demonstration, and experiment. Content mastery is most important, and methodology is a necessary but subordinate means to reach the goal of liberally educating students.

Example of a realist approach

How might a realist high-school physics teacher structure a unit on Isaac Newton's laws of motion? First, the teacher would help students place Newton in context within the history of science and discuss his scientific contributions. Second, the teacher might illustrate the laws of motion in a laboratory demonstration. Third, the students might discuss the demonstration and frame the scientific generalization it illustrates. Finally, students would be tested to assess their understanding of Newton's laws of motion.[13]

✓ Standards & Assessment

Realists would favor setting standards that specify student academic achievement benchmarks, especially in skill areas such as reading and arithmetic and in subject areas such as mathematics, science, and history. Standardized tests provide reliable, objective, and comparable data about how well students are mastering academic subjects and about teachers' effectiveness in instructing students. Standards can keep schools and teachers accountable. However, they would view standardized test scores as only the first rung in measuring academic achievement. While they verify mastery of basic content, students need to proceed to high-level thinking that demonstrates that they are able to apply theory to practice.

Just as realists are open to a variety of methods that facilitate content learning, they would use technology as an aid in developing and testing skills and subject-matter competencies. They would want computer programs to be as "realistic" and effective as possible.

Pragmatism

Founders of pragmatism

Pragmatism emphasizes the need to test the validity or workability of our ideas by acting on them. Among pragmatism's founders were Charles S. Peirce (1839–1914), William James (1842–1910), George Herbert Mead (1863–1931), and John Dewey

---

[13]Philip H. Phenix, *Philosophies of Education* (New York: Wiley, 1961), pp. 22–24.

(1859–1952). Peirce emphasized using the scientific method to validate ideas empirically; he substituted probability, or what is likely to happen, for certainty. Based on statistics, we can formulate an informed—but not a certain—hypothesis of what is likely to happen. Emphasizing a pluralistic universe, James applied pragmatic philosophy to psychology, religion, and education.[14] Mead emphasized that children develop and learn through their experiences in the environment. Advocating democracy, Dewey applied his version of pragmatism, called experimentalism, to education.[15] Whereas Chapter 4, Pioneers of Teaching and Learning, examines Dewey's contributions to education, this chapter focuses on his experimentalist philosophy.

Organism and environment

Influenced by Charles Darwin's theory of evolution, Dewey applied the terms *organism* and *environment* to education. Dewey saw human beings as biological, social, and verbal organisms that use their life-sustaining impulses to promote their growth and development. Every organism, including human beings, lives in a habitat or environment. As people interact with their environments, they have experiences. From these experiences, they construct a usable network of experiential episodes. For Dewey, the purpose of education is to promote experiences for optimum human growth.

Problem solving

Whereas idealist and realist educators emphasize subject-matter disciplines, Dewey sees thinking and learning as problem solving. In his experimental epistemology, the learner, either as an individual or group member, uses the scientific method to test experience by solving personal and social problems. Problem solving is a process method of general intelligence that can transfer to a wide range of problematic situations.[16]

Key Concepts

Experience

Metaphysics and Epistemology   Unlike the idealist and realist philosophies based on a metaphysical foundation of universal and unchanging reality, pragmatism dismisses metaphysics as empirically unverifiable speculation. Pragmatists focus on epistemology, how we construct our knowledge in a constantly changing world rather than on metaphysical certainties. For example, Peirce, who dismissed certainty as unattainable, replaced it with probability, which had practical applications in human affairs.

Experience, defined as the interaction of the person with the environment, is a key pragmatist concept. A person's interaction with his or her social, cultural, and natural environments constitutes the process of living, growing, and developing. This interaction may alter or change both the person and the environment. Knowing comes from a transaction—a process—between the learner and the environment.[17]

Test of experience

Dewey rejects the idealist and realist concepts that reality is *a priori* or antecedent to human involvement in the world. Rather, he is more concerned with how human beings interact with the environment and construct tentative and flexible conceptions about a changing reality. These tentative assumptions about reality are always subject to further testing and validation, which may lead to a revision, or reconstruction, of an existing assumption or to a new one. Ideas do not exist in their pure state as the idealists assert. Ideas to be validated need to be tested in experience, which means we test them by acting on them and determining what consequences they have for us.

---

[14]For William James's *Talks to Teachers and Pragmatism: A New Name for Some Old Ways of Thinking,* access William James at **www.des.emory.edu/mfp/james.html**. Also, see James W. Garrison and Ronald Podeschi, *William James and Education* (New York: Teachers College Press, 2002).

[15]Reprints and recent editions of Dewey's books are John Dewey, *The School and Society & The Child and the Curriculum* (Mineola, NY: Dover Publications, 2001); *Democracy and Education* (New York: Cosimo Classics, 2005); *Schools of Tomorrow* (Mineola, NY: Dover Publications, 2006); *Art as Experience* (New York: Perigee Books, 2005); *Experience and Education: The 60th Anniversary Edition* (West Lafayette, IN: Kappa Delta Pi, 1998).

[16]For Dewey's discussion of thinking and problem solving, see John Dewey, *How We Think,* introduction by Gerald L. Gutek (New York: Barnes and Noble, 2005), originally published in 1910.

[17]For an analysis of Dewey's pragmatic perspective, see Christine L. McCarthy and Evelyn Sears, "Deweyan Pragmatism and the Quest for True Self," *Educational Theory* (Spring 2000), pp. 213–227.

Although each interaction with the environment has generalizable aspects that carry over to the next problem, each episode will differ somewhat. It was this element of difference in the episode that caused the problem. Intelligent people will use the scientific method to solve problems and add the validated features of a particular problem-solving episode to their ongoing experiences.

Dewey argued that we cannot keep on doing the same things over and over in schools just because they are traditional. We need to use the school as an educational laboratory to test what and how we teach to determine if it leads to the learner's understanding and growth. Does an educational program, curricular design, or teaching strategy achieve its anticipated goals and objectives?[18]

Reconstruction of person and environment

Because we and the environment are constantly changing, pragmatists dismiss the idealist and realist curricula based on supposedly antecedent permanent realities or universal truths as empirically untenable. Rather, they assert that our decision making needs to be guided by our experience. Any claim to truth is really a tentative assertion that we can revise as we do more research. What we need, say the pragmatists, is a socially and scientifically intelligent method that gives us a process-oriented direction in a constantly changing reality.

Relativity of values

Axiology and Logic   Pragmatic axiology is highly situational and culturally relative. A constantly changing and pluralistic universe means that values, too, are not universal and eternal as idealists and realists assert, but they are changing and relative to time, place, and circumstance. For pragmatists, whatever contributes to personal and social growth is valuable; what restricts or limits it is unworthy. Rather than blindly accepting inherited traditional and conventional values, we can clarify our values by testing and reconstructing them in our experience.

Inductive logic

Following the scientific method, experimentalist logic is inductive rather than deduced from first principles as in idealism and realism. Any claim to truth is a warranted assertion that is tentative and subject to further testing and revision.

The Basic Questions

Knowledge is tentative

Rather than transmit subject matters of allegedly permanent truths, pragmatists are concerned with the process of constructing, using, and testing ideas.

An experimental process

For pragmatists, education is an experimental process—a method of solving problems that challenges people as they interact with their world. For Dewey, the most intelligent and reflective way of solving problems is to use the scientific method.

Interdisciplinary approach

Pragmatists favor interdisciplinary education rather than a departmentalized subject-matter curriculum. When you face a problem, pragmatists say, you find the information needed to solve it from many sources, not from a single academic subject. For example, to define the problem of environmental pollution and suggest ways of solving it, we must use information that comes from sources that are historical, political, sociological, scientific, technological, and global. A pragmatically educated person knows how to research and apply information from multiple sources to the problem. In contrast, idealists and realists strongly disagree because they believe students must first acquire a knowledge base by studying and mastering organized subjects before they can use interdisciplinary approaches.

School as microcosm of society

Transmitting cultural heritage

Pragmatists such as Dewey see the school as a local community of learners and teachers intimately connected to the larger society. The school exercises three major functions: to simplify, purify, and balance the cultural heritage. To simplify, teachers

---

[18]For interpretations of Dewey's philosophy to contemporary educational issues, see David T. Hansen, ed., *A Critical Engagement with Dewey's Democracy and Education* (Albany: State University of New York Press, 2006).

FROM PRESERVICE TO PRACTICE

The School as a Special Environment

In this scenario, students are meeting to discuss their preservice clinical observations. Professor Alcott, encourages the students to relate their clinical observations to reflections on general concepts about education, schools, curriculum, and methods. Professor Alcott asks, "Now that you have observed classes in schools, what exactly is a school?" Martin Neswich, a student, replies, "Professor, we have all gone to school and have observed classes in schools. We all know what a school is." Professor Alcott replies, "Before we conclude that we know what a school is, I want you to listen to some guests I have invited to the class to answer that question as a panel." A panelist, a member of a veterans' organization, says "Schools are not doing a good job in teaching American history, civic responsibility, and patriotism." Another panelist, a businessman, says, "Schools need to teach salable market skills needed in business. Some of the people I hire don't even know basic math skills." The third panelist says, "I am a mother of three elementary age students but don't send my children to public schools because they do not provide the proper religious education and moral values." Professor Alcott thanks the panelists for their presentations. Then, he says, "We have heard from three members of the community who have very different ideas about what a school is and what it does. Before we end this unit, I want you to read what John Dewey, one of America's leading philosophers, said about schools. As teachers, we all need to go to the source." He passes out a short excerpt from John Dewey's, *Democracy and Education*, and says "Let's read the selection and discuss the questions at the end of the reading next week."

...as soon as a community depends ... upon what lies beyond its own territory and its own immediate generation, it must rely upon ... schools to insure adequate transmission of all its resources.... Hence a special mode of social intercourse is instituted, the school, to care for such matters.

This mode of association has three functions.... First, a complex civilization ... has to be broken up into portions ... and assimilated ... in a gradual and graded way. The relationships of ... social life are so numerous and so interwoven that a child ... could not readily share in many of the most important of them.... There would be no seeing the trees because of the forest. Business, politics, art, science, religion, would all ... clamor for attention; confusion would be the outcome. The first office of the ... school is to provide a simplified environment. It selects the features which are ... fundamental and capable of being responded to by the young.... In the second place, it is the business of the school environment to eliminate, so far as possible, the unworthy features of the ... environment from influence upon mental habitudes. It establishes a purified medium of action. Selection aims not only at simplifying but at weeding out what is undesirable. Every society gets encumbered with what is trivial, with dead wood from the past, and with what is positively perverse. The school has the duty of omitting such things ... and ... doing what it can to counteract their influence.... As a society becomes more enlightened, it ... is responsible not to transmit and conserve the whole of its existing achievements, but only such as make for a better future society....

In the third place, it is the office of the school ... to balance the various elements in the social environment, and to see ... that each individual gets an opportunity to escape from the limitations of the social group in which he was born, and to come into living contact with a broader environment.... It is this situation which has ... forced the demand for an educational institution which shall provide something like a homogeneous and balanced environment for the young....

Source: John Dewey, *Democracy and Education* (New York: MacMillan Co., 1916), pp. 22–26. Abridged by the author.

Case Questions

1. What does Dewey identify as three functions of the school?

2. How do Dewey's functions of the school differ from those of the panelists?

3. How do you define the role and functions of the school in your own personal philosophy of education?

select cultural, political, and economic elements in the society and reduce their complexity to units appropriate to learners' readiness, interest, and prior experience. To purify, they select valuable cultural elements and eliminate those that limit human interaction and growth. To balance, the school helps learners integrate their experiences into a personal and social harmony.

Cultural diversity, but shared learning processes

In a pluralistic multicultural society, the pragmatic school provides experiences that encourage children of one culture to understand and appreciate members of other cultures. Although cultural diversity enriches the entire society, pragmatists want all children to learn to use the scientific method. They believe that schools should build community consensus by emphasizing common problems and using shared processes to solve them. As genuinely integrated and democratic learning communities, schools should be open to all and encourage the widest possible sharing of resources among people of all cultures.

Implications for Today's Classroom Teacher

- Subject matter as instrumental

- Applying the scientific method

- ✓ Standards & Assessment

- Classroom as community

- Teachers as risk takers

- ✓ Standards & Assessment

- A pragmatist lesson

Whereas idealist and realist teachers make teaching subject matter their primary responsibility, pragmatist teachers are more concerned with teaching students to solve problems using an interdisciplinary approach. Rather than transmitting subjects to students, pragmatist teachers facilitate student research and activities, suggesting resources useful in problem solving, such as those accessible through educational technology.[19]

Students in a pragmatist classroom share the experience of applying the scientific method to a full range of personal, social, and intellectual problems. Teachers expect that students will learn to apply the problem-solving method to situations both in and out of school and thus connect the school to society. Social networking can create a larger, perhaps even a global, community with more opportunities to share ideas, insights, and experiences.

Pragmatist teachers want their classrooms to be collaborative learning communities where students share their interests and problems. Recognizing that every culture has something of value to share with other cultures, they stress multicultural communication between students of different cultures so that together they can create more inclusive democratic communities. Instead of transmitting the status quo, pragmatist teachers are risk takers who see education as an open-ended and uncertain process.

Pragmatists would raise serious questions about the standards movement, especially its heavy reliance on standardized testing. Such tests burden students with antecedent goals and expectations that are set by so-called expert adults and agencies rather than those arising from the students' own experiences, issues, and problems. Further, pencil-and-paper tests measure only how well students assimilate prescribed derived content, rather than genuinely testing problem-solving skills. Teachers whose competency is judged by how well students perform on standardized tests are likely to focus instruction on passing tests rather than solving problems.

How might we apply pragmatism to classroom teaching? Let us say a college teacher-education class is examining the use of standardized tests to determine if standards of academic achievement are being achieved, as in the No Child Left Behind Act (NCLB). The class members do the following:

1. Establish the issue's context: What is a standardized test, and how is it used? Why is using standardized tests to measure achievement an issue? Who supports and who opposes using standardized tests to set academic standards?

2. Define the problem's key terms.

3. Conduct interdisciplinary research and locate information about the issue from various sources such as professional educators, educational psychologists, government agencies, parents' organizations, state and federal legislators, and the Web.

4. Conjecture possible solutions, ranging from acceptance to rejection of the proposition.

5. Resolve the issue by reaching consensus and acting—for example, carry out an agreement to write a position paper and send it to newspapers, journals, and decision makers.

REFOCUS *Use these questions to construct your own philosophy of education. What elements of pragmatism appeal to you as a teacher? Which appeal least? Why? Are there elements of pragmatism that you would like to incorporate into your philosophy of education?*

---

[19]For an examination of the philosophical implications of technology, see Larry A. Hickman, *Philosophical Tools for Technological Culture* (Bloomington: Indiana University Press, 2001).

Existentialism

Existentialism is more a process of philosophizing than it is a systematic philosophy (like idealism and realism). Representing feelings of desperation and hope, it calls for a personal examination of one's own life. An existentialist education encourages deep personal reflection on one's identity, commitments, and choices.

Key Concepts

- Personal reflection

The existentialist author Jean-Paul Sartre (1905–1980) stated that "Existence precedes Essence." Sartre, a playwright and philosopher, emphasized the role of human imagination as a way of knowing and feeling.[20] For Sartre, we are born into a world that we did not choose to be in and that we did not make. However, we possess the personal power, the will, to make choices and to create our own purposes for existence. We are thrust into choice-making situations. Some choices are trivial, but those that deal with the purpose and meaning of life lead to personal self-definition. We create our own definition as we make our own essence. We are what we choose to be. Human freedom is total, say the existentialists, as is our responsibility for choice.[21]

- Creating one's essence through choices

- Existential *angst*

The existentialist belief that human beings are responsible for creating their own essences dramatically differs from idealist and realist beliefs that the person is already defined in a universal system. Whereas the idealist or realist sees the individual existing in a meaningful and explainable world, the existentialist believes the universe is indifferent to human wishes, desires, and plans. Existentialism focuses on the concept of *angst,* or dread. We know that our presence in the world is temporary and that our destiny is death and disappearance. With this knowledge about the human situation, each person can make meaningful choices about freedom or subordination, love and hate, peace and war, and justice or injustice. As we make these choices, we ask: "What difference does it make that I am here and that I have chosen to be who I am?"

- Choosing self-determination

According to the existentialists, we must cope with the constant threat that others—persons, institutions, and agencies—pose to our choice-making freedom. Each person's response to life reflects an answer to the question, "Do I choose to be a self-determined person, or am I content to let others define me?" But existentialism does see hope behind the desperation. Each person has the potential for being, loving, and creating. Each can choose to be a free, inner-directed, authentic person who realizes that every choice is an act of personal value creation.[22]

The Basic Questions

- Creating personal values

Rejecting antecedent metaphysical descriptions that define the person at the moment of birth, existentialists assert that we create our own essence by making personal choices in our lives. Epistemologically, the individual chooses the knowledge that he or she wants to appropriate into his or her life. Existentialists consider axiology most important because human beings create their own values through their choices.

- Awakening consciousness of human condition

Recognizing that we live in a world of physical realities, existentialists accept that science provides useful information about the natural environment. However, the most significant personal aspects of our lives are not scientific. Thus, existentialists believe that our personal knowledge about the human condition and the personal choices we make are crucial. Education's purpose is to awaken our consciousness about our freedom to choose and to create our own sense of self-awareness that contributes to our authenticity.

---

[20]Thomas Baldwin, "Jean-Paul Sartre," in Honderich, *The Philosophers,* pp. 245–252.
[21]Gutek, *New Perspectives on Philosophy and Education,* pp. 113–125.
[22]Van Cleve Morris, *Existentialism in Education* (Prospect Heights, IL: Waveland Press, 1990). Also, access Scott Webster, "Existentialism: Providing an Ideal Framework for Educational Research in Times of Uncertainty" at **www.aare.edu.au**.

Same opportunities for all

Questioning and dialogue

Self-expression needed

At school, existentialists say, teachers and students should engage in discussion about their own lives and choices. Because we are all in the same existential predicament, we all should have opportunities for schooling. In the school, both teachers and students should have the opportunity to ask questions, engage in dialogue, and consider alternatives in all areas of life.

An existentialist teacher would encourage students to philosophize, question, and participate in dialogues about the meaning of their hopes and fears; their desires; and living, loving, and dying. There are no correct or incorrect answers to these questions. They are personal and subjective, not measurable by standardized tests, nor reached by group consensus. An existentialist curriculum consists of whatever leads to existentialist philosophizing. Particularly valuable are subjects that vividly portray individuals in the act of making choices, including emotional and aesthetic ones. Literature and biography can reveal people making choices. Students should read books, often autobiographies and novels, and discuss plays, movies, and television programs that vividly portray the human condition and the choice making it requires.

Students should be free to create their own authentic modes of self-expression.[23] They should be free to experiment with music, art, poetry, and literature to dramatize their emotions, feelings, and insights.

Educational technology that portrays personal choice and freedom has a role in an existentialist education. For example, students can design multimedia productions to express themselves. However, technologies that generate conformity in thinking and in accessing information would be viewed with suspicion. The question is—does social media lead to greater freedom of expression or more conformity? For example, individuals in Egypt, Tunisia, and Libya in the "Arab Spring" of 2011 used social media to commutate with each other and to make the choice, at great personal risk, to oppose dictatorships.

Implications for Today's Classroom Teacher

Teacher encourages awareness

External standards depersonalize education

Teaching from an existentialist perspective is always difficult because curricula and standards are often imposed on teachers from external agencies. Further, existentialists warn that teachers cannot specify goals and objectives in advance because students should be free to choose their own educational purposes. They would oppose the standards movement, especially its emphasis on a common core curriculum for all students and standardized testing to measure academic success, as an impediment to personal choice and freedom. Rather than imposing external standards on students, the existentialist teacher seeks to stimulate an intense awareness in each student of ultimate responsibility for her or his own education and self-definition. To do this, the teacher encourages students to examine the institutions, forces, and conditions that limit freedom of choice. Further, existentialist teachers seek to create open classrooms to maximize freedom of choice. Within these open learning environments, instruction is self-directed rather than standardized.

An Existentialist School: Summerhill

 Standards & Assessment

Summerhill: an example of freedom

Although Summerhill defies neat philosophical classification, the philosophy of its founder Alexander Sutherland Neill (1883–1973) illustrates some aspects of existentialism. A British educator, Neill founded Summerhill School, where he encouraged students to make their own choices about their own education. Liberated from a prescribed curriculum and academic requirements, students were free to choose what, when, and how they learned. Neill found his students actually wanted to learn and eagerly pursued their own educational agendas.[24]

[23]For narrative and education, see Mike Haylor, *Autoethnography, Self Narrative, and Teacher Education* (Boston: Sense Publishers, 2011).
[24]A. S. Neill, *Summerhill School: A New View of Childhood* (London: St. Martin's Griffin, 1995); Mark Vaughan, *Summerhill and A.S. Neill* (London: Open University Press, 2006). The website for Neill's Summerhill School is **www.summerhillschool.co.uk/pages/index.html**.

An existentialist lesson

Literature, drama, and film are especially powerful in existentialist teaching. An example of existentialist teaching might be a senior high-school history class that is studying the Holocaust, the genocide of six million Jews in Europe during World War II by the Nazis. The class views Steven Spielberg's movie, *Schindler's List,* in which an industrialist, Oscar Schindler, who initially profits from the forced labor of Jewish concentration camp inmates, makes a conscious decision to save his workers from death in the Nazi gas chambers. The class then probes the moral situation of one man, Schindler, and the choice that he made in a senseless and cruel world.

Postmodernism

Postmodernism contends that the modern period of history has ended and that we now live in a postmodern era. It originated in the philosophies of the German philosophers Friedrich Nietzsche (1844–1900) and Martin Heidegger (1899–1976). Nietzsche dismissed metaphysical claims about universal truth, suggesting that they were contrived to replace worn-out myths and supernatural beliefs with newer but equally false assertions.[25] Formulating a philosophy called phenomenology, Heidegger asserted that human beings construct their own subjective truths about reality from their intuitions, perceptions, and reflections as they interact with phenomena. Postmodernism exerts a pervasive intellectual influence today, especially on contemporary philosophy, education, women's studies, and literature.[26]

Relationship to constructivism

Postmodernism has implications for **constructivism**, a psychology and method of education. Postmodernists and constructivists agree that we make, or construct, our beliefs about knowledge from our experiences of interacting with our environment. As a human construction, our knowledge is always tentative, conjectural, and subject to ongoing revision. Because our statements, or our texts, about knowledge are a construction of how we perceive reality rather than a correspondence with reality, they can be deconstructed, or taken apart. *Collaborative learning,* the sharing of experiences and ideas through language, makes our discourse about knowledge both a personal and a social construction.[27]

Key Concepts

Derrida and Foucault

The French philosophers Michel Foucault and Jacques Derrida were key figures in developing postmodernism. Like Nietzsche, Foucault totally rejected the premodern idealist and realist claims that there are universal and unchanging truths. However, Foucault's major attack was on the modern experts, especially scientists, social scientists, and educators, who claim that they are impartial, objective, and unbiased. He contends that what these experts pronounce to be objective truth is really a disguised rationale for the elites who hold power and want to use it over others, especially the poor, minorities, and women.[28] In their analysis of education, postmodernists use the concepts of subordination (a powerful elite's control of disempowered groups and classes) and marginalization (the social, political, economic, and educational process of pushing powerless groups to the edges of society). An example of subordination occurs when politically powerful groups mandate certain educational requirements, such as

[25]For an incisive and insightful discussion of postmodernism, see Christopher Butler, *Postmodernism: A Very Short Introduction* (Oxford UK: Oxford University Press, 2002). Also, see Dave Hill, Peter McLaren, Mike Cole, and Glen Ritowski, *Postmodernism in Educational Theory: Education and the Politics of Human Resistance* (London: Tufnell Press, 1999).
[26]David E. Cooper, *World Philosophies: An Historical Introduction* (Oxford, UK, and Cambridge, MA: Blackwell, 1996), p. 467.
[27]John A. Zahorik, *Constructivist Teaching* (Bloomington, IN: Phi Delta Kappa Educational Foundation, 1995), pp. 10–13.
[28]For Foucault and education, see Gail McNicol Jardine, *Foucault & Education* (New York: Peter Lang, 2005); and Mark Olssen, *Michel Foucault: Materialism and Education* (Boulder, CO: Paradigm Publishers, 2006).

standardized testing of prescribed subjects, for other less powerful groups. For example, postmodernists would likely see the "Common Core State Standards" developed in 2010 by the Council of Chief State School Officers (CCSSO) and the National Governors Association Center as a top-down imposition on schools and teachers by powerful elite groups. Marginalization takes place when schools teach an official history that focuses on the achievement of white males of the dominant group and either ignores or places the histories of women and minorities as a minor supplement to the story.

■ Deconstruction

Claiming that knowledge as a human construction is expressed by language, Derrida developed **deconstruction** as a method to trace the origin and the meaning of texts or canons.[29] (A *canon* is a work, typically a book, prized as having authoritative knowledge.) A text is often a book, but it might also be a movie, a play, or another type of cultural representation. In education, a text is often a curriculum guide, a video, or a book, including a textbook, such as the one you are reading. The purpose of deconstruction is to show that texts, rather than reflecting metaphysical truths or objective knowledge, are biased historical and cultural constructions that involve political power relationships. For example, you can deconstruct this book or any textbook by answering such questions as: Who are the authors? Why did they write the book? What were their motives? Does the text endorse a particular ideology? Does that ideology support some people, groups, or classes over others?

Proponents of the Great Books curriculum, discussed later in this chapter, elevate certain books of Western culture to a high status, claiming that they provide highly valuable insights into life and society. However, some postmodernists criticize these texts for emphasizing Western culture while marginalizing Asian and African cultures. Postmodernists would say that texts such as Plato's *Republic* and Aristotle's *Nicomachean Ethics,* though exalted as having an enduring universal moral authority, are mere historical pieces that can be deconstructed to determine how they were and are used as rationales for the domination of one group over another.[30]

■ Deconstructing a text

In deconstructing a canon or text, postmodernists ask (1) What people, events, and situations at a particular time gave prominence to the canon? (2) Who gives a canon a privileged status in a culture or society, and who benefits from its acceptance as an authority? (3) Does the canon exclude underrepresented and marginalized individuals and groups? The answers to these questions point to those who hold actual social, economic, political, and educational power in a particular culture and society.

Postmodernists raise questions about who sets the standards for education and determines the skills and subjects found in the curriculum. For example, postmodernists would encourage the deconstruction of the "Common Core State Standards" by asking: Who set the standards and determined the curriculum? What skills and experiences do the standards include or exclude? Do the standards establish official knowledge and set power relationships among groups? (For an affirmation of these standards, see the section on essentialism later in this chapter.)

The Basic Questions

Like existentialists, postmodernist teachers want to raise their students' consciousness. While existentialists focus on consciousness about personal choice, postmodernists focus on consciousness about social inequalities by deconstructing traditional assumptions about knowledge, education, schooling, and instruction. They do not regard the school's curriculum as a repository of objective truths and scientific findings to be transmitted to students. It is an arena of conflicting viewpoints—some of which dominate and subordinate others.

■ Schools reproduce status quo

Postmodernists see American public schools as battlegrounds, as contested sites, in the struggle for social, political, and economic domination. They contend that the

[29]Gert J. J. Biesta, *Derrida and Education* (New York: Routledge, 2011); and Peter P. Trifonas and Michael Peters, *Derrida, Deconstruction, and Education: Ethics of Pedagogy and Research* (Oxford, UK: Blackwell, 2004).
[30]David E. Cooper, "Postmodernism," in Randall Curren, ed., *A Companion to the Philosophy of Education* (Malden, MA: Blackwell Publishing, 2006), pp. 206–217.

official curriculum is full of rationales, constructed by powerful groups seeking to legitimize their own privileged socioeconomic status and to dominate, or socially control, other, less-fortunate people. They dispute such official educational policy claims that public schools (1) fairly and equitably educate all children; (2) facilitate upward social and economic mobility; and (3) are necessary for maintaining a democratic society. In contrast, postmodernists argue that public schools, like other official institutions, help reproduce a society that is (1) patriarchal—it favors men over women; (2) Eurocentric—its so-called official knowledge is largely a construction of white people of European ancestry; and (3) particularly in the United States, capitalist—private property and the corporate mentality are glorified in the free-market ideology. The experiences of other groups, such as people of color, are marginal elements in the curriculum's official narratives.[31]

Struggle over curriculum

If we think of the school as a contested arena, we can see how postmodernists deconstruct the curriculum. Proponents of official knowledge want a standard cultural core curriculum in secondary and higher education that is based on the traditional canons of Western culture. Postmodernists challenge these canons as representing male-dominated, European-centered, Western, and capitalist culture. They argue that the contributions of underrepresented groups—Africans, Asians, Latinos, and Native Americans; women; the economically disadvantaged; and gays and lesbians—should be included in the curriculum, even at its core, if there is still a core. Postmodernists contend that a culturally diverse curriculum would reach all children, especially those marginalized in contemporary schools.

Teaching as representation

Postmodernists refer to instruction as a "representation," which they define as cultural expressions or discussions that use narratives about reality and values, stories, images, music, and other cultural constructions.[32] For example, a teacher in a social studies class who is presenting a unit on the history and controversy relating to immigration needs to be conscious of the textbook's and her own biases. Postmodernists urge teachers to become conscious of their powerful roles and to critically examine their representations to students. Rather than transmit only officially approved knowledge, teachers must critically represent a wider but more inclusive range of human experience.[33] Students are entitled to hear many voices and many stories, including their own autobiographies and biographies. While postmodernists and pragmatists agree that the curriculum should include discussion of controversial issues, postmodernists do not emphasize the scientific method as do pragmatists. The scientific method, for postmodernists, represents another meta-narrative (a narrative or exposition that is claimed to have global authority) used to give an elite group power over others. In this instance, the scientific method as a meta-narrative has been elevated into what its advocates proclaim to be the sole method of arriving at verifiable claims to truth. Postmodernists would contend that the scientific method is only one of many ways to construct claims to truth and that dominant elites have expropriated it to justify their exploitation of people and resources.

Implications for Today's Classroom Teacher

Teacher empowerment

To empower their students, postmodernists argue that teachers must first empower themselves as professional educators. They need to deconstruct official statements about the school's purpose, curriculum, and organization, as well as the teacher's role and mission. Real empowerment means that as teachers proceed from preservice to practice, they take responsibility for determining their own futures and for encouraging students to determine their own lives.

[31]Angeline Martel and Linda Peterat, "Margins of Exclusion, Margins of Transformation: The Place of Women in Education," in Rebecca A. Martusewicz and William M. Reynolds, *Inside/Out: Contemporary Critical Perspectives in Education* (New York: St. Martin's Press, 1994), p. 152.
[32]Elizabeth Ellsworth, "Representation, Self-Representation, and the Meanings of Difference: Questions for Educators," in Rebecca A. Martusewicz and William M. Reynolds, *Inside/Out: Contemporary Critical Perspectives in Education*, p. 100.
[33]Ibid., pp. 100–101.

▶‖ TEACHSOURCE VIDEO ACTIVITY

Philosophical Foundations of American Education: Four Philosophies in Action

Go to the Education CourseMate website to access the video entitled, "Philosophical Foundations of American Education." This video provides an introduction to the four theories of education discussed in the following sections of this chapter: essentialism, perennialism, progressivism, and critical theory. After watching the video, consider the following questions:

❶ How do these theories agree or disagree on the purposes of education?

❷ How do they agree or disagree on the content of the curriculum?

❸ How do they agree or disagree on the relationship between teachers and learners? Use these questions to guide your reading of the rest of the chapter, and then return to them when you construct your own philosophy of education.

■ Site-based philosophy

✓ Standards & Assessment

■ Postmodernists deconstruct standards

The process of empowering teachers and students begins in the schools and communities where they work and live. Postmodernists urge teachers to create their own site-based educational philosophy. Teachers, students, and community members must begin a local, site-based examination of key control issues by examining such questions as (1) who actually controls their school, establishes the curriculum, and sets the academic standards; (2) what motivates those who control the school; and (3) what rationale justifies the existing curriculum? This kind of critical analysis will empower people and transform society by challenging special economic and political interests and privileges.

The postmodernist emphasis on including the stories of marginalized groups encourages multiculturalism in the schools. Postmodernists would question the motives for establishing a curriculum of core subjects. They would deconstruct rationales for standards, asking critical questions about using standardized tests to measure student achievement, as in the NCLB Act. To find the real power relationships, they would ask who mandates the testing, develops the test, interprets the results, and determines how scores will be used.

Similar questions would apply to using technology in the classroom. The Internet, especially social media, can empower people by creating a means of quick communication for people interested in sharing ideas and common concerns with each other. Likewise, technology, if controlled by dominant groups, can indoctrinate people to accept the status quo that marginalizes and subordinates them, and it can be used to generate a rampant consumerism. A postmodernist teacher would examine the representations in software for student use, as well as to consider issues of power related to students' access to technology.

REFOCUS *Use these questions to construct your own philosophy of education.* What elements of postmodernism appeal to you as a teacher? Which appeal least? Why? Are there elements of postmodernism that you would like to incorporate into your philosophy of education?

What would a postmodernist lesson be like? Students in a high-school American history class might examine how Mexicans living in the territories that Mexico was forced to cede to the United States after the Mexican War were marginalized. Next, they might discuss how Latinos and other marginalized groups have made their voices heard throughout U.S. history. The lesson might include a journal assignment in which students examine areas of their own lives where they feel powerful or marginalized and suggest some actions they believe would help make their voices heard in constructive ways.

Educational Theories

In the following sections, we examine four educational theories: essentialism, perennialism, progressivism, and critical theory (see Overview 6.2). Whereas philosophies present highly generalized views of reality, knowledge, and values, theories explain

OVERVIEW 6.2

Theories of Education

Theory	Aim	Curriculum	Educational Implications	Proponents
Perennialism (rooted in realism)	To transmit universal and enduring truth and values	Fundamental skills, the liberal arts and sciences, the great books of Western civilization	Instruction that features transmission, discussion, and reflection on enduring truths and values	Hutchins Adler Maritain
Essentialism (rooted in idealism and realism)	To develop basic skills of literacy and numeracy and subject-matter knowledge	Basic skills, essential subject matter—history, mathematics, language, science, computer literacy	To prepare competent and skilled individuals for the competitive global economy	Bagley Bestor
Progressivism (rooted in pragmatism)	To educate individuals according to their interests and needs	Activities and projects	Instruction that features problem solving and collaborative learnings; teacher acts as a facilitator	Dewey Kilpatrick Parker Johnson
Critical theory (rooted in neo-Marxism and postmodernism)	To raise consciousness about issues of marginalization and empowerment	Autobiographies of oppressed peoples	Focus on social conflicts, empowerment, and social justice	McLaren Giroux

more particular phenomena and processes. Educational theories examine the roles and functions of schools, curriculum, teaching, and learning. Some theories are derived from philosophies, and others are derived from practice. We begin with the more traditional theories of essentialism and perennialism, which are rooted in idealism and realism, and take a subject-matter approach to teaching and learning. Then we move to progressivism, influenced by pragmatism, and critical theory, influenced by existentialism and postmodernism, which relate education to social change.

Essentialism

Essentialism establishes the school's primary or essential function as maintaining the achievements of human civilization by transmitting them to students as skills and subjects in a carefully organized and sequenced curriculum. William C. Bagley (1872–1946), a leading essentialist professor of education, believed that schools should provide all students with the skills and knowledge needed to function in a democratic society.[34] Failure to transmit these necessary skills and subjects puts civilization in peril. This essential knowledge includes the skills of literacy (reading and writing), computation (arithmetic), and the subjects of history, mathematics, science, languages, and literature. Because there is much to learn but only a limited time to learn it, the curriculum needs to emphasize essential knowledge, and teaching needs to be efficient. For effective learning, the curriculum needs to be sequential and cumulative. It is sequential when lower-order skills generate and lead to more complex higher-order ones. It is cumulative when what is learned at a lower grade level leads to and is added to by knowledge in succeeding grades or levels.[35]

Bagley crafted a finely tuned program of teacher education that moved teachers forward from preservice to professional classroom practice. Teachers need a knowledge

---

[34]J. Wesley Null, *A Disciplined Progressive Educator: The Life and Career of William Chandler Bagley* (New York: Peter Lang, 2003).
[35]William C. Bagley, "An Essentialist Platform for the Advancement of American Education," *Educational Administration and Supervision* 24 (April 1938), pp. 241–256.

base in the liberal arts and sciences, mastery of the skills and subjects they teach, and a repertoire of professional education experiences and methods that enables them to transmit essential skills and subjects efficiently and effectively to students. The successful passage from preservice to practice means that teachers can competently organize skills and subjects into units appropriate to students' age and ability levels and competently teach them.

Arthur E. Bestor, Jr., a professor of history, refined and reiterated essentialist beliefs into the theory of basic education and was a founder of the Council on Basic Education. Bestor argued that schools should provide a sound education in the intellectual disciplines, which he defined as the fundamental ways of thinking found in history, science, mathematics, literature, language, and art. These intellectual disciplines were historically developed as people searched for cultural understanding, intellectual power, and useful knowledge.[36]

New approaches neglected basics

Essentialists charge that often popular and supposedly innovative methods that neglect systematic teacher-directed instruction in basic skills of reading, writing, computation, and the essential subjects have caused a decline in students' academic performance and civility. Social-promotion policies, which advance students to higher grades to keep them with their age cohort even if they have not mastered grade-appropriate skills and subjects, have further eroded academic standards. These policies caused a serious decline in student achievement scores on standardized tests such as the SAT and ACT. In addition, a morally permissive environment in the schools has weakened fundamental civic values of civility, social responsibility, and patriotism.

✓ Standards & Assessment

"New basics"

To correct these deficiencies, *A Nation at Risk,* a national report sponsored by the U.S. Department of Education, recommended that all high-school students complete a rigorous curriculum of "new basics" consisting of English, mathematics, science, social studies, and computer science.[37]

✓ Standards & Assessment

Start of standards movement

The criticisms voiced in *A Nation at Risk* generated the "standards movement," which argues that American education will be improved by creating high academic standards, or benchmarks, for students' academic achievement. Proponents also argue that education will be improved by measuring progress toward achievement of those benchmarks via standardized tests.

No Child Left Behind

The Elementary and Secondary Education Act of 2001, the No Child Left Behind Act (NCLB), gave a federal endorsement to setting standards for teaching and learning. NCLB carries the essentialist premise that schools should emphasize key basic skills, such as reading and mathematics, and that standardized tests can objectively measure students' academic achievement. Further, NCLB uses students' scores on standardized tests to determine how well schools and teachers are meeting stated academic outcomes.

Terms of NCLB

To qualify for federal aid under NCLB, states must establish annual assessments in reading and mathematics for every student in grades 3 through 8. NCLB's proponents contend that these test results will identify schools in which large numbers of students fail to meet or surpass the standard. The law holds school districts accountable for improving the performance of disadvantaged students, as well as the overall student population. Schools and districts failing to make adequate yearly progress are to be identified and remediated. If a school fails to meet standards for three years, its students may then transfer to a higher-performing school.[38]

The standards movement launched in the 1980s has continued and gained momentum with the Common Core State Standards and 21st Century Themes initiatives of 2010–2012. The Common Core State Standards recommended by the Council of

---

[36]Arthur E. Bestor, Jr., *Educational Wastelands: The Retreat from Learning in Our Public Schools* (Urbana: University of Illinois Press, 1953); and Bestor, *The Restoration of Learning: A Program for Redeeming the Unfulfilled Promise of American Education* (New York: Alfred A. Knopf, 1956).
[37]National Commission on Excellence in Education, *A Nation at Risk: The Imperative for Educational Reform* (Washington, D.C.: U.S. Department of Education, 1983), pp. 5, 24.
[38]*No Child Left Behind* (Washington, D.C.: U.S. Printing Office, 2001), pp. 1, 8-9.

TECHNOLOGY@SCHOOL

Skills, Subjects, and Standards

The Nation at Risk and No Child Left Behind emphasized that the curriculum needs to place emphasis on basic skills such as reading and mathematics and basic subjects such as the English language, mathematics, science, history, and computer science. It also emphasized that benchmarks need to be set to determine if students are meeting these academic standards. Recent initiatives for skills, subjects, and standards are the Common Core State Standards and the Core Subjects and 21st Century Themes. Although some educators endorse skills, subjects, and standards as necessary to ensuring the academic quality of American education, others fear that the skill and subject emphasis may weaken process- and project-oriented learning and that standards may lead to a classroom standardization that limits creativity and problem solving. Explore this issue by accessing the following websites, and then make up your own mind.

Access the U.S Department of Education at **www.ed.gov** to survey state and national developments related to standards. Access Common Core State Standards at **www.corestandards.org** and the Core Subjects and 21st Century Themes at **www.p21.org**. Access the Council for Basic Education at **www.c-b-e.org** for its perspectives on the teaching of arts, English, geography, history, mathematics, and other subjects. Access the John Dewey Project on Progressive Education at **www.uvm.edu/~dewey** for its perspective. Access *Rage and Hope: Critical Theory and Its Impact on Education* at **www.perfectfit.org/CT/index2.html**.

Chief State School Officers (CCSSO) and the National Governors Association Center for Best Practices in 2010 reveal a modified essentialist orientation. The standards identify English (language arts) and mathematics as basic subjects whose mastery is needed for success in education and in life.[39] (See more discussion of the Common Core State Standards in Chapter 14, Curriculum and Instruction.)

The Basic Questions

Role of school to teach basics

Essentialists want schools and teachers to be committed to their primary academic mission and not be diverted into nonacademic areas. The schools' appropriate role is to teach students the basic skills and subjects that prepare them to function effectively and efficiently in a democratic society. Although social, economic, and political issues may be examined in relevant subjects such as history and social studies, this discussion should be objective and not politicized to promote a particular ideological agenda.

Subject-matter boundaries

Essentialists favor a subject-matter curriculum that differentiates and organizes subjects according to their internal logical or chronological principles. The curriculum's skills and subjects should be well defined as to scope and have a sequence that is cumulative and prepares students for future learning. Curriculum that ignores the past, rejects subject-matter boundaries, and claims to be interdisciplinary unnecessarily confuses students, blurs academic outcomes, and wastes valuable time and resources by failing to establish the necessary knowledge base.

Suspicious of innovations

Essentialists are suspicious of so-called innovative or process learning approaches, such as constructivism, in which students construct their own knowledge in a collaborative fashion, and of authentic assessment in which students evaluate their own progress. For essentialists, civilized people learn effectively and efficiently when they acquire the knowledge base that scientists, scholars, and other experts have developed and organized. We need not continually reinvent the wheel, wasting time and resources by rediscovering what is already known. We need to learn and use what we already know and move forward from that foundation into the future.

---

[39]Common Core State Standards at **www.corestandards.org,** and the Core Subjects and 21st Century Themes at **www.p21.org**.

Although competent teachers always try to stimulate a student's interest, curriculum content should be based on the time-tested experience of the human race. Genuine freedom comes from staying with a task and mastering it. Bagley, for example, in emphasizing teacher-directed instruction, argues that children have the right to expect teachers, as trained professionals, to guide and direct their learning.[40] Similar to the scientific realists, essentialists argue that students need to learn about the objective real world rather than misguidedly following the constructivist view that they should create their own version of reality.

Implications for Today's Classroom Teacher

Transmitting essential skills

For essentialists, the purpose of education is to transmit and maintain the necessary fundamentals of human culture. Schools have the specific mission of transmitting essential human skills and subjects to the young to preserve and pass them on to future generations.[41] As effective professional educators, teachers should (1) adhere to a carefully structured curriculum of basic skills and subjects; (2) inculcate traditional Western and American values of patriotism, hard work, effort, punctuality, respect for authority, and civility; (3) manage classrooms efficiently, effectively, and fairly as spaces of discipline and order; and (4) promote students on the basis of academic achievement, not social considerations.

An essentialist lesson

Essentialist teachers would use deductive logic to organize instruction. They first teach basic concepts and factual information, and then they lead students to make generalizations based upon that knowledge. Consider a high-school American history class studying the controversy between the two African American leaders, Booker T. Washington and W. E. B. Du Bois's. First, the teacher assigns primary sources such as Washington's *Up From Slavery* and Du Bois's *The Souls of Black Folk*. (Washington and Du Bois are discussed in Chapter 5, Historical Development of American Education.) Then she leads a discussion in which the students, based on their reading and research, carefully identify Washington's and Du Bois's differences in background, education, and policy. After such teacher-guided research and discussion, the students develop generalizations about why Washington and Du Bois acted as they did and assess their influence in African American and U.S. history.

REFOCUS *Use these questions to construct your own philosophy of education.* What elements of essentialism appeal to you as a teacher? Which appeal least? Why? Are there elements of essentialism you plan to incorporate into your philosophy of education?

Perennialism

Truth in the classics

Perennialism shares many features with essentialism, such as using subject matter to transmit the cultural heritage across generations. It differs, however, in that perennialism is derived from the realist philosophy of Aristotle and Aquinas, while essentialism is based more on what has worked as a survival skill throughout history. (For more on Aristotle and Aquinas, see Chapter 3, Global Origins of American Education.) Perennialism asserts that education, like the truth it conveys, needs to be universal and authentic during every period of history and in every place and culture. Neither truth, nor education, is relative to time, place, or circumstances.

Continuity & Change

Education's primary purpose is to bring each new generation in contact with truth by exercising and cultivating the rationality each person possesses as a human being. Perennialist epistemology contends that due to common human nature, people possess a potentiality to know and a desire to find the truth. This potentiality is activated when

[40]J. Wesley Null, "Social Reconstruction with a Purpose: The Forgotten Tradition of William Bagley," in Karen Riley, ed., *Social Reconstruction: People, Politics, Perspectives* (Greenwich, CT: Information Age Publishing, 2006), pp. 27–44.
[41]Diane Ravitch, *Left Back: A Century of Failed School Reforms* (New York: Simon and Schuster, 2000), pp. 465–467.

students come in contact with humankind's highest achievements, especially the great books and the classics in art, music, and literature. Truth exists in and is portrayed in the classic, or enduring, works of art, literature, philosophy, science, and history created by earlier generations and passed on to succeeding generations as a cultural inheritance.

Schools cultivate rationality

Perennialism, derived heavily from realism, is also congenial to idealism. However, leading perennialists such as Jacques Maritain, Robert Hutchins, and Mortimer Adler based their educational theories on Aristotle's and Thomas Aquinas's realism. For them, the school's primary role is to develop students' rationality. They oppose turning schools into multipurpose agencies, especially economic ones that emphasize vocational training. Although perennialists understand the need for vocational skills and competencies, they believe that business and industry can provide up-to-date job training more efficiently than schools. Placing nonacademic demands on schools, such as social adjustment or vocational training, diverts time and resources from the school's primary purpose of developing students intellectually.

Perennial curriculum

Because truth is universal and unchanging, the curriculum should consist of permanent, or perennial, studies that emphasize the recurrent themes of human life. It should contain subjects that cultivate rationality and the moral, aesthetic, and religious values that contribute to ethical behavior and civility. Like idealists, realists, and essentialists, perennialists favor a subject-matter curriculum that includes history, language, mathematics, logic, literature, the humanities, and science. Religious perennialists, such as Jacques Maritain, also include religion and theology in the curriculum.

Education develops the mind

Robert Hutchins, a former president of the University of Chicago, described the ideal education as "one that develops intellectual power" and is not "directed to immediate needs; it is not a specialized education, or a preprofessional education; it is not a utilitarian education. It is an education calculated to develop the mind."[42]

Continuity & Change

Hutchins recommended reading and discussing the great books of Western civilization to bring each generation into an intellectual dialogue with the great minds of the past. These classic works, with their reoccurring themes, stimulate intellectual discussion and critical thinking. With the classics, Hutchins urged the study of grammar, rhetoric, logic, mathematics, and philosophy.

Great books of Western civilization

As noted earlier, postmodernists attack Hutchins's Great Books curriculum as an attempt to give Western European canons dominance over other cultures, such as those of Asia and Africa.

Critique of Great Books curriculum

Maritain, a French philosopher, based his perennialist "integral humanism" on Aristotle's natural realism and Thomas Aquinas's theistic realism.[43] Maritain wanted religion to be an integral part of the curriculum.[44] Rejecting cultural relativism and existentialism, Maritain asserted that education needed to be guided by the ultimate direction that religion provides. His religious emphasis fits the contemporary resurgence of faith-based values in American society. Like Hutchins, Maritain endorsed the great books as indispensable for understanding the development of civilization, culture, and science.[45]

For Maritain, elementary education should develop correct language usage, cultivate logical thinking, and introduce students to history and science. Secondary and

---

[42]Robert Hutchins, *A Conversation on Education* (Santa Barbara, CA: The Fund for the Republic, 1963), p. 1; and Robert M. Hutchins, *The Higher Learning in America* (New York: Transaction, 1995). For biographies of Hutchins, see Milton Mayer, *Robert Maynard Hutchins: A Memoir* (Berkeley: University of California Press, 1993); and Mary Ann Dzuback, *Robert Hutchins: Portrait of an Educator* (Chicago: University of Chicago Press, 1991). For a highly readable and engaging discussion of Hutchins, Mortimer Adler, and the Great Books curriculum, see Alex Beam, *A Great Idea at the Time: The Rise, Fall, and Curious Afterlife of the Great Books* (New York: Public Affairs, 2008).
[43]Douglas A. Ollivant, *Jacques Maritain and the Many Ways of Knowing* (Washington, D.C.: American Maritain Association, 2002).
[44]For a reappraisal of Maritain, see Gerald L. Gutek, "Jacques Maritain and John Dewey on Education: A Reconsideration," Madonna Murphy, "Maritain Explains the Moral Principles of Education to Dewey," and Wade A. Carpenter, "Jacques Maritain and Some Christian Suggestions for the Education of Teachers," in Wade A. Carpenter, guest ed., *Educational Horizons* 83 (Summer 2005), pp. 247–263, 282–301.
[45]Jacques Maritain, *Education at the Crossroads* (New Haven, CT: Yale University Press, 1960), pp. 70–73.

undergraduate college education should focus on the liberal arts and sciences.

The Paideia Proposal

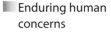

Paideia curriculum

Mortimer J. Adler's ***The Paideia Proposal: An Educational Manifesto*** is a revival of perennialism.[46] *Paideia,* a Greek word, refers to a person's complete educational and cultural formation. Adler, who opposed streaming students into different curricular tracks, wants all students to have the same high quality of schooling. The *Paideia* curriculum includes language, literature, fine arts, mathematics, natural sciences, history, geography, and social studies. These studies are especially useful in helping students develop a repertoire of intellectual skills such as reading, writing, speaking, listening, calculating, observing, measuring, estimating, and problem solving. Together, these skills lead to higher-order critical thinking and reflection.[47]

The Basic Questions

A general education

Perennialists assert that in a democratic society, all students have the right to the same high-quality intellectual education. To track some students into an academic and others into vocational curricula denies them equality of opportunity to a high-quality general education.

Against relativism

Perennialists strongly oppose pragmatism's and postmodernism's **ethical relativism**, which contends that our "truths" are temporary statements based on how we cope with changing circumstances. Perennialists, such as Allan Bloom in *The Closing of the American Mind,* condemn ethical and cultural relativism for denying universal standards by which certain actions are consistently either morally right or wrong.[48]

Implications for Today's Classroom Teacher

For perennialists, the school's primary role is to develop students' reasoning powers. To fulfill this academic mission, teachers in their preservice preparation need an education in the liberal arts and sciences and need to read and discuss the great books. As practicing professionals, teachers need a solid academic foundation to act as intellectual mentors and models for their students.

Enduring human concerns

In primary grades, perennialist teachers would teach fundamental skills, such as reading, writing, computation, and research skills, and stimulate a desire for learning so students are prepared to begin their lifelong quest for truth. Perennialist secondary teachers would emphasize the enduring human concerns explored in the great works of history, literature, drama, art, and philosophy. Like idealists, perennialists emphasize the classics that speak to people across generations.

Standards & Assessment

Emphasis on academic content

Endorsing high academic standards, perennialists want those standards to be based on intellectual content, especially knowledge of the classics. If standards and examinations reflect knowledge of the enduring subjects, perennial issues, and great books, they would favor them.

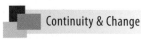

Continuity & Change

A perennialist lesson

Kindle and other electronic and digital versions of the great books and other classics are an effective way of transmitting them to a larger audience. Also, chat rooms and other social networking tools can enhance communication about the classics. Technology, including posts on social media, however, is not a substitute for reading the classic.

An illustration of the perennialist emphasis on recurring human concerns and values can be seen in a middle-school literature class that is reading and discussing

[46]Mortimer J. Adler, *The Paideia Proposal: An Educational Manifesto* (New York: Macmillan, 1982); see also Mortimer J. Adler, *Paideia Problems and Possibilities* (New York: Macmillan, 1983). For the Paideia philosophy, materials, and teaching practices, access the National Paideia Center at **www.paideia.org**.

[47]Adler, *Paideia Proposal,* pp. 22–23.

[48]Allan Bloom, *The Closing of the American Mind* (New York: Simon and Schuster, 1987).

Louisa May Alcott's *Little Women*. The students have discussed the main characters—Marmee, Jo, Beth, Meg, and Amy—and the issues of war, poverty, and illness that the March family faces. The class discussion reveals that the March family's sad and happy times reoccur perennially in family life today. That evening at dinner, the grandmother of Alice, a student in the class, asks, "What are you studying in school?" Alice replies, "We just finished reading *Little Women*." Alice's mother and grandmother say that they, too, read and enjoyed the book when they were girls. In the ensuing conversation, Alice, her mother, and her grandmother share their impressions of the book. In such ways, perennial themes can become memories that speak across time to generations.

REFOCUS *Use these questions to construct your own philosophy of education. What aspects of perennialism appeal to you as a teacher? Which appeal least? Why? Are there elements of perennialism you would like to incorporate into your philosophy?*

Progressivism

A widespread reform movement

Progressivism originated as a general reform movement in American society and politics in the late nineteenth and early twentieth centuries. Although they agreed in opposing traditional education and wanting to reform schools, progressives did not always agree on how to bring about the changes they desired. Whereas child-centered progressives wanted to liberate children from authoritarian schools, social reconstructionists wanted to use schools to reform society.[49] Administrative progressives, who were school superintendents and principals, wanted to make schools more efficient and cost effective by building larger schools that could house more class sections and offer a more diverse curriculum.

In their revolt against traditional schools, progressive educators oppose essentialism and perennialism. Educators such as Marietta Johnson, William H. Kilpatrick, and G. Stanley Hall rebelled against rote memorization and authoritarian classroom management.

Prolonging childhood

Marietta Johnson (1864–1938), founder of the Organic School in Fairhope, Alabama, epitomized child-centered progressive education. Believing that prolonging childhood is especially needed in a technological society, Johnson wanted childhood lengthened rather than shortened.[50] Children, she said, should follow their own internal timetables rather than adults' scheduling. Possessing their own stages of readiness, children should not be pushed by teachers or parents to do things for which they are not ready.

Activity-based curriculum

Anticipating contemporary constructivist learning, Johnson believed children learn most successfully and satisfyingly by actively exploring their environments and constructing their own conception of reality based on their direct experiences. Johnson's activity-based curriculum accentuated physical exercise, nature study, music, crafts, field geography, storytelling, dramatizations, and games. Creative activities such as dancing, drawing, singing, and weaving took center stage, while reading and writing were delayed until the child was nine or ten years old.[51]

Johnson designed a teacher-education program that went from preservice to practice. During preservice, caring and effective teachers needed to develop (1) a sincere affection for and sympathetic interest in children; (2) a knowledge base in child and adolescent development and psychology and in the skills and subjects they taught; and (3) a commitment to social welfare. As in-service practitioners, teachers should create safe, developmentally friendly, and engaging classroom environments in which children, following their own interests, learn at their own pace.

William Heard Kilpatrick (1871–1965), a professor of education at Columbia University's Teachers College, made progressivism an integral part of teacher preparation. In restructuring Dewey's problem solving into the project method, Kilpatrick used three guiding principles: (1) genuine education involves problem solving; (2) learning is enriched as students collaboratively research and share information to formulate and test

---

[49]For social reconstructionism, see Karen L. Riley, ed., *Social Reconstructionism: People, Politics, Perspectives* (Greenwich, CT: Information Age Publishing, 2006).
[50]Marietta Johnson, *Thirty Years with an Idea* (Tuscaloosa: University of Alabama Press, 1974), pp. 20–21.
[51]Johnson, *Thirty Years with an Idea*, pp. 52–55, 62–63, 86–95.

their hypotheses; and (3) teachers can guide students' learning without dominating it. Using these principles, Kilpatrick designed four types of projects: (1) implementing a creative idea or plan; (2) enjoying an aesthetic experience; (3) solving an intellectual problem; and (4) learning a new skill or area of knowledge.[52]

Project method

Kilpatrick believed that teachers who used the project method could transform their classrooms into collaborative, democratic, learning communities. As they worked collaboratively, students, motivated by their own interests, would be engaged in wholehearted, purposeful activity in which they designed and completed a project. Unlike the prestructured objectives of the essentialist and perennialist curricula, the project method was open ended in that its outcomes were not specified in advance but came out of the project.[53]

Standards & Assessment

Visit the Project-Based Learning Space website, found at the Education Course-Mate website, for the background, theory, and application of the project method.

Key Concepts

Practices opposed by progressives

The Progressive Education Association opposed (1) authoritarian teachers, (2) exclusively book-based instruction, (3) passive memorization of factual information, (4) the isolation of schools from society, and (5) using physical or psychological coercion to manage classrooms. These progressive educators positively affirmed that (1) the child should be free to develop naturally; (2) interest, motivated by direct experience, is the best stimulus for learning; (3) the teacher should facilitate learning; (4) there needs to be close cooperation among the school, home, and community; and (5) the progressive school should be a laboratory to test educational ideas and practices.

Practices favored by progressives

Opposing the conventional subject-matter curriculum, progressives experimented with alternative curricula, using activities, experiences, problem solving, and projects. Child-centered progressive teachers sought to free children from conventional restraints and repression. More socially oriented progressives, called social reconstructionists, sought to make schools the centers of larger social reforms.[54] Led by George Counts and Harold Rugg, the social reconstructionists believed that teachers and schools need to investigate and deliberately work to solve social, political, and economic problems. In many ways, **social reconstructionism** anticipated critical theory, discussed in the next section of the chapter.[55]

Progressive reforms in schools

The Basic Questions

For progressives, knowledge is an instrument that does or creates something. Although it can come from many sources—books, experiences, experts, the library, the laboratory, and the Internet—it becomes meaningful when we use it as a tool to accomplish a purpose. Agreeable to using technology in instruction, progressives want it to be an open means to accessing information. For example, social media can be used to share ideas and information with individuals around the world. When students work together collaboratively, especially on projects, the results of learning are open ended in that they lead to more experiences and are socially charged in that they bring individuals into social interaction.

Readiness, interests, and needs

For progressives, children's readiness and interests, rather than predetermined subjects, should shape curriculum and instruction. They resist the imposition of standards from outside of the school by government agencies and special interest groups as a new form of authoritarian control that can block open-ended, problem-based inquiry.

[52]William H. Kilpatrick, "The Project Method: The Use of the Purposeful Act in the Educative Process," *Teachers College Record* (September 1918).
[53]John A. Beineke, *And There Were Giants in the Land: The Life of William Heard Kilpatrick* (New York: Peter Lang, 1998), pp. 106–107.
[54]The definitive history of progressive education remains Lawrence A. Cremin, *The Transformation of the School* (New York: Random House, 1961).
[55]William B. Stanley, "Education for Social Reconstruction in Critical Context," in Karen Riley, ed., *Social Reconstructionism: People, Politics, Perspectives*, pp. 89–110.

Instructionally flexible, progressive teachers use a repertoire of learning activities such as problem solving, field trips, creative artistic expression, and projects. Constructivism, like progressivism, emphasizes socially interactive and process-oriented hands-on learning in which students work collaboratively to expand and revise their knowledge base.[56]

■ Constructing reality

In professional education, progressives warn against separating preservice from practice, which are phases in the same flow, or continuum, of a teacher's experience. Preservice experiences, such as clinical observation, should be directly connected to classroom practice and not regarded as preparatory to it. In turn, practice should be considered as a continuing process of in-service professional development, in which teachers construct innovative and effective teaching strategies. The teacher should guide students to new activities, new projects, and new problems, thus enlarging and broadening their social and cultural relationships.

Implications for Today's Classroom Teacher

■ Example of a progressive strategy

The West Tennessee Holocaust Project, designed by teachers and students at the Whitwell Middle School in Whitwell, Tennessee, offers an excellent illustration of the project method.[57] The project's purpose was to teach respect for different cultures and to understand the consequences of intolerance.[58] Linda Hooper, the school's principal, saw the project as providing an opportunity "to give our children a broader view of the world … that would crack the shell of their white cocoon."[59]

■ Preproject preparation

In preparing for the project, students read Anne Frank's *Diary of a Young Girl* and Elie Wiesel's *Night,* studied aspects of Judaism, and viewed the motion picture *Schindler's List.* Overwhelmed by the immensity of the Holocaust's toll of six million Jews killed in Nazi extermination camps, the students experienced difficulty in understanding why and how this genocide had occurred.

■ Student initiative

The students learned that some courageous Norwegians, expressing solidarity with their Jewish fellow citizens, pinned ordinary paper clips to their lapels as a silent protest against the Nazi occupation. One student reacted, saying, "Let's collect six million paper clips and turn them into a sculpture to remember the victims." The students decided to do so as a memorial to the six million Jewish victims of the Holocaust.

The students collected paper clips from their family and friends, set up a Web page about the project, and asked for donations of clips. Although they collected 100,000 clips in the project's first year, the goal of collecting 6 million paper clips seemed insurmountable. When Lena Gitter, a ninety-four-year-old Holocaust survivor, learned about the project, she contacted two German journalists, Peter Schroeder and Dagmar Schroeder-Hildebrand, who were doing research at the U.S. Holocaust Memorial Museum in Washington, D.C. Intrigued that American children in a small Southern town were engaged in a unique project to honor the victims of the Holocaust, the journalists wrote articles about the project that appeared in Germany and Austria.

■ On-site learning

After that, the school was deluged with paper clips. The Schroeders visited the Whitwell school and community. Their visit was a culturally enriching experience for the students, who met persons from another country for the first time. It was especially significant because the Schroeders were from Germany, the country whose Nazi leaders had perpetrated the Holocaust. The Schroeders wrote a book about *The Paper Clip Project* that was published in Germany.[60]

---

[56]For translating constructivist epistemology into classroom practice, see Peter W. Airasian and Mary E. Walsh, "Constructivist Cautions," *Phi Delta Kappan* (February 1997), pp. 444–449. Also see David J. Martin and Kimberly S. Loomis, *Building Teachers: Constructivist Approach to Introducing Education* (Stamford, CT: Cengage Learning, 2007).

[57]Dita Smith, *Washington Post* (April 7, 2002), p. C01, at **www.truthorfiction.com /rumors/s/studentmemorial.htm.**

[58]**www.whitwellmiddleschool.org/?PageName=bc&n=69256.**

[59]Smith, *Washington Post.*

[60]Peter W Schroeder and Dagmar Schroeder-Hildebrand, *Six Million Paper Clips: the Making of a Children's Holocaust Memorial* (Minneapolis, MN: Kar-Ben Publishing Co., 2004). Also see the DVD, Eliott Berlin and Joe Fab, Directors, *Paper Clips.*

AP Photo/Mark Gilliland

The West Tennessee Holcaust Project is an example of a progressive collaborative learning strategy with community involvement.

Multiple-skill learning

During the project, students developed an array of skills. They recorded correspondence and contributions in a ledger, wrote letters to acknowledge contributions, and responded to e-mails sent to their website.

Although none of Whitwell's students had ever met a Jew when the project began, several Jewish Holocaust survivors visited and spoke to them and residents of the town. In 2005, Whitwell eighth graders visited the Holocaust Museum in Washington, D.C.

The students decided to house their paper clip collection in a German railroad car, like those that transported Jews to the extermination camps. With the help of the Schroeders, an actual German railway car was brought to Whitwell. With the help of the entire community, the students created a permanent museum, in which the paper clips, stored in the car, are a memorial to the Holocaust victims.

Community participation

The Whitwell Holocaust project illustrates the open-endedness of the project method. The project's activities permeated the school and the community, bringing residents and students together in a collaborative effort. It would get the attention of the president and vice president of the United States, become the subject of a book, and become an international cause. When they began the project, the Whitwell students and teachers had no idea how many lives they were to touch. A student, summing up the project, said, "Now, when I see someone, I think before I speak, I think before I act, and I think before I judge."[61]

REFOCUS *Use these questions to construct your own philosophy of education. What elements of progressivism appeal to you as a teacher? Which appeal least? Why? Are there elements of progressivism that you plan to incorporate into your philosophy of education?*

---

[61]Smith, *Washington Post.*

Critical Theory

Critical theory, an influential contemporary theory of education, urges a rigorous critique of schools and society to uncover exploitative power relationships and bring about equity, fairness, and social justice.[62] Many of its assumptions are derived from postmodernist and existentialist philosophies, neo-Marxism, feminist and multicultural theories, and Paulo Freire's liberation pedagogy. (Freire is discussed in Chapter 4, Pioneers of Teaching and Learning.) Henry Giroux and Peter McLaren are leading critical theorist philosophers.[63]

Key Concepts

Neo-Marxist influence

Some of the ideas of Karl Marx, a nineteenth-century philosopher, have influenced critical theory. Arguing that all institutions rest on an economic base, Marx saw human history as a class struggle for social and economic power.[64] Critical theorists often use such Marxist concepts as class conflict and alienation to analyze social and educational institutions. Alienation refers to feelings of powerlessness experienced by people who have been marginalized and pushed to society's edges.

Powerful groups dominate

According to critical theorists, critical consciousness requires recognition that an individual's social status, including educational and economic expectations and opportunities, is largely determined by race, ethnicity, gender, and class. The dominant socioeconomic class that controls social, political, economic, and educational institutions uses its power to maintain, or reproduce, its favored position and to subordinate socially and economically disadvantaged classes.[65] In the United States, historically subordinate groups are the urban and rural poor, African and Native Americans, Latinos, women, and gays and lesbians.[66] Through a critical education, however, subordinated classes and groups can become conscious of their exploitation, resist domination, overturn the patterns of oppression, and empower themselves.

The Basic Questions

A new public philosophy

Critical theorists want to raise consciousness about questions dealing with knowledge, education, the school, and teaching and learning. For them, knowledge is about issues of social, political, economic, and educational power and control. In particular, critical theorists want to raise the consciousness of people who have been forced into marginal and subordinate positions in society because of race, ethnicity, language, class, or gender.[67]

Social control

Critical theorists contend that economically, politically, and socially dominant classes control and use schools to reproduce and maintain their privileged social and economic position. To maintain their commanding status, children of the dominant classes attend prestigious schools and universities that prepare them for high-level

---

[62]Douglas Kellner, "Critical Theory," in Randall Curren, ed., *A Companion to the Philosophy of Education* (Malden, MA: Blackwell Publishing, 2006), pp. 161–175.

[63]Henry Giroux, *Public Spaces, Private Lives* (Lanham, MD: Rowman and Littlefield, 2001); Giroux, *Border Crossings: Cultural Workers and the Politics of Education* (New York: Routledge, 2005).

[64]For a brief introduction to Marx and Marxism, see Peter Osborne, *How to Read Marx* (New York: W. W. Norton, 2005).

[65]Martin Carnoy, "Education, State, and Culture in American Society," in Henry A. Giroux and Peter L. McLaren, eds., *Critical Pedagogy, the State, and Cultural Struggle* (Albany: State University of New York Press, 1998), pp. 6–7.

[66]Angeline Martel and Linda Peterat, "Margins of Exclusion, Margins of Transformation: The Place of Women in Education," in Rebecca A. Martusewicz and William Reynolds, eds., *Inside/Out: Contemporary Critical Perspectives in Education* (New York: St. Martin's Press, 1994), pp. 151–154.

[67]Henry A. Giroux and Peter L. McLaren, "Schooling, Cultural Politics, and the Struggle for Democracy," in Giroux and McLaren, *Critical Pedagogy, the State, and Cultural Struggle*, pp. xi–xii.

careers in business, industry, and government. Children of subordinate groups and classes are indoctrinated to accept the conditions that disempower them as the best of all possible worlds. Schools in economically disadvantaged urban and rural areas, for example, serve mainly the poor, African Americans, and Latinos. Typically underfinanced, these schools are often deteriorating physically and lack needed resources.

■ Teacher empowerment

Inner-city schools, as well as many other schools, are ensnared in large, hierarchical educational bureaucracies. With orders coming down from the top, teachers have little or no decision-making power about how schools will run. Within the school, teachers tend to be isolated from each other in self-contained classrooms. Further, parents and others in the local community are kept at a distance, with little school involvement. The curriculum, too, is determined by higher-level administrators, with little room for local initiatives that relate to the life experiences of students or community members.

✓ Standards & Assessment

NCLB and the "Common Core State Standards" further impose demands on teachers and students that are generated from outside of the school community.

■ Official curriculum

Critical theorists see curriculum as existing in two spheres: the formal official curriculum and the **"hidden" curriculum**. Mandated by state and local districts, the official curriculum requires teachers to teach certain specific skills and subjects to students. For example, the Common Core State Standards and 21st Century Themes initiatives represent a new variation of the official curriculum. Some critical theorists would judge these recommendations by the Council of Chief State School Officers (CCSSO) and the National Governors Association Center as coming from groups that are external to the local on-site school community. The "hidden" curriculum imposes approved dominant group behaviors and attitudes on students through the school environment. The dominant classes use the official curriculum to transmit their particular beliefs and values as the legitimate version of knowledge for all students. Transmission, instead of critical thinking and analysis, reproduces in students the officially sanctioned and mandated version of knowledge. For example, the official version of history portrays the American experience as a largely white, male-dominated, European American series of triumphs in settling and industrializing the nation. Women, African Americans, Native Americans, and Latinos are marginalized afterthoughts to the official narrative.[68]

■ "Hidden" curriculum

The hidden curriculum is a key element in school-based social control. "Hidden" because it is not stated in published state mandates or local school policies, it permeates the public-school milieu. For example, sexist attitudes that males have a greater aptitude than females in mathematics and science maintain and reproduce gender-specific patterns of entry into education and careers in those fields.

Although the privileged classes have historically dominated schools, critical theorists do not see their domination as inevitable.[69] They believe that teachers, as critically minded activists, can transform schools into democratic public spheres in which they raise the consciousness of the exploited and empower the dispossessed.

■ Students' life stories

Critical theorists want students to construct their own meaningful knowledge and values in their local contexts, the immediate situations and communities in which they live and in the schools they attend. Teachers should begin consciousness-raising with the students by examining the conditions in their neighborhood communities. Students can share their life stories to create a collaborative group autobiography that recounts experiences at home, in school, and in the community. They can further connect this group autobiography to the larger histories of their respective economic classes and racial, ethnic, and language groups. For example, *The Freedom Writers Diary* is a compelling narrative of how Erin Gruwell, an English

---

[68]For the tensions between "official" and "nonofficial" history, see Peter N. Stearns, Peter Seixas, and Sam Wineburg, eds., *Knowing, Teaching, and Learning History: National and International Perspectives* (New York: New York University Press, 2000).

[69]Patricia H. Hinchey, *Becoming a Critical Educator: Defining a Classroom Identity, Designing a Critical Pedagogy* (New York: Peter Lang, 2004).

teacher at Woodrow Wilson High School in Long Beach, California, used autobiographical writing as a teaching method. Gruwell's students, categorized as at-risk students, wrote their autobiographies in diaries. They wrote about the conditions that they were experiencing in their own situations—violence, gang warfare, drug abuse, and poverty.[70]

The multicultural society in the United States provides many more versions of the American experience than the officially approved story. Members of each racial, ethnic, and language group can tell their own stories rather than having it told for them. After exploring their own identities, students can develop ways to recognize stereotyping and misrepresentation and to resist indoctrination both in and out of school. They can learn how to take control of their own lives and shape their own futures.[71]

Implications for Today's Classroom Teacher

Teachers must empower themselves

Critical theorists want teachers—in both their preservice preparation and classroom practice—to focus on issues of power and control in school and society. They urge teachers to (1) find out who their real friends are in the struggle for control of schools; (2) learn who their students are by helping them explore their own self-identities; (3) collaborate with local people to improve their school and community; (4) join with like-minded teachers in teacher-controlled professional organizations to empower themselves; and (5) participate in critical dialogues about political, social, economic, and educational issues that confront American society.

✓ Standards & Assessment

External limits on teachers' power

Critical theorists find that teachers' power in determining their own professional lives is severely limited. State boards, not teachers' professional organizations, largely determine entry requirements into the profession. Where standardized tests are used to determine schools' effectiveness and teachers' competency, teachers are judged by criteria mandated by state legislators and prepared by so-called experts external to their own schools and classrooms.

Question uses of technology

Michael Apple, a neo-Marxist curriculum theorist, warns that too much discussion about using educational technology in the classroom is rhetorical rather than motivated by a desire for genuine change. Unless educational technology is used to uncover the root issues of discrimination and poverty, he believes it is likely to bring an externally derived, "impersonal, prepackaged style" to education rather than one based on the schools' real internal conditions.[72]

A lesson with a critical-theory approach

Teachers using a critical-theory approach might design a unit in which middle-school social studies students explore their racial and ethnic heritages. Students begin by sharing their impressions of their heritage by telling stories about their families, their customs, and their celebrations. Then, parents and grandparents are invited in as guest speakers to share their cultural experiences with the students. Students then create a multicultural display that includes family photographs, artifacts, and other items that illustrate the lives and cultures of the people who live in the local community.

REFOCUS *Use these questions to construct your own philosophy of education. What elements of critical theory appeal to you as a teacher? Which appeal least? Why? Are there elements of critical theory that you would like to incorporate into your philosophy of education?*

---

[70]The Freedom Writers, with Erin Gruwell, *The Freedom Writers Diary: How a Teacher and 150 Teens Used Writing to Change Themselves and the World Around Them* (New York: Doubleday/ Random House, 1999). Also see the Freedom Writers Foundation at **www.freedomwritersfoundation.org**.

[71]Rage and Hope: Critical Theory and Its Impact on Education at **www.perfectfit.org/CT/index2.html**.

[72]Michael W. Apple, *Official Knowledge: Democratic Education in a Conservative Age* (New York and London: Routledge, 2000), pp. 132–133.

TAKING ISSUE

Read the brief introduction below, as well as the Question and the pros and cons list that follows, and then answer the question using your own words and position.

Teacher Objectivity or Commitment on Social, Political, and Economic Issues

There have been longstanding debates over the issue of whether teachers should teach matters dealing with society, politics, and the economy as objectively as possible or if they should teach in a way that is committed to deliberate social reform. In particular, the essentialists, progressives, and critical theorists take very different positions on teacher objectivity or commitment to social reform in their classrooms.

Question

Should teachers be objective when they teach about social, political, or economic issues in their classrooms?

Arguments PRO

1. Teachers should not use their classroom to indoctrinate students to accept a particular ideology of social, political, and economic change.

2. Teachers should be objective and present the various opinions on issues as fairly as possible.

3. Teachers should provide students with objective information on social, political, and economic issues, but student action on these issues should take place when they are adults not when they are children or teenagers.

Arguments CON

1. Teaching, like education, represents commitment to certain values; teachers need to endorse democratic and egalitarian values that are committed to social justice.

2. Objectivity or neutrality is not possible for teachers. When teachers claim to be objective, they are really supporting the status quo.

3. If teachers really want to have a voice in curriculum and instruction, they need to be actively not passively engaged in the political and economic decision-making process.

Question Reprise: What Is Your Stand?

Reflect again on the following question by explaining *your* stand on this issue: Should teachers be objective when they teach about social, political, or economic issues in their classrooms?

Constructing Your Personal Philosophy of Education

Throughout the chapter, you have been encouraged in the Refocus questions to reflect on how the philosophies and theories can be used in constructing your own philosophy of education. Now, it is time to bring your thoughts together in a summative experience—in which you sum up your ideas on your philosophy of education. You can return to the questions about knowledge, education, schooling, and teaching and learning, which were raised at the chapter's beginning. You can reconsider your initial beliefs about what is true and valuable. The Refocus questions asked whether you planned to incorporate elements of the philosophies and theories examined in this chapter in your own philosophy of education. Did your encounter with them cause you to revise or rethink your initial philosophical beliefs? In summing up your philosophical project, you can reconsider such questions as the following:

■ Do you believe that knowledge is based on universal and eternal truths, or is it relative to different times and places?

■ What is the purpose of education? Is it to transmit the culture, to provide economic and social skills, to develop critical-thinking skills, or to criticize and reform society?

- What are schools for? Are they to teach skills and subjects, encourage personal self-definition, develop human intelligence, or create patriotic and economically productive citizens?

- What should curriculum contain? Should it include basic skills and subjects, experiences and projects, the great books and the classics, inquiry processes, and/or critical dialogues?

- What should the relationship be between teachers and students? Should it include transmitting the heritage, teaching and learning skills and subjects, examining great ideas, encouraging self-expression and self-definition, constructing knowledge, or solving problems?

Summing Up

1 The chapter defined the terms *metaphysics, epistemology, axiology* (ethics and aesthetics), and *logic,* and discussed how these subdivisions of philosophy relate to questions of education, schooling, knowledge, and teaching and learning.

2 To provide a conceptual framework on education, we examined the philosophies of idealism, realism, pragmatism, existentialism, and postmodernism, as well as the theories of essentialism, perennialism, progressivism, and critical theory.

3 By studying these philosophies and theories of education, you can examine the underlying philosophical bases of curriculum and teaching and learning.

4 The chapter examined the philosophical rationales for education as transmission of the cultural heritage, skill and subject matter curriculum, process and problem-solving instruction, social change; and also standards and core curriculum.

Key Terms

The numbers indicate the pages where explanations of the key terms can be found.

philosophies 179
theories 179
metaphysics 180
epistemology 180
axiology 180
ethics 180
aesthetics 180
deductive logic 181
inductive logic 181
idealism 182

macrocosm 182
microcosm 182
a priori ideas 183
Socratic method 184
realism 185
pragmatism 187
experience 188
existentialism 192
postmodernism 194
constructivism 194

deconstruction 195
essentialism 198
perennialism 201
The Paideia Proposal 203
ethical relativism 203
progressivism 204
social reconstructionism 205
critical theory (critical pedagogy) 208
"hidden" curriculum 209

Certification Connection Activity

This chapter examines the philosophical underpinnings of educational theories. To prepare for Praxis II, use your conceptual framework to analyze the philosophical and theoretical underpinnings of the Common Core State Standards and Core Subjects and 21st Century Themes. You can find information on the Common Core State Standards and on the Core Subjects and 21st Century Themes on the Internet. Answer the following questions:

1 Is there a particular philosophy or theory of education that underlies these standards, subjects, and themes?

2 Or do these standards, subjects, and themes reflect a mixture of several philosophies or theories?

3 Do these standards, subjects, and themes agree or disagree with your personal philosophy?

Discussion Questions

1. Reflect on your ideas about knowledge, education, schooling, and teaching and learning. What is your philosophy of education? Share your ideas with your classmates, and listen to their philosophies. Discuss the agreements and disagreements that emerge. Reflect on strategies you might use to bring your school and teaching into more coherence with your philosophical beliefs.

2. Has your philosophy of education been influenced by significant teachers and mentors in your life or by books, motion pictures, and television programs about teachers and teaching? Share and discuss such influences with your classmates.

3. Identify the underlying philosophical and theoretical orientations in preservice courses in your teacher-education program. For example, is there an emphasis on skills and subjects, process learning, projects, or constructivism?

4. In your clinical observation, what underlying philosophical orientations can you detect in the practice of experienced teachers? Consider if these orientations reflect the philosophies and theories discussed in the chapter. For example, is there an emphasis on skills and subjects, process learning, projects, or constructivism?

5. Are there philosophies and theories or elements of philosophies and theories that you consider unacceptable or incompatible with contemporary American society and public education?

6. Of the philosophies and theories of education discussed in this chapter, which appear to be the most compatible with each other, and which are the most opposed?

7. Focus on a method of instruction that a professor is using in a course in your teacher-education program, and analyze it in terms of its philosophical orientation.

Suggested Projects for Professional Development

1. Access the "Rage and Hope: Critical Theory and Its Impact on Education" website on the Internet. The site provides information on such leaders of critical theory as Michael Apple, Henry Giroux, and Peter McLaren. How do these leaders interpret critical theory's implications for education and society?

2. Access William James's *Talks for Teachers* on the Internet. Analyze and identify James's major ideas on teaching. What philosophy underlies his educational principles?

3. Access the National Paideia Center and the Council for Basic Education on the Internet. Compare and contrast their approaches to education, curriculum, and instruction.

Identify the theories discussed in this chapter that support the Paideia and the Basic Education approaches to education.

4. Consider how autobiographical writing can aid in formulating your ideas about education. Access the Freedom Writers Foundation on the Internet for strategies that you might use in writing your own educational autobiography or the use of autobiographical writing as a teaching method.

5. Organize a working group, an informal seminar of students in this course, who meet periodically to discuss and share their problems and progress in writing their personal philosophies of education.

Suggested Resources

Internet Resources

For the relationship of existentialism to education, access Scott Webster, "Existentialism: Providing an ideal framework for educational researching times of uncertainty," at **www.aare .edu.au**.

For the Paideia philosophy, teaching strategies, and materials, access the National Paideia Center at **www.paideia.org**.

For Movietone News footage on John Dewey and audio excerpts on George Counts and Boyd Bode, access the Education Museum at the University of South Carolina at **www.ed.sc.edu /museum**.

For the publications of William James, access William James at **www.des.emory.edu/mfp/james.html**.

For recent research, projects, and programs on John Dewey and progressive education, consult the John Dewey Project on Progressive Education at the University of Vermont: **www.uvm .edu/~dewey**.

For resources on John Dewey's life and philosophy, consult the Center for Dewey Studies, Southern Illinois University at **www.siuc.edu/~deweyctr**.

For information and materials about basic education, consult the Council for Basic Education at **http://c-b-e.org**.

Publications

Barrow, Robin, and Ronald G. Woods. *An Introduction to Philosophy of Education*. New York: Routledge, 2006. *Provides a useful commentary about philosophy of education as a field.*

Beam, Alex, *A Great Idea at the Time: The Rise, Fall, and Curious Afterlife of the Great Books*. New York: Public Affairs, 2008. *A highly readable and engaging discussion of Hutchins, Mortimer Adler, and the Great Books curriculum.*

Butler, Christopher. *Postmodernism: A Very Short Introduction*. Oxford, UK: Oxford University Press, 2002. *A succinct and clearly written analysis of the major features and development of postmodernism.*

Cahn, Steven M. *Classic and Contemporary Readings in the Philosophy of Education*. New York: Oxford University Press, 2011. *Provides primary source selections from such classic theorists as Plato and Aristotle and contemporary theories such as feminism and multiculturalism.*

Carr, David. *Making Sense of Education: An Introduction to the Philosophy and Theory of Education and Teaching*. New York: Routledge Falmer, 2003. *Examines the philosophical connections between philosophy and teaching and learning.*

Curren, Randall, ed. *A Companion to the Philosophy of Education*. Malden, MA: Blackwell Publishing, 2006. *Contains interpretive essays and bibliographies on historical and contemporary movements in philosophy of education.*

Erneling, Christina E. *Towards Discursive Education: Philosophy, Technology, and Modern Education*. New York: Cambridge University Press, 2010. *Considers the implications of education, philosophy, and psychology for technology.*

Grinberg, Jaime G. A., Lewis Tyson, and Megan Laverty. *Playing with Ideas: Modern and Contemporary Philosophies of Education*. Dubuque, IA: Kendall Hunt Publishing, 2007. *An engaging and lively discussion of significant contemporary educational philosophies.*

Gutek, Gerald. *New Perspectives on Philosophy and Education*. Columbus, OH: Pearson, 2009. *A discussion and commentary on historical and contemporary philosophies of education.*

Gutek, Gerald L. *Philosophical and Ideological Voices in Education*. Boston: Allyn and Bacon, 2004. *Provides discussions of the major philosophies, ideologies, and theories of education with representative primary source selections.*

Hansen, David T. *Ethical Visions of Education: Philosophy and Practice*. New York: Teachers College Press, 2007. *Provides a discussion of how leading philosophers and theorists of education sought to integrate their ideas into classroom practice.*

Hansen, David T., ed. *John Dewey and Our Educational Prospect: A Critical Engagement with Dewey's Democracy and Education*. Albany: State University of New York Press, 2006. *Provides an analysis of Dewey's highly influential book,* Democracy and Education.

Hinchey, Patricia H. *Becoming a Critical Educator: Defining a Classroom Identity, Designing a Critical Pedagogy*. New York: Peter Lang, 2004. *Hinchey's book applies critical theory to schools and classrooms.*

Noddings, Nel. *Philosophy of Education*. Boulder, CO: Westview Press, 2011. *Provides an excellent overview of philosophy of education in relation to teaching, learning, schools, and policy with attention to contemporary issues such as standards and tests.*

Riley, Karen, ed. *Social Reconstruction: People, Politics, Perspectives*. Greenwich, CT: Information Age Publishing, 2006. *Contains analyses of social reconstructionism in historical and educational perspectives.*

Watras, Joseph. *Philosophical Conflicts in American Education, 1893–2000*. Boston, MA: Allyn and Bacon, 2004. *Analyzes major movements in curriculum and instruction from philosophical and historical perspectives.*

Watts, Leonard J., ed. *Leaders in Philosophy of Education: Intellectual Self Portraits*. Boston: Sense Publishers, 2008. *Discusses the work of leading philosophers of education in examining intellectual and practical virtues, women's education, creativity, multiculturalism, and globalization.*

Additional resources for this chapter, including the TeachSource Videos, can be found on the Education CourseMate website. Go to **CengageBrain.com** to access the site.

PART THREE

Political, Economic, and Legal Foundations

Governing and Administering Public Education

Education in the United States is organized on four governmental levels: local, intermediate (in some states), state, and federal. Understanding the formal organization of schools and how they are governed can help you make wise choices and realistic decisions about schools and take appropriate political action. In this chapter, we examine the various governmental levels and how they affect education.

The United States does not have a centralized, national education system like those in Great Britain, France, or Japan. We have fifty different state educational systems and many differences among local school systems even within the same state.

The U.S. Constitution makes no mention of public education, but the Tenth Amendment to the Constitution reserves to the states all powers not specifically delegated to the federal government or prohibited to the states by the Constitution. This amendment is the basis for allocating to the states primary legal responsibility for public education. However, the states have delegated varying degrees of responsibility for day-to-day school system operations to local districts. So we begin our discussion of how schools are governed and administered at the local level. As you read this chapter, think about the following questions:

FOCUS QUESTIONS

- How do local, state, and federal governments influence education?
- How does the local school board work with the district superintendent in formulating school policy?
- Why have many school districts consolidated?

- What are the various roles and responsibilities of the governor, state legislature, state board of education, state department of education, and chief state school officer in determining school policy?
- How has the federal role in education changed over the years?

*This chapter was revised by Dr. David E. Vocke, Towson University.

Local Responsibilities and Activities

Every public school in the United States is part of a local school district. The district is created by the state. The state legislature, subject to the restrictions of the state constitution, can modify a local district's jurisdiction, change its boundaries and powers, or even eliminate it altogether. In most states, the local district encompasses a relatively small geographical area and operates schools for children within specific communities. However, because a school district operates on behalf of the state, local policies must be consistent with policies set forth in the state school code.

Characteristics of Local School Boards

Responsibilities of local boards

Despite the fact that the state limits their prerogatives, **local school boards** have been delegated and assume significant decision-making responsibility. Many school boards have the power to raise money through local tax initiatives. They exercise power over personnel and school property. Most states leave student policy largely to local school boards, but others, by law, impose specific requirements or limitations.

Most school boards elected

Methods of selecting board members are prescribed by state law. The two standard methods are election and appointment. Election is thought to make for greater accountability to the public, but some people argue that appointment leads to greater competence and less politics. Election, by far the most common practice, accounts for more than 94 percent of school-board members nationwide.[1] A few states specify a standard number of board members, others specify a permissible range, and a few have no requirements. Most school boards fall within a five-to-eight-member range.

School board diversity: A continuing concern

Many educators are concerned about whether school boards adequately reflect the diversity of the communities they serve. A recent nationwide survey from the National School Board Association reports that the number of women on local school boards in 2010 stood at 44 percent, up from 33 percent in 1981 (see Figure 7.1). Minority representation increased over the same period, from 8.5 percent to 19.3 percent, but continues to lag behind the rising proportion of minority students in U.S. public schools (44 percent in 2010).[2] Large school systems (those enrolling fifteen thousand or more students) tend to have more racially heterogeneous boards. The survey indicated that minority members constituted approximately 28 percent of the school-board membership in these systems; women made up 51.7 percent.[3]

The majority of school-board members (60 percent) are between 40 and 59 years of age, and 34 percent are over the age of 60. Board members tend to be more educated than the general population (74 percent have had four or more years of college) and wealthier (48.6 percent earn more than $100,000 annually). They are likely to be educators, professionals, or businesspeople (59 percent). Thirty-eight percent have children currently enrolled in school. School districts are aware that whether or not board

[1]Frederick M. Hess and Olivia Meeks, *School Boards Circa 2010: Governance in the Accountability Era* (Alexandria, VA: National School Boards Association, 2010).
[2]Ibid., p. 38; Frederick M. Hess, *School Boards at the Dawn of the 21st Century: Conditions and Challenges of District Governance* (Alexandria, VA: National School Boards Association, 2002); and *Digest of Education Statistics,* 2010, at **http://nces.ed.gov/programs/digest/d10/tables/dt10_021.asp**, Table 21 (October 2011).
[3]Frederick M. Hess and Olivia Meeks, *School Boards Circa 2010: Governance in the Accountability Era.*

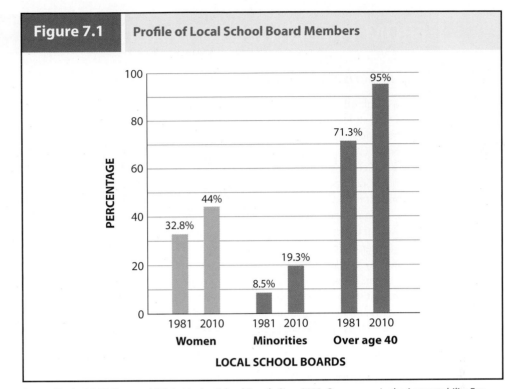

Figure 7.1   Profile of Local School Board Members

Source: Frederick M. Hess and Olivia Meeks, *School Boards Circa 2010: Governance in the Accountability Era* (Alexandria, VA: National School Boards Association, 2010).

members have children in the district's schools can affect the board members' policy-making agendas, although different districts react to this knowledge differently. Some school districts require board members to have school-age children; other districts permit children of board members to attend school *outside* the district.

Age and socioeconomic factors may contribute to board members' political views. Thirty-two percent of board members see their political affiliation as conservative, 47.3 percent claim to be moderate, and 20.4 percent identified themselves as liberal. Board members' general political views may, in turn, contribute to their votes on school issues in their districts.[4]

Types of board meetings

School boards hold three types of meetings: regular, special, and executive. The first two are usually open to the public. The third type, usually closed to the public, deals with personnel issues, acquisition of property, or problems related to individual students. Open board meetings obviously enhance school-community relations and allow parents and other citizens to understand the issues encompassing the system's schools as well as to air their concerns. The use of closed board meetings to reach major policy decisions is often criticized and violates "sunshine laws," the requirement that meetings of government agencies be open to the public, in many states. The "From Preservice to Practice" feature describes an open executive meeting.

Pressure on school boards

School-board members experience considerable pressure as they listen to and weigh the competing demands of citizen advisory groups, the business community, parents with special concerns (such as students with special needs, gifted and talented programs, school discipline, and allocation of resources), the teachers' association, and local and state politicians, who often are key in funding decisions. Some decisions have winners and losers; high priorities take precedence over lower ones, and funding constraints frequently mean difficult (and occasionally unpopular) decisions.

---

[4]Frederick M. Hess and Olivia Meeks, *School Boards Circa 2010: Governance in the Accountability Era.*

FROM PRESERVICE TO PRACTICE

A Partnership in Decision Making?

As everyone assembled for the school board's regular meeting, Dr. Clore, superintendent of schools, nodded to the president of the school board that he was ready for the meeting to commence.

This would be a difficult meeting. They would be considering all administrative contracts, but special concerns had arisen about the contract of Tom Day, the principal of Westside Elementary–Middle School. Many parents and teachers were upset that the school had failed to meet adequate yearly progress, even with the greater flexibility for meeting standards that had been announced by the state department of education, for a second straight year. These groups had generated a small mountain of documentation to support their point of view and had pushed their request for his termination through all of the school district's required steps up to tonight's announcement of the decision. Dr. Clore, too, had recommended that the board not renew Mr. Day's contract. He had worked with him but had seen no improvement. In his mind, Principal Day was not an instructional leader. Day had poor communication with faculty, staff, and parents and seemed to lead from behind the principal's desk rather than through proactive interaction with others.

Other parents and former students, however, continued to support Principal Day and had been lobbying both publicly and privately with individual board members for his retention.

Dr. Clore looked around. On one side of the room sat the parents and teachers who supported Mr. Day, ready to raise their objections if—more like "when," thought Dr. Clore—the board announced Day's departure. On the other side sat those who had worked to remove him. It looked like a no-win situation. "Tonight," Dr. Clore thought, "we are all at a crossroad."

Dr. Clore wished, again, that the state's sunshine laws, designed to encourage openness in governmental decision making, permitted a little more privacy about personnel matters. Although much of the deliberation had already been conducted behind closed doors in executive session, the announcement of contracts had to be made in an open meeting.

"Well," he thought to himself, "at least it will all finally be over with fairly quickly." The policy of this board was to allow a maximum of five minutes of citizen input on any agenda item. Each group with a similar view would have to select a representative to speak. Dr. Clore was certain that the pro and con groups of parents were prepared to have a representative speak before the board, although he was less sure about the teachers. That meant at least ten minutes of unpleasantness.

He hoped nothing got out of hand. The school board president was relatively new to his position, and personnel considerations could become emotional. Dr. Clore knew that if the procedures were not followed exactly, a lawsuit could follow.

Case Questions

1. Ideally, school boards and superintendents work in partnership. How would you define the roles of the superintendent and school board in this situation?
2. What legal issues could arise if the mandated procedures were not followed at this meeting?
3. What role, if any, might teachers have in such personnel decisions?
4. In a larger district, how might central office staff other than the superintendent be involved in an issue such as this?
5. What might be a better way for the school board to handle this potentially explosive situation?

School-board members make up one of the largest groups of elected representatives in the state governance system. It is important to remember that the board's role is to *govern* the local school district, not to micromanage the day-to-day operations of the system. In the following section, the specific responsibilities of the school board are delineated.[5]

School Board Responsibilities

Schools are big business

School administration and management is big business, and school-board members must understand good business practices. Overall, U.S. school boards have fiscal responsibility for $605 billion each year and employ more than 6.3 million teachers,

[5]John Cassel and Tim Holt, "The Servant Leader," *American School Board Journal* (October 2008), pp. 34–35.

administrators, and support staff (such as guidance counselors, librarians, and instructional aides).[6] They constitute the largest nationwide employer. Many school-board members (41 percent) will spend more than twenty-five hours per month on school-board business.[7] Board members must be fair and mindful of the law when dealing with students, teachers, administrators, parents, and other community residents.

The powers and responsibilities of school boards may be classified as follows:

1. *Policy.* School boards set the general rules about what is done in the schools, who does it, and how. The shift to school-based management has changed the what, who, and how, permitting greater involvement of teachers, school-based administrators, and parent groups in day-to-day school operation and direction.

2. *Staffing.* Technically, the board is responsible for hiring all school district employees. In practice, however, school boards usually confine themselves to recruiting and selecting the school superintendent (the district's chief executive officer) and high-ranking members of the central office staff. Decisions on hiring and retaining principals and teachers are usually delegated to the district's administrators.

3. *Employee relations.* School-board members are responsible for all aspects of employee relations, including collective bargaining with teacher unions. Large school districts rely on consultants or attorneys to negotiate with teachers, but small school districts may use the superintendent or a school-board committee.

4. *Fiscal matters.* The board must keep the school district solvent and get the most out of every tax dollar. The school district usually has a larger budget than any other aspect of local government. This is an especially critical responsibility in harsh economic times as we have seen in the past few years.

5. *Students.* The board addresses questions of student rights and responsibilities, requirements for promotion and graduation, extracurricular activities, and attendance.

6. *Curriculum and assessment.* The school board develops curriculum—especially development related to federal and state law and guidelines—and approves textbook selections. Likewise, the board must implement and report on high-stakes state assessments.

7. *Community relations.* The school board must respond not only to parents but also to other members of the community.

8. *Intergovernmental requirements.* Federal and state agencies establish a variety of requirements for local schools, and the local school board is responsible for seeing that these mandates are carried out.[8]

Board members are expected to govern the school system without encroaching on the superintendent's authority. Members, in theory, have no authority except during a board meeting and while acting as a collective group or board.[9] They also must be politically prudent. Eventually, someone will ask for a favor, and members must be able to resist this pressure.

[6]Public Education Finances: 2009—Figure 2. "Percentage Distribution of Total Public Elementary-Secondary School System Expenditure: 2008–2009 (Washington, D.C.: U.S. Census Bureau, May 2011) at **www2.census.gov/govs/school/09f33pub.pdf**; and *Digest of Education Statistics, 2010,* at **http://nces.ed.gov/programs/digest/d10/tables/dt10_085.asp?referrer=list,** Table 85 (October 2011).
[7]Frederick M. Hess and Olivia Meeks, *School Boards Circa 2010: Governance in the Accountability Era.*
[8]Edwin C. Darden, "Responsibility and Obligation," *American School Board Journal* (August 2007), pp. 42–43; Education Commission of the States, "ECS Education Policy Issue Site: School Boards," at **http://ecs.org/html/issue.asp?issueid=103** (October 2011); and National School Boards Association, "Key Work of School Boards," at **www.nsba.org/Board-Leadership/Governance/KeyWork** (October 2011).
[9]Robert L. Zorn, "Educating New Board Members," *American School Board Journal* (August 2008), pp. 26–27; and Jason Cabico and Erica E. Harrison, "Getting on Board," *Kennedy School Review* (2009), pp. 19–24.

The School Superintendent and Central Office Staff

Executive officer of school system

One of the board's most important responsibilities is to appoint a competent **superintendent of schools**.[10] The superintendent is the chief executive officer of the school system, whereas the board is the legislative policy-making body. Sometimes, the superintendent literally is a CEO. Although the vast majority of superintendents are educators, a growing number of school districts, most notably Seattle, New York, Pittsburgh, Providence, and Los Angeles, have hired leaders from the private sector or the military as superintendents.[11]

As with school boards, concerns have emerged that superintendents fail to reflect the diversity of the districts they serve. Currently, 76 percent of school superintendents are men, 24 percent are women—up from 6.6 percent in 1992—and only 6 percent are members of minority groups.[12]

The school board, which consists of laypeople rather than experts in school affairs, is responsible for seeing that schools are properly run by the professional education personnel. The board of education often delegates many of its own legal powers to the superintendent and staff, especially in larger districts, although the superintendent's policies are subject to board approval.

Board reliance on superintendent

A major function of the school superintendent is to gather and present data so that school-board members can make intelligent policy decisions. The superintendent advises the school board and keeps members abreast of problems; generally, the school board refuses to enact legislation or make policy without the school superintendent's recommendation. However, in cases of continual disagreement or major policy conflict between the school board and the superintendent, the latter is usually replaced. The average tenure of superintendents is about 7 years. In large urban districts, the average is lower, at 3.6 years[13] The reasons most superintendents give for losing their jobs are communication breakdowns and micromanagement (interference in school administration) by the board.[14] What would Dr. Clore's feelings be about school-board interference and micromanagement?

Duties of the superintendent

Besides advising the board of education, the superintendent usually is responsible for many other functions, including the following:

1. *Management of professional and nonteaching personnel* (for example, custodians and cafeteria workers)

2. *Leadership in curriculum, instruction, and assessment* (ensuring decisions about curriculum and instruction are based on data derived from district assessments)

3. *Administrative management* (including district organization, budgeting, long-range planning, and complying with directives from state and federal agencies)

In addition, the superintendent oversees day-to-day operation of the district schools and serves as the major spokesperson for the schools.[15]

---

[10]Edgar B. Hatrick, "Searching for Excellence in a Superintendent," *School Administrator* (2010), p. 41.

[11]Caralee Adams, "No Experience Needed?" *Scholastic Administrator* (Winter 2011), pp. 33–36; Ericka Mellon, "Army Strong, Superintendent Savvy," *District Administration* (May 2011), pp. 71–77; and Christina Samuels, "Broad Academy's Growing Reach Draws Scrutiny," *Education Week* (June 8, 2011), pp. 1–13.

[12]Angela Pascopella, "State of the Superintendency," *District Administration* (February 2008), pp. 32–36; Theodore J. Kowalski, Robert S. McCord, George J. Petersen, I. Phillip Young, and Noelle M. Ellerson, *The American School Superintendent: 2010 Decennial Study* (Lanham, MD: Rowman & Littlefield Education, 2010); and Daniel A. Domenech, "AASA's Status Check on the Superintendency," *School Administrator* (December 2010), p. 47.

[13]J. H. Snider, "The Superintendent as Scapegoat," *Education Week* (January 11, 2006), pp. 40–41; and "Urban School Superintendents: Characteristics, Tenure, and Salary Seventh Survey and Report," *Urban Indicator* (Washington, D.C.: Council of the Great City Schools, Fall 2010).

[14]Donald R. McAdams, "Getting Your Board Out of Micromanagement," *School Administrator* (November 2008), p. 6.

[15]Doug Eadie, "Prescription for Success," *American School Board Journal* (August 2008), pp. 46–47; and Lee Mitgang, "Flipping the Script," *School Administrator* (December 2010), pp. 15–18.

Community pressure on superintendents

Superintendents often experience strong pressure from various segments of the community, such as disgruntled parents or organized community groups with their own agendas (sometimes overt, sometimes covert). Much of the superintendent's effectiveness depends on his or her ability to deal with such pressure groups. Only a confident school leader can balance the demands and expectations of parents and community groups with the ultimate goal of improving learning for all students in the district. Experts agree that the key to success as a superintendent is communication—with school-board members, citizen groups, teachers, parents, unions, and elected officials. Failure to build citizen, legislative, and political support quickly leads to discord between the superintendent and the various stakeholders.[16]

Central office organization

A **central office staff** assists the superintendent (see Figure 7.2). Large districts of 25,000 or more students, which represent only 2 percent of all school districts in the United States, may have many levels in the staff hierarchy: a deputy superintendent, associate superintendents, assistant superintendents, directors, department heads, and coordinators and supervisors—each with their own support staffs.[17] Small school districts usually have a less bureaucratic central office.

Critique of bureaucracy

Critics charge that the many-layered bureaucracies of large school districts are inefficient and a waste of taxpayers' money. Actually, the responsibilities of central offices are diverse and complex, including interacting with federal and state education agencies, processing payroll and contracts, monitoring human resources, and overseeing construction, transportation, and purchasing. Additionally, with the mandates since No Child Left Behind (NCLB), central offices have been faced with more pressure to direct the districts' schools.[18]

The Principal and the School

Most schools have a single administrative officer, a **principal**, who is responsible for school operations. Interestingly, 59 percent of elementary-school and 29 percent of secondary-school principals are women. In small schools, the principal may teach part-time as well; large schools may have one or more assistant or vice principals. The administrative hierarchy may also include department chairpersons, discipline officers (for instance, a dean of students), and guidance counselors. Each of these individuals works closely with the school principal and under his or her direction. Furthermore, most principals work with a community-based school improvement group, often a parent-teacher association or a school-based management team.[19]

The principal's role

Traditionally, the most important aspect of the principal's job is the role of manager: dealing with day-to-day school operations, meetings, paperwork, phone calls, and everyday tasks. Today, however, there is increasing pressure to demonstrate improved student performance on mandated assessments. Principals must focus on the cycle of curriculum development, instruction, assessment, and data analysis. The successful principal has to be adept at collaborating with various stakeholders to make "data-driven decisions" that raise student achievement.[20]

---

[16]Donald R. McAdams, "Responding to Board Member Requests for Information," *School Administrator* (March 2008), p. 6; and Edgar B. Hatrick, "Searching for Excellence in a Superintendent," *School Administrator* (October 2010), p. 41.

[17]Kathleen Vail, "The Changing Face of Education," *Education Vital Signs* (2003) at **www.nsba .org**; and *Digest of Education Statistics* (2010) at **http://nces.ed.gov/programs/digest/d10 /tables/dt10_091.asp?referrer=list,** Table 91 (October 2011).

[18]Hayes Mizell, "The Central Office Must Evolve," *Journal of Staff Development* (June 2010), pp. 46–48.

[19]Laura A. Cooper, "The Principal as Instructional Leader," *Principal* (January 1989), pp. 13–16; Allan C. Ornstein, "Leaders and Losers," *Executive Educator* (August 1993), pp. 28–30; and "Indicator 33-2011: Characteristics of School Principals," *The Condition of Education 2011* at **http://nces.ed.gov/programs/coe/indicator_pal.asp** (October 2011).

[20]Kevin Butler, "Principal Preparation Programs," *District Administration* (September 2008), pp. 66–70; Douglas B. Reeves, "Looking Deeper into the Data," *Educational Leadership* (December 2008), pp. 89–90; and Center for the Future of Teaching and Learning, and International SRI, "School Leadership: A Key to Teaching Quality. A Policy Brief on the Role of Principals in Strengthening Instruction," *Center for the Future of Teaching and Learning* (January 1, 2011).

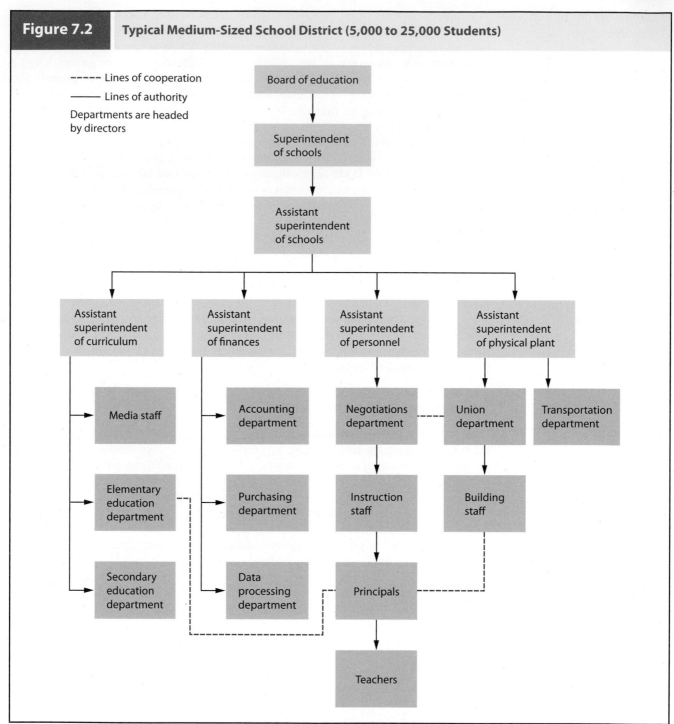

Figure 7.2 Typical Medium-Sized School District (5,000 to 25,000 Students)

This figure shows the organizational chart of a medium-sized school district with 5,000 to 25,000 students, representative of almost 12 percent of school districts nationwide. Small school districts, with 1,000 to 5,000 students—about 38 percent of all districts nationally—have much simpler organizational structures. The organizational hierarchy of larger school districts is cumbersome; a chart of a district with 100,000 or more students would extend off the page.

Source: Digest of Educational Statistics, 2010, Table 91, at http://nces.ed.gov/programs/digest/d10/tables/dt10_091.asp?referrer=list

Continuity & Change

In the past, secondary-school principals were often considered primarily as general managers, whereas elementary-school principals viewed themselves as leaders in curriculum and instruction.[21] This was likely because larger secondary schools create

[21]Lynn K. Bradshaw, "The Changing Role of Principals in School Partnerships," *NASSP Bulletin* (May 2000) pp. 86–96; and Steven M. Kimball, "Human Capital Managers at Every School" *Phi Delta Kappan* (April 2011), pp. 13–18.

Principals have multiple responsibilities but it is probably most important that they view themselves as leaders in curriculum, instruction, and assessment.

Steve Hix/Somos Images/Corbis

more managerial work for the principal. Today, however, because of the mandates of NCLB, all principals must be able to craft a collective school effort to analyze academic data to improve teaching and learning for all students. If a principal is unsuccessful, and the school fails to meet the accountability mandates, it will likely face corrective action, and the principal in the failing school will face surrendering his or her leadership position. As a teacher, how will you interact with your principal? In large secondary schools, a teacher's interaction with the principal might be minimal, consisting of primarily formal observations; faculty meetings; cafeteria, hall, or bus duty; and conversations in the main office. In contrast, many elementary-school teachers have frequent, almost daily, contact with the principal, and these encounters can cover a wide range of school- and student-related issues.

REFOCUS What would be the ideal relationship between you, as a new teacher, and the principal at your school? Do you think you would ever like to serve as a principal?

Customarily, authority concerning school policies flows from the top down, from the school board through the superintendent and central office staff to the principal. In some districts, however, as explained in Chapter 2, The Teaching Profession, *Professional Learning Communities* (PLCs) have provided principals and teachers increased responsibility for such matters as curriculum, professional development, teaching assignments, and classroom practices. Collaboration with teachers and other school staff to create school policies that improve student learning calls for a more participatory governance style among school principals.[22]

■ Influence of Professional Learning Communities

Parent and Community Involvement

Many collaborative school programs go beyond principals and teachers by giving important roles to parents and other community members, as well. In doing so, they build on a movement for increased parent and community involvement evident since the 1970s.

■ Reasons for parent involvement

Many educators have promoted parent involvement for the most basic of reasons: Research indicates that it pays off in higher student test scores, better grades, an

---

[22]NASSP, *Changing Role of the Middle Level and High School Leader: Learning from the Past – Preparing for the Future* (Reston, VA: National Association of Secondary School Principals, 2007); and *The Principal Story* (New York: The Wallace Foundation, 2009) at **www.wallacefoundation.org /principal-story/Pages/default.aspx** (October 2011).

▶❙❙ **TEACHSOURCE VIDEO ACTIVITY**

Parental Involvement in School Culture: A Literacy Project

Go to the Education CourseMate website to access the video entitled, "Parental Involvement in School Culture: A Literacy Project." Does this video show effective examples of parental involvement? As you watch the parents working on this school project, think about other ways parents can be involved, and answer the following questions:

1 What is the motivation of Patricia and Monica, parents of students, to become involved in the literacy project?

2 From the perspective of the classroom teacher, describe both the benefits and challenges of having parents involved in school culture.

Uninvolved parents

Types of community involvement

Types of community participation

---

increase in student attendance, reduced drop-out rates, and improved attitudes toward learning, particularly for inner-city and minority students.[23] Across the nation, polls indicate that the public overwhelmingly supports the idea of parent involvement and believes that parents play a major role in children's education. As a result of this support, parent involvement has been a key component of NCLB and is a major component of the Obama administration's plan to reauthorize the Elementary and Secondary Education Act (ESEA).[24]

Nevertheless, teachers perceive that parents are reluctant to take full advantage of existing opportunities to involve themselves with their children's schooling. In a Department of Education survey of parents, 46 percent of parents claimed that they volunteered at school, while 78 percent reported that they attended a parent-teacher conference.[25] Some parents, according to research, avoid school involvement because of feelings of inadequacy, negative experiences in schools as students, and negative perceptions of administrator and teacher attitudes.[26] However, in a survey of parents with children enrolled in urban schools, 83 percent of respondents indicated they felt respected by school personnel.[27]

The pressure for school reform has produced formal arrangements that give parents and other community members a voice in local educational decisions. For purposes of discussion, we can divide community involvement into three broad categories: community participation, community control, and community schools.

Community Participation The usual form of **community participation** involves advisory committees at either the neighborhood school or central board level. These committees are commonly appointed by school officials and offer the school board help and advice. Citizen groups provide advice and assistance in many areas:

---

[23]Anne T. Henderson, Karen L. Mapp, Vivian R. Johnson, and Don Davies, *Beyond the Bake Sale: The Essential Guide to Family–School Partnerships* (New York: The New Press, 2006); and Jennifer J. Salopek, "Make Parents Your Partners," *Education Update* (February 2011), pp. 1, 4, 5.
[24]Jennifer DePlanty, Russell Coulter-Kern, and Kim A. Duchane, "Perceptions of Parent Involvement in Academic Achievement," *Journal of Educational Research* (July 2007), pp. 361–368; and *Supporting Families and Communities* (Washington, D.C.: United States Department of Education, June 2010) at **www2.ed.gov/policy/elsec/leg/blueprint/faq/supporting-family.pdf**.
[25]*Digest of Education Statistics, 2010,* at **http://nces.ed.gov/programs/digest/d10/tables /dt10_061.asp?referrer=list**, Table 61 (October 2011); and Larry Ferlasso, "Involvement or Engagement?" *Educational Leadership* (May 2011), pp. 10–14.
[26]Gregory Flynn and Barbara Nolan, "What Do School Principals Think About Current School-Family Relationships?" *NASSP Bulletin* (September 2008), pp. 173–190; and Nancy Protheroe, "The School-Family Connection," *Principal* (November 2010), pp. 28–33.
[27]Brian Perkins, *What We Think: Parental Perceptions of Urban School Climate* (Alexandria, VA: National School Boards Association, 2008); and Ann Bradley, "Poll: Urban Parents Find Schools Safe," *Education Week* (May 7, 2008), p. 4.

(1) identification of goals, priorities, and needs; (2) development of curricula and extra-curricular programs; (3) support for financing schools; (4) recruitment of volunteers; and (5) assistance to students in school and in "homework hotline" programs. Nearly every state has a parent involvement law.[28]

Shared power

Community Control In a system of **community control,** an elected community council or board does more than offer advice—it shares decision-making power with the central school board.

Experience in Chicago

Since the 1990s, Chicago Public Schools have practiced a form of community control, known as *local school councils* (LSCs), as part of local educational reform designed to improve academic achievement. Members of LSCs are elected to two-year terms. The councils are responsible for approving how funds and resources are allocated, developing and monitoring school improvement plans, and monitoring and evaluating the school's principal. Though Chicago teachers, administrators, and LSCs generally felt positive about the administrative changes, the larger community of businesspeople, citizens, parents, and legislators did not.[29]

Operation of charter schools

Perhaps the newest major development in community involvement in education is the establishment of **charter schools** (discussed in more detail in Chapter 16, School Effectiveness and Reform in the United States). In this arrangement, the local school board or state board of education grants a community group or private organization a *charter* (a contract listing specific rights, privileges, and expectations) that permits the group to establish and operate a public school. Specific arrangements about finance, school operation, physical location, student enrollment, teacher work conditions, and accountability are negotiated. If the charter school fails to meet prescribed accountability standards, its charter is revoked, and the school is closed.[30] See the Taking Issue box for a discussion of the pros and cons of charter schools.

Partnerships to improve achievement

Community Schools Since the early 1980s, the school has come to be seen as only one of the educational agencies within the community. Under this concept—called **community schools**—the school serves as a partner, or coordinating agency, in providing educational, health, social, family support, recreational, and cultural activities to the community. Such concentrated efforts are designed to increase student achievement and provide a safe and supportive environment. In Providence, Rhode Island, for example, students in the Providence Full Service Community Schools (PFSCS) program had 55 percent fewer incidences of chronic absenteeism among participants than in the general school population. The PFSCS program included a family literacy program, health and wellness services, before- and after-school programs, a summer program, and family engagement initiatives.[31] Programs such as these are especially helpful for low-income families.

Sharing among agencies

As part of the community schools plan, schools share their personnel and facilities with other community agencies or even businesses. In return, schools may expect to share facilities, equipment, and personnel with other community agencies, local businesses, and area universities. This type of sharing is especially important in a period of retrenchment and school budget pressures.

---

[28]Mavis Sanders, "Building Bridges Toward Excellence: Community Involvement in High Schools," *High School Journal* (February–March 2005), pp. 1–9; Kyle Zinth, "Parental Involvement in Education," *State Notes* (Denver, CO: Education Commission of the States, March 2005); Gavin Shatkin and Alec Ian Gershberg, "Empowering Parents and Building Communities," *Urban Education* (November 2007), pp. 582–615; and Kavitha Mediratta, Seema Shah, Sara McAlister, Norm Fruchter, Christina Mokhtar, and Dana Lockwood, *Organized Communities, Stronger Schools* (New York: Annenberg Institute for School Reform at Brown University, March 2008).
[29]Gavin Shatkin and Alec Ian Gershberg, "Empowering Parents and Building Communities," *Urban Education* (November 2007), pp. 582–615; and Chicago Public Schools, *Local School Councils* at **www.cps.edu/pages/Localschoolcouncils.aspx** (October 2011).
[30]Carlee Adams, "Is a Charter School, Right for You?" *Instructor* (November 2008), pp. 23–25; and National Alliance for Public Charter School, *About Charter Schools* at **www.publiccharters .org/About-Charter-Schools.aspx** (October 2011).
[31]Coalition for Community Schools, *Top Community Schools Research* at **www.communityschools .org/aboutschools/top_community_schools_research.aspx** (October 2011).

TAKING ISSUE

Read the brief introduction below, as well as the Question and the pros and cons list that follows. Then, answer the question using your own words and position.

Charter Schools as Public School Reform

As the pressure for school choice increases, so has the public's desire for greater participation in its schools. The Obama administration and Secretary of Education Duncan promote charter schools as an avenue for school choice and a way to spur reform.

Question

Should local boards of education continue to support charter schools as a better way to educate students? (Think about this question as you read the PRO and CON arguments listed below. What is *your* take on this issue?)

Arguments PRO

1. Charter schools provide an alternative vision of schooling that is not realized in the traditional public-school system.

2. Charter schools have increased autonomy from state and local school district regulations.

3. Special populations of students may be served by charter schools.

4. Students, teachers, and parents participate by choice and are committed to making charter schools work; true collaboration is possible. Teachers are given freedom to craft the curriculum in creative ways, as long as standards are met.

5. Charter schools are generally smaller and more manageable in size.

6. Parental involvement and overall communication are increased in charter schools. There is a sense of community among stakeholders.

Arguments CON

1. Accountability goals frequently are not clearly spelled out by sponsors in charter schools, leading to misunderstanding and confusion.

2. State and federal regulations still apply to charter schools and tend to restrain their independence.

3. Charter schools often receive inadequate funding for start-up and operating expenses, especially if they serve special populations that require high expenditures.

4. Charter schools have difficulty finding staff, and there is high teacher attrition.

5. Charter schools tend to "skim" the more talented students for admission, thus ignoring more challenging students.

6. Insufficient planning time for charter school boards, principals, and staff makes for management and communication problems later on.

Question Reprise: What Is Your Stand?

Reflect again on the following question by explaining *your* stand about this issue: Should local boards of education continue supporting charter schools?

Size of Schools and School Districts

Debate about school size

Educators have long debated the question of size: How many students should be enrolled in a single district? How large should a school be? Five decades ago, James Conant argued that the most effective high schools were the ones large enough to offer comprehensive and diversified facilities. More recently, however, other educators have contended that small schools are more effective.[32]

---

[32]James B. Conant, *The American High School Today* (New York: McGraw-Hill, 1959); and Kenneth Leithwood and Doris Jantzi, "A Review of Empirical Evidence about School Size Effects: A Policy Perspective," *Review of Educational Research* (January 1, 2009), pp. 464–490.

> ▶ ❚❚   **TEACHSOURCE VIDEO ACTIVITY**

Effective Schools Correlates Visible in Gates Foundation Schools

After reading this section, go to the Education CourseMate website to watch the ABC News video entitled, "Effective Schools Correlates Visible in Gates Foundation Schools." At the Bronx Engineering and Technology Academy, a strong curriculum, devoted teachers, high expectations, and small classes help students from challenging backgrounds learn the skills and ambition to move forward with big dreams.

❶ The Bronx Engineering and Technology Academy utilizes a small-school strategy to enhance student achievement. What factors go into making this school successful?

❷ How is this school different from/similar to the schools you attended?

_____

** This video reinforces key concepts found in Section IV: Profession and Community of the Praxis II Exam.**

Problems of large schools

In 1987, after reviewing several studies, two researchers concluded that high schools should have no more than 250 students. Larger enrollments, according to this analysis, result in a preoccupation with control and order, and the anonymity of a large school makes it harder to establish a sense of community among students, teachers, and parents.[33] More than twenty years later, school systems are applying these lessons to high schools. For example, a 2010 study of 123 small high schools in New York City, known as small schools of choice (SSCs), which are limited to 100 students per grade, found that the SSCs improved graduation rates and college readiness of disadvantaged students more so than those of comparable schools.[34]

Past studies indicate that learning is best in high schools of 600 to 900 students; learning declines as school size shrinks, and students in very small schools learn less than students in moderate-size schools. Teachers in schools with populations larger than the 600 to 900 range were more likely to report that apathy, tardiness, and drug use were serious problems than were teachers in relatively smaller schools.[35]

Ideal size of districts

The debate about school size parallels similar disputes about the optimum size of school districts. Larger school districts, according to their proponents, offer a broader tax base and reduce the educational cost per student; consequently, these districts can better afford high-quality personnel, a wider range of educational programs and special services, and efficient transportation facilities. Most studies of this subject over the past sixty years have placed the most effective school district size as between 10,000 and 50,000 students.[36]

Advantages of small districts

Today, however, small is often considered better in school districts as well as in individual schools. Proponents of smaller districts contend they are more cost effective and

---

[33]Thomas B. Gregory and Gerald R. Smith, *High Schools as Communities: The Small School Reconsidered* (Bloomington, IN: Phi Delta Kappa, 1987); and Hanna Skandera and Richard Sousa, "Why Bigger Isn't Better," *Hoover Digest* (Summer 2001).

[34] Howard Bloom, Saskia Thompson, Rebecca Unterman, Corinne Herlihy, and Colin Payne. *Transforming the High School Experience: How New York City's New Small Schools Are Boosting Student Achievement and Graduation Rates* (New York: MDRC, June 2010).

[35]David C. Berliner, "By the Numbers: Ideal High School Size Found to Be 600 to 900," *Education Week* (April 24, 1996), p. 10; and *School Size and its Relationship to Achievement and Behavior* (Raleigh, NC: Public Schools of North Carolina, April 2000) at **www.ncpublicschools.org /docs/data/reports/size.pdf** (October 2011); and Board on Children, Youth and Families, *Engaging Schools: Fostering High School Students' Motivation to Learn* (Washington D.C.: The National Academies Press, 2003).

[36]John T. Jones, Eugenia F. Toma, and Ron W. Zimmer, "School Attendance and District and School Size," *Economics of Education Review* (April 2008), pp. 140–148.

Trend toward larger districts

efficient. The small size is more inviting to parental involvement, and management of the system is more transparent to the citizens of the community than in larger districts.[37]

Arguments and counterarguments aside, the trend in American education has been toward larger school districts. By the 2008–2009 school year, 22.63 percent of all public school students were in the one hundred largest districts—.6 percent of all public school districts, each serving 47,000 or more students. In most cases, the larger school systems are located in or near cities, the largest being the New York City system with approximately 982,000 students in more than 1,500 schools, followed by Los Angeles with 687,534 students.[38]

Combining school districts

Consolidation School districts increase enrollment through population growth and through **consolidation**, when several smaller school districts combine into one or two larger ones. As Figure 7.3 illustrates, consolidation dramatically reduced the overall number of districts from more than 130,000 in 1930 to more than 13,800 in 2008, with the bulk of the decline taking place in the thirty years between 1930 and 1960.[39]

Reasons for consolidation

School districts consolidate for a variety of reasons; chief among them are the following:

- *Size.* Larger school districts permit broader, more rigorous curriculum offerings and more specialized teachers.

- *Services.* Larger districts justify hiring counselors, assistant principals, and team leaders not normally found in smaller districts.

- *Economics.* There is an efficiency of scale where purchasing decisions (for example, books, paper, and art supplies) should yield significant cost savings when ordering in bulk. Consolidation also permits older buildings to be retired at considerable cost savings. Redundant high-salaried central-office positions may also be cut when school districts combine.[40]

Push for consolidation continues

Though thousands of districts were consolidated in the earlier part of the previous century as the United States transitioned away from a rural economy, state legislatures today continue the push for consolidation as enrollment numbers in rural districts continue to decline. States such as Arizona, Arkansas, Indiana, Kansas, Maine, Nebraska, New York, and Vermont are enacting merger plans that encourage district consolidation. Arkansas, for example, recently enacted legislation that simply eliminated all districts with enrollments below an arbitrary number (350 students), forcing consolidation.[41] Consolidating districts usually means closing schools, and this has proved to be a serious and emotional matter, especially in small and rural districts where the local school may be a focal point of community identity. A less drastic method of consolidation is for neighboring districts to share programs and personnel.[42]

REFOCUS As you follow various news outlets, what educational issues are discussed at the local school district, state level, and national level? How do these issues affect the local district in which you teach or have field experiences?

[37]Craig Howley and Robert Bickel, "The Influence of Scale," *American School Board Journal* (March 2002), pp. 28–30; and Joshua Bendor, Jason Bordoff, and Jason Furman, *An Education Strategy to Promote Opportunity, Prosperity, and Growth* (Washington, D.C.: The Brookings Institution, 2007), p. 14.
[38]Jennifer Sable, Chris Plotts, and Lindsey Mitchell, *Characteristics of the 100 Largest Public Elementary and Secondary School Districts in the United States: 2008–2009* (Washington, D.C.: U.S. Department of Education, National Center for Education Statistics, 2011), at **www.eric.ed.gov/PDFS/ED512593.pdf** (October 2011).
[39]Nora Gordon, *The Causes of Political Integration: An Application to School Districts* (Cambridge, MA: National Bureau of Economic Research, 2006); and *Digest of Education Statistics, 2010,* Table 90 at **http://nces.ed.gov/programs/digest/d10/tables/dt10_090.asp** (October 2011).
[40]Glenn Cook, "The Challenges of Consolidation," *American School Board Journal* (October 2008), p. 10; and William D. Duncombe and John M. Yinger, "School District Consolidation: The Benefits and Costs and Costs," *School Administrator* (May 2010), pp. 10–17.
[41]Craig Howley, Jerry Johnson, and Jennifer Petrie, *Consolidation of Schools and Districts: What the Research Says and What It Means* (Boulder, CO: National Education Policy Center, 2011) at **http://nepc.colorado.edu/publication/consolidation-schools-districts** (October 2011).
[42]Glenn Cook, "The Long Road to Unity," *American School Board Journal* (September 2008), pp. 48–51; and Glenn Cook, "Rural School Districts Facing Threat of Consolidation," *American School Board Journal* (December 2008), p. 9.

Figure 7.3	Declining Number of Public School Districts, 1930–2008

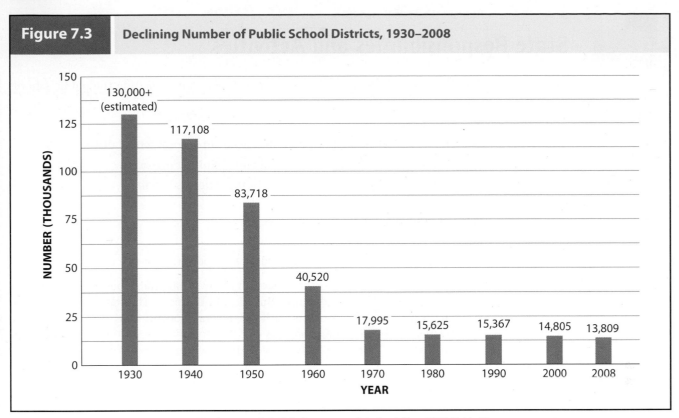

Source: *Digest of Education Statistics*, 2010 (Washington, D.C.: U.S. Government Printing Office, 2011), Table 90.

Intermediate Units

Coordination and supplementary services

The term **intermediate unit** or **regional educational service agency (RESA)** refers to an office or agency in a middle position between the state department of education and local school districts. This agency provides coordination and supplementary services to local districts, and it links local and state educational authorities. The intermediate unit is usually a legal and political extension of the state department of education created by the state legislature. By the 2008–2009 school year, thirty-three states had some form of intermediate unit. Approximately 1,400 intermediate or regional agencies currently provide services to school districts in the United States.[43]

Services provided

In most cases, intermediate units provide widely varied assistance to school districts that are typically rural and have small administrative staffs. In recent years, intermediate units have been instrumental in assisting districts in meeting various requirements of NCLB and other mandates. They have provided support in finding teachers who meet the highly qualified standard, developing assessments, operating data systems, serving the needs of special education students, and providing services for English language learning students.[44] Many educators believe that an intermediate unit covering several districts can economically provide services that many small or financially strapped school districts could not afford on their own.

REFOCUS Does your state have intermediate units or regional educational service agencies? If so, how do they directly affect local schools?

---

[43]*Digest of Education Statistics, 2010*, Table 92 at **http://nces.ed.gov/programs/digest/d10/tables/dt10_092.asp?referrer=list** (October 2011).
[44]AESA Governmental Relations Committee, *Improving American Education through Educational Service Agencies* (Arlington, VA: The Association of Educational Service Agencies, 2010).

State Responsibilities and Activities

Legal responsibility of state

Each state has legal responsibility for supporting and maintaining the public schools within its borders. The state does the following:

- Enacts legislation.
- Determines state school taxes and financial aid to local school districts.
- Sets minimum standards for training and recruiting personnel.
- Develops state curriculum standards (some states also establish approved textbook lists).
- Establishes assessment requirements.
- Makes provisions for accrediting schools.
- Provides special services such as student transportation or free textbooks.

State laws

The **state school code** is the collection of laws that establishes ways and means of operating schools and conducting education in the state. The state, of course, cannot enact legislation that conflicts with the federal Constitution. Many states have quite detailed laws concerning methods of operating the schools. The typical organizational hierarchy, from state to local levels, is shown in Figure 7.4.

The Governor and State Legislature

Powers of the governor

✓ Standards & Assessment

Although gubernatorial powers vary widely, authority on educational matters is spelled out in law. Typical aspects of the governor's role in education are summarized in Overview 7.1 at the Education CourseMate website. Usually a governor is charged with making educational budget recommendations to the legislature. In many states, the governor has legal access to any accumulated balances in the state treasury, and these monies can be used for school purposes. The governor can generally appoint or remove school personnel at the state level and, in some states, even remove local superintendents. But these powers often carry restrictions, such as approval by the legislature. In most states, the governor can appoint members of the state board of education and, in several states, the chief state school officer.[45] Governors can veto educational measures or threaten to veto to discourage the legislature from enacting opposed educational laws.

Powers of the legislature

In most states, the legislature is primarily responsible for establishing and maintaining the public schools and has broad powers to enact laws pertaining to education. These powers are limited by restrictions in the form of federal and state constitutions and court decisions.

The legislature usually decides major financial matters, including the nature and level of state taxes for schools and the taxing powers of local school districts. It may also determine basic parameters of teaching and instruction, including (1) what may or may not be taught, (2) how many years of compulsory education will be required, and (3) the length of the school day and school year. In addition, the legislature may establish testing and assessment procedures, authorize school programs, and set standards for building construction. Where the legislature does not enact these policies, they are usually the responsibility of the state board of education, which we describe in the next section.

New state legislation

As a teacher, you will need to comply with various state laws. State legislatures have had to comply with the accountability mandates under the federal No Child Left

---

[45]NASBE, *State Education Governance Models: 2011* (Arlington, VA: National Association of State Boards of Education, 2011).

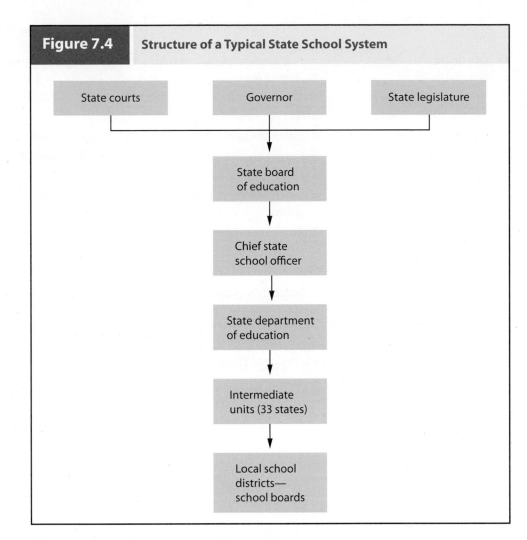

Figure 7.4	Structure of a Typical State School System

Standards & Assessment

Behind Act. As a result, state statutes have been enacted increasing academic standards, mandating assessments, and establishing systems of sanctions for schools failing to meet adequate yearly progress.[46] Not since the wave of school reform that followed the passage of the Elementary and Secondary Education Act (ESEA) of 1965 have state legislatures played such a prominent role in educational policy.

The State Board of Education

The **state board of education** is usually the most influential and important state education agency. With the exception of Wisconsin and Minnesota, all states have some sort of state board of education, which depends on the state legislature for appropriations and authority and serves an advisory function for the legislature. The precise duties and functions of state boards of education vary, but most develop the rules to implement the education statutes enacted by the legislature.[47]

Selection of state board members

As of 2009, governors appointed board members in thirty-three states. The state legislature appointed board members in two states, and eleven states elected members by popular vote. The remaining states used a combination of appointed members and elected members. The number of members on state boards ranges from seven to

---

[46]"K–12 Governance: Shifting Roles in Governance," *National Conference of State Legislatures* (2011), at **www.ncsl.org/IssuesResearch/Education/K12SchoolGovernance/tabid /12870/Default.aspx** (October 2011).
[47]Ibid.

twenty-one, with a seven-member board the most popular.[48] (An odd number of members eliminates tie votes.)

Just as there are a variety of ways to configure and select state school board members, board responsibilities vary among the states. There are, however, some areas of common jurisdiction that state boards share:

- Setting state curriculum standards
- Establishing high school graduation requirements
- Setting certification standards for school personnel
- Developing state accountability and assessment systems
- Setting accreditation policy for local school districts and teacher-preparation programs
- Implementing the mandates of NCLB and administering federal assistance programs
- Administering various state programs[49]

Ultimately, state boards of education are the voice of the citizens in overseeing the operation of public schools within a state. They are an important component in maintaining the quality of education across the United States.

The State Department of Education

State board responsibilities

Functions of state education departments

REFOCUS Talk to teachers and administrators in local schools. In what ways do they see state board of education and state department of education policies affecting day-to-day school operations? Do they see this impact as positive or negative?

Recent responsibilities

Continuity & Change

As a teacher, you are most likely to encounter in day-to-day work the **state department of education**. State departments of education usually operate under the direction of the state board of education and are administered by the chief state school officer. Traditionally, state departments of education primarily collected and disseminated statistics about the status of education within the state. Since the 1950s, however, state departments have taken on many other functions.[50] In short, they implement the laws of the state legislature and the regulations of the state board.

In the latter half of the twentieth century, state departments of education had to grapple with controversial issues such as desegregation, compensatory education, appropriate education for all students, student rights, school finance reform, and minimum competency testing. During the past decade, state departments, in addition to their traditional duties, have been required to develop accountability systems, implement statewide assessments, and even assist with restructuring schools that have not met adequate yearly progress.[51]

The Chief State School Officer

Chief executive officer

The **chief state school officer** (sometimes known as the state superintendent or commissioner of education) heads the state department of education and is also the chief executive of the state school board. He or she is usually a professional educator.

[48]"State Education Governance," *National Association of State Boards of Education* (April 2011), at **www.nasbe.org** (October 2011); and NASBE, *State Education Governance Models: 2011* (Arlington, VA: National Association of State Boards of Education, 2011).
[49]"State Boards of Education," *The National Association of State Boards of Education* at **http://nasbe.org/index.php?option=com_content&view=category&id=32&Itemid=1035** (October 2011).
[50]Fred C. Lunenburg and Allan C. Ornstein, *Educational Administration: Concepts and Practices,* 6th ed. (Belmont, CA: Wadsworth, 2011).
[51]Thomas J. Sergiovanni, Paul Kelleher, Martha McCarthy, and Frances Fowler, *Educational Governance and Administration,* 6th ed. (Boston: Allyn and Bacon, 2008); and Isabel Owen and Daniel Lautzenheiser, "Do You Know Who Your Chief State School Officer Is?" *Education Week* (September 14, 2011), p. 24.

Increasing numbers of women

The office is filled in one of three ways: in 2011, twelve states filled the position through appointment by the governor, twenty-four states through appointment by the state board of education, and fourteen states by popular election. Additionally, as of 2011, four chief state school officers were African American; however, 34 percent of chief officers were women—an increase from earlier decades.[52] The greater number of women in the position represents a departure from the good-old-boy network that once dominated the upper echelons of educational administration.

Duties of the chief state school officer

The duties of chief state school officers and relationships between that position and state boards and state departments vary widely. Generally, an elected chief officer enjoys more independence than one who is appointed. In 2011, nineteen states had new state superintendents take office. The high turnover has been attributed to the trend of state superintendents being held responsible for statewide student achievement results and to the political nature of the position; new governors generally prefer to have like-minded appointees in the position.[53] See Overview 7.1 on the Education CourseMate website for the basic responsibilities of chief state school officers.

The Federal Role in Education

We'll consider the federal government's role in four parts: (1) the federal agencies that promote educational policies and programs; (2) the trend that has shifted many educational decisions between the federal government and the state governments; (3) federal financing of education; and (4) the Supreme Court's decisions concerning education. In this chapter, we focus on the first two parts. Federal spending is examined in Chapter 8, Financing Public Education, and court decisions are discussed in Chapter 9, Legal Aspects of Education.

Federal Educational Agencies

Role of federal government

During most of the nation's first 150 years, between 1787 and 1937, Congress enacted only a handful of significant educational laws. Since passage of the ESEA of 1965, however, we have passed hundreds of significant laws.[54] Traditionally, the major organizations of teachers and administrators, such as the American Federation of Teachers, the National Education Association, and the National School Boards Association, have preferred that the federal government offer financial aid and special services but refrain from interfering in educational policy. Many educators now believe that the federal government has intruded on local and state responsibilities and added numerous unfunded mandates on state and local agencies struggling to improve the schools.[55]

 Continuity & Change

Evolution of the department

The U.S. Department of Education   Although many different federal agencies now encompass educational programs or activities, the **U.S. Department of Education** is the primary federal educational agency. When the Department of Education was founded in 1867, as the Office of Education, its commissioner had a staff of three clerks and a total of $15,000 to spend. From its humble beginnings, the agency has grown to about 4,200 employees, and in 2010, its annual expenditures exceeded $116 billion.

---

[52]NASBE, *State Education Governance Models: 2011* (Arlington, VA: National Association of State Boards of Education, 2011); and "Meet the Chiefs," *Council of Chief State School Officers* at **www.ccsso.org/Who_We_Are/Meet_the_Chiefs.html** (October 2011).

[53]Sean Cavanagh, "State Chiefs' Roster Beset by Turnovers," *Education Week* (July 13, 2011), p. 26.

[54]Don Wolfensberger, "Congress and Education Policy: ESEA at 40—The Evolving Federal Role in Education," *Woodrow Wilson International Center for Scholars* (March 2005) at **www.wilsoncenter.org/sites/default/files/education-intro.pdf** (October 2011).

[55]Kimberly Scriven Berry and Carolyn D. Herrington, "States and their Struggles with NCLB: Does the Obama Blueprint Get It Right?" *Peabody Journal of Education* (2011), pp. 272–290.

The department has the smallest staff of all the cabinet agencies, yet it has the third-largest discretionary budget.[56]

Over time, the Office of Education assumed the responsibilities of (1) administering grant funds and contracting with state departments of education, school districts, and colleges and universities; (2) engaging in educational innovation and research; and (3) providing leadership, consultative, and clearinghouse services related to education.

Cabinet-level status

In 1979, after much congressional debate and controversy, the Office of Education was elevated to the Department of Education. A secretary of education was named, with full cabinet-level status, and the department officially opened in 1980.

Role of the secretary of education

The secretary of education has widespread visibility and influence. Besides advising the president, managing educational policies, and promoting programs to carry out those policies, the secretary can exert persuasion and pressure in political and educational circles. Over the years, secretaries of education—including William Bennett, Lauro Cavazos, Lamar Alexander, Richard Riley, Roderick Paige, Margaret Spelling, and Arne Duncan—have used the limelight to push their own brands of reform.[57] Current Secretary of Education Duncan has been extremely visible as he makes the case to alter provisions of the NCLB through reauthorization of the ESEA.[58] The Technology @ School feature discusses Internet sources of information on the various levels of school governance.

Returning Responsibility to the Federal Government

 **Standards & Assessment**

In 2001, Congress approved President George W. Bush's educational reform initiative, the No Child Left Behind Act (NCLB), and it has remained in place during the Obama administration as policy makers await the reauthorization of the ESEA. NCLB sought to improve low-performing schools and to hold states and local school districts accountable for students meeting high standards as measured by annual performance tests in reading and mathematics. We discuss NCLB's influence on schooling in Chapter 1, Motivation, Preparation, and Conditions for the Entering Teacher, and Chapter 16, School Effectiveness and Reform in the United States. Local school districts that fail to improve student performance, especially in Title I schools, must offer parents the opportunity to choose other public schools or make available free tutoring programs.[59]

In the 1980s, the Reagan administration sought to reduce monetary outlays and shift program responsibility to state and local governments. Twenty years later, the Bush administration, through NCLB, exerted more federal influence on local public schools than at any time in history. Accountability pressure on both state and local school levels has had superintendents, principals, and teachers scrambling to show increased test scores in reading and math to demonstrate that individual schools were making adequate yearly progress (AYP). Despite NCLB's far-reaching implications and somewhat increased funding levels, critics continue to fault NCLB as an "unfunded mandate" and for usurping the authority of state and local educational agencies.[60]

[56]*Digest of Education Statistics*, 2010, "U.S. Department of Education Outlays—Table 384," at **http://nces.ed.gov/programs/digest/d10/tables/dt10_384.asp?referrer=list** (October 2011); "About ED Overview," U.S. Department of Education at **www2.ed.gov/about /landing.jhtml** (October 2011); and "The Federal Role in Education," U.S. Department of Education at **www.ed.gov/about/overview/fed/role.html** (October 2011).

[57]Kenneth A. Dodge, Martha Putallaz, and David Malone, "Coming of Age: The Department of Education," *Phi Delta Kappan* (May 2002), pp. 674–676; and D. T. Stallings, *A Brief History of the United States Department of Education 1979–2002* (Durham, NC: Center for Child and Family Policy—Duke University, 2002) at **www.childandfamilypolicy.duke.edu/pdfs/pubpres /BriefHistoryofUS_DOE.pdf**.

[58]Arthur H. Camins, "Two Roads Diverge for American Education," *Phi Delta Kappan* (February 2011), pp. 44–46.

[59]*Choices for Parents*, U.S. Department of Education, 2010, at **www2.ed.gov/nclb/choice /index.html** (October 2011).

[60]Elizabeth DeBray-Pelot and Patrick McGuinn, "The New Politics of Education: Analyzing the Federal Education Policy Landscape in the Post-NCLB Era," *Educational Policy* (January 2009), pp. 15–42; and Kimberly Scriven Berry and Carolyn D. Herrington, "States and their Struggles with NCLB: Does the Obama Blueprint Get It Right?" *Peabody Journal of Education* (2011), pp. 272–290.

TECHNOLOGY @ SCHOOL

School Governance Information Available on the Internet

As a prospective teacher, you can learn more about the different levels of school governance through research on the Web. Below you will find the websites for the professional organizations of various school leaders that we have described in the chapter. Although the initial focus during your education career will be on classroom teaching and not administrative duties, these sites can be a valuable resource in your development as a professional educator.

Each of the sites provides up-to-date information about current issues that impact their respective constituencies. For example, the American Association of School Administrators (AASA), at its *Policy and Advocacy* page, provides access to its "Legislative Action Center," which describes the organization's position on various pieces of federal legislation, especially the reauthorization of ESEA. Each of the sites listed has a similar link; the National School Boards Association (NSBA) link is *Advocacy and Legislation,* and the Education Commission of the States (ECS) has an *Education Issues* link with an "A" through "Z" index. Examine these links at the various sites to discover which issues are on the radar for school leaders. What positions do the organizations take on the various issues (that is, accountability, charter schools, performance pay, Common Core Curriculum, and so on)? How might these issues impact you as a classroom teacher?

In addition to the links to various reports and updated news, many sites are using different media to keep their membership informed. The National Association of Secondary School Principals (NASSP) has a page, the *School Leader's Review—Podcasts,* that allows you to subscribe to regularly posted discussions of important education topics. The Council of Chief State School Officers (CCSSO) site contains a link to the Common Core Curriculum Implementation Video Series that explains the standards in a series of video vignettes. Monitoring these sites will ensure that you are current with the education policy debates taking place around the country.

- National School Boards Association (**www.nsba.org**)
- National Association of State Boards of Education (**www.nasbe.org**)
- Council of Chief State School Officers (**www.ccsso.org**)
- Education Commission of the States (**www.ecs.org**)
- The American Association of School Administrators (**www.aasa.org**)
- The National Association of Elementary School Principals (**www.naesp.org**)
- National Association of Secondary School Principals (**www.nassp.org**)
- U.S. Department of Education (**www.ed.gov**)
- Public Education Network (PEN) (**www.publiceducation.org/index.asp**)
- The Center for Public Education (**www.centerforpubliceducation.org**)

Recent federal focus

As Secretary of Education Arne Duncan urges changes to NCLB through the reauthorization of the ESEA, it is evident that for the foreseeable future the federal government will be influencing education policy that impacts local schools. The Obama administration is advocating flexibility for schools and districts to design data-based improvement plans to increase achievement, but it assures its critics it will not give districts a "pass" to avoid accountability.[61] Because schools function today in an era of accountability, new teachers will face rigorous expectations almost immediately, regardless of the level at which they teach. The key here is faculty cooperation and sharing, which is necessary for increased student academic achievement.

Nonpublic Schools

The state and nonpublic schools

Although this chapter has focused on public education, nonpublic schools are not exempt from governmental influences. In particular, many state education laws apply to private and parochial schools as well as to public institutions—laws pertaining to

---

[61]Marion Herbert, "Is the Reauthorization of ESEA in Sight?" *District Administration* (May 2011), p. 14; and "ESEA Reauthorization," *ED Review* (June 24, 2011), p. 1.

health standards, building codes, child welfare, student codes, and so forth. In addition, legislative bodies in many states have passed laws to help private schools and to provide public-funded aid in such areas as student transportation, health services, dual enrollment or shared-time plans, school-lunch services, book and supply purchases, student testing services, student tuition, and student loans.

Enrollment in nonpublic schools

As indicated in Chapter 1, Motivation, Preparation, and Conditions for the Entering Teacher, nonpublic schools in 2009–2010 accounted for approximately 10 percent of total enrollments in U.S. elementary and secondary schools, or a total of 5.5 million students. Catholic schools still enroll the most private-school students, although their numbers have declined from 85 percent of all private-school students in 1969 to 39 percent in 2010. Nonsectarian, independent schools increased their share of students from 8 percent of private-school enrollments in 1969 to 23 percent in 2010. Conservative Christian school enrollments now account for 13.4 percent of nonpublic-school enrollment, down from a peak of approximately 16 percent in 2005–2006.[62]

Private schools typically operate differently from public schools. They have a principal or headmaster but generally lack the cadre of support people mentioned earlier in this chapter. They usually derive their authority from a board of directors or school committee, which, unlike a public school board, addresses the operation of one particular private school.

Competition or cooperation?

Many commentators see public and private sectors as competing for students and for funds. Other educators, however, prefer to envision cooperation between public and private schools in an effort to meet the needs of students. In fact, certain distinctions between public and private schools are becoming blurred. For example, programs of *school choice* may include public charter schools; magnet and alternative schools; private independent and religious schools; virtual schools; and, home schooling. In some cases, there is a blending of the public and private by allowing students to apply public funds to a private education.[63] (Privatization is discussed in detail in Chapter 16, School Effectiveness and Reform in the United States, and school choice is covered in Chapter 8, Financing Public Education.)

Summing Up

1. The governance of education is organized on four governmental levels: local, intermediate (in some states), state, and federal.

2. Schools are organized into school districts; approximately 13,800 public school districts currently operate in the United States.

3. At the local level, the school board, the school superintendent, the central office staff, and school principals all take part in governing and administering the schools.

4. Educators have attempted to increase parent and community involvement in the schools. Forms of public involvement include community participation, community control, community schools, and charter schools.

5. Educators have long debated the optimum size for schools and school districts. Many believe that increases in size do not necessarily mean increases in efficiency or effectiveness and might result in the opposite.

6. Small and rural school districts continue to undergo significant consolidation, a movement that began in the 1930s.

7. More than half of the states have one or more intermediate units that support local school districts and assist districts in meeting their needs.

[62]Allan C. Ornstein, "The Growing Popularity of Private Schools," *Clearing House* (January 1990), pp. 210–213; and "Participation in Education: Elementary/Secondary Education," *The Condition of Education 2011* (Washington D.C.: National Center for Education Statistics, Institute of Education Sciences, U.S. Department of Education, 2011) at **http://nces.ed.gov/programs/coe/tables/table-pri-1.asp** (October 2011).
[63]Lamar Alexander, "A Horse-Trade for K–12 Education," *Phi Delta Kappan* (May 2002), pp. 698–699; and Bruno V. Manno, "The New Marketplace of School Choice," *Education Week* (December 1, 2010), pp. 24–25.

8 In most states, the legislature is primarily responsible for establishing and maintaining public schools and has broad powers to enact laws pertaining to school education.

9 All states except Wisconsin and Minnesota have state boards of education. The state boards oversee state departments of education headed by the chief state school officer.

10 Overall, the federal role in education has dramatically expanded since the 1950s. The No Child Left Behind Act is credited with giving even more influence over education to the federal government.

11 Nonpublic schools account for approximately 10 percent of total enrollments in U.S. elementary and secondary schools, with Catholic schools comprising almost 39 percent of these enrollments, and nonreligious, independent schools 23 percent.

Key Terms

The numbers indicate the pages where explanations of the key terms can be found.

local school boards 217
superintendent of schools 221
central office staff 222
principal 222
community participation 225
community control 226

charter school 226
community schools 226
consolidation 229
intermediate unit 230
regional educational service agency RESA 230

state school code 231
state board of education 232
state department of education 233
chief state school officer 233
U.S. Department of Education 234

Certification Connection Activity

This chapter describes the American educational governance system and the role that major stakeholders play within this system. The section of Praxis II, Principles of Learning and Teaching, entitled Profession and Community: The Larger Community, addresses topics such as "partnerships among teachers, parents/guardians, and leaders in the community to support the educational process." After focusing on the section of this chapter on local school boards and community involvement, search for recent articles in your local media that report on local school board actions. In your journal, identify how the local issues you discovered compare to the topics identified in the chapter. Describe how support from the larger community could help make local schools more effective in meeting the needs of all students in the school system.

Discussion Questions

1 What do you consider the advantages and disadvantages of elected, rather than appointed, local school boards? Do the same arguments apply to state boards of education? Would you rather work where school boards are elected or where they are appointed? Explain.

2 React to the following statement critiquing the No Child Left Behind Act (NCLB): "The Obama Administration, in its efforts to reauthorize the Elementary and Secondary Education Act, must radically alter key provisions of NCLB." What are some reasons for and against shifting educational responsibilities from the states to federal government?

Suggested Projects for Professional Development

1 Interview classmates who went to large high schools (more than a thousand students) and those who went to smaller high schools (fewer than a thousand students). List the perceived benefits and drawbacks of each. Where would you rather teach and why?

2 Make a chart listing the advantages and disadvantages of consolidating school districts. Find reports from local news outlets on the Internet where consolidation is taking place. How do these accounts compare to the list you prepared?

3 Talk with teachers and administrators in local schools about ways in which parents and the school community participate in the schools. Prepare a plan that would reach out to and/or involve students' parents in meaningful ways in your classroom and in the school community.

④ Visit the website of your local school district or a district in which you are especially interested. (Use the sites in the Technology @ School section in this chapter to find your state department of education, which will then provide access to the local school districts.) What can you learn from this site about school board activities, such as curriculum issues, state assessment programs, and policy issues? How would this information be useful to you if you were teaching in the school district?

⑤ Attend a school board meeting at one of the local districts near your school. Examine the meeting agenda, and categorize the items according to the school-board responsibilities listed in the chapter. What individuals or community groups were present, and what views did they express? How did the school board respond to these viewpoints? What decisions did the school board make, and how were these reached? Summarize what you learned about school-district governance from your attendance at the meeting.

Suggested Resources

Internet Resources

Visit the U.S. Department of Education's home page at **www.ed.gov** to evaluate the scope of the federal government's involvement in education. The site has easy access to pages for the major stakeholders addressed in this chapter: students, parents, teachers, and administrators. Take the time to fully explore the various pages because in addition to learning about federal policy priorities, there is information about fellowships, lesson plans, ideas for organizing instruction, blogs, online workshops and videos, and answers to FAQs.

You may also find Secretary Duncan's Facebook page (**www.facebook.com/SecretaryArneDuncan**) useful. Follow the Secretary around the country as he promotes the administration's education reform efforts. This resource will assure that you are up to date on the issues being promoted by the Obama administration.

Publications

Berends, Mark, Matthew G. Springer, Herbert J. Walberg, and Ann Primus, eds. *Charter School Outcomes.* New York: Lawrence Erlbaum Associates, 2008. *Contains updated research on multiple aspects of the charter school movement.*

Cornish, Mary M., ed. *Promising Practices for Partnering with Families in the Early Years.* Charlotte, NC: Information Age Publications, 2008. *Looks at family involvement strategies designed to improve stakeholders' skills in partnering effectively.*

Donaldson, Gordon. *Cultivating Leadership in Schools: Connecting People, Purpose, and Practice,* 2d ed. New York: Teachers College Press, 2006. *An excellent book, which presents an overview of the challenge of school leadership in complex and demanding situations.*

Dufour, Richard, Rebecca Dufour, Robert Eaker, and Gayle Karhanek. *Raising the Bar and Closing the Gap: Whatever It Takes.* Bloomington, IN: Solution Tree Press, 2010. *Case studies are utilized to describe how PLCs can enhance learning for students in a variety of schools.*

Epstein, Joyce. *School, Family, and Community Partnerships,* 2nd ed. Boulder, CO: Westview Press, 2010. *Provides assistance to educators and teachers in training to examine comprehensive programs of school, family, and community partnerships.*

Glatthorn, Allan A., and Jerry Jailall. *The Principal as Curriculum Leader: Shaping What Is Taught and Tested,* 3rd ed. Thousand Oaks, CA: Corwin Press, 2009. *An informed discussion of what it means to be a curriculum leader in the era of NCLB.*

Henderson, Anne T. *Beyond the Bake Sale: The Essential Guide to Family–School Partnerships.* New York: The New Press, 2007. *Describes the importance of partnerships and suggests ways to enhance them.*

Houston, Paul D. *No Challenge Left Behind: Transforming American Education through Heart and Soul.* Thousand Oaks, CA: Corwin Press/American Association of School Administrators, 2008. *Reminds educators to keep the focus on students in a time of school reform.*

Lunenburg, Fred C., and Allan C. Ornstein. *Educational Administration: Concepts and Practices,* 6th ed. Belmont, CA: Wadsworth, 2011. *Provides a thorough understanding of educational administration by balancing theory and research with investigations of practical issues administrators face.*

Maeroff, Gene I. *School Boards in America: A Flawed Exercise in Democracy.* New York: Palgrave Macmillan, 2010. *Gives an inside view of local school boards and how they work.*

Manna, Paul. *Collision Course: Federal Education Policy Meets State and Local Realities.* Washington, D.C.: CQ Press, 2011. *Analyzes the relationship between federal education policy makers and state and local education agencies that must implement NCLB mandates.*

Ravitch, Diane. *The Death and Life of the Great American School System: How Testing and Choice Are Undermining Education.* New York: Basic Books, 2010. *Examines issues such as school choice, evaluating the quality of teaching, and charter schools. Ravitch advocates for strong educational values and the revival of strong neighborhood public schools.*

Sergiovanni, Thomas J. *The Principalship: A Reflective Practice Perspective,* 6th ed. Boston: Pearson, 2009. *A comprehensive examination of the role of the principal in the complex schools of today.*

Warren, Mark R., and Karen L. Mapp. *A Match on Dry Grass: Community Organizing as a Catalyst for School Reform.* Oxford: Oxford University Press, 2011. *Based on a national study, the book presents case studies of organizing efforts by* *parents, students, and community members in Chicago, New York City, Los Angeles, Denver, San Jose, and the Mississippi Delta.*

Additional resources for this chapter, including the TeachSource Videos, can be found on the Education CourseMate website. Go to **CengageBrain.com** to access the site.

CHAPTER

8

Financing Public Education

Education in the United States is big business. By 2008, public education (K–12) cost more than $585 billion annually, and elementary and secondary education represented approximately 4.1 percent of the nation's annual gross domestic product.[1] The three major sources of revenue for public schools are local, state, and federal governments. As Figure 8.1 shows, revenues from federal sources have increased from less than half a percent in 1929–1930 to 9.6 percent currently (achieving a high of almost 10 percent in 1979–1980). State contributions also rose from less than 17 percent in 1929–1930 to almost 47 percent by 2009. As state and federal contributions have risen, local revenues have fallen in proportion, from more than 82 percent to 43.7 percent.[2]

Although the percentages of funds provided by these three sources have changed, the total amount of money for schools concerns most local school districts. During times of economic downturns, the business of schooling becomes immersed in serious financial difficulty. In a recent survey of local school board members, almost 92 percent of respondents identified "budget/funding" as an extremely or very urgent issue for their district.[3]

*This chapter was revised by Dr. David Vocke, Towson University.

[1]"Table 3—Gross Domestic Product (GDP), Total Public Revenue in Elementary and Secondary Schools," *Education Finance Statistics Center* (Washington, D.C.: National Center for Education Statistics, U.S. Department of Education, 2010) at **http://nces .ed.gov/edfin/tables/tab_gdp.asp**.

[2]"Table 1—Revenues and Percentage Distribution of Revenues for Public Elementary and Secondary Education," *Revenues and Expenditures for Public Elementary and Secondary Education, School Year 2008–2009* (Washington D.C.: U.S. Department of Education, National Center for Education Statistics, June 2011) at **http://nces.ed.gov/ pubs2011/expenditures/tables/table_01.asp.**

[3]Frederick M. Hess and Olivia Meeks, *School Boards Circa 2010: Governance in the Accountability Era* (Alexandria, VA: National School Boards Association, 2010).

This chapter explores the reasons for both the overall changes in school financing and the current climate of uncertainty. Today's educators must deal with budget constraints, equity and adequacy in school financing, accountability, and various plans to restructure the system of financial support. As you read, think about the following questions:

FOCUS QUESTIONS

■ What proportion of school revenues do local, state, and federal governments contribute?

■ What problems are created by relying on property taxes as school revenue sources?

■ What particular fiscal problems characterize urban schools?

■ Why do significant differences in education spending occur among and within states? How does public opinion affect spending?

■ What major steps have been taken to reform school finance?

■ How has the recent economic downturn affected school finances?

———

*This chapter was revised by Dr. David E. Vocke, Towson University.

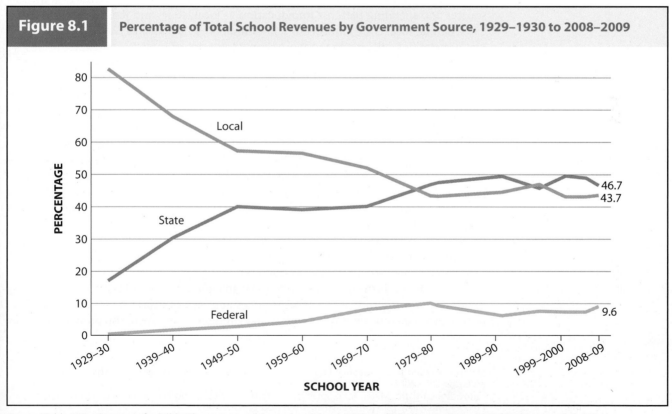

Figure 8.1 | **Percentage of Total School Revenues by Government Source, 1929–1930 to 2008–2009**

Source: "Table 162—Revenues for Public Elementary and Secondary Schools," *Digest of Education Statistics, 2007* (Washington, D.C.: U.S. Department of Education, National Center for Education Statistics, 2008) at **http://www.nces.ed.gov/programs/digest/d07/tables /dt07_162.asp?referrer=report**; "Table 1—Revenues and Percentage Distribution of Revenues for Public Elementary and Secondary Education," *Revenues and Expenditures for Public Elementary and Secondary Education, School Year 2008-2009* (Washington, D.C.: U.S. Department of Education, National Center for Education Statistics, June 2011) at **http://nces.ed.gov/pubs2011/expenditures/tables/table_01.asp**.

Tax Sources of School Revenues

Criteria for evaluating taxes

Progressive versus regressive

Elastic versus inelastic

Public-school funding relies primarily on revenues generated from taxes, especially local property taxes and state sales and income taxes. Certain taxes are considered fairer than others. Most people today accept the following criteria for evaluating taxes:

1. A tax should not *cause unintended economic distortions*. It should not change consumer-spending patterns or cause the relocation of business, industry, or people.
2. *A tax should be equitable.* It should be based on the taxpayer's ability to pay. Those with greater incomes or with greater property worth should pay more taxes. Taxes of this sort are called **progressive taxes**. Inequitable taxes and those that require lower-income groups to pay a higher proportion of their income than higher-income groups are called **regressive taxes**.
3. *A tax should be easily collected.* Administration by the responsible agency and ability to comply with the requirements by the taxpayer should be simple.[4]
4. *The tax should respond to changing economic conditions,* rising during inflation and decreasing in a recession.[5] Responsive taxes are *elastic;* those not responsive are *inelastic.*

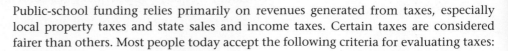

Local Financing for Public Schools

Although states are responsible for education, traditionally much of this responsibility has fallen to local school districts. Overview 8.1 summarizes governmental income sources and spending patterns for education at local, state, and federal levels. As indicated earlier, local contributions to school financing have decreased over the past several decades but still amount to more than 43 percent of total school expenditures.

Property Tax

How property tax is calculated

Problems with property tax

The **property tax** is the main source of revenue for local school districts, accounting for 72.3 percent of local tax revenue received. New Hampshire, New Jersey, and Texas are most reliant on property taxes to generate state and local revenue.[6]

Property taxes are determined by first arriving at the *market value* of a property—the probable selling price for the property. The market value is converted to an *assessed value* using a predetermined index or ratio, such as one-fourth or one-third; for example, a property with a market value of $200,000 might have an assessed value of only $50,000. The assessed value is generally less than the market value. Finally, the local tax rate, often expressed in mills, is applied to the assessed value. A **mill** represents one-thousandth of a dollar; thus a tax rate of 25 mills amounts to $25 for each $1,000 of assessed value (or $25 × 50 = $1,250 tax).

The property tax is not considered to be an equitable tax and is difficult and costly to administer. Differing assessment practices and lack of uniform valuation may lead people owning equivalent properties to pay different taxes. Also, the property tax may

---

[4]Allan R. Odden and Lawrence O. Picus, *School Finance: A Policy Perspective*, 4th ed. (Boston: McGraw-Hill, 2008).
[5]James W. Guthrie, Mathew G. Springer, R. Anthony Rolle, and Eric A. Houck, *Modern Education Finance and Policy* (Boston: Pearson/Allyn and Bacon, 2007).
[6]Paul Johnson and William Kyle Ingle, *Property Taxes and School Funding in Ohio* (Bowling Green, OH: The Institute for Child and Family Policy, 2009), p.1 at **www.bgsu.edu/downloads/ edhd/file65754.pdf** (October 2011); and Jeffrey L. Barnett, *State and Local Government Finance Summary: 2008* (Washington, D.C.: U.S. Census Bureau, 2011) at **www2.census.gov/govs/ estimate/08statesummaryreport.pdf** (October 2011).

OVERVIEW 8.1

Other Income Sources by Level and Spending Pattern

Level	Income Sources	Spending Patterns
Local	■ Property tax ■ Exclusive product rights ■ Special taxes and user fees	Funding goes to local schools in the district. Districts vary widely in their ability to fund their schools, and state aid does not always equalize the discrepancies.
State	■ Personal income tax ■ Sales tax ■ Other taxes: excise taxes, severance taxes ■ Corporate income tax ■ Lotteries	States vary in ability to finance education. Local districts are funded using combinations of four plans: flat grant, foundation, power-equalizing, or weighted student. Many states are striving to provide an adequate education for all students.
Federal	■ U.S. Treasury	Funding is distributed primarily to states for designated purposes, such as assisting student in low-income schools, reading improvement, and special education.

fail to distribute the tax burden according to ability to pay. A retired couple may have a home whose market value has increased substantially, along with their taxes, but because they live on a relatively low fixed income, they cannot afford the increasing taxes. In this respect, the property tax is regressive.[7]

In addition, the property tax is not immediately responsive to changing economic conditions. Some states reassess properties every one to two years, but others reassess only every three to four years. Thus a property's assessed value and actual tax are often based on outdated market conditions.

Other Sources of Local Funding

In addition to the property tax, local school districts can gather revenues through special income taxes and other taxes or fees. Some municipalities, especially small villages and towns, depend on such sources as traffic fines and building permits to help raise revenues.

Rise in user fees

User fees—fees charged to use a certain facility or service—are the most common type of special assessment. User fees can be levied on bus service, textbooks, recreational activities, preschool classes, and after-school centers. School districts are more often charging students to participate in sports, which is a form of a user fee. User fees tend to be utilized more frequently when school districts face budget shortfalls. Because they are not based on ability to pay, user fees are considered a regressive tax.[8]

Exclusive product rights

A growing number of school boards have signed lucrative contracts with corporations for **exclusive product rights** and exclusive naming rights. For example, schools will sign an exclusive product contract with a soft drink company to allow that particular brand to be sold on school property in exchange for a set fee.

[7]William A. Owings and Leslie S. Kaplan, *American Public School Finance* (Belmont, CA: Wadsworth, Cengage Learning, 2006), p. 129.
[8]Robert W. Wassmer and Ronald C. Fisher, "Interstate Variation in the Use of Fees to Fund K–12 Public Education," *Economics of Education Review* (February 2002), pp. 87–100; David L. Baker, "Revisiting User Fees in Challenging Fiscal Times," *Public Manager* (Summer 2010), pp. 66–71; and Stephanie Simon, "Public Schools Charge Kids for Basics, Frills," *Wall Street Journal—Eastern Edition* (May 25), pp. A1–A14.

Jim West/PhotoEdit

Taxes are major sources of both local and state school funding. Property taxes, personal income taxes, and sales taxes provide much school funding. Historically, some citizens in many parts of the country have resisted tax increases.

Other school districts have developed fund-raising campaigns with corporate sponsors, generating everything from cash donations to new stadiums, scoreboards, and equipment purchases. Nevertheless, these contracts are negotiated on a district-by-district basis, with some districts benefiting handsomely while others struggle to fund their school district budgets; one study found that revenues from exclusive agreements with soft drink distributers ranged from $1.5 million per year in one district to $4,800 in another.[9] The Taking Issue box debates school-based commercial activities.

Local Resources and Disparities

Wealthy versus poor districts

Despite state and federal aid, some school districts have greater difficulty supporting education than others do. A school district located in a wealthy area or an area with a broad **tax base** (for example, expensive residential neighborhoods, shopping malls, businesses, and industry) generates more revenue than a poor school district. As a result, in most states, the wealthiest school districts often spend two to three times more per student than the poorest school districts do. As we discuss later in this chapter, state courts and legislatures have attempted to reduce these disparities through reforms in the system of educational finance. In most states, however, substantial disparities in funding persist, and the recent economic downturn is likely to exacerbate the problem.[10]

Municipal overburden

Although financial problems affect many rural and suburban districts, the greatest financial troubles are usually found in large cities. Cities are plagued by what is commonly called **municipal overburden**, a severe financial crunch caused by high population density, a high proportion of low-income citizens, and aging infrastructure. The additional spending needed for social services and upkeep prevents large cities from devoting as great a percentage of their total tax revenues to schools as suburban and rural districts can.

Another problem is that city schools have a greater proportion of special-needs students—namely, English language learners, students in poverty, and students with

[9]Brian O. Brent and Stephen Lunden, "Much Ado About Very Little: The Benefits and Costs of School-Based Commercial Activities," *Leadership & Policy in Schools* (July 2009), pp. 307–336.
[10]Bruce Baker, David Sciarra, and Danielle Fairrie, *Is School Funding Fair? A National Report Card* (Newark, NJ: Education Law Center, 2010).

Urban cycle of financial
strain

disabilities. These students often require programs and related services that might cost
50 to 100 percent more per student than basic programs.[11]

Despite their dire need for more revenues, cities often cannot
realistically raise property taxes. Ironically, tax increases contribute
to the decline of urban schools because they cause businesses and
middle-income residents to depart for the suburbs, which tend to
have a lower tax burden. Thus, the city's tax base is undermined. Declining services due to lack of revenues also cause residents to leave—
a no-win situation.

State Financing of Public Schools

Although the states have delegated many educational powers and responsibilities to
local school districts, each state remains legally responsible for educating its children
and youth, and the states' portion of education funding has increased steadily; elementary and secondary education now account for the largest category in the percentage
of state spending at 26 percent.[12] In this section, we look at the principal types of state
taxes used to finance education, variations in school funding from state to state, methods by which state aid is apportioned among local districts, and the role of state courts
in promoting school finance reform.

State Revenue Sources

Sales taxes and **personal income taxes** are the two major state revenue sources.
Because states currently pay almost 47 percent of the cost of public elementary and
secondary education (see Figure 8.1), these two taxes are important elements in the
overall support of public schools.[13]

Sales Tax   As of 2011, forty-six states had statewide sales taxes, with such taxes making up approximately one-third of state revenues. The average rate was 6.8 percent,
and four states, Louisiana, California, Tennessee, and Washington, had rates at or
above 8.25 percent.[14]

Sales tax evaluated

The sales tax tends to have a regressive effect, especially when placed on essentials
such as food and medical prescriptions. There are thirty-one states that exempt food, and
all but one exempt medicine.[15] In general, low-income groups are penalized through the
sales tax because it takes a larger share of their income than it takes from someone who
is wealthy. The sales tax is, however, easy to administer and collect; it does not require
periodic valuations or entail legal appeals (as the property tax does). The sales tax is also
elastic because the revenue derived from it tends to parallel the economy. When the state

---

[11]Colin K. Armstrong, "The Root Criticism of Urban Schools," *School Administrator* (December
2008), pp. 38–39; Jennifer Sable, Chris Plotts, and Lindsey Mitchell, *Characteristics of the
100 Largest Public Elementary and Secondary School Districts in the United States: 2008–09*
(NCES 2011–301). (U.S. Department of Education, National Center for Education Statistics,
Washington, D.C.: U.S. Government Printing Office, 2010), p. 7–8; and "In Fairness to Cities,"
Scientific American (September 2011), p. 14.
[12]*Policy Basics: Where Do Our Tax Dollars Go?* (Washington, D.C.: The Center on Budget and
Policy Priorities, April 12, 2011) at **www.cbpp.org/files/policybasics-statetaxdollars.pdf**.
[13]"Table 1—Revenues and Percentage Distribution of Revenues for Public Elementary and
Secondary Education," *Revenues and Expenditures for Public Elementary and Secondary Education,
School Year 2008–2009* (Washington D.C.: U.S. Department of Education, National Center for
Education Statistics, June 2011) at **http://nces.ed.gov/pubs2011/expenditures/tables
/table_01.asp**.
[14]"2008 State & Local Tax Collection by Source," *Federation of Tax Administrators* at **www
.taxadmin.org/fta/rate/slsource.html** (October 2011); and "FAQ," *The Sales Tax
Clearinghouse* at **www.thestc.com/FAQ.stm** (October 2011).
[15]Scott McCredie, "The Best and Worst States for Taxes," *MSN Money* (March 27, 2008) at **www
.msn.com/;** and MSN Money Staff, "The Best and Worst States for Taxes," *MSN Money* (April 29,
2011) at **http://money.msn.com/taxes/the-best-and-worst-states-for-taxes.aspx**.

is caught in an economic downturn and consumer spending declines, sales tax revenues decrease to reduce the state's income. States in recent years are finding that this reduction leads to cutbacks in expenditures, which can negatively impact school spending.[16]

Personal Income Tax   The personal income tax is the largest source of state tax revenue, representing more than 33 percent of state revenues. Only nine states do not levy a state personal income tax.[17] Just as the sales tax rate varies among states—from 3 to 8.25 percent—the state income tax, based on a progressive percentage of personal income, also varies and may range from 2 percent to 8 percent of personal income.

Income tax evaluated

A properly designed income tax should cause no economic distortions. Assuming no loopholes, it rates high in terms of equity, reflecting the taxpayer's income and ability to pay. The income tax is also more equitable than other taxes because it usually considers special circumstances of the taxpayer, such as dependents, illness, disability, and the like. In a number of states, state income taxes have become more progressive because of increased standard deductions and personal exemptions, and several states have eliminated taxes on poor families altogether.[18]

The personal income tax is easy to collect, usually through payroll deductions. It is also highly elastic, allowing state government to vary rates according to the economy. However, its elasticity makes it vulnerable to recession, which drives income revenue down.

Other State Taxes   Other state taxes contribute limited amounts to education. These include (1) excise taxes on motor fuel, liquor, and tobacco products; (2) estate and gift taxes; (3) severance taxes (on the output of minerals and oils); and (4) corporate income taxes.

State lotteries

Another trend that emerged in the past forty years has been to establish state lotteries and other gaming enterprises to support education. Although this was a major purpose of the early lotteries, funds have been diverted to meet other social priorities such as health care, social welfare agencies, and road construction. As a result, in most of the forty-three states where lotteries currently exist, twenty-four dedicate a portion of lottery revenues for education, but the lottery contributes less than 5 percent of those states' total revenue allocated to education.[19] Lotteries are somewhat regressive because relatively more low-income individuals play the lottery than do high-income individuals, and they spend larger percentages of their annual income on it.

States' Ability to Finance Education

State variations in spending

Some students are more fortunate than others, simply by geographic accident. State residence has a lot to do with the type and quality of education a child receives. In 2009, eight states spent more than $14,000 per year to educate the average student. In contrast, thirteen states spent less than $9,000 per student. And Utah spent less than $7,000 per student (see Figure 8.2).[20]

---

[16]Institute on Taxation and Economic Policy, "Tax Fairness Fundamentals," *Fair State and Local Taxes* (Washington, D.C.: ITEP, 2011) at **www.itepnet.org/pdf/guide1.pdf**.
[17]"2010 State Tax Collection by Source (2011)," *Federation of Tax Administrators* at **www.taxadmin.org/fta/rate/10taxdis.html** (November 2011); and Institute on Taxation and Economic Policy, "Personal Income Taxes," *Fair State and Local Taxes* (Washington, D.C.: ITEP, 2011) at **www.itepnet.org/pdf/guide1.pdf**.
[18]Carl Davis, Kelly Davis, Matthew Gardner, Robert S. McIntyre, Jeff McLynch, and Alla Sapozhnikova, *Who Pays? A Distribution Analysis of the Tax Systems in all 50 States* 3rd ed. (Washington, D.C.: Institute on Taxation and Economic Policy, November 2009).
[19]O. Homer Erekson, Kimberly DeShano, Glenn Platt, and Andrea L. Ziegert, "Fungibility of Lottery Revenues and Support of Public Education," *Journal of Education Finance* (Fall 2002), pp. 301–311; Clayton B. Reid, "Lottery Money Little Help to Schools," *Newsmax* (January 18, 2008) at **www.newsmax.com/Newsfront/lotteries-and-schools/2008/01/18/id/322684** (November 2011); and Lisa Jeremiah, *State Lotteries' Revenues, Costs, and Impacts* (Cheyenne: Wyoming Legislative Service Office, January 2011).
[20]Frank Johnson, Lei Zhou, and N. Nakamoto, "Table 3," *Revenues and Expenditures for Public Elementary and Secondary Education: School Year 2008–2009* (Washington, D.C.: National Center for Education Statistics, 2011).

TAKING ISSUE

Read the brief introduction below, as well as the Question and the pros and cons list that follows. Then, answer the question using your own words and position.

Expanding Funding for Public Education

Funding public education is a serious burden for state and local governments. School boards have sought new tax revenues and creative ways to meet pressing financial needs. One innovative yet controversial approach to funding is the emergence of corporate–school relationships, also known as *school commercialism*. For example, a local business might pay to renovate the school's gym in exchange for having its name placed on the basketball court floor. Although both schools and businesses stand to gain, these relationships present thorny issues for teachers and administrators, as well as for the public.

Question

Should school boards establish special financial relationships with corporations and businesses to supplement their budgets? (Think about this question as you read the PRO and CON arguments listed here. What is *your* take on this issue?)

Arguments PRO

1. Corporations provide direct financial support to schools and school districts for exclusive use of their product(s), which include soft drinks and snack foods.

2. Some corporations provide sponsored educational materials that can easily be incorporated into the curriculum by classroom teachers.

3. Local corporate sponsors contribute to fund-raising campaigns for needed upgrades to build stadiums, install scoreboards, and build auditoriums.

4. Providing exclusive naming rights for school facilities in exchange for contributions is a way to recognize the philanthropic efforts of the corporate entity.

5. Partnerships between schools and the business community provide an integrated effort to improve the educational program in local schools in a time of funding shortfalls.

Arguments CON

1. Payment for exclusive product use favors one business over others. In addition, many parents and educators worry that food product placement, especially, contributes to unhealthy student eating habits.

2. Sponsored educational materials present a biased point of view or product placement that is nothing more than a marketing tool.

3. Schools and school districts that have access to generous local sponsors receive favored treatment, while others struggle to fund their school district budgets.

4. Businesses engaged in exclusive naming rights are granted a captive audience of young consumers for a relatively small investment.

5. Children are exposed to advertising in all realms of life. School should provide an environment free of marketing messages and implicit endorsements of particular brands.

Question Reprise: What Is Your Stand?

Reflect on the following question by explaining *your* stand about this issue: Should school boards establish special financial relationships with corporations and businesses to supplement their budgets?

What can states afford?

Do these figures mean that some states set their education priorities higher than other states do? No, they reflect what states can afford, which has much to do with the personal incomes and property values of their inhabitants. We must consider what the states spend on all other services and functions, such as medical care, transportation, and human services.

Since the beginning of the recession in 2008, the downturn in the national economy has had a negative impact on state budgets and their ability to fund vital services such as K–12 schooling. As a result, thirty-seven states have provided less funding per student to local school districts, and per-pupil funding has been cut by more than

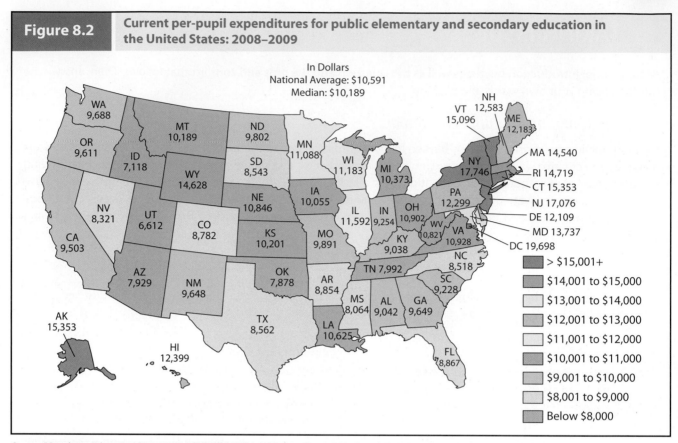

Figure 8.2 Current per-pupil expenditures for public elementary and secondary education in the United States: 2008–2009

In Dollars
National Average: $10,591
Median: $10,189

Legend:
- > $15,001+
- $14,001 to $15,000
- $13,001 to $14,000
- $12,001 to $13,000
- $11,001 to $12,000
- $10,001 to $11,000
- $9,001 to $10,000
- $8,001 to $9,000
- Below $8,000

Source: "Graphs in Education Finance (1 of 17)," Education Finance Statistics Center (Washington, D.C.: National Center for Education Statistics, n.d.) at **http://nces.ed.gov/edfin/graph_topic.asp?INDEX=1**.

10 percent from prerecession levels in seventeen states. Arizona, California, Hawaii, and South Carolina have reduced funding by more than 20 percent from pre-2008 levels.[21]

Aging population and school budgets

Educational Support and Aging Baby Boomers   Another factor that diminishes states' abilities to finance public education is an aging population. The average age of the U.S. population is projected to continue growing as it has since 1900, largely due to the baby boom generation reaching retirement age. The proportion of people older than sixty-five was 4.1 percent in 1900. In 2000, it was 12.4 percent and will likely reach 20 percent or more by 2050.[22] Older people who no longer have children in school are generally more resistant to increased taxes for schools. Yet government spending on the elderly is greater than spending on children as per capita costs for the elderly are more than double those for children. This is due largely to spending on Social Security and Medicare benefits provided to retirees.[23]

Graying of the nation

The increase in average age is a nationwide trend; however, some parts of the country are graying faster than others. According to the 2010 census, fourteen of the twenty "oldest" states are in the Northeast and Midwest, where the graying population is more likely to be reluctant to provide financial and political support for schools.[24]

[21] Phil Oliff and Michael Leachman, *New School Year Brings Steep Cuts in State Funding for Schools* (Washington, D.C.: Center on Budget and Policy Priorities, October 7, 2011).

[22] Administration on Aging, *Projected Future Growth of the Older Population* (Washington, D.C.: Department of Health and Human Services, 2010) at **www.aoa.gov/aoaroot/aging_statistics/future_growth/future_growth.aspx#age** (November 2011).

[23] Grayson K. Vincent and Victoria A. Velkoff, *The Next Four Decades, The Older Population in the United States: 2010 to 2050, Current Population Reports, P25–1138* (Washington, D.C.: U.S. Census Bureau, 2010); and Jeffrey S. Passel, "Demography of Immigrant Youth: Past, Present, and Future," *Future Of Children* (Spring 2011), pp.19–41.

[24] "One Nation, Divisible," *Economist* (November 20, 2010), pp. 33–34.

In contrast, areas with a higher concentration of youth, such as the Sunbelt states, can offset the growing influence of older age groups.

State Aid to Local School Districts

States use four basic methods to finance public education. Some states have financial strategies that combine methods.[25]

The oldest, most unequal method

1. *Flat grant model.* This is the oldest and most unequal method of financing schools. State aid to local school districts is based on a fixed amount multiplied by the number of students in attendance. This fails to consider students with special needs (bilingual students cost more to educate than do native English speakers), special programs (vocational and special education), or the wealth of school districts. The five states that utilize this model do so in conjunction with other funding options.

   The remaining three methods each pursue greater equality of educational opportunity by allocating more funds to school districts in greatest need of assistance.

A minimum per student

2. *Foundation plan.* This most common approach, used by twenty-five states and the District of Columbia, guarantees a minimum annual expenditure per student, to all school districts in the state. However, reformers usually consider the minimum level too low, and wealthy school districts easily exceed it. School districts with a high percentage of children from low-income families suffer with this plan.

Inverse ratio to wealth

3. *Power-equalizing plan.* Twenty-two states have adopted some form of this more recent plan. Each school district retains the right to establish its own expenditure levels, but the state pays a percentage of local school expenditures based on district wealth and taxation effort. Wealthier school districts receive fewer matching state dollars, and poorer districts receive more.

Students weighted by characteristics

4. *Weighted student plan.* Students are weighted in proportion to their special characteristics (that is, special needs, low-income, and so forth) or special programs (for example, vocational or English for Speakers of Other Languages [ESOL]) to determine the cost of instruction per student. For example, a state might provide $4,000 for each regular student, 1.5 times that amount ($6,000) for vocational students, and 2 times that amount ($8,000) for students with special needs. This plan is often used in conjunction with the foundation plan.[26]

The Courts and School Finance Reform

Serrano v. Priest

Efforts to equalize educational opportunities among school districts within a state have been spurred by a series of court decisions that have fundamentally changed the financing of public education in most states. The 1971 landmark decision in *Serrano v. Priest* radically altered the way California allocated education funds. California, like nearly all the states, depended primarily on local property taxes to support the schools, and plaintiffs argued that this system of financing resulted in unconstitutional disparities in expenditures between wealthy and poor school districts. The California Supreme Court agreed and declared the state's funding formula unconstitutional.

San Antonio v. Rodriguez

After the *Serrano* decision, the U.S. Supreme Court ruled in 1973 in *San Antonio v. Rodriguez* that expenditure disparities based on differences in local property taxes between school districts in a state were not unconstitutional under the U.S. Constitution but might be unconstitutional under state constitutions. The *Rodriguez* decision

[25]Amy M. Hightower, Hajime Mitani, and Christopher B. Swanson, *State Policies that Pay: A Survey of School Finance Policies and Outcomes* (Bethesda, MD: Editorial Projects in Education, Inc., 2010).
[26]William A. Ownings and Leslie S. Kaplan, *American Public School Finance* (Belmont, CA: Wadsworth, 2006), pp. 214–218.

FROM PRESERVICE TO PRACTICE

Funding Woes

"Can you believe the budget cuts being proposed by the school board?" Karen asked. "I know the economy is bad, but I didn't think a school district as poor as ours would have to face such cuts to extracurricular activities and technology upgrades, Stuart. We should be getting more state money per pupil than the wealthy districts. I thought that's what the legislature approved last year with the new funding formula!"

"You're right, Karen, it's not fair. But that's the way it is. We both chose to work here," Stuart replied. "With all the layoffs at the defense contractor and other small businesses closing, people are not buying as much, so sales tax revenue is down. On top of that, with all the foreclosures in the area and declining property values, property tax collections are down, too. The board is in a real bind."

Karen sighed. "I just wish that education received the priority it needs to serve all students well. I know that the money comes from local, state, and federal sources, but it seems that the state is unable to keep up with needs of the local districts. It seems the state has done all it can."

"Homeowners here are carrying a large share of the budget through the property tax, too," Stuart noted. "That affects renters, like me. My landlord just sent around a letter asking his tenants to vote against the upcoming school levy that seeks to raise property taxes by 12 percent. That's a huge increase, and he says he will pass along the costs by raising our rent if the levy passes."

"Even with more from local taxes, I think our school district still has less than other area schools," Karen responded. "If the situation gets worse, what will the board's next move be? I'm guessing they'll increase class sizes in the upper grades and begin laying off high school teachers."

"I'll bet you're right, Karen," Stuart agreed. "Wealthy districts have figured out ways to generate local money beyond property taxes. Several of them have established foundations through booster clubs. The businesses that are located in the community contribute heavily each year and get a tax write-off."

"Too bad we don't have a few more generous businesses!" Karen said, laughing. Then, turning serious, she asked, "Do you think I have to worry about my job, as a beginning teacher?"

"Probably not this year because it looks like the primary grade teachers are safe. But you never know; most of a school's budget is in personnel. That's you and me. In the meantime, I guess the best thing we can do is just keep focusing on the students."

Case Questions

1. Why is it important for beginning teachers like Karen and Stuart to have a basic understanding of school finance?

2. How does the current economic situation relate to school financing in your state?

3. How does school-district wealth relate to school financing in your state?

4. What percentages of your local school district's money are derived from local sources? From state sources? From federal sources? If you don't know, estimate the amounts. Then check to see how close your estimates are.

▌ Disparities remained

placed the issue of inequities in school finance in the hands of the state courts and legislatures, where many believed it belonged.[27]

Since *Rodriguez*, certain state courts have ruled that school financing arrangements are unconstitutional if they result in large disparities in per-pupil expenditures based on wealth differences among school districts. For example, in *Rose v. Council for Better Education* (1989), the Kentucky Supreme Court declared the entire state educational system, including the method of funding schools with property taxes, unconstitutional. This decision prompted the legislature to hike average education spending some 30 percent and to undertake an extensive plan of educational reform (described in Chapter 16, School Effectiveness and Reform in the United States).[28] After the Kentucky case, twenty-three states across the nation had their state funding

---

[27]Camille Walsh, "Erasing Race, Dismissing Class: San Antonio Independent School District V. Rodriguez," *Berkeley La Raza Law Journal* (March 2011), pp. 133–171.
[28]David J. Hoff, "The Bottom Line," *Education Week* (January 6, 2005), pp. 28–36; and Anne Rebecca Newman, "Transforming a Moral Right into a Legal Right: The Case of School Finance Litigation and the Right to Education," *Philosophy of Education Society* (2006), pp. 82–90.

▶ ‖ **TEACHSOURCE VIDEO ACTIVITY**

Education and Equity

A fter reading about the courts and school finance reform, go to the Education CourseMate website to access the BBC News video entitled, "Education and Equity." While viewing the video, take note of the differences in educational opportunities available to the profiled students. Think about the efforts that have taken place to reduce the disparities in funding among school districts.

1 Based upon this video and reading the chapter, why is the issue of equity so difficult to resolve?

2 What specific differences exist between the two schools portrayed in the video case?

This video reinforces Key Concepts Found In Section IV: Profession and Community of the Praxis II Exam.

State court decisions

systems ruled unconstitutional on the grounds of inadequate funding[29] The From Preservice to Practice box shows how teachers might be affected by their states' distribution of money to local school districts.

Recent state court decisions have focused on both adequacy, providing adequate resources to help students reach the proficiency level of the state testing system, and equity, the belief that students in low-income school districts have the right to the same educational opportunity as students from high-income districts.[30] In short, states need to close the gap between the best- and worst-financed local school districts.

Some states may also need to factor private schools into their distribution plans. In June 2002, the U.S. Supreme Court, in a five-to-four vote, ruled in favor of the Cleveland voucher program, which is funded by the state of Ohio. This program provides state money in the form of educational vouchers that may be used by the parents of low-income students to attend religious or nonsectarian private schools. The Court declared the voucher program constitutional as long as equivalent remedial services were provided for low-income/remedial students in public schools. Subsequent state legislation (known as EdChoice) passed in 2005, extended the tuition vouchers to Ohio's public-school students in schools categorized as being in "academic emergency." In the 2009–2010 school year, 12,685 students received the Ohio vouchers.[31] Thirty-six states, by 2011, had either passed or had pending bills for funding vouchers, tax credits, or other benefits for private education.[32]

REFOCUS How responsive are the sales tax and the personal income tax in times of recession and economic downturn? Which do you believe has the greater responsibility in funding public education: state or local government? Explain your reasoning.

Does money alone make a difference?

Yet, some critics of school finance reform have argued that money alone makes little difference in the quality of education.[33] They contend that educational improvement

---

[29]Allan R. Odden and Lawrence O. Picus, *School Finance: A Policy Perspective,* 4th ed. (Boston: McGraw Hill, 2008), pp. 42–43; and Lesley A. DeNardis, "From Equity to Adequacy: Evolving Legal Theories in School Finance Litigation: The Case of Connecticut," *International Journal of Education* (2010) at **www.macrothink.org/journal/index.php/ije/article/view/386**.

[30]Peter Hart and Robert M. Teeter, *Equity and Adequacy: Americans Speak on Public School Funding* (Princeton, NJ: Educational Testing Service, 2004) at **www.ets.org/Media/Education_Topics /pdf/2004report.pdf**; and "Systems for Determining Adequacy," *The Education Commission of the States* (2011) at **www.ecs.org/html/issue.asp?issueid=48&subissueID=35** (November 2011).

[31]Mark Walsh, "Supreme Court Upholds Cleveland Voucher Program," *Education Week* (June 27, 2002); "Ohio Legislature Expands School Voucher Program," *Church & State* (September 2005), pp. 3, 21; and Alexandra Usher and Nancy Kober, *Keeping Informed about School Vouchers: A Review of Major Developments and Research* (Washington, D.C.: Center on Education Policy, July 2011).

[32]Peter Schrag, "Vouchers: They're Baaaaaack!" *The Nation* (June 20, 2011), pp. 25–26.

[33]Gerald W. Bracey, "Schools-Are-Awful Bloc Still Busy in 2008," *Phi Delta Kappan* (October 2008), pp. 103–114; and Michelle Rhee, "What I've Learned," *Newsweek* (December 3, 2010), pp. 36–41.

demands commitment and responsibility on the part of students, teachers, and parents. Moreover, unless we address a variety of social and cognitive factors, especially family structure, reform efforts may be useless. With all of these issues unresolved, school finance reform will be hotly debated for years to come.

Federal Education Funding

The evolving federal role

Until the middle of the twentieth century, the federal government gave states (or local schools) little financial assistance in educating American students (see Chapter 5, Historical Development of American Education). This attitude aligned with the majority belief that the federal government should have little to do with education, which was a state responsibility. After the Soviet Union launched the *Sputnik* satellite in 1957, national policy became more closely linked to education, and federal funding dramatically increased and focused on specific, targeted areas; increased federal monies were allocated for improvement of science, mathematics, and foreign language instruction and for teacher education.

Civil Rights Act

From the mid-1960s through the 1970s, the full force of the federal government came into play to enforce U.S. Supreme Court decisions on school desegregation. The impetus came from the Civil Rights Act of 1964, which provided that all programs supported by federal funds must be administered and operated without discrimination or that all federal funds would be withheld.

Programs for diverse groups

In addition to these desegregation efforts, the educational needs of minority groups and women received considerable attention and funding from the mid-1960s to the late 1970s. Diverse groups such as non-English-speaking students, Native Americans, students in low-income schools, and those with special needs were targeted for special programs.

Current Trends in Federal Aid to Education

In the 1980s, the Reagan administration brought its new conservatism to the federal level, and the trend of increasing federal contributions to public schooling ended. Federal education spending declined over the course of the decade (compare Table 8.1 with Figure 8.1). During this time, school funding methods also changed. **Categorical grants** (funds targeted for specific groups and designated purposes) gave way to **block grants** (funds for a general purpose without precise categories). This move was part of the "new federalism" that shifted responsibility for many federal social and educational programs from the national government to state governments based on the theory that states, which were closer to the programs, would know best how to spend the funds.

The 1990s saw another shift in the trend of federal involvement in funding K–12 schooling. The federal *Goals 2000* program, supported by both the G. H. W. Bush and Clinton administrations, reversed the reduction in federal dollars appropriated to support education programs. Gone, too, was the emphasis on block grants as categorical programs began to remerge. A major target for federal dollars that were awarded to the states was the development and implementation of state curriculum standards.[34]

Standards & Assessment

No Child Left Behind

The trend toward more categorical funding gained momentum as we entered the new millennium. The No Child Left Behind (NCLB) Act of 2001 focused federal funding on standards, testing, accountability measures, and teacher quality. States were

---

[34]Gail L. Sundeman, "The Federal Role in Education: From the Reagan to the Obama Administration," VUE (Summer 2009) at **www.annenberginstitute.org/VUE/wp-content/pdf/VUE24_Sunderman.pdf** (November 2011).

Table 8.1	Federal Funds for Elementary and Secondary Education, 1970–2009	
Year	Amount (billions)	Federal Government Share of Funding (percentage)
1970	$3.2	8.0
1972	4.4	8.9
1974	4.9	8.5
1976	6.3	8.9
1978	7.7	9.4
1980	9.5	9.8
1982	8.2	7.4
1984	8.6	6.8
1986	9.9	6.7
1988	10.7	6.3
1990	12.7	6.1
1994	18.3	7.1
1996	22.1	6.8
2000	27.0	7.3
2002	33.1	7.9
2005	44.8	9.2
2009	56.7	9.6

Note: As a result of the Education Consolidation and Improvement Act in 1981, many programs and funds were shifted among various federal departments; the base of comparison has not been exactly the same since then.

Source: Johnson, F., Zhou, L., and Nakamoto, N. (2011). *Revenues and Expenditures for Public Elementary and Secondary Education: School Year 2008-09 (Fiscal Year 2009)*. U.S. Department of Education. Washington, D.C.: National Center for Education Statistics. Retrieved November 25, 2011 from **http://nces.ed.gov/pubsearch**.

required to refine curriculum standards, develop assessments of the standards in reading and math for grades 3 through 8 and once in high school, and establish an accountability plan. Additionally, school systems had to ensure that all teachers were highly qualified.[35]

Since the passage of NCLB, the federal government has become more involved with the state and local education agencies in taking an active role implementing education policy. The law not only required that assessments be developed and administered, it also required that benchmarks for adequate yearly progress (AYP) be established to ensure that all students are proficient in meeting standards as measured by the assessments. Additionally, the achievement results must be categorized by student ethnicity, family income, home language, and disability, and schools only meet AYP when each of the student groups meets AYP.[36]

Over the past decade, critics labeled NCLB an unfunded mandate because federal funding has lagged behind states' ability to cover the costs of developing and administering achievement tests, identifying criteria to determine highly qualified teachers,

[35]Pamela Karwasinski and Katharine Shek, "A Guide to the No Child Left Behind Act," *The Center for Public Education* (March 15, 2006) at **www.education.com/reference/article /Ref_guide_No_Child_Left** (November 2011).
[36]*The No Child Left Behind Act of 2001* at **www2.ed.gov/policy/elsec/leg/esea02/index .html** (November 2011); and Mary Branham Dusenberry, "NCLB: Not as Easy as ABC," *State News* (May 2007), pp. 19–23.

and other provisions of the act. This lack of funding has been frustrating to school officials at both state and local levels, especially as schools' budgets constrict due to the economic downturn.[37]

The Obama administration

The transition from the Bush administration to the Obama administration saw a shift in focus on number of issues related to NCLB. The new administration recognized that parts of the act were problematic and reforms would be forthcoming as work began on the reauthorization of the Elementary and Secondary Education Act (ESEA). The Obama White House also realized that school systems were struggling under the financial restraints brought on by the global recession. The administration secured passage of The American Recovery and Reinvestment Act (ARRA) of 2009, which helped save jobs in school districts across the nation as $77 billion was awarded to strengthen elementary and secondary education. One program within the ARRA was Race to the Top (RTTT), a $4.35 billion competitive education grant designed to encourage states to make improvements in teacher effectiveness, improve achievement in low-performing schools, increase graduation and college enrollment rates, promote charter schools, and enhance data systems. Thirty-five states and Washington, D.C., entered the competition for the grants, but only nine states and D.C. won the competition for the funds. These states will serve as models for education reform based on the administration's priorities. Secretary of Education Arne Duncan has announced that the reauthorization of ESEA will include reforms such as those included in RTTT, but there will be greater flexibility in providing relief from the provisions of NCLB.[38]

REFOCUS Do you believe that the federal government contributes sufficient support to public education in the United States? Explain your position.

School Finance Trends

Financial crises in education often make the headlines. For example, the recent national recession has triggered large state-revenue shortfalls. Coupled with rising costs and other budgetary problems, the loss of state revenue has placed many local school districts in a bleak fiscal situation. Although such crises may have come and gone in the past with changes in the economy and in federal and state budgets, we are still faced with several long-lasting concerns about school finance. As we examine historical trends, keep in mind that educators today are being asked to show proof that they are spending public money wisely. To find out more about current school funding, see the Technology @ School box.

Taxpayer Resistance

Taxpayer initiatives

Beginning in the late 1970s, a tax revolt swept the country, putting a damper on the movement for school finance reform. In California, a 1978 taxpayer initiative called Proposition 13 set a maximum tax of 1 percent on the fair market value of a property and limited increases in assessed valuation to 2 percent a year. By 2006, forty-three states had imposed some type of property tax limitations or caps.[39]

Results of taxpayer resistance

Additionally, as a result of this **taxpayer resistance**, twenty-three states implemented spending limits that are intended to restrain the growth of state budgets.[40]

---

[37]Alyson Klein, "Focus Turns to Congress after High Court's Denial of Challenge to NCLB Law," *Education Week* (June 16, 2010), p. 24.

[38]*Race to the Top: Game Changing Reforms* (Washington, D.C.: U.S. Department of Education, 2010) at **www.ed.gov/open/plan/race-top-game-changing-reforms** (November 2011); and "9 States, D.C. Receive 'Race to the Top' Education Funds," *USA Today* (August 24, 2010).

[39]Isaac Martin, "Does School Finance Litigation Cause Taxpayer Revolt? Serrano and Proposition 13," *Law & Society Review* (September 2006), pp. 525–558; and Nathan B. Anderson, "Property Tax Limitations: An Interpretive Review," *National Tax Journal* (September 1, 2006), pp. 685–694.

[40]Bert Waisanen, "State Tax and Expenditure Limits—2008," *National Conference of State Legislatures* (2008) at **www.ncsl.org/default.aspx?tabid=12633** (November 2011).

TECHNOLOGY @ SCHOOL

Finding School Financing Information on the Internet

As a teacher, you should remain informed about issues and trends in school financing. As discussed in this chapter, financing decisions at every level of government can affect your school community.

One way to stay informed about school finance issues is to monitor the website of the Education Commission of the States (www.ecs.org). This site provides access to a number of relevant resources. From the home page, click on "Education Issues," and then click "Issues A-Z." One more click on "Finance," and you will find a wealth of information about *funding formulas, litigation* related to *adequacy* of funding, and the status of *state budgets*. Also available are research reports, additional articles on school finance issues, and access to other websites.

Another valuable site for school funding information is at the federal government's Education Finance Statistics Center (EDFIN) (**http://nces.ed.gov/edfin/index.asp**). This site is helpful in getting finance information on public elementary/secondary education. Of particular interest is the ability to find longitudinal data for a particular school district anywhere in the country. By using the site's "Data Tools," you can ascertain the school district's total revenue per pupil; its federal, state, or local revenue per pupil; and total revenues for each of the governmental entities. An interesting exercise would be to select the highest and lowest income districts in your state and investigate the site to determine the funding levels from each of the different government sources. As you begin to search for teaching positions, you may want to consult this site about the financial status of school districts you are interested in.

✓ Standards & Assessment

■ Continuity & Change

The late twentieth-century educational reform movement emphasized the need to improve the quality of education. Taxpayers seem willing to support increased education spending for that purpose. They want to know what they are getting for the dollars they spend. This concern has led to increased educator accountability for the use of public funds.

The Accountability Movement

■ Accountable for results

Although definitions of **accountability** vary, the term generally refers to the notion that teachers, administrators, school-board members, and even students themselves must be held responsible for the results of their efforts. Teachers must meet some standard of competency, and administrators must demonstrate that their efforts are improving student academic achievement.

■ Reasons for the accountability movement

The accountability movement stems from various factors. Parents realize that schooling is important for success and that children across the country are failing to learn sufficiently well. As the cost of education has increased, parents demand to know what they are paying for. Eighty percent of Americans believe there is a need for greater accountability in public education. Taxpayers, who want to keep the lid on school spending, want to hold educators responsible for students' academic achievement.[41]

■ Federal and state measures

The NCLB decade has brought the issue of accountability to the forefront of federal education policy. The act required statewide assessment programs in reading and mathematics for all children in grades 3 through 8. The purpose has been to hold schools accountable for the performance of all students on the assessments. If a school fails to meet AYP for a set number of years, sanctions will be placed on the school.[42]

---

[41]Peter Hart and Robert M. Teeter, *Equity and Adequacy: Americans Speak on Public School Funding* (Princeton, NJ: Educational Testing Service, 2004) at **www.ets.org/Media/Education_Topics/pdf/2004report.pdf.**

[42]Allan Odden, "The New School Finance," *Phi Delta Kappan* (September 2001), pp. 85–91; Todd Ziebarth and Bryan Hassel, *ECS Issue Brief—School Restructuring Via the No Child Left Behind Act: Potential State Roles* (Denver, CO: Education Commission of the States, November 2005) at **www.ecs.org.**

Assessment in the Middle Grades: Measurement of Student Learning

After reading about the accountability movement, go to the Education CourseMate website to access the video entitled "Assessment in the Middle Grades: Measurement of Student Learning." Listen carefully to Mr. Somers discuss the assessment of his students' mastery of math content. Also pay attention to the opinions of Karen, his student, on the benefits of assessment.

❶ Based upon this video and reading the chapter, why are the issues of assessment and accountability so critical in American education today?

❷ What specific strategies does this teacher use to promote better results on classroom tests?

This video Reinforces Key Concepts Found In Section II: Instruction and Assessment of the Praxis II Exam.

These changes can have drastic implications for school funding at both the state and local district level.

Reauthorization with flexibility

The Obama administration is proposing a number of adjustments to NCLB through reauthorization of the ESEA. The administration continues to be committed to accountability but is also promoting the concept of flexibility from federal education mandates. States that receive waivers from the Department of Education, instead of meeting the NCLB requirement to meet proficiency measures by the 2014 deadline, will be able to set performance targets to graduate students from high school ready for college and career. Secretary Arne Duncan insists the waivers will only be granted in exchange for rigorous and comprehensive state-developed plans designed to improve educational outcomes for all students and improve the quality of instruction.[43]

REFOCUS How do you feel about plans to link student progress on yearly achievement tests to federal funding? What are the pros and cons of this funding approach?

Tax Credits, Educational Vouchers, and School Choice

Tuition tax credits

Tuition tax credits allow parents to claim a tax reduction for approved education expenses they pay to send their child to nonpublic school. The tax-credit movement reflects the public's desire for increased choice in schools as well as the continuing quest of nonpublic schools for support. Since the 1950s, Minnesota has employed tax deductions for educational expenses; at least five other states also use a type of tax credit for such expenses, and at least 28 states were investigating creating or expanding tuition tax credits.[44] A recent version of the tuition tax credit is the scholarship tax credit program where corporations and individuals can donate a portion of the state taxes that are owed to private nonprofit school tuition organizations that award scholarships to K–12 students. The scholarship can be used for private schools or public schools outside of the student's home district. Eight states currently have scholarship tax credit programs.[45]

[43]Joetta Sack-Min, "What about NCLB?" *American School Board Journal* (February 2009), pp. 26–27; and "11 States Seek Flexibility from NCLB to Drive Education Reforms in First Round of Requests," *U.S. Department of Education* at **www.ed.gov/news/press-releases/11-states-seek-flexibility-nclb-drive-education-reforms-first-round-requests** (November 2011).
[44]Joe Nathan and William L. Boyd, "Lessons about School Choice from Minnesota: Promise and Challenges," *Phi Delta Kappan* (January 2003), pp. 350–355; Krista Kafer, "Choices in Education: 2005 Progress Report," *Backgrounder* (April 25, 2005); and Lawrence Hardy, "The Voucher Revival," *American School Board Journal* (November 11, 2011), pp. 14–18.
[45]"School Choice: Scholarship Tax Credits," *NCLS* (2011) at **www.ncsl.org/?tabid=12950**.

Educational vouchers

Use of **educational vouchers** is another growing trend in school finance reform. Under a voucher system, the state or local school district gives parents of school-age children a tax-subsidized voucher or flat grant, representing a portion of their children's educational cost. Children then use this voucher to attend a school of the family's choosing.[46] At least a dozen voucher programs were operational around the country in 2011, and pro-voucher legislators in thirty states had introduced bills to use tax dollars to send students to nonpublic schools.[47]

Opposition to tax credits and voucher programs

Debates over tax credits and voucher programs have been vigorous and emotional. The NEA, the AFT, and other educational organizations contend that vouchers or tax credits offer no real choice to most students, split the public along socioeconomic lines, and reduce financial support for the public schools.[48] Opponents have also argued that such programs provide unconstitutional support for church-related schools, undermine the public-school system by supporting and encouraging the movement of students to nonpublic schools, and produce a large drain on public-school budgets or state treasuries.[49]

Choice and the "marketplace"

Proponents of tuition tax credits and vouchers generally link the issue with the concept of **school choice**, which is discussed in detail in Chapter 16, School Effectiveness and Reform in the United States. By widening the average person's choices for schooling, supporters contend, we can increase competition among schools and raise the overall level of educational quality. The idea is to depend on education to follow the laws of the marketplace: If students and parents can choose schools, the effective schools will stay in operation, and the less desirable ones will either go out of business or improve.

Arguments in favor

In addition, supporters of tuition tax credits and voucher programs argue that such credits are not unconstitutional and do not seriously reduce federal revenues or hamper public-school tax levy efforts. They also argue that these programs provide wider opportunity for students to attend schools outside the inner city; thus, tax credits or vouchers do not contribute to, and might even reduce, racial and socioeconomic isolation. Many supporters also believe that tax credits or vouchers, besides providing parents with a choice in selecting schools, stimulate public-school improvement, particularly when families have choices within the public-school district.[50]

Charter schools

The call for school choice is most obvious with the growth of *charter schools*, discussed in Chapter 7, Governing and Administering Public Education. Minnesota was first to adopt a charter school law in 1991; by 2010, there were 1.7 million students in 5,500 charter schools across forty states and the District of Columbia. Most charter school organizers contend that they receive less public funding than noncharters. Many school boards counter that they are frugal in allocating operating funds for charter schools, fearing a financial drain on already tight budgets for existing public schools.[51]

---

[46]Bruce D. Baker, Preston Green, and Craig E. Richards, *Financing Education Systems* (New York: Merrill Prentice Hall, 2008), pp. 318–321.

[47]Alexandra Usher and Nancy Kober, *Keeping Informed about School Vouchers: A Review of Major Developments and Research* (Washington, D.C.: Center on Education Policy, July 2011); and Lawrence Hardy, "The Voucher Revival," *American School Board Journal* (November 11, 2011), pp. 14–18.

[48]NEA, *Our Positions & Actions* at **www.nea.org/home/17702.htm** (November 2011); and AFT, *School Vouchers* at **www.aft.org/issues/schoolchoice/vouchers** (November 2011).

[49]Elizabeth Green, "A Libertarian Is Searching for an Education 'Plan B,'" *The New York Sun* (January 14, 2008); and NSBA, *Voucher Strategy Center* at **www.nsba.org/Advocacy/Key-Issues/SchoolVouchers/VoucherStrategyCenter** (November 2011).

[50]Greg Anrig, "An Idea Whose Time Has Gone," *Washington Monthly* (April 2008), pp. 29–33; "Subsidizing Private Education—At Taxpayer Expense," *NEA Policy Brief* (2011) at **www.nea.org/home/49400.htm** (November 2011); and "Vouchers," *Education Week* (August 11, 2011) at **www.edweek.org/ew/issues/vouchers** (November 2011).

[51]Katrina E. Bulkley, "Charter Schools: Taking a Closer Look," *Kappa Delta Pi Record* (March 1, 2011), pp. 110–115.

Shrinking School Budgets

School budget scrutiny

The economic downturn that began with the recession in 2008 has forced school officials to face funding challenges that have been unprecedented for several generations. Most local school boards have been grappling with reduced funding from both the state and local levels. The reliance on the property taxes at the local level makes it difficult to project when the decline in those revenues will turn around because home property values are predicted to remain low for several years. State revenues, which rely on sales and personal income taxes, are, at best, projected to remain flat as long as unemployment stays at its current rate and consumer confidence remains at historically low levels.[52]

The growing fiscal stress on school districts requires that they find additional funding streams or cut spending; there is much greater likelihood the latter will be the only options for most local boards of education. Raising existing tax rates or implementing new taxes does not seem to be an option in the current political climate. The option left to school districts is to reduce spending. Terms such as "efficient spending," "downsizing," and "managing decline" are being used to advise school boards concerning how to balance their school district budgets.[53]

States and local school systems have taken a number of actions to reduce spending while trying not to harm the delivery of educational programs to students. Unfortunately, with about 70 percent of all school districts experiencing funding decreases in 2010–2011, the cuts have been so severe the impact has to be felt in the classroom:

- Forty-eight percent of school districts reported teaching staff reductions, including teachers of core academic subjects.
- Seventy-nine percent of districts with funding decreases reduced the purchase of instructional materials and technology equipment.
- Thirty-eight percent of impacted districts reduced extracurricular programs and activities.
- Fifty-six percent of districts with funding decreases reduced or eliminated professional-development efforts.
- Sixty-six percent of these districts slowed, postponed, or stopped reform efforts that had been planned for the academic year.[54]

These are but a few of the actions taken to balance school districts' budgets. Most economic projections would seem to indicate that for the foreseeable future, school boards will be seeking ways to do more with less.

School Infrastructure and Environmental Problems

Deteriorating facilities

The nation's **school infrastructure** is in critical disrepair. By *infrastructure*, we mean the basic physical facilities of the school plant (plumbing, sewer, heat, electric, roof, carpentry, and so on). Building experts estimate that schools in the United States are deteriorating faster than they can be repaired and faster than most other public facilities. Plumbing, windows, electrical wiring, and heating systems in many schools are dangerously out of date; roofing is below code; and exterior brickwork, stone, and wood are in serious disrepair. Over the past twenty years, school districts have had to

[52]"Cutting to the Bone: At a Glance," *The Center for Public Education* (October 7, 2010) at **www.centerforpubliceducation.org/Main-Menu/Public-education/Cutting-to-the-bone-At-a-glance** (November 2011); and Ron Schachter, "District-Level Downsizing," *District Administration* (June 2011), pp. 29–32.
[53]Michael J. Petrilli and Margerite Roza, *Stretching the School Dollar: A Brief for State Policy Makers* (Washington, D.C.: Thomas B. Fordham Institute, January 2011).
[54]Nancy Kober and Diane Stark Rentner, *Strained Schools Face Bleak Future: Districts Foresee Budget Cuts, Teacher Layoffs and Slowing of Educational Reform* (Washington, D.C.: Center on Education Policy, June 2011).

Rachel Epstein/The Image Works

School boards are being pressed to eliminate unnecessary spending, and school budgets must stand up to close scrutiny. Many districts are trying to "do more with less," in spite of demands for smaller schools, teacher shortages, and deteriorating old school buildings.

defer maintenance of school facilities due to a lack of funds for upkeep and repair. Estimates of the costs of this deferred maintenance range from a conservative $271 billion to a more aggressive $650 billion.[55] When maintenance and repair work is delayed, students are subjected to potentially dangerous conditions: unsafe drinking water, poor air quality from mold, outdated security systems, reduced curricular offerings as specialized spaces like gyms are closed, and danger from structural problems.[56]

More classrooms will be needed

Even as school boards struggle to meet the needs of an aging infrastructure, the U.S. Census Bureau has modified its projections for the growth of the school-age population. Using 2010 census figures as a baseline, the bureau now expects school-age population growth to remain steady through 2020. Elementary and secondary school enrollment is expected to rise by approximately 6 percent during this time frame. Repairs aside, concern is growing about where the money will come from to build the additional classrooms we continue to need.[57]

REFOCUS   Are budget constraints impacting local schools in your area? Is the school infrastructure in local school districts in need of updating?

Summing Up

1. Schools are financially supported by state and local governments and—to a lesser extent—by the federal government. Overall, since the early twentieth century, state support has increased dramatically, and local support has declined; the percentage of federal support grew until the early 1980s, then declined, but has since recovered to earlier levels.

2. Although the property tax is the main local source of school revenue, it is considered a regressive tax.

[55]William D. Eggers and Tiffany Dovey, "Rebuilding America's Schools," *Education Week* (September 26, 2007), p. 30; and 21st Century School Fund, *Through Your Lens: Student and Teacher Views of School Facilities across America* (2010) at **www.eric.ed.gov/PDFS/ED509518.pdf** (November 2011).

[56]21st Century School Fund, *Repair for Success: An Analysis of the Need and Possibilities for a Federal Investment in PK-12 School Maintenance and Repair* (November 16, 2009) at **www.21csf.org/csf-home/Documents/RepairforSuccessAugust2011.pdf** (November 2011).

[57]U.S. Census Bureau, "School Enrollment: 1980 to 2020," *The 2012 Statistical Abstract* (Washington, D.C.: U.S. Census Bureau, 2011) at **www.census.gov/compendia/statab/2012/tables/12s0219.pdf** (November 2011).

❸ There is wide variation in the financial ability among states and within states (at the local district level) to support education. Poorer school districts tend to receive more money from the state than do wealthier school districts, but the amount rarely makes up for the total difference in expenditures per pupil.

❹ School finance reform, initiated by the state courts and carried forward by state legislatures, has attempted to reduce or eliminate funding disparities between poorer and wealthier districts. The basic goal is to provide for adequate educational opportunities and give poorer districts the means to improve their performance.

❺ Since the *Sputnik era*, federal funding of education has become increasingly linked to national policy. As policy emphasis has changed, so has the level of funding.

❻ Controversies over accountability, tuition tax credits, educational vouchers, charter schools, and school choice reflect increasing public concern with the educational system.

❼ Taxpayer resistance, especially to increases in property taxes, results in strong pressure to be more accountable with school revenue.

❽ Deteriorating school infrastructure pose significant financial liabilities for many school districts.

Key Terms

The numbers indicate the pages where explanations of the key terms can be found.

progressive taxes 243
regressive taxes 243
property tax 243
mill 243
user fees 244
exclusive product rights 244

tax base 245
municipal overburden 245
sales tax 246
personal income tax 246
categorical grants 253
block grants 253

taxpayer resistance 255
accountability 256
tuition tax credits 257
educational voucher 258
school choice 258
school infrastructure 259

Certification Connection Activity

This chapter can be linked to Praxis II's Principles of Learning and Teaching section, Profession and Community: The Larger Community. You should be aware of the sources of school funding to be able to advocate for equitable community support for adequate resources to enhance student learning. In your journal, examine your state department of education website to determine the actual levels of funding for the state's school districts. Identify those districts that have the highest per-pupil expenditure and those with the lowest levels of funding. Based on the discussion in the chapter, describe the differences in educational services that are likely to exist among these districts. What special funding needs might inner-city school districts have versus suburban districts? What special needs might rural districts have?

Discussion Questions

❶ How could state school boards and legislatures design a tax structure that is fair and equitable and capable of keeping abreast of changing economic conditions? What specific elements would make up this tax code?

❷ State your reasons for or against the following types of financial support for school choice:

(a) Government vouchers that any student can use to pay tuition in any accredited school, public or private

(b) Vouchers as in (a), but issued only to students whose families demonstrate financial need

(c) No vouchers for private or parochial schools, though students are free to choose any *public* schools they like

❸ What do you see as the pros and cons of corporate–school partnerships, such as naming rights for school facilities and curriculum materials with advertisements?

Suggested Projects for Professional Development

❶ Survey taxpayers (parents, neighbors, classmates, coworkers) about their attitudes toward school taxes. To what extent do they resist such taxes? For what reasons, or under what conditions, might they be willing to pay more for school funding? Do you notice any differences of opinion among various age groups, ethnic groups, income groups, geographic groups, or social classes? Summarize your findings for the class.

2. In your visits to schools this term, be alert to infrastructure concerns. What specific problems do you see, and what do the students and faculty identify as problems? Are circumstances significantly better or worse in neighboring districts? If so, how do people account for these differences? Keep notes on your findings in a journal.

3. Examine several weeks' worth of the state and local news section of your daily paper (hard copy or via the Internet) for articles relating to school finance. Identify the main concerns in the articles. Compare the topics of the articles to issues addressed in the chapter. How does the article complement the text coverage? Share your findings with the class.

4. Examine the websites of several local school districts in your area to find a charter school. After a charter is identified, con-tact the school administrator to discuss the ways in which the school is similar to/different from other schools in the district. Also, determine the charter's financial circumstances in comparison to similar schools in the district. Develop a wiki with the findings that your classmates can review.

5. Interview a local school-board member regarding the following:

■ Concerns about funding and the budget process

■ His or her most important budget priorities

■ Creative ways to address budget problems

■ How public support for the budget is built after the budget is established

Suggested Resources

Internet Resources

The Center on Budget and Policy Priorities (**www.cbpp.org**) conducts research and analysis on budget and tax policies. Its focus is broader than just education issues, but its reports are accessible to the general public and are informative regarding issues of the day. By entering "education" as a keyword in the search box, numerous reports related to education financing are provided. Charts, graphs, and tables are generally incorporated into the reports to illustrate economic issues discussed in the articles. This site is an excellent resource for keeping current with education finance issues. It also provides videos, podcasts, blogs, and slideshows to present its reports.

Publications

Baker, Bruce D., Preston C. Green, and Craig E. Richards. *Financing Education Systems.* New York: Merrill Prentice Hall, 2008. *Gives a comprehensive, contemporary view of school finance and focuses on the concepts of equity, adequacy, and efficiency.*

Carl, Jim. *Freedom of Choice: Vouchers in American Education.* Santa Barbara, CA: Praeger, 2011. *The author proposes that vouchers are linked to the growing conservative movement that focuses on free markets, religious separatism, and consumer choice.*

Feinberg, Walter, and Christopher Lubienski, eds. *School Choice Policies and Outcomes: Empirical and Philosophical Perspectives.* Albany: SUNY Press, 2008. *Provides an examination of varying voices in the choice debate and suggests choice, directed by the appropriate goals, might advance education.*

Guthrie, James W., Mathew G. Springer, R. Anthony Rolle, and Eric A. Houck. *Modern Education Finance and Policy.* Boston: Pearson/Allyn and Bacon, 2007. *A comprehensive examination of educational finance that focuses on accountability, resource allocation, and policy.*

Hanushek, Eric A., and Alfred A. Lindseth. *Schoolhouses, Courthouses, and Statehouses: Solving the Funding-Achievement Puzzle in America's Public Schools.* Princeton, NJ: Princeton University Press, 2009. *The authors suggest that court rulings requiring states to spend more on funding education in the name of equity has not reduced the achievement gap. They propose a performance-based system that offers incentives to raise achievement.*

Hess, Frederick M., and Eric Osberg, eds. *Stretching the School Dollar: How Schools and Districts Can Save Money While Serving Students Best.* Cambridge, MA: Harvard Education Press, 2010. *A number of finance experts offer ideas for ways to deal with the difficult times schools are facing.*

Howell, William G. *The Education Gap: Vouchers and Urban Schools.* Washington, D.C.: Brookings Institute Press, 2006. *A study of the impact of vouchers on urban schools, particularly with regard to finances and school leadership.*

Ladd, Helen F., and Edward B. Fiske, eds. *Handbook of Research in Education Finance and Policy.* New York: Routledge, 2008. *A comprehensive review of the field of education finance; includes a historical evolution of the field.*

Odden, Allen R., and Lawrence O. Picus. *School Finance: A Policy Perspective,* 4th ed. New York: McGraw-Hill, 2008. *An examination of school productivity formulas, fiscal policy, and fiscal federalism.*

Roza, Marguerite. *Educational Economics: Where Do School Funds Go?* Washington, D.C.: Urban Institute Press, 2010. *Considers the sources of school finance–federal block funding, foundation grants, earmarks, set-asides, and union mandates—and how they can easily be diverted from where they are most needed.*

Shelly, Bryan. *Money, Mandates, and Local Control in American Public Education.* Ann Arbor, MI: University of Michigan Press, 2011. *An up-to-date examination of school finance that includes an analysis of unfunded and underfunded mandates and regulations that the author suggests are the true cause of the loss of community control over public education.*

 Additional resources for this chapter, including the TeachSource Videos, can be found on the Education CourseMate website. Go to **CengageBrain.com** to access the site.

9

Legal Aspects of Education

During the past six decades, the courts have increasingly been asked to resolve issues relating to public education in the United States. This rise in educational litigation reflects the fact that education has assumed a greater importance in our society than it had a few decades ago. The growth in litigation has been paralleled and, to some extent, spurred on by an enormous increase in state and federal legislation affecting education. As litigation and legislation regarding the schools continue to increase, teachers and administrators are increasingly responsible for learning about the ins and outs of school law.

This chapter presents a general overview of the U.S. court system and examines the legal topics and court decisions that have most affected today's schools and teachers. The major topics we will consider are (1) the rights and responsibilities of both teachers and students and (2) religion and the schools.[1] Questions to consider as you read this chapter include the following:

FOCUS QUESTIONS

- What legal rights and responsibilities do teachers have?
- What are the legal rights of students?
- Can religious activities be conducted in public schools?
- Can the government assist nonpublic schools?

---

*This chapter was revised by Dan Levine.

[1]Other chapters of this book also discuss selected legal issues in education. For court decisions regarding school finance, see Chapter 8, Financing Public Education. Desegregation law and legislation regarding special education are considered in Chapter 12, Providing Equal Educational Opportunity.

The Court System

Cases involving education-related issues can be heard either in federal or state courts, depending on the allegations of the **plaintiffs** (the persons who sue). Federal courts decide cases that involve federal laws and regulations or constitutional issues. State courts adjudicate cases that involve state laws, state constitutional provisions, school-board policies, or other nonfederal problems. Most cases pertaining to elementary and secondary education are filed in state courts. However, to keep from overburdening court calendars, both federal and state courts usually require that prospective **litigants** (the parties in a lawsuit) exhaust all administrative avenues available for resolution before involving the court system.

State Courts

▌ Types of state courts	State court organization has no national uniformity. The details of each state's judicial system are found in its constitution. At the lowest level, most states have a court of original jurisdiction (often called a municipal or superior court) where cases are tried. The facts are established, evidence is presented, witnesses testify and are cross-examined, and appropriate legal principles are applied in rendering a verdict.

The losing side may appeal the decision to the next higher level, usually an intermediate appellate court. This court reviews the trial record from the lower court and additional written materials submitted by both sides. The appellate court is designed to ensure that appropriate laws were properly applied, that they fit with the facts presented, and that no deprivation of constitutional rights occurred.

If one side remains unsatisfied, another appeal may be made to the state's highest court, often called its supreme court. A state supreme court decision is final unless a question involving the U.S. Constitution has been raised. The side that wants to appeal may then petition the U.S. Supreme Court to consider the case.

Federal Courts

▌ Three tiers of federal courts

Federal courts are organized into a three-tiered system: district courts, circuit courts of appeals, and the Supreme Court. The jurisdiction and powers of these courts are set forth in the Constitution and are subject to congressional restrictions. The lowest level, the district court, holds trials. For appeals at the next federal level, the nation is divided into twelve regions called circuits. Each circuit court handles appeals only from district courts within its particular geographic area. Unsuccessful litigants may request that the U.S. Supreme Court review their case. If four of the nine justices agree, the Supreme Court will take the case; if not, the appellate court ruling stands.[2]

▌ Conflicting rulings

Decisions of a court below the U.S. Supreme Court have force only in the geographic area served by that particular court. For this reason, it is possible to find conflicting rulings in different circuits. Judges often look to previous case law for guidance in rendering decisions, and they might find precedents for a variety of legally defensible positions on a single issue.

▌ First Amendment

The First and the Fourteenth Amendments   Although education is considered a state responsibility, it has produced an abundance of federal litigation, particularly in connection with the First and Fourteenth Amendments to the U.S. Constitution. The First Amendment concerns freedom of religion, speech, press, and assembly and

---

[2]Some case citations in this chapter include the term *cert. denied*. This means that the losing parties petitioned the U.S. Supreme Court for review, but their request was denied.

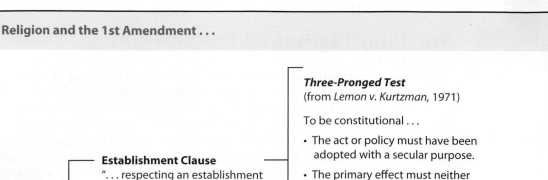

Figure 9.1   Religion and the 1st Amendment . . .

FIRST AMENDMENT

"Congress shall make no law . . ."

Establishment Clause
". . . respecting an establishment of religion . . ."

Free Exercise Clause
". . . or prohibiting the free exercise thereof . . ."

Three-Pronged Test
(from *Lemon v. Kurtzman*, 1971)

To be constitutional . . .

- The act or policy must have been adopted with a secular purpose.
- The primary effect must neither advance nor inhibit religion.
- The law or policy must not result in an excessive entanglement of government and religion.

Two-Pronged Test

- The plaintiffs must prove that their beliefs are sincerely held and that the protested government action truly injures the exercise of those beliefs.
- The government must prove that a truly compelling public necessity requires restricting that free exercise and that no less restrictive means are available.

the right "to petition the government for redress of grievances." Many First Amendment cases have dealt with the role of religion in public education and with the extent of protection guaranteed to freedom of expression by students and teachers. Two First Amendment clauses are frequently cited in lawsuits: the **establishment clause**, which prohibits the establishment of a government-sanctioned religion, and the **free-exercise clause**, which protects rights of free speech and expression. To interpret these clauses, the courts generally use the criteria, or "tests," shown in Figure 9.1.

Court cases involving the Fourteenth Amendment often focus on the section declaring that no state shall "deprive any person of life, liberty, or property, without due process of law; nor deny to any person within its jurisdiction the equal protection of the law." The first part of this passage is known as the **due-process clause**. The second part is known as the **equal-protection clause**. Fourteenth Amendment cases have addressed the issue of school desegregation as well as the suspension and expulsion of students. Litigants citing the Fourteenth Amendment must show that a "liberty" or a "property" interest is a major element in the case. A liberty interest is involved if "a person's good name, reputation, honor or integrity is at stake." A property interest might arise from legal guarantees granted to tenured employees; for instance, teachers beyond the probationary period have a property interest in continued employment. Similarly, students have a property interest in their education. If either a liberty or a property interest is claimed, a school district must provide due process (guaranteeing a fair and impartial hearing and the opportunity to present evidence) to the people involved. The rest of this chapter will explore the use of these and other legal concepts in actual school settings.

Fourteenth Amendment: Liberty and property interests

Teachers' Rights and Responsibilities

As pointed out in Chapter 2, The Teaching Profession, teachers historically were vulnerable to dismissal by local boards of education for virtually any reason and without recourse. Collective negotiation statutes, tenure laws, mandatory due-process procedures, and other legal measures have been established to curb such abuses and to guarantee teachers certain rights. Along with rights come responsibilities, and many of these, too, have been written into law.

Testing and Investigation of Applicants for Certification or Employment

Background checks

Almost everywhere in the United States, individuals who want to teach in grades K–12 must possess teaching certificates, which are usually granted by the state. In recent years, many states have passed legislation requiring thorough background checks of prospective teachers, and some extend this requirement to currently employed teachers seeking recertification. For example, New York and Texas now require that all candidates for certification be fingerprinted as part of a check for criminal histories. Some states electronically share background information about candidates for government positions. Prospective teachers should be careful about what they post online because many districts are examining sites such as Twitter, Myspace, and Facebook for information about job applicants.[3]

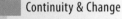

Continuity & Change

Standards & Assessment

These trends have been fueled by two complementary developments. One consideration is that technology has made it more feasible to use fingerprints and other information sources in checking with local, state, and federal law-enforcement agencies. The other is that the public has become increasingly concerned about dangers posed by child molesters and potential school employees with other criminal records.

Nondiscrimination requirements

As described in Chapter 1, Motivation, Preparation, and Conditions for the Entering Teacher, states require, in addition to background checks, that prospective teachers pass one or more competency tests for certification. In some cases, current teachers also must pass competency tests for continued employment. States where minority candidate passing rates are considerably lower than those for nonminorities have faced several lawsuits charging that specific tests discriminate against minority applicants. To answer such a lawsuit, employers must be able to specify the characteristics a test measures, establish that these characteristics are necessary in carrying out the job, and demonstrate that the test correlates with the work behavior in question.

Most lawsuits charging that teacher tests are discriminatory have either failed or been withdrawn because the available data did not demonstrate a clear pattern of discrimination nor an intent to discriminate. On the other hand, worries about possible legal challenges, particularly from minority candidates, undoubtedly have occasionally led states to keep passing scores low. For example, concerns regarding a legal challenge alleging discrimination in part led the Massachusetts State Board of Education to substantially reduce the minimum score required to pass a proposed certification test in that state.[4]

---

[3]"Texas Now Requiring Fingerprints From School Employees," *American School Board Journal* (March 2008), p. 10; and Emily Behlmann, "Social Media Background Checks," *Wichita Business Journal*, May 4, 2011, available at **www.bizjournals.com**.
[4]Mark Walsh, "Court Seeks Justice Dept's Views in Case over N.Y. Teacher Test," *Education Week*, December 12, 2007; and Linda Tyler, "Toward Increasing Teacher Diversity," 2011 paper prepared at the Educational Testing Service, available at **www.ets.org**.

Employment Contracts and Tenure

In choosing which teachers to hire, local school boards must comply with laws that prohibit discrimination with respect to age, sex, race, religion, or national origin. Upon appointment, the teacher receives a written contract to sign. The contract may specify that the teacher must adhere to school-board policies and regulations. If the school district has negotiated with a teacher organization, the provisions of that agreement apply as well.

Breach of contract

Contracts are binding on both parties. When one side fails to perform as agreed—called a **breach of contract**—the contract is broken. In such instances, the party that breached the contract may be sued for damages. Some states permit a teacher's certificate to be revoked if the teacher breaches the contract. If a school district breaks a contract, teachers may be awarded payments for damages or be reinstated to their former positions.

Terms of tenure

Nearly every state also has some type of tenure law. **Tenure** protects teachers from dismissal without cause. Each state defines "cause"; the usual reasons include incompetency, immorality, insubordination, and unprofessional conduct. In addition, as explained in the next section, the school district must follow due process if it wants to dismiss a tenured teacher.

From its inception, the notion of tenure has been controversial. Arguments for and against tenure are presented in this chapter's Taking Issue box.

Continuing employment

Once granted tenure, rather than sign an annual contract, many teachers are employed under a **continuing contract**. The term means that their reemployment for the next year is guaranteed unless school officials give notice by a specific date that the contract will not be renewed.

Probationary period

Most states have a probationary period before teachers achieve tenure. Moreover, many tenured teachers who change districts lose their tenure and must serve another period of probation. The probationary period often consists of three years of consecutive, satisfactory service, but some states have been moving to establish much shorter periods, at the end of which new teachers can be quickly removed from their jobs.

Probationary contracts in some states allow the teacher to be discharged at the end of the contract term for any reason and without explanation—no due process is required, unless the teacher can demonstrate that his or her dismissal involves a constitutionally guaranteed liberty or property interest. (See the next section for information on the meaning of due process.) In other states, probationary teachers have general due-process rights, but the process may be streamlined to expedite dismissal of candidates rated as incompetent.[5]

Due Process in Dismissal of Teachers

Fairness in teacher dismissal

Due process refers to the use of legal rules and principles established to protect the rights of the accused. These principles are especially important to a teacher being dismissed from a job. The core element of due process is fairness. Although requirements vary from state to state, the rules shown in Table 9.1 are generally recognized in teacher dismissal cases.

Assistance for struggling teachers

Other procedures for removing teachers

Firing a teacher for incompetence requires documentation of efforts to help that person improve. Obtaining this documentation can be burdensome for everyone involved, and few tenured teachers are dismissed using formal legal procedures. Instead, administrators sometimes use less formal procedures for excluding incompetent teachers from their school districts. These procedures include counseling incompetent teachers out of the profession and suggesting and financing early retirement.[6]

---

[5]Mark F. Bernstein, "Delaying Teacher Tenure for Education's Good," *School Administrator* (May 2006), available at **www.aasa.org**; Stephen Sawchuck, "AFT Urged to Adopt Streamlined Teacher-Discipline Policy," *Education Week*, January 28, 2011; and "Teacher Tenure is under Increased Attack," 2012 posting by *eSchool News*, available at **www.eschoolnews.com**.
[6]Edwin M. Bridges, *Managing the Incompetent Teacher,* 2nd ed. (Eugene, OR: ERIC Clearinghouse on Educational Management, 1990). See also Zach Miner, "Ratting Out Bad Teachers," *District Administration* (May 2008), p. 12; and Alain Jehlen, "'I Couldn't Believe It Happened to Me'," *NEA Today*, April 11, 2011, available at **www.nea.org/neatoday**.

TAKING ISSUE

Read the brief introduction below, as well as the Question and the pros and cons list that follows. Then, answer the question using your own words and position.

Tenure for Teachers

At one time, many teaching positions in large cities were controlled by political patronage. In some cities, principal-ships were available for a price at the ward committeeman's office, and teaching jobs were won or lost on the basis of precinct work. In general, teachers were afraid to contradict an administrator or an influential parent. Tenure was introduced partly to stop these abuses and to give teachers independence in and out of the classroom. However, some educators now contend that the tenure system has outlived its usefulness.

Question

Should the tenure system for teachers continue? (Think about this question as you read the PRO and CON arguments listed below. What is *your* take on this issue?)

Arguments PRO

1. Teaching is, by its nature, controversial. A good teacher cannot help but offend someone at some level. Teachers can do their jobs properly only with the academic freedom that tenure helps to protect.

2. A tenure system does not protect incompetence. Procedures exist for removing a teacher who is clearly ineffective. The responsibility for teacher incompetence lies with lax state licensing procedures and with administrators who are too reluctant to dismiss teachers during probationary periods.

3. Teachers must cope with pressure from a bewildering array of sources, including parents, other community members, administrators, and legislators. A complaint from any one of these parties might lead to a teacher's dismissal. For this reason, teachers need—and deserve—the special protection offered by tenure.

4. Tenure was originally a response to serious political and administrative abuses, especially in large cities. The same forces that caused these problems still exist, and they will create similar abuses if the protection of tenure is ever removed.

Arguments CON

1. Some teachers use their positions to advance personal, social, or political views under the guise of controversial discussion. Other teachers are simply lazy or incompetent. Often these marginal teachers—not the good teachers—benefit from tenure protection.

2. The procedures for removing a tenured teacher are often so complex and arouse so much resentment among other teachers that administrators are discouraged from trying. Furthermore, even with upgraded screening methods, many ineffective teachers will continue to slip through. The only solution is to give school officials, like private employers, the right to fire an unproductive employee.

3. The many sources of pressure actually enhance a teacher's security. Active parents and community members often use their influence to protect good teachers. The layers of school administration offer avenues of appeal if a teacher's position is threatened. Thus, even without a tenure system, competent teachers will be secure in their jobs.

4. Teachers now have powerful professional organizations that shield them from undue political and administrative interference. With these organizations looking after teachers' rights, the tenure system has become an anachronism.

Question Reprise: What Is Your Stand?

Reflect again on the following question by explaining *your* stand about this issue: Should the tenure system for teachers continue?

Negotiation and Strikes

Most states allow negotiation

Teachers have the right to form and belong to unions and other professional organizations. Since the 1960s, such teacher groups have lobbied for state legislation to permit school boards to negotiate agreements with them. This effort has been successful in

Table 9.1	Due-Process Rules for Dismissing a Tenured Teacher

1. The teacher must be given timely, detailed, written notice of the charges.
2. The teacher must be accorded a hearing and sufficient time to prepare.
3. The teacher has a right to be represented by legal counsel.
4. The teacher may present written and oral evidence, including witnesses.
5. The teacher may cross-examine witnesses and challenge evidence.
6. The hearing is to be conducted before an impartial body. The U.S. Supreme Court has ruled (in *Hortonville District v. Hortonville Education Association*) that, under the U.S. Constitution, a school board may be that impartial body unless bias can be proven.
7. The teacher is entitled to a written transcript of the proceedings.
8. The teacher has the right to appeal an adverse ruling to a higher legal authority, usually the state court system.

Source: See *Hortonville District v. Hortonville Education Association*, 426 U.S. 482 (1976); Richard S. Vacca, "Teacher Evaluation and the Courts," *CEPI Education Law Newsletter* (December 2003), available at **www.cepi.vcu.edu/newsletter**; Benjamin Dowling-Sendor, "When Firing Backfires," *American School Board Journal* (April 2005); Richard S. Vacca, "Public School Teachers," *CEPI Education Law Newsletter* (October 2006), available at **www.cepi.vcu.edu/newsletter**; and Joanne Barkan, "Firing Line," *Dissent*, June 29, 2011, available at **www.dissentmagazine.org**.

most states; however, a few continue to prohibit negotiations between teachers and school boards. Although the laws enacted vary widely, they usually allow the two sides to bargain collectively or at least to "meet and confer." Some states specify the procedure that must be followed if the two sides fail to agree (for example, fact-finding in Kansas; binding arbitration in Maryland).[7]

Penalties for striking

Because education is considered a vital public service, the law generally prohibits employee strikes. (A few states allow teachers to withhold services under specific conditions written into state law.) However, teachers sometimes do strike despite legal prohibitions. In such instances, school officials can seek court injunctions ordering teachers to return to their classrooms. Defiance of a court order can result in penalties. Florida and Minnesota, for example, prohibit striking teachers from receiving salary increases for one year after a strike; New York law allows striking teachers to be penalized two days' pay for each day on strike; and Michigan permits dismissal of striking teachers.

Protection against Assault

Physical assault

In recent decades, physical assault on teachers and administrators has become an important problem at some schools, particularly secondary schools in big cities. In such cases, courts generally have convicted defendants who violated either educational statutes or state criminal codes. Some analysts have concluded that educators can help protect themselves and their fellow employees by vigorously pressing criminal charges and initiating civil suits for assault and battery. In addition, many school districts have developed policies that stress punishment of students, parents, or others who assault teachers and that also assist teachers in pursuing legal responses. On the other hand, due to various legal complications, it often is difficult to prosecute or otherwise punish special-education students who assault teachers.[8]

[7]Tom Loveless, ed., *Conflicting Missions* (Washington, D.C.: Brookings Institution, 2000); Steven Klein, "Hammer It Out," *American School Board Journal* (April 2008), pp. 31–35; and Stephen Sawchuck, "States Eye Curbs on Collective Bargaining by Teachers," *Education Week*, February 20, 2011.
[8]Kevin Bushweller, "The Return of Laura Marks," *Teacher Magazine* (November/December 2001), pp. 22–29; Perry A. Zirkel, "Assaults on School Personnel," *Principal* (September/October 2002); and Susan Snyder, "Violence Targets Teachers, Staff," *Philadelphia Inquirer*, March 30, 2011, available at **www.philly.com**.

OVERVIEW 9.1

Selected U.S. Supreme Court Decisions Affecting Teachers' Rights and Responsibilities

Case	Summary of Decision
Pickering v. Board of Education (1968)	Teachers may speak their opinions as long as the school's regular operation is not disrupted.
Board of Regents of State Colleges v. Roth (1972)	After the probationary period, teachers have a property interest in continued employment.
Cleveland Board of Education v. LeFleur (1974)	Boards of education may establish leave policies for pregnant teachers, but these policies may not contain arbitrary leave and return dates.
Hortonville District v. Hortonville Education Association	In a due-process hearing, a school board may be the impartial body conducting the hearing.
Washington v. Davis (1976)	Underrepresentation of a group in the work force does not, in itself, prove unconstitutional employment discrimination, but the employer in this situation must prove that hiring has not been discriminatory.
School Board of Nassau County v. Arline (1987)	Dismissing a teacher because of a physical impairment or contagious disease is unconstitutional.
Lehnert v. Ferris Faculty Association (1991)	Employees who are not union members cannot be required to pay dues used for political purposes unrelated to collective bargaining agreements.

Protection against Unreasonable Search and Surveillance

Open-ended property search

Teachers have Fourth Amendment privacy rights that protect them against unreasonable open-ended search of their property, such as a locked desk in their classroom or a car in the school parking lot. School officials, police, or others must have some kind of evidence that provides a reasonable basis to support their search.

In several instances, administrators have installed video and/or audio in classrooms to provide surveillance of actions that allegedly might be dangerous to students. In one case in which audio recording devices were placed in special-education classrooms, a federal court ruled that this did not violate teachers' rights because a classroom is a public-use area subject to constant scrutiny. However, a state court subsequently found the district in violation of that state's eavesdropping laws.

Freedom of Expression

Courts have tended to uphold teachers' rights to express themselves in public or in school (see Overview 9.1). However, in determining whether the expression is protected under the First Amendment, the court considers the effects on school operation, teacher performance, teacher–superior relationships, and coworkers, as well as the appropriateness of the time, place, and manner of the teacher's remarks.

Pickering: protection of free expression

An example is the case of Marvin Pickering, a tenured high-school teacher who published a letter to the editor of the local newspaper criticizing the board and superintendent about bond proposals and expenditures. The letter resulted in his termination. In *Pickering v. Board of Education,* the U.S. Supreme Court held that publishing the letter did not impede the "proper performance of his daily duties in the classroom or . . . [interfere] with the regular operation of schools generally." For this reason, Pickering's dismissal was found to be improper. Similarly, the court system awarded $1 million to a Portland, Oregon, teacher whose district fired her for speaking out against the insufficient opportunities provided for her special-education students.[9]

On the other hand, two teachers in Alaska were dismissed for writing a letter that was highly critical of their superintendent and contained many false allegations. Reaction to the letter was immediate and prolonged. The Alaska Supreme Court held that the teachers' effectiveness had been impaired by their remarks and that their ability to work closely with colleagues had been diminished.[10]

A comparison of these cases shows that the decision rested not just on the behavior itself but also on its results. The courts have developed a three-step analysis for assessing teachers' rights to freedom of expression: (1) Did the teacher's expression of opinion involve a public matter of political, social, or other concern to the community? (2) If yes, courts still must weigh First Amendment rights against the employer's responsibility to promote a productive and harmonious climate for the delivery of education. The latter consideration led the courts to reject teachers' rights to wear political buttons if that might affect their communicating the curriculum. Finally, (3) the teacher is entitled to judicial relief only if his or her expression of opinion can be shown to be a motivating factor in dismissal or other punitive action. The Supreme Court largely reaffirmed this line of reasoning in the *Garcetti v. Ceballos* decision in 2006.[11]

Pickering and similar decisions would not be applicable to teachers in schools not publicly funded. The civil rights of private- and parochial-school teachers—tenure, freedom of expression, due process, and the like—depend primarily on the terms of their individual contracts with the school.

Verbal and Emotional Abuse of Students   Teachers' rights to freedom of expression do not extend, of course, to verbal or emotional abuse of students. Teachers can be sued and/or suspended or dismissed for engaging in such behavior. A teacher who also served as a basketball and football coach was accused of using terms (while coaching) such as "tontos" in dealing with Native American students and "jungle bunnies" in referring to African American students. Although allowed to continue teaching science and physical education, he was suspended from coaching for unprofessional conduct. Other teachers have had their employment terminated or interrupted for directing obscene curses at students they perceived as troublesome or for persistently using sarcasm and ridicule to pressure or embarrass students. Teachers also can be sued personally under civil liability or criminal statutes by parents who believe their children have been injured by verbal or emotional abuse or even by allegedly vulgar materials assigned by the teacher.[12]

Sidenotes (left margin):

- Impaired teacher effectiveness
- Three-step analysis
- Nonpublic teachers not necessarily protected
- Verbal abuse not condoned

---

[9]*Pickering v. Board of Education*, 391 U.S. 563 (1968). See also Sara Kennedy, "One Teacher's Voice," 2005 posting available at **www.handsandvoices.org**: search for "Settlegoode"; Richard S. Vacca, "Teacher First Amendment Speech 2006," *CEPI Education Law Newsletter* (January 2006), available at **www.cepi.vcu.edu/newsletter**; Justin M. Bathon and Kevine P. Brady, "Teacher Free Speech and Expression in a Digital Age," *NASSP Bulletin* (September 2010), pp. 213–226; and "Teachers' Different Freedoms and Laws," 2011 posting by FindLaw, available at **http://public.findlaw.com**.

[10]*Watts v. Seward School Board*, 454 P. 2d 732 (Alaska 1969), cert. denied, 397 U.S. 921 (1970). See also Edwin C. Darden, "When Speech Isn't Free," *American School Board Journal* (December 2007), pp. 42–43; and Priscilla Winslow, "Garcetti Four Years Later," *CPER Journal* (March 2011).

[11]Benjamin Dowling-Sendor, "Is Speaking Out Cause for Dismissal?" *American School Board Journal* (March 1990), pp. 8, 46; Richard. S. Vacca, "*Garcetta v. Ceballos*," *CEPI Education Law Newsletter* (October 2007), available at **www.cepi.vcu.edu/newsletter**; and Joan Del Fattore, "Defending Academic Freedom in the Age of Garcetti," *Academe* (January/February 2011), available at **www.aaup.org**.

[12]Perry A. Zirkel and Ivan B. Gluckman, "Verbal Abuse of Students," *Principal* (May 1991), pp. 51–52; Mark Walsh, "'Slave Ship' Case Settled," *Education Week*, July 8, 1998; Edwin C. Darden, "The Words That Wound," *American School Board Journal* (March 2008), pp. 42–43; Margaret King and Gregory Janson, "First Do No Harm," *Early Childhood Education Journal* (August 2009), pp. 1-4; and Pete Wright, "Dealing with a Verbally Abusive Teacher," 2011 posting by Wrightslaw, available at **www.wrightslaw.com**.

Academic Freedom

Challenges to books and other materials

Academic freedom refers to the teacher's freedom to choose subject matter and instructional materials relevant to the course without interference from administrators or outsiders. Recent years have witnessed hundreds of incidents in which parents or others have tried to remove or restrict use of public-school materials, including allegedly immoral or unwholesome works such as *Little Red Riding Hood,* the Harry Potter series, *Snow White, Huckleberry Finn,* and the *Goosebumps* series. There have been nearly nine thousand attempts to ban materials from U.S. schools and libraries since 1990. Several courts have ruled that materials can be eliminated on the basis of vulgarity but not to censor ideas. In general, teachers should have a written rationale for the materials they select, explaining how they fit into the curriculum, and they should give students a choice of alternate materials if the students or their parents object to the materials selected.[13]

Teachers upheld

Appeals courts have upheld a high-school teacher's right to assign a magazine article containing "a vulgar term for an incestuous son"; another teacher's use of a film in which citizens of a small town randomly killed one person each year; school library inclusion of books involving witchcraft and the occult; and elementary-school teachers' use of a literary anthology in which students were instructed to pretend they were witches and write poetic chants.[14]

Restrictions upheld

On the other hand, decisions of school officials to restrict teachers' academic freedom have sometimes been upheld. For example, a West Virginia art teacher was suspended for (unwittingly) distributing sexually explicit cartoons, an Ohio English teacher was prohibited from assigning the books *One Flew over the Cuckoo's Nest* and *Manchild in the Promised Land* to juvenile students unless their parents consented, a North Carolina teacher was disciplined after her students performed a play containing adult language in a state drama competition, and an Ohio teacher was dismissed for inappropriate religious activities that included branding crosses electrically onto students' arms.

Issues courts consider

In general, courts have considered the following issues: (1) students' age and grade level, (2) the relevancy of the questioned material to the curriculum, (3) the duration of the material's use, (4) the general acceptance of a disputed teaching method within the profession, (5) the prior existence of board policy governing selection of materials and teaching techniques, (6) whether the materials are required or optional, and (7) whether actions against the teacher involved retaliation for free expression.[15]

Teacher as Exemplar or Role Model

Morality standards

Decades ago, teachers' behaviors were closely scrutinized because communities believed they should be exemplars—that is, examples to their students of high moral standards and impeccable character, conservative dress and grooming, and polished manners. Although these standards have relaxed, in some places teachers may still be dismissed under immorality statutes for a drunk-driving incident, homosexuality, or for living

---

[13]*Board of Education v. Pico,* 102 S. Ct. 2799 (1982); "More Than a Book a Day Challenged in U.S. Schools, Libraries," 2006 posting at **www.ala.org/bbooks**; Jack L. Nelson, "The Need for Courage in American Schools," *Social Education* (November/December 2010), pp. 298–303; and Gordon Flegg, "So It Goes," *American Libraries,* August 3, 2011, available at **www .americanlibrariesmagazine.org**.

[14]*Keefe v. Geanakos,* 418 F. 2d 359 (1st Cir. 1969); *Pratt v. Independent School District No. 831,* 670 F. 2d 771 (8th Cir. 1982); and *Brown v. Joint Unified School District,* 42-15772 (9th Cir. 1994). See also Todd A. DeMitchell and John J. Carney, "Harry Potter and the Public School Library," *Phi Delta Kappan* (October 2005), pp. 159–165; and Lewis Beale, "Book Banners Finding Power in Numbers," *Miller-McCune,* February 10, 2011, available at **www.miller-mccune.com**.

[15]*DeVito v. Board of Education,* 317 S.E. 2d 159 (W. Va. 1984). See also Benjamin Dowling-Sendor, "Who Has the Right to Choose?" *American School Board Journal* (March 2002); Michael D. Simpson, "Defending Academic Freedom," *Social Education* (November/December 2010), pp. 310–315; and Greg Laden, "Creationist Teacher Fired," 2011 posting by Science Blogs, available at **www.scienceblogs.com**.

unmarried with a member of the opposite sex. Seemingly less weighty behaviors have also become grounds for dismissal, such as engaging in a water fight in which a student suffered mild skin irritations or joking about testes and menstrual periods when these topics were not part of the curriculum being taught by a science teacher.[16]

Renewed emphasis on role-model responsibilities

Recent years have seen a movement toward reemphasizing teachers' responsibilities as moral exemplars in and out of school. Many parents have demanded that schools reinforce traditional values among students, and many schools have introduced character education programs. School district policies generally still require that teachers serve as positive role models. Based in part on such requirements, Indiana courts upheld the dismissal of a teacher who drank beer in the presence of students at a local restaurant and then drove them home. A number of teachers have been reprimanded, suspended, or even fired for posting sexually oriented material on the Internet. According to attorneys for the National School Boards Association, misbehavior outside the school that reduces teachers' capacity to serve as positive role models can justify reprimands or dismissals as long as rights to free speech and free association (with friends or acquaintances of one's choice) are not violated. Some courts have followed this line of reasoning in allowing school districts to carry out random drug testing of teachers and other staff. However, teachers are much less likely than professionals in general to be found or accused of using illegal drugs, and teacher groups have tended to view random testing as an invasion of privacy. At least one federal court has ruled that such testing unconstitutionally violates teachers' rights to be free of unreasonable searches.[17]

Prohibiting gay discrimination

Moral standards are also subject to changing social mores. In the past few years, for example, some states and numerous jurisdictions have passed laws prohibiting discrimination against gay or lesbian individuals. Several courts have cited such laws in rejecting job termination and other actions that may have been directed against gay or lesbian teachers.[18]

Dress and grooming cases

Courts also have decided cases in which teachers' dress and grooming conflicted with school district policies or traditions. One California court ruled that women teaching at "back-to-basics" schools in Pomona could not be required to wear dresses if they preferred to wear outfits with pants. Another California court ruled that Paul Finot's wearing of a beard was symbolic expression protected by the First Amendment as well as a liberty protected under the Fourteenth Amendment. On the other hand, when Max Miller's contract was not renewed because of his beard and long sideburns, the circuit court upheld the dismissal. "As public servants in a special position of trust," the judges stated, "teachers may properly be subjected to many restrictions in their professional lives which would be invalid if generally applied." In any case, proper attire and grooming are important considerations in the profession of teaching whether or not they are legally required.[19]

---

[16]*Everett Area School District v. Ault,* 548 A. 2d 1341 (Pa. Cmwlth. 1988); *Baldrige v. Board of Trustees,* No. 97–230 (Washington 1997); Richard S. Vacca, "Public Trust and the Role of Classroom Teachers," *CEPI Education Law Newsletter* (March 2005), available at **www.cepi.vcu.edu/newsletter**; Edwin C. Darden, "Conduct Unbecoming," *American School Board Journal* (October 2007); Wendy Owen, "Fashion Doesn't Make the Teacher, But It Gets Respect from Students," *Oregon Live,* October 12, 2009, available at **www.oregonlive.com**; and "Using Facebook Can Get School Employees Fired," *Education News,* February 1, 2012.
[17]Perry A. Zirkel, "My Space?" *Phi Delta Kappan* (January 2009), pp. 388–389; and Richard S. Vacca, "Teacher Dismissal for Unprofessional Conduct," *CEPI Education Law Newsletter* (January 2011), available at **www.cepi.vcu.edu/newsletter**.
[18]Michael D. Simpson, "Big Legal Victories for Gay Students and Teachers," *NEA Today* (January 2003); Karen Graves, "Doing the Public's Business," *Educational Studies* (February 2007), pp. 7–32; Suzanne E. Eckes and Martha M. McCarthy, "GLBT Teachers," *American Educational Research Journal* (No. 3, 2008), pp. 530–554; Holly N. Bishop, Chadwick Caraway, and David L. Stader, "A Case for Legal Protection for Sexual Minority Educators," *Clearing House* (March 2010), pp. 84–88; and Alex Blaze, "When Students Harass Gay Teachers," *The Bilerico Project,* January 31, 2011.
[19]*Miller v. School District No. 167 of Cook County, Illinois,* 495 F. 2d 65 (7th Cir. 1974); *Finot v. Pasadena City Board of Education,* 58 Cal. Rptr. 520 (1976); June Million, "Dress Codes for Teachers?" *Education Digest* (January 2004), pp. 59–61; and "May a Teacher Wear Clothing Not Approved by a Teacher Dress Code?" 2011 posting by the First Amendment Center," available from **www.firstamendmentschools.org/freedoms/faq.aspx?id=13027**.

Legal and Ethical Dimensions of Teaching: Reflections from Today's Educators

Go to the Education CourseMate website to access the video entitled, "Legal and Ethical Dimensions of Teaching: Reflections from Today's Educators." Think about what aspects of the law will be relevant to you as a teacher. The video covers issues that teachers face every day, such as ethical dilemmas, concerns about child abuse, and how the law affects courses of action. After watching the video, answer the following questions:

1 Discuss your thoughts about the issue of academic freedom. Do you think that teachers should be able to assign learning materials that others (such as parents) may find controversial? Explain your answer.

2 This video introduces the viewer to a variety of legal and ethical issues that confront teachers on a day-to-day basis. Choose a particular vignette or story told within the video and explain how you might handle the situation if you were the classroom teacher. Use the chapter content to inform your decision making about the issue.

This video case reinforces key concepts found in Section IV: Profession and Community of the Praxis II exam.

Tort Liability and Negligence

Student injuries

Torts are civil wrongs. Under tort law, individuals who have suffered through the improper conduct of others may sue for damages. For example, educators may be found guilty of negligence when students are injured during classes, on the playground, or elsewhere if the injury resulted from failure to take appropriate preventive action. Of course a case won't be filed every time a child is accidentally injured, but when injury results from negligent or intentional action, legal remedies can be pursued.

Decline of immunity

A generation ago, nearly every school district was immune from tort liability. This immunity had its origins in English common law, under which the king, as sovereign, could not be sued. Since 1960, most states have eliminated or modified this view of governmental immunity. In states that permit suits, the parties sued may include the school district as well as specific school administrators, teachers, and other staff. For example, school districts can be held liable for their employees' negligent or malicious actions (such as sexual abuse, neglect of hazing or bullying among students, or failure to report students' suicidal intentions) if school officials have provided little or no supervision or ignored persistent complaints. These responsibilities even extend to malicious or neglectful action or inaction by volunteers who donate time to work with a school.[20]

Standards of proper care

Teachers are required by law to protect their students from injury or harm. In nearly all states, the traditional standard of care is what a reasonable and prudent person would do under similar circumstances. In one case, a kindergarten teacher was charged with negligence when a child fell from a playground structure while the teacher was attending to other children. The court ruled that the teacher was not required to have all children in sight at all times. Her presence in the immediate area was sufficient

[20]Rebecca Jones, "Schools and the Law," *American School Board Journal* (April 2000); Richard S. Vacca, "Tort Liability and School Staff," *CEPI Education Law Newsletter* (January 2008), available at **www.cepi.vcu.edu/newsletter**; and Mark Walsh, "Court Upholds Law Protecting Teachers and Administrators," *Education Week*, February 23, 2011.

Teachers must try to foresee potentially dangerous situations and prevent injuries to their students.

to establish that the teacher was fulfilling her duty. The New York State Supreme Court reached a similar conclusion in overturning a jury award to an injured high-school athlete, on grounds that school officials had exercised "reasonable care" in operating their school's football program. In other cases, however, school districts or their employees have been found partially or wholly responsible for students' injuries that a reasonable person should have been able to foresee.[21]

Can danger be foreseen?

An important principle is whether the injury could have been foreseen and thus prevented. An overweight student expressed concern to her physical education teacher about a class requirement to perform a back somersault. The teacher insisted the somersault be done, and the student's neck snapped in the attempt. The court said the teacher showed utter indifference to the student's safety, and the jury awarded $77,000 in damages. Similarly, a high-school student in an introductory chemistry class blew away his hand while completing an assignment to make gunpowder. The court ruled that the injury was foreseeable, and the teacher was negligent. Typically, courts will take into account the age and maturity of students, the degree of difficulty and inherent danger of activities, the proper use of protective devices, and related considerations in determining whether adults were negligent in not foreseeing the likelihood of injuries.[22]

Parental consent forms

School districts require parents to sign consent forms when students are involved in activities such as field trips or athletic competition. The form generally has two purposes: to inform parents of their children's whereabouts and to release school personnel from liability in case of injury. However, because parents cannot waive a child's

[21]*Clark v. Furch*, 567 S.W. 2d 457 (Mo. App. 1978); Benjamin Dowling-Sendor, "Friday Night Tragedy," *American School Board Journal* (September 2004); Kelley R. Taylor, "Misplaced Blame?" *Principal Leadership* (March 2010), pp.8–10; and Brittany Smith, "Fighting Back," *Valparaiso University Law Review* (No. 2, 2011).
[22]*Landers v. School District No. 203, O'Fallon*, 383 N.E. 2d 645 (Ill. App. Ct. 1978). See also George R. Schaefer and Colleen McGlone, "Negligence and Sovereign Immunity," *Journal of Physical Education, Recreation & Dance* (August 2006), pp. 10–11; Edwin C. Darden, "A Slippery Slope," *American School Board Journal* (April 2007); and Richard S. Vacca, "Student Safety," *CEPI Education Law Newsletter* (February 2011), available at **www.cepi.vcu.edu/newsletter**.

AP Photo/Jim Cole

right to sue for damages if an injury occurs, these forms actually serve only the first purpose. Obtaining a parental waiver does *not* release teachers from their legal obligations to protect the safety and welfare of students.

Recent years have brought what some observers describe as an explosion in litigation related to liability and negligence. In addition, rather than accepting the exercise of reasonable precautions as a defense against negligence, recent judicial decisions have frequently emphasized "strict liability." In this situation, teachers cannot be too careful, for negligence might occur in numerous school settings. Physical-education instructors, counselors, sponsors of extracurricular activities, and shop and laboratory teachers must take special care. Prudent safeguards include a clear set of written rules, verbal warnings to students, regular inspection of equipment, adherence to state laws and district policies regarding hazardous activities, thoughtful planning, and diligent supervision.[23]

Reporting Child Abuse

Laws require reporting abuse

Because a high percentage of abuse is directed at school-age children, schools play an important role in protecting them. In most states, laws require educators to report suspected cases of child abuse to authorities or designated social service agencies. As a result, increasing numbers of school districts have written policies describing how teachers should proceed when they suspect abuse.

Copyright Laws

Fair-use guidelines

A *copyright* gives authors and artists control over the reproduction and distribution of works they create; consequently, permission for reproduction usually must be obtained from the owner. Beginning in the 1970s, widespread use of copy machines bred serious and regular violations of copyright laws. To address this problem, in 1976 Congress amended the original 1909 copyright laws to include photocopying and the educational use of copyrighted materials. In addition, a committee of librarians, publishers, authors, and educators developed "fair-use" guidelines. **Fair use** is a legal principle that allows use of copyrighted materials without permission from the author under specific, limited conditions. New restrictions on the fair use of copyrighted materials are emerging in connection with the Internet and other digital media. Table 9.2 summarizes fair-use restrictions on copying for classroom use or other educational purposes.[24]

Continuity & Change

Plays and musicals

Authors usually copyright plays and musical productions, and schools must obtain permission from the author or the author's agent before presenting such works. Often a royalty fee is charged to secure permission, the amount of which may depend on whether or not admission is charged.

Video recordings

Videotapes and DVDs also fall within the fair-use guidelines of the copyright laws. These guidelines specify that educational institutions may not keep the recordings they make of copyrighted television programs for more than forty-five days without a license. During the first ten days, an individual teacher may use the recorded program once and may show it once again after that period when "instructional reinforcement is necessary." After forty-five days, the tape or DVD must be erased. Video recording may occur only when a faculty member requests it in advance; thus, it may not be done on a regular basis in anticipation of faculty requests.

---

[23]Robert J. Shoop, "Identifying a Standard of Care," *Principal Leadership* (March 2002); Mark S. Kapocius, "Sound Advice," *American School Board Journal* (March 2006); and Jack Zemlicka, "Tough Cases to Tackle," *Wisconsin Law Journal*, February 14, 2011, available at **www.wislawjournal.com**.
[24]Linda Starr, "Copyrights and Copying Wrongs," 2010 paper posted at the Education World Internet site, available at **www.educationworld.com/a_curr/curr280a.shtml**; Preston Parker, "Copyright Future in the Digital World," *Tech Trends* (May 2011), pp. 16–18; and U.S. copyright legislation and practices at **www.loc.gov/copyright**.

Table 9.2	**Fair-Use Guidelines on Copying Materials for Educational Use**

- Copying of prose is limited to excerpts of no more than 1,000 words.
- Copies from an anthology or encyclopedia cannot exceed one story or entry, or 2,500 words.
- A poem may be copied if it is less than 250 words, and an excerpt of no more than 250 words may be copied from a longer poem.
- Distribution of copies from the same author more than once a semester or copying from the same work or anthology more than three times during the semester is prohibited.
- Teachers may make one copy per student for class distribution; if charges are made, they may not exceed actual copying costs.
- It is illegal to create anthologies or compilations by using photocopies as a substitute for purchasing the same or similar materials.
- Consumable materials, such as workbooks, may not be copied.
- Under the fair-use doctrine, single copies of printed materials may be made for personal study, lesson planning, research, criticism, comment, and news reporting.
- Most magazine and newspaper articles may be copied freely. However, items in weekly newspapers and magazines designed for classroom use by students may not be copied without permission.
- Individual teachers must decide independently to copy material; they may not be directed to do so by higher authorities.
- There are three categories of material for which copies may be freely made: writings published before 1978 that have never been copyrighted, published works for which copyrights are more than seventy-five years old, and U.S. government publications.
- It is safer to link to a source than to provide a full download if you are not sure you have fair use.

Software

Computer software is subject to the same fair-use restrictions as other copyrighted materials. For example, teachers may not copy a protected computer program and distribute it for use on school computers. Downloading computer files from another source may require permission and/or fees. For example, after it was found that a Los Angeles school allegedly possessed pirated copies of hundreds of software programs, district officials agreed to pay $300,000 to rectify this infringement and to develop a multimillion-dollar plan to pay for violations at other schools.[25]

Internet

Copyright Policy and New Media   **Copyright** policy involving the Internet and other new media is becoming an increasingly difficult concern for teachers, students, and administrators. On the one hand, copyright holders have taken action to prohibit unauthorized use of text or images, to correct or restrict posting of incomplete or erroneous materials, or otherwise to reduce or eliminate potentially illegal publication of their materials on the Internet and other platforms. Business and commercial groups led by the entertainment and software industries worked with federal legislators to develop the No Electronic Theft Act of 1997, the Digital Millennium Act of 1998, the Technology, Education, and Copyright Harmonization Act of 2002, and the Enforcement of Intellectual Property Rights Act of 2008, which provide hefty penalties for possessing or distributing illegal electronic copies.

---

[25]Information on the complex issues involving copyright of digital materials is provided at **www.wustl.edu/policies/computing.html**.

On the other hand, new technologies are enabling individuals to draw on a multitude of sources and mix all or part of them with their own creations, in an almost endless variety of forms and transformations that are extremely difficult for copyright owners to discern or police. Concerned that many educators are interpreting guidelines such as those we offer in this text too fearfully and restrictively to allow for many lawful uses of copyrighted materials, a working group of media-literacy specialists, legal experts, and concerned educators has prepared a "Code of Best Practices in Fair Use for Media Education Literacy." The code states the following:[26]

REFOCUS What areas of caution did the preceding material suggest to you as a teacher? What topics might require further study to make sure you do not violate the law but can also defend your rights as a teacher?

1. Educators can make illustrative material from copyright sources available to learners in class or in workshops or mentoring sessions, but they should select only material relevant to the project or topic and use only what is necessary for the educational goal.

2. Educators can integrate copyrighted material into books, podcasts, DVD collections, websites, and other curriculum materials, but whenever possible should provide attribution for quoted material.

3. Educators should be able to share good examples of meaning and media, but in doing so should select only as much illustrative material as is necessary to attain the educational goals.

4. Educators should be free to enable learners to incorporate, change, and re-present media objects in their own classroom work, but students should be able to demonstrate how their use of copyrighted material transforms or repurposes the original.

5. Educators should work with learners to reach a reasoned decision about distribution that reflects good pedagogy and ethical values.

Students' Rights and Responsibilities

Decline of *in loco parentis*

During the 1960s, students increasingly began to challenge the authority of school officials to control student behavior. Before these challenges, students' rights were considered limited by their status as minors and by the concept of ***in loco parentis***, according to which school authorities assumed the powers of the child's parents during the hours the child was under the school's supervision. Use of this concept has declined, however, and the courts have become more active in identifying and upholding students' constitutional rights. Student responsibilities have been increasingly recognized as well—that is, understanding that students' educational rights are tied in with responsibilities on the part of both students and educators to ensure effective operation of the school.

Nonpublic-school students not necessarily protected

The following sections and Overview 9.2 summarize some of the most important court decisions involving students' rights and responsibilities. These apply primarily to public schools. As with teachers, students in nonpublic schools may not enjoy all of the constitutional guarantees discussed in this chapter. Unless a substantial relationship between the school and the government can be demonstrated, private-school activity is not considered action by the state and therefore does not trigger state constitutional obligations. However, the movement toward voucher plans (see Chapter 8, Financing Public Education) and other school choice arrangements (discussed in Chapter 16, School Effectiveness and Reform in the United States) that provide public funds for students who are attending nonpublic schools has begun to blur this distinction.

---

[26]Linda Howe-Stiger and Brian C. Donohue, "Technology Is Changing What's Fair Use in Teaching—Again," *Education Policy Analysis Archives*, 2002 posting available at **http://epaa.asu. edu**; Star Lawrence, "Copy Wrongs," *Edutopia* (April 2008), available at **www.edutopia.org**; "The Code of Best Practices in Fair Use for Media Education Literacy," 2009 posting by the Center for Social Media, available at **www.centerforsocialmedia.org**; and Edwin C. Darden, "Copyright Rules for Schools," *American School Board Journal* (April 2011), available at **www.asbj.com**.

OVERVIEW 9.2

Selected U.S. Supreme Court Decisions Affecting Student's Rights and Responsibilities

Case	Summary of Decision
Tinker v. Des Moines Independent Community School District (1969)	Students are free to express their views except if conduct disrupts class-work, causes disorder, or invades the rights of others.
Goss v. Lopez (1975)	Suspension from school requires some form of due process for students.
Ingraham v. Wright (1977)	Corporal punishment is not cruel or unusual punishment and is permitted where allowed by state law.
New Jersey v. T.L.O. (1985)	To be constitutional, searches of students and students' property must meet a two-pronged test.
Bethel School District No. 403 v. Fraser (1986)	Schools need not permit offensive or disruptive speech.
Hazelwood School District v. Kuhlmeier (1988)	A school newspaper is not a public forum and can be regulated by school officials.
Honig v. Doe (1988)	Disabled students who are disruptive must be retained in their current placement until official hearings are completed.
Gebser v. Lago Vista Independent School District (1998)	School districts are not legally at fault when a teacher sexually harasses a student unless the school acted with "deliberate indifference" in failing to stop it.

Freedom of Expression

Tinker: guarantees of free speech

In 1965, John Tinker, fifteen, his sister Mary Beth, thirteen, and friend Dennis Eckhardt, sixteen, were part of a small group planning to wear black armbands to school as a silent, symbolic protest against the war in Vietnam. Hearing of this plan and fearing problems, administrators responded by adopting a policy prohibiting the wearing of armbands; the penalty was suspension until the armbands were removed. The Tinkers and Eckhardt wore the armbands as planned, refused to remove them, and were suspended. Their parents filed suit. In finding for the plaintiffs, the U.S. Supreme Court outlined the scope of student rights, so that this case, *Tinker v. Des Moines Independent Community School District,* became the standard for examining students' freedom of speech guarantees.[27]

Bethel/Fraser: limits of free speech

To justify prohibition of a particular expression of opinion, the Court ruled, school officials must be able to show that their actions were caused by "something more than a mere desire to avoid the discomfort and unpleasantness that always accompany an unpopular viewpoint." Student conduct that "materially disrupts classwork or involves substantial disorder or invasion of the rights of others" could be prohibited. In the absence of such good reasons for restraint, the students' constitutional guarantees of free speech would apply. But as the preceding statements suggest, free expression in public schools has limits. In *Bethel School District No. 403 v. Fraser,* the U.S. Supreme Court confirmed that students may be punished for offensive or disruptive speech. In 2007, the Court added that administrators may prohibit student speech they view as promoting illegal drugs.[28]

---

[27]*Tinker v. Des Moines Independent Community School District,* 393 U.S. 503 (1969). See also Benjamin Dowling-Sendor, "The Boundaries of Law," *American School Board Journal* (March 2005); Robert M. O'Neil, "Legal Issues in the Protection of Student Freedoms," *Social Education* (November/December 2010), pp. 322–325; and Beth Hawkins, "Tinker Case Guides Court," *Minnesota Post,* June 15, 2011, available at **www.minnpost.com**.
[28]*Bethel School District No. 403 v. Fraser,* 106 S. Ct. 3159 (1986). See also Josh Dunn and Martha Derthick, "Doubtful Jurisprudence," *Education Next* (Winter 2008), available at **www.educationnext.org**; and Richard S. Vacca, "Student Expression and Assaultive Speech," *CEPI Education Law Newsletter* (March 2011), available at **www.cepi.vcu.edu/newsletter**.

FROM PRESERVICE TO PRACTICE

Advising a Student Newspaper

Sara Rodriguez couldn't believe that she had been assigned to be the faculty adviser for the student newspaper. After all, she was just a beginning teacher. Sara had written for her high-school and university student newspapers, but she had never been in charge of such a project. Now Sara found herself supervising and directing eighteen-year-old students, just three years her junior.

Sara, twenty-one, had recently graduated with an English major and journalism minor. She would be teaching English II and English III, and the student newspaper would be an extracurricular activity.

Bob Cartwright, the student editor, was a member of the senior class who was frequently outspoken about his beliefs and views. Just one month into the school year, all students attended a required assembly for an anti-drug program. The next day, Bob came to her and said that he was going to write an editorial emphasizing student rights. He was tired of being forced to attend presentations when he had more important things to do with his time.

The next day Sara found this editorial written by Bob on her desk.

Student Rights Ignored!

Drug-free schools! Just say no!

Slogans without meaning were once again presented to an audience that was more knowledgeable about drugs than any of the presenters. Every year we have to submit to this inane practice. What a colossal waste of time and energy! If the presenters were knowledgeable, they would already know that some drugs are being grown right on this very campus.

This editor just says NO to more assemblies about drug-free schools. Students are encouraged to walk out should another of these so-called educational opportunities present itself as a requirement. Let's stand up for our right to have a voice in determining what we must suffer. Write letters to this paper. Write to the principal and to the superintendent. Let them know what you think about this assembly and demand to have students involved in the planning process for all assemblies in the future.

Sara decided she must respond quickly, yet she did not want to cause a problem where there was none. She wondered if this editorial would cause trouble and thought she had better seek assistance from the principal. Her English classes were going well, but she wondered if problems serving as student newspaper adviser and dealing with this situation and other similar situations might jeopardize her chances for tenure or a continuing contract.

Case Questions

1. What responsibilities and authority does Sara have as faculty adviser for the student newspaper?

2. What should Sara have determined before accepting such a position?

3. Should the student editor's action affect her evaluation?

4. What rights and responsibilities does the student newspaper editor have?

Hazelwood/Kuhlmeier: regulating student publications

Student publications may also raise problems. For example, in one case, school policy required the principal to review each proposed issue of *The Spectrum,* the school newspaper written by journalism students at Hazelwood East High School in St. Louis County, Missouri. The principal objected to two articles scheduled to appear in one issue. The principal claimed the articles were deleted not because of the subject matter but because he considered them poorly written and there was insufficient time to rewrite them before the publication deadline.

Three student journalists sued, contending that their freedom of speech had been violated. This case, *Hazelwood School District v. Kuhlmeier,* reached the U.S. Supreme Court, which upheld the principal's action. The justices found that *The Spectrum* was not a public forum; rather, it was a supervised learning experience for journalism students. As long as educators' actions were related to "legitimate pedagogical concerns," they could regulate the newspaper's contents in any reasonable manner. The ruling further stated that a school could disassociate itself not only from speech that directly interfered with school activities but also from speech that was "ungrammatical, poorly written, inadequately researched, biased, prejudiced, vulgar or profane, or unsuitable for immature audiences." This decision was a clear restriction on student rights as previously understood.[29]

Legitimate regulation

Controversies concerning publications written or distributed by students have prompted many school boards to develop regulations that can withstand judicial scrutiny. Generally, these rules specify a time, place, and manner of distribution; a method of advertising the rules to students; a prompt review process; and speedy appeal procedures. Students may not distribute literature that is by legal definition obscene or libelous or that is likely to cause the substantial disruption specified in *Tinker*. School boards also have considerable leeway in determining whether nondisruptive material will be published in school newspapers and yearbooks. This chapter's "From Preservice to Practice" case study involves a teacher concerned about her responsibilities as the school newspaper adviser.

Cyberbullying and Other Electronic Misdeeds   The Internet and the development of other electronic devices have generated legal issues that educators will be contending with for a long time to come. Among the actions generating issues for educators are cyberbullying, disparagement of school or staff, gaining access to prohibited materials, and sexting. In the case of all four types of activity, students' negative actions more often than not take place outside the school, though they sometimes happen in the classroom or make use of school equipment or resources. Regarding all these types of activities, there is tension between students' rights to free speech and expression, and educators' duty to protect and enhance the welfare of students and staff.

Definition and consequences

Cyberbullying   Cyberbullying involves the use of electronic means to torment, threaten, harass, humiliate, embarrass, or otherwise target another person. The consequences of cyberbullying have been of growing concern as individuals, particularly young people, seem to be frequently using their electronic devices to transmit materials that can be perceived as harmful or damaging to others' status, health, or reputation. In several incidents highly publicized in the mass media, children and youth who perceived themselves as targets or victims of such materials have proceeded to kill themselves or have suffered damaging mental- or physical-health effects. School officials generally have been reluctant to punish the originators or transmitters of cyberbullying materials, partly because doing so might be viewed as exposing their institutions to legal liability for violating students' free speech.[30]

In a few cases, however, schools have taken action against alleged cyberbulliers, and have been taken to court for doing so. In a California case, for example, an eighth-grade girl reported that a classmate had posted a YouTube video calling her a "brat" and a "slut." The classmate was suspended for two days, after which her family sued the district for violation of free-expression rights. The presiding federal judge said that to allow a school to suspend a student "simply because another student takes offense to their speech, without any evidence that such speech caused a substantial disruption of the school's activities, runs afoul of the law," and ruled against the district. Fortunately, such restrictions do not prevent schools from implementing comprehensive policies to help students understand and avoid negative consequences of cyberbullying, and many districts are introducing such policies.[31]

[29]*Hazelwood School District v. Kuhlmeier*, 86-836 S. Ct. (1998). See also Richard S. Vacca, "Student Speech and Expression 2004," *CEPI Education Law Newsletter* (February 2004), available at **www.cepi.vcu.edu/newsletter**; Perry A. Zirkel, "Bong Hits?" *Phi Delta Kappan* (October 2007), pp. 158–159; Perry A. Zirkel, "*Tinker* Redux," *Phi Delta Kappan* (December 2008), pp. 308–309; and Aileen Abrams, "Some U.S. Supreme Court Decisions Every School Official Should Know," 2011 posting by the New York State School Boards Association, available at **www.nyssba.org**.
[30]Richard S. Vacca, "Student Expression and Electronic Communication," *CEPI Education Law Newsletter* (April 2007), available at **www.cepi.vcu.edu/newsletter**; and Justin W. Patchin and Sameer Hinduja, *Cyberbullying Prevention and Response* (New York: Routledge, 2012).
[31]Victoria Kim, "For Students, A Right to be Mean Online?" *Los Angeles Times*, December 13, 2009; "State Stifling Free Speech," 2011 posting at Education News, available at **www.ednews.org**; Kenneth S. Trump, "Managing Bullying in Politically Charged Climates," *District Administration* (January 2011); Nancy Krent, "Disciplining Student Misconduct in Cyberspace," *School Administrator* (February 2012), available at **www.aasa.org**; and information available from the Cyberbullying Research Center at **www.cyberbullying.us**.

Continuity & Change

Changing definitions of bullying and cyberbullying may be raising issues and problems for educators more frequently than in the past. Several analysts believe there is an emerging tendency to define even small acts of hostility and social exclusion as examples of bullying. For example, some children have been accused of bullying for not inviting others to their birthday parties, or for indicating dislike of particular classmates. Continuation or magnification of such a trend may make life more difficult for teachers and administrators.

Disparagement of school or staff

Disparagement of School or Staff   Some students have been punished for sending e-mail or other material that school officials considered disparaging of the school or staff, to the extent that the material was potentially disruptive or destructive. Such punishment may be legal even if the computers involved are off school property. However, electronic materials that might fit in these categories have the same legal standing as printed documents, which may require finding a delicate balance between legally protected individual rights on the one hand, and prohibitions on harming individuals and institutions on the other. Incidents that have gone to courts include the following:

- An Ohio school district had to pay $30,000 to a high-school student after it lost a court case in which the student challenged his suspension for posting material that ridiculed his band teacher.

- A Florida school district had to pay monetary damages to a student it had suspended for posting negative material about a teacher on Facebook.

- The Third Circuit Court of Appeals ruled that two students who created Myspace profiles ridiculing their principals were protected by the First Amendment in the absence of disruptive effects within the schools.

On the other hand, some courts have upheld school officials who punished students for distributing derogatory cell-phone videos of teachers, and some judges have allowed administrators to ban use of cell phones in classrooms, provided evidence was presented concerning negative effects on discipline or morale.[32]

▶❚❚ TEACHSOURCE VIDEO ACTIVITY

Cyberbullying

G o to the Education CourseMate website to access the BBC News video entitled "Cyberbullying." This video briefly describes an instance of cyberbullying that was taken care of within a social network, but it also mentions several possible technological steps to address the problem.

1 Was bullying in general a significant problem at the high school you attended? Had cyberbullying become an evident problem? Do you know any young people who have been victimized by cyberbullying? How much of a priority do you think schools and teachers should give to reducing or preventing cyberbullying?

2 The video presents several steps that might be taken to combat cyberbullying. Are there others you think might be equally or more effective? Are there legal impediments that might work against their implementation?

---

[32]Michael D. Simpson, "No More Classroom Paparazzi," *NEA Today* (October 2008); Joe Dwinell, "School Cell Phone Ban Pushes the Right Buttons," *Boston Herald*, February 8, 2011; and Vivian Nereim, "Appeals Court Rules Myspace Parodies Protected by First Amendment," *Pittsburgh Post-Gazette*, June 13, 2011, available at **www.post-gazette.com**.

Gaining access to
prohibited materials

Gaining Access to Prohibited Materials Since the **Children's Internet Protection Act (CIPA)** went into effect in 2001, schools and libraries receiving discounts on electronic equipment and media have been required to install a "technology protection measure" that prevents minors from using computers with Internet capabilities to access "visual depictions that are obscene, child pornography, or harmful to minors." After CIPA was challenged in court, the U.S. Supreme Court ruled that the law is a constitutional condition imposed on institutions in exchange for government funding. But the Court also said that institutions must adopt a policy for unblocking the Internet for adults, without requiring the user to offer reasons for disabling the filter. However, CIPA requirements sometimes have been interpreted by educators and the public as virtually prohibiting all access to YouTube and other sites that offer some prohibited material. Thus, classroom use of YouTube and similar sites frequently has been viewed as unacceptable. The U.S. Department of Education has provided the following guidance to help teachers handle YouTube and other sites while complying with CIPA:[33]

- Accessing YouTube does not necessarily violate CIPA.
- Websites blocked for students are not always denied to teachers for use in school.
- "Brute force technologies" that shut down wide swaths of the Web, such as all of YouTube, are not required.

Definition and legal
response

Sexting Sexting frequently is defined as the act of using a cell phone or comparable electronic device to transmit sexually explicit images of oneself to individuals known to or in media contact with the sender. A growing number of jurisdictions have been passing laws against sexting, generally raising child-pornography charges if the sender or recipient is not yet an adult. Depending on the jurisdiction, sexters or transmitters of the images can be charged with either misdemeanors or felonies, and can receive significant fines or jail sentences. Most often, teenagers engaged in consensual sexting are charged with misdemeanors rather than felonies.

Because sext messages can be sent easily to numerous classmates and acquaintances and sometimes create conflicts as well as damage reputations and social relationships, educators have become increasingly concerned with this type of behavior among their students. In general, school officials dealing with sexting should follow legal principles and guidelines described elsewhere in this chapter with respect to search (for example, of cell phones), discipline, and harassment.[34]

This chapter's Technology @ School feature offers more information on legal issues involved with student computer use.

Mixed rulings

Dress Codes and Regulations
Many courts have had to determine whether dress codes and regulations constitute an unconstitutional restriction on students' rights to free expression. In some instances, as in a Louisiana case dealing with requirements that football team members shave their mustaches, judges have ruled that the Constitution allows school boards to impose dress and grooming codes to advance their educational goals. Similarly, a U.S. district court upheld a ban on boys' earrings as part of a policy prohibiting display of gang emblems.

In other cases, however, judges have ruled that prohibitions against long hair were arbitrary and unreasonable and that girls' wearing of pantsuits or slacks could not be prohibited. Several courts have stopped school districts from banning rosary beads that allegedly indicate gang membership, concluding that there are better ways to limit gangs than this restriction on student expression. A federal court ruled that a school district could not prevent students from wearing bracelets stating they love Boobies because the bracelets might be expressing support for breast-cancer awareness. Much depends on the arguments and evidence regarding the educational purposes served by such restrictions,

---

[33]Tina Barseghian, "Straight From the DOE," *Mind/Shift*, April 26, 2011.
[34]Jason S. Long and Jennifer S. Caradine, "Tips for School Administrators on How to Handle 'Sexting'" 2011 posting by the National Law Review, available at **www.natlawreview.com**.

TECHNOLOGY @ SCHOOL

Legal Issues Involving Technology in Schools

The widespread and still growing emphasis on using technology in education increases the likelihood that you, as a teacher, will face legal issues involving use of computers and other electronic media. Some of these issues are spelled out in a paper titled "Navigate the Legal Maze" by Rita Oates (**www2.scholastic.com/browse**). Among the technology-related issues dealt with are teachers' acceptable use of material (taking copyright laws into account), surveillance and privacy concerns when using cameras or other recorders, students misappropriation of text or images from websites, and educators' obligations to filter digital material accessible to students. Oates points out that teachers do not have privacy protections when using district computers and that teachers can check with their district's legal counsel if there are serious questions about their responsibilities regarding lawful use of technology.

Another good source on this topic is the Center for Safe and Responsible Internet Use (**www.csriu.org**), which provides a portal to learn about basic issues, including legal issues, involving technology and safety for students, cyberbullying, responsible usage, and related matters.

the likelihood that violations will be disruptive, and the extent to which dress codes and restrictions are intended to accomplish a valid constitutional goal.[35]

A rational basis

In general, school officials must demonstrate a rational basis for prohibiting language or symbols they think may contribute to school problems. Applying this test, several courts also have ruled that public schools can require students to wear a designated uniform if school officials present evidence indicating that uniforms could help make schools safer or more productive. In several cases, dress codes have been upheld under this standard, but, in some cases, dress codes have been challenged successfully on the grounds that they were arbitrary or capricious.[36]

Suspension and Expulsion

The issue of expulsion is illustrated in the case of nine students who received ten-day suspensions from their Columbus, Ohio, secondary schools for various alleged acts of misconduct. The suspensions were imposed without hearings but in accordance with state law; the school board had no written procedure covering suspensions. The students filed suit, claiming deprivation of their constitutional rights. In defense, school officials argued that without a constitutional right to education at public expense, the due-process clause of the Fourteenth Amendment did not apply.

Minimum due process

When this case, *Goss v. Lopez*, reached the Supreme Court in 1975, a majority of the Court disagreed with the school officials, reasoning that students had a legal right to public education. In other words, students had a property interest in their education that could not be taken away "without adherence to the minimum procedures" required by the due-process clause. Further, the justices said that students facing suspension "must be given some kind of notice and afforded some kind of hearing," including "an opportunity to explain [their] version of the facts." Also, "as a general

---

[35]Benjamin Dowling-Sendor, "A Matter of Disruption, Not Dress," *American School Board Journal* (August 1998); Wendell Anderson, "School Dress Codes and Uniform Policies," *Policy Report* (Fall 2002), available at **www.eric.ed.gov**; Kelly R. Taylor, "What Not to Wear," *Principal Leadership* (February 2009); David L. Hudson Jr., "Students Should Be Free to Wear Rosary Beads," 2011 posting by the First Amendment Center, available at **www.firstamendmentcenter.org**; and James R. Marsh, "Court Reverses Boobies Bracelet Ban," 2011 posting by Childlaw Blog, available at **www.childlaw.us**.

[36]Perry A. Zirkel, "A Uniform Policy," *Phi Delta Kappan* (March 1998), pp. 550–551; Benjamin Dowling-Sendor, "What Not to Wear," *American School Board Journal* (August 2005); Mark Walsh, "U.S. Appeals Court Backs District's Rules on School Uniforms," *Education Week*, May 21, 2008, p. 8; and Angela Walmsley, "What the United Kingdom Can Teach the United States about School Uniforms," *Phi Delta Kappan* (March 2011), pp. 63–66.

rule notice and hearing should precede removal of the student from school." Applying these principles to suspensions of up to ten days, the Court added that longer suspensions or expulsions might require more elaborate due-process procedures.[37]

In response to such court decisions, most school districts have developed policies governing suspensions and expulsions. These policies usually distinguish between short- and long-term suspensions. Short-term suspension rights typically include oral or written notice describing the misconduct, the evidence on which the accusation is based, a statement of the planned punishment, and an opportunity for the student to explain his or her version or refute the stated facts before an impartial person. Expulsions require full procedural due process similar to that necessary for teacher terminations.[38]

Controversy Regarding Students with Disabilities   Recent court decisions have limited school officials' authority to suspend or expel disabled students who are disruptive or violent. In the case of *Honig v. Doe*, the Supreme Court ruled that such students must be retained in their current placement pending the completion of lengthy official hearings. The Individuals with Disabilities Education Act (IDEA) of 1990 specified additional rights that make it difficult to suspend or expel students with disabilities, including those who may be severely disruptive or prone to violence. As a result, educators are seeking new ways to guarantee the rights of students while dealing with disruptive pupils who are classified as disabled. Congress has passed legislation aimed at making it less cumbersome for administrators to suspend disabled students who violate school discipline rules, but educators report that practical issues are still murky.[39]

Protection from Violence

Educators have a duty to protect students against violent actions that occur at school or at school-sponsored events, which frequently extends to off-campus events such as graduations, proms, and parties. Depending on the circumstances, the courts or other government agencies may find school districts or their employees legally liable for failing in this duty. For example, a Louisiana court held a school district partly responsible for the gunshot wound suffered by a student after a school security guard warned the student of trouble but refused to escort him to his car. Virginia Tech University was fined $55,000 by the U.S. Department of Education for its slow response in moving to protect students under gunfire from a mentally ill attacker. By contrast, an Illinois appellate court held Chicago high-school officials not liable for the shooting of a student because they did not know that the weapon had been brought into school. In general, if the chance of harm to students is highly foreseeable, the educator's "duty to care" becomes a "duty to protect." Of course, regardless of questions involving legal culpability, educators should do everything possible to protect their students from violence.[40]

Written policies

Rights of students with disabilities

Schools may be liable for violence

---

[37]*Goss v. Lopez*, 419 U.S. 565 (1975). See also Perry A. Zirkel, "Supporting Suspenders," *Phi Delta Kappan* (November 1994), pp. 256–257; Richard S. Vacca, "Student Procedural Due Process," *CEPI Education Law Newsletter* (February 2006), available at **www.cepi.vcu.edu/newsletter**; and "Student Discipline," 2011 posting by the Missouri Department of Elementary Education, available at **www.dese.mo.gov**.

[38]Perry A. Zirkel and Ivan B. Gluckman, "Due Process for Student Suspensions," *NASSP Bulletin* (March 1990), pp. 95–98; Richard S. Vacca, "Student Discipline 2010," *CEPI Education Law Newsletter* (March 2010), available at **www.cepi.vcu.edu/newsletter**; and Matthew Lynch, "Due Process in Suspension and Expulsion," *Education News*, August 12, 2011, available at **www.ednews.org**.

[39]Mitchell L. Yell, "*Honig v. Doe*," *Exceptional Children* (September 1989), pp. 60–69; Richard S. Vacca, "Student Procedural Due Process 2006," *CEPI Education Law Newsletter* (February 2006), available at **www.cepi.vcu.edu/newsletter**; and Robert K. Crabtree, "Discipline," 2011 posting by Wrightslaw, available at **www.wrightslaw.com**.

[40]Perry A. Zirkel, "Safe Promises?" *Phi Delta Kappan* (April 2000), pp. 635–636; Richard S. Vacca, "The Duty to Protect Students from Harm," *CEPI Education Law Newsletter* (November 2002), available at **www.cepi.vcu.edu/newsletter**; and Robbie Brown, "Virginia Tech Faces a Fine for Its Delays after Shooting," *New York Times*, March 29, 2011.

Gun-Free Schools Act

Zero tolerance

Zero tolerance sometimes
out of control

Zero Tolerance and Its Effects on Schools　Although school laws and policies dealing with school safety are primarily the responsibility of state and local governments (including public-school districts), growing national concern with violence in and around schools helped stimulate passage of the federal Gun-Free Schools Act of 1994. This legislation prohibits districts from receiving federal grants to improve performance among disadvantaged students unless their respective state governments have legislated "zero tolerance" of guns and other potentially dangerous weapons. By 1995, all fifty states had introduced such legislation, which in general provides for automatic suspension of students who possess objects that school officials decide are dangerous. Most districts have policies specifying how the legislation will be implemented and any additional grounds, such as possession of illegal substances, for automatic suspension.[41]

Zero-tolerance laws and policies have made schools safer than before but have also had negative effects. A study by the Harvard University Civil Rights Project found that zero-tolerance practices frequently had spun out of control in dishing out harsh punishments for minor infractions. For example, certain items leading to student suspensions or involvement of the police have generated a great deal of public ridicule of school districts, including a broken bb-gun a 10-year-old found outside his school, a kitchen knife in a lunch box, a belt buckle with a sharp edge, the finger of a kindergarten student who used it as a play gun during recess, a strong rubber band that could make a powerful sling shot, and a drawing of a student attacking a teacher. A more serious problem, according to the Advancement Project, headquartered in Washington, is that many disadvantaged students are derailed from schooling into incarceration by minor infractions of zero-tolerance policies. To avoid such outcomes and improve school climate through actions involving safety in schools, analysts urge educators to do the following:[42]

- Make sure students have opportunities to talk with and connect with caring adults.
- Provide flexibility and consider alternatives to expulsion.
- Clearly define what constitutes a weapon, a misbehavior, or a drug.
- Comply with due-process laws.
- Tailor policies to local needs and review them annually.

Search and Seizure

Fourth Amendment
rights

A legal search usually requires a lawfully issued search warrant. But rising drug use in schools and accompanying acts of violence have led some school officials (particularly in big-city high schools) to install metal detectors or X-ray machines to search for weapons. They have banned beepers and cell phones (sometimes used in drug sales), required students to breathe into alcohol-analysis machines, searched students' book bags, and systematically examined lockers. Court challenges of such practices have usually centered on the Fourth Amendment, which states: "The right of the people to be secure in their persons, houses, papers, and effects, against unreasonable searches and seizures, shall not be violated, and no warrants shall issue, but upon probable cause, supported by oath or affirmation, and particularly describing the place to be searched, and the person or things to be seized."

---

[41]Chris Pipho, "Living with Zero Tolerance," *Phi Delta Kappan* (June 1998), pp. 725–726; "Disturbing Trends of 'Zero Tolerance,'" *Education Reporter* (October 2006), available at **www .eagleforum.org**; and Gara Lamarche, "The Time Is Right to End 'Zero Tolerance'" *Education Week*, April 6, 2011.

[42]Judith A. Browne, *Derailed: The Schoolhouse to the Jail Track* (Washington, D.C.: Advancement Project, 2003), available at **www.advancementproject.org/home**; Tim Lockette, "Zero Tolerance, Zero Justice," *Teaching Tolerance*, May 13, 2009, available at **www.tolerance.org**; and "Still Haven't Shut Off the School-to-Prison Pipeline," 2011 report by ACLU of Florida Advancement Project available at **www.advancementproject.org/home**.

Reasonable cause

Legal terms express suspicion in differing degrees. The "probable" cause mentioned in the Fourth Amendment means that searchers believe it is more probable than not that evidence of illegal activity will be found. This is the degree of suspicion required for police searches. In contrast, where school searches have been upheld, courts have said "reasonable" cause was sufficient for school officials to act. Searches usually are conducted because administrators have reason to suspect that illegal or dangerous items are on the premises.

T.L.O.: searching a purse

These principles were considered in a case involving a teacher who discovered two girls in a school restroom smoking cigarettes. This was a violation of school rules, and the students were taken to the vice principal's office and questioned. One of the girls admitted smoking, but T.L.O., age fourteen, denied all charges. The vice principal opened T.L.O.'s purse and found a pack of cigarettes. While reaching for the cigarettes he noticed some rolling papers and decided to empty the purse. The search revealed marijuana, a pipe, some empty plastic bags, a large number of dollar bills, and a list entitled, "People who owe me money." T.L.O.'s mother was called, and the evidence was turned over to the police. T.L.O. confessed to the police that she had been selling marijuana at school.

Two-pronged standard

After she was sentenced to one year's probation by the juvenile court, T.L.O. appealed, claiming the vice principal's search of her purse was illegal under the Fourth Amendment. In finding for school authorities in *New Jersey v. T.L.O.*, the U.S. Supreme Court set up a two-pronged standard to be met for constitutionally sanctioned searches. Courts consider (1) whether the search is justified at its inception, and (2) whether the search, when actually conducted, is "reasonably related in scope to the circumstances which justified the interference in the first place." Using these criteria, the Court found the search of T.L.O.'s purse justified because of the teacher's report of smoking in the restroom. This information gave the vice principal reason to believe that the purse contained cigarettes. T.L.O. denied smoking, which made a search of her purse necessary to determine her veracity. When the vice principal saw the cigarettes and came across the rolling papers, he had reasonable suspicion to search her purse more thoroughly.[43]

Drug-sniffing dogs

Courts have also ruled that the suspicions of school officials sometimes were not sufficiently reasonable to justify the searches that followed. Using trained dogs to sniff student lockers and cars for evidence of drugs has been accepted because it occurred when the lockers and cars were unattended and in public view. The use of such dogs with students, however, can raise problems. In Highland, Indiana, 2,780 junior- and senior-high students waited for hours in their seats while six officials using trained dogs searched for drugs. A school official, police officer, dog handler, and German shepherd entered the classroom where Diane Doe, thirteen, was a student. The dog went up and down the aisles sniffing students, reached Diane, sniffed her body, and repeatedly pushed its nose on and between her legs. The officer interpreted this behavior as an alert signaling the presence of drugs. Diane emptied her pockets as requested, but no drugs were found. Finally, Diane was taken to the nurse's office and strip-searched. No drugs were found. Before school, Diane had played with her own dog, and this smell remaining on her body had alerted the police dog.

Strip-search unconstitutional

The Does filed suit. Both the district court and the appeals court concluded that although the initial procedures were appropriate, the strip search of Diane was unconstitutional. The court of appeals said, "It does not require a constitutional scholar to conclude that a nude search of a thirteen-year-old child is an invasion of constitutional rights of some magnitude. More than that: It is a violation of any known principle of human decency." In a similar ruling in 2009, the Supreme Court ruled that a strip search of a girl accused of providing ibuprofen to a friend was unconstitutional because

---

[43]*New Jersey v. T.L.O.*, 105 S. Ct. 733 (1985). See also Andrew Trotter, "The Perils of Strip Searches," *Executive Educator* (June 1995), pp. 29–30; Perry A. Zirkel, "Outstripping Students Again," *Phi Delta Kappan* (March 2008), pp. 538–541; Nathan Essex, "The U.S. Supreme Court Raises the Bar for Strip Searches in Public Schools," *Clearing House* (March 2010), pp. 105–108; and Emily G. Waldman, "Students' Fourth Amendment Rights in Schools," 2011 posting at the Pace University Digital Commons, available at **http://digitalcommons.pace.edu**.

"directing a 13-year-old girl to remove her clothes, partially revealing her breasts and pelvic area, for allegedly possessing ibuprofen, was excessively intrusive."[44]

In sum, when searches are conducted without a specific warrant, the following guidelines seem appropriate:[45]

Guidelines for searches

- Searches must be particularized. Reasonable suspicion should exist that *each student* being searched possesses specific contraband or evidence of a particular crime.
- Lockers are considered school property and may be searched if reasonable cause exists.
- Dogs may be used to sniff lockers and cars. Generalized canine sniffing of students is permitted only when the dogs do not touch them.
- Strip searches usually are unconstitutional and should not be conducted unless available evidence clearly indicates a significant threat to student safety is present.
- School officials may perform a pat-down search for weapons if they have a reasonable suspicion that students are bringing dangerous weapons to school.
- School officials may conduct searches on field trips, but the usual standards for searches still apply.
- School officials' judgments are protected by government immunity if the search is not knowingly illegal.

Constitutionality of video surveillance

Video Surveillance and Search   Because videos can allow for searching to identify persons who have threatened or might threaten the safety of students and staff, school officials increasingly have been installing cameras and other means of surveillance. On the other hand, extensive video surveillance can violate Fourth Amendment protections against unreasonable search and seizure. Thus, the constitutionality of video surveillance hinges on its continuing reasonableness in a given situation. Few cases examining this issue have reached the courts, but, in one instance, the Sixth Circuit Court of Appeals has ruled that it was not permissible to have ongoing scrutiny of athletic locker rooms.[46]

Testing athletes for drugs

Drug Testing as a Form of Search   Some school-board members and other policy makers have urged administrators to introduce random testing of student athletes' urine to detect marijuana, steroids, and other illegal substances. Historically, such testing was viewed as a potentially unconstitutional search. In 1995, however, the U.S. Supreme Court ruled that this type of drug search is not necessarily unconstitutional even without specific reason to suspect a particular individual. A majority of the justices concluded that school officials have reasonable grounds to be especially concerned with drug use among athletes, who presumably set an example for other students. Since then, the Supreme Court has also permitted drug testing of students engaged in other activities. Students in violation of disciplinary policies involving the possession, or sale, or use of prohibited substances on school property or at school-sponsored or school-sanctioned activities can be subject to appropriate disciplinary sanctions.[47]

[44]*Doe v. Renfrou,* 635 F. 2d 582 (7th Cir. 1980), cert. denied, 101 U.S. 3015 (1981). See also Perry A. Zirkel, "Searching Students," *Principal Leadership* (September 2005), pp. 64–68; David L. Stader et al., "Drugs, Strip Searches, and Educator Liability," *Clearing House* (March 2010), pp. 109–113; and Perry A. Zirkel, "You Can't Touch Me," *Phi Delta Kappan* (May 2011), pp. 76–77.
[45]Kate Ehlenberger, "The Right to Search Students," *Educational Leadership* (December 2001/January 2002), pp. 31–36; Edwin C. Darden, "Trouble on the Line," *American School Board Journal* (January 2007); and Emily J. Nelson, "Custodial Strip Searches of Juveniles," *Boston College Law Review* (Issue 1 2011), available at **http://lawdigitalcommons.bc.edu**.
[46]Richard S. Vacca, "Student Search and Seizure," *CEPI Education Law Newsletter* (March 2008), available at **www.cepi.vcu.edu/newsletter**; Ellen Kollie, "Video Surveillance Keeps School Users Safe," *School Planning and Management* (August 2010), pp. 62–65; and "Wyoming Teacher Evaluation Bills Contain Provisions for Video Cameras in Classrooms," 2011 posting by the National School Boards Association, available at **http://legalclips.nsba.org**.
[47]Richard S. Vacca, "Search and Seizure," *CEPI Education Law Newsletter* (April 2010), available at **www.cepi.vcu.edu/newsletter**; and Kern Alexander and David M. Alexander, *American Public School Law,* 8th ed. (Belmont, CA: Wadsworth, 2012).

Classroom Discipline and Corporal Punishment

Classroom discipline was the issue in a case involving a sixth grader who was placed in a time-out area of the classroom whenever his behavior became disruptive. The student had a history of behavioral problems, and the teacher had tried other methods of discipline without success. While in time out, the boy was allowed to use the restroom, eat in the cafeteria, and attend other classes. His parents sued, charging that the teacher's actions (1) deprived their son of his property interest in receiving a public education; (2) meted out punishment disproportionate to his offense, in violation of his due-process rights; and (3) inflicted emotional distress.

The district court said that school officials possess broad authority to prescribe and enforce standards of conduct in the schools, but this authority is limited by the Fourteenth Amendment. In this case, the student remained in school and thus was not deprived of a public education. "Time out" was declared to be a minimal interference with the student's property rights. The court noted that the purpose of a time out is to modify the behavior of disruptive students and to preserve the right to an education for other students in the classroom. All of the student's charges were dismissed.[48]

A particularly controversial method of classroom discipline is corporal punishment, which has a long history in American education dating back to the colonial period. Although there has been a steady decline in the number of states allowing corporal punishment in schools since the *Ingraham v. Wright* case in 1977, it remains legal in twenty states. It is unacceptable to many educators, although it enjoys considerable support within some segments of the community and is administered more frequently than educators like to admit. Recent surveys indicate that hundreds of thousands of children are spanked or paddled each school year, and thousands sustain injuries that require medical attention.[49]

Certain state legislatures have prohibited all corporal punishment in public schools. In states where the law is silent on this issue, local boards have wide latitude and may ban physical punishment if they choose. However, where a state statute explicitly permits corporal punishment, local boards may regulate but not prohibit its use. In this context, many school boards have developed detailed policies restricting the use of corporal punishment. Violations of policy can lead to dismissal, and legal charges are possible for excessive force, punishment based on personal malice toward the student, or unreasonable use of punishment.

Florida is an example of a state that allows corporal punishment. In 1977, the U.S. Supreme Court, in *Ingraham v. Wright*, ruled on the constitutionality of this law from two federal perspectives: (1) whether use of corporal punishment was a violation of the Eighth Amendment barring cruel and unusual punishment, and (2) whether prior notice and some form of due process were required before administering punishment.

In this case, James Ingraham and Roosevelt Andrews were junior-high students in Dade County, Florida. Because Ingraham had been slow to respond to the teacher's instructions, he received twenty paddle swats administered in the principal's office. As a consequence, he needed medical treatment and missed a few days of school. Andrews was also paddled, but less severely. Finding that the intent of the Eighth Amendment was to protect those convicted of crimes, the justices said it did not apply to corporal punishment of schoolchildren. As to due process, the Court said, "We conclude that

---

[48]*Dickens v. Johnson County Board of Education*, 661 F. Supp. 155 (E.D. Tenn. 1987). See also Josh Dunn and Martha Derthick, "Timeout," *Education Next* (Spring 2009), available at **www.educationnext.org**; Courtney Mitchell, "Corporal Punishment in the Public Schools," *Law and Contemporary Problems* (Spring 2010), pp. 321–341; and Nervi Shah, "Lt. Governors Say Spare the Rod," *Education Week*, April 6, 2011.

[49]Perry A. Zirkel and David W. Van Cleaf, "Is Corporal Punishment Child Abuse?" *Principal* (January 1996), pp. 60–61; Martha M. McCarthy, "Corporal Punishment in Public Schools," *Educational Horizons* (Summer 2005), pp. 235–240; and Richard Korman, "Is It Ever OK to Spank My Child?" *Miller-McCune*, March 28, 2011, available at **www.miller-mccune.com**. See also material available at **www.stophitting.com**.

the Due Process clause does not require notice and a hearing prior to the imposition of corporal punishment in the public schools, as that practice is authorized and limited by common law."[50]

Possible liability

Despite this ruling, the Court also commented on the severity of the paddlings. In such instances, the justices stated, school authorities might be held liable for damages to the child. Moreover, if malice is shown, the officials might be subject to prosecution under criminal statutes. In a later action, the Court also indicated a role for the due-process clause discussed earlier in this chapter. By declining to hear *Miera v. Garcia,* the Court let stand lower-court rulings that "grossly excessive" corporal punishment may constitute a violation of students' due-process rights. Thus, teachers can be prosecuted in the courts for using excessive force and violating students' rights.[51]

Indeed, lower courts have ruled against teachers or administrators who have used cattle prods to discipline students, slammed students' heads against the walls, or spanked students so hard they needed medical attention, and the Supreme Court will probably continue to uphold such rulings. Overall, recent judicial decisions, together with the ever-present possibility of a lawsuit, have made educators cautious in using corporal punishment.

Sexual Harassment or Molestation of Students

Unwelcome sexual advances

The Supreme Court's decision in *Ingraham v. Wright* regarding physical punishment and a later decision in *Franklin v. Gwinnett* strengthened prohibitions against sexual harassment and sexual molestation. Definitions of these terms vary, but for interactions between students and teachers, the terms generally include not only sexual contact that calls into question the teacher's role as exemplar but also unwelcome sexual advances or requests for favors, particularly when the recipient might believe that refusal will affect his or her academic standing. Recent years have seen a dramatic increase in court cases involving school employees accused of sexually harassing students. Although the courts have been vague on what constitutes illegal sexual harassment of students, it is clear that both staff members and the districts that employ them can be severely punished if found guilty in court.[52]

Proactive action against sexual harassment

School officials' legal responsibilities regarding teachers' sexual harassment of students were somewhat clarified in a 1998 Supreme Court decision (*Gebser v. Lago Vista Independent School District*) that involved a ninth grader who was seduced by a science teacher but never informed administrators about this sexual relationship. Her parents sued for damages from the school district using the argument that Title IX of the Education Amendments of 1972 requires schools to proactively take action to identify and eliminate sexual harassment. The Supreme Court ruled that school officials are not legally liable unless they know of the harassment and then proceed with "deliberate indifference." Some analysts were unhappy because they believed this decision allowed officials to avoid identifying and combating harassment, but others

---

[50]*Ingraham v. Wright, 430* U.S. (1977). See also Perry A. Zirkel, "You Bruise, You Lose," *Phi Delta Kappan* (January 1990), pp. 410–411; Benjamin Dowling-Sendor, "A Shock to the Conscience," *American School Board Journal* (April 2001); Doriane L. Coleman, Kenneth A. Dodge, and Sarah K. Campbell, "Where and How to Draw the Line Between Reasonable Corporal Punishment and Abuse," *Law and Contemporary Problems* (Spring 2010), pp. 107–165; and Valerie Strauss, "Teachers Hitting Kids?" *Washington Post,* February 13, 2011.
[51]*Miera v. Garcia,* 56 USLW 3390 (1987); Benjamin Dowling-Sendor, "When Teachers Get Too Tough," *American School Board Journal* (May 2000); Edwin C. Darden, "Legal Problems with Corporal Punishment," *School Administrator* (January 2009); and Dan Frosch, "Schools Under Pressure to Spare the Rod Forever," *New York Times,* March 29, 2011.
[52]Martha M. McCarthy, "The Law Governing Sexual Harassment in Public Schools," *Phi Delta Kappa Research Bulletin* (May 1998), pp. 15–18; Benjamin Dowling-Sendor, "What Did They Know?" *American School Board Journal* (August 2002); Jeremy Beck, "Entity Liability for Teacher-on-Student Sexual Harassment," *Journal of Law & Education* (January 2006), pp. 141–151; and Cecilia L. Real, "Sexual Harassment in School," *Smart Parenting,* May 16 2011, available at **www.smartparenting.com.ph**.

believed it reinforced administrators' resolve to implement policies that demonstrate their concern about harassment.[53]

Touching students unlawful?

Despite the relief from liability that *Gebser* provides for school officials, individual staff members must be wary of any action a student or parent might interpret as sexual harassment or assault. Given the numerous allegations brought against teachers in recent years, many teacher organizations have been advising their members to avoid touching students unnecessarily. They also recommend that teachers make sure that doors are open and/or that other persons are present when they meet with a student. Legal advisers recognize the necessity for or benefits of touching or even hugging a student, as when a kindergarten teacher helps students put on coats or comforts a distressed pupil or a teacher grabs the aggressor in a fight between students, but many advise teachers to avoid physical contact as much as possible, particularly with older students.

Guidelines for dealing with potential harassment

Sexual abuse or harassment of one student by another is also a serious problem. As in the case of students allegedly harassed by teachers, the law regarding harassment by other students is poorly defined and murky. Name calling and teasing with sexual overtones have been interpreted as illegal harassment that educators have a legal obligation to suppress, but in certain situations, school staff have been absolved of legal responsibility. Some school districts' anti-harassment policies have prohibited so-called unwelcome statements about gays and lesbians, but a federal appeals court prevented punishment of students who made such statements when it ruled they were exercising First Amendment rights to religious expression. On the other hand, several districts have paid settlements to gay or lesbian students who were harassed by peers. The following guidelines have been suggested for educators who think sexual harassment may be occurring:[54]

1. Don't ignore the situation or let it pass unchallenged.
2. Don't overreact; find out exactly what happened.
3. Don't embarrass or humiliate any party to an incident.
4. Initiate steps to support the alleged victim.
5. Apply consequences in accordance with school behavior codes.
6. Don't assume that the incident is an isolated occurrence.
7. Provide comprehensive awareness programs for students, teachers, parents, and administrators.
8. School psychologists, counselors, and social workers should be available on request to the victim and his or her parents.

Student Records and Privacy Rights

FERPA curbs abuses

Until 1974, students or their parents could not view most student records kept by schools. However, prospective employers, government agencies, and credit bureaus could do so. As might be guessed, abuses occurred. In 1974, Congress passed the **Family Educational Rights and Privacy Act** (also called either FERPA or the **Buckley Amendment**) to curb possible abuses in institutions receiving federal funds.

---

[53]*Gebser v. Lago Vista Independent School District,* 98-1866 S. Ct. (1998). See also *Revised Sexual Harassment Guidance* (Washington, D.C.: U.S. Department of Education Office of Civil Rights, 2001), available at **www.ed.gov**; Edward F. Dragan, "Setting Boundaries for Sexual Harassment," *School Administrator* (December 2006), available at **www.aasa.org**; Allison Fetter-Harrott, "Staff-to-Student Sexual Harassment," *District Administration* (March 2010), available at **www.districtadministration.com**; and Michael Keany, "Molestation and Rumors of Molestation," 2011 posting by School Leadership 2.0, available at **www.schoolleadership20.com**.
[54]Perry A. Zirkel, "Student-to-Student Sexual Harassment," *Phi Delta Kappan* (April 1995), pp. 448–450; Richard S. Vacca, "Student-Peer Sexual Harassment 2009," *CEPI Education Law Newsletter* (February 2009), available at **www.cepi.vcu.edu/newsletter**; and Frances E. Rogers, "Student-on-Student Sexual Harassment," *Education Digest* (April 2011), pp. 35–38.

The Buckley Amendment requires public-school districts to develop policies allowing parents access to their children's official school records. The act prohibits disclosure of these records to most third parties without prior parental consent. Districts must have procedures to amend records if parents challenge the accuracy or completeness of the information they contain. Hearing and appeal mechanisms regarding disputed information must also be available. Parents retain rights of access to their child's school records until the child reaches age eighteen or is enrolled in a postsecondary institution.

However, the Buckley Amendment allows several exceptions. Private notes and memoranda of teachers and administrators (including grade books) are exempt from view. In addition, records kept separate from official files and maintained for law-enforcement purposes (for example, information about criminal behavior) cannot be disclosed, and nothing may be revealed that would jeopardize the privacy rights of other pupils. On the other hand, many schools have become more open to making information available about students who may threaten security on campus.[55]

Student-privacy policies also are affected by the **Protection of Pupil Rights Amendment** to the federal General Education Provisions Act of 1978. This Amendment specified that instructional materials used in connection with "any research or experimentation program or project" must be "available for inspection" by participating students' parents and guardians. In addition, no student can be required to participate in testing, psychological examination, or treatments whose "primary purpose is to reveal information" concerning political affiliations, sexual behaviors or attitudes, psychological or mental problems, income, and other personal matters. It has been difficult to define terms such as "instructional materials" and "research program," and many parents have used the Protection of Pupil Rights Amendment to object to school activities that probe students' feelings or beliefs. Consequently, teachers and other staff must consider carefully whether collecting information on students' background or beliefs serves a legitimate goal.[56]

Compulsory Attendance and Homeschooling

Every state has a law requiring children to attend school, usually from age six or seven to age sixteen or seventeen. In the past two decades, these compulsory-attendance laws have received increased attention because of a revival of interest in homeschooling. A growing number of parents who object to subject matter taught in public schools, the teaching methods used, or the absence of religious activities have chosen to teach their children at home. State governments allow for homeschooling, but depending on state legislation, they impose regulations dealing with hours of study, testing, whether homeschooled children can participate in extracurricular activities at nearby public schools, and other matters.[57]

Homeschooling parents brought to court for violating compulsory-attendance laws have usually been asked to demonstrate the home program's essential equivalence to public-school offerings with respect to subject matter covered, adequacy of texts

[55]Perry A. Zirkel, "A D-Grading Experience?" *Phi Delta Kappan* (November 2000), pp. 253–254; Richard S. Vacca, "Student Records 2004," *CEPI Education Law Newsletter* (May 2004), available at **www.cepi.vcu.edu/newsletter**; Edwin C. Darden, "A School Board's Guide to FERPA," *American School Board Journal* (February 2009); and Meris Stansbury, "Feds Take Huge Steps to Protect Student Privacy," *eSchool News*, April 7, 2011, available at **www.eschoolnews.com**.
[56]Benjamin Dowling-Sendor, "A Matter of Privacy," *American School Board Journal* (November 2004); Perry A. Zirkel, "Parental Discretion Advised?" *Phi Delta Kappan* (March 2006), pp. 557–558; "School Flouts Parental Consent," *Education Reporter* (June 2011), available at **www.eagleforum.org**; and information available at **www2.ed.gov/policy/gen/guid/fpco/ppra**.
[57]Josh Dunn and Martha Derthick, "Home Schoolers Strike Back," *Education Next* (Fall 2008), available at **www.educationnext.org**; Milton Gaither, "Home Schooling Goes Mainstream," *Education Next* (Winter 2009), available at **www.educationnext.org**; Stacy T. Khadaroo, "N.H.: Can a Divorced Parent Veto Home Schooling?" *Christian Science Monitor*, January 6, 2011; and information from the Home School Legal Defense Association, available at **www.hslda.org**.

used, and hours of daily instruction. In some states, they also must show test results indicating that their children's education is comparable to that of school-educated peers. Parents have often prevailed in such cases, but courts have consistently upheld the right of state legislatures to impose restrictions and requirements.[58]

Need for Balance between Rights and Responsibilities

Critique of courts

During the past several decades, as courts have upheld the constitutional rights of students and placed restrictions on school officials, many educators and parents have decided that the legal process is out of balance. They believe that the courts place too much emphasis on student rights and too little on the need for school discipline. The result, said former AFT president Albert Shanker, "is schools where little or no learning goes on because teachers have to assume the role of warden."[59]

Focus on reasonableness

However, some scholars believe that since the mid-1980s, the Supreme Court has moved to redress the balance. In this view, the Court's decisions in *New Jersey v. T.L.O.* (1985), *Bethel v. Fraser* (1986), and *Hazelwood v. Kuhlmeier* (1988) place fewer burdens on school officials than the 1969 *Tinker* decision. Rather than demonstrating that certain rules are necessary, school officials now need to show only that the rules are reasonable. This emphasis on reasonableness indicates that the Court "is placing considerable confidence in school officials," trusting those officials to maintain a proper balance between student rights and the school's needs.[60]

Religion and the Schools

Neutral government

The framers of our Constitution were acutely aware of religious persecution and sought to prevent the United States from experiencing the serious and often bloody conflicts that had occurred in Europe. As noted at the beginning of this chapter, the First Amendment, adopted in 1791, prohibits the establishment of a nationally sanctioned religion (the establishment clause) and government interference with individuals' rights to hold and freely practice their religious beliefs (the free-exercise clause). Judge Alphonso Taft succinctly stated the position of government toward religion more than one hundred years ago: "The government is neutral, and while protecting all, it prefers none, and it disparages none."[61]

[58]Perry A. Zirkel, "Home Sweet.... School," *Phi Delta Kappan* (December 1994), pp. 332–333; and Richard Yeakley, "Court Rejects Mother's Religious Home-School Arguments," *Belief Net News*, March 18, 2011, available at **www.beliefnet.com**.

[59]Albert Shanker, "Discipline in Our Schools," *New York Times*, May 19, 1991, p. E7. See also Benjamin Dowling-Sendor, "Balancing Safety with Free Expression," *American School Board Journal* (December 2001); Perry A. Zirkel, "Handcuffing Discipline," *Phi Delta Kappan* (March 2010), pp. 76–77; and "68% Say School Discipline Is Too Easy These Days," 2011 posting by Rasmussen Reports, available at **www.rasmussenreports.com**.

[60]Lowell C. Rose, "Reasonableness—The Court's New Standard for Cases Involving Student Rights," *Phi Delta Kappan* (April 1988), pp. 589–592. See also Richard S. Vacca, "The Roberts Court," *CEPI Education Law Newsletter* (December 2008), available at **www.cepi.vcu.edu /newsletter**; Ron Schachter, "Discipline Gets the Boot," *District Administration* (January 2010), available at **www.districtadministration.com**; and Douglas E. Abrams, "Recognizing the Public Schools' Authority to Discipline Students' Off-Campus Cyberbullying of Classmates," 2011 posting by the Social Science Research Network, available at **www.ssrn.com**.

[61]Quoted by Justice Tom Clark in *School District of Abington Township v. Schempp*, 374 U.S. 203 (1963). See also Benjamin Dowling-Sendor, "Trouble in Paradise," *American School Board Journal* (June 2002); Richard S. Vacca, "Free Exercise of Religion in Public Schools," *CEPI Education Law Newsletter* (November 2006), available at **www.cepi.vcu.edu/newsletter**; and Thomas C. Berg, "The Story of the School Prayer Decisions," 2011 posting by the Social Science Research Network, available at **www.ssrn.com**.

Prayer, Bible Reading, and Religious Blessings and Displays

State-written prayer unconstitutional

Before 1962, students in New Hyde Park were required to recite daily this nondenominational prayer composed by the New York State Board of Regents: "Almighty God, we acknowledge our dependence upon thee, and we beg thy blessings upon us, our parents, our teachers and our Country." Although exemption was possible upon written parental request, the U.S. Supreme Court in *Engle v. Vitale* (1962) ruled the state-written prayer unconstitutional. According to the Court, "Neither the fact that the prayer may be denominationally neutral nor the fact that its observance on the part of students is voluntary can serve to free it from the limitations of the Establishment Clause."[62]

The decision created a storm of protest that has barely subsided to this day. A year later, the Court again prohibited religious exercises in public schools. This time, the issue involved oral reading of Bible verses and recitation of the Lord's Prayer. These were clearly religious ceremonies and "intended by the State to be so," even when student participation was voluntary. In 2000, the Court excluded student-led prayer at a football game because the game and therefore the prayer were officially sponsored by the school. On the other hand, the courts have ruled that students can lead or participate in prayers at commencement ceremonies, as long as decisions to do so are made by students without the involvement of clergy.[63]

Invocations and benedictions

The Supreme Court also has ruled against invocations and benedictions in which a clergyman opens or closes a public-school ceremony by invoking blessings from a deity. In a 1992 decision, the Court concluded that such blessings violate the standards established in *Lemon v. Kurtzman* (see Figure 9.1), which prohibit the government from advancing religion. However, Justice Anthony Kennedy's majority opinion noted that state actions implicating religion are not necessarily unconstitutional because some citizens might object to them and that the decision was not meant to require a "relentless and pervasive attempt to exclude religion from every aspect of public life."

Moment-of-silence policies

One effect of the decision was to postpone full constitutional review of several important questions, such as whether schools can implement "moment of silence" policies that allow voluntary silent prayer in classrooms, whether a school choir can perform clearly Christian songs at a graduation ceremony, and whether private groups can distribute free Bibles on school premises.

A secular atmosphere

Displaying religious symbols (such as a cross or a menorah) in public schools in a manner that promotes a particular religion is clearly unconstitutional. However, the Supreme Court has ruled that religiously oriented artifacts such as a Nativity scene can be displayed in public settings if the overall atmosphere is largely secular. The interpretation of this ruling is controversial. In one nonschool case, the Court banned a Nativity scene in front of the Allegheny County (Pennsylvania) Courthouse because it had not been "junked up" (in the words of a county official) with Santa Claus figures or other secular symbols. After that decision, a federal judge required the removal of a crucifixion painting from the Schuylerville (New York) School District, on the grounds that the painting lacked any "meaningful" secular features. In 2002, an Ohio school district was prohibited from posting the Ten Commandments in front of four high

---

[62]*Engle v. Vitale*, 370 U.S. 421 (1962). See also "Guidelines on Constitutionally Protected Prayer," 2003 paper available at **www.ed.gov**; Perry A. Zirkel, "Friday Night Rites," *Phi Delta Kappan* (October 2008), pp. 146–147; David M. Schimmel, "The Battle over School Prayer," *American Journal of Educ*ation (May 2010), pp. 453–457; and John H. McElroy, "Understanding the First Amendment's Religion Clauses," *Intercollegiate Review* (Spring 2011), available at **www .firstprinciplesjournal.com**.
[63]*School District of Abington Township v. Schempp and Murray v. Curlett*, 374 U.S. 203 (1963). See also Benjamin Dowling-Sendor, "A Defeat for Pregame Prayer," *American School Board Journal* (August 2000); Richard S. Vacca, "Graduation Prayer Revisited," *CEPI Education Law Newsletter* (May 2008), available at **www.cepi.vcu.edu/newsletter**; and "Moment of Silence Returns to Illinois," *Education Week*, January 26, 2011.

Federal judges have concluded that students who refuse to stand and recite the pledge of allegiance cannot be compelled to do so if participation violates their religious or other personal beliefs.

schools. Since then, the Supreme Court ruled that government institutions may display the Ten Commandments as part of an historical exhibit, but not as a lone display of religious messages.[64]

Access to Public Schools for Religious Groups

School meetings of religious groups

Bridget Mergens, an Omaha high-school senior, organized a group of about twenty-five students who requested permission to meet on campus before school every week or so to read and discuss the Bible. Although similar Bible clubs were allowed to meet at other schools, administrators refused the request, partly to avoid setting a precedent for clubs of Satanists, Ku Klux Klanists, or other groups the school would find undesirable. Bridget's mother brought suit, and in 1990, the U.S. Supreme Court found in her favor. Public high schools, the Court ruled, must allow students' religious, philosophical, and political groups to meet on campus on the same basis as other extracurricular groups. Permitting such meetings, the Court stated, does not mean that the school endorses or supports them. Courts have since ruled that this equal access applies not only before and after school but also during noninstructional time during the school day, and that it also applies to gay and lesbian groups formed by students.[65]

Options for schools

Implications of the *Mergens* case have aroused great uncertainty. Schools apparently must choose between allowing practically any student group to meet or dropping all extracurricular activities. Similar considerations apply concerning the distribution of flyers about religious activities. A third option would be to permit meetings only by groups whose activities relate directly to the curriculum, but difficult problems arise in defining such activities. Recent Supreme Court cases have failed to fully clarify the

[64]Rob Boston, "The Klan, a Cross, and the Constitution," *Church and State* (March 1995), pp. 7–9; Benjamin Dowling-Sendor, "The Ten Commandments Ruling," *American School Board Journal* (October 2005); Charles J. Russo, "Religious Music and Public Schools," *School Business Affairs* (March 2010), pp. 38-40; and Charles C. Haynes, "County Can Uphold Religious Freedom by Taking Commandments Down," 2011 posting by the First Amendment Center, available at **www.firstamendmentcenter.org**.
[65]*Board of Education of the Westside Community Schools v. Mergens*, 88 S. Ct. 1597 (1990). See also Haven B. Gow, "Students, Teachers, and Religious Freedom," *Liberty Online* (January/February 2006), available at **www.libertymagazine.org**; J. K. Williams, "God's Country," *American Educational History Journal* (No. 2, 2010), pp. 437–454; and Tom Pierpont, "A Far-Reaching E-Mail from the ACLU," 2011 posting by Inside Nova, available from **www2.insidenova.com**.

issue, but it is clear that religious and other groups and activities must satisfy criteria such as the following:[66]

- The activity must be student initiated.
- The school may not sponsor the activity, but its employees may attend meetings, and it may pay incidental costs such as heating.
- Outsiders may not direct the group or regularly attend meetings.

Pledge of Allegiance

Religious objections to pledge

The separation of church and state also applies to statements of allegiance to the state. In one case, several Jehovah's Witnesses went to court over a West Virginia requirement that their children recite the pledge of allegiance at school each morning. The parents based their objection on religious doctrine. The U.S. Supreme Court supported school officials' actions in expelling students who would not recite the pledge and salute the flag. However, three years later, after Witnesses in several locations had been accosted in the streets and forced to salute the flag, the Court reversed itself and concluded that students could be excused from reciting the pledge. The court ruled that the children could be exempted because the requirement to pledge conflicted with their religious beliefs. Subsequent decisions have provided further support for this conclusion.[67]

In 2002, a federal court of appeals ruled the Pledge of Allegiance unconstitutional because it includes the words "under God." This decision predictably sparked nationwide controversy; however, final disposition of the issue has yet to be determined by the Supreme Court and other courts.[68]

Religious Objections Regarding Curriculum

Basal readers challenged

In Tennessee in the mid-1980s, fundamentalist Christian parents brought suit against the Hawkins County School District, charging that exposure of their children to the Holt, Rinehart and Winston basal reading series was offensive to their religious beliefs. The parents believed that "after reading the entire Holt series, a child might adopt the views of a feminist, a humanist, a pacifist, an anti-Christian, a vegetarian, or an advocate of a one-world government." The district court held for the parents, reasoning that the state could satisfy its compelling interest in the literacy of Tennessee schoolchildren through less-restrictive means than compulsory use of the Holt series. However, an appellate court reversed this decision, stating that no evidence had been produced to show that students were required to affirm their belief or disbelief in any idea mentioned in the Holt books. The textbook series, the court said, "merely requires recognition that in a pluralistic society we must 'live and let live.'"[69]

---

[66]Benjamin Dowling-Sendor, "Opening Your Schools," *American School Board Journal* (May 1999); "A Question of Equity," *American School Board Journal* (February 2003); Colby M. May, "Religion's Legal Place in the Schoolhouse," *School Administrator* (October 2006), available at **www.aasa.org**; Tony Mauro, "Christian Group's Case Marshals Past Plaintiffs," 2010 posting by the First Amendment Center, available at **www.firstamendmentcenter.org**; and Dana Rudolph, "Schools Have Right to Form GSAs," 2011 posting by the Keen News Service, available at **www.keennewsservice.com**.

[67]*West Virginia State Board of Education v. Barnette*, 319 U.S. 624 (1943); *Lipp v. Morris*, 579 F. 2d 834 (3rd Cir. 1978); Perry A. Zirkel and Ivan B. Gluckman, "Pledge of Allegiance," *NASSP Bulletin* (September 1990), pp. 115–117; Garrett Epps, "Beware," *American Prospect* (October 2011), available at **www.prospect.org**; and "Fined for Not Saying Pledge of Allegiance," 2011 posting by Ask the Judge, available at **www.askthejudge.info**.

[68]Margaret M. McCarthy, "Controversy Continues over the *Pledge of Allegiance,*" *Educational Horizons* (Winter 2005), pp. 92–97; Grace Y. Kao and Jerome E. Coplulsky, "The Pledge of Allegiance and the Meanings and Limits of Civil Religion," *Journal of the American Academy of Religion* (March 2007), pp. 121–149; and "Eleventh Circuit Ruled Florida Pledge of Allegiance Law Constitutional," *Jurist*, July 23, 2011.

[69]*Mozert v. Hawkins County Board of Education*, 86-6144 (E.D. Tenn. 1986); *Mozert v. Hawkins County Board of Education*, 87-5024 (6th Cir. 1987); Michael P. Farris, "A Dangerous Path," *Home School Court Report* (July/August 2006), available at **www.hslda.org**; and Vivian E. Hamilton, "Immature Citizens and the State," *BYU Law Review* (No. 4 2010), available at **www.lawreview.byu.edu**.

■ Secular humanism

In somewhat similar cases, district judges upheld a group of parents in Alabama who contended that school textbooks and activities advanced the religion of secular humanism[70] and a New York group that contended that Bedford Public Schools were promoting pagan religions when students recited a liturgy to the Earth or sold worry dolls. The first decision was reversed by a federal appeals court, which held that the textbooks did not endorse secular humanism or any other religion, but rather attempted to instill such values as independent thought and tolerance of diverse views. The appeals court noted that if the First Amendment prohibited mere "inconsistency with the beliefs of a particular religion there would be very little that could be taught in the public schools." The second case also was resolved in favor of the schools. Similar conclusions have been reached by courts hearing complaints about New Age classroom materials in California and several other states.[71]

■ The evolution controversy

In 1987, the U.S. Supreme Court considered *Edwards v. Aguillard,* a case that challenged Louisiana's Balanced Treatment for Creation-Science and Evolution-Science Act. Creation science, or creationism, is the belief that life has developed through divine intervention or creation rather than through biological evolution. The Louisiana act required that creation science be taught wherever evolution was taught, and that appropriate curriculum guides and materials be developed. The Supreme Court ruled this law unconstitutional. By requiring "either the banishment of the theory of evolution . . . or the presentation of a religious viewpoint that rejects evolution in its entirety," the Court reasoned, the Louisiana act advanced a religious doctrine and violated the establishment clause of the First Amendment.[72]

■ Criticism of evolutionary theory

Intelligent Design   Controversy sometimes associated with the creationist point of view escalated in the twenty-first century as the **intelligent design** concept was introduced in a growing number of schools. This point of view argues that life is too complex to be formed through natural selection as portrayed by Darwin, therefore, it must be directed by a so-called intelligent designer. Many advocates of intelligent design avoid explicit references to divine creation, instead emphasizing what they view as flaws (including lack of valid evidence) in the theories developed by Darwinists.[73]

■ Teach outside of science

Actions initiated by advocates of intelligent design included a Cobb County (Ga.) school-board requirement that biology texts have stickers stating that "This textbook contains material on evolution. Evolution is a theory, not a fact. . . . This material should be approached with an open mind, studied carefully, and critically considered," and a similar curriculum-statement in which the Dover, Pennsylvania, school board suggested that students learn about intelligent design. These and several comparable actions have been challenged in federal courts, where judges have concluded that intelligent design involves support for particular religions and is not a scientific theory that can be required or inserted in the science curriculum. However, some analysts have noted that intelligent design still might be studied appropriately in social studies or elsewhere in the curriculum.[74]

---

[70]The secular humanism philosophy deemphasizes religious doctrines and instead emphasizes the human capacity for self-realization through reason.

[71]*Smith v. Board of School Commissioners of Mobile County,* 87-7216, 11th Cir. (1987); and Matthew Lynch, "The Separation of Religion and School," *Education News,* May 16, 2011, available at **www.ednews.org**.

[72]*Edwards v. Aguillard,* 197 S. Ct. 2573 (1987); "ACLU Warns Louisiana Officials Not to Open Door to Creationism," *Church and State* (February 2010), pp. 18–19; and David Sessions, "What If Public Schools Were Mandated to Teach Islamic Creation in Science Class?" *Christian Science Monitor,* May 16, 2011, available at **www.csmonitor.com**.

[73]Elizabeth Culotta, "Is ID on the Way Out?" *Science,* February 10, 2006, p. 570; and Nicholas Bakalar, "On Evolution, Biology Teachers Stray from Lesson Plan," *New York Times,* February 7, 2011.

[74]Joseph Dunn and Martha Derthick, "A Setback in Dover," *Education Next,* no. 2 (2006), available at **www.educationnext.org**; Benjamin Dowling-Sendor, "Drawing the Line between Science and Religion," *American School Board Journal* (March 2006); Sandhiya Bathija, "Creationism's Evolving Strategy," *Church and State* (January 2011), pp. 11–13; and "Judgment Day," PBS Nova videos, available at **www.pbs.org**.

Teaching about Religion

Promoting understanding
of religious traditions

Guarantees of separation between church and state do not prohibit public schools from teaching *about* religion or about controversial topics involving religion. Some states and school districts have been strengthening approaches for developing an understanding of religious traditions and values while neither promoting nor detracting from any particular religious or nonreligious ideology. In addition, many scholars have been preparing materials for such constitutionally acceptable instruction.[75]

Federal guidelines

According to guidelines issued in 1995 and reissued in 1998 by the U.S. Department of Education, schools can teach subjects such as "the history of religion, comparative religion, the Bible (or other scripture) as literature, and the role of religion in the history of the United States and other countries." These federal guidelines, which also touched on many other controversies concerning religion and schools, are summarized in Overview 9.3. However, courts may not necessarily support what the executive branch deems correct.[76]

Government Guidelines Regarding Prayer and Religion in Schools

Teachers may neither
encourage nor
discourage

In 2003, the Department of Education issued more detailed guidelines involving prayer and related activities in public schools. Guidelines and commentary included the following:[77]

- Students may organize prayer groups and religious clubs before school to the same extent that students are permitted to organize other noncurricular student-activity groups. . . .

- Teachers may . . . . take part in religious activities where the overall context makes clear that they are not participating in their official capacities. Before school or during lunch, for example, teachers may meet with other teachers for prayer or Bible study to the same extent that they may engage in other conversation or nonreligious activities. . . .

- If a school has a "moment of silence" or other quiet periods during the school day, students are free to pray silently, or not to pray. . . . Teachers and other school employees may neither encourage nor discourage students from praying during such time periods. . . .

- Students may express their beliefs about religion in homework, artwork, and other written and oral assignments, free from discrimination based on the religious content of their submissions. Such home and classroom work should be judged by ordinary academic standards of substance and relevance and against other legitimate pedagogical concerns.

---

[75]For example, see Susan Black, "Teaching about Religion," *American School Board Journal* (June 2003); Carrie Kilman, "One Nation, Many Gods," *Education Digest* (November 2007), pp. 14–20; "American Academy of Religion on Teaching Creationism," 2010 posting by the National Center for Science Education, available at **www.ncse.com**; and C. M. Bailey, "Teaching the Bible in Public Schools," 2011 posting by Blog Critics, available at **www.blogcritics.org**.
[76]Charles C. Haynes, "Religion in the Public Schools," *School Administrator* (January 1999), available at **www.aasa.org**; Thomas Hutton, "Does the Bible Have a Place in Your Classrooms?" *American School Board Journal* (June 2008); Martha McCarthy, "Beyond the Wall of Separation," *Phi Delta Kappan* (June 2009), pp. 714–719; "Religion in the Public Schools," 2011 posting by the Anti-Defamation League, available at **www.adl.org**; and information at **www .teachingaboutreligion.org**.
[77]Rod Paige, "Guidance on Constitutionally Protected Prayer in Public Elementary and Secondary Schools," 2003 paper posted at the U.S. Department of Education Internet site, available at **www.ed.gov**. See also Edwin C. Darden, "Pause and Ponder," *American School Board Journal* (May 2008), pp. 48–49; and Randy Aust, "How Is Teaching Religion Different?" *Education, Technology and Religion*, April 20, 2011, available at **www.randyaust.com**.

OVERVIEW 9.3

Guidelines on Religion in the Schools, from the U.S. Department of Education

Student prayer and religious discussion: The U.S. Constitution does not prohibit purely private religious speech by students. Students therefore have the same right to engage in individual or group prayer and religious discussion during the school day as they do to engage in other comparable activity.

Generally, students may pray in a nondisruptive manner when not engaged in school activities or instruction and subject to the rules that normally pertain in the applicable setting.

Graduation prayer: Under current Supreme Court decisions, school officials may not mandate or organize prayer at graduation nor organize religious baccalaureate ceremonies.

Official neutrality: Teachers and school administrators . . . are prohibited by the Constitution from soliciting or encouraging religious activity and . . . from discouraging activity because of its religious content.

Teaching about religion: Public schools may not provide religious instruction, but they may teach about religion . . . , the history of religion, comparative religion, the Bible (or other scripture) as literature, and religion's role in the history of the United States and other countries, are all permissible public-school subjects.

Although public schools may teach about religious holidays . . . and may celebrate the secular aspects of holidays, schools may not observe holidays as religious events or promote such observance by students.

Student assignments: Students may express their beliefs about religion in the form of homework, artwork, and other written and oral assignments. . . . Such home and classroom work should be judged by ordinary academic standards.

Religious literature: Students have a right to distribute religious literature to their schoolmates on the same terms as they are permitted to distribute other literature that is unrelated to school curriculum or activities.

Religious exemptions: Schools enjoy substantial discretion to excuse individual students from lessons that are objectionable to the student or the student's parents on religious or other conscientious grounds.

Released time: Schools have the discretion to dismiss students to off-premises religious instruction, provided that schools do not encourage or discourage participation. . . . Schools may not allow religious instruction by outsiders on school premises during the school day.

Teaching values: Though schools must be neutral with respect to religion, they may play an active role with respect to teaching civic values and virtue.

Student garb: Students may display religious messages on items of clothing to the same extent that they are permitted to display other comparable messages.

The Equal Access Act: Student religious groups have the same right of access to school facilities as is enjoyed by other comparable student groups.

Source: Richard W. Riley, "Secretary's Statement on Religious Expression" (released by the U.S. Department of Education, Washington, D.C., 1998).

Government Regulation and Support of Nonpublic Schools

States can regulate

In 1925, *Pierce v. Society of Sisters* established that a state's compulsory school-attendance laws could be satisfied through enrollment in a private or parochial school. Attention then turned to the question of how much control a state could exercise over the education offered in nonpublic schools. A 1926 case, *Farrington v. Tokushige,* gave nonpublic schools "reasonable choice and discretion in respect of teachers, curriculum and textbooks." Within that framework, however, states have passed various kinds of legislation to regulate nonpublic schools. Some states have few regulations; others require the employment of certified teachers, specify the number of days or hours the school must be in session, or insist that schools meet state accreditation standards. One current controversy involves the application of state standards for special education.[78]

[78]*Pierce v. Society of Sisters*, 268 U.S. 510 (1925); and *Farrington v. Tokushige*, 273 U.S. 284 (1926). See also David F. Salisbury, "Lessons From Florida," *Cato Institute Briefing Papers*, March 20, 2003, available at **www.cato.org**; F. Diarmuid, "The Curious Case of Free Exercise," *First Things* (December 2007), pp. 35–40; and "Pierce v. Society of Sisters," *The Burns Brief*, June 1, 2011.

State aid for transportation

On the other side of the coin, states have offered many types of support for nonpublic schools, including transportation, books, and health services. In the 1947 case *Everson v. Board of Education of Erving Township*, the Supreme Court considered a provision in the New Jersey Constitution that allowed state aid for transportation of private and parochial students. The Court held that where state constitutions permitted such assistance, they did not violate the U.S. Constitution. Since the Everson decision, the distinction between permissible and impermissible state aid to nonpublic schools has usually been based on the **child benefit theory:** aid that directly benefits the child is permissible, whereas aid that primarily benefits the nonpublic institution is not.[79]

Wolman: permissible state aid

In *Wolman v. Walter* (1977), *Agostini v. Felton* (1997), *Mitchell v. Helms* (2000), and *Zelman v. Simmons-Harris* (2002), the Supreme Court went further. Addressing state support for nonpublic schools permitted by the Ohio and New York constitutions, the Court decided specific questions by applying the three-pronged *Lemon v. Kurtzman* test illustrated previously in Figure 9.1. The Court's decisions were as follows:[80]

- Providing for the purchase or loan of secular textbooks, standardized tests, and computers is constitutional.

- Providing speech, hearing, and psychological diagnostic services at the nonpublic-school site is constitutional.

- Providing for the purchase and loan of other instructional materials and equipment, such as projectors, science kits, maps and globes, charts, media players, and so on, was ruled unconstitutional because this involves excessive government entanglement with religion.

- Providing funds for field trips is unconstitutional because "where the teacher works within and for a sectarian institution, an unacceptable risk of fostering religion is an inevitable byproduct."

- Providing Title 1 remedial services from public-school staff located at neutral facilities does not constitute excessive entanglement of church and state.

- Providing students with vouchers used to pay for tuition at nonpublic schools is constitutional if no financial incentives skew the program toward religious schools and such vouchers do not violate the state constitution.

A legal muddle

The material just outlined shows why many legal scholars believe that constitutional law regarding government aid to nonpublic schools is something of a muddle. Why should government purchase of textbooks, tests, and computers for nonpublic schools be constitutional but not purchase of maps, globes, charts, and media players? Why can government-supported psychological services be provided at nonpublic schools, whereas remedial services must be provided at a neutral site? How can vouchers to attend nonpublic schools be legal in some states but not others? Questions as convoluted as these help explain why Court attempts at clarification have been only partly successful.

REFOCUS Do you think controversies involving church and state will affect you directly as a teacher? Which aspects are most relevant in your subject field? What difficulties or challenges relating to religion might arise in the schools in your community?

What school policies have sometimes drawn student and parental opposition on religious grounds?

[79]Barbara Miner, "A Brief History of Milwaukee's Voucher Program," *Rethinking Schools* (Spring 2006), available at **www.rethinkingschools.org**; "Shifting Boundaries," 2009 paper posted by the Pew Forum, available at **www.pewforum.org**; and Adam B. Schaeffer, "A Strategic Defeat for Educational Freedom," 2011 posting by the Cato Institute, available at **www.cato.org**.

[80]Clint Bolick, "The Promise of Choice," *Hoover Digest* (Spring 2003); Clint Bolick, "Voting Down Vouchers," *Education Next* (Spring 2008), available at **www.educationnext.org**; and Dan Laitsch, "Taking Stock of Private School Vouchers," 2011 posting by the Horace Mann League, available at **www.horacemannleague.blogspot.com**.

Summing Up

1 Education-related court cases have significantly increased in the past few decades. Such cases can be heard in both federal and state courts, depending on the issues involved. Only decisions of the U.S. Supreme Court apply nationally.

2 Tenure protects teachers from dismissal, except on such specified grounds as incompetence, immorality, insubordination, and unprofessional conduct. Teachers accused of such conduct are entitled to due-process protections.

3 Teachers have the right to form and belong to unions and other professional organizations, but most states prohibit teachers from striking.

4 Teachers' rights regarding freedom of expression and academic freedom depend on a balance between individual and governmental interests. Teachers have rights guaranteed to individuals under the Constitution, but school boards have obligations to ensure the "proper" and "regular" operation of the schools, taking into account the rights of parents, teachers, and students.

5 Restraints on teachers' behavior outside school and on their dress and grooming are not as stringent as they once were in the United States, but teachers still are expected to serve as role models and to behave in an exemplary manner.

6 Schools must uphold definite safety standards to avoid legal suits charging negligence when students are injured. In addition, teachers must obey copyright laws.

7 Educators must observe the rights of copyright owners but have much leeway to use parts of copyrighted properties or even entire short works for educational purposes.

8 The courts have clarified and expanded such students' rights as freedom of expression, due process in the case of suspension or expulsion, prohibition against bodily searches in the absence of specific grounds, limitations on corporal punishment, and privacy of records.

9 With regard to cyberbullying, or the use of digital media to disparage the school or the staff, gain access to prohibited materials, or circulate intimate images of oneself or classmates, students' negative actions more often than not take place outside the school, though they sometimes happen in the classroom or make use of school equipment or resources. Regarding all these types of activities, there is tension between students' rights to free speech and expression, and educators' duty to protect and enhance the welfare of students and staff.

10 Organized and mandated prayer and Bible reading are not allowed in public schools. School curricula do not automatically constitute unconstitutional discrimination against religion when they ignore religious points of view or explanations.

11 The legal basis for government support for nonpublic schools is mixed. For example, government may provide textbooks, tests, and psychological services for students at nonpublic schools, but providing funds for field trips, projectors, science kits, or maps is thought to entangle church and state.

Key Terms

The numbers indicate the pages where explanations of the key terms can be found.

plaintiffs 264
litigants 264
establishment clause 265
free-exercise clause 265
due-process clause 265
equal-protection clause 265
breach of contract 267
tenure 267

continuing contract 267
due process 267
academic freedom 272
torts 274
fair use 276
copyright 277
in loco parentis 278

Children's Internet Protection Act (CIPA) 283
Family Educational Rights and Privacy Act (Buckley Amendment) 291
Protection of Pupil Rights Amendment 292
intelligent design 297
child benefit theory 300

Certification Connection Activity

This chapter introduces the legal aspects of education. It is vital for every teacher to understand how the law affects them and their students. There are two aspects of law that all teachers should know. One involves confidentiality and treatment of student records. Praxis II, Principles of Learning and Teaching, is likely to pose direct questions about confidentiality and privacy. The other aspect is the topic of "fair use" with respect to copyright, software piracy, and individual privacy in the Internet age. In your journal, record your local school district's policies regarding confidentiality and student records. In addition, investigate the district's policy on fair use of copy machines, computers, and the Internet.

Discussion Questions

1 Should teachers be required to meet higher or different standards of personal morality than other citizens? Why or why not?

2 Debate the pros and cons of prayer, Bible reading, and religious observances in public schools. Should current laws change regarding these activities?

3 Should students' due-process rights differ from those of adults outside the school? Why or why not? What differences may be most justifiable?

4 To what extent are academic freedom issues in elementary schools different from those in secondary schools? How might this distinction be important for you as a teacher?

5 Think of a situation in which your personal views might conflict with your school's policies regarding corporal punishment, student dress codes, or some other legal issue. To what extent would you find it difficult to comply with official policies? If you refused to comply, might this make it difficult to work with colleagues, students, or parents? What might you do to modify the policies or otherwise resolve the problem?

Suggested Projects for Professional Development

1 Research the teacher-tenure regulations in your state and in one or two nearby states. Do the states differ with respect to probationary period, cause for dismissal, or other matters? Are teachers in your community aware of these policies?

2 From a nearby school district, collect and analyze information about teachers' responsibilities for identifying and reporting child abuse. What are the district's explicit policies? Have any teachers been released or otherwise disciplined for failure to meet these responsibilities?

3 Survey several nearby school districts regarding their policies on student and teacher dress codes. Find out whether

and how these policies have changed in the past ten or fifteen years. Do you expect to see further changes in the near future?

4 For your portfolio, prepare a lesson plan dealing with religious holidays in a manner that neither unconstitutionally promotes nor inhibits religion.

5 Go to FindLaw to search for and download the Department of Education's report "Discipline of Students with Disabilities." What conclusions and responsibilities are likely to be most important and perhaps most problematic to you as a teacher?

Suggested Resources

Internet Resources

You can find useful sources dealing with material in this chapter at **http://library.findlaw.com**. Hear sound clips of arguments in Supreme Court cases at **www.oyez.org**. Many Supreme Court cases can be examined at **www.thisnation.com**. The American Civil Liberties Union at **www.aclu.org** gives considerable attention to education-related cases.

"The Code of Best Practices in Fair Use for Media Education Literacy," available at **www.centerforsocialmedia.org**, describes many situations in which educators can utilize the fair-use doctrine to appropriately defend drawing on copyrighted materials while recognizing the rights of owners to legal protection of their property.

A wealth of law-related material involving school safety and student discipline is available at **www.keepschoolssafe.org**.

"School Law Topics" is a useful site updated by the Missouri Department of Elementary and Secondary Education at **http://dese.mo.gov/schoollaw**.

Publications

Alexander, Kern, and David M. Alexander. *American Public School Law,* 8th ed. Belmont, CA: Wadsworth, 2012. *This venerable*

text has been providing solid and reliable information and analysis regarding school law for decades.

Essex, Nathan L. *School Law and the Public Schools,* 5th ed. Upper Saddle River, NJ: Prentice Hall, 2011. *Addresses both contemporary and historical legal issues involving the organization and functioning of public schools.*

Schimmel, David, and Leslie R. Stellman. *Teachers and the Law,* 8th ed. Upper Saddle River, NJ: Prentice Hall, 2010. *A nontechnical, question-and-answer format considers a wide and comprehensive range of topics.*

Yudof, Mark G. et al. *Educational Policy and the Law,* 5th ed. Belmont, CA: Wadsworth, 2012. *Provides extensive background material, analysis, and discussion on a comprehensive set of school law topics.*

 Additional resources for this chapter, including the TeachSource Videos, can be found on the Education CourseMate website. Go to **CengageBrain.com** to access the site.

PART FOUR

Will & Deni McIntyre/Corbis

Social Foundations

Culture, Socialization, and Education

We are all aware that the world is changing rapidly. Communications and the economy are becoming globalized, career success requires increasingly advanced skills, immigration has accelerated in the United States and many other countries, and family patterns today differ greatly from those thirty years ago. Each such change has a major impact on education from elementary school through the university level.

Nevertheless, certain underlying imperatives and influences regarding how we rear children and youth necessarily remain important. Student development still is strongly influenced by families, neighborhoods, and friends, as well as by wider cultural and social forces such as the mass media, just as it was thirty or sixty or ninety years ago.

On the other hand, the specific ways in which such forces exert their influence on children and youth change over time. For example, you, as a teacher, may have increasing difficulty capturing students' attention in a digitized world that offers myriad competing stimuli. To respond adequately, you must understand what is happening in the family, the mass media, and the peer group, and how cultural and social trends are influencing the behaviors and ideas that students bring to the classroom.

As you read the chapter, keep these questions in mind:

FOCUS QUESTIONS
- What cultural patterns influence instruction in schools?
- How does school culture socialize the young?
- How have television and other mass media affected students?
- Do sex roles and sex differences influence learning and achievement? If so, how?
- How do aspects of youth culture affect the schools?

*This chapter was revised by Dan Levine.

Aspects of culture

A society ensures its unity and survival by means of culture. The term **culture** has been broadly defined to encompass all the continually changing patterns of acquired behavior and attitudes transmitted among the members of a society. Culture is a way of thinking and behaving; it is a group's traditions, memories, and written records, its shared rules and ideas, and its accumulated beliefs, habits, and values. No individual, group, or entire society can be understood without reference to culture. Habits of dress, diet, and daily routine—the countless small details of ordinary life that seem to require little reflection—all constitute cultural patterns and identities. **Socialization**, which prepares children to function first as young people and then as adults, transmits culture and thereby allows society to function satisfactorily.

School as cultural agent

Many individuals and institutions play a part in socializing children and youth. The family, of course, is most important for young children, but in modern societies, formal institutions also help determine what a child learns and how well he or she is prepared to function in society. The school serves as perhaps the major institution (other than the family) devised by the adult generation for maintaining and perpetuating the culture. It supplies the tools necessary for survival and ensures the transmission of knowledge and values to future generations. Schools uphold and pass on the society's values, beliefs, and **norms** (rules of behavior), not only in lesson subject matter but also through the very structure and operation of the educational system.

In a diverse society such as our own, schools are responsible for helping young people learn to participate in a national culture, but they also must be sensitive to cultural differences and make sure that students from minority groups have equal opportunities to succeed in education. We discuss the challenges posed by this imperative in the multicultural education sections of Chapter 12, Providing Equal Educational Opportunity.

Agents of Socialization

Major socializing institutions

Various social institutions help to transmit culture to children and youth. For many societies, the most important historically have been the church, peer group, school, and, of course, family. Some of these institutions, such as the church, have become less influential in Western societies, while others, such as the mass media, have emerged as a socializing force. In this section, we discuss several issues concerning the influence of family patterns on education. We then go on to consider the peer group's socializing role and educational implications, school culture, and the influences of television and other mass media. Overview 10.1 summarizes the socializing contributions of each of these institutions.

The Family

Early influence of family

Although its organization varies, the family is the major early socializing agent in every society. As such, it is the first medium for transmitting culture to children. Because the family is the whole world to young children, its members teach a child what matters in life, often without realizing the enormous influence they wield. The behaviors adults encourage and discourage and the ways in which they provide discipline also affect a child's orientation toward the world.

Home environment and preparation for school

Many children do well in school because their family environments have provided them with good preparation for succeeding in the traditional classroom. Others do poorly, in part because they have been poorly prepared, and the schools generally have failed to help them overcome this disadvantage. (We'll describe possibilities for modifying instruction and other ways of helping unsuccessful students in later chapters.) Recent changes in the nature of the family have important implications for children's educational development and success in school. This section discusses several of the most important changes affecting families, including increases in poverty,

OVERVIEW 10.1

Effects of Major Socializing Institutions

Institution	Trends and Characteristics	Socializing Effects
Family	■ Poverty ■ Single-parent families ■ Increase in working mothers ■ Cohabitation ■ Latchkey children ■ Pressures on children ■ Overindulged children ■ Homelessness	Some trends, such as increasing numbers of working mothers and expanding options for before- and after-school activities, hold positive potential, but most put children at risk for difficulty in school.
Peers	■ Popularity, athletics, attractiveness more important than academics ■ Extracurricular activities ■ Bullying ■ Active learner role carries risks	Cooperative activities can reduce bullying and foster peer relationships that promote academics. Extracurricular activities tend to promote academic achievement.
School culture	■ Hidden curriculum diverse with frequently important impacts ■ Classroom cultures stress ■ Accommodations, bargaining, compromise ■ Teacher overload leading to rationing attention	School often teaches students to reduce their enthusiasm and to prefer passive learning.
Television and digital media	■ Unclear relationship of television to achievement ■ Television may socialize aggression, undesirable attitudes ■ Internet promising for active learning ■ Electronic social networking becoming more important but might pose problems for students	Television and other media can contribute to academic achievement, but their content and use must be carefully planned or they can become agents of negative socialization and mislearning.

single-parent families, working mothers, and cohabitation. We'll also discuss how families may create educational difficulties by pressuring or overindulging children. Finally, we'll examine the severe problems some children face in their home situations, including abuse and homelessness.

Children in Poverty   Poverty is a major problem for many families. More than 20 percent of American children live in poverty. Poverty rates are particularly high for children from minority groups; more than one-third of African American and Latino children and youth are growing up in families below the poverty line. Poor children often face educational difficulties. We'll discuss the relationship between social class and educational achievement in more detail in Chapter 11, Social Class, Race, and School Achievement.

Single-parent families

Single-Parent Families   Many observers connect the substantial poverty rates among children and youth with the high incidence of single-parent families. Recent decades have seen a large increase in the percentage of households with a single parent, usually a never-married, divorced, or separated woman. Overall, single-parent families now constitute about a third of all households with children under age eighteen. More than 40 percent of female-headed families are below the poverty line, compared with a little more than 10 percent for two-parent families.[1]

Some observers conclude that modern marriage is a roulette game, as likely as not to land children in single-parent families. For example, of all non-Hispanic white children, 22 percent were living in single-parent households in 2010, compared with less than 10 percent in 1960. The figures for African American children and youth are even more startling: 62 percent were living in single-parent households in 2010. Overall, more than half of all young people below the age of eighteen live in a single-parent family for some part of their childhood.[2]

Impact on children

Much research has concentrated on the specific effects of growing up in a home where the father is absent. A few studies assess little measurable impact on children, but most others find a variety of negative effects, including a greater likelihood that families will fall into poverty and that children will suffer serious emotional and academic problems. The major reason this research may lack conclusiveness is the difficulty in controlling for the effects of social class. A large percentage of families that had lost a father also declined in social class, and this change in status makes it difficult to identify the separate effects of each factor.[3]

To help you, as a teacher, respond to the trend toward single-parent families, analysts have recommended steps such as the following:[4]

Recommendations for schools

- Do not assume that all or even most children from single-parent families have unusual problems.
- Send copies of communications to the noncustodial parent.
- Include representation of single-parent families in the curriculum, add library materials that show varied lifestyles, and help children cope with divorce.
- Cooperate with other agencies in improving child-care arrangements before and after school.
- Conduct workshops to help teachers avoid any negative expectations they may have developed for children from single-parent families.
- Assign school counselors to help students succeed in academic and social tasks.
- Serve as advocates in providing appropriate help for individual students.
- Schedule meetings and events at times convenient for single parents.
- Form school-sponsored support groups for single parents and their children.
- Assist parents in learning how to supervise their children successfully.

Mothers who work

Increase in Working Mothers   The percentage of U.S. working mothers with children under age eighteen has increased steadily since 1950. Several reasons account for this increase: better employment opportunities for women, rising divorce rates, family financial pressures that require a second income, increase in the age at first

[1]Steven L. Nock, "Marriage as a Public Issue," *The Future of Children* (Fall 2005), available at **www.futureofchildren.org**; Jane Waldfogel, Terry-Ann Craigie, and Jeanne Brooks-Gunn, "Fragile Families and Child Wellbeing," *The Future of Children* (Fall 2010), available at **www.futureofchildren.org**; *Statistical Abstract of the United States* (Washington, D.C.: U.S. Government Printing Office, 2012); and information available from **www.childstats.gov**.
[2]Kristin F. Seefeldt and Pamela J. Smock, "Marriage on the Public Policy Agenda," *Poverty Research Insights* (Winter 2004), available at **www.npc.umich.edu**; Joy Jones, "State of the Black Marriage," *Ebony* (March 2011), pp. 72–73; and Suzy Khimm, "The Richer You Are, the Greater Chance You'll Marry," *Washington Post*, February 6, 2012.
[3]David Blankenhorn, *The Future of Marriage* (New York: Encounter, 2009); and Robert Mare, "A Multigenerational View of Inequality," *Demography* (February 2011), pp. 1–23.
[4]Adele M. Brodkin and Melba Coleman, "Teachers Can't Do It Alone," *Instructor* (May–June 1995), pp. 25–26; and Kayla Milstead and Gerra Perkins, "Family Structure Characteristics and Academic Success," *Academic Leadership* (Winter 2011), available at **www.academicleadership.org**.

marriage, and changes in traditional cultural attitudes dictating that mothers stay home. Schools, which traditionally relied on unemployed mothers for volunteer help, need to adjust their expectations of when their students' parents will be available for meetings and volunteering. Most schools have also adjusted their programs to help address the need to supervise children of working parents after the end of the regular school day.

Cohabitation Increase and Effects   In recent years, an increasing number and percentage of children have been growing up in cohabiting households in which their parent or parents have a sexual relationship but are not legally married. The incidence of cohabiting households has increased more than ten times since 1970. By 2012, about 25 percent of children born were to cohabiting couples—more than were born to single mothers living alone. Relatively little research has examined the effects on children, but analysts have begun to provide support for the following conclusions:[5]

- On many social and educational indicators, children in cohabiting households score poorly compared with children from intact, married families.

- Children in cohabiting households are more likely to suffer from child abuse than children in married or single-parent families.

- Cohabitation initially became prominent in low-income communities in the 1970s but has since been growing in working-class and lower-middle-class communities. In the words of a report prepared for The National Marriage Project and the Institute for American Values, the United States is "devolving into a separate-and-unequal family regime, where the highly educated and the affluent enjoy strong and stable families, and others are consigned to increasingly unstable, unhappy, and unworkable ones." Nonmarried parents also have much greater fertility than married couples, who are significantly middle class. This means that nonmarried parents are now producing a majority of the nation's children, many of whom will inherit the difficult economic and social circumstances of their parents.

Latchkey Children and Community Learning Centers   The situation of **latchkey children** who return to unsupervised homes after school is particularly problematic because many of these children spend much of their time watching television or roaming the streets. National data indicate that millions of latchkey children return to empty homes or go to community locations such as malls or street corners. Partly for this reason, many school officials as well as civic and political leaders have taken action to expand opportunities for children and youth to participate in extended-day programs at school or in recreational and learning activities at community centers after school. After-school programs thus have become an important aspect of services for young people in many locations, and you are likely to find that many of the students you teach will attend before- or after-school programs. However, an overemphasis on academics in after-school or other out-of-school programs can make for "hurried children," described in the next section.[6]

---

[5]Quote is from W. Bradford Wilcox, "When Marriage Disappears," 2010 report prepared for The National Marriage Project and the Institute for American Values, available at **www .stateofourunions.org**. See also Richard Fry and D'Vera Cohn, "Living Together," 2011 report prepared for the Pew Foundation, available at **www.pewresearch.org**; Sharon Lerner, "Knocked Up and Knocked Down, 2011 posting by Slate, available at **www.slate.com**; W. Bradford Wilcox, ed., "Why Marriage Matters," 2011 report prepared for The National Marriage Project and the Institute for American Values, available at **www.americanvalues .org**; and Charles Murray, *Coming Apart* (New York: Crown Forum, 2012).
[6]Brian Libby, "Fourteen Million Kids, Unsupervised," *Edutopia*, January 16, 2007, available at **www.edutopia.org**; Frances K. Alston, "All About Latch Key Children," 2011 posting by Afterschooling.org, available at **www.afterschooling.org**; "Guidelines for Latch Key Kids," January 2012 posting by I'm Not an Octopus, available at **www.imnotanoctopus.com**; and information available at **www.afterschoolalliance.org**.

"Superbabies"

School responses to "hurried" children

An epidemic of overindulgence

Reports of abuse and neglect increasing

Subsequent problems of abused children

Hurried and/or Overparented Children   Awareness of the growing importance of education in contemporary society has stimulated many parents to push their children to excel in learning beginning in infancy. The desire to raise so-called "superbabies" appears particularly prevalent among middle-class parents, for whom the ABCs of childhood frequently center on "Anxiety, Betterment, [and] Competition." According to some analysts, these children are "overparented." To meet the demands of such parents, many preschool and primary classrooms might focus so systematically on formal instruction that they harm children in a misplaced effort to mass-produce little Einsteins. Some developmental psychologists characterize such parental pressure as a type of "miseducation" that creates **hurried children** and deprives young people of childhood. Responses to this problem include raising the age for enrolling in kindergarten and retaining five-year-olds not ready to advance to first grade for an additional year in kindergarten.[7]

Overindulged Children   Whereas many children might be pressured to meet parental demands for early learning, others are overindulged by parents who provide them with too many material goods or protect them from challenges that would foster emotional growth. (Of course, some children may be simultaneously overly pressured and overindulged.) Many observers believe that overindulgence is a growing tendency, particularly among young middle-class parents trying to provide their children with an abundance of advantages. Some psychologists argue that overindulgence is an epidemic afflicting as many as 20 percent of the children in the United States. These "cornucopia kids" may find it hard to endure frustration, and thus may present special problems for their teachers and classmates.[8]

Child Abuse and Neglect   Children from any social class may suffer abuse or neglect by their parents or other household members. As we noted in Chapter 9, Legal Aspects of Education, as a teacher, you will have a major responsibility to report any evidence that a student has been maltreated. Our society has become more aware of the extent and consequences of child abuse and neglect, and the number of children confirmed as victims of abuse and neglect has reached nearly one million a year. More than half of these cases involve neglect of such needs as food, clothing, or medical treatment; about one-seventh involve sexual mistreatment; and approximately one-fourth involve beatings or other physical violence. Many child-welfare agencies have been overburdened by the extent of the problem. Although they work to keep families together when safe for children, such agencies often must remove children from their homes and place them in foster care.[9]

Research on child abuse indicates that its victims tend to experience serious problems in emotional, intellectual, and social development. As adults, they have relatively high rates of alcohol and drug abuse, criminal behavior, learning disorders, and psychiatric disturbance. However, this research is difficult to interpret because a relatively large proportion of abuse victims are low-income children. The links between poverty and developmental problems and delinquent or criminal behavior make it harder to

---

[7]Walter Kirn and Wendy Cole, "What Ever Happened to Play?" 2001 paper at the *Time* Internet site, available at **www.hyper-parenting.com/time.htm**; Amanda Morin, "The Benefits of Under-Scheduling Your Child," *Education.Com*, August 25, 2008, available at **www.education .com/magazine**; Lenore Skenazy, *Free-Range Kids* (San Francisco: Jossey-Bass, 2010); and Richard Weissbourd, "The Overpressured Student," *Educational Leadership* (May 2011), available at **www.ascd.org.**

[8]Bruce A. Baldwin, *Beyond the Cornucopia Kids* (New York: Direction Dynamics, 1988); Joan Acocella, "The Child Trap," *New Yorker*, November 17, 2008, available at **www.newyorker.com**; Karin Klein, "Are You Raising Cornucopia Kids?" 2010 posting by the Association of Christian Schools International, available at **www.acsi.org**; and Preston Carlson, "Spoiled Brats Becoming More Violent," 2011 posting by The Imperfect Parent, available at **www.imperfectparent.com.**

[9]"Children, Families, and Foster Care," *The Future of Children* (Winter 2004), available at **www .futureofchildren.org**; Richard S. Vacca, "Parent Rights and Child Abuse Issues," *CEPI Education Law Newsletter* (October 2008), available at **www.cepi.vcu.edu/newsletter**; and "Children Hospitalized at Alarming Rate Due to Abuse," *Science Newsline*, February 6, 2012. See also material at **www.childhelp.org** and **www.childabuse.com.**

separate out the influence of abuse. The relationship is by no means simple; in fact, many abused children manage to avoid serious emotional and behavioral problems.[10]

School and teacher responses

In any case, educators must recognize that abused or seriously neglected students might not only have a difficult time learning but might also behave in ways that interfere with other students' learning. For this reason, organizations such as the Children's Television Workshop and the National Education Association have developed materials to help teachers deal with abused children, and they are working with other agencies to alleviate abuse and neglect.

Implications for the schools

Homelessness   Several studies indicate that homeless children disproportionately suffer from child abuse and physical ill health. As we would expect, they also are relatively low in school attendance and achievement. The federal government has done relatively little to provide for homeless adults and children, and many local governments have been unwilling or unable to provide much assistance. However, many schools are striving to provide appropriate help. Some districts and schools, for instance, hire additional counselors, sponsor after-school programs, employ a full-time person to coordinate services with shelters for homeless families, or try to avoid transferring homeless children from one school to another.[11]

Problems related to homeless children were greatly magnified when the economic decline began in 2008. In Minneapolis, for example, nearly one in ten students were thought to be homeless at some point in 2009. School districts are required by federal law to help homeless children stay in one school continuously, but following this policy can greatly expand costs for transportation and other necessities such as supplies and counseling. The National Center on Family Homelessness reported that more than 1.5 million children were homeless nationally in 2010, and urged communities to do more to overcome the multiple difficulties caused by this undesirable situation.

Overall effects on children

Assessment of Trends Related to the Family   The various interrelated trends we have been discussing have produced a significant change in the structure and function of families in the United States. Research does not conclusively establish that all of the results are damaging to children; in some respects, maternal employment and other related trends lead to gains for children. However, many studies indicate that maternal employment and life in a single-parent or divorced family have detrimental effects for many children. Trends such as the rise in homelessness and poverty are obviously even more damaging.

Decline of the nuclear family

Historically, according to many analysts, our system of universal education drew support from the development of the **nuclear family** (two parents living with their children), which grew to prominence in Western societies during the past two centuries. The nuclear family has been described as highly child centered, devoting many of its resources to preparing children for success in school and later in life. With the decline of the nuclear family since World War II, the tasks confronting educators appear to have grown more difficult.[12]

---

[10]David P. Farrington, "Childhood Origins of Antisocial Behavior," *Clinical Psychology & Psychotherapy* (May/June 2005), pp. 177–199; "Child Abuse," 2010 paper at the Jim Hopper Internet site, available at **www.jimhopper.com/abstats**; and Jared K. McIntyre and Cathy S. Widom, "Childhood Victimization and Crime Victimization," *Journal of Interpersonal Violence* (March 2011), pp. 640–663.

[11]John H. Holloway, "Addressing the Needs of Homeless Students," *Educational Leadership* (December 2002/January 2003); John C. Buckner, "Understanding the Impact of Homelessness on Children," *American Behavioral Scientist* (February 2008), pp. 721–736; Lucy Nicholson, "Homeless in America," *The Fiscal Times*, February 1, 2012, available at **www.thefiscaltimes.com**; and information available at **www.homelesschildrenamerica.org**.

[12]Edward Shorter, *The Making of the Modern Family* (New York: Basic Books, 1975). See also Lawrence Stone, *Road to Divorce: England 1537–1987* (New York: Oxford University Press, 1991); David Popenoe, *War over the Family* (Piscataway, NJ: Transaction, 2008); Carolyn Moynihan, "The Marriage Gap That's Destroying Middle America," 2011 posting by Mercator Net, available at **www.mercatornet.com**; Derek Thompson, "The Death (and Life) of Marriage in America," *Atlantic* (February 2012), available at **www.atlantic.com**; and material posted by the National Marriage Project, available at **www.stateofourunions.org**.

■ The postnuclear family

David Popenoe, examining family trends in highly industrialized countries such as Sweden and the United States, concluded that these trends are creating the *postnuclear* family, which emphasizes individualism (individual self-fulfillment, pleasure, self-expression, and spontaneity), as contrasted with the nuclear family's child-centered familism. Adults, Popenoe further concluded, "no longer need children in their lives, at least not in economic terms. The problem is that children . . . still need adults . . . who are motivated to provide them with . . . an abundance of time, patience, and love." Many social scientists also worry about the "total contact time" between parents and children. Some research indicates that this time has declined as much as 40 percent during the past few decades.[13]

■ Agencies overloaded

In the context of these family changes and the problems they create, social agencies established to help children and youth sometimes become too overloaded to provide services effectively. For example, one Maryland social worker, when asked why a six-year-old had not been removed from a known crack house run by his mother, responded that he had "twenty similar cases on his desk, and that he didn't have time to go through the time-consuming process of taking a child from a parent" unless there was an immediate emergency. Overload of social-service agencies seems to have widely increased in recent years due to economic recession and resulting cuts in state and local budgets.[14]

■ Many children in jeopardy

According to the National Commission on Children, although most American children remain "healthy, happy, and secure," many are now "in jeopardy." Even those children free from extreme misfortune may confront difficult conditions. "They too attend troubled schools and frequent dangerous streets. The adults in their lives are often equally hurried and distracted . . . The combined effects are that too many children enter adulthood without the skills or motivation to contribute to society."[15] The From Preservice to Practice box describes the efforts of two teachers to motivate children with difficult home lives.

■ **REFOCUS** What steps might you take as a teacher to work effectively with children whose families differ from the traditional two-parent family?

The Peer Group

■ Peer group influence

Whereas family relationships may constitute a child's first experience of group life, peer-group interactions soon begin to make their powerful socializing effects felt. From playgroup to teenage clique, the peer group affords young people many significant learning experiences—how to interact with others, how to be accepted by others, and how to achieve status in a circle of friends. Peers are equals in a way that parents and their children or teachers and their students are not. A parent or a teacher sometimes can force young children to obey rules they neither understand nor like, but peers do not have formal authority to do this; thus children can learn the true meaning of exchange, cooperation, and equity more easily in the peer setting.

Peer groups increase in importance as the child grows, and they reach maximum influence in adolescence, by which time they sometimes dictate much of a young person's behavior both in and out of school. Some researchers believe that peer groups are more important now than in earlier periods—particularly when children have little close contact with their parents and few strong linkages with the larger society.

■ Qualities that students esteem

Peer Culture and the School Educators are particularly concerned with the characteristics of student culture within the school. **Peer culture** frequently works against

[13]David Popenoe, *Disturbing the Nest* (New York: Aldine de Gruyter, 1988), pp. 329–330; David Popenoe, *Families without Fathers* (New York: Transaction, 2009); and Christina Gibson-Davis, "Mothers but Not Wives," *Journal of Marriage and Family* (February 2011), pp. 264–278.
[14]William Zinsmeister, "Growing Up Scared," *Atlantic Monthly* (June 1990), p. 67; and Christy Gutowski, "High DCFS Caseloads Raise Red Flags," *Chicago Tribune*, March 4, 2012.
[15]National Commission on Children, *Beyond Rhetoric* (Washington, D.C.: U.S. Government Printing Office, 1991), pp. xvii–xviii. See also Traci Cook et al., "America's Children," 2011 report posted by the Federal Interagency Forum on Child and Family Statistics, available at **www .childstats.gov**.

FROM PRESERVICE TO PRACTICE

Tuning In

Mark and Claudia have students in their classes who are dealing with difficult home lives and other issues. The two teachers are discussing ways to motivate these children and support their learning.

Mark: Claudia, what else can I be doing to motivate these kids? I have tried everything we were taught in our methods class. What do you do to attract and hold your students' attention?

Claudia: Early in the year, I try and find out what their favorite TV programs are. Then I use the programs' dilemmas and our discussions of the characters to introduce major units. It seems to work, but you have to do your homework on the students first. You might give that a try, Mark.

Mark: How do I even begin to figure out their favorite TV programs? What do you do, have them fill out a survey form on the first day of class?

Claudia: No, I just talk to them as they come in and ask if they saw this or that program last night. They tell me what programs they watched, and in a week, I have a pretty good list of programs that most of the kids watch. Just talk to them and ask them. They'll tell you.

Mark: I wonder how much TV they actually watch. I hardly have time to turn my TV on, but if I'm going to use this approach, I guess I'd better start making it part of my own homework assignment. What else do you think would help, Claudia?

Claudia: By now, you should know which students are your potential troublemakers. Find out what they like. And ask

their guidance counselor what he or she can share about the student. Many of our students come from troubled families, families in poverty, homeless families. As the economy worsens, we're seeing more qualifiers for free and reduced-price breakfast and lunches. That's just one small indicator that we are dealing with many students who lack the advantages we had when we were growing up.

Mark: Some of my students want to sleep most of the time. Do you think drugs have much to do with their inattention in class?

Claudia: Maybe in a few cases, but there's no single answer. I'm betting some of your students have bad home situations and possibly poor nutrition, and others are over-scheduled with sports and jobs, besides school. They get less sleep than they need for many reasons. Plus, I've read recent research that suggests the brain chemistry of adolescents changes their sleep schedules. Teachers deal with all of this. Also, I don't want to make you feel bad, but when *all* of my students seem sleepy, the first thing I check is whether I could be boring them.

Mark: Okay, I'll make sure it isn't me! But I'll talk to the counselor about some of these kids, and the athletic director, too. She and the other coaches have a pretty good handle on students who go out for sports. Maybe some of my underachievers or troublemakers are playing volleyball or football this fall. Maybe between us, we can benefit everyone—the students, the coaches, and the teacher.

Case Questions

1. Do you think teachers should use television programs to help promote attention to concepts they teach? Explain your answer.
2. Why is it important that teachers understand the backgrounds of students in their classrooms?
3. What other steps do you think Mark should take to help his effectiveness as a teacher?

academic goals at school. For example, a landmark 1961 study by James Coleman found that high-school students gained the esteem of their peers by a combination of friendliness and popularity, athletic prowess, an attractive appearance and personality, or possession of valued skills and objects (cars, clothes, a music collection). Scholastic success was not among the favored characteristics; in general, the peer culture hindered rather than reinforced the school's academic goals.[16]

Importance of friends, looks, athletics

More than two decades later, John Goodlad and his colleagues asked more than seventeen thousand students, "What is the one best thing about this school?" The most frequent response by far was "my friends." Respondents also were asked to identify the types of students they considered most popular. Only 10 percent of respondents in

[16]James S. Coleman, *The Adolescent Society* (New York: Free Press, 1961). See also "The Adolescent Society," *Education Next*, no. 1 (2006), available at **www.educationnext.org**; and Paul Cooper and Barbara Jacobs, "Pupils Making a Difference," *Emotional and Behavioural Difficulties* (March 2011), pp. 5–13.

Teachers should help students develop positive peer relationships conducive to learning.

Richard G. Bingham II/Alamy Limited

Continuity & Change

Suggestions for teachers

junior and senior high schools selected "smart students"; instead, 70 percent of students selected either "good-looking students" or "athletes." Pondering these data, Goodlad concluded that "physical appearance, peer relationships, and games and sports" are more than mere concerns students carry into the school; these phenomena "appear to prevail" there. Noting that Coleman and others reported similar findings in earlier decades, he further wondered "why we have taken so little practical account of them in schools."[17]

To foster peer relationships that support rather than impede learning, some educators recommend conducting activities that encourage students to learn cooperatively. In addition, teachers should promote children's interaction with peers, teach interpersonal and small-group skills, assign children responsibility for the welfare of their peers, and encourage older children to interact with younger children. Such steps may help counteract peer pressure for antisocial behavior. However, each of these approaches requires considerable planning and dedication in implementation.[18]

Participation in Extracurricular Activities   Polls continually show that students consider their cooperation and interaction with peers in extracurricular activities a highlight of their school experience. Many educators believe this participation is a positive force in the lives of students, but the effect has been difficult to measure. The difficulty lies in determining whether participation in extracurricular activities is a cause or an effect of other aspects of students' development. It is known, for example, that students who participate in many extracurricular activities generally have higher grades than those who do not participate, other things being equal. It may also be true, however, that students with higher grades are more likely to participate than are those with lower grades.

Positive impact on educational aspirations

Despite these difficulties, research suggests that participation—especially in athletics, service, leadership activities, and music—fosters emotional and physical health as well as students' aspirations to higher educational and occupational attainment (for

[17]John I. Goodlad, *A Place Called School* (New York: McGraw-Hill, 1984), p. 75. See also K. M. Pierce, "Posing, Pretending, Waiting for the Bell," *High School Journal* (December 2005/January 2006), pp. 1–15; and Brett Laursen et al., "Opposites Detract," *Journal of Experimental Child Psychology* (August 2010), pp. 240–256.
[18]Erik E.J. Thoonen et al., "Can Teachers Motivate Students to Learn?" *Educational Studies* (July 2011), pp. 345–360.

▶ | | TEACHSOURCE VIDEO CASE

Social and Emotional Development: The Influence of Peer Groups

Go to the Education CourseMate website to access the video entitled, "Social and Emotional Development The Influence of Peer Groups." In this video, a drama teacher, Voncille Ross, examines the issue of peer pressure head on with her sixth graders. As you're watching, you'll notice how Voncille draws her students out on their experiences with peer pressure (such as feeling the need to identify with a particular social group) through open discussion. Then you'll see how students use drama to gain perspective on the real-life situations they encounter, the different choices they can make, and the potential consequences. After watching the video, answer the following questions:

❶ This chapter states that schools should foster positive peer relationships that support student learning. How does Voncille Ross, the teacher in this video case, achieve this? Cite some specific examples.

❷ In the video, the students and teacher discuss the issue of peer pressure through drama and class discussion. What insights did you gain about peer culture within schools today after watching this video case?

** This video reinforces key concepts found in Part I: Students as Learners of the Praxis II Exam.**

example, more years of school completed later). The research also suggests that positive effects are more likely in small schools than in large schools.[19]

Importance for teachers

These conclusions have great significance for educators. Participation outside the academic curriculum probably is more *manipulable* (alterable by the school) than most other factors related to educational outcomes. For example, home environments may cause problems, but educators can rarely change a student's home environment. Nevertheless, teachers and administrators can promote student participation in extracurricular activities, and this may be one of the most effective ways to improve students' performance.

REFOCUS How might you, as a teacher, shape your students' peer relationships in positive directions?

Continuity & Change

Research on Bullying and Its Prevention In recent years, research has begun to address the problems caused by bullies—youngsters who severely harass their peers either inside or outside the school. Most schools have implemented policies to reduce bullying, particularly with respect to sexual orientation and to bullying involving the use of computers, cell phones, and other new media (cyberbullying). Factors frequently cited as causing some children to behave as bullies include neglect and abuse in their homes, the influence of television, and a lack of social skills that leads to a cycle of aggressive behavior. The majority of bullies are male, but the incidence of bullying by girls has been rising. Educators are concerned about not only the harm bullies do to others but also the tendency of bullies to exhibit criminal behavior as adults. Approaches you might apply to modify bullying behaviors include behavioral

Causes and prevention of bullying

---

[19]Alyce Holland and Thomas Andre, "Participation in Extracurricular Activities in Secondary Schools," *Review of Educational Research* (Winter 1987), pp. 437–466; Sarah J. Donaldson and Kevin Ronan, "The Effects of Sports Participation on Young Adolescents' Emotional Well-Being," *Adolescence* (Summer 2006), pp. 369–389; and Lisa A. Kort-Butler and Kellie J. Hagewen, "School-Based Extracurricular Activity Involvement and Adolescent Self-Esteem," *Journal of Youth and Adolescence* (May 2011), pp. 568–581.

contracts, instruction in peaceful conflict resolution, classroom activities designed to reduce teasing, and enlisting parental involvement in supervising behavior.[20]

Adolescent Culture as a Determinant of Later Success, or Not   Some scientists studying adolescent culture in the schools have reported that it frequently has negative consequences for the futures of students who feel or are perceived as different from most other students. For example, Robert Crosnoe has found that feelings of not fitting in among students who were bullied because they were obese or gay sometimes led not only to depression, drug use, or other dysfunctions, but also to increased risk of not obtaining postsecondary educations. Related research indicates that lack of popularity in adolescence is associated with the subsequent emergence of career and adjustment problems in young adulthood.[21]

On the other hand, some analysts point out that many students who are excluded or are otherwise treated as outsiders in their high schools experience much success in college and later life. For example, Alexandra Robbins has studied the culture in a large high school and found that many "geeks," "nerds," and other outsiders are not popular and frequently are ridiculed and even bullied. But later in life, her "quirk theory" speculates, many are successful, in part because they are viewed as refreshingly different and interesting. Thus, there is considerable uncertainty about possible effects of high-school culture on subsequent careers, and much variation in how it may affect particular students.

School Culture

▌ Aspects of school culture

Education in school, compared with learning experiences in family or peer-group contexts, occurs in relatively formal ways. Group membership is not voluntary but determined by age, aptitudes, and, frequently, gender. Students are tested and evaluated; they are told when to sit, when to stand, how to walk through hallways, and so on. The rituals of school assemblies, athletic events, and graduation ceremonies—as well as the school insignia, songs, and cheers—all convey the school culture and socialize students. Less-ritualized activities and teacher behaviors also acculturate students to the school.

Student Roles and the Hidden Curriculum   Gita Kedar-Voivodas has examined teacher expectations for student roles—that is, desired student behaviors and characteristics—in the elementary classroom. She identified three main types of expected student role: the pupil role, the receptive learner role, and the active learner role.

▌ Three major student roles

The *pupil role* is one in which teachers expect students to be "patient, docile, passive, orderly, conforming, obedient and acquiescent to rules and regulations, respectful to authority, easily controllable, and socially adept." The *receptive learner role* requires students to be "motivated, task-oriented, . . . good achievers, and as such, receptive to the institutional demands of the academic curriculum." In the *active learner role*, according to Kedar-Voivodas, students go "beyond the established academic curriculum both in terms of the content to be mastered and in the processes" of learning. Traits of the active learner include "curiosity, active probing and exploring, challenging authority, an independent and questioning mind, and insistence on explanations." Kedar-Voivodas noted

[20]Matthew S. Robinson, "Scared Not to Be Straight," *Edutopia* (February 2008), available at **www.edutopia.org**; Kenneth S. Trump, "Managing Bullying in Politically Charged Climates," *District Administration* (January 2011). Also see material at **www.bullyonline.org**, **www .stopbullyingnow.com**, and **www.cyberbullying.us**.

[21]Antonius H. Cillessen, David Schwartz, and Lara Mayeux, eds., *Popularity in the Peer System* (New York: Guilford, 2011); Robert Crosnoe, *Fitting In, Standing Out* (New York: Cambridge University Press, 2011); Robert Crosnoe, "The Burden of the Bullied," 2011 paper posted by The University of Texas, available at **www.utexas.edu/features**; Monica K. Johnson, Robert Crosnoe, and Glenn H. Elder, "*Insights on Adolescence From a Life Course Perspective,*" *Journal of Research on Adolescence* (Issue 1, 2011), pp. 273–280; Adele Melander-Dayton, "Why It's Good to be a High School Loser," Salon, May 1, 2011, available at **www.salon.com**; and Alexandra Robbins, *The Geeks Shall Inherit the Earth* (New York: Hyperion, 2011).

▶II TEACHSOURCE VIDEO ACTIVITY

Developing Student Self-Esteem: Peer-Editing Process

Go to the Education CourseMate website to access the video entitled, "Developing Student Self-Esteem: Peer Editing Process." In this video, the teacher demonstrates how she sets up a peer-editing session that helps student's become better writers and increases their self-esteem in the process. While watching the video, think about what happens when high-school students critique the writing of their classmates. After watching the video, answer the following questions:

1 How does the peer-editing process shown in this video case support positive peer relationships and increase student motivation?

2 From a teacher's perspective, what are the pros and cons of using the peer-editing strategy? If you were a teacher, would you employ this strategy in your classroom? Why or why not?

** This video reinforces key concepts found in Part I: Students as Learners of the Praxis II Exam.**

---

that many educational philosophers, among them John Dewey and Maria Montessori, have stressed the value of active learning.[22]

Rejecting the active learner

Kedar-Voivodas also found, however, that students exemplifying the active learner role sometimes are rejected by teachers. That is, many teachers respond negatively to active, independent, and assertive children. The difference is large, Kedar-Voivodas said, between the school's academic curriculum, which demands successful mastery of cognitive material, and its "hidden" curriculum, which demands "institutional conformity."[23]

Effects of the hidden curriculum

The **hidden curriculum**—a term used by many critics of contemporary schools—is what students learn, other than academic content, from what they do or are expected to do in school. In addition to teaching children to passively conform in the classroom, the hidden curriculum may be preparing economically disadvantaged students to be docile workers later in life. It can communicate negative racial and sexual stereotypes through material included in (or omitted from) textbooks. It can lead children to believe that bullying is acceptable or that copying others' work is expected and excusable. Excessive emphasis on competition for grades may create a hidden curriculum that teaches students that beating the system is more important than anything else.[24]

Routine classroom activities

Classroom Culture   In his study of classroom processes in elementary schools, Philip Jackson found relatively few different types of classroom activity. The terms *seatwork, group discussion, teacher demonstration,* and *question-and-answer period* described most of what happened in the classroom. Further, these activities were performed according to well-defined rules such as "no loud talking during seatwork" and "raise your hand if

---

[22]Gita Kedar-Voivodas, "The Impact of Elementary Children's School Roles and Sex Roles on Teacher Attitudes," *Review of Educational Research* (Fall 1983), p. 417. See also Regina D. Langhout and Cecily A. Mitchell, "Engaging Contexts," *Journal of Community & Applied Social Psychology* (November/December 2008), pp. 593–614.

[23]Ibid., p. 418. See also Michael Apple, *Education and Power,* 2nd ed. (New York: Routledge, 1995); Craig D. Jerald, "School Culture," *CSRI Issue Brief* (December 2006), available at **www.center-forcsri.org**; Michael Apple, ed., *Global Crises, Social Justice, and Education* (New York: Routledge, 2010); and Joe L. Kincheloe, *Key Works in Critical Pedagogy* (Boston: Sense, 2011).

[24]Maggie Rosen, "The Hidden Curriculum," *Principal* (September 1995), p. 60; Jonathan Martin, "Pedagogy of the Alienated," *Equity and Excellence in Education* (March 2008), pp. 31–34; and Mary Breuing, "Problematizing Critical Pedagogy," *The International Journal of Critical Pedagogy* (May 25, 2011).

you have a question." The teacher served as a "combination traffic cop, judge, supply sergeant, and timekeeper." In this cultural system, the classroom often becomes a place where events happen "not because students want them to, but because it is time for them to occur."[25]

Stress on order, obedience

The rules of order that characterize most elementary-school classrooms, Jackson concluded, focus on preventing disturbances. Thus, the prevailing socialization pattern in the culture of the school and classroom places its greatest emphasis on what Kedar-Voivodas called the obedient pupil role. Other studies have reached essentially the same conclusion. For example, "A Study of Schooling" conducted by John Goodlad and his colleagues described the following widespread patterns:[26]

Enthusiasm controlled

1. The classroom is generally organized as a group that the teacher treats as a whole. This pattern seems to arise from the need to maintain orderly relationships among twenty to thirty people in a small space.

2. "Enthusiasm and joy and anger are kept under control." As a result, the general emotional tone is flat or neutral.

3. Most student work involves "listening to teachers, writing answers to questions, and taking tests and quizzes." Textbooks and workbooks generally constitute the media of instruction.

4. These patterns become increasingly rigid and predominant as students proceed through the grades.

Curiosity not encouraged

5. Instruction seldom goes beyond "mere possession of information." Relatively little effort is made to arouse curiosity or to emphasize thinking.

In summary, Goodlad wrote, students "rarely planned or initiated anything, read or wrote anything of some length, or created their own products. And they scarcely ever speculated on meanings."[27]

Passive learning in working-class schools

As we discuss elsewhere in this book, such systematic emphasis on passive learning by rote is in opposition to most contemporary ideas of what education should accomplish. Much has changed since Goodlad and his colleagues collected their data, but many classrooms still exemplify passive, rote learning. In particular, passive learning is more likely to be emphasized in schools with low-achieving, working-class students than in schools with high-achieving, middle-class students. To study this topic, Jean Anyon examined five elementary schools that differed markedly in social class. In the two predominantly working-class schools, Anyon found that instruction emphasized mostly mechanical skills such as punctuation and capitalization. In contrast, instruction in the schools she categorized as predominantly middle-class or "affluent professional" emphasized working independently and developing analytical and conceptual skills. Similar patterns have been reported by other researchers.[28]

Continuity & Change

---

[25]Philip W. Jackson, *Life in Classrooms* (New York: Holt, 1968), pp. 8–9, 13. See also Philip W. Jackson, *The Practice of Teaching* (New York: Teachers College Press, 1986); David T. Hansen, Mary E. Driscoll, and Rene V. Arcilla, eds., *A Life in Classrooms* (New York: Teachers College Press, 2007); and Amy Novotney, "Rooting Out Problem Behaviors," *Monitor on Psychology* (May 2011), available at **www.apa.org**.
[26]Goodlad, *A Place Called School*, pp. 123–124, 236, 246. See also Donald J. Willower and William L. Boyd, *Willard Waller on Education and Schools* (Berkeley, CA: McCutchan, 1989); Antonia Lewandowski, "Seen and Heard," *Teacher Magazine* (March 2006); and Akevy Greenblatt, "Technology Does Not Equal 21st Century Learning," 2011 posting by Connected Principals, available at **www.connectedprincipals.com**.
[27]John I. Goodlad, "A Study of Schooling," *Phi Delta Kappan* (March 1983), p. 468. See also Edgar H. Schuster, "The Persistence of the 'Grammar of Schooling,'" *Education Week*, April 30, 2003; and Paul E. Barton and Richard J. Coley, "The Mission of the High School," *ETS Policy Information Perspective* (July 2011), available at **www.ets.org**.
[28]Jean Anyon, "Social Class and the Hidden Curriculum of Work," *Journal of Education* (Winter 1980), pp. 67–92; Jean Anyon, *Ghetto Schooling* (New York: Teachers College Press, 1997); Jean Anyon, *Theory and Social Research* (New York: Routledge, 2008); and Ken McGrew, "To Bravely Speak," *Education Review*, May 2, 2011.

Why do classrooms so often function in this way? This is an important question, and many analysts have addressed it. Reasons they have offered include the following:

1. *Institutional requirements to maintain order.* As Jackson points out, a multitude of routines seek to govern interactions between twenty or thirty students and a teacher. Researchers use terms such as *institutional realities* and *organizational dynamics* to describe the forces that translate a need for order into an emphasis on passive learning.[29]

2. *Student preferences for passive learning.* We should not underestimate the degree to which many students resist active learning. As Walter Doyle writes, students may "restrict the amount of output they give to a teacher to minimize the risk of exposing a mistake." By holding back, students can also persuade other students or the teacher to help them. As one older student said, "Yeah, I hardly do nothing. All you gotta do is act dumb, and Mr. Y will tell you the right answer. You just gotta wait, you know, and he'll tell you."[30]

3. *Accommodations, bargains, and compromises between students and teachers.* In a context that combines institutional requirements for order with student preference for passive learning, the teacher and students may reach an *accommodation* or *bargain* by which they *compromise* on a set of minimal standards. For example, Martin Haberman has observed what he calls "the Deal" in many urban classrooms: students are nondisruptive as long as the teacher ignores the fact that they are not diligent in their classwork. The widespread existence of such "ABCs" has been documented in major studies. Michael Sedlak and his colleagues called such an arrangement "a complex, tacit conspiracy to avoid rigorous, demanding academic inquiry."[31]

4. *Teachers' allocation of attention.* Many teachers feel compelled to give most of their time and attention to a few students. In some cases, these will be the slowest students—whomever the teacher believes most need help. In many other cases, however, attention goes primarily to the brightest students, who teachers frequently believe will benefit the most from extra attention. This attitude is particularly prevalent when teachers have so many "slow" students that helping them all seems impossible.

Helen Gouldner and her colleagues found these dynamics in an inner-city, all-black elementary school with a large proportion of students from low-income home environments that failed to prepare them to function well in the classroom. The few well-prepared students (generally from relatively high-status families) were the "pets"—those whom teachers helped throughout their school careers. The largest group of students (the "nobodies") received relatively little teacher attention and generally was neither disruptive nor particularly successful. The remaining students, a small group of "troublemakers," were unable or unwilling to conform to the routine demands of the classroom. These patterns were well in line with the school's "sorting and selecting" function because the teachers, most of

[29]Goodlad, "A Study of Schooling," pp. 469–470; Max Angus, *The Rules of School Reform* (London: Falmer, 1998); Daniel U. Levine and Rayna F. Levine, "Considerations in Introducing Instructional Interventions," in Barbara Presseisen, ed., *Teaching for Intelligence,* 2nd ed. (Thousand Oaks, CA: Corwin, 2007); and Nancy J. Ratcliff et al., "The Elephant in the Classroom," *Education* (Winter 2010), pp. 306–314.

[30]Walter Doyle, "Academic Work," *Review of Educational Research* (Summer 1983), pp. 184–185. See also David Ferrero, "Tales from the Inside," *Education Next* (No. 2, 2006), available at **www.educationnext.org**; and Roxy Harris, "Urban Classroom Culture," *Education Review* (Winter 2011–2012).

[31]Michael W. Sedlak et al., *Selling Students Short* (New York: Teachers College Press, 1986), p. 13; Martin Haberman, "The Ideology of Nonwork in Urban Schools," *Phi Delta Kappan* (March 1997), pp. 499–503; Jeffrey Mirel, "The Traditional High School," *Education Next* (No. 1, 2006), available at **www.educationnext.org**; and Martin Haberman, "The Pedagogy of Poverty versus Good Teaching," 2011 posting by Dallas Friends of Public Education, available at **www.dfpe.org**.

whom were African American, could feel they were promoting success for at least some black students in a difficult learning environment.[32]

Conformity as a social demand

5. *Society's requirement that students learn to conform.* Underlying schools' emphasis on passive learning is the reality that young people must learn to function in social institutions outside the school. Because most people in contemporary society must cope with large economic, political, and social institutions, children must be socialized to follow appropriate routines and regulations. Philip Jackson summarizes this part of a school's socialization mission as follows: "It is expected that children will adapt to the teacher's authority by becoming 'good workers' and 'model students.' The transition from classroom to factory or office is made easily by those who have developed 'good work habits' in their early years." This goal of schooling is part of the hidden curriculum mentioned earlier.[33]

Burdens on teachers

6. *Teacher overload.* It is difficult for teachers to provide active, meaningful learning experiences when they must cope with the demands of large classes and class loads, a variety of duties and tasks outside their classrooms, pressures to cover a wide range of material and skills, and other such responsibilities.[34] As we document elsewhere in this book, recognition is growing of the heavy burdens on teachers, and many reformers are working to reduce teacher overload.

We could offer many additional reasons why classroom instructional patterns have been relatively unaffected by contemporary learning theory, but most of them in some way involve institutional constraints that favor passive, rote learning.[35] Overcoming such constraints requires significant innovations in school organization and pedagogy, as we will see in Chapter 16, School Effectiveness and Reform in the United States.

Positive aspects

Our focus in this section on negative aspects of school culture merits a reminder regarding the many positive aspects of elementary and secondary schools in the United States. Most schools provide an orderly learning environment, and most students learn to read and compute at a level required to function in our society. Relationships among teachers, students, and parents are generally positive. Most students receive a high-school diploma, and many proceed to various postsecondary educations. We describe in greater detail many successful aspects of the U.S. education system in Chapter 5, Historical Development of American Education; Chapter 11, Social Class, Race, and School Achievement; Chapter 15, International Education; Chapter 16, School Effectiveness and Reform in the United States; and elsewhere in this book.

> **REFOCUS** To what extent did your high-school teachers emphasize active learning? Do you recall any obvious obstacles to active learning that emphasized higher-order goals?

More television time than school time

Television and Digital Media

Some social scientists refer to television as the "first curriculum" because it appears to affect the way children develop learning skills and orient themselves toward acquiring knowledge and understanding. Because using television and other media may require

---

[32]Helen Gouldner, *Teachers' Pets, Troublemakers, and Nobodies* (Westport, CT: Greenwood, 1978), pp. 133–134. This self-fulfilling prophecy and the way it operated at the school studied by Gouldner and her colleagues are described at greater length in Ray C. Rist, *The Urban School* (Cambridge, MA: MIT Press, 1973). See also Cris Tovani, "I Got Grouped," *Educational Leadership* (March 2010), available at **www.ascd.org**; and Michell Garcia, "Students Beware," 2011 posting by Teaching Tolerance, available at **www.tolerance.org**.

[33]Jackson, *Life in Classrooms*, p. 32. See also David M. Schimmel, "Collaborative Rule-Making and Citizenship Education," *American Secondary Education* (Summer 2003), pp. 16–35; and Allen Mendler and Brian Mendler, "What Tough Kids Need from Us," *Reclaiming Children and Youth* (Spring 2010), pp. 27–31.

[34]Linda M. McNeil, *Contradictions of School Reform* (New York: Routledge, 2000); Mark J. Garrison and Hank Bromley, "Social Contexts, Defensive Pedagogies, and the (Mis)uses of Educational Technology," *Educational Policy* (September 2004), pp. 589–613; and Linda M. McNeil, "Teaching Boldly in Timid Schools," in M. C. Fehr and D. E. Fehr, eds., *Teach Boldly!* (New York: Peter Lang, 2010).

[35]Other frequently cited reasons include the tendency for teachers to teach the way they were taught, the high costs involved in introducing new approaches, and the lack of adequate preservice and in-service training.

little in the way of effort and skills, educators face a formidable challenge in maintaining students' interest and motivation in schoolwork. The average eighth grader spends more than three times as much time viewing television, surfing the Internet, and playing video games as doing homework and reading outside school. In addition, a large proportion of children and youth believe their peers' values are significantly influenced by what they see in the media. For more on the influence of television, see the Taking Issue box.

Television and school achievement

Although research shows a relationship between school achievement and television viewing, the nature of this relationship is not entirely clear. Some studies suggest that viewing television may reduce students' reading activities, but this conclusion is not well documented, and international studies show that students in some countries that rank high on television viewing among children also have relatively high achievement scores. It is difficult to separate cases in which television causes reduced attention to reading from those in which low-performing students turn to television for escape. Nevertheless, many educators are concerned that use of television and other media may lower achievement for many students, particularly because surveys indicate that millions of children watch television and use other media late into the night and then yawn their way through school the next day.[36]

General mass media effects

Apart from their possibly negative effects on school achievement, television and other media—such as movies, video games, and the music industry—deeply influence the socialization of children and youth. Research indicates that bombardment by the media contributes to such undesirable childhood outcomes as obesity and fragmented attention spans. The media both stimulate and reflect fundamental changes in attitudes and behaviors that prevail in our society, from recreation and career choices to sexual relationships, consumerism, and drug use. Unfortunately, no conclusive data determine just how much the media affect children and youth or whether overall developments and effects are positive or negative (depending, of course, on what one values as positive or negative). For example, twenty-four-hour-a-day rock-music programming on cable television has been viewed both as a means to keep young people off the streets and as the beginning of the end of Western civilization.[37]

Correlation with aggression

Many adults are particularly worried that television, video games, and other media may encourage aggressive or violent behavior. The average child now witnesses thousands of simulated murders and tens of thousands of other violent acts by the time he or she completes elementary school. The effects depend in part on situational factors: for example, the child's degree of frustration or anger, potential consequences such as pain or punishment, previous receptivity to violence, and opportunity to perform an act of violence. Overall, however, according to a committee of behavioral scientists, "television violence is as strongly correlated with aggressive behavior as any other behavioral variable that has been measured." The American Academy of Pediatrics and the American Psychological Association also have concluded that repeated exposure to violence on television and in other media promotes violent behavior.[38]

---

[36]*Survey of Sixth Grade School Achievement and Television Viewing Habits* (Sacramento: California State Department of Education, 1982); Amy Azzam, "Teaching the Tweens," *Educational Leadership* (April 2006), available at **www.ascd.org**; "Children and Electronic Media," *The Future of Children* (Spring 2008), available at **www.futureofchildren.org**; Rob Nugent, "The Decline of Reading in an Age of Ignorance," *Quadrant* (January 2011), pp. 6–12; and Ron Kaufman, "The Impact of Television and Video Entertainment on Student Achievement in Reading and Writing," undated posting at the "Kill Your Television" site, available at **www.turnoffyourtv.com**.
[37]Mark Bauerlein, *The Dumbest Generation* (New York: Tarcher, 2008); Mark Bauerlein, "The Anti-Intellectual Environment of American Teens," *Education Next* (Spring 2009), available at **www.educationnext.org**; and Mark Bauerlein, "Too Dumb for Complex Texts?" *Educational Leadership* (February 2011), available at **www.ascd.org**.
[38]U.S. Department of Health and Human Services, *Television and Human Behavior: Ten Years of Scientific Progress and Implications for the Eighties*, vol. 1, Summary Report (Washington, D.C.: U.S. Government Printing Office, 1982), pp. 6, 38–39; "Violent Video Games Poison the Teenage Brain," *American School Board Journal* (February 2007); Edward A. Swing and Craig A. Anderson, "Television and Video Game Exposure and the Development of Attention Problems," *Pediatrics* (August 2010), available at **www.aap.org**; and Christopher J. Ferguson, "Video Games and Youth Violence," *Journal of Youth and Adolescence* (April 2011), pp. 377–391.

TAKING ISSUE

Read the brief introduction below, as well as the Question and the pros and cons list that follows. Then, answer the question using your own words and position.

The Influence of Television

Television is a fixture in almost every home; its influence is so pervasive that it has been called another parent. Because most children spend more time watching television than attending school, debate continues over television's effect on student learning and behavior.

Question

Does television's influence on students generally benefit the teacher? (Think about this question as you read the PRO and CON arguments listed here. What is *your* take on this issue?)

Arguments PRO

1. Television enriches students' background knowledge so that they can understand much instruction more readily. Teachers who take advantage of what students already have learned from television can accelerate subject matter presentation.

2. In addition to providing useful information, television awakens interest in a wide range of topics. Teachers can draw on the interests that television arouses and involve students more deeply in many parts of the curriculum.

3. Television assists teachers by making learning palatable at an early age. Programs such as *Sesame Street* have increased student achievement in the early years by showing children that learning can be fun.

4. Television provides a catharsis for feelings of hostility and anger. Children who watch television dramas can work out potentially violent impulses that might otherwise be directed at classmates, parents, or teachers.

5. Television can provide a good socializing experience. Research has shown that programs like *Sesame Street* can increase cooperative behavior among children. Furthermore, many children's shows offer their viewers a welcome relief from the world of adults.

Arguments CON

1. Most often, the information that students gain from television is a superficial collection of facts, not useful background knowledge. Moreover, television may delude students into thinking that these scattered facts represent genuine understanding.

2. Television viewing creates mental habits that teachers must try to counteract. Although television may provoke a fleeting interest in a topic, it accustoms students to learning through passive impressions rather than thoughtful analysis. In addition, extensive television viewing by children is associated with a reduced attention span.

3. Early exposure to "fun" learning often raises false expectations about school. The teacher cannot be as entertaining as Big Bird. The need to compete with such television shows makes the teacher's job more difficult.

4. Research on modeling indicates that many children, confronted with a situation parallel to one they have seen on television, respond with the same behavior used by the television characters. In other words, violent television programs often encourage violent behavior.

5. For every *Sesame Street*, dozens of television programs tend to alienate children from the values of the school and the wider society. For example, some programs reinforce negative peer attitudes toward social institutions; some present simplistic or distorted notions of right and wrong; and many encourage dangerous fantasies.

Question Reprise: What Is Your Stand?

Reflect again on the following question by explaining *your* stand about this issue: Does television's influence on students generally benefit the teacher?

Social scientists also are becoming particularly concerned about media effects on the socialization of girls. Recent research indicates that the depiction of sex in the media is implicated in increasing teen pregnancies. In addition, a task force of the

American Psychological Association has examined research on the influence of television, music videos, music lyrics, magazines, movies, video games, and the Internet, as well as advertising and merchandising, and concluded that effects include damage to girls' self-image and healthy development. The Association deplored the "sexualization" of children and youth, which it defined as "occurring when a person's value comes only from her/his sexual appeal or behavior, to the exclusion of other characteristics, and when a person is sexually objectified, e.g., made into a *thing* for another's sexual use."[39]

Positive uses of television

It also is true, however, that television and digital media can be an important force for positive socialization. For example, research shows that the children's television program *Sesame Street* has helped both middle-class and working-class youth academically, and children can become more cooperative and nurturing after viewing programs emphasizing these behaviors. Research also indicates that computer software programs such as *Cyberchase* can help elementary students improve in mathematics. Some analysts believe that video games, computer games, and other digital media are helping children and youth develop many kinds of problem-solving and motor skills. Several analysts also believe that the ease of digital learning is creating a cognitive surplus that will enable great advances in living and working among young people and adults.

Continuity & Change

Recognizing both the good and the damaging effects media can have on children and youth, many people are working for improvements. The Parent-Teacher Association has made television reform—particularly reduction in sex, commercialism, and violence during prime time—one of its major national goals, and organizations such as the National Citizens Committee for Broadcasting have lobbied for change.

Reform efforts

However, progress has been slow. A typical afternoon of "kidvid" still can be a mind-numbing march of cartoon superheroes, and many programs insistently instruct children to demand another trip to the nearest toy store. In 1990, the federal government introduced a requirement that television stations broadcast at least three hours per week of educational and informational programs for children, but much of this programming has few viewers, and programs emphasizing sex and/or violence continue mostly unabated.[40]

Different from television

Net Generations in the Digital Age   Some analysts have begun to examine possible changes as children and youth grow up in an environment permeated by digital communications and information sources such as interactive video and the increasingly ubiquitous Internet. One of the first books that addressed these developments was Don Tapscott's *Growing Up Digital*. Tapscott, who refers to young people growing up in the emerging digital age as the "net generation," believes the Internet is quite different from television—it stimulates interactive participation rather than passive viewing. Tapscott predicts that the Internet will produce "a generation which increasingly questions the implicit values contained in information . . . [and in so doing forces

---

[39]Eileen L. Zurbriggen et al., "Report of the APA Task Force on the Sexualization of Girls," 2007 paper prepared for the American Psychological Association, executive summary available at **www.apa.org**; Anita Chandra et al., "Does Watching Sex on Television Predict Teen Pregnancy?" *Pediatrics* (November 2008), pp. 1047–1054, available at **www.aap.org**; and Vicki Courtney, "Preventing the Sexualization of Girls," 2011 posting by Vicki Courtney, available at **www.vickicourtney.com**.

[40]Daniel R. Anderson, "Educational Television Is Not an Oxymoron," *Annals of the American Academy of Political and Social Science* (May 1998), pp. 24–38; Steven Johnson, *Everything Bad Is Good for You* (New York: Riverhead, 2006); Marc Prensky, "Young Minds, Fast Times," *Edutopia* (May 31, 2008), available at **www.edutopia.org**; Clay Shirky, *Here Comes Everybody* (London: Penguin, 2008); Jenny Levine, "Gaming and Libraries," *Library Technology Reports* (July 2009), pp. 5–35, available at **www.alatechsource.org**; Judy Willis, "A Neurologist Makes the Case for the Video Game as a Learning Tool," *Edutopia* (April 20, 2011), available at **www.edutopia.org**; and Ron Kaufman, "How Television Images Affect Children," undated posting at the "Kill Your Television" site, available at **www.turnoffyourtv.com**.

children] to exercise not only their critical thinking but their judgment . . . [and thus contributes] to the relentless breakdown of the notion of authority."[41]

Liberating and productive

Tapscott believes that the digital revolution's primary effects will be liberating for individuals and productive for society. Individuals will find information and knowledge easily accessible and opportunities vastly expanded. In addition, familiarity with digital media is preparing young people to function effectively at the multitasking required in complicated jobs. Society will find that a knowledge-based economy improves efficiency and productivity and that technology will enable the educational system to function successfully in preparing young persons for skilled employment. Like other analysts, however, Tapscott is concerned that digital media and learning will increase the already troublesome gap between the haves and the have-nots, that is, between middle-class youth who have good access to new technologies and low-income youth who have relatively poor access and thus may be further disadvantaged.

Social networking issues

Web 2.0 and Social Networking   Tapscott and other leading analysts such as Urs Gasser, John Palfrey, and Clay Shirky have become particularly concerned with young peoples' experience in connection with Web 2.0—the increasingly interactive and social networking aspects of the Internet. They point out that, by age twenty, many youth will have been on the Internet for 30,000 hours or more, much of it in contact with other participants from around the world. Even very young children are logging on to sites where they communicate with others who comprise expanding communities of interconnected users. Most observers worry about apparent negatives in this situation, such as dangers posed by anonymous online "friends," over-reliance on occasionally unreliable sources found on Google or elsewhere, and time-consuming distractions from schoolwork and learning. But they also point out that Web 2.0 aspects of the Internet provide enormous opportunities for improving the lives of children and adults, as well as the functioning of social, political, and economic institutions. Some of the suggestions they have made regarding actions that should be emphasized in the schools include the following:[42]

- Teach about the safe and appropriate use of Web 2.0 tools, rather than blocking them out and leaving students to fend for themselves.

- Draw not just on popular sites such as Facebook and Twitter, but also specialized social-networking sites such as GlobalSchoolNet.

- Make sure students are learning and writing acceptable English rather than truncated versions used in text messaging.

- Change instruction from a teacher-focused model to one based on students' skills in using the Internet and communications patterns inherent in Web 2.0.

- Emphasize skills, such as group projects carried out on the Web, that will be beneficial in future employment.

- Encourage students in using video games or computer games that emphasize art, history, or science rather than violence or sex.

- Help students balance relationships and contacts they have on the computer with real-life activities, such as sports and clubs.

- Develop media competence, including digital literacy, visual literacy, and other aspects.

See the Technology @ School box for more on "media literacy."

---

[41]Don Tapscott, *Growing Up Digital* (New York: McGraw-Hill, 1998), p. 26. See also Clay Shirky, *Cognitive Surplus* (New York: Penguin, 2010); and Larry D. Rosen, "Teaching the iGeneration," *Educational Leadership* (February 2011), available at **www.ascd.org**.
[42]Naomi Dillon, "Protecting Students Online," *American School Board Journal* (December 2008); Don Tapscott, *Grown Up Digital* (New York: McGraw-Hill, 2008); Adam D. Thierer, "Understanding Our Digital Kids," *City Journal* (October 10, 2008), available at **www.city-journal.com**; Greg Downey, "Is Facebook Rotting Our Children's Brains?" *Neuroanthropology* (March 2, 2009); and Stan Bumgardner and Kirk Knestis, "Social Networking as a Tool for Student and Teacher Learning," *District Administration* (May 2011), available at **www.districtadministration.com**.

Gender Roles and Sex Differences and Outcomes

Early reinforcement of gender roles

Not only does society demand conformity to its fundamental values and norms; it also assigns specific roles to each of its members, expecting them to conform to certain established behavioral patterns. Socialization is particularly forceful regarding **gender roles**—ideas about the ways boys and girls and men and women are "supposed" to act. Gender roles vary from culture to culture, but within a given culture they are rather well defined, and children are socialized in them through an elaborate schedule of selective reinforcement. For example, a preschool boy may be ridiculed for playing with dolls, and young girls may be steered away from activities considered too physically rough. By age 3, as Robert Havighurst has remarked, there is already a "noticeable difference in behavior between boys and girls." Even at such an early age, boys are more "active," and girls are more "dependent" and "nurturant."[43]

Gender roles and school problems for boys

When children go to school, they discover that it is dominated by traditional norms of politeness, cleanliness, and obedience. Teachers generally suppress fighting and aggressive behavior. This can be a problem for boys because, as research indicates, on the average they are more aggressive than girls almost from the time they are born, probably because of hormone differences. Some scholars believe that teachers' tendency to reward passive behavior and discourage aggressiveness helps account for boys' relatively high rates of alienation and violation of school rules. Boys receive many more reprimands from teachers than do girls, and by the time students enter the secondary grades, boys greatly outnumber girls in remedial classes and in classes for those with emotional disturbances.[44]

Gender roles and school problems for girls

By way of contrast, the problems that girls encounter in the educational system generally reflect their socialization for dependence rather than assertiveness. Historically, most girls were not encouraged to prepare for high-status fields such as law or medicine or high-paying technical occupations. Instead, they were expected to prepare for roles as wives and homemakers. The few occupations women were encouraged to consider, such as elementary teacher, social worker, and nurse, tended to have relatively low pay and low status. This type of socialization did not motivate girls to acquire skills useful for later economic success. Furthermore, verbal skills of the kind in which girls tend to excel failed to prepare them for success in mathematics and science. As a result, many girls were excluded from educational opportunities.[45]

Girls not encouraged in competition or leadership

Although socialization in the elementary school frequently intends to make boys obedient and cooperative, in high school, the emphasis placed on athletics means that boys have often received more opportunities than girls to learn leadership and competitive skills that can be useful in later life. Girls, expected to be cooperative and even docile, traditionally have had relatively little encouragement to learn such skills, and those who did were perceived as violating proper norms for female behavior in American society.

---

[43]Robert J. Havighurst, "Sex Role Development," *Journal of Research and Development in Education* (Winter 1983), p. 61. See also Timothy J. Lensmire, "Learning Gender," *Educational Researcher* (June–July 1995), pp. 31–32; Harriet R. Tenenbaum, "You'd Be Good at That," *Social Development* (May 2009), pp. 447–463; and Darip Cvencek, Andrew N. Meltzoff, and Anthony G. Greenwald, "Math-Gender Stereotypes in Elementary School Children" *Child Development* (March 2011).
[44]Christina H. Sommers, *The War against Boys* (New York: Simon and Schuster, 2000); Gerry Garibaldi, "How the Schools Shortchange Boys," *City Journal* (Summer 2006), available at **www.city-journal.org**; Janet Mulvey, "The Feminization of Schools," *Education Digest* (April 2010), pp. 35–38; and Michael Thompson, "Why Do So Many Boys Not Care about School?" 2011 posting by PBS, available at **www.pbs.org/parents/experts/archive**.
[45]Susan L. Gabriel and Isaiah Smithson, eds., *Gender in the Classroom* (Urbana: University of Illinois Press, 1990); Karyn M. Plumm, "Technology in the Classroom," *Computers and Education* (April 2008), pp. 1052–1068; Richard Whitmire and Susan M. Bailey, "Gender Gap," *Education Next* (Spring 2010), available at **www.educationnext.org**; and Susan Fisk, "Negative + Math + Stereotypes = Too Few Women," *Gender News*, February 14, 2011, available at **www.stanford.edu**.

TECHNOLOGY @ SCHOOL

Helping Students Develop Media Literacy

Media literacy involves skill in learning from and critically evaluating different forms of electronic and print media. Helping students develop media literacy will be an important part of your job as a teacher. Most of your students will not only spend time watching television, they also will play computer games and video games and use the Internet for many purposes. One way to avoid negative outcomes, such as potential school achievement problems, unfavorable socialization, and unquestioning acceptance of media values, is to encourage active listening, viewing, and surfing.

You can teach about many aspects of media literacy. For example, you might help your students understand basic issues regarding the functioning and effects of mass media. Renee Hobbs offers suggestions in the article "Teaching Media Literacy: YO! Are You Hip to This?" (and in other articles) at **www.mediaeducationlab.com**. The CML Media-Lit Kit at **www.medialit.org** provides advice for implementing media literacy instruction that addresses a wide range of curriculum standards.

Boys' versus girls' peer groups

Raphaela Best found that school peer groups also help communicate traditional expectations for boys and girls. Best reported that boys' peer groups stress "canons" such as "always be first" and "don't hang out with a loser," whereas girls' peer groups place relatively more emphasis on having fun rather than winning and on cooperation rather than competition. Best also reported that as the students she studied grew older, they made some progress in overcoming stereotypes that limited the aspirations of girls and restricted the emotional growth of boys. Similarly, Barrie Thorne studied elementary-school students and concluded that gender roles are socially constructed at an early age. She also concluded that teachers should try to counteract gender stereotypes by facilitating cooperative behaviors and enhancing opportunities to participate in diverse activities.[46]

Sex Differences in Achievement and Ability

Reading and mathematics

Recent studies in the United States indicate that sex differences in academic achievement are relatively small to nonexistent. For example, data on the reading performance of nine-, thirteen-, and seventeen-year-olds indicate that girls score only a little higher than boys. Conversely, among seventeen-year-olds, boys score slightly higher than girls in higher-order mathematics achievement, but this difference is smaller than it was in 1970; nine- and thirteen-year-olds show little meaningful difference in mathematics scores for girls and boys. Research also indicates that female gains in mathematics probably are partly due to greater participation in math courses during the past few decades.[47]

Innate differences?

Though sex differences in achievement are narrowing or disappearing, much controversy remains about possible differences in innate ability. These arguments often focus on whether a larger proportion of boys than girls have unusually strong innate ability for higher-order mathematics or abstract thinking in general. Research on this

---

[46]Raphaela Best, *We've All Got Scars: What Boys and Girls Learn in Elementary School* (Bloomington: Indiana University Press, 1983); and Barrie Thorne, *Gender Play* (New Brunswick, NJ: Rutgers University Press, 1993). See also Eva Anggard, "Barbie Princesses and Dinosaur Dragons," *Gender and Education* (December 2005), pp. 539–553; and Jill D. Kelter and Alice W. Pope, "The Effect of Child Gender on Teachers' Responses to Oppositional Defiant Disorder," *Child and Family Behavior Therapy* (January-March 2011), pp. 49–57.

[47]Yupin Bae et al., *Trends in Educational Equity of Girls and Women* (Washington, D.C.: National Center for Education Statistics, 2000), available at **www.nces.ed.gov**; and Christianne Corbett, Catherine Hill, and Susan J. Colley, "The Mathematics of Sex," *American Mathematical Monthly* (April 2011), pp. 379–382.

▶️❚❚ TEACHSOURCE VIDEO ACTIVITY

Gender Equity in the Classroom: Girls and Science

G o to the Education CourseMate website to access the video entitled, "Gender Equity in the Classroom: Girls and Science," and think about how you, as a teacher, can promote learning for all students—girls and boys. In this video, the teacher discusses how he keeps the girls in his classroom interested in science. He stresses the importance of role models and mentors who can help sustain their interest in science through adolescence and beyond. After you watch the video, answer the following questions:

❶ How do programs like the Girls Science Club (shown in the video case) benefit girls in today's schools?

❷ Watch the classroom teacher in this video case. How does he try to keep his students engaged—especially the female students? Note some specific strategies he uses.

** This video reinforces key concepts found in Section III: Communication Techniques of the Praxis II Exam.**

topic shows more variability in ability among boys than among girls: boys are more likely to be either markedly high or markedly low in ability. However, some recent research indicates that girls and women are constituting a growing percentage of the highest-ability students.[48]

Different brain functioning

Those who believe that ability differences between the sexes are present at birth point to differences in brain function between boys and girls. For most people, the left hemisphere of the brain specializes in verbal tasks, whereas the right hemisphere specializes in nonverbal ones, including spatial functions important in mathematics. In this respect, brain research suggests some differences associated with sex hormones that begin to function at birth or even earlier. Among right-handed people (the majority), women handle spatial functions more with the *left* hemisphere than do men. Women also use the *right* hemisphere more in verbal functions. Numerous other differences have also been reported.[49]

Math anxiety and fear of success

Other observers, however, argue that differences in experience and expectations account for most or all of the learning and achievement differences between boys and girls. Particular attention has been paid to "math anxiety" among women—the possibility that the relatively poor performance of certain women in math (and therefore in science and other fields dependent on math) stems from socialization practices that make them anxious and fearful about mathematical analysis. A related line of argument is that women fear success in traditionally male activities and occupations because succeeding would violate sex stereotypes, thereby inviting ridicule. Still other analysts believe that girls tend to divert their attention more toward social relationships

[48]Elizabeth Fennema et al., "New Perspectives on Gender Differences in Mathematics," *Educational Researcher* (June–July, 1998), pp. 19–21; Doreen Kimura, *Sex and Cognition* (Cambridge, MA: MIT Press, 2000); Eugene A. Geist and Margaret King, "Different, Not Better," *Journal of Instructional Psychology* (March 2008), pp. 43–52; Heather MacDonald, "Math *Is* Harder for Girls," *City Journal*, July 28, 2008, available at **www.city-journal.com**; Hanna Rosin, "The Genius Gap," *New York*, June 4, 2010, available at **www.nymag.com**; and Maia Szalavitz, "The Math Gender Gap," *Time Healthland*, August 30, 2011.

[49]Richard M. Restak, "The Other Difference Between Boys and Girls," *Educational Leadership* (December 1979), pp. 232–235; Louann Brizendine, *The Female Brain* (New York: Morgan Road Books, 2006); Louann Brizendine, *The Male Brain* (New York: Three Rivers Press, 2011); and Eka Roivainen, "Gender Differences in Processing Speed," *Learning and Individual Differences* (April 2011), pp. 145–149.

Rhoda Sidney/The Image Works

Though sex differences in achievement are narrowing, much controversy remains about possible sources of sex differences and ways to address them.

as they enter adolescence. But the situation is complex, and few large-scale generalizations can be made.[50]

Educational and Occupational Attainment of Women

Educational gains for women

Throughout most of U.S. history, women completed fewer years of schooling than did men. In 1979, however, women for the first time outnumbered men among college freshmen. Since 1992, more than half of all bachelor's and master's degrees have been awarded to women. Women now constitute nearly 60 percent of college enrollment.[51]

Occupational gains

Related gains have also been registered in the occupational status of women. For example, in 1950, only 15 percent of accountants were women, compared to over 50 percent in 2011; the comparable percentages for female lawyers were 4 percent in 1950 and 31 percent in 2011. In addition, about half of first-year law students are now female. Both our schools and the wider society are seeing the effects of efforts to eliminate sexism from school curricula, by encouraging girls to attend college and prepare for the professions, providing support for girls and women to enter scientific fields and computing, and other actions to equalize opportunity.[52]

Much to be accomplished

Ways to improve gender equity in education

Nevertheless, much remains to be achieved. Despite recent gains, many women still are concentrated in low-paying, low-status occupations. Although the percentage of female scientists and engineers with doctoral degrees has more than doubled since 1973, women still constitute less than one-quarter of the total. Researchers'

[50]Lynn Friedman, "The Space Factor in Mathematics," *Review of Educational Research* (Spring 1995), pp. 22–50; Janet S. Hyde, "The Gender Similarity Hypothesis," *American Psychologist* (September 2005), pp. 581–592; "Do Synapses Vary with Gender?" *New Scientist* (September 18, 2008), p. 17; Sarah D. Sparks, "Researchers Probe Causes of Math Anxiety," *Education Week* (May 18, 2011); and "The Theory behind the Research," undated posting at the Girls Tech site, available at **www.girlstech.douglass.rutgers.edu**.
[51]Brenda Feigen, *Not One of the Boys* (New York: Knopf, 2000); Kelvin Pollard, "The Gender Gap in College Enrollment and Graduation," 2011 posting by the Population Reference Bureau, available at **www.prb.org**; and Stephanie Coontz, "The M.R.S. and the P.H.D.," *New York Times* (February 11, 2012).
[52]Catherine Hill, Christianne Corbett, and Andresse St. Rose, "Why So Few?" 2010 paper posted at the American Association of University Women Internet site, available at **www.aauw.org**; and Julie Clayton, "Fix the System, Not the Women," *Science* (January 21, 2011), pp. 349–351.

suggestions for further improving educational opportunities and equity for girls and women include the following:[53]

- Increase teacher training dealing with gender issues.
- Attend more closely to gender equity in vocational education.
- Protect the rights of pregnant girls and teenage parents.
- Introduce "gender-fair" curricula that accommodate learning-style differences.
- Introduce special programs to encourage girls to participate in math, computing, and science programs.
- Work to counteract the decline in self-esteem that many girls experience as they become concerned with their appearance.

The Increasing Plight of Working–Class and Low–Skilled, Middle–Class Men

Difficulties of working-class men

We noted previously that traditional socialization practices in the classroom have created problems for many boys and that women have been gaining in education and employment, particularly when compared with men. Associated with but beyond these patterns, there is widespread concern regarding the status and future of working-class men and of low-skilled middle-class men—those who have not acquired technical skills in higher education and were in the middle class mainly because of relatively high income. As a group, men in these categories have faced difficult circumstances as our economy has moved away from manufacturing and construction. Such circumstances have been apparent in data on the following trends and patterns:[54]

- Many men are seeking work in a dwindling number of manual-labor jobs outside the service sector.
- After adjusting for inflation, the wages of men have fallen significantly since 1973.
- Among men who did not attend college, unemployment increased from 5–10 percent in the 1960s to 20–25 percent in 2000, before recession pushed it even higher.
- As marriage rates for the working class have fallen rapidly, many more less-educated men have become absent fathers who have child-support payments deducted from their already-low wages.

Possible actions to help

Some of the educational reforms and innovations described in this book and elsewhere may produce improvements in students' opportunities, including those of working-class males. A few, such as high-school career academies, can be particularly helpful for working-class and poverty students. But widespread national efforts to address the plight of working-class and low-skilled, middle-class segments of the population necessarily will involve complicated programs involving on-the-job training, family support, accelerated job creation, and related efforts. No programs along these lines are likely to be inexpensive or easy to implement.

REFOCUS   What might you do as a teacher to encourage girls, or boys, for that matter, to overcome overly passive tendencies?

[53]Ibid.
[54]Hanna Rosin, "The End of Men," *Atlantic* (July/August 2010), available at **www.theatlantic. com**; Richard Whitmire, *Why Boys Fail* (New York: Anacom, 2010); "Decline of the Working Man," *Economist* (April 28th, 2011); Kay Hymowitz, *Manning Up* (New York: Basic Books, 2011); Don Peck, "Can the Middle Class Be Saved?" *Atlantic* (September 2011), available at **www.theatlantic.com**; Adam Serwer, "The Bell Swerve," *American Prospect* (May 2011), available at **www.prospect.org**; and information provided by The Boys Initiative (**www.theboysinitiative.org**).

Adolescent and Youth Problems

In many traditional, nonindustrialized cultures, the young are initiated into adult life after puberty. This initiation sometimes takes place through special rituals designed to prove the young person's worthiness to assume adult roles. In such societies, one is either a child or an adult; only a brief gap—if any gap at all—separates the two.

In modern technological societies, the young are forced to postpone their adulthood for a period of time called adolescence or youth. A major reason is that modern society no longer has an economic need for young people in this age group. One unfortunate result is that youth have become more and more isolated from the rest of society. In recent decades, this isolation has intensified many youth-centered problems, such as drug use, drinking, suicide, early pregnancy, and delinquency. At the same time, the isolation of youth hampers efforts of schools and other social institutions to prepare young people for adulthood.[55]

Drugs and Drinking

General usage of drugs and alcohol among youth has grown markedly over the past half-century, and recently, after a decade or more of decline, the use of some drugs has begun to rise again. Many high-school students are regular users of alcohol and/or marijuana, and small percentages use cocaine, crack, methamphetamines, and other drugs. Regular use of alcohol has remained fairly stable, but research indicates that alcohol use has been increasing among students younger than fifteen years old, that many teenagers have driven an automobile while intoxicated, and that an alarming number of teenagers frequently drink alone when they are bored or upset. The National Center on Addiction and Substance Abuse surveyed high-school students and found that nearly half reported use of cigarettes, alcohol, marijuana, cocaine, or other addictive substances within the previous thirty days.[56]

Educators worry that young people's use of alcohol, marijuana, and other relatively mild drugs may reinforce or stimulate alienation from social institutions or otherwise impede the transition to adulthood. This is not to say that drug use invariably leads to problems such as low academic performance, rebelliousness, and criminal activity; it is just as likely that the problems arise first and lead to the drug use. Many young people are using drugs and alcohol to escape from difficulties they encounter in preparing for adult life. But whatever the sequence of causation, usage rates among U.S. youth remain higher than in any other industrialized nation. Moreover, contrary to much earlier opinion, some authorities believe that mild drugs such as marijuana are often a stepping-stone to stronger drugs such as methamphetamine, cocaine, and heroin. Young people themselves believe that drugs and alcohol are a negative influence in their lives. National surveys consistently show that many high-school students cite either drugs or alcohol as the "single worst influence" in their lives.[57]

[55]James S. Coleman, "Families and Schools," *Educational Researcher* (August–September 1987), pp. 32–38; James E. Cote, *Arrested Adulthood* (New York: New York University Press, 2000); and Wendy Troop-Gordon, Kari J. Visconti, and Kayla J. Kuntz, "Perceived Popularity During Early Adolescence," *Journal of Early Adolescence* (April 2011), pp. 125–151.
[56]"America's #1 Public Health Problem," 2011 report prepared for the National Center on Addiction and Health Abuse," available at **www.casacolumbia.org**. Information about trends and prevention of substance abuse among youth is available at **www.jointogether.org**.
[57]Diane Ravitch, "Sex, Drugs—and More Sex and Drugs," *Education Next*, no. 1 (2006), available at **www.educationnext.org**; and Jeff R. Temple and Daniel H. Freeman, "Dating Violence and Substance Abuse among Ethnically Diverse Adolescents," *Journal of Interpersonal Violence* (March 2011), pp. 701–718.

Suicide

Rise in suicide rate

Educators have become increasingly concerned about suicide among young people. The suicide rate among children and youth has about quadrupled since 1950, and some surveys suggest that as many as one in ten school-age youth may attempt suicide. Reasons for this increase appear to include a decline in religious values that inhibit suicide, influence of the mass media, bullying by peers—particularly of gay and lesbian students, perceived pressures to excel in school, uncertain effects of commonly prescribed medications, failed relationships with peers, and pressures or despondency associated with divorce or other family problems.[58]

Teachers should learn warning signs

Teachers and other school personnel need to be alert to the suicide problem. Warning signs include the following: withdrawal from friends, family, and regular activities; violent or rebellious behavior; running away; alcohol or drug abuse; unusual neglect of personal appearance; radical change in personality; persistent boredom; difficulty in concentrating; decline in schoolwork quality; and emotional or physical symptoms such as headaches and stomachaches. Teachers also should keep in mind a U.S. District Court ruling that found school officials partly responsible for a student's suicide when they failed to provide reasonable care and help for a young man who had displayed suicidal symptoms.[59]

Teenage Pregnancy

Rise in births out of wedlock

Among teenagers as a whole, the number and rate of births have fallen substantially during the past half-century, partly because of the availability of contraceptives and abortion and the success of abstinence campaigns in some communities. On the other hand, the percentage of births to teenage mothers that occur out of wedlock has skyrocketed from 15 percent in 1960 to almost 90 percent in the past decade. Researchers have linked this trend to various social problems. For example, families headed by young mothers are much more likely than other families to live below the poverty line, and teenage mothers are much less likely to receive prenatal care than are older mothers. Not surprisingly, then, children of teenage mothers tend to have poor health and to perform poorly in school. Moreover, society spends billions of dollars each year to support the children of teenage mothers.[60]

Reasons for increase

Teenage births constitute a substantially higher percentage of births in the United States than in most other industrialized nations. According to social scientists who have analyzed fertility data, high incidence of out-of-wedlock births among teenagers results from such interrelated factors as social acceptance of teenage sexuality, earlier and more frequent sexual intercourse, a decrease in early marriages, lack of potential marriage partners, a decline in community and parental influence over the young, encouragement from the media, and the assumption by social agencies of responsibility for helping younger mothers.[61]

School responses

Many schools have responded by establishing school-based clinics for pregnant teenagers and new mothers and by expanding courses that focus on sex education,

[58]Douglas Fisher, "Keeping Adolescents 'Alive and Kickin' It,'" *Phi Delta Kappan* (June 2006), pp. 784–786; and Anat B. Klomek, Andre Sourander, and Madelyn S. Gould, "Bullying and Suicide," *Psychiatric Times* (February 2011), pp. 27–31.

[59]Burr Snider, "Loss Prevention," *Edutopia* (October 2006), available at **www.edutopia.org**; Carolyn M. Rutledge, Don Rimer, and Micah Scott, "Vulnerable Goth Teens," *Journal of School Health* (September 2008), pp. 459–464; and Stephen D. Whitney, et al., "Principals' Perceptions of Benefits and Barriers to School-Based Suicide Prevention Programs," *Children and Youth Services Review* (June 2011), pp. 869–867. See also "Teen Suicide Theme Page" and links provided at **www.cln.org/themes/suicide.html**.

[60]Kay S. Hymowitz, "It's Morning After in America," *City Journal* (Spring 2004), available at **www.city-journal.org**; and Anita Babbit, "Teen Pregnancy on the Rise," 2011 posting by The College Network, available at **www.uwire.com**.

[61]Kingsley Davis, "A Theory of Teenage Pregnancy in the United States," in Catherine S. Chilman, ed., *Adolescent Pregnancy and Childbearing* (Washington, D.C.: U.S. Government Printing Office, 1980); Kristin A. Moore, "Teen Births," *Child Research Briefs* (March 2009), available at **www.childtrends.org**; and Olivia Marshall, "The Drop Out Crisis and Teen Pregnancy," *P-Fix*, June 29, 2011, available at **www.progressivefix.com**.

health, personal development, and family life. Although early data on these activities were generally negative, recent studies indicate that they can be effective in preventing or at least alleviating problems associated with teenage pregnancy. Positive results also have been reported for a variety of approaches implemented since 1996 as part of the federally sponsored National Campaign to Prevent Teen Pregnancy. In addition, organizations such as Girls, Inc. have conducted projects that provide girls with a combination of assertiveness training, health services, communications skills, personal counseling, and information about sexuality. Recent data show that these efforts appear to have helped in substantially reducing the incidence of teenage pregnancies.[62]

Delinquency and Violence

Continuity & Change

Overall trends

Juvenile delinquency has increased in recent decades, paralleled by related increases in single-parent families, peer culture influence, drug and alcohol use, and the growth of low-income neighborhoods in big cities. Problems connected with violence and delinquency are particularly acute among young African American males, whose rate of death from homicide has more than tripled since 1985. Even among young white males, however, homicide rates are more than twice as high as in any other industrialized country.

Research on delinquency and violence among youth supports several generalizations:[63]

- Significant delinquency rates appear among youth of all social classes. However, violent delinquency is much more frequent among working-class youth than among middle-class youth.

- Although a large proportion of crimes are committed by people under age 25, most delinquents settle down to a productive adult life.

- An increase in gangs has helped generate greater violence among youth.

Unemployment

- Delinquency is associated with unemployment. From this point of view, delinquency is a partial response to the restricted opportunities available to some young people in modern society.

- Family characteristics related to delinquency include lack of effective parental supervision and lack of a father.

School performance

- Delinquency is related to learning disabilities and low school achievement.

- One of the strongest predictors of delinquency is peer influence, but this influence interacts with the family, the neighborhood, and other factors.

Influence of peers

- Violent youth crime has increased substantially in suburban and rural areas.

Effects on Schools

Major consequences for schools

As we have seen, young people do not simply leave larger cultural patterns behind when they enter the schoolhouse door. Like the other topics discussed in this chapter, the characteristics of youth culture have enormous consequences for the U.S. educational system. The most direct problems are drugs and alcohol in the schools, and violence, theft, and disorder on school grounds. Indicators of antisocial behavior in and around the schools have been a continuing topic of debate during the past thirty years.[64]

---

[62]Dean F. Miller, *The Case for School-Based Health Clinics* (Bloomington, IN: Phi Delta Kappa, 1990); Janice D. Key et al., "Effectiveness of an Intensive, School-Based Intervention for Teen Mothers," *Journal of Adolescent Health* (April 2008), pp. 394–400; and Todd Melby, "Federal Funds Create Sexuality Educator Jobs," *Contemporary Sexuality* (March 2011), pp. 1–6.
[63]Paul V. McNulty, "Natural Born Killers," *Policy Review* (Winter 1995), pp. 84–87; Kay S. Hymowitz, "The Children's Hour," *City Journal* (Winter 2009), available at **www.city-journal .com**; and Susan L. Wynne and Hee-Jong Joo, "Predictors of School Victimization," *Crime and Delinquency* (May 2011), pp. 458–488.
[64]James N. Loque, "Violent Death in American Schools in the 21st Century," *Journal of School Health* (January 2008), pp. 58–61; and Rebecca Bondu, Dewey G. Cornell, and Herbert Scheithauer, "Student Homicidal Violence in Schools," *New Directions for Youth Development* (Spring 2011), pp. 13–30.

Although violence and vandalism are most common at low-income schools in big cities, they are serious problems at many schools outside the inner city, especially when the schools are afflicted by teenage and young-adult gangs, by crime connected with substance abuse and drug sales, and by trespassers who infiltrate school buildings. Nearly two hundred students have been killed in or around schools during the past ten years, some of them in the highly publicized shootings at Columbine and Santee High Schools. In recent years, elaborate security plans have been put in place, zero-tolerance policies (described in Chapter 9, Legal Aspects of Education) have been introduced, and schools have implemented multiple programs to reduce bullying and intergroup hostilities.

Social service personnel in schools

In response to youth problems in general, schools now employ many more counselors, social workers, and other social service personnel than they did in earlier decades. Urban high schools, for example, use the services of such specialized personnel as guidance and career counselors, psychologists, security workers, nurses, truant officers, and home–school coordinators. Many of these specialists help conduct programs that target alcohol and drug abuse, teenage sex, school dropout, suicide, intergroup relations, and parenting skills.

In addition, many schools are cooperating with other institutions in operating school-based clinics and/or in providing coordinated services that help students and families receive assistance with mental and physical health problems, preparation for employment, and other preoccupations that detract from students' performance in school. Thousands of schools also are implementing programs to improve school-wide discipline, teach students conflict-resolution skills, develop peer-mediation mechanisms, and control gang activities. Related chapters of this book provide additional information on efforts to improve school climates and environments.

REFOCUS   How do you think your teaching will be affected by problems of adolescence such as violence, drug use, and pregnancy? What kind of help might you need in dealing with such problems?

Summing Up

1 Changes in family composition may be detrimentally influencing children's behavior and performance in school. Although the situation is complicated, increases in single-parent families and in the number of working mothers appear to be having a negative effect on many students. In recent years, cohabitation has become much more frequent, particularly among less-wealthy and less-educated parents whose children frequently perform poorly in school and subsequently in the economy.

2 Peer culture becomes more important as children proceed through school, but it has an important influence on education at all levels of schooling. Educators should be aware of the potentially positive effects of participation in extracurricular activities.

3 The school culture (that is, regularities in school practice) appears to stress passive, rote learning in many elementary and secondary schools, particularly in working-class schools and mixed-class schools with relatively large numbers of low-achieving students. This happens in part because schools, as institutions, must maintain orderly environments; because many students prefer passive learning; because teachers generally cannot adequately attend to the learning needs of all students; and because society requires that students learn to function within institutions.

4 Television probably increases aggressiveness and violent behavior among certain children and youth, and it may tend to detract from achievement, particularly in reading. Analysts have also been studying the social and cultural effects of digital technologies. Recommendations are being made to teach Internet skills and promote media literacy.

5 Girls traditionally have not been encouraged to seek education that prepares them for full participation in the larger society, and both girls and boys have experienced gender-role pressures in the school. Even so, educational and occupational opportunities for women have been improving rapidly. Although gender differences in school achievement have been declining, certain differences in ability may persist in verbal skills (favoring females) and advanced mathematics (favoring males). Working-class males are facing increasingly difficult economic and social conditions as manufacturing and construction declines in importance for citizens with relatively low education levels.

6 Youth has become a separate stage of life marked by immersion in various subcultures. Teenage drug use and drinking, suicide, pregnancy, delinquency, and violence raise serious concerns about the development of adolescents and youth both inside and outside the school.

Key Terms

The numbers indicate the pages where explanations of the key terms can be found.

culture 305
socialization 305
norms 305

latchkey children 308
hurried children 309
nuclear family 310

peer culture 311
hidden curriculum 316
gender roles 324

Certification Connection Activity

This chapter discusses a variety of factors that influence the growth and development of children. As the United States becomes an increasingly fragmented society with changing expectations and norms, child-rearing practices vary. Every state has laws regarding child abuse and neglect. Most of the laws require professionals who work with children to report suspected abuse and neglect. Different states have different reporting requirements and different interpretations of what constitutes child abuse and neglect. The Praxis II, Principles of Learning and Teaching, may ask questions regarding the major laws related to education and teaching. Child abuse reporting is a significant law directly relating to teachers. Investigate your state's laws regarding child abuse and neglect. In your journal, record how to report suspected abuse and neglect.

Discussion Questions

1 How do adolescents' socialization experiences differ in urban and rural communities? Are such differences declining over time, and if so, why?

2 How does "schooling" differ from "education"? As a prospective teacher, what implications do you see in this line of analysis?

3 In your experience, which types of students are most popular? Do you believe that popularity patterns have changed much in recent decades? If so, why?

4 What might the schools do to alleviate problems of drug use, violence, and teenage pregnancy? What should they do? Do you believe the "might" and "should" are different? Why or why not?

Suggested Projects for Professional Development

1 Write a description of the regularities of schooling as you remember them at the high school you attended. Compare your description with those of your classmates. Do these patterns seem to vary much from one school to another? If so, how?

2 Contact local government officials in a nearby city, or use the Internet to obtain data on changes occurring in family life and family composition. Does the city have any data showing how such changes have affected the schools? What can you learn or predict from the data?

3 Interview local school district officials to determine what their schools are doing to reduce drug use and abuse. Cite any evidence that these efforts have been effective. What might be done to make them more effective?

4 Based on library and Internet sources cited in this chapter, develop a plan that could help a school or a teacher respond effectively and appropriately to challenges posed by students who have difficult home situations. Consider including this plan in your personal portfolio.

Suggested Resources

Internet Resources

A series of articles discussing "The Digital Learner" is available at **www.edutopia.org**.

The Spring 2008 issue of *The Future of Children,* available at **www.futureofchildren.org**, is devoted to "Children and Electronic Media."

The theme of the February 2011 issue of *Educational Leadership* (**www.ascd.org**) is "Teaching Screenagers."

Possibilities for improving media literacy among children and youth are explored in the Temple University Media Education Lab at **http://mediaeducationlab.com** and the Center for Media Education at **www.medialit.org**. These sites review projects underway at media labs where developers are devising interactive learning experiences that can foster students' skills in constructing meaning, solving problems, and generally learning to learn. Such projects have great potential for shaping children's growth in a positive direction. In an article titled "In Defense of Distraction" (**www.nymag.com**), Sam Anderson describes many ways in which new technologies may be limiting the attention span and ability to concentrate of young persons but concludes that youth also may be learning to function in a "Zenlike state of focused distraction."

Publications

Cillessen, Antonius H., David Schwartz, and Lara Mayeux, eds., *Popularity in the Peer System*. New York: Guilford, 2011. *Research-based contributions regarding many aspects of youth culture and its consequences.*

Hansen, David T., Mary E. Driscoll, and Rene V. Arcilla, eds., *A Life in Classrooms*. New York: Teachers College Press, 2007. *A collection of essays on Philip Jackson's work, including his classic studies of school culture.*

Lareau, Annette. *Unequal Childhoods*. Berkeley: University of California Press, 2003. *An ethnographic study of family cultures and parenting practices in low-income, working-class, and middle-class families.*

Sedlak, Michael W., Christopher W. Wheeler, Diana C. Pullin, and Philip Cusick. *Selling Students Short*. New York: Teachers College Press, 1986. *Evaluates classroom "bargains" that result in low-level learning and analyzes the weaknesses of bureaucratic school reform that takes little account of these classroom realities.*

Tapscott, Don. *Grown Up Digital*. New York: Basic Books, 2008. *Describes how the Internet is affecting the attitudes and behavior of children and youth, and examines implications for education, the economy, and other institutions.*

Additional resources for this chapter, including the TeachSource Videos, can be found on the Education CourseMate website. Go to **CengageBrain.com** to access the site.

CHAPTER

11

Social Class, Race, and School Achievement

We begin this chapter by briefly explaining social class and examining relationships among students' social class, racial and ethnic background, and performance in the educational system. Then we discuss why students with low social status, particularly disadvantaged minority students, typically rank low in educational achievement and attainment. We conclude the chapter by examining the implications of these relationships in the context of our nation's historic commitment to equal educational opportunity.

This chapter, like Chapter 10, Culture, Socialization, and Education, offers no easy answers; nevertheless, we hope it will provide you with a deeper understanding. We will show how inadequate achievement patterns have become most prevalent among students with socioeconomic disadvantages, especially if those students also belong to minority groups that have experienced widespread discrimination. Other chapters will look at efforts to change the prevailing patterns and improve the performance of disadvantaged students. First, however, we must focus on the multiple root causes of the problem and their implications for teaching and learning. As you read this chapter, think about these questions:

FOCUS QUESTIONS

- What is the relationship between social class and success in the educational system?
- After accounting for social class, are race and ethnicity associated with school achievement?
- How do environment and heredity affect low achievement levels?

- What are the major reasons for low achievement among students with low socioeconomic status?
- What roles do home and family environment play in encouraging or discouraging high achievement?
- How does the relationship between social class and school achievement affect the national goal of providing equal educational opportunities for all students?

*This chapter was revised by Dan Levine.

Social Class and Success in School

American society is generally understood to consist of three broad classes: working, middle, and upper. A well-known and strong relationship exists between social class and educational achievement. Traditionally, working-class students have performed less well than middle- and upper-class students. As you read the analysis in this section, you should ask yourself why it has been so difficult to improve the achievement of working-class students and what can be done to improve their achievement in the future.

Categories of Social Class

Class and SES

In the 1940s, W. Lloyd Warner and his colleagues used four main variables—occupation, education, income, and housing value—to classify Americans and their families into five groups: upper class, upper middle class, lower middle class, upper lower class, and lower lower class. Individuals high in occupational prestige, amount of education, income, and housing value ranked in the higher classes. Such people are also said to be high in **socioeconomic status (SES)**; that is, others see them as upper-class persons, and they are influential and powerful in their communities. Conversely, people low in socioeconomic status are considered low in prestige and power.[1]

Social classes defined

Today, the term *working* class is more widely used than lower class, but social scientists still identify three to six levels of SES, ranging from upper class at the top to lower working class at the bottom. The **upper class** is usually defined as including wealthy persons with substantial property and investments. The **middle class** includes professionals, managers, and small-business owners (upper middle) as well as technical workers, technicians, sales personnel, and clerical workers (lower middle). The **working class** is generally divided into upper working class (including skilled crafts workers) and lower working class (unskilled manual workers). Skilled workers may be either middle class or working class, depending on their education, income, and other considerations such as the community in which they live.[2]

Intergenerational poverty

In recent years, observers have identified an **underclass** group within the working class. The underclass has been growing; the population of U.S. neighborhoods with at

[1] W. Lloyd Warner, Marcia Meeker, and Kenneth Eells, *Social Class in America* (Chicago: Science Research Associates, 1949). See also Douglas S. Massey, *Categorically Unequal* (New York: Sage, 2007); Annette Lareau and Dalton Conley, eds., *Social Class* (New York: Sage, 2008); Sarah Lubienski and Corinna C. Crane, "Beyond Free Lunch," *Education Policy Analysis Archives* (Vol. 18, 2010), available at **http://epaa.asu.edu/ojs**; "What Is Socioeconomic Status (SES)?" 2011 posting by Peter Levine, available at **www.peterlevine.ws**; and Susan T. Fiske and Hazel R. Markus, *Facing Social Class* (New York: Russell Sage, 2012).

[2] Will Barratt, "Barratt Simple Measure of Social Status," 2006 paper prepared by Will Barratt, available at **wbarratt.indstate.edu**; and Diana T. Sanchez and Julia A. Garcia, "Social Class in America," *RSF Review* (May 7, 2012). A bibliography is at **www.pbs.org/peoplelikeus**. At the latter site, you can also participate in an interactive game to characterize your home furniture preferences in social-class terms.

least 40 percent of their inhabitants in poverty has increased by about a third since 2000. The underclass generally resembles the lower working class, but many of its members are the third or fourth generation to live in poverty and depend on public assistance to sustain a relatively meager existence. Usually concentrated in the inner slums of cities or in deteriorated areas of rural poverty, many members of the underclass frequently have little hope of improving their economic and social situations. Recent data indicate that many immigrant children and youth will be entering or are in danger of becoming part of an underclass. In particular, there is growing concern about the achievement of children whose parents or grandparents came to the United States from Mexico or elsewhere in the Americas. The percentage of Hispanic children in the United States is expected to about double in the next forty years, making it imperative that their relatively low achievement be raised and their high level of school dropout be lowered.[3]

Also, some analysts have identified an "overclass" that they believe is prospering in a competitive international economy at the same time that much of our population is stagnating economically. Alternatively, some analysts have identified a "creative class" or "cognotariat" consisting of highly educated urban dwellers whose work involves an emphasis on creativity. As do observers studying underclass development, these analysts generally emphasize the importance of education in determining one's social status and income.[4]

Research on Social Class and School Success

One of the first systematic studies investigating the relationship between social class and achievement in school was Robert and Helen Lynd's study of "Middletown" (a small Midwestern city) in the 1920s. The Lynds concluded that parents, regardless of social class, recognize the importance of education for their children; however, many working-class children come to school unequipped to acquire the verbal skills and behavioral traits required for success in the classroom. The Lynds' observations of social class and the schools were repeated by W. Lloyd Warner and his associates in a series of studies of towns and small cities in New England, the Deep South, and the Midwest. Thousands of studies have since documented the close relationship between social class and education in the United States and, indeed, throughout the world. Furthermore, research also confirms that transmission of status often is multigenerational. That is, higher-status parents generally transmit educational and related advantages to their children, who in turn frequently transmit advantages to their own children.[5]

For example, we have a clear picture of this relationship from the **National Assessment of Educational Progress (NAEP)** and other agencies that collect achievement information from nationally representative samples of students. As shown in Table 11.1, mathematics and reading proficiency scores of groups of students vary directly with their social class. Students with well-educated parents (one primary

Continuity & Change

"Middletown" study

Standards & Assessment

NAEP

[3]Christopher Jencks and Paul E. Peterson, eds., *The Urban Underclass* (Washington, D.C.: The Brookings Institution, 1991); Dalton Conley, "The Geography of Poverty," *Boston Review* (March/April 2007), available at **www.bostonreview.net**; Ron Haskins, "Immigrant Children Falling Behind," 2011 presentation at the Brookings Institution, available at **www.brookings.edu**; Elizabeth Kneebone, Cary Nadeau, and Alan Berube, "The Re-Emergence of Concentrated Poverty," 2011 posting by the Brookings Institution, available at **www.brookings.edu**; Andrew J. Rotherham, "The Education Crisis No One Is Talking About," *Time*, May 12, 2011, available at **www.time.com**; and Nicholas D. Kristof, "The White Underclass," *New York Times*, February 8, 2012.
[4]David Brooks, *Bobos in Paradise* (New York: Simon and Schuster, 2000); and Christopher Newfield, "The Structure and Silence of the Cognotariat," *Globalization, Societies and Education* (June 2010), pp. 175–189.
[5]Robert S. Lynd and Helen M. Lynd, *Middletown: A Study in American Culture* (New York: Harcourt, Brace and World, 1929); Ludger Woessman, "How Equal Are Educational Opportunities?" March 2004, CESIFO Working Paper No. 1162, available at **www.ksg.harvard.edu/pepg/PDF/events/Munich/PEPG-04-15Woessman.pdf**; and John Ermisch, Markus Jantti, and Timothy M. Smeeding, eds., *From Parents to Children* (New York: Russell Sage, 2012).

Table 11.1	Average Scores of Eighth Graders, by Parental Education and by Type of Community	
	Mathematics	Reading
Parental Education		
Not graduated high school	265	248
Graduated high school	271	254
Some education after high school	285	267
Graduated college	295	275
Type of Community		
Central city	273	257
Urban fringe/large town	283	266
Rural/small town	279	263

Note: Scores are from testing by the National Assessment of Educational Progress, which defines community type as follows: "Central city" includes central cities in metropolitan areas. "Urban fringe/large town" generally includes other locations in metropolitan areas. A "large town" is a place with at least 25,000 people outside metropolitan areas. Scores are for 2011.

Source: 2011 posting by Child Trends Data Bank; and extractions from National Center for Education Statistics data sets at **www.nces.ed.gov/nationsreportcard/naepdata**.

measure of social class) score much higher than students whose parents have less education. This holds to such an extent that nine-year-olds whose parents had at least some college had average scores not far below those for thirteen-year-olds whose parents had not completed high school. Income is another component of social class that is correlated with school performance. Recent data showed that whereas 46 percent of eighth graders at low-poverty schools (with 25 percent or fewer of students eligible for free or reduced-price lunch) scored at the Proficient level or above on the NAEP reading test, only 12 percent of eighth graders at high-poverty schools with 75 percent of their students eligible attained those levels.

✓ Standards & Assessment

▮ Achievement correlated with community

School achievement also correlates with the type of community, which reflects the social class of people who reside there. As shown in Table 11.1, the average mathematics and reading scores of students in "urban fringe/large town" areas (with a relatively high proportion of residents in professional or managerial occupations) are higher than those of students in "central city" areas, which have a high proportion of residents who receive public assistance or are unemployed.[6]

✓ Standards & Assessment

▮ Concentrated poverty schools

Further evidence of the relationship between social class and school achievement can be found in studies of poverty neighborhoods in large cities. For example, Levine and his colleagues examined sixth-grade achievement patterns at more than a thousand predominantly low-income schools (which they called *concentrated poverty schools*) in seven big cities and reported that all but a few had average reading scores more than two years below the national average. They also pointed out that at least one-fourth of the students at these schools cannot read well enough when they enter high school to be considered functionally literate. This pattern can be found at concentrated poverty schools in big cities throughout the United States.[7]

---

[6]Tess Stovall and Deirdre Dolan, "Incomplete," 2011 report prepared for Third Way, available at **www.thirdway.org**; Sean Reardon, "The Widening Academic-Achievement Gap between the Rich and the Poor," in Richard M. Murnane and Greg J. Duncan, eds., *Whither Opportunity?* (New York: Sage, 2011); and Sabrina Tavernise, "Education Gap Grows Between Rich and Poor, Studies Say," *New York Times*, February 10, 2012.

[7]Daniel U. Levine and Rayna F. Levine, *Society and Education,* 9th ed. (Needham Heights, MA: Allyn and Bacon, 1996). See also Richard D. Kahlenberg, "Back to Class," *American Prospect* (January/February 2007), available at **www.prospect.org**; Richard Rothstein, "Whose Problem Is Poverty?" *Educational Leadership* (April 2008), pp. 8–13; and Susan Popkin, "The Costs of Concentrated Poverty," 2011 posting by Metrotrends Blog, available at **www.metrotrends.org**.

Rural poverty

Many educators also are concerned about the achievement of rural students, especially those who live in low-income regions and pockets of rural poverty. Although rural students generally achieve near the national average, research indicates that poverty and inequality can hamper their progress, and that two-thirds of rural educators believe the academic performance of their low-income students is in either "great need" or "fairly strong need" of improvement.[8]

Effective schools

We also should emphasize, however, that methods exist for improving the achievement of students with low socioeconomic status. In particular, the "effective schools" movement that came to prominence in the 1980s showed that appropriate school-wide efforts to enhance instruction can produce sizable gains in the performance of disadvantaged students, even in concentrated poverty schools in big cities and rural schools in poor areas. It is easier today than only ten or fifteen years ago to find schools that have improved achievement among their low-income students. We describe the effective schools movement and other efforts to improve performance among disadvantaged students in other chapters, particularly Chapter 16, School Effectiveness and Reform in the United States.

Percentages attending college

Social Class, College Participation, and National Problems   Social class is associated with many educational outcomes in addition to achievement in reading, math, and other subjects. On the average, working-class students not only have lower achievement scores but also are less likely than middle-class students to complete high school or to enroll in and complete college. Only about 25 percent of high-school graduates from the lowest two socioeconomic quartiles (the lowest 50 percent of students measured in terms of family income) enter college and attain a postsecondary degree, compared with more than 80 percent of high-school graduates in the highest quartile. (Each "quartile" contains one-quarter of the population.) Researchers find that social class relates to college attendance and graduation even when they compare students with similar achievement levels. For example, one study showed that low-status high-school seniors were nearly 50 percent less likely to enter a postsecondary institution than were high-status seniors with similar reading achievement scores. Limitations in federal financial aid, among other reasons, have caused this discrepancy to grow in recent years.[9]

> **REFOCUS**   Have you visited schools where many students were from a different social class from most students in schools you attended? What differences did you observe? How do you think these differences would affect achievement?

One team of researchers studying international literacy patterns recently concluded that "inequality is deeply rooted in the education system and in the workplace in the United States . . . our nation concentrates on producing and rewarding first-class skills and, as a result, is world class at the top; however it . . . accepts in fact, if not in rhetoric, a basic skills underclass." These patterns also led a senior researcher at the Educational Testing Service to observe that the United States has not adequately "recognized the need to eliminate barriers to achievement that arise in the family, and how lack of resources affect achievement."[10]

---

[8]Alan J. DeYoung and Barbara K. Lawrence, "On Hoosiers, Yankees, and Mountaineers," *Phi Delta Kappan* (October 1995), pp. 104–112; and Marty Strange, "Finding Fairness for Rural Students," *Phi Delta Kappan* (March 2011), pp. 8–15.

[9]Paul L. Barton and Richard J. Coley, *Windows on Achievement and Inequality* (Princeton, NJ: ETS Policy and Research Center, 2008), available at **www.ets.org**; David L. Kirp, "College For the Few," *American Prospect* (December 2008), pp. 40–41, available at **www.prospect.org**; and Russell W. Rumberger, "Education and the Reproduction of Economic Inequality in the United States," *Economics of Education Review* (April 2010), pp. 246–254.

[10]Paul L. Barton and Richard J. Coley, *Windows on Achievement and Inequality* (Princeton, NJ: ETS Policy and Research Center, 2008), available at **www.ets.org**; David L. Kirp, "College For the Few," *American Prospect* (December 2008), pp. 40–41, available at **www.prospect.org**; Russell W. Rumberger, "Education and the Reproduction of Economic Inequality in the United States," *Economics of Education Review* (April 2010), pp. 246–254; and Martha J. Bailey and Susan M. Dynarski, "Gains and Gaps," 2011 NBER paper number 17633.

Race, Ethnicity, and School Success

Race and ethnicity
defined

Patterns of social class and educational achievement in the United States are further complicated by the additional factors of race and ethnicity. **Race** identifies groups of people with common ancestry and physical characteristics. **Ethnicity** identifies people who have a shared culture. Members of an **ethnic group** usually have common ancestry and share language, religion, and other cultural traits. Because no pure races exist, some scholars avoid referring to race and instead discuss group characteristics under the heading of ethnicity.

Status of minority groups

As we saw in Chapter 5, Historical Development of American Education, the U.S. population is a mix of many races and ethnicities. Some racial and ethnic minority groups in this country have experienced social and economic oppression as a *group* despite the accomplishments of many individuals. For example, African Americans have a lower average socioeconomic status than that of the white majority, even though many individual African Americans may be of higher SES than many whites. Other major ethnic minority groups, such as Mexican Americans and Puerto Ricans, are also disproportionately low in socioeconomic status. (These two groups, combined with Cuban Americans and citizens with Central and South American ancestry, constitute most of the Hispanic/Latino population, which is growing rapidly and now outnumbers the African American population. This chapter uses the term *Hispanic* in reporting data from government publications employing this terminology and generally uses *Latino* elsewhere.) An ongoing concern for educators is the fact that these racial and ethnic minority groups are correspondingly low in academic achievement, high-school and college graduation rates, and other measures of educational attainment.[11]

✓ Standards & Assessment

Eighth-grade samples

We can see the close association among social class, race or ethnicity, and school performance in Figure 11.1, which presents average math and reading scores attained by nationally representative samples of eighth graders. African American students have the lowest SES scores (as reflected by higher percentages in poverty). They also have the lowest math and reading scores. In contrast, non-Hispanic whites are highest in SES, second-highest in math, and just below the highest in reading. In general, school achievement scores parallel scores on socioeconomic status; the higher the SES score, the higher the achievement scores.[12]

Gains by minorities

Data collected by the NAEP indicate that the gap between African American and Latino students on the one hand and white students on the other may be narrowing. African American and Latino students have registered gains in reading, math, and other subjects. Some observers attribute these improvements partly to the federal Title I and No Child Left Behind (NCLB) programs and/or to increases in desegregation. (See Chapter 12, Providing Equal Educational Opportunity, for discussions of Title I, NCLB, and desegregation.) The gap is by no means closed, however. African American and Latino students still score far below whites in reading and other subjects, and African American and Latino seventeen-year-olds still have approximately the same average reading scores as white thirteen-year-olds.[13]

---

[11]Melissa Kearney, "Intergenerational Mobility for Women and Minorities in the United States," *The Future of Children* (Fall 2006), available at **www.futureofchildren.org**; Ana Rojas-LeBouef and John R. Slate, "Reading and Math Differences between Hispanic and White Students in Texas," 2011 paper posted for the National Council of Professors of Educational Administration, available at **www.cnx.org**; and Heather MacDonald, "California's Demographic Revolution," *City Journal* (Winter 2012), available at **www.city-journal.com.**

[12]Further analysis of these and other data also indicates considerable variation within broad racial and ethnic classifications. For example, among Hispanics, Cuban Americans have much higher SES and achievement scores than do Mexican American and Puerto Rican students. Among Asian American subgroups, Hmong and Vietnamese students tend to be relatively low in status and achievement.

[13]Jens Ludwig, "Educational Achievement and Black–White Inequality," *Education Next* (Summer 2003), available at **www.educationnext.org**; and "Reading Gaps," *The Condition of Education* (Washington D.C.: National Center for Education Statistics, 2011).

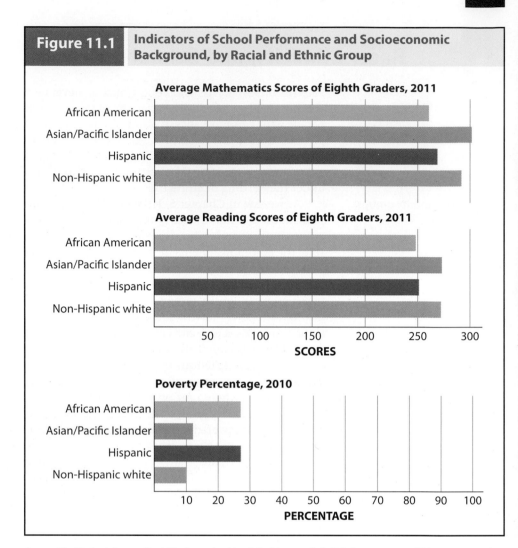

Figure 11.1 Indicators of School Performance and Socioeconomic Background, by Racial and Ethnic Group

Source: The Nation's Report Card: Mathematics 2011 (Washington, D.C.: U.S. Department of Education, 2011); *The Nation's Report Card: Reading 2011* (Washington, D.C.: U.S. Department of Education, 2011); and *Statistical Abstract of the United States 2012* Washington, D.C.: U.S. Government Printing Office, 2012).

▌ Dropout rates

As you might expect from the achievement data shown in Figure 11.1, non-Hispanic white and Asian students (other than Vietnamese Americans) are more likely to complete high school than are African American and Latino students. Figure 11.2 shows that the high-school completion rate for African American students has been rising since 1975, but it remains a little below the rate for whites, and the rate for Latinos has been so low that national leaders are gravely concerned about the future of Latino youth. In addition, high-school dropout rates are still extremely high among African American and Latino students in big-city poverty areas. Knowledgeable observers estimate that dropout rates range from 40 to 60 percent in some big cities and may exceed 75 or 80 percent at schools enrolling mostly underclass students.[14]

▌ College attendance

African American and Latino students are also less likely to enter and complete college and other postsecondary institutions. Postsecondary enrollment rates for African American and Latino high-school graduates rose substantially in the 1960s and early 1970s, but they have increased slowly since then. As a result, African American and Latino students constitute less than 30 percent of enrollment in higher education, well below their percentage in the college-age population. The causes cited for these patterns include rising tuition, reductions in federal funds, and cuts in special recruiting

---

[14]"Dropout Factories Declining," *American School Board Journal* (April 2011), pp. 7–16.

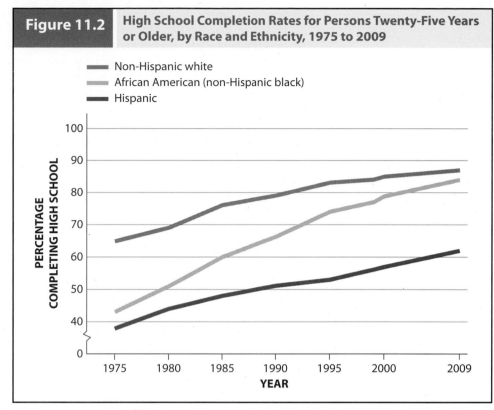

Figure 11.2 | High School Completion Rates for Persons Twenty-Five Years or Older, by Race and Ethnicity, 1975 to 2009

Source: Statistical Abstract of the United States 2012 (Washington, D.C.: U.S. Government Printing Office, 2012).

and assistance programs. Some educators also note that participation in drug cultures may have disabled many minority youth. Reports from major educational agencies have referred to the rate of minority enrollment in higher education as "shockingly low" and "intolerable." The reports generally conclude that colleges, universities, and government officials should take steps to increase minority enrollment.[15]

The Special Problem of Minority Status Plus Urban Poverty

Segregated inner cities

As we have documented, educational achievement generally is distressingly low at schools in poor inner-city neighborhoods. We have also pointed out that although high-school completion rates for African American students have been rising nationally, the dropout problem remains severe in big cities. These problems reflect the fact that the inner cores of many large U.S. urban areas have become segregated communities populated by working-class and underclass African American and Latino residents. Causes and results of this socioeconomic and racial/ethnic stratification include the following:

Polarization among African Americans

1. *The African American population of the United States has become more economically polarized.* The overall socioeconomic status and income of this population have increased substantially since 1950. For example, the average income (in real dollars) of married couples among African Americans has approximately doubled since 1950,

---

[15]The agencies mentioned include the Education Commission of the States, the State Higher Education Executive Officers, the United States Commission on Civil Rights, and the American Council on Education. See, for example, *Empty Promises* (Washington, D.C.: Advisory Committee on Student Financial Assistance, 2002); "Demography as Destiny," 2006 paper prepared for the Alliance for Excellent Education, available at **www.all4ed.org**; and "Winning the Future," 2011 report posted by the White House Initiative on Educational Excellence for Hispanics, available at **www.ed.gov**.

and the number of black families earning $50,000 or more has about quadrupled. However, many other African Americans still live in urban poverty, in neighborhoods where most families are headed by single women, and where rates of crime, delinquency, drug abuse, teenage pregnancy, and other indicators of social disorganization remain extremely high. Similarly for Hispanics, in many communities, there is a substantial split that divides a growing middle-class segment and a large segment residing in big-city poverty neighborhoods. Rates of social disorganization in these latter neighborhoods are high.[16] The From Preservice to Practice feature in this chapter shows challenges that teachers face in these neighborhoods.

Dysfunctional institutions

2. *Social institutions such as the family, the school, and the law-enforcement system often appear to have collapsed in the inner city.* Parents find it difficult to control their children, and law-enforcement agencies are unable to cope with high rates of juvenile delinquency and adult crime.[17]

Rising social isolation

3. *The concentration of low-income minority populations in big-city poverty areas has increased their isolation from the larger society.* In contrast to the urban slums and ghettos of fifty or a hundred years ago, today's concentrated poverty areas are larger geographically, and, in many cases, their residents are more homogeneous in (low) socioeconomic status. Unskilled and semiskilled jobs are more difficult to obtain, and many jobs have been moved overseas or to the suburbs, where they are practically inaccessible to central-city residents. Andrew Hacker observed that the contemporary "mode of segregation, combining poverty and race, is relatively new. To reside amid so many people leading desultory lives makes it all the harder to break away."[18]

Problems for young black males

4. *The problems experienced by young black males have escalated enormously.* Some knowledgeable observers believe that the plight of young males in inner-city poverty areas is at the root of a series of other serious problems: high rates of out-of-wedlock births, the persistence of welfare dependency, and violent crime and delinquency. The growth in female-headed families in urban poverty areas relates directly to the high rates at which young African American men drop out of the labor force, are incarcerated in prisons or placed on parole, or otherwise are excluded or exclude themselves from mainstream institutions. The result is a great reduction in the pool of men available to participate in stable families and accumulate resources for upward mobility.[19]

Comparing the Influence of Social Class and Ethnicity

Social class as the primary factor

The close interrelationship among social class, race and ethnicity, and school achievement leads researchers to frequently ask whether race and ethnicity are associated with performance in the educational system even after one takes into account the low socioeconomic status of African Americans and other disadvantaged minority groups. In general, the answer has been that social class accounts for much of the variation in educational achievement by race and ethnicity. That is, if you know the social class of a

---

[16]Bart Landry, *The New Black Middle Class* (Berkeley: University of California Press, 1987); William J. Wilson, *The Truly Disadvantaged* (Chicago: University of Chicago Press, 1987); George J. Borjas, "Making It in America," *The Future of Children* (Fall 2006), available at **www.futureofchildren.org**; Bart Landry and Kris Marsh, "The Evolution of the New Black Middle Class," *Annual Review of Sociology* (August 2011); and Robin E. Smith, "How to Evaluate Choice and Promise Neighborhoods," 2011 paper prepared for the Urban Institute, available at **www.urban.org**.
[17]Richard J. Coley and Paul E. Barton, "Locked Up and Locked Out," 2006 report prepared for the Educational Testing Service, available at **www.ets.org**; and William J. Wilson, "Being Poor, Black, and American," *American Educator* (Spring 2011), available at **www.aft.org**.
[18]Andrew Hacker, *Two Nations* (New York: Ballantine, 1995); and Sarah A. Stoddard et al., "Social Connections, Trajectories of Hopelessness, and Serious Violence in Impoverished Urban Youth," *Journal of Youth and Adolescence* (March 2011), pp. 278–295.
[19]Ronald B. Mincy, *Black Men Left Behind* (Washington, D.C.: Urban Institute, 2006); Douglas S. Massey and Robert J. Sampson, *The Moynihan Report Revisited* (Thousand Oaks, CA: Sage, 2009); and Timothy M. Smeeding, Irwin Garfinkel, and Ronald B. Mincy, "Young Disadvantaged Men," *Annals of the American Academy of Political and Social Science* (May 2011), pp. 6–21.

FROM PRESERVICE TO PRACTICE

Hoping for Success

David Rusciatti looked over his first class in eighth-grade English. He had agreed to teach in this inner-city school because that's where he began his own schooling, but the neighborhood was a different place now from just a few years ago when he had lived here.

David knew that this would be a challenging first year. In fact, a couple of the more experienced teachers had told him that they wouldn't like to be in his shoes. His schedule was full, with five classes of eighth-grade English. This first class seemed to have a mix of students of differing ethnicities and vastly different backgrounds. According to the guidance counselor, most of the students were low achievers. He knew that at least four of the boys and two of the girls had already attended eighth grade last year.

David heard quite a bit of giggling and chatting. As he took roll call, he noted back and hand slapping as each student raised his or her hand to indicate they were present. He remembered what his supervising professor had told him last year, "Remember, David, the first day and the first week are all-important. You must set the pace and lay down the rules then or you are finished for the year."

David had prepared the first day's class with his professor's advice about setting the tone in mind. Following the premise that he must involve the students in their own active learning, he had developed a series of questions and activities. Before he could implement his plan of action, however, the assistant principal came in and took him aside. He whispered, "Don't rile Thomas Davis, over there. I've been told that he has a small pistol concealed under his shirt. I've called the campus police, and they'll nab him as soon as class is dismissed. He's upset about something to do with his girlfriend. If you have trouble before then, you can call me at the office using that phone on the wall. Think you'll be okay?"

"I'll be okay. I have the day well planned." As the assistant principal left, David wondered if he actually would be okay. All went well until he asked the students to write a short paragraph telling about their best experiences of the summer. Several students began commenting to each other, joking and laughing. David was unsure how much of this he should allow, so he smiled and encouraged those who were writing to continue. At the same time, he began to walk around the class to talk to each student not writing.

He scanned the class, noting the different levels of involvement. He would have to learn more about how to teach a group of students with such varying backgrounds. And about each individual, too. Maybe that should come first.

Case Questions

1. Should first-year teachers be assigned difficult classes such as this one? Justify your answer.
2. What obstacles must David hurdle to be considered an effective teacher?
3. How would you prepare for and handle a class such as this?
4. What instructional policies might David want to introduce?

group of students, you can predict with a good deal of accuracy whether their achievement, ability scores, and college attendance rates are high or low. Information about their racial or ethnic group generally does relatively little to improve such a prediction. This also means that working-class white students as a group are low in achievement and college attainment, whereas middle-class minority students, as a group, rank relatively high on these variables.[20]

Disadvantaged minorities in the United States remain disproportionately working class and underclass, and their children remain much less successful in the educational system than are the children of the middle class. Moreover, because education is an important channel for gaining access to the job market, minority students with low socioeconomic status have relatively less opportunity for economic success later in their

[20]Cecilia E. Rouse and Lisa Barrow, "U.S. Elementary and Secondary Schools," *The Future of Children* (Fall 2006), available at **www.futureofchildren.org**; Nikki L. Aikens and Oscar Barbarin, "Socioeconomic Differences in Reading Trajectories," *Journal of Educational Psychology* (May 2008), pp. 235–251; and Naomi Gerstel, "Rethinking Families and Community," *Sociological Forum* (March 2011), pp. 1–20.

lives. From this point of view, the schools' ineffectiveness in educating students from working-class homes helps to perpetuate the current class system—and the burden of poverty and low achievement falls disproportionately on the nation's racial and ethnic minority groups.

A divided population

> **REFOCUS** If the middle-income segment of the population is shrinking, and the low-income segment is growing, chances are good that, as a teacher, you will have low-income students in your classes. What are you doing to prepare yourself to teach children from all social classes effectively?

For educators, the challenge is to improve the performance of all low-status students, from whatever ethnic group. The U.S. population as a whole has become more divided, with a growing high-income segment, a growing low-income segment, and a shrinking middle segment. Many commentators share the alarm of former Secretary of Labor Robert Reich: "If we lose our middle class and become a two-tiered society, we not only risk the nation's future prosperity but also its social coherence and stability. As the economy grows, people who work the machines and clean the offices and provide the basic goods and services are supposed to share in the gains, but that hasn't been happening."[21]

Reasons for Low Achievement among Low-Status Students

Over the past forty years, much research has been aimed at understanding and overcoming the academic deficiencies of low-achieving students in general and low-achieving students from working-class or poor families in particular. Although the explanations are not necessarily mutually exclusive, we will group them under the following major factors: home environment, heredity versus environment, and obstacles in the classroom, also summarized in Overview 11.1.

Home Environment

Chapter 10, Culture, Socialization, and Education, points out that children's families are the most important agent in their early socialization and education. We also noted that characteristics of the home environment closely reflect the family's social class. Thus, social-class differences in home environment associate with educational performance and student attainment. Many working-class students grow up in homes that fail to prepare them well for school. Even though their parents may stress the importance of education, these students tend to function poorly in the typical classroom.

Knowledge and understandings

Children's home environments cultivate three key sets of characteristics important to their school achievement: (1) knowledge and understandings, (2) cognitive and verbal skills, and (3) values and attitudes. Regarding *knowledge and understandings,* middle-class children are more likely than working-class children to acquire a wide knowledge of the world outside the home through access to books and cultural institutions (for example, museums), parental teaching, and exploration of diverse environments. Knowledge and understandings acquired through exposure to the wider world are helpful to children when they enter school. Working-class students today may experience even greater disadvantages than in earlier eras because they tend to have less access to computers at home than do middle-class students.[22]

Continuity & Change

[21]Quoted in Keith Bradsher, "Productivity Is All, But It Doesn't Pay Well," *New York Times,* June 25, 1995, p. 4E. See also Christopher Jencks and Joseph Swingle, "Without a Net," *American Prospect,* January 3, 2000, available at **www.prospect.org**; and Richard M. Murnane and Greg J. Duncan, eds., *Whither Opportunity?* (New York: Sage, 2011).

[22]Annette Lareau, "Social Class Differences in Family–School Relationships**,**" *Sociology of Education* (April 1987), pp. 73–85; Betty Hart and Todd R. Risley, "The Early Catastrophe," *American Educator* (Spring 2003), available at **www.aft.org**; "Meaningful Differences in the Language Learning Environments of Young American Children," 2006 PBS interview with Todd Risley, available at **www.childrenofthecode.org/interviews/risley.htm**; and Jacob E. Cheadle and Paul R. Amato, "A Quantitative Assessment of Lareau's Qualitative Conclusions about Class, Race, and Parenting," *Journal of Family Issues* (May 2011), pp. 679–706.

OVERVIEW 11.1

Obstacles to Achievement for Working-Class Students by Area of Influence

Area of Influence	Potential Obstacles to Achievement for Working-Class Students
Home	Disadvantages in home environment of some working-class students, especially in the first few years of life, may leave children unprepared to learn in school. Specifically: ■ *Knowledge and understandings.* Lack of exposure to the cultural and technological world may limit understandings needed in school. ■ *Cognitive and verbal skills.* Restricted language does not help prepare children for school. ■ *Values and attitudes.* Focus on control does not encourage higher-order thinking or independent problem-solving skills needed in school.
Heredity versus Environment	Working-class children average lower scores on intelligence tests, which may be related to environment or heredity, or both. The debate over why scores are low includes at least three views: ■ *Hereditarian.* Differences in intellectual capacity are inborn, affected little by environment. ■ *Environmentalist.* Family, school, and cultural environments are major factors in determining IQ test performance. ■ *Synthesis.* Both environment and heredity contribute to IQ and school performance. Teachers and parents should provide the best possible environment for each child to make the most of their inherited abilities.
Classroom	Obstacles in the classroom that can contribute to low achievement by working-class students include the following: ■ Inappropriate curriculum and instruction ■ Lack of previous success in school ■ Ineffective fixation on low-level learning ■ Difficult teaching conditions in working-class schools ■ Teacher perceptions of student inadequacies ■ Ineffective homogeneous grouping ■ Delivery-of-service problems ■ Overly large classes ■ Lack of teacher preparation and experience ■ Negative peer pressure ■ Differences between teacher and student backgrounds ■ Incompatibility between classroom expectations and students' behavioral patterns/learning styles ■ Accumulating effects of information-poor homes and neighborhoods

■ Cognitive and verbal skills   Students' *cognitive and verbal skills* also reflect social-class differences in family language environments. Basil Bernstein has found that both middle- and working-class children develop adequate skills with respect to "ordinary" or "restricted" language, but middle-class children are superior in the use of "formal" or "elaborated" language. Ordinary, restricted language is grammatically simple, relying on gestures and further explanations to clarify meaning. Elaborated, formal language is grammatically complex and provides greater potential for organizing experience within an abstract

Middle-class children are more likely than working-class children to attain a wide knowledge of the world through books and parental teaching.

meaning system. Many scholars believe that facility in using elaborated language helps middle-class children excel in cognitive development.[23]

Values and attitudes

Regarding *values and attitudes,* socialization practices in many working-class homes ill-prepare children to function independently in the school and classroom. Many children from lower socioeconomic backgrounds are at a disadvantage because their socialization appears to emphasize obedience and conformity, whereas middle-class families tend to stress independent learning and self-directed thinking. After an intensive study of seven hundred families in Nottingham, England, John and Elizabeth Newson summarized these different socialization patterns as follows:[24]

> Parents at the upper end of the social scale are more inclined on principle to use democratically based, highly verbal means of control, and this kind of discipline is likely to produce personalities who can both identify successfully with the system and use it for their own ends later on. At the bottom end of the scale . . . [many] parents choose on principle to use a highly authoritarian, mainly non-verbal means of control, in which words are used more to threaten and bamboozle the child into obedience than to make him understand the rationale behind social behavior. . . . Thus the child born into the lowest social bracket has everything stacked against him including his parents' principles of child upbringing.

---

[23]Basil Bernstein, *The Structuring of Pedagogic Discourse* (New York: Routledge, 1990); Jeanne S. Chall and Vicki A. Jacobs, "Poor Children's Fourth-Grade Slump," *American Educator* (Spring 2003), available at **www.aft.org**; James Atherton, "Language Codes," 2011 paper posted at the Doceo Internet site, available at **www.doceo.co.uk/background**; and Jessi Streib, "Class Reproduction by Four Year Olds," 2011 online publication at **www.springerlink.com**.
[24]John Newson and Elizabeth Newson, *Seven Years Old in the Home Environment* (London: Allen and Unwin, 1976), p. 406. See also Felix Montes, "Study Shows That Model Learning Community Bears Fruit for Young Children," *IDRA Newsletter* (September 2006), available at **www.idra.org**; Gary W. Evans and Jennifer Rosenbaum, "Self-Regulation and the Income-Achievement Gap," *Early Childhood Research Quarterly* (December 2008), pp. 504–514; Robert Weis and Erin E. Toolis, "Parenting Across Cultural Contexts in the USA," *Early Child Development and Care* (August 2010), pp. 849–867; and Annette Lareau, *Unequal Childhoods*, 2nd ed. (Berkeley: University of California Press, 2011).

Differences in child-rearing practices reflect the fact that many working-class environments are relatively dangerous for children, and parents use methods that do not help at school but do prepare their children to function in this hostile environment. Other differences arise from parents' own limits in education, resources, and knowledge of what practices help children develop intellectually.

Stimulation by home environment

The importance of the home and family environment for general intellectual development has also been documented in studies by J. McVicker Hunt, Martin Deutsch, and other researchers. These studies generally indicate that environmental stimulation in working-class homes is less conducive to intellectual development, on the average, than it is in middle-class homes. Deutsch outlined factors, such as lack of productive visual and tactile stimulation, that limit learning readiness in many disadvantaged children. Deutsch and others developed indexes of environmental disadvantage that correlate even more closely with IQ scores and school success than do social-class indicators.[25]

Early cognitive development

The environmental disadvantage theory holds that early developmental years are more important than later years. As pointed out by Benjamin Bloom, David Hamburg, and others, the most rapid development of many human characteristics, including cognitive skills, occurs during the preschool years. Furthermore, the child's intellectual development is affected even during the prenatal stages by the mother's general health, her diet, her alcohol intake and drug usage, and stress and other emotional factors. Although we can counteract learning deficits that arise from disadvantaged early environments, it is, as this implies, more difficult to produce changes for older children; we need a more powerful environment to bring about these changes. It further implies that, as a society, we should use more of our resources to address early environmental problems and disadvantages. These understandings helped lead to the development of *compensatory education*, which, as described in Chapter 12, Providing Equal Educational Opportunity, tries to remedy the effects of environmental disadvantages by providing preschool education and improved instruction in elementary and secondary schools.[26] We will further describe compensatory education in the next chapter.

Early brain development

Concern is growing regarding the negative effects on cognitive performance that impoverished environments can produce as scientists learn more about how the brain develops and what this knowledge might mean for educators. In general, neurologists and other investigators have reinforced Bloom's conclusions about the importance of a positive home environment in the first two or three years of life, when the brain is growing rapidly and establishing billions of neural connections. In addition to emphasizing the value of good preschools, many educators are exploring the implications for devising instructional methods that take into account how the brain works. However, it may be some time before we know enough to anticipate substantial improvements in curriculum and instruction based on an understanding of how the brain functions and develops.[27]

[25]Martin Deutsch, "The Role of Social Class in Language Development and Cognition," in A. H. Passow, M. I. Goldbery, and A. J. Tannenbaum, eds., *Education of the Disadvantaged* (New York: Holt, 1967), pp. 214–224; Richard J. Coley, "An Uneven Start," 2002 paper prepared for the Educational Testing Service, available at **www.ets.org/research/perc/pic**; Hyunjoon Park, "Home Literacy Environments and Children's Reading Performance," *Educational Research and Evaluation* (December 2008), pp. 489–505; and James Heckman, "The Economics of Inequality," *American Educator* (Spring 2011), available at **www.aft.org**.
[26]Benjamin S. Bloom, *Stability and Change in Human Characteristics* (New York: Wiley, 1964); Benjamin S. Bloom, *Human Characteristics and School Learning* (New York: McGraw-Hill, 1976); Jens Ludwig and Isabel Sawhill, "Success by Ten," *Hamilton Project Discussion Paper* (February 2007), available at **www.brookings.edu**; Douglas Besharov and Craig Ramey, "Preschool Puzzle," *Education Next* (Fall 2008), available at **www.educationnext.org**; and Greg Duncan et al., "The Long Reach of Early Childhood Poverty," 2011 paper prepared for the Harvard Center on the Developing Child, available at **www.developingchild.harvard.edu**.
[27]Judy Willis, "Which Brain Research Can Educators Trust?" *Phi Delta Kappan* (May 2007), pp. 697–699; and Jack P. Shonkoff et al., "Building the Brain's 'Air Traffic Control' System," 2011 paper prepared for the National Scientific Council on the Developing Child, available at **www.developingchild.harvard.edu**.

Average differences are
not universal patterns

Socialization differentials like those we have discussed in this section reflect *average* differences across social-class groups. As a teacher, you must remember that no universal patterns distinguish all middle-class families and students from all working-class families. Many children from working-class families do well in school, and many middle-class children do not. Many families with low socioeconomic status do provide a home environment conducive to achievement, and the great majority of low-income parents try to offer their children a positive learning environment. It also appears that the child-raising methods of working-class families probably are becoming more like those of middle-class families. Nevertheless, children from low-income, working-class homes are still disproportionately likely to grow up in an environment that inadequately prepares them to succeed in contemporary schools.

REFOCUS How could you, as a teacher, make low-income parents feel comfortable talking to you about things they could do at home to support their child's school achievement?

The Heredity-versus-Environment Debate

The past century has seen heated controversy about whether intelligence, which relates strongly to school achievement, is determined primarily by heredity or by environment.

Early IQ tests

Hereditarian View When IQ tests were undergoing rapid development early in the twentieth century, many psychologists believed that intelligence was determined primarily by heredity. Those who took this **hereditarian view of intelligence** thought that IQ tests and similar instruments measured innate differences, present from birth, in people's capacity. When economically disadvantaged groups and some minority groups, such as African Americans, scored considerably below other groups, the hereditarians believed that the groups with the lower scores were innately inferior in intellectual capacity.

The hereditarian view underwent a major revival in the 1970s and 1980s, based particularly on the writings of Arthur Jensen, Richard Herrnstein, and a group of researchers conducting the Minnesota Study of Twins. Summarizing previous research as well as their own studies, these researchers identified heredity as the major factor in determining intelligence—accounting for up to 80 percent of the variation in IQ scores.[28]

Jensen and his critics

Jensen published a highly controversial study in the *Harvard Educational Review* in 1969. Pointing out that African Americans averaged about 15 points below whites on IQ tests, Jensen attributed this gap to a genetic difference between the two races in learning abilities and patterns. Critics have countered Jensen's arguments by contending that a host of environmental factors that affect IQ, including malnutrition and prenatal care, are difficult to measure and impossible to separate from hereditary factors. IQ tests are biased, they said, and do not necessarily even measure intelligence.[29]

After his 1969 article, Jensen continued to cite data that he believed link intelligence primarily to heredity. His critics continue to respond with evidence that environmental factors, schooling in particular, have a major influence on IQ.[30]

---

[28]Arthur R. Jensen, "How Much Can We Boost IQ and Scholastic Achievement?" *Harvard Educational Review* (Winter 1969), pp. 1–123; Richard J. Herrnstein and Charles Murray, *The Bell Curve* (New York: Free Press, 1994); J. Phillipe Rushton and Arthur R. Jensen, "Race and IQ," *Open Psychology Journal* (No. 2, 2010), available at **www.benthamscience.com/open/topsyj**; and Michael Balter, "What Does IQ Really Measure?" 2011 posting by Science magazine, available at **http://www.sciencemag.org**.

[29]Jensen, "How Much Can We Boost IQ and Scholastic Achievement," pp. 273–356; H. Nyborg, ed., *The Scientific Study of Human Intelligence* (New York: Pergamon, 2003); Carl Zimmer, "The Nature of Intelligence," *Scientific American* (October 2008), pp. 68–75; Steven Rose, "Darwin 200," *Nature*, February 12, 2009, available at **www.nature.com**; Peter Taylor, "Three Puzzles and Eight Gaps," *Biology and Philosophy* (January 2010), pp. 1–31; and Charles Murray, "The Debate about Heritability of General Intelligence Radically Narrows," *The American* (August 11, 2011), available at **http://blog.american.com**.

[30]Arthur R. Jensen, *The g Factor* (Westport, CT: Praeger, 1998); Arthur R. Jensen, "Race Differences, G, and the 'Default Hypothesis,'" *Psychology*, January 1, 2000; Stephen Ceci and Wendy M. Williams, "Darwin 200," *Nature*, February 12, 2009, available at **www.nature.com**; and Robert Plomin and Denise Daniels, "Why Are Children in the Same Family So Different from One Another?" *International Journal of Epidemiology* (June 2011), pp. 563–582.

Stress on compensatory
help

Environmentalist View By the middle of the twentieth century, numerous studies had contradicted the hereditarian view, and most social scientists took the position that environment is as important as or even more important than heredity in determining intelligence. Social scientists who stress the **environmentalist view of intelligence** generally emphasize the need for continual compensatory programs beginning in infancy. Many also criticize the use of IQ tests on the grounds that these tests are culturally biased. Many attribute the differences in IQ scores between African Americans and whites, for example, to differences in social class and family environment and to systematic racial discrimination.

IQ gains

Sandra Scarr and Richard Weinberg studied differences between African American children growing up in their biological families and those growing up in adopted families. They concluded that the effects of environment outweigh the effects of heredity. Thomas Sowell, after examining IQ scores collected for various ethnic groups between 1920 and 1970, found that the scores of certain groups, including Italian Americans and Polish Americans, have substantially improved. Other studies indicate that the test scores of African Americans and Puerto Ricans have risen more rapidly than scores in the general population in response to improvements in teaching and living conditions.[31]

Cause of IQ gains

James Flynn, who collected similar data on other countries, found that massive gains in IQ scores in fourteen nations have occurred during the twentieth century. These improvements, according to Flynn's analysis, largely stemmed not from genetic improvement but from environmental changes that led to gains in the kinds of skills assessed by IQ tests. Research also indicates that IQ has been increasing even in previously high-scoring populations, suggesting that there may be multiple causes such as early-childhood education, challenging media environments, and increasingly complex work assignments. Torsten Husen and his colleagues have concluded, after reviewing large amounts of data, that improvements in economic and social conditions, and particularly in the availability of schooling, can produce substantial gains in average IQ from one generation to the next. In general, educators committed to improving the performance of low-achieving students find these studies encouraging.[32]

A middle position

Synthesizers' View Certain social scientists have taken a middle, or synthesizing, position in this controversy. The **synthesizers' view of intelligence** holds that both heredity and environment contribute to differences in measured intelligence. For example, Christopher Jencks, after reviewing a large amount of data, concluded that heredity is responsible for 45 percent of the IQ variance, environment accounts for 35 percent, and interaction between the two ("interaction" meaning that particular abilities thrive or wither in specific environments) accounts for 20 percent. Robert Nichols reviewed all these and other data and concluded that the true value for heredity may be anywhere between .40 and .80, but that the exact value has little importance for policy.

Interaction of heredity
and environment

In general, Nichols and other synthesizers maintain that heredity determines the fixed limits of a range; within those limits, the interaction between environment and heredity yields each individual's actual intelligence. This view has been supported by recent studies indicating that in impoverished families much of the IQ variation correlates with quality of environment, whereas in wealthier families (which presumably provide

---

[31]Sandra Scarr and Richard A. Weinberg, "I.Q. Test Performance of Black Children Adopted by White Families," *American Psychologist* (July 1976), pp. 726–739. See also Lee M. Butcher and Robert Plomin, "The Nature of Nurture," *Behavior Genetics* (July 2008), pp. 361–371; Lambert M. Surhome, Mariam T. Tennoe, and Susan F. Hessenow, eds., *Robert Plonim* (Mauritius, Africa: Betascript, 2011); and Richard E. Nisbett et al., "Intelligence," *American Psychologist* (January 2012).
[32]Marguerite Holloway, "Flynn's Effect," *Scientific American* (January 1999); Tomoe Kanaya, Matthew H. Scullin, and Stephen H. Cecci, "The Flynn Effect and U.S. Policies," *American Psychologist* (October 2003); James R. Flynn, *What Is Intelligence?* (Cambridge, MA: Cambridge University Press, 2007); and Jonah Lehrer, "Are Smart People Getting Smarter?" *Wired* (August 2, 2011), available at **www.wired.com**.

> **REFOCUS** How might you, as a teacher, establish a classroom environment that can facilitate full development of a broad range of student abilities?

an adequate environment) heredity exerts a greater influence on children's intelligence. In this view, even if interactions between heredity and environment limit our ability to specify exactly how much of a child's intelligence reflects environmental factors, teachers (and parents) should provide each child with a productive environment in which to realize her or his maximum potential.[33]

Obstacles in the Classroom

We have noted that the home and family environment of many working-class students lacks the kind of educational stimulation needed to prepare students for success in the classroom. However, certain school and classroom dynamics also foster low achievement. The following list highlights some of the most important classroom obstacles to achievement that working-class students face.

■ Concepts increasingly abstract

1. *Inappropriate curriculum and instruction.* Curriculum materials and instructional approaches in the primary grades frequently assume that students are familiar with vocabulary and concepts to which working-class students have had little or no exposure. After grade 3, much of the curriculum requires advanced skills that many working-class students have not yet acquired; hence, they fall further behind in other subject areas.[34]

■ Students' perceptions of inadequacy

2. *Lack of previous success in school.* Lack of academic success in the early grades not only detracts from learning more difficult material later but also damages a student's perception that he or she is a capable learner who has a chance to succeed in school and in later life. Once students believe that they are inadequate learners and lack control over their future, they are less likely to work vigorously at overcoming learning deficiencies.[35]

■ Insufficient higher-order instruction

3. *Ineffective fixation on low-level learning.* When a student, or group of students, functions far below grade level, teachers tend to concentrate on remediating basic skills in reading, math, and other subjects. This reaction is appropriate for some low achievers who need intensive help in acquiring initial skills, but it is damaging for those who could benefit from more challenging learning experiences and assignments. Although helping low-achieving students master higher-order learning skills presents a difficult challenge to teachers, certain instructional strategies make it possible to move successfully in this direction.[36]

■ Problems for teachers

4. *Difficulty of teaching conditions in working-class schools.* As students fall further behind academically and as both teachers and students experience frustration and discouragement, behavior problems increase in the classroom. Teachers have more difficulty

---

[33]Robert C. Nichols, "Policy Implications of the IQ Controversy," in Lee S. Shulman, ed., *Review of Research in Education* (Itasca, IL: Peacock, 1978); Eric Turkheimer et al., "Socioeconomic Status Modifies Heritability of IQ in Young Children," *Psychological Science* (November 2003), pp. 623–628, available at **www.people.virginia.edu/~ent3c/papers2/papers.htm**; David L. Kirp, "Nature, Nurture, and Destiny," *American Prospect* (November 2007), available at **www.prospect.org**; and Elliot M. Tucker-Drob et al., "Emergence of a Gene X Socioeconomic Status Interaction on Infant Mental Ability Between 10 Months and Two Years," *Psychological Science* (January 2011), pp. 125–133.

[34]Lisa Delpit, "Lessons from Teachers," *Journal of Teacher Education* (May/June 2006), pp. 220–231; Elizabeth Bondy and Dorene D. Ross, "The Teacher as Warm Demander," *Educational Leadership* (September 2008), available at **www.ascd.org**; Barbara McClanahan, "Help! I Have Kids Who Can't Read in My World History Class!" *Preventing School Failure* (Winter 2009), pp. 105–112; and Allan Luke, Annette woods, and Karen Dooley, "Comprehension as Social and Intellectual Practice," *Theory Into Practice* (Issue 2, 2011), pp. 157–164.

[35]Jim Wright, "Learning Interventions for Struggling Students," *Education Digest* (January 2006), pp. 35–39; Kay S. Hymowitz, "The Children's Hour," *City Journal* (Winter 2009), available at **www.city-journal.com**; and John Kiernan, "Teaching Math to Diverse Learners," 2011 posting by the Essential Educator, available at **www.essentialeducator.org**.

[36]Allison Zmuda, "Springing into Active Learning," *Educational Leadership* (November 2008), pp. 38–42; and Christine S. Beck, "No More Lost Ground," *Educational Leadership* (April 2011), available at **www.ascd.org**.

providing a productive learning environment. Some give up trying to teach low achievers or leave the school to seek less-frustrating employment elsewhere.[37]

Gaps in language and culture

5. *Teacher perceptions of student inadequacy.* Teachers in working-class schools may see low achievement in their classrooms and conclude that many of their students cannot learn. This view easily becomes a self-fulfilling prophecy because teachers who question their students' learning potential are less likely to work hard to improve academic performance, particularly when improvement requires an intense effort that consumes almost all of a teacher's energy.[38]

Separate groups for "slow" learners

6. *Ineffective homogeneous grouping.* Educators faced with large groups of low achievers frequently address the problem by setting them apart in separate classes or subgroups where instruction can proceed at a slower pace without detracting from the performance of high achievers. Unfortunately, both teachers and students tend to view concentrations of low achievers as "slow" groups for whom learning expectations are low or nonexistent.

Less support for the "slow"

Ray Rist studied this type of arrangement, called **homogeneous grouping**, at a working-class school in St. Louis. A kindergarten class was divided into groups, the "fast learners" and the "slow learners." The fast group received "the most teaching time, rewards, and attention from the teacher." The slow group was "taught infrequently, subjected to more control, and received little if any support from the teacher." Naturally, by the end of the year, differences had emerged in how well prepared these children were for first grade, and the first-grade teacher grouped the students on the basis of their perceived readiness.[39]

Instructional alternatives

Situations like the one Rist described might benefit from keeping the students in heterogeneous classes (that is, groups with a diversity of previous achievement) but giving them individualized instruction so that each can progress at his or her own rate. However, individualization is extremely difficult to implement and often requires such system-wide change in school practices that it becomes almost an economic impossibility. Thus, teachers in schools with mostly low-income students, confronted with heterogeneous classes, generally have failed to work effectively with their numerous low achievers.

One solution is to group low achievers homogeneously for blocks of instruction in reading, mathematics, or other subjects but to make sure that the groups are small and temporary and are taught by highly skilled teachers who work well with such students. This alternative aligns with research indicating that restrictive settings (that is, separate arrangements for low achievers) may have either positive or negative outcomes, depending on what educators do to make instruction effective. An approach of this kind frequently is called "flexible grouping." We further discuss the issue of homogeneous versus heterogeneous grouping in Chapter 16, School Effectiveness and Reform in the United States, and in this chapter's Taking Issue box.[40]

---

[37]Stanley Pogrow, "Making Reform Work for the Educationally Disadvantaged," *Educational Leadership* (February 1995), pp. 20–24; Richard D. Kahlenberg and Bernard Wasow, "What Makes Schools Work?" *Boston Review* (October–November 2003), available at **www.bostonreview.net**; Paul Tough, *Whatever It Takes* (Boston: Houghton Mifflin, 2008); and Stanley Pogrow, *Teaching Content Outrageously* (New York: Wiley, 2011).

[38]Charles M. Payne, *Getting What We Ask For* (Westport, CT: Greenwood, 1984); Lisa Delpit, *Other People's Children* (New York: New Press, 1995), pp. 173–174; Charles M. Payne, *So Much Reform, So Little Change* (Cambridge, MA: Harvard Education Press, 2008); and Charles M. Payne, "Demanding and Supporting Success," *American Educator* (Spring 2011), available at **www.aft.org**.

[39]Ray C. Rist, *The Urban School: A Factory for Failure* (Cambridge, MA: MIT Press, 1973), p. 91. See also Ray C. Rist, "Student Social Class and Teacher Expectations," *Harvard Education Review* (Fall 2000), pp. 257–266; Sharon Cromwell, "Homogeneous or Heterogeneous," 1999 paper with links prepared for *Education World*, available at **www.educationworld.com**; and Cris Tovani, "I Got Grouped," *Educational Leadership* (March 2011), available at **www.ascd.org**.

[40]Michael Scriven, "Problems and Prospects for Individualization," in Harriet Talmage, ed., *Systems of Individualized Education* (Berkeley, CA: McCutchan, 1975), pp. 199–210; Gaea Leinhardt and Allan Pallay, "Restrictive Educational Settings: Exile or Haven?" *Review of Educational Research* (December 1982), pp. 557–558; Laura Robb, "But They All Read at Different Levels," *Instructor* (January/February 2008), pp. 47–51; Michael Petrilli, "All Together Now?" *Education Next* (Winter 2011), available at **www.educationnext.org**; and Dina Brulles and Susan Winebrenner, "Clustered for Success," *Educational Leadership* (February 2012).

TAKING ISSUE

Read the brief introduction below, as well as the Question and the pros and cons list that follows. Then, answer the question using your own words and position.

Homogeneous Grouping

Many schools and classrooms group students by ability in specific subjects, separating the slower learners from the faster ones or the more advanced from the less advanced. Advocates of homogeneous grouping argue that it is both fair and effective, but critics have charged that it harms students, particularly low achievers.

Question

Is placing students in homogeneous groups by ability a generally effective approach for classroom instruction?

Arguments PRO

1. In a large, heterogeneous class with students at many different levels, the teacher cannot give the slowest learners the special attention they need. In fact, teachers may begin to see students who struggle to master the lesson as problems and quicker students as favorites. Therefore, it makes sense to separate students into ability groups for specific subjects.

2. It is unfair to high-achieving students who are capable of learning quickly to slow the pace of instruction to suit average students. The high achievers may become bored and discouraged unless they are separated into groups that can proceed at a faster rate.

3. Homogeneous grouping encourages the growth of an esprit de corps among group members. With cooperation and friendly competition, students at similar levels can spur each other forward.

4. Many teachers are more effective with certain kinds of students than with others. Homogeneous grouping allows teachers to spend more time with groups they enjoy teaching and are best suited to teach.

5. Homogeneous grouping indicates to parents that the school recognizes differences in learning styles. The school is seen as making a commitment to each child's individual needs.

Arguments CON

1. Research has shown that ability grouping tends to stereotype slower learners and hamper their progress. The instruction offered to such groups is often inferior. Because little is expected of them, they are seldom challenged, and thus they fall further behind the more advanced students. In general, slower learners will do better in heterogeneous classes.

2. Although high-achieving students may be hindered somewhat in a heterogeneous setting, they will remain motivated as long as they sense that the teacher appreciates their talents. Moreover, it is important for them to learn that students of all academic levels have something of value to contribute.

3. A group spirit may develop among high achievers who feel a special honor in being placed together, but low achievers will feel stigmatized, often leading to negative group attitudes. They may become increasingly alienated from school and society.

4. Only a few extraordinary teachers have the necessary skill, patience, and enthusiasm to work effectively with an entire group of low achievers. Other teachers assigned to such groups may become frustrated and demoralized.

5. Parents of low achievers are rarely pleased at seeing their children separated from others. A heterogeneous setting is the best indication that the school cares about all of its students.

Question Reprise: What Is Your Stand?

Reflect again on the following question by explaining your stand about this issue: Is placing students in homogeneous groups by ability a generally effective approach for classroom instruction?

■ Overload on teachers and schools

7. *Service-delivery problems*. The problems we have described suggest the great difficulty in delivering educational services effectively in classes or schools with a high percentage of low achievers. For example, a teacher in a working-class school who has ten or twelve low-achieving students in a class of twenty-five

▶❚❚ TEACHSOURCE VIDEO ACTIVITY

Inclusion: Grouping Strategies for Inclusive Classrooms

Go to the Education CourseMate website to access the video entitled, "Inclusion: Grouping Strategies for Inclusive Classrooms." In this video, you'll observe an inclusive classroom and see how teacher Sheryl Cebula works with an inclusion specialist and additional support staff to make sure each child succeeds. After watching the video, think about the following questions:

❶ Based upon reading the Taking Issue Box and watching this video, where do you stand on the issue of heterogeneous versus homogeneous grouping strategies? Explain your position and opinions.

❷ In this video, we see firsthand the benefits of heterogeneous grouping (that is, including all kinds of children in one classroom). Describe the positive aspects of heterogeneous grouping that you observe within the video.

_____

** This video reinforces key concepts found in Section I: Students as Learners of the Praxis II Exam.**

has a many times more difficult task of providing effective instruction than does a teacher who has only four or five low achievers in a middle-class school. Not only may teachers in the former situation need to spend virtually all of their time overcoming low achievers' learning problems, but the negative dynamics that result from students' frustration and misbehavior make the task much more demanding. These problems are particularly acute for new teachers, who lack the experience to deal with them expeditiously. Administrators, counselors, and other specialized personnel in working-class schools experience the same predicament: the burden of addressing learning and behavior problems may leave little time for improving services for all students. The serious problems endemic in such **overloaded schools** make it difficult for educators to function effectively.[41]

Benefits of small classes

8. *Overly large classes.* As suggested previously, classes too large for teachers to provide sufficient help to overcome learning problems often lead to ineffective instruction for low-achieving students. Teachers of large classes find it particularly hard to help low achievers master complex skills such as critical thinking, reading comprehension, mathematics problem solving, and other higher-order skills.[42]

The effects of class size were assessed in a major study of students in Tennessee. The researchers found that students in small classes scored substantially higher in reading and math in kindergarten and first grade than did students in average-sized classes. They also maintained their advantage in later grades. Effects were particularly impressive at schools that enrolled large proportions of students from low-income

_____

[41]David F. Feldon, "Cognitive Load and Classroom Teaching," *Educational Psychologist* (Summer 2007), pp. 123–137; and Christian Bruhwiler and Peter Blatchford, "Effects of Class Size and Adaptive Teaching Competency on Classroom Processes and Academic Outcome," *Learning and Instruction* (February 2011), pp. 95–108.

[42]Barbara A. Nye, "Do the Disadvantaged Benefit More from Small Classes?" *American Journal of Education* (November 2000), pp. 1–25; and Tim Weldon, "Reducing Class Size," 2011 posting by The Council of State Governments, available at **http://knowledgecenter.csg.org/kc**.

Conditions such as over-crowded classes, inexperienced teachers, or mismatches between the expectations of schools and teachers and the backgrounds and learning styles of students can contribute to lower achievement.

Jon Naso/Star Ledger/Corbis News/Corbis

minority backgrounds. Several subsequent smaller studies have arrived at similar conclusions.[43]

Upgrading teacher training helps students achieve

9. *Teacher preparation and experience.* Studies of high-poverty schools in big cities have shown that teachers at schools with concentrations of low-SES students tend to have less preparation and experience in teaching their subjects than teachers at schools with mostly middle-class students. For this reason, many analysts believe that upgrading teacher training and preparation and hiring teachers with appropriate experience should be priority goals in efforts to improve the achievement of low-income and working-class students.[44]

Ridiculing high achievers

10. *Negative peer pressure.* Several researchers have reported that academically oriented students in predominantly working-class schools are often ridiculed and rejected for accepting school norms. John Ogbu and Signithia Fordham, among others, have described negative peer influences as being particularly strong among working-class African American students. At some inner-city schools where significant numbers of students react in this way, high achievers who work hard are often labeled "brainiacs" and accused of "acting white."[45] Commenting on these phenomena, an African American professor concluded that the "notion that someone with a hunger for knowledge would be regarded as a 'traitor to his race' . . . would seem

[43]Jeremy D. Finn and Charles M. Achilles, "Answers and Questions about Class Size," *American Educational Research Journal* (Fall 1990), pp. 557–577; Frederick M. Hess and Juliet Squire, "From Research to Policy," *American School Board Journal* (August 2008), pp. 38–41; Spyros Konstanto-poulos, "How Consistent Are Class Size Effects?" *Evaluation Review* (February 2011), pp. 71–92; and materials available at **www.classsizematters.org**.

[44]Linda Darling-Hammond, "Teacher Quality and Student Achievement," *Education Policy Analysis Archives* (January 2000), available at **http://epaa.asu.edu/ojs**; Richard J. Murnane and Jennifer L. Steele, "What Is the Problem?" *The Future of Children* (Spring 2007), available at **www.futureofchildren.org**; and Stephen Sawchuck, "Teacher Distribution," *Education Week*, April 20, 2011.

[45]Paul Willis, *Learning to Labour* (Westmead, England: Saxon House, 1977); Signithia Fordham, "Racelessness as a Factor in Black Students' School Success," *Harvard Educational Review* (February 1988), pp. 54–84; Roland G. Fryer, "'Acting White,'" *Education Next* (No. 2, 2006), available at **www.educationnext.org**; Myron Magnet, "The Great African-American Awakening," *City Journal* (Summer 2008), available at **www.city-journal.com**; Stuart Buck, *Acting White* (New Haven, CT: Yale, 2010); James Causey, "What's Wrong with Acting White?" *Jsonline* February 21, 2011, available at **www.jsonline.com**; and Jean Moule, *Cultural Competence*, 2nd ed. (Belmont, CA: Wadsworth, 2012).

like some kind of sinister white plot. In a society where blacks had to endure jail-ings, shootings, and lynchings to get an education, it seems utterly unbelievable that some black youngsters now regard . . . academic failure as a sign of pride."[46]

Recognizing education's importance

Some researchers have reported that such attitudes appear to be much less prevalent or nonexistent among middle-class black students or those who attend desegregated schools. In addition, research by Lois Weis and her colleagues suggests that antischool peer pressures among working-class students lessen as they realize that education is im-portant for future success. Although working-class adolescents historically tended to view academic learning as irrelevant to their future employment, the high-school boys in her study perceived schooling as offering "utilitarian opportunities" for acquiring skilled jobs and thus were willing to "put in their time" in school and even go to college.[47]

Diversity in learning style and behavior

11. *Differences in teacher and student backgrounds.* Teachers from middle-class back-grounds might have difficulty understanding and motivating disadvantaged pupils. Particularly in the case of white teachers working with disadvantaged mi-nority students, differences in dialect, language, or cultural background may make it difficult for the teachers to communicate effectively with their students. Such mismatches may also hamper the work of middle-class minority teachers in low-income schools. In any case, many teachers are reluctant to accept assignment or to remain in high-poverty schools, to the extent that many such schools are left with numerous inexperienced teachers who have not learned to work well with low-income students and to teach them effectively.[48]

12. *Incompatibility between classroom expectations and students' behavioral patterns and learn-ing styles.* Teachers may also be unprepared for diversity in their students' learning styles and behavior. Numerous analysts have concluded that the behavioral patterns and learning styles of many working-class students and some groups of minority stu-dents differ from those of middle-class or nonminority students. When teachers gear their classroom expectations to the learning styles and behavior of high-achieving, middle-class students, such style differences can lead to school failure.

For example, some researchers suggest that the following patterns of behaviors ex-ist, and they recommended the following ways for teachers to adapt their instruction to help students who display these styles:[49]

■ Many African American students tend to behave energetically in class (a pattern researchers refer to as having high "activation" levels). These students do not per-form well if teachers require them to sit in one place for extended periods of time or prohibit impulsive responses. If, as a teacher, you have highly active students, you should plan learning activities that allow students some physical movement.

■ Some low-income African American students tend to become confused when teach-ers fail to act forcefully and authoritatively. Researchers therefore suggest that, as a teacher, you maintain authority and avoid treating students as "buddies."

---

[46]Greg Wiggan, "From Opposition to Engagement," *Urban Review* (November 2008), pp. 317–349; and John McWhorter, "Color Blind," *New Republic*, April 22, 2011, available at **www.tnr.com**.
[47]Maxine Seller and Lois Weis, *Beyond Black and White* (Albany: State University of New York Press, 1997). See also Lois Weis, *Class Reunion* (New York: Routledge, 2004); Lois Weis, ed., *The Way Class Works* (New York: Routledge, 2007); Doug Noon, "Class Not Dismissed," 2008 posting at Borderland, available at **www.borderland.northernattitude.org**; and Nicola Ingram, "Within School and Beyond the Gate," *Sociology* (No. 2, 2011), pp. 287–302.
[48]Betty Achenstein and Julia Aguire, "Cultural Match or Culturally Suspect?" *Teachers College Record* (August 2008), pp. 1505–1540; Uvaney Maylor, "'They Do Not Relate to Black People like Us,'" *Journal of Education Policy* (January 2009), pp. 1–21; and Donald Boyd et al., "The Effect of School Neighborhoods on Teacher Career Decisions," 2010 report prepared for the Brookings Institution, available at **www.teacherpolicyresearch.org**, click on "Research Papers."
[49]LaVonne Neal et al., "The Effects of African American Movement Styles," *Journal of Special Edu-cation* (Spring 2003), pp. 49–58; Jawanza Kunjufu, *Understanding Black Male Learning Styles* (Sauk Village, IL: African American Images, 2010); and Augusta Mann, Touching the Spirit," 2011 posting by Successful Urban Teachers, available at **www.successfulteachers.com**.

■ African American and Latino students may tend to be "field dependent"—that is, they learn poorly when instruction begins with abstract, decontextualized concepts. You can help field-dependent students by presenting concrete material before moving to abstract analysis. Providing opportunities for students to learn in pairs or cooperative groups may also help.

We should emphasize that research has not conclusively established the existence of such distinctive behavioral patterns or learning styles among working-class or minority students. Learning differences between low-income African American, Latino, or other minority students and nonminority students may stem mostly from socioeconomic status rather than from race or ethnicity. Nevertheless, numerous studies do support the conclusion that you can help improve performance among your low-achieving students if you adjust for the various behavioral and learning styles of *all* your students. We'll discuss such alternative teaching practices in the multicultural education section in Chapter 12, Providing Equal Educational Opportunity.[50]

■ Middle-class expectations for behavior

> **REFOCUS** Which reasons for low achievement among many low-income students seem most important to you? Can you identify other possible explanations not listed in this chapter? (Hint: Many low-income parents move around a lot.)

13. *Accumulating effects of information-poor homes and neighborhoods.* Disadvantages associated with growing up in an impoverished environment (for more information on home influences, see the "Home Environment" section earlier in this chapter) not only accumulate just in infancy and early childhood but also cascade further as children proceed through school. Research indicates that students in poverty neighborhoods and schools have relatively limited access to high-quality print and digital materials, and thus during summer vacations and other time away from school, they fall further and further behind middle-class students in achievement.[51]

Our analysis so far makes it clear that many students are economically disadvantaged and also experience educational disadvantages in schools and classrooms. Recent research indicates that disadvantaged students can increase their success in the educational system with outstanding teachers and appropriate instructional strategies.[52] But the discouraging facts of achievement and social class have raised questions about whether or not schools do indeed make a difference—do they generally help in significant ways in counteracting the disadvantages students experience? The rest of this chapter confronts this issue. Related chapters, particularly Chapter 16, School Effectiveness and Reform in the United States, will discuss ways to bolster student achievement by improving the organization and delivery of instruction.

Do Schools Equalize Opportunity?

The research discussed in the preceding sections indicates that disproportionate numbers of students from low-income backgrounds enter school poorly prepared to succeed in traditional classrooms and in later years rank relatively low in school achievement and other indicators of success. If we define equal opportunity in terms of overcoming

---

[50]Madge G. Willis, "Learning Styles of African American Children," *Journal of Black Psychology* (Fall 1989), pp. 47–65; A. Wade Boykin and Caryn T. Bailey, "The Role of Cultural Factors in School Relevant Cultural Functioning," 2000 paper prepared for the Center for Research on Students Placed at Risk, available at **www.csos.jhu.edu/crespar/reports.htm**; Karolyn Tyson and William Darity, Jr., "It's Not 'a Black Thing,'" *American Sociological Review* (August 2005), pp. 582–605; and A. Wade Boykin and Pedro Noguera, *Creating the Opportunity to Learn* (Washington, D.C.: ASCD, 2011).

[51]Donna Celano and Susan B. Neuman, "When Schools Close, the Knowledge Gap Grows," *Phi Delta Kappan* (December 2008), pp. 256–262; and Susan J. Bodily et al., "Hours of Opportunity," 2010 report prepared for the Rand Corporation, available at **www.rand.org**.

[52]Daniel U. Levine and Beau Fly Jones, "Mastery Learning," in Richard Gorton, Gail Schneider, and James Fischer, eds., *Encyclopedia of School Administration and Supervision* (Phoenix, AZ: Oryx, 1988); Stanley Pogrow, "Teacher Feature," *Teachers.Net Gazette* (January 2002), available at **www.teachers.net/gazette/JAN02**; Nathan Glazer, "Inside the Testing Factory," *Education Next* (Winter 2008), available at **www.educationnext.org**; and Charles A. Hughes and Douglas D. Dexter, "Response to Intervention," *Theory into Practice* (Issue 1, 2011), pp. 4–11.

disadvantages associated with family background so that students on the average perform equally well regardless of socioeconomic status, one must conclude that the educational system has failed to equalize opportunity.

Coleman's study

Equal educational opportunity has received considerable attention since the 1966 publication of a massive national study conducted by James Coleman and his colleagues. Titled *Equality of Educational Opportunity,* this federally supported study collected data on approximately six hundred thousand students at more than four thousand schools. Its congressional sponsors expected it to show that low achievement among low-socioeconomic students stemmed from low expenditures on their education, thus justifying increased school funding.

Influence of school spending versus social class

As expected, Coleman and his colleagues reported that achievement related strongly to students' socioeconomic background and that schools with high proportions of working-class and underclass students generally received less funding than did middle-class schools. However, they also found that expenditures for reduced class size, laboratories, libraries, and other aspects of school operation were fundamentally unrelated to achievement after one took into account (1) a student's personal socioeconomic background and (2) the social-class status of other students in the school. Many readers incorrectly interpreted the data to mean that schools cannot improve the performance of economically disadvantaged students. In reality, the results supported two conclusions: (1) simply spending more on education for disadvantaged students was unlikely to substantially improve their achievement, and (2) moving students from mostly working-class schools to middle-class schools *could* improve achievement.[53]

Jencks's conclusions

In the next decade, two influential books by Christopher Jencks and his colleagues bolstered this analysis. After examining a great deal of data, Jencks and his colleagues reached the following conclusions:[54]

1. School achievement depends substantially on students' family characteristics.

2. Family background accounts for nearly half the variation in occupational status and up to 35 percent of the variation in earnings.

3. The schools accomplish relatively little in terms of reducing the achievement gap between students with higher and lower socioeconomic status.

International parallels

Studies from many other countries support similar conclusions. For example, scholars at the World Bank, after reviewing several decades of international research, reported that family background has an "early and apparently lasting influence" on achievement. Likewise, a review of studies in Great Britain concluded that schools there have served as "mechanisms for the transmission of privileges from one generation of middle-class citizens to the next."[55]

---

[53]James S. Coleman et al., *Equality of Educational Opportunity* (Washington, D.C.: U.S. Government Printing Office, 1966); Frederick Mosteller and Daniel P. Moynihan, eds., *On Equality of Educational Opportunity* (New York: Random House, 1972); and James S. Coleman, *Equality and Achievement in Education* (Boulder, CO: Westview, 1990). See also Adam Gamoran and Daniel A. Long, "Coleman Report, Forty Years On," 2007 paper prepared for the Wisconsin Center for Education Research, available at **www.wcer.wisc.edu**; Geoffrey D. Borman and Maritza Dowling, "Schools and Inequality," *Teachers College Record* (May 2010), pp. 1201–1246; and Laura B. Perry and Andrew McConney, "Does the SES of the School Matter?" January 2012 posting by the Horace Mann League, available at **http://horacemannleague.blogspot.com**.
[54]Christopher Jencks et al., *Inequality* (New York: Basic Books, 1972); and Christopher Jencks et al., *Who Gets Ahead?* (New York: Basic Books, 1979). See also Daniel P. McMurrer and Isabel V. Sawhill, *Getting Ahead* (Washington, D.C.: Urban Institute, 1998); Debopam Bhattacharya and Bhashkar Mazumder, "A Nonparametric Analysis of Black-White Differences in Intergenerational Income Mobility in the United States," 2011 paper prepared for the Federal Reserve Bank of Chicago, available at **www.chicagofed.org**; and "Christopher Jencks Interview," undated Internet posting by the Public Broadcasting System, available at **www.pbs.org/fmc/interviews/jencks.htm**.
[55]Marlaine E. Lockheed, Bruce Fuller, and Ronald Nyirongo, *Family Background and School Achievement* (Washington, D.C.: World Bank, 1988), p. 23; Yossi Shavit and Hans-Peter Blossfeld, eds., *Persistent Inequality* (Boulder, CO: Westview, 1993); Patrick Heuveline, Honqxing Yang, and Jeffrey M. Timberlake, "It Takes a Village (Perhaps a Nation)," *Journal of Marriage and Family* (October 2010), pp. 1362–1376; and "How Do Some Students Overcome Their Socio-Economic Background?" *PISA in Focus* (June 2011), available at **www.pisa.oecd.org**.

This does not mean, however, that all or even most students from low-income families will be unsuccessful as adults or that the schools should be viewed as mostly unsuccessful in helping provide opportunities for students with diverse socioeconomic backgrounds. Research supports the following general conclusions:

Significant socioeconomic mobility

1. *Although students with low socioeconomic status tend to perform poorly in school and later have restricted employment opportunities, a substantial proportion of working-class children and some from families living in poverty do eventually attain middle-class status.* For example, although nearly two-thirds of men in the U.S. labor force grew up in working-class families or on a farm, more than 50 percent are in middle- or high-status jobs; nearly 40 percent are in upper-middle-class jobs even though less than 25 percent were raised in upper-middle-class families. Socioeconomic mobility of this kind has been present throughout U.S. history. However, it may have diminished somewhat in recent years.[56]

Role of education

2. *The educational system has helped many people surpass their parents' status.* Its role in promoting socioeconomic mobility has grown more central as middle- and high-status jobs have become more complex and dependent on specialized educational skills and credentials, and technological and economic changes have eliminated many unskilled jobs.[57]

College as the dividing line

3. *As education increasingly determines socioeconomic status and mobility, college attendance and graduation constitute a kind of dividing line between those likely to attain high socioeconomic status and those not.* One hundred years ago, enrollment in high school probably was the best educational indicator of socioeconomic status. As of fifty or sixty years ago, high-school graduation was the clearest dividing line. Today, postsecondary education is almost a prerequisite for middle- or high-status jobs.

Continuing disadvantages of underclass

4. *Despite the success of many working-class students, opportunities—educational, social, and economic—are too few to overcome the disadvantages of the underclass.* Children who attend low-achieving poverty schools remain disproportionately likely to stay low in socioeconomic status.

Traditional versus Revisionist Interpretations

Opposite views of U.S. schools

Growing recognition of the strong relationship between social class and school achievement has led to a fundamental disagreement between two groups of observers of U.S. education. According to the **traditional view of schools**, the educational system succeeds in providing economically disadvantaged students with meaningful opportunities for social and economic advancement. The **revisionist view of schools**, in contrast, holds that the schools fail to provide most disadvantaged students with a meaningful chance to succeed in society. You may hear **critical theory or critical pedagogy** used as synonyms for the revisionist view. The following sections explore the ramifications of these two arguments.[58]

---

[56]David L. Featherman and Robert M. Hauser, *Opportunity and Change* (New York: Academic Press, 1978); Michael Hout, "More Universalism, Less Structural Mobility," *American Journal of Sociology* (May 1988), pp. 1358–1400; Isabel V. Sawhill, "Still the Land of Opportunity?" 1999 paper prepared for the Urban Institute, available at **www.urban.org**; Emily Beller and Michael Hout, "Intergenerational Social Mobility," *The Future of Children* (Fall 2006), available at **www.futureofchildren.org**; Isabel V. Sawhill, "Opportunity in America," *The Future of Children* (Fall 2006), available at **www.futureofchildren.org**; Michael Hout, "Intergenerational Class Mobility and the Convergence Thesis," *British Journal of Sociology* (January 2010), pp. 221–224; and Scott Winship, "Mobility Impaired," *National Review*, November 14, 2011, and "The President's Suspect Statistics," *National Review*, January 2, 2012, both available at **www.nationalreview.com**.
[57]Hout, "More Universalism"; and Robert Mare, "A Multigenerational View of Inequality," *Demography* (February 2011), pp. 1–23.
[58]Revisionists are sometimes referred to as neo-Marxists if they believe that the capitalist system must be abolished or fundamentally changed for schools to provide truly equal opportunity for all students.

The Traditional View

Education as balancing excellence with opportunity

Proponents of the traditional view acknowledge the relationships among social class, educational achievement, and economic success, but they emphasize existing opportunities and data indicating that many working-class youth do experience social mobility through schools and other institutions. Most traditionalists believe that our educational and economic institutions balance a requirement for excellence with provision of opportunity. From this perspective, each individual who works hard, no matter how disadvantaged, has the opportunity to succeed in elementary and secondary schools and to go to college.

Multiple chances

Traditionalists point out that the U.S. educational system gives the individual more chances to attend college than do the educational systems of many other countries (see Chapter 15, International Education). Students in this country do not, as in some nations, face an examination at age eleven or twelve that shunts them into an almost inescapable educational track. Even if American students do poorly in high school, they can go to a community college and then transfer to a university. Furthermore, admission standards at many four-year colleges permit enrollment of all but the lowest-achieving high-school graduates.

Schools as screening devices

Traditionalists admit that schools serve as a screening device to sort different individuals into different jobs, but they do not believe that this screening is systematically based on race, ethnicity, or income. Instead, they believe, better-educated people obtain better jobs primarily because schools have made them more productive. Additional years of schooling are an indication of this greater productivity. The employer needs criteria to guide hiring choices, and in a democratic society that values mobility and opportunity, quality of education counts, not the applicant's family connections, race, ethnic origin, or social class.

The Revisionist View and Critical Pedagogy

Education as maintaining elite dominance

Revisionists contend that elite groups control the schools and thus channel disadvantaged students into second-rate secondary schools and programs, third-rate community colleges, and fourth-rate jobs. Many critical pedagogists also believe that the educational system has been set up specifically to produce disciplined workers at the bottom of the class structure. This is accomplished in part by emphasizing discipline in working-class schools, just as the working-class family and the factory labor system emphasize discipline.[59]

Why students resist

Much analysis in critical pedagogy has been referred to as **resistance theory**, which attempts to explain why some students with low socioeconomic status refuse to conform to school expectations or to comply with their teachers' demands. The students' resistance, in this view, arises partly because school norms and expectations contradict the traditional definitions of masculinity and femininity these students hold. In addition, an "oppositional peer life" stimulates students to resist what they perceive as the irrelevant middle-class values of their teachers. Some research indicates that oppositional behaviors are particularly prevalent among male students. As described in Chapter 6, Philosophical Roots of Education, resistance theorists have further concluded that the traditional curriculum marginalizes the

---

[59]Major writings of the revisionist scholars and critical pedagogists include the following: Martin Carnoy, ed., *Schooling in a Corporate Society* (New York: McKay, 1975); Joel H. Spring, *The Sorting Machine* (New York: McKay, 1976); Samuel Bowles and Herbert Gintis, *Schooling in Capitalist America* (New York: Basic Books, 1976); Michael W. Apple and Lois Weis, eds., *Ideology and Practice in Schooling* (Philadelphia, PA: Temple University, 1983); Henry A. Giroux, *Cultural Workers and the Politics of Education* (New York: Routledge, 1991); Michael W. Apple, *Ideology and Curriculum* (New York: Routledge, 1994); Henry A. Giroux, "The Fall of Public Education," 2011 paper available at **www.truthout.org**; and materials available at **www.henryagiroux.com**.

everyday knowledge of such students, thereby reinforcing anti-intellectual tendencies in working-class cultures.[60]

What teachers should do

Critical theorists have been devoting considerable attention to ways educators can improve the situation. Using a variety of related terms such as *critical discourse, critical engagement,* and *critical literacy,* they have emphasized the goal of teachers becoming "transformative intellectuals" who work to broaden schools' role in developing a democratic society. For example, Pauline Lipman believes that teachers should promote not just the "personal efficacy" but also the "social efficacy" of working-class and minority students, and they should help them prepare to become leaders in their local communities. She also believes that teachers should pursue this type of goal as part of a larger effort to reform public schools. Some analysts believe that computers and other technologies can help low-income students overcome many of their disadvantages.[61] As the Technology @ School box discusses, however, students from some groups lack sufficient access to these technologies.

An Intermediate Viewpoint

This chapter provides data indicating that working-class students as a group underperform middle-class students. After examining reasons offered to account for this difference, we summarized several decades of research concluding that elementary and secondary schools frequently fail to overcome the disadvantages that working-class students bring to school. Although recent studies have pointed to a number of more successful schools, the overall pattern offers support for some of the revisionists' conclusions.

Schools' failures versus successes

On the other hand, not all working-class students and minority students fail in the schools, and not all middle-class students succeed. An accurate portrayal of the relationships between social class and achievement lies somewhere between the revisionist and the traditional views. Schools do not totally perpetuate the existing social-class structure into the next generation; neither do they provide sufficient opportunity to break the general pattern in which a great many working-class students perform at a predictably low level. Levine and Levine, reviewing the research on each side of the debate, have offered an intermediate view that stresses the following:[62]

Lowest class positions are most frozen

- Research on status mobility in the United States indicates that people at the bottom level mostly tend to freeze into their parents' status. Despite considerable intergenerational movement up the socioeconomic ladder and some movement down, large proportions of Americans with the lowest social-class backgrounds do not progress beyond the status of their parents.

Minorities and concentrated poverty schools

- Social and demographic trends have concentrated many children in low-income urban and rural communities in schools extremely low on achievement measures.

[60]Robert W. Connell et al., *Making the Difference* (Boston: George Allen and Unwin, 1982); Henry A. Giroux, "Youth and the Politics of Representation," *Educational Researcher* (May 1997), pp. 27–30; Kathleen K. Abowitz, "A Pragmatist Revisioning of Resistance Theory," *American Educational Research Journal* (Winter 2000), pp. 877–907; Peter McInerney, "Toward a Critical Pedagogy of Engagement for Alienated Youth," *Critical Studies in Education* (February 2009), pp. 29–35; Alexander M. Gurn, "Critical Pedagogy in the Classroom and the Community," *Curriculum Inquiry* (January 2011), pp. 143–152; and Geneva Gay, "Our Children Need . . . Education for Resistance," *Journal of Educational Controversy* (Fall 2011/Winter 2012), available at **www.wce.wwu.edu/resources/IASEC**.
[61]Henry A. Giroux, *Teachers as Intellectuals* (Granby, MA: Bergin and Garvey, 1988); Pauline Lipman, *Race, Class, and Power in School Restructuring* (Albany: State University of New York Press, 1998); and Henry A. Giroux, *Twilight of the Social* (Boulder, CO: Paradigm, 2012).
[62]Levine and Levine, *Society and Education*. See also Gary N. Marks, "Cross-National Differences and Accounting for Social Class Inequalities in Education," *International Sociology* (December 2005), pp. 483–505; Richard Breen, "Educational Expansion and Social Mobility in the 20th Century," *Social Forces* (December 2010), pp. 365–388; David Grusky and Szonja Szelenyi, eds., *The Inequality Reader* (Boulder, CO: Westview, 2011); and P. L. Thomas, "Universal Public Education—Our (Contradictory) Missions," *Journal of Educational Controversy* (Fall 2011/Winter 2012), available at **www.wce.wwu.edu/resources/IASEC**.

TECHNOLOGY @ SCHOOL

Dealing with the Digital Divide

Recent years have brought much attention to the extent and implications of the digital divide—the gap between advantaged and disadvantaged Americans in access to digital media. For example, a report titled "Connected to the Future" on children's Internet use stated that 66 percent of high-income children had Internet access at home, compared with only 29 percent of low-income children. The report is available at **www.cpb.org**. Similarly, federal government data state that 48 percent of black students and 50 percent of Latino students use a computer at home, compared to 81 percent of white students.

As a teacher, you will encounter students who have had extensive computer exposure and other students with little, if any. You will need ways to help all of them become more proficient with computers, just as you address other individual differences. Your school may or may not have widespread and fast access to the Internet, but in either case, you should help all your students use the Internet and other digitized resources to improve their learning.

You'll find discussion and proposals regarding possibilities for narrowing the digital divide in society in a report titled "Falling through the Net: Toward Digital Inclusion" at **www.ntia.doc.gov/ntiahome/fttn00/contents00.html**.

A disproportionately high percentage of students in these schools are from racial or ethnic minority groups.

Equal opportunity, past and present

- Although many working-class students attend predominantly working-class schools that reinforce their initial disadvantages through ineffective instruction, many others attend mixed-status schools with teaching and learning conditions more conducive to high performance. In addition, a growing number of working-class schools appear to be emphasizing higher-order learning.

- Although we cannot pinpoint the exact percentage of working-class students who succeed in the schools or who use their education to advance in social status, the schools do serve as an important route to mobility for many economically disadvantaged children.

Continuity & Change

REFOCUS Where does your position on equality of opportunity best fit—with a traditionalist, revisionist, or intermediate viewpoint? Why?

Historically, educational leaders such as Horace Mann worked to establish and expand the public-school system partly because they believed this would help give all American children an equal chance to succeed in life, regardless of the circumstances of their birth. The data cited in this chapter suggest that the traditional public-school function of providing equal educational opportunity has taken on a more charged meaning, at a time when educational attainment is becoming an increasing prerequisite for success in the economy. Provision of equal opportunity in society now depends on improving the effectiveness of instruction for children—particularly those from minority backgrounds—who attend predominantly poverty schools. This issue will be discussed further in succeeding chapters.

Summing Up

1. Social class relates both to achievement in elementary and secondary schools and to entry into and graduation from college. Students with low socioeconomic status tend to rank low in educational attainment; middle-class students tend to rank high. Low achievement is particularly a problem in poverty areas of large cities.

2. Low-income minority groups generally are low in educational achievement, but little or no independent relationship exists between race or ethnicity and achievement after taking account of social class.

3. Major reasons for low achievement include the following: (a) students' homes and family environments poorly

prepare them for success in the traditional school; (b) genetic considerations (that is, heredity) may interact with environment in some cases to further hamper achievement; and (c) traditionally organized and operated schools have failed to provide effective education for economically disadvantaged students.

④ Many problems in the schools tend to limit achievement: inappropriate curriculum and instruction, lack of previous success in school, difficult teaching conditions, teacher perceptions of student inadequacy, ineffective homogeneous grouping, delivery-of-service problems, overly large classes, negative peer pressures, differences in teacher and student backgrounds, and incompatibility between classroom expectations and students' behavioral patterns.

⑤ Research on social class and education has somewhat supported the revisionist view that schools help perpetuate the existing social-class system. This contrasts with the traditional view that U.S. society and its educational system provide children and youth with equal opportunity to succeed regardless of their social-class background.

⑥ Because recent research indicates that the schools can be much more effective, we may move closer to the ideal of equal educational opportunity in the future.

Key Terms

The numbers indicate the pages where explanations of the key terms can be found.

socioeconomic status (SES) 336
upper class 336
middle class 336
working class 336
underclass 336
National Assessment of Educational Progress (NAEP) 337

race 340
ethnicity 340
ethnic group 340
hereditarian view of intelligence 349
environmentalist view of intelligence 350
synthesizers' view of intelligence 350

homogeneous grouping 352
overloaded schools 354
traditional view of schools 359
revisionist view of schools 359
critical theory (critical pedagogy) 359
resistance theory 360

Certification Connection Activity

This chapter, Social Class, Race, and School Achievement, aligns with the Praxis II's topic of Students as Diverse Learners. The social class, home environment, and ethnicity influences on school performance are three of the main topics in this chapter. In your journal, reflect on the reasons provided in this chapter for the achievement gap among groups of students in American schools. After generating a list of possible explanations for the gap, propose strategies schools and teachers can use to combat the achievement gap.

Discussion Questions

① What can teachers and schools do to overcome each of the school-related obstacles and problems that contribute to low achievement among economically disadvantaged students? What might you accomplish in working to overcome these obstacles and solve these problems?

② Which revisionist arguments are the most persuasive? Which are most vulnerable to criticism?

③ Imagine that you have been hired as a new teacher in a school with a racial, economic, and linguistic composition quite unlike your own background. What can you do to improve your chances to succeed, and whom might you ask for assistance?

④ What was your own experience with homogeneous and heterogeneous grouping in high school? Were these arrangements beneficial for both high- and low-achieving students? What might or should have been done to make them more effective?

⑤ To what extent would you be willing to contact parents of low-achieving students when you become a teacher? Do you think this should be part of the classroom teacher's responsibilities?

Suggested Projects for Professional Development

1 For your portfolio, prepare an analysis of unusually effective schools, those whose students achieve more than students with similar social background at most other schools. What are the characteristics or correlates of these unusually effective schools? Searching the Internet for "effective schools" will give you access to sites that focus on effective schools.

2 Contact a nearby elementary school to determine what steps teachers are taking to improve achievement among low-income and/or minority students. Compare your findings with those of your classmates. You may want to work together in identifying ideas and approaches to use in your own classroom.

3 Interview someone from a low-income background who has been successful in the educational system. To what does he or she attribute this success? What special obstacles did the person encounter, and how were they overcome?

4 Compile articles from newspapers, magazines, and the Internet discussing low achievement in the public schools. Do these sources consider the kinds of material presented in this chapter? How? What solutions do the authors propose? What is your assessment of the likely effectiveness of these solutions?

Suggested Resources

Internet Resources

Useful sites to explore regarding topics in this chapter include home pages of professional organizations such as the American Psychological Association (**www.apa.org**) and the National Education Association (**www.nea.org**). Sites sponsored by the Brookings Institution (**www.brook.edu**), the Institute for Research on Poverty (**www.ssc.wisc.edu/irp**), and the Rand Organization (**www.rand.org**) also provide information on relevant topics.

The Spring 2011 issue of the *American Educator* (available at **www.aft.org**) is devoted to the theme of "Equalizing Opportunity" and includes articles by William J. Wilson on being poor and black, James Heckman on early childhood education, and Charles Payne on demanding and supporting high expectations.

Several papers portraying patterns of racial/ethnic segregation and socioeconomic stratification in the United States are available at **http://mumford1.dyndns.org/cen2000**.

The theme of the January 2011 issue of Education Northwest Magazine (**www.educationnorthwest.org/edunw-magazine**) is "Looking for Answers to the Dropout Problem."

Educational Testing Service (ETS) offers information on equality of educational, economic, and social opportunity at its Policy Information Center, **www.ets.org/research/pic**.

Publications

Brooks, David. *Bobos in Paradise.* New York: Simon and Schuster, 2000. *Brooks describes how the countercultural "bohemians" of the 1960s entered the middle class and thereby changed cultural attitudes and practices. An excerpt is available at* **www.pbs.org/peoplelikeus/essays**.

Grusky, David, and Szonja Szelenyi, eds. *The Inequality Reader,* 2nd ed. Boulder: Westview, 2011. *Provides access to source material regarding a diverse and comprehensive set of topics involving mobility, inequality, and social status.*

Herndon, James. *The Way It Spozed to Be.* New York: Bantam, 1968. *A classic account of the way education works, or doesn't work, in inner-city schools.*

Payne, Charles M. *So Much Reform, So Little Change.* Cambridge, MA: Harvard Education Press, 2008. *Subtitled "The Persistence of Failure in Urban Schools," this volume examines the intense problems of high-poverty schools but in doing so also suggests how some schools have begun to counteract the roots of failure.*

 Additional resources for this chapter, including the TeachSource Videos, can be found on the Education CourseMate website. Go to **CengageBrain.com** to access the site.

CHAPTER 12

Providing Equal Educational Opportunity

U.S. schools were the world's first to aim at providing all students with educational opportunity through high-school and postsecondary levels. Nonetheless, as Chapter 11, Social Class, Race, and School Achievement, indicated, effective education all too rarely extends to economically disadvantaged and minority students. Stimulated by the civil rights movement, many people have recognized the need to improve educational opportunity, not just for disadvantaged students but also for students with disabilities.

In this chapter, we examine desegregation, compensatory education for economically disadvantaged students, multicultural education (including bilingual education), and education for students with disabilities. These topics reflect four significant movements that have attempted to enlarge and equalize educational opportunities for our students. You may agree that our schools should provide equal opportunity but consider this a matter for the government, the school board, and civil rights groups. How would it affect you in the classroom? There are several ways:

- First, wherever you teach, you will find yourself professionally and morally obligated to furnish specific help for low-achieving students.

- Second, the increasing racial and ethnic diversity in student populations means that you will probably need to accommodate students from a variety of ethnic groups, cultural backgrounds, and languages.

- Third, more students than ever before are being classified as having disabilities, and increasingly these students are included in regular classrooms. As a teacher, you will be at least partly responsible for addressing their special needs.

To begin formulating your own philosophy and approach to equal educational opportunity, think about the following questions as you read this chapter:

FOCUS QUESTIONS

- What are the rationales for desegregation, compensatory education, multicultural education, and education of children with disabilities?
- What are the major obstacles and approaches in desegregating the schools?
- What are the major approaches to compensatory education?
- What is multicultural education? What forms does it take in elementary and secondary schools? What are its major benefits and dangers?
- What does the law say about providing education for students with disabilities? What are the major issues in their education?

*This chapter was revised by Dan Levine.

Desegregation

Desegregation and integration

Desegregation of schools is the practice of enrolling students of different racial groups in the same schools. **Integration** generally means more: not only that students of different racial groups attend schools together but also that effective steps are taken to accomplish two of the underlying purposes of desegregation: (1) overcoming the achievement deficit and other disadvantages of minority students and (2) developing positive interracial relationships. During the past five decades, attention has turned increasingly from mere desegregation to integration, with the goal of providing equal and effective educational opportunity for students of all backgrounds. However, we have much to do to fully achieve either of these goals.

A Brief History of Segregation in American Education

Discrimination and oppression by race were deeply embedded in our national institutions from their very beginnings. The U.S. Constitution, for example, provided for representation of the free population but allowed only three-fifths representation for "all other persons," generally meaning slaves. ("Representation" refers to distribution of seats in the U.S. House of Representatives.) In most of the South before the Civil War, it was a crime to teach a slave to read and write.

Slavery and the Constitution

Segregated facilities

After the Civil War, the Thirteenth, Fourteenth, and Fifteenth Amendments to the Constitution attempted to extend rights of citizenship irrespective of race. During Reconstruction, African Americans made some gains, but, after 1877, legislative action segregated blacks throughout the South and in other parts of the country. They were required to attend separate schools, were barred from competing with whites for good employment, and were denied the right to vote.[1] Victimized by these so-called Jim Crow laws, African Americans were required to use separate public services and facilities (for instance, transportation, recreation, restrooms, and drinking fountains) and frequently had no access at all to private facilities such as hotels, restaurants, and theaters. Many were lynched or severely beaten by members of the Ku Klux Klan and other extremist associations.

Asian Americans, Latinos, Native Americans, and some other minority groups experienced similar, though generally less virulent, discriminatory practices. For

---

[1]In this chapter, the term *whites* refers to non-Hispanic whites, that is, citizens not classified as members of a racial or ethnic minority group for the purposes of school desegregation.

Bettmann/Corbis

Since 1957, when the National Guard escorted African American students to a formerly all-white public high school in Little Rock, Arkansas, considerable progress has been made in desegregating the country's public schools in medium-sized cities and towns in rural areas.

example, some states excluded Chinese Americans by law from many well-paid jobs and required their children to attend separate schools.[2]

Separate, unequal schools

On any measure of equality, schools provided for African Americans seldom equaled schools attended by whites. As an example, in the early 1940s, school officials in Mississippi spent $52.01 annually per student in white schools but only $7.36 per student in black schools. In many cases, African American students had to travel long distances at their own expense to attend the nearest black school, and, in many instances, black senior high schools were a hundred miles or more away from a black student's home.[3]

Legal suits challenged segregation in elementary and secondary schools in the early 1950s. The first to be decided by the U.S. Supreme Court was a case in which lawyers for Linda Brown asked that she be allowed to attend white schools in Topeka, Kansas. Attacking the legal doctrine that schools could be "separate but equal," the plaintiffs argued that segregated schools were inherently inferior, even if they provided equal expenditures because forced attendance at a separate school automatically informed African American students that they were second-class citizens and thus destroyed many students' motivation to succeed in school and in society. In May 1954, in a unanimous

The *Brown* case

decision that forever changed U.S. history, the Supreme Court ruled in *Brown v. Board of Education* that "the doctrine of separate but equal has no place" in public education. Such segregation, the Court said, deprived people of the equal protection of the laws guaranteed by the Fourteenth Amendment.[4]

Effects of the *Brown* decision soon were apparent in many areas of U.S. society, including employment, voting, and all publicly supported services. After Mrs. Rosa

---

[2]Gwen Kin Kead, "Chinatown-1," *New Yorker,* June 10, 1991, pp. 45–83; Greg Barrios, "Walkout in Crystal City," *Teaching Tolerance* (Spring 2009), available at **www.tolerance.org**; and Collin Tong, "Lessons from Infamy," 2011 posting by Crosscut, available at **www.crosscut.com**.
[3]National Research Council, *Common Destiny* (Washington, D.C.: National Academy Press, 1989); Peter McCormick, "How a Band of High School Students Influenced Desegregation," *Brown Quarterly* (Winter 2009), available at **www.brownvboard.org**; and Kern Alexander and David M. Alexander, *American Public School Law,* 8th ed. (Belmont, CA: Wadsworth, 2012).
[4]William L. Taylor, "The Role of Social Science in School Desegregation Efforts," *Journal of Negro Education* (Summer 1998), pp. 196–203; and Cobolsky, "Featured U.S Supreme Court Case that Helped Shape the United States," 2011 posting by Lawinfo.com, available at **www.blog.lawinfo.com**.

Parks refused in December 1955 to sit at the back of a bus in Montgomery, Alabama, protests against segregation were launched in many parts of the country. Dr. Martin Luther King Jr. and other civil rights leaders emerged to challenge deep-seated patterns of racial discrimination. Fierce opposition to civil rights demonstrations made the headlines in the late 1950s and early 1960s as dogs and fire hoses were sometimes used to disperse peaceful demonstrators. After three civil-rights workers were murdered in Mississippi, the U.S. Congress passed the 1964 Civil Rights Act and other legislation that attempted to guarantee equal protection of the laws for minority citizens.[5]

Initial reaction among local government officials to the *Brown* decision was frequently negative. The Supreme Court's 1955 *Brown II* ruling that school desegregation should proceed with "all deliberate speed" met massive resistance in much of the United States. This resistance took such forms as delaying reassignment of African American students to white schools, opening private schools with tuition paid by public funds, gerrymandering school boundary lines to increase segregation, suspending or repealing compulsory attendance laws, and closing desegregated schools. In 1957, Arkansas governor Orval Faubus refused to allow school officials at Central High in Little Rock to admit five African American students, and President Dwight Eisenhower called out the National Guard to escort the students to school. As of 1963, only 2 percent of African American students in the South were attending school with whites.

The Progress of Desegregation Efforts

After the early 1960s, school districts in medium-sized cities and towns and in rural areas made considerable progress in combating both **de jure segregation** (segregation resulting from laws, government actions, or school policies specifically designed to bring about separation) and **de facto segregation** (segregation resulting from housing patterns rather than from laws or policies). In response to court orders, school officials have reduced African American attendance in racially isolated minority schools (often defined as either 50 percent or more minority, or 90 percent or more minority).[6] As shown in Figure 12.1, the national percentage of African American students attending schools with an enrollment consisting of 90 percent or more minority decreased from 64 percent in 1969 to 33 percent in 1988. (Progress was greatest in the South, where the percentage of African American students in schools 90 percent or more minority decreased from 78 percent in 1969 to less than 35 percent early in the 1980s.) However, this improvement was not entirely sustained: the percentage of African American students in schools with an enrollment consisting of 90 percent or more minorities increased from 33 percent to nearly 40 percent between 1988 and 2011.[7]

For Hispanic students, however, the percentage attending predominantly minority schools has increased since 1969 (see Figure 12.1). In that year, 23 percent of Latinos attended schools with an enrollment consisting of more than 90 percent minority; by 2011, more than one-third of Latino students attended such schools. This trend reflects the movement of Latino people into inner-city communities in large urban areas, particularly the migration of Mexicans into cities in Arizona, California, and

---

[5]Brian Willoughby, "Brown v. Board," *Teaching Tolerance* (Spring 2004), available at **www.tolerance.org**; Marian S. Holmes, "The Freedom Riders," *Smithsonian* (February 2009), available at **www.smithsonian.org**; and "The Whole World Was Watching," 2011 posting by The Menil Collection, available at **www.menil.org**.

[6]The term *minority* in this context refers to African Americans, Asians, Latinos, Native Americans, and several other smaller racial or ethnic groups as defined by the federal government. In 2010, the government began counting students as "multiracial" if they or their parents choose this category when asked to designate race/ethnicity.

[7]Gary Orfield and Erica Frankenberg, "Where Are We Now?" *Teaching Tolerance* (Spring 2004), available at **www.tolerance.org**; and Kristin Senty, "Measuring School Segregation," 2011 posting by Iowa State University, available at **www.econ.iastate.edu**.

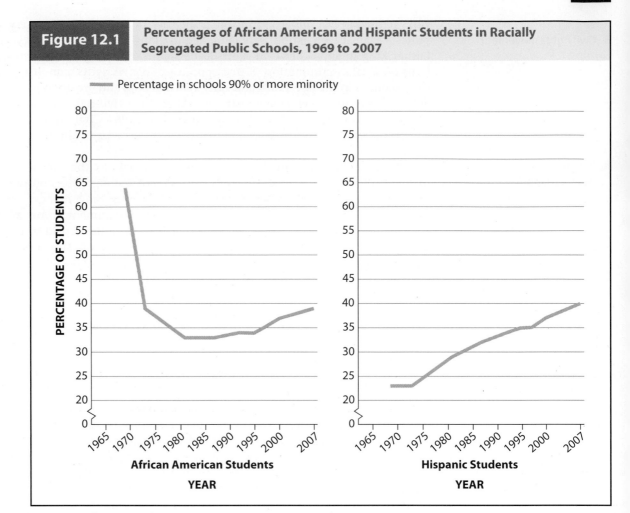

Figure 12.1 Percentages of African American and Hispanic Students in Racially Segregated Public Schools, 1969 to 2007

Source: Data adapted from Gary Orfield and Chungmei Lee, "Racial Transformation and the Changing Nature of Segregation," 2006 paper prepared for the Harvard University Civil Rights Project; and Gary Orfield, "Reviving the Goal of an Integrated Society," 2009 paper prepared for The Civil Rights Project/Proyecto Derechos Civiles at the University of California at Los Angeles, available at **www.civilrightsproject.ucla.edu**.

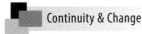

Continuity & Change

Big-city segregation remains

Middle-class withdrawal

Texas, and of Puerto Ricans into New Jersey, New York, Chicago, and other eastern and midwestern cities.[8]

At the same time that small-town and rural districts have significantly desegregated, segregation in large metropolitan regions has increased. A main cause has been increasingly pronounced housing segregation in those areas. Today, the large majority of public-school students in big cities such as Atlanta, Chicago, Detroit, New York, and Philadelphia are minority students, and most attend predominantly minority schools. A major stumbling block to desegregation of schools has been the desire of most whites, and of many minority parents, to maintain neighborhood schools. Highly segregated residential patterns in most metropolitan areas produce highly segregated neighborhood schools.

In many instances, predominantly minority neighborhoods also have high poverty rates and rank extremely low in socioeconomic status. Opposition to desegregation is strong in school districts where a high percentage of minority students are from low-income families. As noted in Chapter 11, Social Class, Race, and School Achievement, schools in

---

[8]Gary Orfield and Erica Frankenberg, "The Last Have Become First," 2008 paper prepared for The Civil Rights Project, available at **www.civilrightsproject.ucla.edu**; and William H. Frey, "Census Shows Challenge of America's Children," 2011 posting by the Brookings Institution, available from **www.brookings.edu**.

these neighborhoods struggle with the effects of concentrated poverty, and most have failed to provide effective education. White parents and middle-class parents generally are quick to withdraw their children from schools in which desegregation has substantially increased the proportion of low-income students. The net result is that city school districts and schools have become increasingly low income and minority in their student composition.[9]

In the 1990s and 2000s, many school districts ceased all or part of the desegregation plans they had introduced in previous decades. They cited various reasons for their decisions:

Trend toward cessation

- Some urban districts had predominantly minority enrollment in all their schools and found it difficult or impossible to maintain desegregated schools even with substantial student busing.

- In some districts, courts ruled that the district had accomplished enough to overcome discriminatory effects attributable to the original constitutional violations.

- In other districts, public and school officials concluded that desegregation efforts did little to actually help minority students.

- In 2007, the Supreme Court ruled that school districts could no longer use race as the sole or major factor in devising a desegregation plan.

Desegregation Plans

Components of desegregation plans

Plans to accomplish desegregation usually involve one or more of the following actions:

- Alter attendance areas to include a more desegregated population.

- Establish **magnet schools**—schools that use specialized programs and personnel to attract students throughout a school district.

- Bus students involuntarily to desegregated schools.

- Pair schools, bringing two schools in adjacent areas together in one larger zone. For example, School A enrolls all students from grades 1 through 4; School B enrolls all students from grades 5 through 8.

- Allow **controlled choice**, a system in which students may select the school they want to attend as long as such choice does not result in segregation.

- Provide voluntary transfer of city students to suburban schools.

Milwaukee as a desegregation example

Means such as these at least temporarily led to substantial school desegregation in many small or medium-sized cities. A good example is Milwaukee. At a time when African American students made up approximately 40 percent of the city's school population, Milwaukee increased the number of its desegregated schools (defined as 25 to 50 percent black) from 14 in 1976 to 101 in 1978. Most of this increase was achieved through (1) establishing magnet schools, (2) implementing a voluntary city-suburban transfer plan, and (3) redrawing school boundaries. The number of desegregated students fell greatly when the city-suburban program ended, but the pattern illustrates what voluntary desegregation might accomplish in all but the largest, most segregated cities. Inter-district magnet schools are being operated in several metropolitan areas.[10]

---

[9]Barry A. Gold, *Still Separate and Unequal* (New York: Teachers College Press, 2007); Beth Tarasawa, "New Patterns of Segregation," *Southern Spaces*, January 19, 2009, available at **www.southernspaces.org**; and Julianne Hins, "Still Separate and Unequal, Generations After Brown v. Board," 2011 posting by Color Lines, available at **www.colorlines.com**.

[10]Robert S. Peterkin, "What's Happening in Milwaukee?" *Educational Leadership* (January 1991), pp. 50–52; Thomas Pettigrew, "Justice Deferred," *American Psychologist* (September 2004), pp. 521–529; and Douglas N. Harris, "Lost Learning, Forgotten Promises," 2006 paper prepared for the Center for American Progress, available at **www.americanprogress.org**. See also Dana Goldstein, "Across District Lines," *American Prospect* (June 2009), available at **www .prospect.org**; and Aida Tefera et al., *Integrating Suburban Schools* (Los Angeles: Civil Rights Project, 2011), available at **www.civilrightsproject.ucla.edu**.

| | Large central-city districts—especially those with 50 percent or higher minority enrollment—find desegregated schooling extremely difficult to attain. For example, in a big city with 80 percent minority students, action to eliminate predominantly single-race schools may involve hour-long bus rides and transporting students from one largely minority school to another. For these and similar reasons, desegregation plans in many big cities generally concentrate on trying to improve the quality of instruction. |

■ Big-city obstacles

■ Emphasizing quality of instruction

■ Magnet schools

Large central-city districts—especially those with 50 percent or higher minority enrollment—find desegregated schooling extremely difficult to attain. For example, in a big city with 80 percent minority students, action to eliminate predominantly single-race schools may involve hour-long bus rides and transporting students from one largely minority school to another. For these and similar reasons, desegregation plans in many big cities generally concentrate on trying to improve the quality of instruction.

According to research, even large and heavily segregated cities can produce more desegregation by expanding magnet schools than through large-scale, involuntary busing that transports students to predominantly minority schools. The most frequently used themes include arts, business, foreign languages, health professions, international studies, Montessori early childhood, science and mathematics, and technology. Districts that operate or have operated a substantial number of magnet schools include Buffalo, Dallas, Houston, Jacksonville, and Minneapolis.[11] The Taking Issue box explores the effectiveness of magnet schools.

Nonblack Minorities

■ What is a minority group?

Another aspect of desegregation that deserves special attention is the status of non-black minority groups. Depending on regional and local circumstances and court precedents, various racial minority groups may or may not be counted as minority for the purposes of school desegregation. For example, in the 1970s, the courts determined that Mexican American students in the Southwest were victims of the same kinds of discrimination as were African American students. However, in some cities, the courts did not explicitly designate Mexican American and other Latino students to participate as minorities in a desegregation plan, even though many or most attend predominantly minority schools.[12]

Movement to Charter Schools Reinforcing Segregation

As we describe in Chapter 16, School Effectiveness and Reform in the United States, and elsewhere in this book, charter schools are public schools that are released from some state or local regulations regarding teachers' credentials and dismissals, staff unionization, hours of operation, enrollment restrictions, or other matters. They can be authorized by school boards or by outside agencies such as for-profit consulting firms. By 2012, more than 5,000 charter schools had been established, enrolling more than 1.5 million students. A majority of charters have been created in urban areas, often in big cities where achievement is low and officials hope to reform unsuccessful practices. In some big cities, such as Kansas City and New Orleans, there are now more charters than regular public schools.[13]

Elsewhere in this book, we discuss charters' success (or lack of success) in improving student outcomes. Here we should acknowledge that many are small schools that enroll mostly low-income minority students who are potential dropouts; as such, they may be as segregated or even more segregated than the regular schools they came from.

---

[11]Christine H. Rossell, "The Desegregation Efficiency of Magnet Schools," *Urban Affairs Review* (May 2003); "Report Explores Educational Consequences of Segregation," *American School Board Journal* (February 2007); "Creating and Sustaining Successful K–8 Magnet Schools," 2008 WestEd report prepared for the U.S. Department of Education, available at **www.ed.gov**; and Genevieve Siegel-Hawley and Erica Frankenberg, "Magnet School Student Outcomes," *Research Brief of the National Council on School Diversity* (No. 6, 2011).

[12]However, federal data collection activities are standardized and have required that student enrollments be reported separately for the following groups: "Black," "American Indian," "Spanish-Surnamed American," "Portuguese," "Asian," "Alaskan Natives," "Hawaiian Natives," and "Non-Minority."

[13]Jim Horn, "Charter Schools," 2011 posting by Schools Matter, available at **www .schoolsmatter.info**; and Corey G. Johnson, "Charter Schools Perpetuating Racial Segregation," 2011 posting by California Watch, available at **www.californiawatch.org**.

TAKING ISSUE

Read the brief introduction below, as well as the Question and the pros and cons list that follows. Then, answer the question using your own words and position.

Magnet Schools and Desegregation

In recent years, many city school districts have established desegregation plans that rely in part on magnet schools. Magnet schools offer a specialized program in a particular field of interest to attract students from all parts of a city or region, thereby creating a mix of ethnic and racial groups. Critics have argued, however, that magnet schools often cause more problems than they solve.

Question

Are magnet schools an effective means of promoting desegregation and achieving related school-improvement goals? (Think about this question as you read the PRO and CON arguments listed here. What is *your* take on this issue?)

Arguments PRO

1. Research in various cities has shown that a coordinated plan involving magnet schools can lead to substantial gains in desegregation. Milwaukee and Buffalo, for example, are using magnet schools effectively.

2. Magnet schools' specialized, high-level programs attract middle-class and college-bound students to the public-school system, thus helping reverse the white, middle-class exodus that has long plagued desegregation efforts.

3. In addition to attracting various ethnic and racial groups, magnet schools create a mixture of socioeconomic classes. Working-class and middle-class students gather in a setting that encourages beneficial socialization.

4. Concentration of resources allows magnet schools to offer a better education than a system of nonspecialized schools. Most important, they make this high-quality education available to everyone, regardless of racial, social background, or cultural background.

5. As students gain recognition for academic excellence at the magnet schools, community pride will grow. The schools will become a means of promoting community identity, bringing together all races and classes in a common endeavor.

Arguments CON

1. Only limited evidence supports the idea that magnet schools make a significant contribution to desegregation. Because magnets frequently are expensive to develop and maintain, they may well become unjustifiable financial burdens for school districts.

2. Magnets often drain away the best students, leaving other public schools in the district with high concentrations of low achievers. These other schools find it increasingly difficult to maintain teacher and student morale and deliver a good education.

3. Converting a local school into a magnet has sometimes led to increased tension between socioeconomic groups. Local students distrust the "outsiders" (generally of a different social class) who come into the neighborhood to attend the school.

4. Many magnet schools are in fact not for everyone. Instead, they are selective: students must meet certain achievement standards to be admitted. Thus low-achieving students—the ones most in need of help— are less likely to benefit from magnet schools than are other students.

5. Their elitist nature prevents magnet schools from fostering a sense of community. They are more likely to provoke resentment among parents whose children are excluded—especially when taxes are raised to support the magnet program.

Question Reprise: What Is Your Stand?

Reflect again on the following question by explaining *your* stand about this issue: Are magnet schools an effective means of promoting desegregation and achieving related school-improvement goals?

Yet there generally has not been as much public concern about their segregated status as there has been for racial and economic isolation in regular public schools.

The situation is further complicated by the relatively large number of Asian American groups in many big cities. With a rapidly growing population of Filipino, Korean, and Vietnamese students added to the many students of Chinese and Japanese ancestry, city school districts face considerable uncertainty in devising multiethnic desegregation plans. The court order for San Francisco, for example, required multiethnic enrollment and busing of four groups: Asian American, African American, Hispanic, and non-Hispanic white.

Difficult issues

Questions regarding the desegregation of nonblack minority groups might multiply in the future as more Asian and Latino students move into many localities. Many of these students need bilingual services, which are easiest to deliver to a group of students together. Grouping them together, however, will conflict with desegregation goals that emphasize dispersal and multiethnic enrollment.

Effects on Student Performance and Attitudes

Inconsistent data

To what extent do students benefit from integrated schools? The voluminous research on this subject is somewhat contradictory. Some studies show a positive relationship between desegregation and academic achievement, but other studies show little or no relationship. Several analysts have concluded that desegregation seldom detracts from the performance of white students and frequently contributes to achievement among minority students. Achievement among low-income minority students is most likely to improve when they attend schools with middle-income nonminority students. This can only happen, however, when desegregation plans are well implemented and schools take substantial action to improve the effectiveness of instruction.[14]

Importance of implementation

What about students' attitudes toward people from other racial and ethnic groups? As with achievement, some data show that desegregation has positive effects on interracial attitudes, while other studies indicate no effect or even a negative effect. Positive intergroup relationships develop only if desegregation is implemented well and if educators promote equal-status contact between minority and nonminority students.

Studies on students' aspirations are much more consistent, indicating that desegregation frequently improves the educational aspirations and college enrollment of minority students by making those aspirations more realistic and better informed. Several studies also indicate that desegregated schooling helps minority students enter the mainstream network of social and cultural contacts useful for success in later life.[15]

Implications for minority students at poverty schools

The complexities of desegregation and its effects on achievement and attitudes leave many people perplexed: What does desegregation imply for minority students who attend predominantly minority, low-achieving schools in low-income neighborhoods? Assigning such students to a desegregated school with a substantially higher percentage of high-achieving students places them in a potentially much less

---

[14]Ronald A. Krol, "A Meta Analysis of the Effects of Desegregation on Academic Achievement," *Urban Review* (December 1980), pp. 211–224; Daniel U. Levine, "Desegregation," in Torsten Husen and T. Neville Postlethwaite, eds., *International Encyclopedia of Education,* 3rd ed. (Oxford: Pergamon, 1994), pp. 1483–1486; Richard D. Kahlenberg, "The New Brown," *Legal Affairs* (May–June 2003), available at **www.legalaffairs.org**; Richard Kahlenberg, "Race, Class and Education," 2006 presentation prepared for the Century Foundation, available at **www.tcf.org**; Richard D. Kahlenberg, "The New Look of School Integration," *American Prospect* (June 2, 2008), available at **www.prospect.org**; and Jamelle Bouie, "The Sad Return to Segregated Schools in Raleigh, N.C." *American Prospect,* January 12, 2011, available at **www.prospect.org**.
[15]Janet Schofield, "School Desegregation and Intergroup Relations," in Gerald Grant, ed., *Review of Research in Education* 17 (Washington, D.C.: American Education Research Association, 1991), pp. 335–412; Richard D. Kahlenberg, "Back to Class," *American Prospect* (January/ February 2007), available at **www.prospect.org**; and Philip Tegeler, Roslyn A. Mickelson, and Martha Bottia, "What We Know about School Integration, College Attendance, and the Reduction of Poverty," 2010 posting by Spotlight on Poverty and Opportunity, available at **www.spotlightonpoverty.org**.

dysfunctional educational environment. Provided that they receive appropriate support and teaching, their academic performance can substantially improve. We emphasize elsewhere—particularly in Chapter 16, School Effectiveness and Reform in the United States—that some high-poverty schools are unusually successful and that many more should be equally successful. Until that happens, effective instruction at desegregated schools is an important alternative for helping low-achieving minority students.

Characteristics of well-desegregated schools

Unfortunately, only a few studies focus on schools in which desegregation seems to have worked. One of the most comprehensive of such studies evaluated the Emergency School Aid Act, which provided hundreds of millions of dollars between 1972 and 1982 to facilitate desegregation. This study indicated that desegregation aided African American students' achievement in schools in which (1) resources were focused on attaining goals, (2) administrative leadership was outstanding, (3) parents were more heavily involved in the classroom, and (4) staff systematically promoted positive interracial attitudes.[16]

Moral and political imperatives

Despite the mixed evidence, perhaps the most compelling reasons for integration are moral and political. Morally, our national education policy must reflect a commitment to American ideals of equality. Politically, two separate societies, separately educated, cannot continue to exist in America without serious harm to the body politic.

Compensatory Education

Another aspect of our nation's commitment to equal educational opportunity is the **compensatory education** movement, which has sought to overcome (that is, compensate for) disadvantaged background and thereby improve the performance of low-achieving students, particularly those from low-income families. Stimulated in part by the civil rights movement in the 1960s, compensatory education was expanded and institutionalized as part of President Lyndon Johnson's War on Poverty.

Title I

The Elementary and Secondary Education Act (ESEA), passed in 1965, among other provisions immediately provided $1 billion to improve the education of economically disadvantaged children. (A disadvantaged student was defined as a student from a family below the government's official poverty line.) The moneys are known as **Title I** funds, named after the portion of the ESEA that describes them. The federal government distributes the funds to the states, which, along with school districts, identify schools with sufficient disadvantaged students to receive a share. More than $200 billion were spent on Title I between 1965 and 2012. By 2009, Title I funding of more than $14 billion annually provided assistance to more than five million students, and many additional students participated in other compensatory programs. Schools and districts use the money to establish substantial compensatory education programs that provide tutoring, longer school days, early childhood learning, instructional technology, and many other services and activities. Some of the important services and activities of compensatory education are listed next. The Technology @ School box also tells you how to learn more about successful Title I schools.

Compensatory education services

1. *Parental involvement and support.* Programs have ranged from helping parents learn to teach their children to improving family functioning and parents' employability.

2. *Early childhood education.* **Head Start** and **Follow Through** have been the largest programs of this kind. Head Start generally attempts to help disadvantaged

[16]J. E. Coulson, *National Evaluation of the Emergency School Aid Act* (Washington, D.C.: System Development Corporation, 1976). See also Janet W. Schofield and Leslie R. M. Hausmann, "School Desegregation and Social Science Research," *American Psychologist* (September 2004), pp. 536–546; Richard D. Kahlenberg, "Middle-Class Schools for All," *Democracy* (Spring 2008), available at **www.democracyjournal.org**; and Susan Eaton and Steven Rivkin, "Is Desegregation Dead?" *Education Digest* (February 2011), pp. 24–31.

TECHNOLOGY @ SCHOOL

An Internet Site about Successful Title I Schools

Go to www2.ed.gov/PDFdocs/urbaned.pdf to read a study of "high-performing, high-poverty" urban schools. Select a school from the list, and read the description of developments and outcomes at the school. As you read, ask yourself the following questions:

■ What seems to have improved achievement the most?

■ Are the described practices "transportable," that is, easy to use at other schools?

■ How were special education and/or bilingual programs and teachers involved?

■ How were Title I funds spent?

■ Would you want to teach at this school?

You might also want to share your conclusions and material with classmates who selected other schools.

---

four- and five-year-olds achieve readiness for the first grade. Follow Through concentrated on improving achievement in the primary grades.

3. *Reading, language, and math instruction.* Most Title I projects have concentrated on improvement in reading, language, and math.

4. *Bilingual education.* Latino children constitute the largest group in bilingual programs, but programs have been provided in more than sixty languages. Bilingual programs are discussed in the following section on multicultural education.

5. *Guidance, counseling, and social services.* Various psychological and social services have been provided for disadvantaged students.

6. *Dropout prevention.* Services that include vocational and career education have aimed at keeping students from dropping out of school.

7. *Personnel training.* Many preservice and in-service training programs have been funded to help teachers improve instruction.

8. *After-school programs.* These provide academic-improvement services or general enrichment activities, or both.

9. *Computer laboratories and networks.* In recent years, compensatory funds have helped many schools establish computer laboratories and in-school networks.

Early Childhood Compensatory Education

Discouraging early results

During the first decade of compensatory education, most interventions appeared to be relatively ineffective in raising student achievement levels and cognitive development. Despite the expenditure of billions of dollars per year, students generally were not making long-range academic gains.

Improved procedures and funding

This discouraging start led to corrections. The federal and state governments improved monitoring procedures, required more adequate evaluation, and sponsored studies to improve compensatory education. Some states also began to provide additional money for compensatory programs. By the early 1980s, research suggested that compensatory education in preschool and the primary grades could indeed improve the cognitive development and performance of disadvantaged students.[17]

---

[17]Thomas W. Fagan and Camilla A. Heid, "Chapter 1 Program Improvement," *Phi Delta Kappan* (April 1991), pp. 582–585; and Nancy Korber, Jennifer McMurrer, and Malini R. Silva, "State Test Score Trends," 2011 report prepared for the Center on Education Policy, available at **www.cep-dc.org**.

Exemplary early childhood programs

In particular, several studies of outstanding early childhood education programs demonstrated that such efforts can have a long-lasting effect if they are well conceived and effectively implemented. Positive long-range achievement results have been reported for disadvantaged students in outstanding preschool programs in Ypsilanti, Michigan; Syracuse, New York; and several other locations. Compared with nonparticipants, students who participate in such programs are less likely to be placed later in special education or to repeat grades (both costly). Participants are also more likely to graduate from high school and to acquire the skills and motivation needed for rewarding employment, thereby increasing tax revenues and reducing reliance on public assistance.[18]

Overall pluses and minuses

These impressive results, however, usually come from programs that researchers consider exemplary. Most preschool programs have been less well funded or less well implemented and have produced fewer gains. In general, Title I programs still fail to ensure that most low-achieving students will acquire the academic and intellectual skills necessary to obtain good jobs in a modern economy.

Comprehensive Ecological Intervention

Importance of early family environment

Educators face great difficulty working to overcome the extreme disadvantages of students who grow up in particularly harmful environments, such as concentrated poverty neighborhoods. For this reason, policy makers and educators increasingly support **ecological intervention**—comprehensive efforts to improve the home and neighborhood environment of young children.[19]

Features of successful programs

Advocates of ecological intervention point to research on the important cognitive development that occurs during infancy, as well as to the frequently disappointing results of Head Start interventions that do not begin until age four or five. Comprehensive psychological, social, and economic support can be successful, the research indicates, if it begins when children are younger than two or three years old. Some effective programs of this type enroll young children in educationally oriented day care or preschool classes. The successful programs also typically include nutrition and health care, as well as counseling on parenting. Some particularly comprehensive programs also include assistance in obtaining adequate housing, improvement of neighborhood services involving community centers and public safety, and close coordination among educational institutions ranging from preschool to the postsecondary level. Examples of such programs that are beginning to report positive results include the Harlem Children's Zone and the Purpose-Built Communities efforts described in Chapter 16, School Effectiveness and Reform in the United States.[20]

Standards & Assessment

The No Child Left Behind Act

Reauthorization of ESEA

In 2001, Congress reauthorized the ESEA and Title I but, in so doing, established sweeping new requirements for all elementary and secondary schools. The revised law,

---

[18]W. Steven Barnett and Colette M. Escobar, "The Economics of Early Educational Intervention," *Review of Educational Research* (Winter 1987), pp. 387–414; W. Steven Barnett and Clive R. Belfield, "Early Childhood Development and Social Mobility," *The Future of Children* (Fall 2006), available at **www.futureofchildren.org**; Douglas Besharov and Craig Ramey, "Preschool Puzzle," *Education Next* (Fall 2008), available at **www.educationnext.org**; and James J. Heckman, "The Economics of Inequality," *American Educator* (Spring 2011), available at **www.aft.org**.
[19]Lisbeth Schorr, *Within Our Reach* (New York: Anchor Doubleday, 1989); Richard Colvin, "Minding Young Minds," *Education Sector,* March 8, 2007, available at **www.educationsector.org**; Paul Tough, "Learning Zone," *Edutopia*, November 19, 2008, available at **www.edutopia.org**; and Arthur J. Reynolds et al., "Cost-Benefit Analysis of the Chicago Child-Parent Center Early Education Program," *Child Development* (January–February 2011), pp. 379–404.
[20]National Commission on Children, *Beyond Rhetoric* (Washington, D.C.: U.S. Government Printing Office, 1991); Susan B. Neuman, "The Science of What Works to Change the Odds for Children at Risk," *Phi Delta Kappan* (April 2009), pp. 582–587; M. Angela Nievar et al., "Impact of HIPPY on Home Learning Environments of Latino Families," *Early Childhood Research Quarterly* (September 2011), pp. 268–277; and information available from the National Institute for Early Education Research at **www.nieer.org**.

known as the **No Child Left Behind Act (NCLB)**, has affected not only schools that receive Title I funding, but nearly all public schools. In addition to policies described in our discussion of rules for teachers in Chapter 1, Motivation, Preparation, and Conditions for the Entering Teacher, NCLB includes regulations in the following key areas:[21]

Challenging standards and annual tests

Standards and testing. States and school districts are required to develop challenging academic content and achievement standards for all students in reading/language arts, mathematics, and science, with the goal of having all students attain proficiency by the 2013–2014 school year. To assess progress toward these standards, states must test students, including annual tests for students in grades 3–8 in reading/language arts and mathematics, and at least two tests for students in grades 9–12. At least 95 percent of students overall and in each special-needs subgroup (see the next listed item) must be tested.

Disaggregated data

Students with special needs. The performance of different special-needs subgroups of students (including English Language Learner [ELL] students, students with disabilities, poverty students, and racial/ethnic minorities) must be *disaggregated,* that is, reported separately from the total for all students at a school.

Schools needing improvement

Adequate yearly progress. A key provision of NCLB is that all schools and districts must make **adequate yearly progress (AYP)** toward their 2013–2014 goals. Schools and districts that fail to make sufficient progress are designated as "needing improvement." The school is identified as needing improvement if the school as a whole or any disaggregated subgroup has achievement scores below those the state government has determined are required in moving forward to meet its 2013–2014 goals. Because many schools compile scores for fifty or more subgroups, it is easy for a school to be identified as needing improvement.

Supplemental services and restructuring

Schools needing improvement are to receive special help from their district or state, such as consultants, professional development, or other additional resources. Students at Title I schools needing improvement also are to receive "supplemental services" such as tutoring, after-school help, or summer school. If, after several years, a school still fails to meet yearly progress goals, its students are eligible to transfer to another public school in the district. Still further failure to make adequate progress subjects schools to "corrective action" or "restructuring," which may include replacing all or part of the faculty and administration, conversion to charter-school status, or takeover by an outside organization, along with a variety of instructional and curricular innovations selected by a school or district.[22]

Confusion and uncertainty

Variation in defining proficiency

States, school districts, teachers, students, and parents have all experienced a great deal of confusion and uncertainty concerning how to implement NCLB requirements. (The NCLB involves nearly seven hundred pages of law and thousands of pages of regulations.) Part of the confusion involves the fact that states create their own definitions of most terms and concepts in the legislation. States not only decide which skills and concepts are tested and which tests are administered but also define what is considered proficient or acceptable achievement. These definitions vary widely from state to state and even within states. For example, one study indicated that eighth graders with the same skills would be at the thirty-sixth percentile in Montana but the eighty-ninth percentile in Wyoming. The same study showed that in Washington, the fourth-grade

---

[21]Diane Ravitch and John Chubb, "The Future of No Child Left Behind," *Education Next* (Spring 2009), available at **www.educationnext.org**; Abby Rapoport, "The Coming Battle over NCLB Exemptions," *The American Prospect* (February 2012), available at **www.prospect.org**; and material available at **www.ed.gov/nclb**.
[22]Nancy Kober, "The AYP Blues," *American Educator* (Spring 2005), available at **www.aft.org**; Basha Krasnoff, "Turning around Chronically Underperforming Schools," *Northwest Education* (Summer 2009), available at **www.educationnorthwest.org/edunw-magazine**; and Sarah Karp, "Last-Ditch Efforts Aim to Stop School Closings, Turnarounds," *Catalyst Chicago,* February 21, 2012, available at **www.catalyst-chicago.org**.

proficiency level was set at the fifty-third percentile in reading but at the seventy-sixth percentile in mathematics.[23]

The states also determine what type and how much yearly progress is adequate for schools. Some states define acceptable achievement in terms of closing gaps among different subgroups of students, others in terms of absolute performance levels. But all states were required to specify that all students would be proficient in 2014, and many "back-ended" goals in the sense that rapidly expanding percentages of students would become proficient as 2014 approached. As a result, by 2012, many thousands of schools were classified as not making AYP. Furthermore, officials at the U.S. Department of Education estimated that by 2014, 82 percent of public schools would be deficient with respect to AYP.[24]

The desire to avoid being labeled as failures apparently induced many school officials to try to "game the system," that is, use statistical and organizational manipulations to increase the likelihood that their schools and districts will attain AYP. Many analysts assert that students are hurt by such practices, which include the following:

- Some critics believe that NCLB has frequently resulted in lowering standards and student performance. Several states, for example, have reset scores needed to achieve proficiency at levels lower than before NCLB.

- A subgroup must generally include a minimum of students—say, thirty or fifty—before test scores of those students are counted in determining a school's AYP. This led some school officials to identify fewer students with disabilities to keep this subgroup below the minimum number. Conversely, some districts included students with disabilities in larger subgroups for which their low scores could be masked by the higher scores of nondisabled students. Some schools and districts may be encouraging or facilitating dropouts or transfers among students whose low achievement might detract from AYP status, or the schools/districts may be retaining some students in middle school or the ninth grade if their promotion might damage high schools' classification on AYP.

- Faculty have been reported to be discouraging gifted students from attending special schools or programs elsewhere because their withdrawal would reduce AYP scores.

- Many schools and teachers are thought to be concentrating teaching resources on students with scores near the proficient level and thereby neglecting or reducing efforts to help their lowest and highest achievers.

- Many analysts also believe that more teachers and schools are emphasizing low-level skills of the kind likely to be tested on state assessments since the passage of the NCLB.

Status of NCLB and Movement toward Waivers

Before 2012, the U.S. Department of Education made several relatively small modifications in response to complaints about NCLB regulations. For example, it exempted scores of new ELL students from AYP calculations, and it allowed a few states to experimentally use students' growth in achievement rather than a point-in-time snapshot of students' proficiency status in calculating AYP. But critics remained stridently unhappy. In particular, many observers believe the use of a single paper-and-pencil test encourages teachers to overemphasize rote-learning skills, and many believe that schools are drastically underfunded if they are to meet NCLB requirements. In addition, the prospect of rapid growth in the number of schools classified as making inadequate

[23]G. Gage Kingsbury et al., "The State of State Standards," 2003 report published by the Northwest Evaluation Association, summary available at **www.nwea.org/research/national.asp**; and George Miller, "NCLB," *Education Week*, January 9, 2012.

[24]Stan Karp, "Taming the Beast," *Rethinking Schools* (Summer 2004), available at **www .rethinkingschools.org**; and Michael Muskal, "No Child Left Behind," *Los Angeles Times*, February 9, 2012.

AYP raised the possibility that most schools nationally would be required to engage in significant restructuring, even in the case of otherwise high-achieving schools with only one or a few number of relatively small nonproficient subgroups.

Requirements for waivers

In this context, government officials sought ways to improve NCLB policies and practices. When it became apparent that Congress was unlikely to modify NCLB before 2013, if then, the Department of Education acted to allow states to obtain waivers from NCLB requirements. States receiving waivers are allowed to develop alternate approaches to assess and classify student performance but must also set and meet targets for graduating students and for assuring their career-readiness. States must also create systems for evaluating teachers that go beyond test scores to include such components as principal observation, peer review, student work, and parent and student feedback. Waiver states must continue disaggregating data for subgroups of students and must take action to improve the achievement of low performers, but they are allowed to define larger subgroups partly to increase accountability for students in groups previously too small to trigger AYP sanctions.[25]

Questions about Compensatory Education

Although data collected since the 1980s suggest that compensatory education can help disadvantaged students, many questions remain about its nature and effectiveness:

Ineffective pullout

1. *How can we make Title I more effective?* Research indicates that Title I has been relatively ineffective in many schools partly because most programs have used a **pullout approach**—that is, they take low achievers out of regular classes for supplementary reading or math instruction. Pullout approaches generally have struggled because they tend to generate much movement of students and therefore confusion throughout the school.

Recent improvements

In recent years, federal legislation, including NCLB, has made it much easier to replace Title I pullout with school-wide approaches that allow for coordinated, in-class assistance for low achievers. In addition, organizational changes such as Response to Intervention (described later in the "The Discrepancy Model, Response to Intervention and Incentives to Mislabel" section) are improving achievement in numerous schools, the Effective Schools model (see Chapter 16, School Effectiveness and Reform in the United States) has produced improved performance in many schools, and expanded staff development has helped teachers learn how to broaden compensatory instruction beyond mechanical subskills. On the other hand, data we cited in Chapter 11, Social Class, Race, and School Achievement, indicate that millions of low-income children continue to achieve at unacceptably low levels.[26]

Behavioristic versus cognitive approaches

2. *What type of early instruction should we provide?* Much uncertainty in early compensatory education surrounds whether programs should use a behavioristic direct-instruction approach, which focuses on basic skills such as decoding of words or simple computation in math, or instead should emphasize conceptual development and abstract thinking skills. Some direct-instruction programs have had excellent results through the third grade, but performance levels often fall when participating children enter the middle grades. Results in cognitive-oriented programs stressing independent learning and thinking skills generally have been less successful in terms of mastery of mechanical skills in the primary grades, but some of the best cognitive approaches have resulted in gains that show up later.[27]

---

[25]Anne C. Lewis, "Think Ahead to Red Penciling," *Phi Delta Kappan* (January 2009), pp. 315–316; and Stan Karp, "NCLB Waivers Give Bad Policy New Lease on Life," 2012 posting at Rethinking Schools Blog, available at **www.rethinkingschoolsblog.wordpress.com**.
[26]John M. Weathers, "Teacher Community in Urban Elementary Schools," *Education Policy Analysis Archives* (Vol. 19, 2011), available at **epaa.asu.edu**.
[27]Sharon L. Kagan, "Early Care and Education," *Phi Delta Kappan* (November 1993), pp. 184–187; Daniel J. Weigel and Sally S. Martin, "Identifying Key Early Literacy and School Readiness Issues," *Early Childhood Research and Practice* (Fall 2006), available at **ccrp.uiuc.edu**; and Jack Snowman, Rick McCown, and Robert Biehler, *Psychology Applied to Teaching*, 13th ed. (Belmont, CA: 2012).

Uncertainty about
secondary schools

3. *What should we do in high schools?* High schools have achieved moderate success in individual classrooms and in "schools within a school," in which a selected group of teachers work intensively with relatively few low-achieving students. However, researchers still know little about the best compensatory approaches for secondary-school students.[28]

Between assimilation and
separation

How Much Can the Schools Accomplish in the Absence of Major Social and Economic Reforms?

In view of the low achievement levels still characteristic of many schools and groups of students, some educators question whether compensatory education by itself can significantly improve a student's chances of succeeding in school and in later life—especially a minority student living in a neighborhood of concentrated poverty. As described in Chapter 11, Social Class, Race, and School Achievement, revisionist critics argue that in the absence of fundamental reforms in society as a whole, U.S. public schools will continue to marginalize disadvantaged students. Thus, some observers believe that we may need to improve low-income parents' economic and social circumstances before their children's school achievement will rise significantly on a widespread basis. It remains to be seen whether efforts to improve education for disadvantaged students carried out in isolation from much larger efforts to improve their families and communities can be sufficiently effective to disprove these skeptics' pessimism.[29]

> **REFOCUS** Do you think you are or will be well prepared to teach students who receive or should receive compensatory services? What might you do to be better prepared?

Multicultural Education

Multicultural goals for all
students

Multicultural education refers to the various ways in which schools can take productive account of cultural differences among students and improve opportunities for students with cultural backgrounds distinct from the U.S. mainstream. Certain aspects of multicultural education focus on improving instruction for students who have not learned Standard English or who have other cultural differences that place them at a disadvantage in traditional classrooms. As a teacher, you should also be concerned with the larger implications of multicultural education that make it valuable for *all* students. By fostering positive intergroup and interracial attitudes and contacts, multicultural education may help all students function in a culturally pluralistic society. (From this point of view, the movement toward desegregation can be considered a part of multicultural education.)

Historical emphasis on
assimilation

Although the U.S. population always has been pluralistic in composition, the emphasis throughout much of our history, as noted in Chapter 4, Pioneers of Teaching and Learning, has been on assimilating diverse ethnic groups into the national mainstream rather than on maintaining group subcultures. In educating diverse groups of immigrants, the public-school system has stressed the development of an American identity. Students learned how Americans were supposed to talk, look, and behave, sometimes in classes of fifty or sixty pupils representing the first or second generation of immigrants from ten or fifteen countries. Although this approach succeeded in "Americanizing" and allowing social mobility for many immigrants, observers have pointed out that African Americans, Asian Americans, Latinos, Native Americans, and

---

[28]Daniel U. Levine, "Educating Alienated Inner City Youth: Lessons from the Street Academies," *Journal of Negro Education* (Spring 1975), pp. 139–149; Emily A. Hassel and Bryan C. Hassel, "The Big U-Turn," *Education Next* (Winter 2009), available at **www.educationnext.org**; and Matthew S. Urdan, "High School Reform," 2011 posting by Inside Government, available at **www.insidegov.org**.

[29]Alex Kotlowitz, "Should We Really Expect Schools to Cure Poverty?" *Reuters*, August 24, 2011, available at **www.reuters.com/search/blog**; and Diane Ravitch, "Schools We Can Envy," *The New York Review of Books*, March 8, 2012, available at **www.nybooks.com**.

Culturally Responsive Teaching: A Multicultural Lesson for Elementary Students

After reading this section, go to the Education CourseMate website to access the video entitled, "Culturally Responsive Teaching: A Multicultural Lesson for Elementary Students." In today's world of high-stakes testing, many teachers find it difficult to find time to weave diversity lessons into the coursework, but in this clip, you'll see how Dr. Hurley, a psychologist, includes a lesson on multiculturalism in a traditional lesson on the five-paragraph essay. After watching this video, answer the following questions:

1 After watching this video and reading the chapter, explain why Dr. Hurley's lesson is a good example of successful multicultural (and multiethnic) instruction.

2 Based on what you read about the goals and aims of multicultural education, what specific skills do you think Dr. Hurley's students gained as a result of participating in this lesson?

** This video reinforces key concepts found in Section III: Communication Techniques of the Praxis II Exam.**

certain European ethnic groups were systematically discriminated against in a manner that revealed the shortcomings of the melting-pot concept.[30]

Valuing diversity

In the 1960s, civil rights leaders fought to reduce the exclusion of minority groups and to shift emphasis from assimilation to diversity and cultural pluralism. In place of the melting-pot metaphor, **cultural pluralism** introduced new metaphors such as "tossed salad" or "mosaic" that allow for distinctive group characteristics within a larger whole. According to the American Association of Colleges for Teacher Education (AACTE), "to endorse cultural pluralism is to endorse the principle that there is no one model American." From this viewpoint, the differences among the nation's citizens are a positive force.[31]

Remember, emphasizing cultural pluralism does not mean you support a philosophy aimed at cultural, social, or economic separation. Depending on how we define cultural pluralism, it may or may not stress integration in cultural, social, or economic matters. Generally, it lies somewhere between total assimilation and strict separation of ethnic or racial groups. Cultural pluralism, particularly in education, is more important than ever before as the United States becomes transformed into what observers call the first "universal nation."

Multicultural Instruction

One key area in multicultural education concerns instructional approaches for teaching students with differing ethnic and racial backgrounds. Several of the most frequently discussed approaches address student learning styles, recognition of dialect differences, bilingual education, and multiethnic curriculum.

---

[30]Min Zhou and Carl L. Bankston III, *Growing Up American* (New York: Russell Sage, 1998); and Suzanne Fields, "A Melting Pot Gone Cold," *Real Clear Politics*, April 22, 2011, available at **www.realclearpolitics.com**.
[31]"No One Model American: A Statement of Multicultural Education" (Washington, D.C.: American Association of Colleges for Teacher Education, 1972), p. 9. See also Christopher Clausen, *Faded Mosaic* (Chicago: Ivan R. Dee, 2000); and Amy Kiley, "Many Nations under God," *U.S. Catholic* (May 2011), pp. 18–22.

Accommodating cultural learning patterns

Student Learning Styles In Chapter 11, Social Class, Race, and School Achievement, we briefly described behavioral patterns and **learning styles** that appear to correlate with students' socioeconomic status and, perhaps, with their race or ethnicity. We also mentioned attempts to modify instruction to accommodate different learning styles. One good example of research on this subject was provided by Vera John-Steiner and Larry Smith, who worked with Pueblo Indian children in the Southwest. They concluded that schooling for these children would be more successful if it emphasized personal communication in tutorial (face-to-face) situations. Other observers of Native American classrooms have reported that achievement rose substantially when teachers interacted with students in culturally appropriate ways (that is, social control was mostly indirect); integrated tribal culture into the curriculum while emphasizing mastery of state standards; and/or avoided putting students in competitive situations. Similarly, several researchers have reported that cooperative learning arrangements are particularly effective with some Mexican American students whose cultural background deemphasizes competition.[32]

Model minority stereotype

Analysts also have examined research on the performance of Asian American students. Several observers believe that certain subgroups of Asian students (for example, Koreans and Vietnamese) tend to be nonassertive in the classroom and that this reluctance to participate may hinder their academic growth, particularly with respect to verbal skills. (However, research suggests that such behavioral patterns diminish or disappear as Asian American students become more assimilated within U.S. society.) In addition, Asian American students can be harmed by a stereotype indicating that they are all part of a model minority who have no serious problems in school.[33]

Black English

Recognition of Dialect Differences Teachers generally have tried to teach so-called proper or Standard English to students who speak nonstandard dialects. Frequently, however, a simplistic insistence on proper English has caused students to reject their own cultural background or else to view the teachers' efforts as demeaning and hostile. In recent years, educators have been particularly concerned with learning problems among students who speak Black English. Some have developed "code-switching" techniques that use students' dialects to provide a bridge to Standard English. But research shows that Black English is not simply a form of slang; it differs systematically from Standard English in grammar and syntax. Because Black English seems to be the basic form of English spoken by many low-income African American students who are floundering academically, educators have proposed that schools use Black English as the language of instruction for these students until they learn to read. Although this approach seems logical, little research has provided support for it.[34]

Ebonics in Oakland

Analysis of the dialect of many African American students (that is, Black English) frequently is referred to as **Ebonics**. An important controversy regarding Ebonics and its possible use in improving instruction for African American students arose in

[32]Vera John-Steiner and Larry Smith, "The Educational Promise of Cultural Pluralism," 1978 paper prepared for the National Conference on Urban Education, St. Louis, MO: Paulette Running Wolf and Julie A. Rickard, "Talking Circles," *Journal of Multicultural Counseling & Development* (January 2003), pp. 39–43; Bracken Reed, "Finding Success in Indian Country," *Northwest Education* (Winter 2008), available at **www.educationnorthwest.org/edunw-magazine**; and Jean Moule, *Cultural Competence*, 2nd ed. (Belmont, CA: Wadsworth, 2012).

[33]Benji Chang and Wayne Au, "You're Asian, How Could You Fail Math?" *Rethinking Schools* (Winter 2007/2008), available at **www.rethinkingschools.org**; Yong Zhao and Wei Qiu, "How Good Are the Asians?" *Phi Delta Kappan* (January 2009), pp. 338–343; and Helen Gym, "Tiger Mom and the Model Minority Myth," *Rethinking Schools* (Summer 2011), available at **www.rethinkingschools.org**.

[34]J. R. Harber and D. N. Bryan, "Black English and the Teaching of Reading," *Review of Educational Research* (Summer 1976), pp. 397–398; Charles J. Fillmore, "A Linguist Looks at the Ebonics Debate," 1997 posting at the Center for Applied Linguistics site, available at **www.cal.org/ebonics**; Abha Gupta, "What's Up wif Ebonics, Y'All?" 1999 posting at Reading Online, available at **http://readingonline.org/articles/gupta**; "Why Would We Teach Ebonics?" *Filthy Lucre*, January 19, 2009, available at **www.filthylucre.com**; and Owen G. Mordaunt, "Bidialectalism in the Classroom," *Language, Culture and Curriculum* (Issue 1, 2011), pp. 77–87.

1997 after the Oakland, California, school board declared that Black English is a distinctive language. The board requested state and federal bilingual education funds to help teachers use Black English in implementing approaches for improving black students' performance with respect to Standard English and reading. After television sound bites allowed for the interpretation that Oakland schools were abandoning the goal of teaching "good" English, numerous national figures (including Reverend Jesse Jackson) criticized the board for its policies regarding the use of Ebonics in teaching. Although the Linguistic Society of America declared that Oakland's policy was "linguistically and pedagogically sound," the Oakland Board of Education responded by removing terminology involving Ebonics from its policies and setting aside $400,000 for a "Standard English Proficiency" program designed to help teachers understand and build on dialect characteristics in instructing students whose language patterns strongly emphasize Black English.[35]

■ *Lau v. Nichols* requirements

■ Rise of bilingual programs

Bilingual Education   **Bilingual education**, which provides instruction in their native language for students not proficient in English, has been expanding in U.S. public schools as immigration has increased. In 1968, Congress passed the Bilingual Education Act, and, in 1974, the Supreme Court ruled unanimously in *Lau v. Nichols* that the schools must take steps to help students who "are certain to find their classroom experiences wholly incomprehensible" because they do not understand English. Although the federal and state governments fund bilingual projects for more than sixty language groups speaking various Asian, Indo-European, and Native American languages, the majority of children served by these projects are native speakers of Spanish. Overview 12.1 summarizes several approaches for helping children whose first language is not English.

The Supreme Court's unanimous decision in the *Lau* case, which involved Chinese children in San Francisco, did not focus on bilingual education as the only remedy. Instead, the Court said, "Teaching English to the students of Chinese ancestry is one choice. Giving instruction to this group in Chinese is another. There may be others." In practice, early federal regulations for implementing the *Lau* decision tended to focus on bilingual education as the most common solution for ELL students. The regulations generally suggested that school districts initiate bilingual programs if they enrolled more than twenty students of a given language group at a particular grade. Bilingual programs proliferated accordingly. Since 1983, however, the federal government has accepted, and sometimes even encouraged, English-as-a-second-language (ESL) instruction or other nonbilingual approaches for providing help to ELL students.

Researchers agree that ELL students should be given special help in learning to function in the schools. "Submersion" approaches, which simply place ELL students in regular classrooms without any special assistance or modifications in instruction, frequently result in failure to learn. Data collected by the Council of Chief State School Officers and other organizations indicate, moreover, that significant numbers of ELL students are receiving little specialized assistance to help them learn English and other subjects.[36]

---

[35]Wayne O'Neill, "If Ebonics Isn't a Language, Then Tell Me, What Is?" *Rethinking Schools* (Fall 1997), available at **www.rethinkingschools.org**; John H. McWhorter, "Throwing Money at an Illusion," *Black Scholar* (January 1997); Mary E. Flannery, "Yo! From Tupac to the Bard," *NEA Today* (November/December 2008), available at **www.nea.org/neatoday**; G. L. "Do It Be Makin' Sense?" 2010 posting by the *Economist*, available at **www.economist.com**; and James R. Coffey, "The Ebonics (Black Vernacular) Language," 2011 posting by Yahoo, available at **www.associatedcontent.com**.
[36]*Meeting the Needs of Students with Limited English Proficiency* (Washington, D.C.: U.S. Government Accounting Office, 2001); "English-Language Learners," 2004 posting at Education Week Research Center, available at **www.edweek.org/rc/issues**; and Margarita Calderon, Robert Slavin, and Marta Sanchez, "Effective Instruction for English Language Learners," *The Future of Children* (Spring 2011), available at **www.futureofchildren.org**.

OVERVIEW 12.1

Approach	Variations	Pros	Cons
Bilingual Education	First-language maintenance—emphasis on teaching in the native language over a long time	■ Might sustain a constructive sense of identity among ethnic or racial minority students. ■ Can provide a better basis for learning higher-order skills such as reading comprehension while students acquire basic English skills.	■ Requires many speakers of native languages as teachers. ■ Separates groups from one another. ■ Might discourage students from mastering English well enough to function successfully in the larger society.
	Transitional bilingual education (TBE)—providing intensive English instruction and then proceeding to teach all subjects in English as soon as possible.	■ Supported by federal and most state governments. ■ Moves students relatively quickly into regular classes. ■ Requires relatively few native language speakers as teachers.	■ Students may not sufficiently master English before moving to regular classes, hurting their ability to learn other subjects.
	Universal bilingual education—instruction in two languages for all students, native and nonnative English speakers.	■ All students learn more than one language, increasing their competence in a global society.	■ Requires many trained staff members. ■ Expensive to provide adequate materials.
English Language Instruction	Submersion—placing ELL students in regular classrooms with no modifications.	No or little extra cost to school.	Students generally may fail to learn English or other subjects.
	Structured immersion—placement in regular classes with special assistance provided inside and outside of class.		
	Sheltered immersion—using principles of second-language learning in regular classrooms.		

Controversies: How much English, how soon?

Controversies over bilingual education have become increasingly embittered. As in the case of teaching through dialect, arguments erupt between those who would immerse children in an English-language environment and those who believe initial instruction will be more effective in the native language. Educators and laypeople concerned with ELL students also argue over whether to emphasize teaching in the native language over a long period of time, called **first-language maintenance**, or provide intensive English instruction and teach all subjects in English as soon as possible, called **transitional bilingual education (TBE)**. Those who favor maintenance believe that this will help sustain a constructive sense of identity among ethnic or racial minority students and provide a better basis for learning higher-order skills, such as reading comprehension, while they acquire basic English skills. Their opponents believe that maintenance programs are harmful because they separate groups from one another or discourage students from mastering English well enough to function successfully in the larger society.[37] TBE has been supported by federal guidelines and by legislation in certain states. Studies indicate that approximately 75 percent of Hispanic students and nearly 90 percent of other groups such as Asian and Russian students exit transitional programs within three years. NCLB regulations generally are pushing schools toward fewer years outside the regular classroom.

Staffing disputes

Adherents and opponents of bilingual education also differ on staffing issues. Those who favor bilingual and bicultural maintenance tend to believe that the schools need many adults who can teach ELL students in their own language. Advocates of transitional or ESL programs, on the other hand, tend to believe that a legitimate program requires only a few native language or bilingual speakers. Some critics of bilingual education go so far as to claim that bilingual programs are primarily a means of providing teaching jobs for native language speakers who may not be fully competent in English.

How much improvement?

Among scholars who believe that bilingual education has produced little if any improvement, several have reviewed the research and concluded that "structured immersion" (placement in regular classes with special assistance provided inside and outside of class) and "sheltered immersion" (using principles of second-language learning in regular classrooms) are more successful than TBE.[38] Other scholars disagree, arguing that well-implemented bilingual programs do improve achievement, and several reviews of research have reported that bilingual education worked significantly better than immersion or other mostly monolingual programs.[39] (Part of the reason for these differences in conclusions involves disagreements about which studies should be reviewed and the criteria for selecting them.)

Conclusions for bilingual instruction

Claude Goldenberg reviewed much of the research and concluded that " . . . primary-language instruction enhances English-language learners' academic achievement . . . [but] certain accommodations must be made when ELL students are instructed in English, and these accommodations probably must be in place for several years, until students reach sufficient familiarity with academic English to permit them to be successful in mainstream instruction." He cited a number of important accommodations such as strategic use of the native language, extended explanation, and extensive opportunities for practice. He also presented the following conclusions that he believes can be drawn from multiple studies on instruction for ELL students:

- *If feasible, children should be taught reading in their primary language. . . .*

- *As needed, students should be helped to transfer what they know in their first language to learning tasks presented in English. . . .*

---

[37]Rosalie P. Porter, *Forked Tongue* (New York: Basic Books, 1990); Jill K. Mora, "A Road Map to the Bilingual Education Controversy," 2003 paper prepared at San Diego State University, available at **http://coe.sdsu.edu/people/jmora**; Kelly D. Salas, "Defending Bilingual Education," *Rethinking Schools* (Spring 2006), available at **www.rethinkingschools.org**; Herman Badillo, *One Nation One Standard* (New York: Sentinel, 2007); Rob Manning, "Measure 58 Draws National Attention," 2008 essay prepared for Oregon Public Broadcasting, available at **www.opb.org**; "Attacks on Bilingual Education," 2011 posting by Socyberty, available at **www.socyberty .com**; and Kenji Hakuta, "Educating Language Minority Students and Affirming Their Equal Rights," *Educational Researcher* (May 2011).

[38]Rosalie P. Porter, "The Case against Bilingual Education," 2007 paper prepared for the Center for Equal Opportunity, available at **www.ceousa.org**; and Rosalie P. Porter, *American Immigrant* (New York: 2011).

[39]Ann C. Willig, "A Meta-Analysis of Selected Studies on the Effectiveness of Bilingual Education," *Review of Educational Research* (Fall 1985), pp. 269–317; Stephen Krashen, "Bilingual Education Works," *Rethinking Schools* (Winter 2000/2001), available at **www.rethinkingschools.org**; Claude Goldenberg, "Teaching English Language Learners," *American Educator* (Summer 2008), p. 42, available at **www.aft.org**; Rhoda Coleman and Claude Goldenberg, "Promoting Literacy Development," *Education Digest* (February 2011); pp. 14–18; Matthew Lynch, "Debating Efficacy of Bilingual Ed Programs," *Education News*, October 15, 2011, available at **www.educationnews .org**; and Angela Pascopella, "Successful Strategies for English Language Learners," *District Administration* (February 2011), available at **www.districtadministration.com**.

■ *Teaching in the first and second languages can be approached similarly. However, adjustments or modifications will be necessary, probably for several years and at least for some students, until they reach sufficient familiarity with academic English to permit them to be successful in mainstream instruction. . . .*

■ *ELLs need intensive oral English language development (ELD), especially vocabulary and academic English instruction. . . .*

■ *ELLs also need academic content instruction, just as all students do; although ELD is crucial, it must be in addition to—not instead of—instruction designed to promote content knowledge.*

California and Arizona restrict bilingual education

The arguments are not confined to academic researchers. In recent years, voters in California, Arizona, and Massachusetts supported legislation designed to reduce or eliminate bilingual education. Each vote was accompanied by heated debate. Supporters of the legislation argued that, although bilingual education was attractive in theory, it generally was not working in practice. Opponents emphasized the difficulties that ELL students experience when taught in a language they do not understand. Time will tell how successful the new laws prove. Meanwhile, these developments appear to be having minimal influence on bilingual programming in most other states.

Bilingual education for everyone

Many scholars believe that all students, regardless of their ethnic group, should receive bilingual education. In part, this argument stems from the international economic advantages of a nation's citizens knowing more than one language. Programs that provide education in both English and another language for all students at a multiethnic school are sometimes referred to as "two-way" or "dual" bilingual immersion. To make this type of education a positive force in the future, several groups of civic leaders have recommended stressing multilingual competence, rather than just English remediation, as well as insisting on full mastery of English.[40]

New multiethnic materials and methods

Multiethnic Curriculum and Instruction   Since the mid-1960s, educators have been striving to take better account of cultural diversity by developing multiethnic curriculum materials and instructional methods. Many textbooks and supplemental reading lists have been revised to include materials and topics relating to diverse racial and ethnic groups. In-service training has helped teachers discover multiethnic source materials and learn to use instructional methods that promote multicultural perspectives and positive intergroup relations.

Approaches for Native Americans

Efforts to implement multiethnic curricula have been particularly vigorous with respect to Native American students. For example, educators at the Northwest Regional Education Laboratory have prepared an entire Indian Reading Series based on Native American culture. Mathematics instruction for Native American students sometimes uses familiar tribal symbols and artifacts in presenting word and story problems, and local or regional tribal history has become an important part of the social studies curriculum in some schools. Many observers believe that such approaches can help Native American students establish a positive sense of identity conducive to success in school and society.[41]

---

[40]Rhonda Barton, "Creating Believers," *Northwest Education* (Spring 2006), available at **www.educationnorthwest.org/edunw-magazine**; Carrie Kilman, "Lonely Language Learners?" *Teaching Tolerance* (Spring 2009), available at **www.tolerance.org**; "The Benefits of Dual-Immersion Education," 2011 posting by Imagine This, available at **www.imaginelearning.com**; and "Frequently Asked Questions about Two-Way Immersion," undated posting at **www.cal.org/twi/FAQ.htm**.

[41]Lee Little Soldier, "Is There an Indian in Your Classroom?" *Phi Delta Kappan* (April 1997), pp. 650–653; Buffy Sainte-Marie, "Beyond Autumn's Stereotypes," *Education Week*, October 27, 1999, pp. 37, 39; Mindy Cameron, "In the Language of Our Ancestors," *Northwest Education* (Spring 2004), available at **www.educationnorthwest.org/edunw-magazine**; Cindy Long, "Save the Indian, Save the Child," *NEA Today* (November/December 2008), available at **www.nea.org/neatoday**; Bracken Reed, "First Nation, Next Generation," *Northwest Education* (Winter 2009), available at **www.educationnorthwest.org/edunw-magazine**; and "Charting a New Course for Native Education"; 2010–2011 posting by the National Education Association, available at **www.nea.org**.

However, multiethnic curricula are not intended merely to bolster the self-image and enhance the learning of minority students. A crucial purpose is to ensure that all students acquire knowledge and appreciation of other racial and ethnic groups.

Reducing Eurocentrism

Recent Controversies   In recent years, particular attention has been given to ensuring that curriculum and instruction are not overwhelmingly *Eurocentric* (reflecting the culture and history of ethnic groups of European origin) but incorporate the concerns, culture, and history of ethnic and racial groups of different origins. Such approaches not only introduce materials dealing with the history and status of minority groups but also involve activities such as community-service assignments and cooperative learning tasks designed to acquaint students with minority cultures.

Most such curricula include the contributions of many groups; others focus on a single group. For example, *Afrocentric* programs focus on the history and culture of African Americans. Efforts to introduce Afrocentric and other minority-oriented themes have provoked controversy in California, New York, and other states, as well as in individual school districts. Critics suggest that such programs reject Western culture and history, leaving students lacking knowledge common in U.S. society. Some also suggest that many such curricula include historical inaccuracies. Another concern is that minority-oriented curricula can isolate minority students in separate schools or classes. An additional criticism is that emphasis on minority culture and history sometimes becomes a substitute for other difficult actions required to improve minority students' academic performance.[42]

Responses to the critiques

Supporters of Afrocentric and other minority-oriented themes respond by pointing out that few advocates of these approaches want to eliminate Western culture and history from the curriculum. Molefi Asante argues that the Afrocentric movement strives to de-bias the curriculum by adding appropriate Afrocentric materials, not by eliminating Western classics. In addition, they note that few, if any, supporters of Afrocentric or related approaches minimize the importance of academic achievement or advocate its de-emphasis in the curriculum.

Multiculturalism for the Future

Worries about multicultural education

The controversies about multicultural education as a whole follow lines similar to the specific arguments about Afrocentric and other minority-oriented curricula. Critics worry that multicultural education may increase ethnic separatism, fragment the curriculum, and reinforce the tendency to settle for a second-rate education for economically disadvantaged or minority students. To avoid such potential dangers, multiculturalists have provided useful guidelines for you, as a teacher, to use in providing instruction:

- *Find out what positive aspects of Western civilization are being taught.* If students are not learning that constitutional government, the rule of law, and the primacy of individual rights are among the hallmarks of Western civilization, then they are not learning the essential features of their heritage. . . .

- *Find out if students are being taught that racism, sexism, homophobia, and imperialism are characteristics of all cultures and civilizations at some time—not culture-specific evils.* . . . America's failings should not be taught in isolation from the failings of other countries—no double standard.

[42]Molefi Asante, *The Afrocentric Idea* (Philadelphia, PA: Temple University Press, 1987); Charles Devarics, "Afro-Centric Program Yields Academic Gains," *Black Issues in Higher Education,* December 6, 1990, pp. 1, 34; Molefi Asante, "Afrocentric Curriculum," *Educational Leadership* (January 1992), pp. 28–31; Dennis Byrne, "Afrocentric Curriculum Divisive, Not Unifying," 2006 essay prepared for Real Clear Politics, available at **www.realclearpolitics.com**; Kim Shockley and Rona M. Frederick, "Constructs and Dimensions of Afrocentric Education," *Journal of Black Studies* (July 2010); and Kim G. Shockley, "Reaching African American Students," *Journal of Black Studies* (March 2011).

■ *Insist that all students study both Western and non-Western cultures.* Students need solid academic courses in Latin American, African, and Asian history, in addition to European history.[43]

■ REFOCUS In what ways are you preparing to work with students from a variety of cultural and linguistic backgrounds? How might you benefit as a teacher from knowing more about the cultural background of students different from yourself?

Despite the controversies, most influential educators believe there is an urgent need for comprehensive multicultural approaches that give attention to minority experiences. "If children are to do well academically," said former New York State Commissioner of Education Thomas Sobol, "the child must experience the school as an extension, not a rejection, of home and community." A central goal, Sobol contends, should be to "develop a shared set of values and a common tradition" while also helping "each child find his or her place within the whole."[44]

Education for Students with Disabilities

■ Growth of special education

Major developments in education in the past thirty years have involved schooling for children with disabilities. (Placement in special education usually means that a disabled student receives separate, specialized instruction for all or part of the day in a self-contained class or a resource room.) Table 12.1 shows the numbers of students with selected disabilities served in or through public education in 2010. Analysis conducted by the U.S. Department of Education indicates that almost three-quarters of students with disabilities receive most or all of their education in regular classes (with or without assignment to part-time resource rooms); approximately 25 percent are in self-contained classes; and the rest are in special schools or facilities. Since 1988, the proportion of students with disabilities who spend 80 percent or more of their time in regular education classrooms has increased from less than one-third to more than half.[45]

■ PL 94-142 and IDEA

Federal requirements for educating students with disabilities have been enumerated through a series of federal laws, including the **Education for All Handicapped Children Act** of 1975 (often known by its public law number, PL 94-142), the **Individuals with Disabilities Education Act (IDEA)** of 1990, and the **Individuals with Disabilities Education Improvement Act (IDEIA)** of 2004. The basic requirements spelled out in these acts, as well as by other laws and judicial interpretations, are as follows:

■ Basic requirements for special services

1. Children cannot be labeled as disabled or placed in special education on the basis of a single criterion such as an IQ score; testing and assessment services must be fair and comprehensive.

2. If a child is identified as disabled, school officials must conduct a functional assessment and develop suitable intervention strategies.

3. Parents or guardians must have access to information on diagnosis and may protest decisions of school officials.

[43]Jynotsa Pattnaik, "Learning about the 'Other,'" *Childhood Education* (Summer 2003), pp. 204–211; Paul C. Gorski, "Equity and Social Justice From the Inside-Out," 2011 posting by the Canadian Federation for the Humanities and Social Sciences, available at **http://blog.fedcan.ca**; and Mary Hanley, "The Scope of Multicultural Education," undated posting by New Horizons for Learning, available at **www.education.jhu.edu/newhorizons**.
[44]Thomas Sobol, "Understanding Diversity," *Educational Leadership* (February 1990), pp. 27–30. See also Karen M. Teel and Jennifer E. Obidah, eds., *Building Racial and Cultural Competence in the Classroom* (New York: Teachers College Press, 2008); Leah Davies, "Learning the Value of Diversity," *Teachers Net Gazette*, January 1, 2009, available at **www.teachers.net**; and Christine E. Sleeter, "Are Standards and Multicultural Education Compatible?" *ASCD Express* (No. 15 2011), available at **www.ascd.org**.
[45]U.S. Department of Education, *To Assure the Free Appropriate Education of All Handicapped Children* (Washington, D.C.: U.S. Department of Education, 1996); Terri Mauro, "What Special-Education Placement Works for Your Child?" 2008 essay prepared for About.com, available at **www.specialchildren.about.com**; and Thomas D. Snyder and Sally Dillow, *Digest of Education Statistics 2010* (Washington, D.C.: U.S. Government Printing Office, 2011).

Table 12.1	Number of Students Receiving Public Special-Education Services in 2010, by Type of Disability
Type of Disability	
Learning disabled	2,431,000
Speech or language impaired	1,416,000
Other health impaired	689,000
Intellectual disability	478,000
Emotional disturbance	407,000
Developmental delay	368,000
Autistic	378,000
Hearing impaired	78,000
Orthopedically impaired	70,000
Visually impaired	29,000
Traumatic brain injury	26,000
Total	6,483,000

Note: Numbers do not add to the total because not all categories are shown.

Source: Thomas D. Snyder and Sally Dillow, *Digest of Education Statistics 2010* (Washington, D.C.: U.S. Government Printing Office, 2011), Table 46.

4. Every student eligible for special-education services must be taught according to an **individualized education program (IEP)** that includes both long-range and short-range goals. Because it is an agreement in writing regarding the resources the school agrees to provide, the IEP is a cornerstone of a school's efforts to help students with disabilities. It must specify special and related services that will be provided in accordance with the needs of the student. The IEP must be prepared within thirty days of when the child is declared eligible for special services, by a committee that must include the student's teacher, parent or guardian, and an administrator's designee.

5. Educational services must be provided in the **least restrictive environment**, which means that children with disabilities should be in regular classes to the extent possible. They may be placed in special or separate classes only for the amount of time judged necessary to provide appropriate services. If a school district demonstrates that placement in a regular educational setting cannot be achieved satisfactorily, the student must be given adequate instruction elsewhere, paid for by the district.

Mainstreaming and inclusion

As a result of these legal mandates, school districts throughout the country have made efforts to accommodate students with disabilities in regular class settings for all or most of the school day. The term *mainstreaming* was originally used to describe such efforts. More recently, the term *inclusion* has been applied. Inclusion usually denotes an even more strenuous effort to include disabled students in regular classrooms as much as is possible and feasible. Even if a disability is severe enough that a child needs to spend a substantial amount of time *away* from the regular classroom, he or she can still be encouraged to take part in activities open to other children, such as art or music.

Neither mainstreaming nor inclusion approaches are necessarily intended to eliminate special services or classes for children with exceptional needs. Children in these arrangements may receive a wide range of extra support, from consultation by specialists skilled in working with a particular disability to provision of special equipment.[46]

[46]Patrick A. Schwarz, "Special Education," *Educational Leadership* (February 2007); Cindy Long, "Going Mainstream," *NEA Today* (February 2008), available at **www.nea.org/neatoday**; and James McLeskey et al., "Learning Disabilities and the LRE Mandate," *Learning Disabilities Research and Practice* (May 2011), pp. 60–66.

▶❚❚ **TEACHSOURCE VIDEO ACTIVITY**

Including Students with Physical Disabilities: Best Practices

After reading this section, go to the Education CourseMate website to access the video entitled "Including Students with Physical Disabilities: Best Practices." In this clip, you'll see how Lisa Kelleher, a classroom teacher, works with others in her classroom to support and teach a student with spina bifida. After watching this video, answer the following questions:

❶ Did working with the student appear to take an overwhelming amount of time and attention? If yes, what might be done to reduce drain on the teacher? If no, what supports were in place to help the teacher?

❷ Who do you think is responsible for paying for the kind of supports to carry out inclusive education shown in the video? Ask one or more administrators of schools practicing inclusion to explain the financial arrangements in local schools.

▌ **Ambiguous studies**

Research on mainstreaming and inclusion has produced ambiguous results. Early studies generally failed to find evidence that placement of disabled students in regular classes for most or all of the day consistently improved their academic performance, social acceptance, or self-concept. Few classrooms examined in that early research, however, provided a fair test because too little had been done to train teachers, introduce appropriate teaching methods, provide a range of suitable materials, or otherwise ensure that teachers could work effectively with heterogeneous groups of disabled and nondisabled students. Reflecting such criticism, several studies were conducted that were limited to districts and states considered outstanding in providing mainstreamed or inclusive opportunities for students with disabilities. But mainstreaming/inclusion is very difficult to implement effectively, and, again, relatively few indications emerged that mainstreaming/inclusion has been consistently beneficial for disabled students.[47]

▌ **Model efforts based on systematic reforms**

On the other hand, several assessments of individual schools have been more promising. In general, these schools have been described as models of restructuring. They made systematic reforms to prepare teachers to work with heterogeneous groups; they provided special resources to assist both students and teachers who need help; they had administrators who promoted collaboration between special-education teachers and regular faculty, and they kept class size relatively small. In addition, teachers were effective at individualizing instruction and introducing cooperative learning. The researchers tend to agree that successful mainstreaming or inclusion on a national basis will require similar effective restructuring of schools throughout the United States.[48] From Preservice to Practice presents concerns that you and others entering the teaching profession might have about inclusion.

---

[47]Andrew R. Brulle, "Appropriate, with Dignity," *Phi Delta Kappan* (February 1991), p. 487; Ann C. Dybvik, "Autism and the Inclusion Mandate," *Education Next* (No. 1 2004), available at **www.educationnext.org**; and Michelle Diament, "Educators Support Inclusion But Find Students Ill-Prepared," 2011 posting by Disability Scoop, available at **www.disabilityscoop.com**.
[48]Allan Gartner and Dorothy Kerzner Lipsky, "Beyond Special Education," *Harvard Educational Review* (November 1987), pp. 367–395; Julie Causton-Theoharris and George Theoharris, "Creating Inclusive Schools for All Students," *School Administrator* (September 2008), available at **www.aasa.org**; Barbara McClanahan, "Help! I Have Kids Who Can't Read in My World History Class!" *Preventing School Failure* (Winter 2009), pp. 105–112; Sherry L. Hicks-Monroe, "A Review of Research on the Educational Benefits of the Inclusive Model of Education for Special Education Students," *Journal of the American Academy of Special Education Professionals* (Winter 2011); and "Special Education Inclusion," undated posting by Education World, available at **www.educationworld.com**.

Marmaduke St. John/Spencer Grant/Alamy Limited

Effective mainstreaming of students with disabilities into regular classroom settings requires a variety of special resources, relatively small classes, and educators skilled in and dedicated to creating an effective learning environment and acceptance for all students.

The legal requirements for educating students with disabilities create several challenges for teachers and administrators, beginning with determining who qualifies. After an appropriate determination has been made, schools must assess which services children need and how well they can fulfill those needs. We'll explore these challenges, as well as other questions about special education.

Continuity & Change

Increase in Autism Since about 1980, the incidence of autism among children has been increasing rapidly, from one in several thousand to as much as one in five hundred. A developmental disability that affects verbal and nonverbal communication and interaction, autism can range from mild to severe problems in functioning. Although most of the escalating diagnosis probably is due to changes or advances in diagnosing mild impairments, some may be due to environmental causes such as pollution or to increased associative mating—the tendency for people with similar skills or backgrounds to marry or live with one another. The growing incidence of mild autism means that future teachers will be confronted with many children who have diagnosed disabilities and are placed in inclusive classrooms.[49]

Classification and Labeling of Students

Educators face many difficulties in identifying students who require special-education services. It is hard to be certain, for example, whether a child with very low achievement is intellectually disabled and could benefit from special services or is simply a slow learner who requires more time and guidance to learn. Similarly, it is difficult to

[49]Tina T. Dyches, "Assessing Diverse Students with Autism Spectrum Disorders," *The ASHA Leader*, January 18, 2011; Judith Warner, "Autism's Lone Wolf," *Time*, August 29, 2011, pp. 44–47.

FROM PRESERVICE TO PRACTICE

Meeting All Needs

Josh and Rob are graduating this year and heading for their first year of classroom teaching. Josh looks over at Rob. "I don't know about you, Rob, but I'm pretty overwhelmed by what we're expected to do with and for special-needs students in an inclusion program. I know it's important for special-needs students to spend as much time as possible in the least restrictive environment, but just dealing with the requirements for normal students will be plenty of responsibility for me in my first year of teaching."

Rob nods. "I agree. I suspect that inclusion helps the school district's financial situation. Look at the state formula for funding special education. More money comes to the districts that practice inclusion. But I'm not at all sure that inclusion is the best practice for most students with disabilities. I certainly don't have the training to deal with emotionally disabled students. If a disabled student becomes disruptive, how does a teacher proceed normally?" Rob taps his finger on the table. "I am also really wondering how all of this affects learning for regular students. We'll have to follow Individual Education Plans for all disabled students. Couldn't following the IEP sometimes lead regular students to suspect unfairness? Before I took 'Overview of Special Education' this year, even I kind of thought special-education students could get away with doing almost nothing and call it 'adapting the curriculum.' How can I explain the differences to my class?"

Josh sighs. "I was only worried about meeting the special ed needs. But I can see potential problems in developing or maintaining effective education for regular students, too. In the effort to serve disabled students, I might be tempted to ease up on my preparation for regular students, and vice versa. And behavior problems of just one student can easily distract a whole class, causing all of us to waste valuable time. I wonder how new teachers feel about this after their first year."

Rob makes a note on a notepad. "Let's ask Professor Jackson if we could have a panel discussion. She would know which of last year's graduates are teaching in a school using full inclusion. Then we could ask all our questions about this issue."

Josh looks over at the notepad. "I think we should include teachers who have lots of experience and who have seen how other arrangements work, as well. I remember the old resource rooms where they used to send most of the disabled students. That setup may have worked better for some kids, but I also remember the disruption in class when they gathered up their stuff to go for their special sessions.

"Maybe the working teachers can talk about team teaching," Josh adds. "We don't necessarily have to work alone, you know. I've heard of shared teaching responsibilities, where a special-education teacher teams with the regular teacher. I would definitely like to learn more about that. And there are always aides. Some of them serve as teachers even though they're not certified. Let's ask about all these questions—and more."

Case Questions

1. What arrangements do local schools use to provide services to special-education students?

2. What do you see as the most effective way to serve disabled students?

3. Do you have concerns about working with certain classes of disabled students?

4. Arrange to talk to regular and special-education teachers. What arrangements do special-education teachers believe serve special-education students best? How do regular classroom teachers answer the same question?

determine whether a child who is working below capacity has a learning disability or is performing inadequately because he or she is poorly motivated, poorly taught, or culturally unprepared for assessment materials. Although "learning disability" is currently the most used label—covering students with deficits in reading, math, writing, listening, or other abilities—experts disagree among themselves not only on what constitutes such a disability but also on what services should be provided to ameliorate it. Experts encounter similar problems in distinguishing between severe and mild emotional disturbances or between partial and complete deafness. Children who appear borderline in disability status (a potentially fuzzy borderline) are especially difficult to classify.

IDEIA requirements   **The Discrepancy Model, Response to Intervention and Incentives to Mislabel**
Since passage of the IDEIA, students are not to be classified using the Discrepancy Model; that is, they should not be classified as learning disabled on the basis of

discrepancies between their achievement scores and their scores on IQ tests, but instead they should receive help with specific problems and then be classified as learning disabled only if they do not respond satisfactorily to that intervention. This approach is called **Response to Intervention** (RTI), and dictates leaving a child in the regular school program while providing him or her with suitable interventions; only if that does not work is the child referred for special education or disability services. The RTI approach was developed largely in the 1990s. It has since morphed into an approach to whole-school improvement that we will describe in Chapter 16, School Effectiveness and Reform in the United States.[50]

Many analysts have suggested that the vagueness of the learning disabilities (LD) category has encouraged school districts to use this classification as a way to obtain federal funds to improve educational services for low-achieving students. Because most LD students spend much of their time in regular classes but receive extra assistance in resource rooms, LD services often provide compensatory education for disadvantaged or low-achieving students who do not qualify for Title I services. This may help to explain why the number of U.S. students classified as learning disabled has more than tripled since the 1970s. Research indicates that half or more LD students may not meet criteria commonly accepted by special-education experts. On the other hand, analysts believe that some schools and districts are avoiding classifying students as LD so that their low achievement scores can be obscured among large numbers of regular students rather than counted as part of an NCLB subgroup (see the "The No Child Left Behind Act" section concerning adequate yearly progress earlier in this chapter), where low scores can result in failure to make adequate yearly progress.

Effects of Labeling   Critics also are concerned that classification may become a self-fulfilling prophecy. Students labeled as "disturbed," for example, may be more inclined to misbehave because the label makes unruly behavior acceptable and expected. Researchers have tried to determine whether placement in a special class or program has either a positive or a detrimental effect on students. Among the variables they have considered are peer acceptance and effects on self-concept. On the whole, the research is inconclusive. (Difficulties in conducting this type of research include defining terms, measuring program effects, and allowing for students' differing reactions to a given program.) Although some researchers report that special-education classes limit the progress of many students, others have found that special-class placement can be beneficial when instruction is well planned and appropriate.[51]

Disproportionate Placement of Minority Students

Data on special-education placement show that students from some racial minority groups are much more likely to be designated for programs enrolling students with

Margin notes:
- Finding interventions before labeling
- Growth of the vague "LD" category
- Dangers in labeling
- Inconclusive research
- Use of "retarded" label for minorities and poor

---

[50]Perry A. Zirkel, "Sorting Out Which Students Have Learning Disabilities," *Phi Delta Kappan* (April 2001), pp. 639–641; Rhonda Barton, "Teaching to the Child," *Northwest Education* (Fall 2008), available at **www.educationnorthwest.org/edunw-magazine**; Judy Elliott, "Response to Intervention," *School Administrator* (September 2008), available at **www.aasa .org**; Jennifer Stepanek, "Response to Intervention," *Northwest Education* (Fall 2008), available at **www.educationnorthwest.org/edunw-magazine**; Charles A. Hughes and Douglas D. Dexter, "Response to Intervention," *Theory into Practice* (Issue 1, 2011); and Mary E. Little, "Action Research and Response to Intervention," *Educational Forum* (No. 1, 2012).
[51]Gaea Leinhardt and Allan Pallay, "Restrictive Educational Settings," *Review of Educational Research* (Winter 1982), pp. 557–578; Douglas Fuchs and Lynn S. Fuchs, "Sometimes Separate Is Better," *Educational Leadership* (December 1994–January 1995), pp. 22–26; Naomi Zigmond, Amanda Kloo, and Victoria Volonino, "What, Where, and How," *Exceptionality* (Issue 4, 2009), pp. 189–204; Susan Baglieri et al., "Disability Studies in Education," *Remedial and Special Education* (July 2011), pp. 267–278; and Naomi Zigmond et al., "Special Education in Restructured Schools," undated paper posted at the New Horizons site, available at **www.education.jhu .edu/newhorizons**.

severe intellectual disabilities than are non-Hispanic white students. African American students, for example, are nearly three times as likely as white students to be in "educable mentally retarded" classes. In addition, black students in special education are approximately twice as likely to spend 60 percent or more of their time outside regular classrooms than are white students with disabilities. Placement in intellectual-disability categories also correlates highly with students' socioeconomic background and poverty status.

Causes and effects

Many analysts believe that placement in classes for the intellectually disabled has been too dependent on intelligence tests, which have been constructed for use with middle-class whites. Some also believe that disproportionate numbers of minority students are shunted into classes for emotionally disturbed or "retarded" children mainly to alleviate teachers' problems in dealing with culturally different children and youth. Many educators and parents worry that such placements may constitute a new version of segregation and discrimination, by which minority students are sentenced to special classes with low or nonexistent educational expectations.[52]

Issues and Dilemmas

We have touched on several issues involved in special education, mainstreaming, and inclusion. In this section, we focus on four issues or dilemmas that may have particular prominence in the next several years. How these issues are resolved will affect your day-to-day life as a teacher.

Financial dilemmas

1. *How will we handle the costs?* Legal rulings that schools must provide an appropriate free education for children with disabilities have often been interpreted to mean that schools must provide the services necessary to help children with special needs derive as much benefit from education as do other students—perhaps establishing an optimal learning environment for every student who requires special assistance. However, providing an optimal learning environment for students with severe disabilities (or, perhaps, for any student) can be expensive. The federal government, while raising academic standards for disabled students under the NCLB, has provided only a fraction of the funds needed to support these services. Upon studying this issue, one legislator confessed that federal failure to fully fund implementation of disability regulations "has to be the mother of all unfunded mandates in this country."[53]

Rights versus expenses

Arguments have arisen between school officials, who claim they cannot afford to provide maximally effective education for all students with disabilities, and parents or other advocates who believe that such students have a constitutional right to whatever services ensure maximum educational gains. Administrators face a series of dilemmas here. Although key court cases have suggested that schools must provide only the level of services that give disabled students "a basic floor of opportunity," federal laws seem to require increasing levels of support. Administrators must not only determine their legal obligations but also decide whether additional services beyond the minimal obligations—and additional costs—are worth the educational payoff for the child. Then they must decide how to pay those costs.

One possible response is to divert local funds. Another is to classify more students as LD to receive additional federal funding. Still another possibility involves including

---

[52]Kevin Welner, "The Overrepresentation of Culturally and Linguistically Diverse Students in Special Education," *Teaching Exceptional Children* (July/August 2006), pp. 60–62; Beth Harry and Janette Klingner, "Discarding the Deficit Model," *Educational Leadership* (February 2007); and Dara Shifrer, Chandra Muller, and Rebecca Callahan, "Disproportionality and Learning Disabilities," *Journal of Learning Disabilities* (May–June 2011), pp. 246–257.
[53]Julie Raw and Rita Healy, "Who Pays for Special Ed?" *Time*, September 25, 2006, pp. 62–63; and Charles K. Trainor, "Special Education Plans," *American School Board Journal* (January 2011), pp. 63–64.

disabled students in regular classes *without* providing costly additional services there or undertaking systematic restructuring. Although any of these approaches can compromise education for both students with disabilities and without, such responses have been common in many school districts.[54]

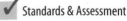 Standards & Assessment

2. *How should special-education students prepare for state testing?* Until recently, most states allowed testing exemptions for special-education students, but this has changed as decision makers realized that many schools increased enrollment in disabled categories to protect their scores and as NCLB began to penalize schools for not testing or reporting scores of disabled students. However, as we discussed earlier in this chapter, many educators are concerned that applying statewide standards may prove disastrous for LD students and other students in special education.[55]

Potential effects on nondisabled students

3. *To what extent do arrangements and services for educating disabled students detract from the education of nondisabled students?* If school officials divert substantial amounts of money from regular budgets to pay for separate placements or special services for disabled students, or if school officials assign students with severe disabilities to regular classes where teachers cannot address their problems efficiently, will classroom conditions for nondisabled students suffer? Observers disagree. Some believe that mainstreaming and inclusion have not substantially detracted from opportunities and outcomes for nondisabled students. Other observers believe that because regular classroom teachers often receive little or no help in dealing with students who have severe mental or emotional problems, some now have more difficulty delivering effective instruction for all students.[56]

Many questions about implementation

4. *What services should we provide for which students, where, when, and how?* Posing this omnibus question indicates that many issues we have discussed remain unresolved. For example, to what extent should we make differing arrangements for severely and mildly disabled students, or for differing students within either category? To what extent should schools implement "full inclusion" arrangements for all or most of the day, as contrasted with "partial inclusion" that assigns students to resource rooms or separate schools for significant amounts of time? To what extent should such decisions rest with parents, who may have little understanding of their school-wide effects, or by professionals, who may lack sensitivity to the particular problems of an individual student? To what extent is it desirable—and feasible—to provide regular classroom support services, such as a sign language interpreter for deaf students or a nurse to assist incontinent students? Does using resource rooms complicate and disrupt the operation of the school as a whole—or is it more disruptive to bring a range of support services into the regular classroom? Will school-wide restructuring carried out partly to accommodate full inclusion result in substantially improved schooling for all students, or is it unreasonable and unrealistic to expect effective widespread restructuring in the foreseeable future? These are a few of the questions for which educators still need good answers.

---

[54]Jordan Cross, "25 Years without Paying the Bills," *School Administrator* (November 2000), available at **www.aasa.org**; Joseph Shapiro, "Recession Hurting Kids with Developmental Delays," 2009 essay prepared for National Public Radio, available at **www.npr.org**; and Christina Samuels, "Finding Efficiencies in Special Education Programs," *Education Week*, January 5, 2011.
[55]Jennifer Randall and George Englehard Jr., "Performance of Students with and without Disabilities under Modified Conditions," *Journal of Special Education*, February 12, 2009; and Michelle Diament, "Duncan Calls for End to Inflated Special Education Scores," 2011 posting by Disability Scoop, available at **www.disabilityscoop.com**.
[56]Naomi Dillon, "Lost in Translation," *American School Board Journal* (March 2007); Rachel Holler and Perry A. Zirkel, "Legally Best Practices in Section 504 Plans," *School Administrator* (September 2008), available at **www.aasa.org**; and Lynn K. Spradlin, *Diversity Matters* (Belmont, CA: Wadsworth, 2012).

Suggested policies and guidelines

School officials struggling with the uncertainties of providing equal opportunity for students with disabilities could benefit from policies and guidelines for deciding what to do. Many informed observers believe that successfully educating students with disabilities will require changes at all levels of the U.S. educational system, including the following:[57]

- Congress should provide more funds to help schools implement its mandates.
- Legislation should require that teachers receive adequate training.
- States and school districts should find ways to quickly identify classrooms or schools where full inclusion or other arrangements are not working well.
- States should pass legislation to expedite quick removal from regular classes of disabled students who are violent or extremely disruptive.
- Schools opting to pursue full inclusion should receive whatever technical help is necessary.
- Teachers and staff in inclusive classrooms should receive training and support in using appropriate instructional strategies that will help all of their students master basic and advanced learning skills, including peer-mediated instruction, mastery learning, differentiated instruction, and cooperative teaching.

REFOCUS What aspects of working with inclusion students do you believe will be most challenging for you as a teacher? What are you doing now to prepare for the challenges?

Summing Up

1 Concern for equal educational opportunity has been expanding to emphasize issues involving racial and ethnic desegregation, achievement levels of students from low-income families, introduction of bilingual education and other aspects of multicultural education, and inclusion of students with disabilities in regular classrooms. Each of these and related sets of issues involve sizable expenditures to enlarge opportunities and ensure that the benefits of education are realistically available to all students. As you enter the education field in the next decade, you will play an important role in determining the extent to which such efforts succeed or fail.

2 Although much desegregation has occurred in smaller school districts, big-city districts, with their concentration of minority students and economically disadvantaged students, have found stable desegregation difficult.

3 Compensatory education seemed unsuccessful until evidence accumulating in the 1980s began to justify a more positive conclusion. However, many serious questions remain concerning the degree to which compensatory

education can have large-scale, substantial, and lasting results. The No Child Left Behind Act (NCLB) has caused sweeping changes not only in compensatory education but also in public schooling for all students.

4 Efforts toward constructive cultural pluralism through education include multicultural education approaches that take account of student learning styles, recognize differences in dialect, provide for bilingual education, and introduce methods and materials involving multiethnic curriculum and instruction. These approaches can help improve the performance of economically disadvantaged minority students and otherwise promote a productive pluralistic society.

5 Legislative and court mandates have led to large expansions in education for students with disabilities. As part of this process, educators are trying to mainstream these students as much as possible to avoid the damaging effects of labeling and separation. Research, however, is unclear concerning the overall gains and losses associated with mainstreaming or inclusion, and many questions remain.

---

[57]Thomas R. Guskey, "Closing Achievement Gaps," *Journal of Advanced Academics* (Fall 2008), pp. 8–31; and Andrew Cangemi et al., "Implementing Inclusive Education," 2011 posting by NY Teachers, available at **www.nyteachers.wordpress.com**.

Key Terms

The numbers indicate the pages where explanations of the key terms can be found.

desegregation 366
integration 366
de jure segregation 368
de facto segregation 368
magnet school 370
controlled choice 370
compensatory education 374
Title I 374
Head Start 374
Follow Through 374
ecological intervention 376
No Child Left Behind Act (NCLB) 377

adequate yearly progress (AYP) 377
pullout approach 379
multicultural education 380
cultural pluralism 381
learning styles 382
Ebonics 382
bilingual education 383
first-language maintenance 384
transitional bilingual education
    (TBE) 384
Education for All Handicapped Children
    Act 388

Individuals with Disabilities Education Act
    (IDEA) 388
Individuals with Disabilities Education
    Improvement Act (IDEIA) 388
individualized education program
    (IEP) 389
least restrictive environment 389
mainstreaming 389
inclusion 389
Response to Intervention (RTI) 393

Certification Connection Activity

This chapter discusses the important concept of equal educational opportunity. Preparing for diverse learners is an important part of becoming a teacher. In the Praxis II, Principles of Learning and Teaching, you will find several questions that cover topics such as gender differences, how culture and community affect learning, and how multicultural backgrounds affect learning. A recent trend in education has been the disaggregation of testing data.

In disaggregating the data, many schools report an achievement gap between whites and Asians on the one hand and African Americans and Hispanics on the other. For the educational system to be successful in addressing No Child Left Behind (NCLB) and to provide educational equity, it is critical for the achievement gap to be closed. In your journal, describe the programs instituted by a local school district to close the achievement gap..

Discussion Questions

1. What actions and policies are most important in bringing about successful desegregation? In what situations is it most difficult to implement desegregation effectively?

2. Why is compensatory education an important national issue? What approaches are most promising for improving the achievement of low-income students?

3. What are some major goals and components of multicultural education? What can teachers in predominantly nonminority schools do to advance its goals?

4. How can you, as a regular classroom teacher, help disabled students in your classes? What difficulties are they likely to encounter? How might you help overcome these difficulties? If you are planning to become a special-education teacher, how can you help your students who are included, fully or partially, in regular classrooms?

Suggested Projects for Professional Development

1. Interview teachers in nearby elementary schools to determine whether they are using or considering inclusion arrangements. What are their attitudes toward inclusion? What can you learn from them that may be useful in your own career?

2. Talk with administrators in nearby schools to find out what school districts are doing to implement Title I and NCLB. Are improvements occurring? What changes have taken place during the past few years? Are similar changes taking place in districts in which you may apply for a position?

3. If a nearby school district operates magnet schools, visit one of them. Ask students and faculty what the magnet

school is accomplishing and how it differs from a regular, nonmagnet school. Ask administrators how the school district defined the school's goals. Does the school seem to be successful in meeting these goals? Do you think you would enjoy working there? Why or why not?

4. Organize and participate in a debate about the desirability of bilingual education. As part of your preparation for the debate, identify articles, books, and websites that help you reach valid conclusions.

5. For your portfolio, begin preparing a section that will show your experience and studies with respect to topics considered in this chapter.

Suggested Resources

Internet Resources

In addition to federal government and ERIC sites and other more specialized Internet locations identified elsewhere in this text, you can research the important policy issues introduced in this chapter at the websites of organizations that conduct public-policy analysis. These include the Brookings Institution (**www.brook.edu**), Education Sector (**www.edsector.org**), the Heritage Foundation (**www.heritage.org**), and the Rand Corporation (**www.rand.org**). Electronic journals such as *Educational Policy Analysis Archives* (**http://epaa.asu.edu/ojs**) also address issues reviewed in this chapter. You can also visit many sites related to specific chapter topics.

Desegregation

The Century Foundation's *Equality & Education* site (**www.tcf.org/education**) provides information about desegregation, school choice, unequal resources, and related topics.

Multicultural Education

A series of essays addressing multicultural education is available in the "Teaching and Learning" section at **www.education.jhu.edu/newhorizons**. Much of the Fall 2000 issue of *Rethinking Schools*, available at **www.rethinkingschools.org**, is devoted to multicultural education. Numerous research reports dealing with bilingual and multicultural education can be accessed at **www.ncela.gwu.edu**. *Education Week's* Research Center provides a summary of issues involving English Language Learners at **www.edweek.org/rc/issues/english-language-learners**.

The theme of the Spring 2011 issue of *The Future of Children* (**www.futureofchildren.org**) is "Immigrant Children."

Materials and practices involving multicultural education are described at the site of the National Center for Culturally Responsive Educational Systems (**www.nccrest.org**).

The November 2008 issue of *The School Administrator* (**www.aasa.org**) focuses on "English Language Learners."

The National Association for Multicultural Education (**www.nameorg.org**) has made a number of papers and publications available on the Internet.

The Spring 2004 issue of *Northwest Education* at **www.educationnorthwest.org/edunw-magazine** (click on "Archive" at bottom right) includes a series of articles dealing with educating Native American students. The Spring 2006 issue describes and analyzes approaches for improving the achievement of ELLs.

Materials and methods for providing culturally responsive instruction to underperforming African American students are available at the website of Successful Urban Teachers, **www.successfulteachers.com**.

Special Education

The theme of the Fall 2008 issue of *Northwest Education* (**www.educationnorthwest.org/edunw-magazine**) is "Response to Intervention."

The September 2008 issue of *The School Administrator* (**www.aasa.org**) focuses on "Inclusion and Intervention" involving special education.

Compensatory Education

The Summer 2009 issue of *Northwest Education* (**www.educationnorthwest.org/edunw-magazine**) is devoted to "Turnaround" schools that successfully restructured after failing to make adequate progress, and the issues they faced in confronting this NCLB requirement.

Publications

Banks, James A., and Cheryl A. M. Banks, eds. *Handbook of Research on Multicultural Education*, 7th ed. New York: Allyn & Bacon, 2009. *A wide variety of research-based chapters deal with cultural diversity and learning, effective instruction for low-income students, desegregation, the history and performance of minority groups, multicultural instruction, and related topics.*

Gibson, Margaret A., and John U. Ogbu, eds. *Minority Status and Schools*. New York: Garland, 1991. *In addition to analyzing the experience of minority students in several countries, this book deals specifically with African American, Korean, Latino, Sikh, Ute Indian, and West Indian students in the United States.*

Kahlenberg, Richard D. Rescuing Brown v. Board of Education. New York: Century Foundation, 2007. *Profiles and analyzes developments in twelve school districts that have been trying to bring about or maintain socioeconomic integration.*

Kirp, David L. Kids First. Jackson, TN: Public Affairs, 2011. *Subtitled "Five Big Ideas for Transforming Children Lives and America's Future," this book describes possibilities for providing strong support for parents, linking schools and communities, high-quality early education, caring and stable adult mentors for disadvantaged students, and nest eggs to help pay for college or kick-start careers.*

Pransky, Ken. *Beneath the Surface*. Portsmouth, NJ: Heinemann, 2008. *Subtitled "The Hidden Realities of Teaching Culturally and Linguistically Diverse Young Learners, K–6," this volume provides strategies and a framework for teaching English language learners.*

 Additional resources for this chapter, including the TeachSource Videos, can be found on the Education CourseMate website. Go to **CengageBrain.com** to access the site.

PART FIVE

Bob Daemmrich/The Image Works

Curricular Foundations

The Changing Purposes of American Education

Contemporary society is constantly changing and evolving. As it changes, we must adapt to meet the challenges of new times and circumstances. Throughout our history, Americans have looked to the schools to help cope with the ebb and flow of change. As a society, we react to change and social pressures by revising our educational purposes and demanding that schools respond by changing their instructional programs.

As a nation, what goals do we have for our education system? As teachers and educators, what are our real purposes, how are these influenced by established educational philosophies and theories, and how should they be guiding our work?

This chapter will begin to focus your thinking on the interaction between our dynamic society and the role that the education system plays in responding to and affecting societal change. As you read, think about the following questions:

FOCUS QUESTIONS

- What should the purpose of education be in American society in the twenty-first century?
- What is the relationship among educational goals, standards, and objectives?
- How have educational goals shifted throughout American history since the end of the nineteenth century?
- What groups of students have been targeted for special attention as goals have changed during the past century?
- What were the themes of major policy reports on education at the end of the twentieth century?
- Which philosophy or theory of education is likely to influence the next swing of the curriculum pendulum?

---

*This chapter was revised by Dr. David E. Vocke, Towson University.

Continuity & Change

As society has changed in response to world events, scientific innovations, political shifts, and social movements, the philosophies and theories examined in Chapter 6, Philosophical Roots of Education, have held varying degrees of influence on the goals for America's schools and ultimately classroom instruction. Certain eras in American education have been dominated by particular philosophical approaches. As times change, the dominant philosophy or theory often changes, and the impact is felt in classrooms across the country—classrooms like those you are about to enter. As a new teacher, you will be entering schools that are influenced by current social conditions, and you will need to look for a fit between your philosophy of education and the educational values of the school district and school in which you teach. Examine your school district's goals as well as those of your school. How do these goals translate into curriculum and teaching methods, and, most importantly, how comfortable are you philosophically with the answers to these questions?

REFOCUS What current examples of changes in society, knowledge, or beliefs about the nature of learners do you believe will affect your goals as a teacher?

This chapter describes the relationship between the philosophies and theories of education and the purposes that have prevailed at different times in the history of American education. We then examine the important changes in educational goals of recent years that have been promoted by influential policy reports. First, however, the chapter shows how we define educational purposes in terms of goals, standards, and objectives.

Establishing Goals and Objectives

Standards & Assessment

Levels of educational purpose

When we talk about the purposes of education, we may be referring to purposes at one or more of the following levels: nation, state, school district, school, subject/grade, unit plan, or lesson plan. Despite mixed opinions, most educators use the terms **goals**, **standards**, and **objectives** to distinguish among levels of purpose, with goals being broader statements of intent, standards being more focused statements, and objectives being more specific guides to classroom instruction. These terms describe a direction— what we are seeking to accomplish. Educators often refer to these terms as "ends" or "endpoints" of education.

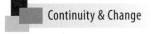
Continuity & Change

Three influential forces

All endpoints, however, reflect the influences of social forces and prevailing philosophies or theories of education. Social forces and philosophies combine to shape the goals adopted at the national or state level; these goals in turn affect the standards and objectives that guide school systems, schools, and classrooms. Over time, changes in social forces can also lead to modifications in prevailing philosophies and theories. The three main types of influential forces are (1) society in general, (2) developments in knowledge, and (3) beliefs about the nature of the learner.[1]

Changes in *society* include shifts in emphasis among the various influences examined in Chapter 10, Culture, Socialization, and Education, and in Chapter 11, Social Class, Race, and School Achievement, such as the family, peer groups, social class, and the economy. Changes in *knowledge* include new developments in science and technology, new methods of processing and storing information, and new methods of defining or organizing fields of study. Finally, changes in beliefs about the nature of the *learner,* such as new discoveries in cognitive science, may also produce changes in educational theories and purposes.

Goals

Goals as broad statements of purpose

Although goals are important guides in education, we cannot directly observe them; rather, they are broad statements of intent that denote a desired and valued competency,

[1]The concept of three sources of change is rooted in the ideas of Boyd Bode and John Dewey, who wrote approximately eighty-five years ago. These ideas, popularized by Ralph Tyler in 1949, have been developed by contemporary curriculum theorists such as Allan Ornstein, J. Galen Saylor, and Robert Zais.

a theme or concern that applies to education in general. The most general goals are often called *aims*.

National or state goals

Goals or aims are formulated at national and state levels, often by prestigious commissions or task forces. An example of a goal at the national level that was influential during the 1990s, from the **National Education Goals Panel Report**, stated, "All children in America will start school ready to learn."[2] Another national or state goal present throughout our history is to prepare students for democratic citizenship. Although these are admirable goals, it is unclear how local school districts or individual schools might achieve them. They merely suggest a general direction to follow.

District goals

Goals at the school district level begin to narrow in focus. For example, a school district goal related to the national goal of school readiness might be "all children will have access to high-quality and developmentally appropriate preschool programs that help prepare children for school." A more sharply focused example of the national citizenship goal might be "students will participate actively in the political and social life of the community." Each of these goals helps to point teachers, principals, and superintendents toward certain general ends.

School goals

Goals at the school level usually narrow in focus even more, translating national, state, and district goals into statements that coincide more closely with the philosophy and priorities of the local school community.[3] School-level goal statements often appear in documents known as *school improvement plans,* which are usually developed by school improvement teams. These goal statements flow from an overall school *mission statement,* which articulates the school's role in educating the community's youth.[4]

Tyler's four questions

In the late 1940s, Ralph Tyler developed an outline for the development and implementation of school goals that remains useful today. Tyler identified four fundamental questions to consider:

1. What educational purposes should the school seek to attain?
2. What educational experiences can be provided to help attain these purposes?
3. How can these educational experiences be effectively organized?
4. How can we determine whether [and to what extent] the purposes have been attained?[5]

▶II TEACHSOURCE VIDEO ACTIVITY

Common Core Standards: A New Lesson Plan for America

Go to the Education CourseMate website to access the BBC News video entitled "Common Core Standards: A New Lesson Plan for America." In this video, set in Atlanta schools, the impact of adopting national standards is discussed. After viewing, think about the following questions:

❶ What are the benefits for students and teachers to adopting the new Common Core State Standards (CCSS)?

❷ What argument could be made against adopting the new CCSS?

[2]*National Education Goals* (Archived Information, 1995), at **www.ed.gov/pubs/CommInvite/neg.html** (January 2012).
[3]Allan C. Ornstein and Francis P. Hunkins, *Curriculum: Foundations, Principles, and Issues,* 5th ed. (Boston: Allyn and Bacon, 2008); and Hugh Burkett, *The School Improvement Planning Process* (Washington, D.C.: The Center for Comprehensive School Reform and Improvement) at **www.centerforcsri.org/files/presentations/SchImpPlanningProcess.pdf** (January 2012).
[4]"School Mission Statements: Where Is Your School Going?" *Education World* (2011) at **www.educationworld.com/a_admin/admin/admin229.shtml** (February 2012); and Susan Black, "Mission Critical," *American School Board Journal* (July 2011), pp. 34–35.
[5]Ralph W. Tyler, *Basic Principles of Curriculum and Instruction* (Chicago: University of Chicago Press, 1949).

FROM PRESERVICE TO PRACTICE

Standards and Objectives

"What did your students learn from the lesson I just observed, Joanne?" Professor Yates asked.

"In this case, Dr. Yates, I would like to have all students learn to appreciate the many different ways that birds adapt to various environments," Joanne replied. "Then I would like them to apply the concept of adaptation to one or more of our local birds. If they can do that, they ought to be able to understand adaptation as an important concept in science."

"I am not sure the students learned what you just described. What came across to me is that birds are found in many sizes, colors, and places. Adaptation didn't seem to be a main point. It would be helpful if you would project your objective for the lesson on the whiteboard at the start of the lesson. What skills and attitudes did you want to link with this knowledge?"

"Well," Joanne said. "I want them to learn to observe, to reflect on what they observe, and to appreciate nature's remarkable variety of adaptations, particularly in birds. I can start tomorrow's lesson with a review and ask some pointed questions about today's lesson. That should tell me pretty quickly if the kids didn't understand the concept of adaptation in birds. What do you think of that, Professor Yates?"

Professor Yates nodded. "That might be one strategy to try. I would also like you to talk with your mentor teacher here at the school. Ms. Butler may have ideas to help you.

You need to develop specific objectives when preparing a lesson. If you know what learning you expect from students, it will help guide your lesson. And, you'll be sure the class is following your thought pattern as you teach the lesson if you ask questions as you go along that relate back to the objective. Now I have some more leading questions for you to consider about your lesson. With which state science standard does this objective align?"

"Gosh, I didn't even think about that," Joanne said, a little disconcerted. "I thought it was enough to try to prepare the lesson with the specifics on the birds. I guess I need to expand my vision about how all of this ties together. This semester of interning has really been tough for me, but I can see that having a vision of how everything fits together might help me keep on target. I want to rethink my lesson for tomorrow. Can you give me some leads, Professor Yates?"

"I could, but I won't," Dr. Yates replied. "I want you to work with Ms. Butler and think out these things for yourself. Your students' responses will tell you if you are successful or not. Be sure that you know the standards that will structure the organization of your curriculum objectives and the specific lesson objectives. I'll be back to observe another lesson next week. Meanwhile, concentrate on developing specific objectives as you prepare your lessons."

Case Questions

1. Why is Professor Yates pushing Joanne to consider specific objectives as well as links to the state standards in science?

2. If Joanne were teaching in your state, what resources could Joanne take advantage of to find the state standards for her teaching area?

3. If schools are particularly concerned with helping students adapt to changing life conditions, how might Joanne expand her lesson beyond biology?

Citizen input

The process of developing goals for a school district or individual school should permit citizens, parents, and (at times) students to give meaningful input. Working in partnership with professional educators who understand child development and the learning process, citizens can provide a valuable perspective in helping to decide the emphasis of the public school's direction.[6]

Whether formulated at the national, state, school district, or school level, goals are usually written in nonbehavioral terms as general statements of intent. They are intended to be long-lasting guides. Goals provide a direction by describing what schooling is intended to accomplish, but they are too broad and long term for teachers and students to apply them directly in classroom lessons.

[6]"School Boards and Student Achievement: A Comparison of Governance in High- and Low-Achieving Districts," *ERS Spectrum* (Winter 2001), pp. 38–40; and Ronald S. Brant and Ralph W. Tyler, "Goals and Objectives," cited in Allan C. Ornstein, Edward F. Pajak, and Stacey B. Ornstein, *Contemporary Issues in Curriculum,* 5th ed. (Upper Saddle River, NJ: Pearson, 2011).

Standards

In recent years, standards have been developed as intermediate steps in translating goals or aims into more specific direction for classroom instruction. Standards define what students should know and be able to do as a result of studying an academic subject at specific points in their schooling. Academic or content standards emphasize the facts, ideas, concepts, and information of the disciplines and the skills needed to apply that knowledge.[7] They are designed to provide a description of the organizational structure of the subject and aid educators in developing curriculum, classroom experiences, and assessments that enable learners to gain a deep understanding of subject matter.[8] Because they have a more narrow focus than goals, standards provide direction for the development of a rigorous curriculum and priorities for what should be taught in individual subjects at each grade level. For example, the following standard from the National Standards for Civics and Government could be linked to the goal mentioned earlier about preparing students for democratic citizenship: "Civic responsibilities. Students should be able to evaluate, take, and defend positions on the importance of civic responsibilities to the individual and society."[9]

One of the primary motivations for the development of standards can be linked to Tyler's fundamental questions listed earlier in the chapter—standards provide specific (more so than goals or aims) "educational purposes that the school seeks to attain." Because the standards list the content and skills necessary to master each subject, it becomes possible to develop assessments to measure student progress, thus determining "whether the purposes have been attained." This idea of assessment-based accountability, whereby the standards are linked to assessments that measure student and school level of success mastering the content standards, has driven school reform efforts for the past twenty years.[10]

Professional organizations such as the National Council of Teachers of Mathematics and the National Science Teachers Association initially developed content standards beginning in the late 1980s as a result of the reform reports that will be discussed later in the chapter. As a result of subsequent federal statutes, states were required to develop standards that would guide the development of curriculum within each state.

Objectives

Objectives are the tools that make goals and standards operational in classroom instruction. Although objectives are more specific than goals and standards, educators disagree about how detailed they ought to be. Some prefer fairly general objectives; others advocate objectives precise enough to be measured in behavioral or performance terms—that is, by an observable student behavior.

In practice at the classroom level, you will most likely organize instruction with a combination of general and specific objectives in mind. General objectives are characterized by "end" terms such as to *know, learn, understand, comprehend,* and *appreciate.* Such objectives will help you develop a sequenced curriculum for a grade level or a unit.

Continuity & Change

Classroom objectives

[7]Diane Ravitch, *National Standards in American Education: A Citizen's Guide* (Washington, D.C.: Brookings, 1995); and Laura Lefkowits and Kirsten Miller, "Fulfilling the Promise of the Standards Movement," *Phi Delta Kappan* (January 2006), pp. 403–407.
[8]AFT, "The American Federation of Teachers' Criteria for Setting Academic Standards," *Setting Strong Standards* (Washington, D.C.: American Federation of Teachers, 2003) at **www.aft.org /pdfs/teachers/settingstrongstandards0603.pdf** (January 2012); and Commission on No Child Left Behind, *State Standards: Assessing Differences in Quality and Rigor and How They Impact NCLB* (Washington, D.C.: The Aspen Institute, 2006) at **www.aspeninstitute.org /policy-work/no-child-left-behind/reports/state-standards-assessing-differences -qual** (January 2012).
[9]*National Standards for Civics and Government,* Center for Civic Education at **www.civiced.org /index.php?page=58erica#10** (January 2012).
[10]Lorrie Shepard, Jane Hannaway, and Eva Baker, eds. *Standards, Assessments, and Accountability— Education Policy White Paper* (Washington, D.C.: National Academy of Education, 2009).

OVERVIEW 13.1

Goals and Objectives of Education

Ends	Level of Direction	Developed By	Example(s)
National and state goals	Nation, state	Commissions, task force groups, U.S. Department of Education, state departments of education, professional associations of the disciplines	Improving basic literacy skills
Standards	Nation, state	State departments of education, professional associations of the disciplines/educators, nonprofit educational organizations, political organizations	"Identify and use text features to facilitate understanding of informational texts." (http://mdk12.org/instruction/curriculum/reading/standard2/grade4.html)
Local goals	School district, school	Groups of administrators, teachers, and/or community members; professional associations	Acquiring information and meaning through reading, writing, speaking, and mathematical symbols
General objectives	Subject/grade	Subject-centered professional associations; curriculum departments or committees of state departments of education; large school districts' curriculum specialists	Improving reading comprehension; appreciating the reading of whole books
	Unit plan	Textbook authors; teams of teachers of specific subjects or grade levels, individual teachers	Developing word recognition skills; listening to stories read
Specific objectives	Lesson plan	Textbook authors; teachers	Identifying the main ideas of the author; describing the characteristics of a leader

■ Lesson plan objectives

At the level of the individual lesson plan, objectives usually become specific, as recommended by Robert Mager. They use precise wording (often action words) such as *describe in writing, state orally, compare, list, identify,* and *solve.* Sometimes called *behavioral* or *performance* objectives, these statements are content or skill specific, require particular student behavior or performance, and are observable and measurable.[11] Both teacher and learner can evaluate the amount or degree of learning because the objective establishes the task the students will perform to demonstrate their learning.[12] The From Preservice to Practice box gives one example of how teachers and their students can benefit from preparing clear objectives.

[11]Robert F. Mager, *Preparing Instructional Objectives,* 3rd ed. (Atlanta, GA: Center for Effective Performance, 1997).
[12]Anne R. Reeves, *Where Great Teaching Begins: Planning for Student Thinking and Learning,* (Alexandria, VA: Association for Supervision and Curriculum Development, 2011).

Standards & Assessment

Examples of objectives

REFOCUS How will you find out about the goals of your state and school district when you, as a teacher, plan your lesson objectives?

As a prospective teacher, you have already been introduced to the curriculum standards for your state. The local school districts and teachers have aligned their curricula, and thus their objectives, with these state standards.[13]

An example of a general unit objective might be that "students will understand why American colonists wanted to separate from Great Britain in the 1770s." Transposing this general objective into a specific lesson objective, we might obtain "Students will describe in writing three reasons American colonists gave in favor of separation from Great Britain." This objective refers to a specific kind of knowledge, states what is expected of students, and gives a precise criterion of three reasons.

Overview 13.1 summarizes the differences among the various levels of goals and objectives. As we move from national goals to lesson objectives, the examples become more specific—that is, easier to observe and/or measure.

Historical Perspective

As an educator, you will discover that policy makers and the public at large are continually questioning the purposes of American education. What should our schools be trying to do? The answers are varied, and the debate has often been heated. To understand this debate, we need to know how educational aims have developed and changed over the years. As the following sections illustrate, the goals of American education have undergone many transformations.

Mental discipline: exercising the mind

Before the twentieth century, the perennialist theory generally dominated American education. Subject matter was organized and presented as an accounting of information. Proponents of the **mental discipline approach** believed that the mind is strengthened through mental activities, just as the body is strengthened by exercising. Traditional subjects, such as languages (Latin, Greek, French, and German), mathematics, history, English, physics, chemistry rhetoric, and logic, were valued for their cultivation of the intellect; the more difficult the subject and the more the student had to exercise the mind, the greater the value of the subject.[14]

Progressive demands for reform

Gradually, demands were made for various changes in schooling to meet the needs of a changing social order. The accelerated pace of immigration and industrial development led a growing number of educators to question the classical curriculum and the emphasis on mental discipline and repetitive drill. Adherents of the new pedagogy represented the progressive voice in education. They emphasized school subjects designed to meet the needs of everyday life for all children in the contemporary world. By the early twentieth century, the effort to reform the schools along more progressive lines was well under way.

Concern for the whole child

In contrast to the perennialist philosophy and mental discipline approach that prevailed before World War I, the period from World War I to post–World War II was dominated by the philosophy of progressivism and the science of child psychology. These emphasized the **whole-child concept** and life adjustment. The prevailing view held that schools must be concerned with the growth and development of the entire child, not just with certain selected mental aspects. The life-adjustment movement was concerned with addressing the needs of all students, especially the students in the middle, those not in the college track or the vocational track.[15] Goals related to cognitive or mental growth had to share the stage with other important purposes of

---

[13]"State Standards and Assessment Systems," *What States Can Learn about State Standards & Assessment Systems from No Child Left Behind Documents & Interviews* (March 2008), pp. 2–5; Matthew Tungate, "Standard Bearers," *Kentucky Teacher* (March 2010), pp. 4–5; and Wangui Njuguna, "Teachers Extol Planning with Standards as Best Practice," *Education Daily* (November 16, 2010), pp.1–3.

[14]Ellwood P. Cubberley, *Public Education in the United States,* rev. ed. (Boston: Houghton Mifflin, 1947).

[15]"Challenge to Schools—Factors Involved in Curriculum Changes," *Congressional Digest* 37, (August 1958), pp. 199–224; and Sister Mary Janet, "Life Adjustment Opens New Doors to Youth," *Educational Leadership* (December 1954), pp. 137–141.

Table 13.1	Goals of Education: Two Major Statements of the Progressive Approach

Cardinal Principles of Secondary Education (1918)	Ten Imperative Needs of Youth (1944)
1. *Health:* provide health instruction and a program of physical activities; cooperate with home and community in promoting health. 2. *Command of fundamental processes:* develop fundamental thought processes to meet needs of modern life. 3. *Worthy home membership:* develop qualities that make the individual a worthy member of a family. 4. *Vocation:* equip students to earn a living, to serve society well through a vocation, and to achieve personal development through that vocation. 5. *Civic education:* foster qualities that help a person play a part in the community and understand international problems. 6. *Worthy use of leisure:* equip people to find "recreation of body, mind, and spirit" that will enrich their personalities. 7. *Ethical character:* develop ethical *character* both through instructional methods and through social contacts among students and teachers.	Develop skills and/or attitudes that enhance the following: 1. Productive work experiences and occupational success 2. Good health and physical fitness 3. Rights and duties of a democratic citizenry 4. Conditions for successful family life 5. Wise consumer behavior 6. Understanding of science and the nature of man 7. Appreciation of arts, music, and literature 8. Wise use of leisure time 9. Respect for ethical values 10. The ability to think rationally and communicate thoughts clearly

Source: Commission on the Reorganization of Secondary Education, *Cardinal Principles of Secondary Education,* Bulletin no. 35 (Washington, D.C.: U.S. Government Printing Office, 1918), pp. 11–15; and Educational Policies Commission, *Education for All American Youth* (Washington, D.C.: National Education Association, 1944).

Continuity & Change

Return to academic essentials

National legislation

education such as goals involving social, psychological, physical, vocational, moral, and civic development. The goal was to present students with a meaningful and relevant curriculum.[16] Table 13.1 describes the two most important statements of goals of this era. The whole-child concept and the corresponding growth of child psychology had a tremendous impact on schools that we still feel today.

During the era of the Cold War and the Soviet *Sputnik* flight (1957), international events gave major impetus to challenge the life-adjustment curriculum and to reexamine academic disciplines as the focus of schooling. The country was appalled at the notion of losing technological superiority to the Soviets; national pride was challenged, and national goals were perceived as threatened.

Influenced by the perennialist and essentialist theories of education, critics called for a return to academic essentials, intellectual rigor, and mental discipline. Thus, hard on the heels of *Sputnik* came national legislation to support training and programs in fields considered vital to defense. The National Defense Education Act of 1958 targeted science, mathematics, modern languages, and guidance (often considered a way to steer youth into the three former fields and into college). The scientific community, university scholars, and curriculum specialists were called upon to reconstruct subject-matter content,

---

[16]Robert V. Bullough and Craig Kridel, "Adolescent Needs, Curriculum and the Eight-Year Study," *Journal of Curriculum Studies* (March 2003), pp. 151–169; and Thomas D. Fallace, "The Effects of Life Adjustment Education on the U.S History Curriculum, 1948–1957," *History Teacher* (August 2011), pp. 569–589.

Educational approaches influenced by progressive philosophies emphasize focusing on educating the "whole child," rather than strictly on imparting academic content. Which approach is closer to your personal philosophy of education?

Spencer Grant/PhotoEdit

especially on the high-school level, while government and philanthropic foundations provided the funds.[17] The new educational climate also included an increasing emphasis on providing enriched educational opportunities for the academically talented child.

Concern for non–college-bound students

The 1960s saw a shift in focus as increased concern about poverty, racial discrimination, and civil rights brought new educational priorities, often related to the progressive and social reconstructionist theories of education. Educators noted that most students did not go on to college and that many failed to graduate or graduated as functional illiterates. Under those circumstances, serious problems could be anticipated if educational goals continued to be narrowly directed toward the most able students, thus equal educational opportunity became a goal of newly expanding federal education programs.[18]

Student diversity

The focus on students who were then characterized as "disadvantaged" extended into the 1980s and expanded to include limited English proficient (LEP) students and students with disabilities. The nation's expanding multicultural and bilingual efforts were characterized by increased federal funding for Hispanic, Asian American, and Native American students, and by legal support for students with limited English skills (*Lau v. Nichols*, U.S. Supreme Court, 1974).[19]

From the 1970s through the 1990s, much concern also surfaced for special education, especially for students with learning disabilities or other special needs. Two landmark pieces of legislation, the Education for All Handicapped Children Act (PL 94-142, 1975) and the Individuals with Disabilities Education Act (IDEA, 1990), detailed policies and procedures for including students with disabilities in regular classrooms, to the extent possible.[20] This approach came to be known as "inclusion" (see Chapter 12, Providing Equal Educational Opportunity, for more on this topic).

[17]Mary M. Harris and James R. Miller, "Needed: Reincarnation of National Defense Education Act of 1958," *Journal of Science Education & Technology* (June 2005), pp. 157–171; and Kathleen Anderson Steeves, Philip Evan Bernhardt, James P. Burns, and Michele K. Lombard. "Transforming American Educational Identity after Sputnik," *American Educational History Journal* (Spring 2009), pp. 71–87.
[18]John W. Gardner, *Excellence: Can We Be Equal and Excellent Too?* (New York: Harper and Row, 1961), pp. 28–29, 77; and Virginia R. L. Plunkett, "From Title I to Chapter 1: The Evolution of Compensatory Education," *Phi Delta Kappan* (April 1985), pp. 533–537.
[19]Maria E. Brisk, *Bilingual Education: From Compensatory to Quality Schooling* (Mahwah, NJ: Lawrence Earlbaum, 2005); and "ELLs and the Law: Statutes, Precedents," *Education Week* (January 8, 2009), pp. 8–9.
[20]"Special Education Milestones," *Congressional Digest* 84 (January 2005), p. 9.

In the 1990s, however, conservative reactions against these trends increased. As noted Chapter 11, Social Class, Race, and School Achievement, multicultural and bilingual programs have been heavily criticized as contributing to fragmentation and separatism rather than cultural unity. Several states approved statutes signifying English as the official state language, leading some to attack funding of bilingual programs. Educators also split into factions over the most effective way to conduct special education. Some wanted full inclusion (elimination of self-contained classrooms for special-education students and assignment of special-education teachers to co-teach regular classrooms). Others supported partial inclusion (whereby students with learning disabilities are placed in general-education classrooms as much as possible). Still others favored maintaining mostly separate, or self-contained, classes for special-education students.[21]

Focus on outcomes

The end of the twentieth century also brought increased demands for educational accountability (demands expressed by elected officials and business leaders as well as by laypeople). Many argued that education should focus more clearly on *outcomes* or outputs—that is, measurable academic results—rather than on inputs such as money, programs, efforts, and intentions. According to some of these critics, mere completion of a curriculum means little if students cannot use their education in real-life contexts. As a result of this focus, a majority of states developed an **outcomes-based education (OBE)** approach to curriculum development. Although many educators believed the focus on student outcomes was a sensible way to look at educational goals, OBE was not without its critics. Some feared that it emphasized affective outcomes (that is, values) and critical-thinking processes to the detriment of religious faith and family values. Others claimed that OBE promoted vague, minimal academic standards, dumbing down the curriculum because of the focus on process rather than content. Still other critics claim that OBE involved higher costs without corresponding results.[22]

 **Standards & Assessment**

State standards

While some educators focused on student performance outcomes, the first decade of the twenty-first century found other educators and policy makers calling for clear **state standards** focusing on content to which all students would be taught. Advocates for state standards wanted to assess proficiency. State standards in school subjects and assessment of progress would help hold students, teachers, schools, and school districts accountable for learning by every student. The federal 2001 **No Child Left Behind Act (NCLB)** required standards and yearly assessment of student progress (known as adequate yearly progress, AYP).

High-stakes testing

Your state's standards will heavily influence your instructional planning as a teacher. As required by NCLB, state standards have been accompanied by accountability systems that affix praise or censure based on the level of performance that measures mastery of the standards. One concern expressed by many observers has been that the assessments are linked to such high-stakes outcomes that they become intimidating for those taking the tests. Another critique has been that each of the fifty states sets its own 'cut-scores' to determine mastery, thus there is no reliable way to determine how the nation as a whole is progressing in meeting standards. Even so, test results, in many states, have helped support decisions about promotion, graduation, and school curriculum, and they are related to a range of consequences for the school districts and professionals preparing students for those exams, including school sanctions, pay raises, and bonuses.[23]

---

[21]Devery R. Mock and James M. Kauffman, "Preparing Teachers for Full Inclusion: Is It Possible?" *Teacher Educator* (Winter 2002), pp. 202–215; Mary Ann Zehr, "Classroom Ban on Spanish Protested," *Education Week* (October 29, 2003), pp. 1–18; and Myrna Mandlawitz, *What Every Teacher Should Know about IDEA 2004 Laws and Regulations* (Boston: Allyn and Bacon, 2007).
[22]Bill Zlatos, "Outcomes-Based Outrage Runs Both Ways," *Education Digest* (January 1994), pp. 26–27; Bruno V. Manno, "The New School Wars: Battles over Outcome-Based Education," *Phi Delta Kappan* (May 1995), pp. 720–726; and Bruno V. Manno, "Outcome-based Education," *Current* (July 1995), p. 3.
[23]James W. Popham, "Content Standards: The Unindicted Co-conspirator," *Educational Leadership* (September 2006), pp. 87–88; and Sandra Myers, "High-Stakes Testing," *Research Starters* (Toledo, OH: Great Neck Publishing, 2008).

▶‖ TEACHSOURCE VIDEO ACTIVITY

Foundations: Aligning Instruction with Federal Legislation

Go to the Education CourseMate website to access the video entitled "Foundations: Aligning Instruction with Federal Legislation." In this video, you'll see teachers and a principal discuss how federal legislation affects the classroom teaching experience. As you're watching, think about your future teaching career. How do you think legislation will affect you and your students? After watching the video, think about the following questions:

1 This chapter discusses the purposes and goals of public education. Based on reading this chapter and watching the video, do you agree with the educational goals targeted by IDEA and NCLB?

2 According to the educators in the video, what are the pros and cons of assessing standards as required by NCLB? If students are not meeting standards, what should teachers do?

** This video reinforces key concepts found in Principles of Teaching and Learning—Section IV: Profession and Community of the Praxis II Exam.**

Continuity & Change

REFOCUS Over the decades, educational goals have targeted different groups of students, such as the academically talented or special needs students. Which group of students now appears to be the target of most educational goals?

Common Core State Standards (CCSS)

In spite of these and other stumbling blocks that confronted states, NCLB advocates have suggested that standards are worth sustaining. They claim that for the first time in the history of American public education, rigorous goals have been established for all children, and schools are paying more attention to the achievement gap and learning needs of children who have historically been left behind.[24]

As mentioned in the previous section, one of the major criticisms of the NCLB accountability measures targets the fragmented system that exists because each state has its own set of standards and corresponding assessments. In an effort to reform this situation, in 2010, the National Governors Association Center for Best Practices (NGA Center) and the Council of Chief State School Officers (CCSSO) released the Common Core State Standards (CCSS) in English/language arts and mathematics for grades K–12.[25] Developing the CCSS has been a voluntary, state-led effort, and by the beginning of 2012, forty-five states and the District of Columbia had formally adopted them for use. These standards are intended to define the knowledge and skills students should gain during their climb of the educational ladder so that by the time they graduate high school, they will be able to succeed in academic college courses and in future career training programs.[26]

Those promoting a common set of standards for schools across the country that are internationally benchmarked with other top-performing countries on international assessments contend this will make education in America more competitive in global comparisons. They say more rigorous standards that require deeper understanding and

---

[24]Jack Jennings and Diane Stark Rentner, "How Public Schools Are Impacted by No Child Left Behind," *Education Digest* (December 2006), pp. 4–9; and Paul Parkison, "Political Economy and the NCLB Regime: Accountability, Standards, and High-Stakes Testing," *Educational Forum* (Winter 2009), pp. 44–57.

[25]David T. Conley, Kathryn V. Drummond, Alicia de Gonzalez, Jennifer Rooseboom, and Odile Stout, *Reaching the Goal: The Applicability and Importance of the Common Core State Standards to College and Career Readiness* (Eugene, OR: Educational Policy Improvement Center, 2011).

[26]"About the Standards," *Common Core Standards Initiative* (2010) at **www.corestandards.org /about-the-standards** (January 2012); and "In the States," *Common Core Standards Initiative* (2010) at **www.corestandards.org/in-the-states** (January 2012).

TECHNOLOGY @ SCHOOL

Finding and Assessing State Standards

Teachers, both new and experienced, must be well informed about national, state, and local educational goals and how these goals will affect their work in the classroom.

For state curriculum standards, you can visit your state department of education website. A number of sites provide access to the appropriate pages of the various departments of education, but two are especially helpful. The first is the "National Standards" page at the *Education World* site (**www.education-world.com/standards**). In addition to access to the state standards by subject, it also provides easy accessibility to each state's entire set of standards and to links for the CCSS in English/language arts and mathematics. Also provided are links to the voluntary National Education Standards for most subject areas; these were developed by the respective professional organizations of each discipline and preceded the development of the state standards.

A second site that provides access to the curriculum standards of each of the fifty states is "Links to All 50 States'

Content Standards Plus CCSS" at **http://patternbasedwriting.com/elementary_writing_success/all-50-states-content-standards**. Provided are links to each state's content standards page and their "Common Core State Standards" page. As an aspiring teacher, you can examine these two resources to get an idea of what states across the nation have developed as standards to guide the K–12 curriculum. What similarities might be found among a random sample of state standards in the same subject area? What impact would these findings have for schools in the United States?

As you enter the teaching profession, the CCSS will be influencing curricula in schools across the country. Monitor this progress at the *Common Core State Standards Initiative* web page (**www.corestandards.org**). In addition to accessing the standards, you can follow news about their implementation in states across the nation and examine various resources with information about the standards.

better alignment of content and skills have to be an improvement over the diverse system of standards and assessments that currently exist.[27]

The common standards are intended to ensure consistency in the quality of education from state to state and school to school. Some educators are concerned, however, that the standards will simply encourage the development of a college-preparatory curriculum for all students, and the common assessments that are being designed to accompany the standards will be especially costly to implement.[28]

The Call for Excellence

Continuity & Change

Keeping in mind how American educational goals have changed over time, we can look more closely at the recent history of the demand for reform in the schools. How have the various proposals from the past three decades reflected important changes in American educational purposes? How well do particular reforms fit your own ideas about the purpose of education?

Overview of Policy Reports

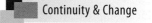
National reports call for reform

By the early 1980s, national attention was focused on the need for educational excellence and higher academic standards for all students—particularly the neglected average student—and not just the needy or the talented. During the past thirty years, national policy reports, most of which reflected a so-called neoessentialist perspective,

[27]"Myths vs. Facts," *Common Core Standards Initiative* (2010) at **www.corestandards.org/about-the-standards/myths-vs-facts** (January 2012); and Matthew Tungate, "Standard Bearers," *Kentucky Teacher* (March 2010), pp. 4–5.
[28]"Are You Ready to Implement Common Core Standards," *District Administration* (March 2011), p. 16; and, Daniel Orlich, "Educational Standards—Caveat Emptor," *Kappa Delta Pi Record* (Winter 2011), pp. 52–57.

urged reforms to improve the quality of education in the United States. Six of the most influential were as follows:

- ■ *Action for Excellence* (1983)
- ■ *Educating Americans for the 21st Century* (1983)
- ■ *High School* (1983)
- ■ *A Nation at Risk* (1983)
- ■ *First Lessons: A Report on Elementary Education in America* (1986)
- ■ *The National Education Goals* (1990, 1994, 1997)

To support their proposals, the reports presented discouraging details and statistics indicating a serious decline in American education. For example:

Declining achievement and competency

1. Average achievement scores on the Scholastic Aptitude Test (SAT) declined steadily from 1963 to 1980. Average verbal scores fell more than 50 points, and mathematics scores dropped almost 40 points.[29]

2. *Educating Americans for the 21st Century* bemoaned the low level of student participation in math and science courses, which had been on the decline for twenty years. The need for improved professional development for math and science teachers was also noted.[30]

International comparisons

3. As we looked toward the new century, U.S. fifteen-year-olds still performed below their peers in twenty (math) and fifteen (science) other industrialized nations (out of a total of twenty-eight countries)—hardly the performance at "world class standards" called for in the *National Education Goals*.[31] (See Chapter 15, International Education, for further discussion of international comparisons.)

Functional illiteracy

4. According to *A Nation at Risk*, "Some 23 million American adults are [in 1983] functionally illiterate by the simplest test of everyday reading, writing, and comprehension."[32]

5. It was reported that many seventeen-year-olds did not possess the critical-thinking skills that should be expected of them, nearly 40 percent could not draw inferences from written material, and only 20 percent could write a persuasive essay. Forty percent of seventeen-year-olds lacked the intermediate reading skills they needed to be successful in lessons at the seventh- or eighth-grade levels.[33]

✔ Standards & Assessment

Importance of technology

All of these reports emphasized the need to strengthen the curriculum in the core subjects of English, math, science, foreign language, and social studies. Technology and computer courses were mentioned often, and at the beginning of the twenty-first century, the need to improve students' technology skills and to upgrade schools technologically was almost a mantra. High-level cognitive and thinking skills were also stressed.

Higher standards, more rigorous requirements

The reports further emphasized tougher standards and tougher courses, and a majority proposed that colleges raise their admission requirements. Most of the reports also talked about increasing homework, time for learning, and time in school, as well as instituting more rigorous grading, testing, homework, and discipline. They mentioned upgrading teacher certification, increasing teacher salaries, increasing the number of science and math teachers and paying them higher salaries, and providing merit pay

---

[29]National Commission on Excellence in Education, *A Nation at Risk: The Imperative for Educational Reform* (Washington, D.C.: U.S. Department of Education, 1983).
[30]Katherine K. Merseth, "From the Rhetoric of Reports to the Clarity of Classrooms," *Educational Leadership* (December 1983), pp. 38–42.
[31]Mariann Lemke and Patrick Gonzales, "Special Analysis: U.S. Student and Adult Performance on International Assessments of Educational Achievement," *The Condition of Education—2006* (Washington, D.C.: National Center for Education Statistics, 2006).
[32]National Commission on Excellence in Education, *A Nation at Risk: The Imperative for Educational Reform* (Washington, D.C.: U.S. Department of Education, 1983).
[33]Ibid.; and William J. Bennett, *First Lessons: A Report on Elementary Education in America*, (Washington, D.C.: U.S. Department of Education, 1986).

Bill Freeman/Alamy Limited

Recent shifts in educational goals have brought a new emphasis on assessment and accountability for students, teachers, and schools, including the use of controversial "high-stakes" testing used to make decisions about outcomes such as graduation and promotion.

Schools play too many roles

for outstanding teachers. Overall, the reports stressed academic achievement, not the whole child, and increased productivity, not relevancy or humanism.

Most of the reports expressed a popular concern that the schools are pressed to play too many social roles; that the schools cannot meet all these expectations; and that the schools are in danger of losing sight of their key purpose—teaching basic skills and core academic subjects, new skills for computer use, and higher-level cognitive skills for the world of work and technology.[34] Many of the reports, concerned not only with academic productivity but also with national productivity, linked human capital with economic capital. Investment in schools would be an investment in the economy and in the nation's future stability. If education failed, so would our workforce and nation. Hence business, labor, and government pledged to work with educators to help educate and train the U.S. population.

In the following sections, we will look more closely at the two most popularized and influential reports: **A Nation at Risk**, published in 1983, and **The National Education Goals**, a 1994 revision of a report first published in 1990.

Rising tide of mediocrity

A Nation at Risk   The report by the National Commission on Excellence in Education, compiled by a panel appointed by the U.S. Department of Education, indicated that a "rising tide of mediocrity" was eroding the well-being of the nation.[35] This mediocrity was linked to the foundations of our educational institutions and was spilling over into the workplace and other sectors of society. The report listed several aspects of educational decline that were evident to educators and citizens alike in the late 1970s and early 1980s: lower achievement scores, lower testing requirements, lower graduation requirements, lower teacher expectations, fewer academic courses, more remedial courses, too many electives, and higher illiteracy rates. It stated that the United States compromised its commitment to educational quality as a result of conflicting demands placed on the nation's schools and concluded that the schools attempted to tackle too many social problems that the home and other agencies of society either would not or could not resolve.

---

[34]G. T. Sewall, "Against Anomie and Amnesia: What Basic Education Means in the Eighties," *Phi Delta Kappan* (May 1982), pp. 603–606.

[35]National Commission on Excellence in Education, *A Nation at Risk: The Imperative for Educational Reform* (Washington, D.C.: U.S. Department of Education, 1983); Gerald W. Bracey, "April Foolishness: The 20th Anniversary of *A Nation at Risk*," *Phi Delta Kappan* (April 2003), pp. 16–21; and Jennifer Borek, "A Nation at Risk at 25," *Phi Delta Kappan* (April 2008), pp. 572–574.

TAKING ISSUE

Read the brief introduction below, as well as the Question and the pros and cons list that follows. Then, answer the question using your own words and position.

Common Core State Standards

The mission statement of the CCSS initiative states:

"The Common Core State Standards provide a consistent, clear understanding of what students are expected to learn, so teachers and parents know what they need to do to help them. The standards are designed to be robust and relevant to the real world, reflecting the knowledge and skills that our young people need for success in college and careers."

Question

Are the CCSS likely to improve American education? (Think about this question as you read the PRO and CON arguments listed here. What is *your* take on this issue?)

Arguments PRO

1. A common set of standards will benefit a highly mobile society where children move from state to state. Students will be more likely to experience the same curriculum regardless of their state of residence under the common standards.

2. If students from the United States are to compete with their peers from around the world on international assessments, only common standards that are internationally benchmarked will transform our education system to be competitive.

3. It will be less expensive and more efficient to develop assessments that measure performance on the common standards than it has been to assess the fifty separate sets of assessments (that tend to be weak and disjointed) under NCLB mandates.

4. With common standards in place, it will be more economical to align digital media and textbooks to address the standards and thus support instruction.

Arguments CON

1. A common set of standards for the United States cannot address the educational needs of students in the fifty individual states that have such diverse economic, demographic, political, and social characteristics.

2. Not all countries that do well on international assessments operate under one set of common standards; more comprehensive educational reforms must be considered if we are to become competitive on the global stage.

3. The federal government will ultimately become involved in the direction of the standards-driven reform and co-opt the idea of state and local control of schooling.

4. Though much effort and collaboration has gone into developing the common standards in English/language arts and math, there is no evidence to support the claim that these efforts will improve the quality of education in the United States.

Question Reprise: What Is Your Stand?

Reflect again on the following question by explaining *your* stand about this issue: Are the CCSS likely to improve American education?

Recommendations of *A Nation at Risk*

The report called for, in part, tougher standards for graduation, including more courses in science, mathematics, foreign language, and the "new basics" such as computer skills; a longer school day and school year; far more homework; improved and updated textbooks; more rigorous, measurable, and higher expectations for student achievement; higher teacher salaries based on performance and career ladders that distinguish among the beginning, experienced, and master teacher; demonstrated entry competencies and more rigorous certification standards for teachers; accountability from educators and policy makers; and greater fiscal support from citizens.[36]

Reports such as *A Nation at Risk* often spring from a broad-based concern about the quality of public education in changing times. The goal of such reports is to make what are perceived as practical recommendations for educational improvement and, as such, provide guidance to state and local boards of education, school districts, and ultimately teachers as they plan for instruction. The changes that took place during the 1980s and 1990s—increases in high-school graduation requirements, increases in required mathematics and science courses, a return to academic basics, more emphasis on technology, and increased college entrance requirements—have been attributed to the recommendations made in *A Nation at Risk*.[37] It has also been suggested that the subsequent "standards movement," which has greatly influenced schooling in the first decade of the twenty-first century, was sparked by the report's criticism of low expectations for student performance.[38]

Continuity & Change

NCLB continued in the tradition of national reports in its concern about the general quality of public education in changing times and its recommendations for educational improvement. It differs in that it provides explicit directives, partially supported by federal funds, to state and local boards of education and to school districts.

Sweeping changes demanded

The National Education Goals   In 1994, Congress passed the **Goals 2000: Educate America Act**. The complete set of goals, published as *The National Education Goals* and often referred to simply as Goals 2000, is listed in Table 13.2. The overriding theme of those goals was the push for an educated citizenry, well trained and responsible, capable of adapting to a changing world, knowledgeable about its cultural heritage and the world community, and willing to accept and maintain America's leadership position in the twenty-first century. The Goals Panel stated that educators must be given greater flexibility to devise teaching and learning strategies that serve all students, regardless of abilities or interests; at the same time, they should be held responsible for their teaching. Parents must become involved in their children's education, especially during the preschool years. Community, civic, and business groups all have a vital role to play in reforming education. Finally, students must accept responsibility for their education, and this means they must work hard in school.[39]

Developing national standards

In 2001, the National Education Goals Panel made its final major report on the progress on the eight goals and twenty-six indicators in Goals 2000. Although the nation as a whole did not meet the national goals by the year 2000, many states made progress, especially in improving opportunities in early childhood education and in the use of student data in instructional decision making. It has been noted that the work of the Goals Panel led to forty-nine states developing their own content standards by 2000.[40] With the suspension of the National Educational Goals Panel in 2002 and the advent of NCLB, America's educational expectations changed to a more specific focus on improved student performance in reading and math, having highly qualified teachers in every classroom, and identifying and improving schools where students were not meeting these standards.

REFOCUS   The national reports of the 1980s emphasized core curriculum subjects, tougher standards, and accountability. Which of these do you believe has most affected your career as a student? Which will be of most importance to you as a teacher?

---

[36]Thomas A. Kessinger, "Efforts toward National Educational Reform: An Essentialist Political Agenda," *Mid-Western Educational Researcher* (Spring 2007), pp. 16–23.
[37]James W. Guthrie and Matthew G. Springer, "A Nation at Risk Revisited: Did 'Wrong' Reasoning Result in 'Right' Results? At What Cost?" *Peabody Journal of Education* (January 2004), pp. 7–35.
[38]Sally Blake, "A Nation at Risk and the Blind Men," *Phi Delta Kappan* (April 2008), pp. 601–602.
[39]*HR 1804—Goals 2000: Educate America Act* (January 24, 1994) at **www.ed.gov/legislation /GOALS2000/TheAct/index.html**.
[40]*National Education Goals Panel—Building on the Momentum (1999)* at **http://govinfo.library .unt.edu/negp/reports/essays.pdf**; and David J. Hoff, "Mission Imponderable: Goals Panel to Disband," *Education Week* (January 9, 2002), p. 21.

Table 13.2	The National Education Goals

Goal 1 School Readiness

By the year 2000, all children in America will start school ready to learn.

Goal 2 School Completion

By the year 2000, the high-school graduation rate will increase to at least 90 percent.

Goal 3 Student Achievement and Citizenship

By the year 2000, all students will leave grades 4, 8, and 12 having demonstrated competency over challenging subject matter, including English, mathematics, science, foreign languages, civics and government, economics, arts, history, and geography, and every school in America will ensure that all students learn to use their minds well, so they may be prepared for responsible citizenship, further learning, and productive employment in our nation's modern economy.

Goal 4 Teacher Education and Professional Development

By the year 2000, the nation's teaching force will have access to programs for the continued improvement of their professional skills and the opportunity to acquire the knowledge and skills needed to instruct and prepare all American students for the next century.

Goal 5 Mathematics and Science

By the year 2000, U.S. students will be first in the world in mathematics and science achievement.

Goal 6 Adult Literacy and Lifelong Learning

By the year 2000, every adult American will be literate and will possess the knowledge and skills necessary to compete in a global economy and exercise the rights and responsibilities of citizenship.

Goal 7 Safe, Disciplined, and Alcohol- and Drug-Free Schools

By the year 2000, every school in the United States will be free of drugs, violence, and the unauthorized presence of firearms and alcohol and will offer a disciplined environment conducive to learning.

Goal 8 Parental Participation

By the year 2000, every school will promote partnerships that will increase parental involvement and participation in promoting the social, emotional, and academic growth of children.

Source: Goals 2000: Educate America Act (March 31, 1994); *The National Education Goals* (Washington, D.C.: U.S. Department of Education, 1994).

Swings of the Pendulum

Old themes reemerge

Continuity & Change

In examining educational goals from the turn of the twentieth century until today, we see considerable change but also old ideas reemerging in updated versions. For example, a stress on rigorous intellectual training, evident in the early twentieth century, reappeared in the 1950s during the Cold War, and again from the 1980s through the early twenty-first century, as a result of concern over economic competition with foreign countries. Similarly, as the social ferment of the 1960s and 1970s brought increasing concern for the rights and aspirations of low-income and minority groups, the ideas of the early progressive educators resurfaced, and a renewed stress was placed on educating the disenfranchised. In an era that has stressed accountability, assessment, and common standards, can you decide where the pendulum is swinging at this point in time?

<table>
<tr><td>

■ Too much expected
   of schools?

</td><td>

In looking at the broad sweep of American educational purposes, you might ask yourself whether schools are expected to do more than is feasible. The schools are often seen as ideal agencies to solve the nation's problems, but can they do so? Many people throughout society refuse to admit their own responsibility for helping children develop and learn. Similarly, parents and policy makers often expect teachers and school administrators to be solely responsible for school reform. In fact, without significant cooperation from parents and community members, schools are likely to struggle, and reform efforts are likely to be frustrated.

</td></tr>
</table>

■ Coping with change

Unquestionably, the goals of education must be relevant to the times. If the schools cannot adapt to changing conditions and social forces, how can they expect to produce people who do? Today we live in a highly technical and bureaucratic society, and we are faced with pressing social and economic problems—aging cities, deteriorating schools and educational infrastructure, the effects of centuries of discrimination, an aging population, economic dislocations, terrorism, and the pollution of the physical environment. Whether we allow the times to engulf us, or whether we can cope with our persistent problems will depend to a large extent on what kinds of skills are taught to our present-day students—and on the development of appropriate priorities for education.[41]

> **REFOCUS** What is your primary goal as a teacher? Ask this same question of several other educators and prospective educators. Compare and contrast your answer with theirs.

Summing Up

① The purposes of education are influenced by changing social forces as well as by educational philosophies and theories.

② Broad statements of educational purpose, generated at the national or state level, are usually translated into more specific goals by the school district or individual school. These goals, in turn, are developed into standards and even more specific objectives at the subject, grade, unit plan, and lesson plan levels.

③ Since the turn of the past century, the goals of American education have gone through numerous shifts in emphasis: academic rigor and mental discipline; the whole child; academically talented students, students in poverty, minority students, and children with disabilities; tougher academic

requirements for all students; and holding schools accountable for all students meeting standards.

④ Most of the major reports released since 1983 have emphasized the need for educational excellence and higher standards. Although educators disagree about many of the recommendations, most states implemented changes based on these reports.

⑤ We must learn to live with some disagreement about the purposes of schooling. Various groups of people need to work together in formulating future educational priorities.

⑥ We often expect schools to be a key instrument for solving our technological or social problems and preparing our workforce for the future. The years ahead will severely test these expectations.

Key Terms

The numbers indicate the pages where explanations of the key terms can be found.

goals 401
standards 401
objectives 401
mental discipline approach 406

whole-child concept 406
outcomes-based education (OBE) 409
state standards 409
No Child Left Behind Act (NCLB) 409

A Nation at Risk 413
The National Education Goals 413
Goals 2000: Educate America Act 415

---

[41]Charles Nevi, "Saving Standards," *Phi Delta Kappan* (February 2001), pp. 460–461.

Certification Connection Activity

This chapter is linked to the Praxis Planning Instruction section of Principles of Learning and Teaching. Relevant topics include society's influence on the purposes of education, establishing goals for educational programs, objectives for the classroom, and influences of national legislation and state standards on the development of local curriculum. You should examine the published national standards of your chosen teaching field and those from your state. After you review these documents, compare them to the local scope and sequence of the school system in which you are interning. In your journal, describe how the CCSS and your state standards seem to influence the local scope and sequence. Assess whether this influence (or lack thereof) is beneficial or detrimental to the educational program of the school. Consider talking with teachers and school administrators to sample their opinions on state versus local scope and sequence.

Discussion Questions

1. After reflecting on your own elementary and secondary education experience, what do you see as the primary goal for education, based on those personal experiences?

2. Are the goals of the progressive approach, as summarized in Table 13.1, desirable for education today? Based on your personal philosophy of education, should these be infused into today's educational goals?

3. What should the top five goals of K–12 education be? Why? What philosophical leanings and social forces influence your answer to the question?

4. What is your opinion of the goals implicit in NCLB? Discuss your thinking with other students in class. What relationship do you see between NCLB and the 1983 report, *A Nation at Risk?*

Suggested Projects for Professional Development

1. As you visit schools during your internships, ask to examine any available goal statements such as mission statements and school improvement plans. Document these in your journal. How do teachers and administrators believe the goals will be implemented? What evidence can you see of the stated goals influencing the school's day-to-day operations?

2. Select a school with yearly goals and ask to see its goal statements. Talk with teachers and administrators to find out the following: the process for developing the goals, who developed them, how parents and the community participated in the process, and how goals assessment takes place. How would you feel about this process if you were participating? What would you see as your role?

3. Write Goals 2025. Be as idealistic as you like but also realistic. How do you believe you, as a teacher, would work toward your Goals 2025?

4. Interview several current teachers in the schools about the influence of the Common Core State Standards (CCSS) in their schools. Structure the interviews to determine what changes in the curriculum they have seen in recent years. How has the role of the state department of education and the central office of the school district changed? What perceptions do the teachers have about the influence of the CCSS on their teaching?

Suggested Resources

Internet Resources

As explained in this chapter, *A Nation at Risk* was a seminal report that influenced school reform throughout the close of the twentieth century. Take some time to analyze the actual report at **http://teachertenure.procon.org/sourcefiles /a-nation-at-risk-tenure-april-1983.pdf**. Closely examine its analysis of schools in the 1980s and its recommendations for remedying the shortcomings. As you look at schools from your personal experiences, how have they changed based on what is portrayed in the report?

Examine the websites of contemporary reform-minded groups. Based on your review of their websites, create a list of goals that these groups have for schools in the second decade of the twenty-first century. Some of the websites to review are Achieve (**www.achieve.org** or **www.facebook .com/pages/Achieve/46050812271**), created by the nation's governors and corporate leaders as an independent, bipartisan, nonprofit education reform organization; The Education Trust (**www .edtrust.org** or **www.facebook .com/edtrust?v=app_4949752878**), established by the

American Association for Higher Education to encourage colleges and universities to support K–12 reform efforts; and Public Education Network (**www.publiceducation.org/index. asp**), an association of local education funds and individuals working to advance public-school reform in low-income communities.

Publications

Bracey, Gerald. *Education Hell: Rhetoric vs. Reality* Alexandria, VA: Educational Research Service, 2009. *Critics continually call for reform due to reports that call into question performance of U.S. students. Bracey provides facts needed to counter this widely held misconception.*

Conant, James B. *The American High School Today*. New York: McGraw-Hill, 1959. *A classic written during the* Sputnik *era, this book offers many recommendations for upgrading the high-school curriculum.*

Darling-Hammond, Linda. *The Flat World and Education: How America's Commitment to Equity Will Determine Our Future.* New York: Teachers College Press, 2010. *Offers remedies for what schools must do to respond to the learning needs of the twenty-first-century.*

Gardner, John W. *Excellence: Can We Be Equal and Excellent Too?* New York: Harper and Row, 1961. *Another classic text, this book remains relevant today. The questions and issues it raises are still of deep concern in American schools and society.*

Goodlad, John I., Roger Soder, and Bonnie McDaniel, eds. *Education and the Making of a Democratic People.* Boulder, CO: Paradigm Publishers, 2008. *Claims we must refocus on the ultimate mission of public schooling—education for democratic citizenship.*

Gordon, David, ed. *A Nation Reformed? American Education 20 Years after A Nation at Risk*. Cambridge, MA: Harvard Education Press, 2003. *A comprehensive look at the impact of* A Nation at Risk. *Did it really engender school reform?*

National Commission on Excellence in Education. *A Nation at Risk: The Imperative for Educational Reform*. Washington, D.C.: U.S. Department of Education, 1983. *Among reports on American education, this one had the most significant impact.*

Provenzo, Eugene F., ed. *Critical Issues in Education*. Thousand Oaks, CA: Sage Publications, 2006. *A selection of writings on the purposes of education throughout the history of the United States.*

Spring, Joel. *American Education*. 15th ed. Columbus, OH: McGraw-Hill, 2011. *A concise look at the purposes of public schooling and current issues that shape education.*

Zhao, Yong. *Catching Up or Leading the Way: American Education in the Age of Globalization*. Alexandria, VA: Association for Supervision & Curriculum Development, 2009. *Questions whether recent reform efforts and goals are preparing students for success in the twenty-first century global society.*

Additional resources for this chapter, including the TeachSource Videos, can be found on the Education CourseMate website. Go to **CengageBrain.com** to access the site.

Curriculum and Instruction

It is easy to see throughout the chapters of this textbook that Americans demand the utmost from their schools. We ask the schools to teach children to think, to socialize them, to alleviate poverty and inequality, to reduce crime, to perpetuate our cultural heritage, and to produce intelligent, democratic citizens. Inevitably, American schools struggle to meet these obligations. Nonetheless, the demands persist, and the resulting impact ultimately focuses on the *curriculum*—the planned experiences provided through instruction—which is continuously modified as education goals are revised, new innovations are developed, social issues are debated, and new interest groups emerge.

We described in Chapter 13, The Changing Purposes of American Education, how the goals of education have shifted with changing national priorities and social pressures. In this chapter, we will look at several major curricular approaches used in recent decades to help meet our changing national goals. You will see that the curriculum approaches also relate closely to the philosophies and theories discussed Chapter 6, Philosophical Roots of Education.[1] Reflect on how these curricular approaches relate to your own emerging philosophy of education.

As we examine various topics related to curriculum, we will also examine recent instructional activities and curricular trends that relate to it. This chapter will help you answer the following questions:

---

*This chapter was revised by Dr. David Vocke, Towson University.

[1]See R. Freeman Butts, *The Revival of Civic Learning* (Bloomington, IN: Phi Delta Kappa, 1980); Lawrence A. Cremin, *American Education: The National Experience* (New York: Harper and Row, 1980); and Lawrence A. Cremin, *The Transformation of the School* (New York: Random House, 1964).

FOCUS QUESTIONS

- What evidence of subject-centered and student-centered curricula can be found in today's schools?
- How might the use of cooperative learning or differentiated instruction influence your work as a teacher?
- How can you use technology or direct instruction in the classroom to improve instruction?
- What trends seem likely to affect curriculum and instruction in the future?

Curriculum Organization

Subject matter versus student needs

We can view the various types of curriculum organization in American schools from two perspectives. One emphasizes the subject to be taught; the other perspective emphasizes the student. The first perspective views **curriculum** as a body of content, or subject matter, that leads to certain achievement outcomes or products. The second defines curriculum in terms of student needs and interests; it is most concerned with process—in other words, how the student develops her ability to acquire new knowledge. Few schools employ pure subject-centered or pure student-centered approaches in the development of school curriculum and the teaching–learning process. You will find that even though most teachers tend to emphasize one approach over the other, they incorporate both choices in their professional decision making about what goes on in the classroom.

Subject-Centered Curricula

Organization by subjects

Subject matter is both the oldest and most commonly practiced framework of curriculum organization. It is a deeply ingrained approach primarily because it is convenient, as you can tell from the departmental structure of secondary schools and colleges. Even in elementary schools, where self-contained classrooms force the teachers to be generalists, curricula are usually organized by the various subjects or academic disciplines.

Arguments pro and con

Proponents of **subject-centered curricula** argue that subjects present a logical basis for organizing and interpreting information, that teachers are trained as subject matter specialists, and that textbooks and other teaching materials are usually organized by subjects. Critics claim that subject-centered curricula often are a mass of facts and concepts learned in isolation. They see this kind of curriculum as de-emphasizing contemporary life experiences and failing to consider the needs and interests of students. In subject-centered curricula, the critics argue, the teacher is the authority and dominates classroom discourse, allowing little student input.

The following sections discuss several variations of subject-centered approaches to curricula, such as the subject-area approach, back-to-basics, and the core curriculum. These represent neither the only possible variations nor hard-and-fast categories. Many schools and teachers mix these approaches, drawing from more than one of them.

Drawing on the classical tradition

Subject-Area Approach to Curriculum   The subject-area approach is the most widely used form of curriculum organization.[2] This long-standing approach has

---

[2]Peter F. Oliva, *Developing the Curriculum*, 7th ed. (Boston: Pearson Education, 2009), p. 257.

its roots in the seven liberal arts of classical Greece and Rome: grammar, rhetoric, dialectic, arithmetic, geometry, astronomy, and music. Advocates of the modern subject-area curricula trace its origins to the work of William Harris, superintendent of the St. Louis school system in the 1870s and U.S. Commissioner of Education at the end of the 1800s.[3] Steeped in the classical tradition, Harris established a subject orientation that has virtually dominated U.S. curricula from his day to the present. As a student, you were most likely introduced to "algebra" and "English grammar," "reading" and "writing," as well as "geography" and "history" in one form or another.

Categories of subjects

The modern **subject-area curriculum** treats each subject as a specialized and largely autonomous body of knowledge. Subjects referred to as the "basics" are considered essential for all students; these usually include the three Rs at the elementary level, and English, history, science, and mathematics at the secondary level. Other specialized subjects develop knowledge and skills for particular vocations or professions—for example, business mathematics and physics. Finally, elective content affords the student optional offerings, often tailored to student interests and needs.

Exploratory subjects

Exploratory subjects refer to subjects that students may choose from a list of courses designed to suit a wide range of learning styles, abilities, and interests. These courses, which can include such subjects as dance, technology, creative writing, career exploration, and drama, allow the school to diversify its offerings and allow students the opportunity to explore topics that might stimulate their interests outside of the realm of the traditional subjects. They appear most often in middle school and late elementary-school curricula.[4] Schools that include exploratory subjects in the curriculum tend to be more progressive in outlook than schools that still favor the traditional academic subjects.

Perennialism: the best of the past

Perennialist and Essentialist Influence on Curriculum   Two of the educational theories described in Chapter 6, Philosophical Roots of Education, are fundamentally subject centered: perennialism and essentialism.[5] Believing that the main purpose of education is the cultivation of the intellect, the perennialists concentrate their curriculum on the three Rs, Latin, grammar, rhetoric, and logic at the elementary level, adding study of the classics at the secondary level. The assumption of the **perennialist-influenced curriculum**, according to Robert M. Hutchins, is that the best of the past—the so-called permanent studies, or classics—remains equally valid for the present because they deal with fundamental questions that are relevant throughout time.[6]

Essentialism: major disciplines, cultural literacy

Essentialists believe that the elementary curriculum should consist of the three Rs, and the high-school curriculum should consist of five or six major disciplines: English (grammar, literature, and writing), mathematics, the sciences, history, foreign languages, and geography.[7] Adherents of the **essentialist-influenced curriculum** believe these subjects constitute the best way of organizing information and keeping up with today's explosion of knowledge. They argue that there is essential information that

[3]Henry Warren Button, "Committee of Fifteen," *History of Education Quarterly* (December 1965), pp. 253–263.
[4]Allan C. Ornstein, Thomas Lasley, and Gail Mindes, *Secondary and Middle School Methods* (New York: Allyn and Bacon, 2005); Steven Scarpa, "A Shift in Middle School," *District Administration* (April 2005), p. 19; and Patrick Akos, Pajarita Charles, Dennis Orthner, and Valerie Cooley, "Teacher Perspectives on Career-Relevant Curriculum in Middle School," *Research In Middle Level Education Online* (January 2011), pp. 1–9.
[5]Theodore Brameld, *Patterns of Educational Philosophy* (New York: Holt, 1950).
[6]Robert M. Hutchins, *The Higher Learning in America* (New Haven, CT: Yale University Press, 1936); and Robert M. Hutchins, "The Organization and Subject Matter of General Education," in Forrest W. Parkay, Eric J. Anctil, and Glen Hass, *Curriculum Planning: A Contemporary Approach* (Boston: Pearson Education, 2006), pp. 31–34.
[7]Arthur Bestor, *The Restoration of Learning* (New York: Knopf, 1956); and James B. Conant, *The American High School Today* (New York: McGraw-Hill, 1959).

adults have learned over time that must be passed on to society's young. Students need an academic knowledge base—"essential knowledge"—to deal with new ideas and challenges that will confront them in the future.[8] Teachers should be held accountable for teaching the essentials of the curriculum through a systematic program of study.[9]

Essentialism shares with perennialism the notion that curriculum should focus on rigorous intellectual training, training that is possible only through the study of certain subjects. Both perennialists and essentialists advocate educational meritocracy. They favor high academic standards and a stringent system of grading and testing to help schools sort students by ability. Today, many parochial schools and academically oriented public schools stress various aspects of the perennialist and essentialist curricula.

Back-to-Basics Approach to Curriculum

In the 1980s, many educators and laypeople called for a **back-to-basics curriculum**.[10] Like the essentialist curriculum influence, "back-to-basics" connotes a heavy emphasis on reading, writing, and mathematics. So-called solid subjects—English, history, science, and mathematics—are required in all grades, and the back-to-basics proponents are even more suspicious than the essentialists of attempts to expand the curriculum beyond this solid foundation; electives or exploratory subjects are not encouraged. Critics of this approach worry that a focus on basics will suppress students' creativity and shortchange other domains of learning, encouraging conformity and dependence on authority.[11]

Back-to-basics proponents insisted on the need to maintain minimum standards, and much of the state school reform legislation enacted from the late 1970s through the 1990s reflects this popular position. As a major component of the back-to-basics movement, minimum competency tests (MCT) were implemented in a majority of states during this time. These statewide tests to demonstrate mastery of minimum skills were required of students to graduate from high school. Advocates claimed such tests validated the high-school diploma; high-school graduates would be seen as having a useful set of minimum skills needed to enter the world of work. The MCT would serve as the precursor to the school-wide assessment programs required after the turn of the twentieth century by the No Child Left Behind Act (NCLB) and the high-stakes exit exams for high-school students.[12] For more on high-stakes exit exams, see the Taking Issue box.

Core Approach to Curriculum

The importance of basic subjects in the curriculum is also expressed by the term *core curriculum*. Unfortunately, in the post–World War II era, this term has been used to describe two different approaches to organizing curricula.

The first approach, which we will call *core curriculum*, gained popularity in the 1930s and 1940s and had its greatest influence at the junior high-school level. In this

Margin notes:

 Standards & Assessment

High academic standards

Public opinion favoring basics

Standards & Assessment

Minimum competency tests

The first core curriculum

---

[8]William C. Bagley, "The Case for Essentialism in Education," *Today's Education: Journal of the National Education Association* (October 1941), pp. 201–202; and G. T. Sewall, "Against Anomie and Amnesia: What Basic Education Means in the Eighties," *Phi Delta Kappan* (May 1982), pp. 603–606.

[9]Wesley J. Null, "William C. Bagley and the Founding of Essentialism: An Untold Story in American Educational History," *Teachers College Record* (April 2007), pp. 1013–1055.

[10]"Back-to-Basics Stifling Creativity?" *Newsweek*, January 27, 1986, p. 59; and Anne Wescott Dodd, "Curriculum Mood Swings," *Education Week*, June 9, 1993, pp. 26, 46.

[11]Elliot W. Eisner, "What Really Counts in School," *Educational Leadership* (February 1991), pp. 10–17; and David W. Jardina, "Back to Basics: Rethinking What Is Basic to Education," *Alberta Journal of Educational Research* (Summer 2001), pp. 187–190.

[12]James S. Catterall, "Standards and School Dropouts: A National Study of Tests Required for High School Graduation," *American Journal of Education* (November 1989), pp. 1–34; Allan C. Ornstein, "National Reform and Instructional Accountability," *High School Journal* (October–November 1990), pp. 51–56; and Marie Gould, "Minimum Competencies," *Research Starters Education* (June 2008), pp. 1–7.

TAKING ISSUE

Read the brief introduction below, as well as the Question and the pros and cons list that follows. Then, answer the question using your own words and position.

High-Stakes Exit Exams for Graduation

Many states have developed high-stakes exit exams as a high-school graduation requirement. To obtain a high-school diploma, students must pass a battery of tests aligned with state content standards. Failure to achieve a passing score on the assessment can mean denial of the high-school diploma.

Question

Are high-stakes exit exams beneficial to students and schools? (Think about this question as you read the PRO and CON arguments listed here. What is *your* take on this issue?

Arguments PRO

1. When the tests are aligned to the state curriculum standards, the exit exams focus the curriculum and ensure that classroom instruction covers key content deemed appropriate for high-school graduates.

2. The rise in requirements for graduation brought about by exit exams is especially important for students from schools that are economically disadvantaged. To break the cycle of poverty and joblessness, these students must be given the skills needed for productive employment ensured by the exit exam.

3. Testing for graduation shows the public that schools are being held accountable for their performance. The test results help to identify schools that are not doing their jobs properly

4. With increased rigor and accountability, students will be provided a quality education that prepares them to pass the test. For the few who have difficulty, alternative pathways to graduation can be implemented, such as alternative assignments or waivers.

5. Using the data provided by the exit exams, educators can discover where the overall problems lie. Policies can be modified accordingly, and curricula can be designed to address the problem areas.

Arguments CON

1. Statewide exit exams are cumbersome, costly, and might not lead to much improvement in the quality of education. The effort must come from the local level, where educators know the strengths and weaknesses of their own schools.

2. Exit exams unfairly penalize students from low-income, underperforming schools. These students fail the tests in disproportionate numbers, which stigmatizes them unjustly and further damages their prospects for employment

3. For systems with exit exams, there is a decrease in the flexibility of curriculum offerings during high school. Students are required to focus on those courses or subjects that are included in the requirements for graduation, which may entail taking numerous remedial courses.

4. Exit exams place one more hurdle for students to clear prior to graduation, and, for some, this may prove to be too formidable. As a result, more students are likely to drop out prior to their senior year.

5. Most teachers already know where the problems lie with student performance. Moreover, soon after an exit exam is established, many teachers begin to teach the test. Thus, the data obtained from such examinations become meaningless and misleading.

Question Reprise: What Is Your Stand?

Reflect again on the following question by explaining *your* stand about this issue: Are high-stakes exit exams beneficial to students and schools?

approach, students study subject matter in an integrated fashion, usually through the study of social-personal issues or themes that cut across subjects (for example, an interdisciplinary examination of a local environmental problem). The teachers organize instructional units in an interdisciplinary manner, showing how diverse subjects relate to one another. This approach, often organized in extended blocks of time,

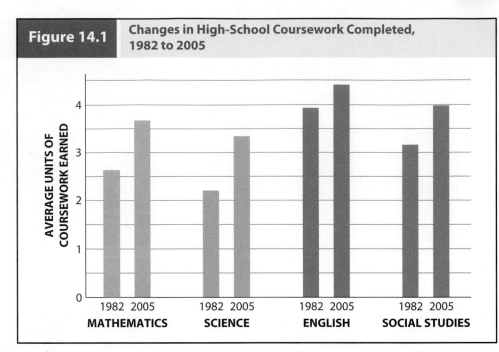

Figure 14.1 | Changes in High-School Coursework Completed, 1982 to 2005

Source: Digest of Education Statistics, 2010 (Washington, D.C.: U.S. Government Printing Offices, 2010), Table 157.

sometimes consisting of two or three periods of the school day, uses problem solving as the primary method of instruction and is tied to a progressive theory of education.[13]

▌ The new core curriculum

The second approach, in contrast, was born out of the 1980s educational reform movement and reflects the more conservative theory of essentialism. In this version, which we will call the **new core curriculum (core subjects approach)**, students experience a common body of required subjects—subjects that advocates consider central to the education of all students.[14] As described in Chapter 13, The Changing Purposes of American Education, the impetus for this new core curriculum was the reform report, *A Nation at Risk*. Students were seen as being inadequately prepared for life beyond high school, whether it be college or the world of work. The report criticized the cafeteria-style curriculum, where students favored desserts and appetizers (that is, less rigorous elective courses) rather than the solid, core subjects. The remedy for this deficiency was an increase in course requirements for graduation; the recommendation for the minimum requirements for high school included four years of English, three years of math, three years of science, three years of social studies, and one-half year of computer science.[15]

▌ Stiffer requirements

The proponents of this new core curriculum helped make subject-matter requirement changes in states and districts nationwide that have certainly impacted you as a student.[16] Those changes are summarized in Figure 14.1. From 1982, just prior to publication of the *At Risk* report, until 2005, the percentage of high-school graduates

[13]Miki M. Caskey, "The Evidence for the Core Curriculum—Past and Present," *Middle School Journal* (January 2006), pp. 48–54; and Peter F. Oliva, *Developing the Curriculum*, 7th ed. (Boston: Pearson Education, 2009), p. 248–251.
[14]John I. Goodlad, "A New Look at an Old Idea: Core Curriculum," *Educational Leadership* (December 1986–January 1987), pp. 8–16; and Richard W. Riley, "World Class Standards: The Key to Educational Reform" (Washington, D.C.: Department of Education, 1993).
[15]National Commission on Excellence in Education, *A Nation at Risk: The Imperative for Educational Reform* (Washington, D.C.: U.S. Government Printing Office, 1983); and ACT, *Rigor at Risk: Reaffirming Quality in the High School Core Curriculum* (Iowa City, IA: ACT, 2007).
[16]*Digest of Education Statistics, 2010* (Washington, D.C.: U.S. Government Printing Office, 2010), Table 157 at **http://nces.ed.gov/programs/digest/d10/tables/dt10_157 .asp?referrer=list**.

who completed a basic curriculum in the core subjects recommended in the report increased from 2 percent to more than 36 percent.[17]

Critiques of the new core curriculum

The new core curriculum approach, which is evident in schools today through the state assessment systems, has drawn criticisms similar to those aimed at the back-to-basics curriculum. These days, more students are college bound, yet a recent study suggests that the traditional core curriculum fails to adequately prepare high-school students for college. The study on college readiness from ACT suggests that core requirements should be more rigorous than is currently the case. Students may be taking the right number of courses in high school, but the quality of the core courses must be upgraded to provide students an opportunity for success, whether in college or at work.[18] The call for rigor in the core curriculum continues today as we transition to the Common Core State Standards (CCSS).[19]

Still other critics would argue that the core curriculum, by focusing only on courses and content, ignores an important component of the education equation—the student. The next section will examine approaches and theories that place considerations about the student at the center of the curriculum.

Student-Centered Curricula

Emphasizing student needs

In direct contrast to subject-centered curricula, **student-centered curricula** of various types emphasize student interests and needs, including the affective aspects of learning. At its extreme, the student-centered approach is rooted in the philosophy of Jean Jacques Rousseau, who encouraged childhood self-expression. Implicit in Rousseau's philosophy is the necessity of leaving the children to their own devices, allowing them the creativity and freedom essential for growth.

Influence of progressivism

Progressive education gave impetus to the modern student-centered curricula. Progressive educators believed that when the interests and needs of learners were incorporated into the curriculum, students would be intrinsically motivated and learning would be more successful. This does not mean that students' whims or passing fads should dictate the curriculum. However, one criticism of student-centered curricula is that proponents sometimes overlook important academic content.

Dewey's call for balance

John Dewey, a champion of student-centered curricula, attempted to establish a curriculum that balanced subject matter with student interests and needs. As early as 1902, he pointed out the fallacies of either extreme. The learner was neither "a docile recipient of facts" nor "the starting point, the center, and the end" of school activity.[20] Dewey tried to emphasize the need for balance while creating a curriculum that would prepare children for the modern, democratic world.

Continuity & Change

Over time, at least five major approaches to organizing student-centered curricula have been identified: activity-centered approaches, relevant curriculum, the humanistic approach, alternative or free schools, and values-centered curricula.

Lifelike, purposeful activities

Continuity & Change

Activity-Centered Approaches   The movement for an **activity-centered curriculum** has strongly affected the public elementary schools. William Kilpatrick, one of Dewey's colleagues, was an early leader. In contrast to Dewey, Kilpatrick believed that teachers could not anticipate the interests and needs of children, which made any preplanned curriculum impossible. Thus, he attacked the traditional school curriculum as detached and unrelated to the problems of real life. Instead, he advocated purposeful activities as relevant and lifelike as possible and tied to a student's needs and interests, such as group games, dramatizations, story projects, field trips, social enterprises,

---

[17]*Digest of Education Statistics: 2010,* Table 161.
[18]ACT, *Rigor at Risk: Reaffirming Quality in the High School Core Curriculum* (Iowa City, IA: ACT, 2007).
[19]Ron Schachter, "The Road to Rigor," *District Administration* (September 2011), pp. 50–60.
[20]John Dewey, *The Child and the Curriculum* (Chicago: University of Chicago Press, 1902), pp. 8–9; and William J. Reese, "The Origins of Progressive Education," *History of Education Quarterly* (Spring 2001), pp. 1–24.

and interest centers.[21] All of these facets of the activity-centered curriculum involved problem solving and active student participation. They also emphasized socialization and the formation of stronger school–community ties. Thus, they have relevance even today.

Constructivism

The recent development of *constructivist learning theory,* described in Chapter 6, Philosophical Roots of Education, draws on similar concepts. Constructivists might use an activity-centered curriculum in which students actively (mentally and physically) interact with knowledge and each other to construct meaning and new knowledge for themselves.[22]

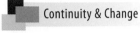

Continuity & Change

Relevant Curriculum   By the 1930s, some progressive reformers complained that the traditional school curriculum had become irrelevant because it had failed to adjust to social change and therefore emphasized skills and knowledge not pertinent to a modern democratic society in crisis. The 1960s and 1970s saw a renewed concern for a **relevant curriculum** but with a somewhat different emphasis. Critics expressed less concern that the curriculum reflect changing social conditions and more concern that the curriculum be relevant to the students' personal needs and interests.

Implementation options

Proponents of this approach today suggest it could best benefit students who are alienated from the traditional curriculum. Educators could implement the approach in a number of ways: (1) individualize instruction through such teaching methods as independent inquiry and special projects; (2) revise existing courses and develop new courses on such topics of student concern as environmental protection, poverty, and intolerance; (3) provide educational alternatives (such as electives and open classrooms) that allow more freedom of choice and meet the needs of students in special circumstances, such as those from homeless families; and (4) extend the curriculum beyond the school's walls, through such means as community service projects and field trips.[23]

Psychological foundation

Humanistic Approach to Curriculum   A **humanistic approach to curriculum** emphasizes affective outcomes, those that address attitudes or emotions, in addition to cognitive outcomes. Such a curriculum draws heavily on the work of psychologists Abraham Maslow, Carl Rogers, and Arthur Combs.[24] Advocates of humanistic education contend that the contemporary school curriculum has failed miserably and that teachers and schools are determined to stress academic achievement and to control students, *not* for students' good but for the benefit of adults. Humanistic educators emphasize more than affective processes; they seek higher domains of spirit, consciousness, aesthetics, and morality. They stress more meaningful relationships between students and teachers, student independence and self-direction, and greater acceptance of self and others. The teacher's role from a humanistic approach is to help learners cope with their psychological needs, to develop a positive classroom environment that fosters positive self-esteem, and to facilitate self-understanding among students to make more effective learning possible.[25]

---

[21]William H. Kilpatrick, "The Project Method," *Teachers College Record* (September 1918), pp. 319–335; Leonard J. Waks, "The Project Method in Postindustrial Education," *Journal of Curriculum Studies* (July 1997), pp. 391–406.

[22]Lois T. Stover, Gloria A. Neubert, and James C. Lawlor, *Creating Interactive Environments in the Secondary School* (Washington, D.C.: National Education Association, 1993), pp. 20–23; and William J. Matthews, "Constructivism in the Classroom: Epistemology, History, and Empirical Evidence," *Teacher Education Quarterly* (Summer 2003), p. 51.

[23]Velma Menchase, "Providing a Culturally Relevant Curriculum for Hispanic Children," *Multicultural Education* (Spring 2001), pp. 18–20; and Julie Landsman, "Bearers of Hope," *Educational Leadership* (February 2006), pp. 26–32.

[24]Abraham H. Maslow, *Toward a Psychology of Being* (New York: Van Nostrand Reinhold, 1962); Arthur W. Combs, *A Personal Approach to Teaching: Beliefs That Make a Difference* (Boston: Allyn and Bacon, 1982); and Carl Rogers, *Freedom to Learn,* 2nd ed. (Columbus, OH: Merrill, 1983).

[25]Carol Witherell and Nel Noddings, *The Challenge to Care in Schools* (New York: Teachers College Press, 1992); Elliot Eisner, *The Educational Imagination,* 3rd ed. (New York: Macmillan, 1993); Vincent A. Anfara Jr., "Advisor-Advisee Programs: Important But Problematic," *Middle School Journal* (September 2006), pp. 54–60; and Allan C. Ornstein, "Critical Issues in Teaching," in Allan C. Ornstein, Edward F. Pajak, and Stacey B. Ornstein, eds., *Contemporary Issues in Curriculum,* 4th ed. (Boston: Pearson Education, 2007).

Freedom for students

Alternative or Free Schools Programs   You are likely to find student-centered curriculum programs in **alternative** or **free schools**, often private, experimental institutions, some organized by parents and teachers dissatisfied with the public schools. These schools typically feature much student freedom, noisy classrooms, and a learning environment, often unstructured, where students are free to explore their interests. Most are considered radical and antiestablishment, even though many of their ideas are rooted in the well-known student-centered doctrines of progressivism.

Controversy about free schools

Paulo Freire, Ivan Illich, Herbert Kohl, and John Holt have stressed the need for, and in many cases have established, student-centered alternative or free schools.[26] Critics, however, condemn these schools as places where little cognitive learning takes place and little discipline and order are provided. Proponents counter that children do learn in student-centered alternative schools, which—instead of stressing conformity—are made to fit the students and address their needs.

Public alternative schools

A second type of alternative school is that which public-school systems run for students who experience persistent discipline problems or exhibit at-risk behaviors. These schools, estimated to number 11,000, start from the premise that school systems must change to provide a more flexible approach to learning. They generally stress greater collaboration among staff members and between staff and students in terms of both innovative curriculum and varied instructional methods. Students are generally reassigned to these schools until their behavior improves, at which time they are likely to return to their traditional school.[27]

Character education

Values–Centered Curriculum   A **values-centered curriculum**—more popularly known as *character education*—places special emphasis on moral and ethical development. Character-education advocates contend that a growing number of children are exhibiting problematic behaviors and attitudes and that, for this reason, programs to instill a climate of respect within the classroom are necessary.[28] A much broader view of the purpose of character education recognizes the character-related problems that exist in contemporary society—corporate greed, apathy, corrupt politicians—and calls for character education to develop active citizens who act in ethical ways. To this end, at least thirty-one states have passed legislation encouraging or mandating character education.[29]

Positive virtues

School practices that are incorporated in character-education programs include building a sense of community and respect for other students in the development of bullying prevention programs.[30] Some character-education programs visually display positive virtues throughout the school, such as self-discipline, respect, or honesty.[31]

---

[26]See, for instance, Paulo Freire, *Pedagogy of the Oppressed* (New York: Herder and Herder, 1970); Ivan Illich, *Deschooling Society* (New York: Harper and Row, 1971); Henry A. Giroux, *Teachers as Intellectuals* (Granby, MA: Bergin and Garvey, 1988); Ron Miller, "John Holt: His Prophetic Voice," *Education Revolution* (Autumn 2002), pp. 28–33; and Camilla A. Lehr and Cheryl M. Lange, "Alternative Schools Serving Students with and without Disabilities: What Are the Current Issues and Challenges?" *Preventing School Failure* (Winter 2003), pp. 59–65.

[27]Mary Magee Quinn, Jeffrey M. Poirier, Susan E. Faller, Robert A. Gable, and Steven W. Tonelson, "An Examination of School Climate in Effective Alternative Programs," *Preventing School Failure* (Fall 2006), pp. 11–17; and Lionel H. Brown and Kelvin S. Beckett, "Chapter 1: Alternative Schools: Portraits in Black and White," in *Building Community in an Alternative School: The Perspective of an African American Principal* (New York: Peter Lang Publishing, 2007), pp. 1–16.

[28]Diana Brannon, "Character Education: It's a Joint Responsibility," *Kappa Delta Pi Record* (Winter 2008), pp. 62–65.

[29]Sanford N. McDonnell, "America's Crisis of Character—And What to Do About It," *Education Week* (October 08, 2008), p. 25.

[30]Eric Schaps, "Creating Caring School Communities," *Leadership* (March 2009), pp. 8–11.

[31]Sara Efron and Pamela Joseph, "Seven Worlds of Moral Education," *Phi Delta Kappan* (March 2005), pp. 525–533.

FROM PRESERVICE TO PRACTICE

Curriculum Choices

Sandra Helenski, Bobby Owens, and Laura Rittilini are new to Frederick Douglass Middle School and the teaching profession. All are on the team assigned to teach seventh-grade students. Sandra teaches English, Bobby teaches life science, and Laura teaches band. All would say they teach students first and the subject second.

Discussion in the teachers' lounge is warming up today as they debate a few of their concerns with the most experienced teachers at Frederick Douglass.

Mrs. Whipper, one of the veterans in the profession, says, "I don't see how you can take the time to teach 'character' if you want them to pass the state assessments in March. You have to stay focused on math and reading—the test content. If you want to last a few years here, I think you should stick to making sure your students can write correctly, read well, and do math. Also, you have to be very careful: Are you sure you know the values of the community or of the parents? If you teach tolerance of diversity that includes gays and lesbians, many conservative religious parents won't be happy. It's all too easy to be misunderstood and to step on someone's toes."

"But, when I have a perfectly good opportunity to use student needs and interests in teaching concepts in the state curricula that relate to values, perhaps through special projects or book assignments, why shouldn't I do that?" responds Sandra. "For example, why can't students learn to search for and evaluate authors' statements about honesty just as easily as they can learn to search for and evaluate metaphors?"

"I'm including some activities that emphasize respect for the environment," said Bobby. "Students will test water and take air samples near the county landfill. They'll analyze their lab results in teams and send reports to the county commissioners. Certainly we can include values with this approach." He turned to the veterans. "What do you think?"

A more experienced teacher responded. "Well, I would be sure that my time was wisely used. That sort of activity can get away from you, and before you know it, March is here and your students aren't ready for the state assessments. So, just be careful in how you plan and implement your objectives."

Laura chimed in with her observation that the skills, knowledge, and dispositions of each band member were important to her. She wanted to be sure that each student valued being part of a team and also valued the discipline and hard work it took from all members to form a championship band. "Certainly," she said, "each of us in our own way is teaching values anyway. Perhaps we need to reflect on what values we teach just doing everyday things."

Case Questions

1. What do all three new teachers hold in common? What kinds of curriculum organization are really under discussion here?

2. How do you react to the experienced teachers' comments to Sandra? How would you reply?

3. What curriculum approach do you favor? Why?

4. Do you agree with Laura's comment that all teachers teach values? How do you expect the experienced teachers to react to Laura's comment?

Critics' concerns

One concern about efforts to infuse character education into the curriculum is that such programs developed for schools might simply be attempts at indoctrination. Students are drilled in how to act ethically rather than engaging in analytical thought about what goes into being ethical. Often, school character programs are grounded in incentives that critics claim encourage students to perform for the reward instead of investigating the process for making conscious decisions about ethically appropriate actions.[32] An additional criticism is that attempts at incorporating character education in the curriculum are ineffective and divert time from the academic mission of the school.[33]

---

[32]Alfie Kohn, "A Critical Examination of Character Education," in Allan C. Ornstein, Edward F. Pajak, and Stacey B. Ornstein, *Contemporary Issues in Curriculum*, 5th ed. (Boston: Pearson Education, 2011), pp. 164–181; and David Light Shields, "Character as the Aim of Education," *Phi Delta Kappan* (May 2011), pp. 40–53.

[33]Kenneth Godwin, Carrie Ausbrooks, and Valerie Martinez, "Teaching Tolerance in Public and Private Schools," *Phi Delta Kappan* (March 2001), pp. 542–546; and Debra Viadero, "Proof of Positive Effect Found for Only a Few Character Programs," *Education Week* (June 20, 2007), p. 20.

Table 14.1	"Character Objectives," as Identified by the Baltimore County (Md.) Public Schools

1. To develop the wisdom and good judgment to make reasoned decisions.

2. To develop a sense of justice that is informed by fairness, honesty, and civility.

3. To develop and demonstrate respect for self, respect for others, and respect for property.

4. To demonstrate tolerance and understanding of others regardless of race, gender, ethnicity, disability, national origin, religion, creed, socioeconomic status, marital status, pregnancy, personal record, sexual orientation, or political belief.

5. To demonstrate compassion for others through the development of empathy, kindness, and service.

6. To demonstrate discipline and responsibility by exhibiting self-control and the willingness to admit mistakes and correct them.

7. To develop a positive attitude that reflects hope, enthusiasm, flexibility, and appreciation.

8. To demonstrate pride in oneself and others by doing the best for self, family, school, and community and by respecting the achievement of others.

9. To exhibit personal and academic integrity through honesty, expressing beliefs in appropriate ways, and working to one's full potential.

Questions

1. Which of the character objectives in Table 14.1 do you consider most important and why?

2. What character objectives would you add to this table?

Source: The Baltimore County Public Schools Student Handbook 2011–2012 (Towson, MD: Baltimore County Public Schools, 2011).

Common core of values

Despite these criticisms, many educators contend that it is possible—even with our diverse society—to incorporate character-education programs into our schools and establish a set of values that represent an American consensus. Table 14.1, for example, lists "character objectives" included by the school system in Baltimore County, Maryland, in its student handbook. Many educators believe that developing such character traits is an urgent responsibility of American schools.

Curriculum Contrasts: An Overview

As we noted earlier, subject-centered and student-centered curricula represent the opposite ends of a continuum. You will find that most schooling in the United States falls somewhere between the two—keeping a tenuous balance between subject matter and student needs, between the cognitive and affective dimensions of students' development.

Influence of school philosophy

Decisions about what you should teach and how your teaching curriculum is organized will be influenced by the philosophical orientation of your school system or school. More traditional schools that subscribe to a perennialist or essentialist philosophy lean toward a subject-centered curriculum. Schools oriented more toward progressive education tend to use a student-centered approach. Overview 14.1 summarizes the various subject-centered and student-centered approaches to curricula and their corresponding philosophies, content emphases, and instructional emphases. As you begin to think seriously about in which district and school you want to teach, consider asking interviewers questions about curricular organization to ensure a fit between your philosophy and that of the district or school. In the next section, we move on to the curriculum development process and the main issues it raises.

REFOCUS One of the questions at the beginning of the chapter asked you to focus on which approach, subject-centered or student-centered, can be found in today's schools. Which approach do you believe has been most important in driving curriculum emphases at the schools you visit? In your opinion, which approach *should* be most important? Why?

OVERVIEW 14.1

Curriculum Organization Approaches

Curriculum Approach	Corresponding Philosophy or Theory	Content Emphasis	Instructional Emphasis
Subject-Centered			
Subject-area	Perennialism, essentialism	Three Rs; academic, vocational, and elective subjects	Knowledge, concepts, and principles; specialized knowledge
Perennialist	Perennialism	Three Rs; liberal arts; classics; timeless values; academic rigor	Rote memorization; specialized knowledge; mental discipline
Essentialist	Essentialism	Three Rs; liberal arts and science; academic disciplines; academic excellence	Concepts and principles; problem solving; essential skills
Back-to-basics	Essentialism	Three Rs; academic subjects	Specific knowledge and skills; drill; attainment of measurable ends or competencies
New core curriculum (core subjects)	Perennialism, essentialism	Common curriculum for all students; focus on academics	Common knowledge; intellectual skills and concepts; values and moral issues
Student-Centered			
Activity-centered	Progressivism	Student needs and interests; student activities; school–community activities	Active, experimental environment; project methods; effective living
Relevant	Progressivism, social reconstructionism	Student experiences and activities; felt needs	Social and personal problems; reflective thinking
Humanistic	Progressivism, social reconstructionism, existentialism	Introspection; choice; affective processes	Individual and group learning; flexible, artistic, psychological methods; self-realization
Alternative or free schools	Progressivism	Student needs and interests; student experiences	Play oriented; creative expression; free learning environment
Values-centered (character education)	Social reconstructionism, existentialism	Democratic values; ethical and moral values; cross-cultural and universal values; choice and freedom	Feelings, attitudes, and emotions; existentialist thinking; decision making

Issues in Curriculum Development

Whether the curriculum is subject centered or student centered, the process of developing it involves (1) assessing the needs and capabilities of all learners and (2) selecting or creating the instructional materials and activities that will address those needs.

Curriculum at national and state levels

At the national level, curriculum making has taken on a more influential role due to the recent emphasis on standards and assessment. Curriculum development at the state level has intensified over the past decade with the requirement by NCLB to develop state standards, assessments, and, by implication, corresponding curriculum realignment. These were prepared by a professional staff in the states' departments of education, assisted by curriculum consultants and experts in the disciplines. The curriculum guidelines have become specific, including lists of "core learning goals" or "state learning outcomes" and instructional materials, either mandated or recommended, that have been aligned with state-developed standards.[34]

Curriculum at the local level

The greatest responsibility for curriculum development has generally fallen on the local school district—or on the schools themselves. Large school districts have the resources to employ personnel who specialize in curriculum development, including subject-matter specialists and assessment coordinators. Smaller school districts generally assign curriculum development to a group of teachers organized by subject or grade level; sometimes parents, administrators, and even students participate.

College admission standards exerted a strong influence on curriculum choices for high schools for several decades. Efforts were made in recent years to align the curriculum from preschool through the four years of college. This has been referred to as P–16 alignment, and it envisions a seamless, articulated curriculum in which what is learned in primary, elementary, and secondary schools builds to prepare students for success in college. This concept is consistent with the emphasis of the new federal initiatives to graduate students who are "college and career ready."[35]

Influence of textbooks

Another major influence on curriculum—one whose importance is often underrated—has been the textbook. Textbooks have long been the most frequently used instructional medium at all levels beyond the primary grades. As such, they can dominate the nature and sequence of a course and profoundly affect students' learning experiences. Because courses often are aligned with the topics addressed in the textbook, especially in districts lacking curriculum specialists, they reflect the textbook author's knowledge and biases. For this reason, it is important for you to understand factors that govern textbook writing and publication.

Standards & Assessment

Limitations of textbooks

To have wide application and a large potential market, textbooks have been criticized as being general, noncontroversial, and bland. Because they are usually written for the largest book-markets, they have disregarded many local or regional issues. Aiming for the greatest number of average students, they may fail to meet the needs and interests of any particular group or individual. In an attempt to address the standards that have been established by multiple state departments of education, publishers have included a wide range of topics and volumes of facts that leave little room for conceptual thinking, critical analysis, and evaluation. Because they are expensive, textbooks

---

[34]James W. Popham, "Curriculum Matters," *American School Board Journal* (November 2004), pp. 30–33; and Barbara Reys and Glenda Lappan, "Consensus or Confusion?" *Phi Delta Kappan* (May 2007), pp. 676–680.

[35]John R. Hoyle and Timothy M. Kutka, "Maintaining America's Egalitarian Edge in the 21st Century: Unifying K–12 and Postsecondary Education for the Success of All Students," *Theory into Practice* (Fall 2008), pp. 353–362; Shepherd Siegel, "A Meaningful High School Diploma," *Phi Delta Kappan* (June 2009), pp. 740–744; and Education Commission of the States, *P–16*, at **www.ecs.org/html/issue.asp?issueid=76** (February 2012).

have made up a large portion of a district's discretionary spending, and they often are used long after they should have been replaced.[36]

Advantages of textbooks

Considering these criticisms, why do teachers rely so heavily on textbooks? The answer is that textbooks also have many advantages. A textbook provides teachers with an outline for planning lessons; summarizes a great deal of pertinent information; enables the student to take home most of the course material in a convenient package; provides a common resource for all students to follow; includes pictures, graphs, maps, and other illustrative material that facilitate understanding; and frequently includes other teaching aids, such as summaries and review questions.[37] Furthermore, textbook authors and publishers have created materials that help teachers reach state standards.

By the time you enter the classroom, two factors are likely to greatly reduce the influence of the textbook on the curriculum you are asked to teach to your students. First, the Common Core State Standards (CCSS) will be in place, thus providing a more focused influence on curriculum development across the country. Secondly, many state legislatures and departments of education are encouraging the utilization of digital content and electronic materials to replace the traditional textbook. Digital material is projected to be more efficient in aligning the curriculum to the new standards and is also more economical than expensive textbooks.[38]

Censorship trends

Another issue in curriculum development is the question of **censorship**. The American Library Association (ALA) defines censorship as "the suppression of ideas and information that certain persons—individuals, groups or government officials—find objectionable or dangerous."[39] In states that prepare approved lists of instructional materials for their schools, the trend is growing to "limit what students shall read." The list of objectionable works has recently included such works as *Water for Elephants* and *The Chocolate War.* Today, almost any instructional material that contains political or economic messages, obscenity, sex, nudity, profanity, slang or questionable English, ethnic or racially sensitive material, or any material that could be interpreted as anti-family, antireligious, or anti-American is subject to possible censorship.[40] Additionally, students' online access to various websites and social networks, as discussed in the Technology @ School box, is of much concern to teachers and parents.[41]

Subtle censorship

Although censorship is often overt, it can operate in subtle ways as well. Curriculum developers may quietly steer away from issues and materials that would cause controversy in the community. Moreover, textbooks might omit topics that could potentially upset specific audiences or interest groups. Even pictures are important; some organizations count the number of pictures of one ethnic group versus another group, of boys versus girls, of business versus labor. Professional associations can also exert a type of censorship when they recommend certain changes in subject content and implicitly discourage other approaches. You must be sensitive to censorship because it is an issue you will likely encounter during your career as an educator. In dealing with

[36]Harvey Daniels and Steven Zemelman, "Out With Textbooks, in with Learning," *Educational Leadership* (December 2003/January 2004), pp. 36–40; Gilbert T. Sewall, "Textbook Publishing," *Phi Delta Kappan* (March 2005), pp. 498–502; and Christian R. Hirsch and Barbara J. Reys, "Mathematics Curriculum: A Vehicle for School Improvement," *ZDM* (November 2009), pp. 749–761.
[37]Allan C. Ornstein, "The Textbook-Driven Curriculum," *Peabody Journal of Education* (Spring 1994), pp. 70–85; and Jess E. House and Rosemarye T. Taylor, "Leverage on Learning: Test Scores, Textbooks and Publishers," *Phi Delta Kappan* (March 2003), pp. 537–541.
[38]Geoffrey H. Fletcher, "A Revolution on Hold," *T.H.E. Journal* (June 2010), pp. 21–23; and "Legislatures Alter Textbook Adoption Landscape," *Educational Marketer* (June 6, 2011), pp. 5–6.
[39]American Library Association, "Intellectual Freedom and Censorship Q and A" (ALA, n.d.) at **www.ala.org/advocacy/intfreedom/censorshipfirstamendmentissues /ifcensorshipqanda#ifpoint3** (January 2012).
[40]Fran Falk-Ross and Jeannetta Caplan, "The Challenge of Censorship," *Reading Today* (April 2008), p. 20; and National Coalition Against Censorship, *Classrooms* at **http://ncac.org /Classrooms** (January 2012).
[41]Mary Ann Bell, "The Elephant in the Room," *School Library Journal* (January 2007), pp. 40–42; and Mike Nantais and Glenn Cockerline, "Internet Filtering in Schools: Protection or Censorship?" *Journal of Curriculum & Pedagogy* (Winter 2010), pp. 51–53.

TECHNOLOGY @ SCHOOL

Safety Issues and Social Media

Educators and parents alike agree that adult supervision of students' Internet use, both at home and at school (a form of censorship), is critical. As a teacher, you need to educate your students about responsible online behavior and safety issues. An excellent website for this is Media Awareness Network at **www.media-awareness.ca/english/teachers/wa_teachers/index.cfm**. This site alerts teachers and students to safety issues associated with websites, social networking/virtual environments, texting, and e-mail. It includes information on the benefits and risks of these activities and offers practical advice on how you can ensure that your students have safe and rewarding experiences. The site also includes a link for parents with much the same information. Additionally, the Federal Trade Commission provides advice for the responsible use of social networking sites, such as Facebook, at Protect Kids Online—**http://onguardonline.gov/articles/0012-kids-and-socializing-online**.

An important issue that deserves attention and that has perhaps been facilitated by social networks is **cyberbullying**, a form of online taunting meant to intimidate a particular child. The National Crime Prevention Council website at **www.ncpc.org/cyberbullying** includes audio messages and videocasts about combating cyberbullying and creating safe environments for students.

A site with resources for teachers interested in appropriately incorporating social networking and Web 2.0 applications in their classroom instruction is Classroom 2.0 at **www.classroom20.com**. This beginner-friendly site aims to assist novices into the digital dialogue. There are numerous ongoing blogs and opportunities to participate in helpful webinars that are supported by **PBS Teachers**. Another feature is a page of starting tips and a webcast video entitled "Tour of Classroom 2.0." Even the most technology-savvy educator could browse for hours on this site.

such issues, we often find that Herbert Spencer's fundamental question, "What knowledge is of most worth?" becomes "*Whose* knowledge is of most worth?"[42]

As teaching becomes more professionalized, teachers are increasingly expected to make curriculum choices and deal with the complex and controversial issues they present. To preserve your academic freedom to make decisions that best address the learning needs of your students, you will need a full understanding of community concerns, statewide standards, and school policies to exercise your professional judgement.[43]

> **REFOCUS** How will you, as a teacher, respond if you feel pressured to censor materials or to follow a textbook-defined curriculum?

Instructional Approaches

Interrelationship of curriculum and instruction

Although educators recognize there are multiple definitions of curriculum, most agree that curriculum and instruction are interrelated. To carry out the curriculum, one must rely on instruction—the strategies, materials, and methods used to teach students. Even more than with curriculum approaches, most teachers incorporate a variety of instructional strategies in their classes. The search for new programs and methods of instruction is continual. The past four decades, in particular, have witnessed a major effort to improve learning outcomes and have students become more efficient and effective learners.

Although we cannot survey all of the major instructional innovations, the following sections describe a few that have influenced classrooms. Chapter 16, School Effectiveness and Reform in the United States, treats the subject of instructional approaches in the context of school reform and school effectiveness.

---

[42]David L. Martinson, "School Censorship: It Comes in a Variety of Forms, Not All Overt," *Clearing House* (May 2008), pp. 211–214; and Kenneth Kidd, "Not Censorship but Selection: Censorship and/as Prizing," *Children's Literature In Education* (September 2009), pp. 197–216.
[43]National Coalition against Censorship, *First Amendment in Schools: Introduction* at **http://ncac.org/education/schools/index.cfm** (January 2012).

Differentiated Instruction

Maximizing learner potential

Differentiated instruction describes an approach to designing lessons that addresses the wide range of differences that exist among students in today's classrooms.[44] Differentiated instruction is a form of personalized instruction with the goal of maximizing each learner's potential. It has also been described as matching teaching to the needs of individual learners.[45]

Multiple paths to learning

A key requirement of differentiated instruction is a curriculum focus that emphasizes constructing understanding rather than accumulating facts. The teacher clearly establishes what students should know and understand, as well as the skills they are to develop. She then plans classroom experiences that are engaging and challenging for students; incorporating a variety of media likely to appeal to the learners, providing students with choices for assignments to complete, and drawing upon an array of instructional methods. It is common that options also be provided for the grouping of students when completing instructional tasks. In other words, students are offered multiple paths to reach a lesson's preset learning objectives. This method of instruction is designed to be engaging because it shows students the connections between their experiences and the curriculum they are studying. Ultimately, the teacher has to be cognizant of the learners' knowledge and skill levels to differentiate instruction to meet the objectives of the planned curriculum.[46]

Proponents suggest that differentiated instruction is a particularly appropriate strategy for classrooms in the twenty-first century. As NCLB has required that all students achieve success in school, classrooms are likely to become more heterogeneously grouped. Students who may have been sorted into lower tracked classes in the past are likely to be mixed into more advanced classes to be prepared to attain higher academic standards. Additionally, classrooms are likely to be more diverse as schools continue to incorporate the inclusion of students with special needs and the number of English Language Learners (ELLs) increases. Based on the varying needs of learners as they strive to master the curriculum, instruction needs to be differentiated to address their varied achievement levels, learning styles, and interests. The goal through such instruction is that all students should reach mastery of the intended outcomes.[47]

Difficult to implement

Critics of differentiated instruction contend that it is too time-consuming and impossible to implement on top of the other requirements that teachers face. Some parents have complained that their children might be neglected while the teacher works with different groups of students during classroom instruction.[48]

Cooperative Learning

Competition versus cooperation

Cooperative rather than competitive learning has also gained acceptance as a best practice for instructing students.[49] In the traditional classroom structure, students compete

[44]Donald C. Orlich, Robert J. Harder, Richard C. Callahan, Michael S. Trevisan, Abbie H. Brown, and Darcy E. Miller, *Teaching Strategies: A Guide to Effective Instruction*, 10th ed. (Belmont, CA: Wadsworth Cengage Learning, 2013), pp. 57–58.

[45]Carol Ann Tomlinson, "Mapping a Route toward a Differentiated Instruction," *Educational Leadership* (September 1999), pp. 12–16; and Julie Anna Hartwell, "ABCs of Differentiating Instruction," *New Teacher Advocate* (Winter 2006), pp. 6–7, 12.

[46]Lori Tukey, "Differentiation," *Phi Delta Kappan* (September 2002), pp. 63–65; and Jennifer Carolan and Abigail Guinn, "Differentiation: Lessons from Master Teachers," *Educational Leadership* (February 2007), pp. 44–47.

[47]James H. VanSciver, "Motherhood, Apple Pie, and Differentiated Instruction," *Phi Delta Kappan* (March 2005), pp. 534–535; and Carol Tomilinson, "This Issue," *Theory into Practice* (Summer 2005), pp. 183–184.

[48]Jennifer Carolan and Abigail Guinn, "Differentiation: Lessons from Master Teachers," *Educational Leadership* (February 2007), pp. 44–47; and Douglas B. Reeves, "From Differentiated Instruction to Differentiated Assessment," *ASCD Express* (July 2011) at **www.ascd.org/ascd-express/vol6/620-reeves.aspx** (January 2012).

[49]Elizabeth G. Cohen, Celeste M. Brody, and Mara Sapon-Shevin, eds., *Teaching Cooperative Learning: The Challenge for Teacher Education* (Albany: State University of New York Press, 2004); David W. Johnson and Roger T. Johnson, "An Educational Psychology Success Story: Social Interdependence Theory and Cooperative Learning," *Educational Researcher* (June 2009), pp. 365–379.

Cooperative learning offers students new chances to experience success in school and helps them develop a range of interpersonal and individual skills.

for teacher recognition and grades. The same students tend to be labeled as winners and losers over the years because of differences in ability and achievement. In the typical school setting, high-achieving students continually receive rewards and are motivated to learn, whereas low-achieving students continually experience failure (or near failure) and frustration. The idea of **cooperative learning** is to change the traditional structure by reducing competition and increasing cooperation among students, thus diminishing possible hostility and tension among students and raising the academic achievement of all.

Motivation to participate

In cooperative learning, students work in groups and thus address the need for human interaction. Also, because they are contributing to the group by working toward a common goal, students are motivated to participate in an active learning experience.[50]

In general, cooperative learning strategies are structured so that there is positive interdependence among group members, typically in heterogeneous groups, wherein each must contribute to accomplish the group's task. It is also necessary for each group member to make an individual contribution to the group, so individual accountability is required. At the culmination of any cooperative learning activity, the final product the group creates must contain input from every member, thus ensuring group accountability. To be successful at these cooperative efforts, students must develop positive interpersonal skills and experience face-to-face interactions.[51]

[50]Nancy Protheroe, "How Children Learn," *Principal* (May/June 2007), pp. 41–44.
[51]Martin Hanze and Roland Berger, "Cooperative Learning, Motivational Effects, and Student Characteristics: An Experimental Study Comparing Cooperative Learning and Direct Instruction in 12th Grade Physics Classes," *Learning and Instruction* (2007), pp. 29–41; and Ceri B. Dean, Elizabeth Ross Hubbell, Howard Pitler, and B. J. Stone, *Classroom Instruction that Works: Research-Based Strategies for Increasing Student Achievement,* 2nd ed. (Alexandria, VA: ASCD, 2012).

Tim Platt/Iconica/Getty Images

Benefits of cooperative learning

According to a review of the research, cooperative learning has been found to (1) increase self-esteem; (2) lead to positive academic gains; (3) reduce racial conflict; (4) encourage listening, engagement, and empathy; (5) increase acceptance of special needs students in the included classroom; and (6) increase active involvement in classes. The data also suggest that cooperative learning is effective in fostering positive interpersonal attitudes, behaviors, values, and skills.[52]

A popular approach

The Jigsaw Classroom An approach that has been popular in contemporary practice is known as the **jigsaw strategy**. In the jigsaw activity, a class is divided into heterogeneous groups of five to six students to complete a task. Each member of the group is designated to become an expert on one segment of the larger group task; that is, each group member holds one piece of the larger jigsaw puzzle, so that students are dependent on their fellow group members to complete the puzzle. The experts will ultimately teach their fellow team members their segment of information, and together the group members will compile the pieces of the puzzle to complete the assigned task. It should be noted that to increase accuracy, prior to teaching one's fellow group members about their segment of information, students with the same segment of information from the other groups in the class will meet in expert groups to review the information and prepare the presentation that they will use to teach their original group members about their particular puzzle piece. In a final activity, the groups are assessed to see how well they put the puzzle together.[53] To be successful in the jigsaw classroom, students must cooperate to complete the assigned task.

▶❚❚ TEACHSOURCE VIDEO ACTIVITY

Cooperative Learning in the Elementary Grades: Jigsaw Model

Go to the Education CourseMate website to access the video entitled, "Cooperative Learning in the Elementary Grades: Jigsaw Model." In this video, the veteran teacher uses the jigsaw model as a cooperative learning strategy to increase student learning and ultimately make her a better teacher. After watching the video, answer the following questions:

❶ There is evidence that cooperative learning can reduce competition and increase cooperation among students. What evidence of this statement do you see within the video case?

❷ The text suggests that there must be positive interdependence and individual accountability built into cooperative learning activities. How do the students in this video case demonstrate these?

** This video reinforces key concepts found in Section II: Instruction and Assessment of the Praxis II Exam.**

---

[52]Robert E. Slavin, *Cooperative Learning: Theory, Research, and Practice* (Boston: Allyn and Bacon, 1995); David W. Johnson and Roger T. Johnson, "Making Cooperative Learning Work," *Theory into Practice* (Spring 1999), pp. 67–73; Judy Willis, "Cooperative Learning Is a Brain Turn-On," *Middle School Journal* (March 2007), pp. 4–13; and Donald C. Orlich, Robert J. Harder, Richard C. Callahan, Michael S. Trevisan, Abbie H. Brown, and Darcy E. Miller, *Teaching Strategies: A Guide to Effective Instruction*, 10th ed. (Belmont, CA: Wadsworth Cengage Learning, 2013), pp. 260–261.
[53]Martin Hanze and Roland Berger, "Cooperative Learning, Motivational Effects, and Student Characteristics: An Experimental Study Comparing Cooperative Learning and Direct Instruction in 12th Grade Physics Classes," *Learning and Instruction* (2007), pp. 29–41; and Elliott Aronson, *Jigsaw Classroom* (n.d.) at **www.jigsaw.org/overview.htm** (January 2012).

Direct Instruction

Carefully prescribed
lessons

The **direct instruction** model has been incorporated in classrooms, especially at the elementary level. According to its advocates, direct instruction "emphasizes well-developed and carefully planned lessons designed around small learning increments and clearly defined and prescribed teaching tasks."[54] Information is conveyed by the teacher in a way that is explicit and extremely scaffolded in highly organized presentations, through scripted lessons. It is teacher directed, and lessons are systematically sequenced with guided student practice and teacher feedback. Instruction is deliberately guided and precisely explicit for the learner to know the content and skills that need to be learned and performed.[55]

 Standards & Assessment

Direct instruction
and NCLB

Use of direct instruction has been fostered by NCLB and the U.S. Department of Education. NCLB, which has focused on improving all students' scores on standardized tests, has targeted underperforming schools in which students fall below expectations; a number of direct-instruction programs target a similar audience. School districts, eager to comply with NCLB requirements, have incorporated direct-instruction programs that have been developed by commercial publishers for a wide array of subjects in the school curriculum, including reading, mathematics, language, science, social science, and handwriting, as well as for special-education programs.[56] The common denominator of these programs is the teacher-directed curriculum that is highly explicit, scripted, and includes intense teacher-student interaction.

Evidence-based
instruction

Direct instruction has gained recognition for increasing the standardized reading scores of students, especially those in low-income settings. Programs using the model have been endorsed by the National Reading Panel and the U.S. Department of Education, often linking the term "evidence-based reading instruction" to direct instruction because of the improvement in students' test scores. Other proponents have suggested that direct instruction is the optimal way to teach and learn science and other subjects. Claims have also been made that affective behaviors such as self-esteem, a sense of responsibility, and positive attitudes toward school have been enhanced as a result of direct-instruction implementation.[57]

Critics affiliated with a more student-centered approach have challenged direct instruction and the studies that suggest its effectiveness. Generally, direct-instruction reading programs incorporate systematic and explicit phonics instruction that is heavily scripted. This approach has been criticized for being overly prescriptive and focusing on isolated skills that might help children become "word readers" but does little to develop comprehension or the ability to read for meaning. Additionally, advocates of problem-based learning in science contend that direct instruction is untenable because students must be engaged in inquiry to become "inquirers," a primary goal of science instruction.[58]

---

[54]"What Is Direct Instruction," *National Institute for Direct Instruction* (n.d.) at **http://nifdi .org/index.html#what** (January 2012).

[55]Nancy Protheroe, "NCLB Dismisses Research Vital to Effective Teaching," *Education Digest* (April 2004), pp. 27–30; and Deanna Kuhn, "Is Direct Instruction an Answer to the Right Question?" *Educational Psychologist* (Spring 2007), pp. 109–113.

[56]"What Is Direct Instruction," *National Institute for Direct Instruction* (n.d.) at **http://nifdi .org/index.html** (January 2012); and Rebecca Harris, "Reading Fundamentals," *Catalyst Chicago* (Summer 2011), pp. 16–19.

[57]Paul A. Kirschner, John Sweller, and Richard D. Clark, "Why Minimal Guidance during Instruction Does Not Work," *Educational Psychologist* (2006), pp. 75–86; Elaine Bukowiecki, "Teaching Children How to Read," *Kappa Delta Pi Record* (Winter 2007), pp. 58–65; Tricia Smith, "Direct Instruction," *Research Starters—Education* (Toledo, OH: Great Neck Publishing, 2008), pp. 1–7; and "General FAQs," *ADI—Association for Direct Instruction* (n.d.) at **www.adihome.org/faqs /general-faqs** (January 2012).

[58]Pat G. Wilson, Prisca Martens, Poonam Arya, and Bess Altwerger, "Readers, Instruction, and the NRP," *Phi Delta Kappan* (November 2004), pp. 242–246; Randall J. Ryder, Burton, Jennifer Lyn, and Anna Silberg, "Longitudinal Study of Direct Instruction Effects From First through Third Grades," *Journal of Educational Research* (January 2006), pp. 180–191; Sandra S. West and Gerald Skoog, "The Current Science Education War: Inquiry or Direct Instruction," *Texas Science Teacher* (April 2006), pp. 8–10; and Barak Rosenshine, *Five Meanings of Direct Instruction* (Lincoln, IL: Center on Innovation & Improvement, 2008).

Twenty-First Century Skills

✔ Standards & Assessment

■ Preparing students for a global future

■ Necessary skills

Secretary of Education Arne Duncan states that schools in the United States need to "dramatically improve teaching and learning" to prepare students for the twenty-first century.[59] The advocacy group, Partnership for 21st Century Skills, represents educators who are promoting a more comprehensive curriculum and instruction effort to prepare students to be successful in the competitive global job market and to fulfill roles as active citizens equipped to solve problems in a democratic society.[60] To master the recommended twenty-first century set of outcomes, classroom instruction will have to become more interactive and engaging than it currently is.

The skills deemed necessary for students in the modern interdependent global society are:

■ Learning and innovation skills (for example, creativity and innovation, critical thinking, and problem solving)

■ Core subjects and twenty-first century themes (for example, global awareness; financial, economic, business, and entrepreneurial literacy; environmental literacy)

■ Information, media and technology skills (for example, information, communications and technology literacy)

■ Life and career skills (for example, initiative and self-direction, flexibility and adaptability)[61]

In contrast to traditional practice in American high schools, these recommendations focus more on processes rather than content, and, as a result, such skill development will have to be infused into the current curriculum and classroom instruction.

For example, within the skill of critical thinking, students should be given opportunities to make judgments and reach decisions because productive adults must possess such valuable, real-world skills. This will require students to evaluate evidence, analyze alternative points of view, synthesize information, draw conclusions, and reflect on the experience.[62] Traditional classroom instruction will not suffice to fulfill this requirement. Classroom instruction that fosters such critical-thinking skills requires teamwork and collaborating with peers—sometimes with those in other countries via electronic media. Furthermore, it involves employing problem-based learning, in which students investigate challenging issues and topics by using real-world contexts that they are likely to encounter in daily life.[63] Instruction to foster **twenty-first century skills** attainment must take place in engaging, flexible, and active environments.

■ Another fad?

Continuity & Change

Fourteen states have made a commitment to infusing twenty-first century skills into their high schools, and proponents of the skills are encouraging a fusion of the twenty-first century skills and the CCSS.[64] Although advocates see this as progress for

---

[59]Tim Walker, "Duncan: Technology Will Transform Student Learning," *NEA Today* (November 23, 2010) at **http://neatoday.org/2010/11/23/duncan-technology-will-transform-student-learning**.

[60]"Poll: U.S. Students Need 21st Century Skills," *Reading Today* (December 2007), p. 7; and Lotta C. Larson and Teresa Northern Miller, "21st Century Skills: Prepare Students for the Future," *Kappa Delta Pi Record* (Spring 2011), pp. 121–123.

[61]Partnership for 21st Century Skills, *Framework for 21st Century Learning* (Washington, D.C.: Partnership for 21st Century Skills, 2011) at **www.p21.org/storage/documents/1._p21 _framework_2-pager.pdf**.

[62]Partnership for 21st Century Skills, *P21 Framework Definitions* (Washington, D.C.: Partnership for 21st Century Skills, 2009) at **www.p21.org/storage/documents/P21_Framework _Definitions.pdf**.

[63]Partnership for 21st Century Skills, *21st Century Learning Environments* (Washington, D.C.: Partnership for 21st Century Skills, n.d.) at **www.p21.org/storage/documents/le_white_ paper–1.pdf**.

[64]Partnership for 21st Century Skills, *Policy Makers* (Washington, D.C.: Partnership for 21st Century Skills, 2011) at **www.p21.org/tools-and-resources/policy-maker#LearningEnvironments**; and Partnership for 21st Century Skills, *P21 Common Core ToolKit* (Washington, D.C.: Partnership for 21st Century Skills, 2011) at **www.p21.org /storage/documents/P21CommonCoreToolkit.pdf**.

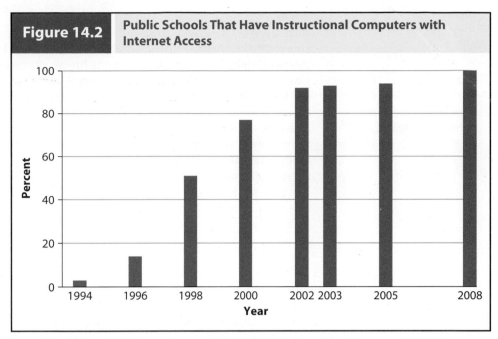

| Figure 14.2 | Public Schools That Have Instructional Computers with Internet Access |

Source: John Wells and Laurie Lewis, *Internet Access in U.S. Public Schools and Classrooms: 1993–2005* (Washington, D.C.: National Center for Education Statistics, 2006) at **http://nces.ed.gov/pubs2007 /2007020.pdf**; Lucinda Gray, Nina Thomas, and Lauries Lewis, *Educational Technology in U.S. Public Schools: Fall 2008* (Washington, D.C.: U.S. Department of Education, National Center for Education Statistics. U.S. Government Printing Office, 2010) at **http://nces.ed.gov/pubs2010/ 20010034.pdf**

the evolution of curriculum and instruction as we move toward a more competitive global society, critics of the approach contend it is just a fad that is being recycled from the past. They maintain that current state standards and the new common core have begun to refocus the curriculum where it should be, on the content, and to be distracted by these soft skills, those that focus on process rather than specific content knowledge, will only water down the recent emphasis on standards and assessment. [65]

Technology–Enhanced Instruction

Connected classrooms

Technology as an instructional tool has become as commonplace in America's classrooms as traditional instructional methods. In 1980, the nation's schools were equipped with about fifty thousand microcomputers. By 1994, computer access increased greatly, yet only 35 percent of the nation's schools and 3 percent of classrooms were connected to the Internet. By 2008, virtually every school and the vast majority of classrooms (97 percent) were connected to the Internet, as illustrated by Figure 14.2, and the number of students sharing access to an Internet-connected computer was approximately three students per machine. [66]

Technology is widespread

Classroom instruction today includes typical technology-enhanced activities such as word processing, concept mapping, spreadsheet applications, Internet research,

[65]Stephen Sawchuk, "Backers of 21st Century Skills Take Flak," *Education Week* (March 4, 2009), pp. 1, 14; and Andrew J. Rotherham and Daniel Willingham, "21st Century Skills: The Challenge Ahead," *Educational Leadership* (September 2009), pp. 16–21.
[66]"Percent of All Public Schools and Instructional Rooms Having Internet Access: Fall 1994 to Fall 2001—Figure 31," *Digest of Education Statistics, 2002,* at **http://nces.ed.gov/programs /digest/d02/fig_31.asp** (January 2012); Carole Vinograd Bausell, "Tracking U.S. Trends," *Education Week* (March 27, 2008), pp. 39, 40; and Lucinda Gray, Nina Thomas, and Laurie Lewis, *Educational Technology in U.S. Public Schools: Fall 2008* (Washington, D.C.: U.S. Department of Education, National Center for Education Statistics. U.S. Government Printing Office, 2010) at **http://nces.ed.gov/pubs2010/2010034.pdf** (January 2012).

PowerPoint presentations, and illustrative graphics.[67] Course management systems, such as WebCT, Blackboard, and Moodle, often support middle- and high-school courses.[68] Personalized instruction that is customized to the student's abilities can be delivered through interactive e-learning literacy interventions rather than a traditional textbook. Such lessons address state standards and employ data diagnostics to guide the progress of individual students' skill acquisition.[69]

Examples of technology-enhanced infusion

More recently, teachers in America's schools are implementing instructional strategies that draw upon **technology-enhanced learning** in a variety of ways. For example, to enhance literacy abilities at the middle-school level, where students enjoy communicating with others, virtual reading groups from distant schools can meet face-to-face via Skype to collaborate on analyzing works of literature. Also, to tap into students' fascination with text messaging, instruction has been designed where threaded electronic discussion forums encourage students to exchange ideas about a particular story.[70] Students can also use their smartphones to search the mobile Internet or text their opinions on course issues to a class brainstorming board.[71]

In technology-enhanced science classes, students are able to view experiments on digital videos and take part in science simulations or real-life virtual labs. On an environmental science field trip, a tablet computer is used to conduct water-quality analysis. After the field trip, students return to the classroom and print out graphs that are used for data analysis to include in their final lab reports. In an astronomy class, the software program *Starry Nights* allows students to observe the night sky during the middle of the school day.[72]

Online courses expand

Online Instruction and Virtual Schools   Additional areas related to e-learning that have experienced growth in recent years have been online courses and virtual schools. It has been estimated that more than four million K–12 students were enrolled in an online course in 2010, and 250,000 students, an increase of 40 percent in the past three years, take all of their coursework online at a virtual public school.[73] Forty states have a virtual school or similar state initiative and 55 percent of school districts have students who were enrolled in distance education courses in 2009–2010. Proponents contend this approach is student-centered, highly personalized, and more efficient than the brick-and-mortar school.[74] Examples of such programs include the Florida

[67]Terri Duggan Schwartzbeck and Mary Ann Wolf, *The Digital Learning Imperative: How Technology and Teaching Meet Today's Education Challenges* (Washington, D.C.: Alliance for Excellent Education, 2012).
[68]Bryan Alexander, "Web 2.0 and Emergent Multiliteracies," *Theory into Practice* (March 2008), pp. 150–160; and *San Diego Unified School District—Moodle* (n.d.) at **http://moodle.sandi.net** (January 2012).
[69]Darrell M. West, *Using Technology to Personalize Learning and Assess Students in Real Time*, (Washington, D.C.: Center for Technology Innovation at Brookings, 2011) at **www.brookings.edu/~/media/Files/rc/papers/2011/1006_personalize_learning_west/1006_personalize_learning_west.pdf**.
[70]Maren Aukerman and Heather Weisse Walsh, "Getting 'Real' in Virtual Talkabout Text," *Middle School Journal* (March 2009), pp. 53–61.
[71]Liz Kolb, "Adventures with Cell Phones," *Educational Leadership* (February 2011), pp. 39–43.
[72]Vaishalli Honawar, "Learning to Teach with Technology," *Education Week* (March 27, 2008), pp. 28–31; and Ian Quinlan, "Technology Evolves to Offer a Clearer View of Science," *Education Week* (June 15, 2011), pp. 2,3.
[73]Alan Dessoff, "The Rise of the Virtual Teacher," *District Administration* (February 2009), pp. 23–26; David Nagel, "More Than Half of U.S. Districts Have Students in Distance Learning Programs," *T.H.E. Journal* (December 1, 2011); and Leslie Brody, "Online Schools Are Largely Untested," *NorthJersey.com* (December 11, 2011) at **www.northjersey.com/news/135423563_Online_schools_are_largely_untested.html**.
[74]Heather Staker, *The Rise of K–12 Blended Learning* (Mountain View, CA: Innosight Institute, 2011) at **www.innosightinstitute.org/innosight/wp-content/uploads/2011/05/The-Rise-of-K-12-Blended-Learning.pdf** (January 2012); and John Watson, Amy Murin, Lauren Vashaw, Butch Gemin, and Chris Rapp, *Keeping Pace with K–12 Online Learning: A Review of State-Level Policy and Practice 2011* (Evergreen, CO: Evergreen Education Group, 2011).

Virtual School and the Idaho Digital Learning Academy, virtual schools that receive state funding and serve a rapidly growing student population.[75]

Benefits of online courses

Online instruction is especially beneficial for students in rural or poor school districts that might not have access to advanced courses. Fewer than 70 percent of rural high schools offer Advanced Placement courses and those that do might only offer one or two. A recent study found that rural middle-school students who took a virtual Algebra I course outperformed their peers in control schools who took the traditional Algebra I course through whole-group instruction. This is especially significant considering 24 percent of rural middle schools nationwide are not able to offer the course. As long as a school has Internet access, it could potentially offer Web-based courses to those students willing to take the challenge. For schools suffering from systems deficiencies, government or private foundation grants may assist in providing needed technology upgrades.[76]

Effective online learning experiences can benefit students because they can work at their own pace, be encouraged to work collaboratively with other students on projects, participate in online discussions, and submit drafts of writing assignments to obtain frequent instructor feedback.[77] Because 95 percent of teenagers are on the Internet and 82 percent have access to broadband at home, this is a resource that has to be incorporated into today's educational environment.

The future and Web-based communities

Continuity & Change

Web 2.0 and Beyond As we have seen, just over a quarter of a century ago, today's educational technology was virtually nonexistent in the American classroom. It will be interesting to see where technology takes us in the next twenty-five years. The future journey, it seems, will certainly involve the continually expanding environment known as **Web 2.0**. The online encyclopedia *Webopedia* defines Web 2.0 as, "focused on the ability for people to collaborate and share information online [and] includes open communication with an emphasis on Web-based communities of users, and more open sharing of information. . . . **Blogs**, wikis, and **Web services** are all seen as components of Web 2.0."[78]

Instead of providing a venue for simply consuming information, as in the past, this version of the Internet allows participants to create, share, and react to the digital information they encounter. An example of a popular user-generated site is YouTube.com, where individuals can go beyond just watching videos from the Internet to actually producing media for a worldwide audience and engaging in discussions about site content.

Literacy 2.0

Because students are so adept at interacting in this digital environment through social networking sites such as Facebook, Myspace, Twitter, and Flickr (76 percent of all teenagers participate in social-networking sites), educators are developing strategies for incorporating what has been termed "Literacy 2.0" into classroom instruction.[79] Blogs

---

[75]John Watson, Amy Murin, Lauren Vashaw, Butch Gemin, and Chris Rapp, *Keeping Pace with K–12 Online Learning: A Review of State-Level Policy and Practice 2011* (Evergreen, CO: Evergreen Education Group, 2011); *Florida Virtual High School* at **www.flvs.net/Pages/default.aspx**; and *Idaho Digital Learning* at **www.idahodigitallearning.org**.

[76]Wallace H. Hannum, Matthew J. Irvin, Jonathan B. Banks, and Thomas W. Farmer, "Distance Education Use in Rural Schools," *Journal Of Research In Rural Education* (January 2009), pp. 1–15; Meris Stansbury, "Rural Schools Need More Federal Attention," *eSchoolNews* (March 9, 2010), at **www.eschoolnews.com/2010/03/09/rural-schools-need-more-federal-attention** (January 2012); Andrea Beesley, "Keeping Rural Schools Up to Full Speed," *T.H.E. Journal* (October 2011), pp. 26–27; and Sarah D. Sparks, "Online Algebra I Class Can Boost Rural Students' Access, Skills," *Education Week*, December 13, 2011, at **http://blogs.edweek.org/edweek/inside-school-research/2011/12/online_algebra_i_class_can_boo.html** (January 2012).

[77]Julie Z. Aronson and Mike J. Timms, "Net Choices, Net Gains: Supplementing High School Curriculum with Online Courses," *Knowledge Brief* (San Francisco: WestEd, 2004); and John K. Waters, "Broadband, Social Networks, and Mobility Have Spawned a New Kind of Learner," *T.H.E. Journal* (December 13, 2011).

[78]Webopedia at **www.webopedia.com/TERM/W/Web_2_point_0.html** (January 2012).

[79]Amanda Lenhart and Mary Madden, *Teens, Privacy & Online Social Networks* (Washington, D.C.: Pew Internet & American Life Project, April 28, 2007); Michele Knobel and Dana Wilber, "Let's Talk 2.0," *Educational Leadership* (March 2009), pp. 20–24; and John K. Waters, "Broadband, Social Networks, and Mobility Have Spawned a New Kind of Learner," *T.H.E. Journal* (December 13, 2011).

or Twitter, similar to personal journals, are examples of this and can provide students a forum to write for an authentic audience and may encourage greater care in writing.[80] English teachers can establish book talks as blogs where students post reactions to literature they've read and to the postings of their classmates. In this forum, thought-provoking discussions can take place, and students can engage in writing for a specific purpose to an authentic audience of peers.[81]

Wikis and the classroom

Wikis, websites that multiple contributors can edit and add to, are another resource for involving students in creating collaborative products through classroom instruction. The *Flat Classroom Project* wiki is an example of this collaboration in a multimodal learning environment. Students from around the world team with partners from different countries to create thematic wiki pages on topics related to Thomas L. Friedman's best-selling book, *The World Is Flat: A Brief History of the Twenty-First Century*. In addition to discussing key concepts in the book, students also learn lessons about working with others with different cultural perspectives.[82] On a more local scale, a social studies class could be given a task of creating a wiki about a specific historical event. Photographs, primary documents, video clips, hyperlinks to other resources, and podcasts of stories students develop could all be part of the group wiki.[83]

To some educators, our rapid technological advances spell the eventual demise of pencil technology. In the twenty-first century, the textbook seems destined to be transformed to online offerings. Experts do agree, however, that technological knowledge and skills will be essential components in the preparation and repertoire of all teachers. The role of technology in school reform is discussed further in Chapter 16, School Effectiveness and Reform in the United States, with an emphasis on teacher training when introducing technology.

REFOCUS Which of the instructional methods listed in this section (differentiated instruction, cooperative learning, twenty-first century skills, and various methods of electronic instruction) do you feel most comfortable with as a teacher? Why? How can you prepare to make effective use of methods with which you are not yet comfortable?

►❚❚ TEACHSOURCE VIDEO ACTIVITY

Using Blogs to Enhance Student Learning: An Interdisciplinary High-School Unit

Go to the Education CourseMate website to access the video entitled, "Using Blogs to Enhance Student Learning: An Interdisciplinary High-School Unit" to see how three high-school teachers use technology in the classroom to encourage student engagement and aid in student understanding of important concepts. After watching the video, answer the following questions:

❶ According to the teachers in the video, what are the advantages to using blogs with high-school students?

❷ Many teachers might be leery of blogging in their classrooms and lessons. Based on watching the video, what are your thoughts about the pros and cons of using this format in lessons?

** This video reinforces key concepts found in Section II: Instruction and Assessment of the Praxis II Exam.**

[80]Rena Shifflet and Cheri Toledo, "Extreme Makeover: Updating Class Activities for the 21st Century," *Learning & Leading with Technology* (June 2008), pp. 34–35.
[81]Heather Gruenthall, "21st Century Booktalks!" *CSLA Journal* (Spring 2008), pp. 23–24; and Will Richardson, "Publishers, Participants All," *Educational Leadership* (February 2011), pp. 22–26.
[82]Margaret Weigel and Howard Gardner, "The Best of Both Literacies," *Educational Leadership* (March 2009), pp. 38–41; and Julie Lindsay and Vicki Davis, "Navigate the Digital Rapids," *Learning and Leading with Technology* (March 2010), pp. 12–15.
[83]Michele Knobel and Dana Wilber, "Let's Talk 2.0," *Educational Leadership* (March 2009), pp. 20–24.

Developing Curriculum Trends

In discussing instructional communications technology, we have already begun to look into the future. Student learning will increase through interaction with expanding technologies. Not all learning will be centered in the school or classroom, and use of computers and the Internet, both in school and at home, will greatly expand how you and your students access information and, just as importantly, what information you access. What other trends will continue to develop and influence American classrooms? In the next section, we describe several that are emerging as important issues.

The Importance of the Arts

Less time for the arts

Schools have increased instructional time for reading, math, and science, especially at the elementary level, because these subjects are the ones that are being tested to measure adequate yearly progress under NCLB requirements. As a result, many schools have had to cut time devoted to the arts and other creative activities, especially in schools labeled as needing improvement and those with higher percentages of low-income students.[84] A RAND Corporation study proposes that narrowing the curriculum to core subjects does a disservice to students because it fails to prepare them for participation in a rich cultural life that is essential preparation for public life. Even though states mandate arts content standards, policies fail to provide time and resources to implement these standards. Concern is growing that if the arts are ignored in the school curriculum, students will miss out on vital experiences to which they would not otherwise be exposed. Advocates for increasing the amount of time devoted to the arts in the school curriculum cite additional evidence to support their cause. They note that a study published in 2011 suggests that integrating arts with other subjects has a positive effect on mathematic and reading achievement in early childhood and adolescence.[85]

Positive impact of arts education

Another recent study examined the development of specific reading subskills and found that second-grade students who were routinely trained in music performed significantly better on tests of the subskills than did the group that was not trained in music.[86] Research from the Guggenheim Museum posits that studying about paintings and sculpture enhances students' abilities in other subjects.[87] Additionally, in the Tucson Unified School District, an interdisciplinary elementary school curriculum that fuses academics and the arts, known as Opening Minds through the Arts (OMA), has been credited with significantly increasing test scores in reading, math, and writing. Low-income students, ELLs, and children from transient families comprised the student populations of the schools that participated in OMA.[88]

---

[84]Peter Levine, Mark Hugo Lopez, and Karlo Barriou Marcelo, *Getting Narrower at the Base: The American Curriculum after NCLB* (Medford, MA: The Center for Information & Research on Civic Learning & Engagement, December 2008); Michael Sikes, *AEP Summary and Analysis of GAO Report, "Access to Arts Education"* (Reston, VA: Arts Education Partnership, March 6, 2009); and Erik Robelen, "Arts Education Sees Decline, Especially for Minorities, Report Suggests," *Education Week* blog, February 28, 2011, at **http://blogs.edweek.org/edweek /curriculum/2011/02/new_study_suggests_arts_ed_for.html**.
[85]Laura Zakaras and Julia F. Lowell, *Cultivating Demand for the Arts: Arts Learning, Arts Engagement, and State Arts Policy* (Santa Monica, CA: RAND Corporation, 2008); and "10 Salient Studies on the Arts in Education," *Online Colleges* (September 6, 2011) at **www.onlinecolleges. net/2011/09/06/10-salient-studies-on-the-arts-in-education**.
[86]SAGE Publications/Psychology of Music, "Music Education Can Help Children Improve Reading Skills," *ScienceDaily* (March 16, 2009) at **www.sciencedaily.com/ releases/2009/03/090316075843.htm**.
[87]"Statistics, the Arts, and Exit Exams," *American School Board Journal* (October 2006), pp. 57–60.
[88]Fran Smith, "Tucson Schools Enhance Learning with the Arts," *Edutopia.org* (The George Lucas Education Foundation, January 28, 2009) at **www.edutopia.org/print/6103** (January 2012).

The evidence continues to mount that the arts deserve to be included in the day-to-day PK–12 curriculum. Although there are those who still suggest that the arts should be taught for their own merit, the preceding discussion bolsters their case that the arts are more than a luxury to be tacked onto the existing curriculum.[89] Secretary of Education Arne Duncan, in discussing reauthorization of the Elementary and Secondary Education Act (ESEA), has often stated that the arts "can no longer be treated as a frill" and must be included in the everyday school curriculum.[90]

Education of English Language Learners

Increasing number of English Language Learners

The number of ELLs (national-origin minority students who are limited in English proficiency) entering U.S. public schools has grown in recent years and will continue to grow in the future. Nationally, 21 percent of the population speaks a language other than English at home—up from just under 18 percent in 2000—and 80 percent of ELLs speak Spanish at home.[91] ELLs represented 17 percent of Texas' public-school students in 2007, and Texas, California, Florida, and New York are considered the "immigration gateway states" that account for the majority of ELL students across the nation. It is estimated that 5.3 million students in the United States can be classified as ELLs, and during the past decade, children entering U.S. schools unable to speak English has grown by 40 percent. Collectively, there are more than four hundred different home languages spoken by ELL students in America's schools.[92]

Almost one-quarter of all children in the United States are from immigrant-origin households representing a wide range of cultures and ethnic backgrounds.[93] Tibet, Nigeria, Yemen, Bangladesh, Liberia, Ethiopia, and Macedonia are just a few of the countries of birth of students in schools across the nation. Many students have emigrated from environments that provided little opportunity for formal schooling, or their schooling was interrupted by political unrest, and they have come to the United States via refugee camps. The New York City school system has classified such students as Students with Interrupted Formal Education, and it is providing programs to assist such students succeed in the school setting. It is, however, a difficult task to prepare such students to meet rigorous graduation requirements when they have had limited experience with the school environment.[94] In many cases, students who are not proficient English speakers may feel alienated from their school and community.[95]

Schools' concerns

A number of concerns face school officials who provide services for ELL students, especially those who have recently immigrated. The fundamental question is, how can

---

[89]Anne C. Grey, "No Child Left Behind in Art Education Policy: A Review of Key Recommendations for Arts Language Revisions," *Arts Education Policy Review* (March 2010), pp. 8–15.

[90]Heather Noonan, "Understanding the Big Picture, Claiming a Seat at the Table," *TRIAD* (October/November 2010), pp. 66–69.

[91]U.S. Census Bureau, "New Census Bureau Data Reveal More Older Workers, Homeowners, Non-English Speakers," *U.S. Census Bureau News* (Washington D.C.: U.S. Department of Commerce), September 12, 2007; and "Participation in Education: Elementary/Secondary Education—Table A-6-2," *The Condition of Education—2011* (Washington, D.C.: National Center for Education Statistics, 2011) at **http://nces.ed.gov/programs/coe/tables/table-lsm-2.asp**.

[92]*State Test Score Trends Through 2007–2008, Part 6: Has Progress Been Made in Raising Achievement for English Language Learners?* (Washington, D.C.: Center On Education Policy, April 10, 2010); and Margarita Calderón, Robert Slavin, and Marta Sánchez, "Effective Instruction for English Learners," *Future Of Children* (Spring 2011), pp. 103–127.

[93]Carola Suarez-Orozco and Marcelo M. Suarez-Orozco, "Education Latino Immigrant Students in the Twenty-First Century: Principles for the Obama Administration," *Harvard Educational Review* (Summer 2009), pp. 327–340.

[94]Mary Ellen Flannery, "Almost from Scratch," *NEA Today* (May 2007), pp. 31–33; and Jennifer Medina, "In School for the First Time, Teenage Immigrants Struggle," *The New York Times*, January 25, 2009, at **http://nytimes.com/2009/01/25/education/25ellis.html** (January 2012).

[95]Natalie M. Russell, "Teaching More Than English: Connecting ESL Students to Their Community through Service Learning," *Phi Delta Kappan* (June 2007), pp. 770–771.

schools effectively educate students who do not speak English? This basic question is confounded by a number of factors: What is the appropriate program for serving ELL students; how do we assess these students on high-stakes tests; and how can we find highly qualified teachers for a diverse ELL population?[96]

Another concern is the impact that the assessment and accountability mandates have had on ELL students and their schools. Current practice has been that ELLs who have resided in the United States for at least one year are required to take the same assessments of content as those taken by native speakers. A few states have been able to offer tests in the native language of the ELLs for up to three years if the tests are aligned with state standards. Most states avoid native-language tests because such tests are difficult to develop and are costly. Advocates for ELLs claim that requiring ELLs to take tests that are written in English becomes an English proficiency test instead of content knowledge based on standards. On average, ELLs score twenty to fifty percentage points below native English speakers on state assessments of English/language arts.[97] Because the ELL population is projected to grow, school officials will continue to grapple with this issue for the foreseeable future.

Continuity & Change

Education for Healthy Youth

Youth health crisis

The news media has trumpeted the rise in health-related issues for America's youth in recent years. Most of the focus has been targeted on the problem of childhood obesity. Since 1980, the percentage of children aged six to eleven who are obese has doubled. Moreover, one-third of teenagers are overweight or obese, and it is estimated that by 2018, obesity-related medical expenses will cost Americans $344 billion in direct health care. Unfortunately, increased risks of cardiovascular disease, hypertension, and Type 2 diabetes are linked to obesity.[98] A National Institute of Child Health and Human Development study confirmed that as children get older, there is a decrease in physical activity that plays a critical role in the rising rates of childhood obesity. According to the study, nine-year-olds engaged in three hours of moderate-to-vigorous physical activity per day while fifteen-year-olds averaged less than fifty minutes of similar activity.[99]

It has been suggested that schools have reduced the time devoted to physical education because more time must be allocated to tested areas such as reading and mathematics. Additionally, existing physical education programs have been challenged for providing inadequate amounts of physical activity for maintaining good health.[100] A study of Oregon schools found that elementary students averaged twelve minutes of physical education a day, and only 4 percent of the state's elementary schools met the target of thirty minutes of physical education daily.[101] Other studies suggest that only four minutes of every thirty allocated to physical-education class time involves

[96]"Research Center: English-Language Learners," *Education Week* (June 16, 2011) at **http://edweek.org/ew/issues/english-language-learners**.

[97]Kate Menken, "NCLB and English Language Learners: Challenges and Consequences," *Theory Into Practice* (March 2010), pp. 121–128; and *State Test Score Trends Through 2007–2008, Part 6: Has Progress Been Made in Raising Achievement for English Language Learners?* (Washington, D.C.: Center on Education Policy, April 10, 2010).

[98]National Association for Sport and Physical Education & American Heart Association, *2010 Shape of the Nation Report: Status of Physical Education in the USA* (Reston, VA: National Association for Sport and Physical Education, 2010); and Ross C. Brownson, Jamie F. Chriqui, Charlene R. Burgeson, Megan C. Fisher, and Roberta B. Ness, "Translating Epidemiology Into Policy to Prevent Childhood Obesity," *Annals of Epidemiology* (June 2010), pp. 436–444.

[99]"Early Teens Lack Exercise as Never Before," *Running & FitNews* (July/August 2008).

[100]*Physical Education Matters: A Full Report* (Los Angeles, CA: The California Endowment, 2008); and Kenneth W. Harris, "Why Education Must Get Physical," *Futurist* (January 2009), pp. 30–32.

[101]Betsy Hammond, "Oregon Students Get Scant PE Classes, State Documents," *The Oregonian* (March 11, 2009) at **www.oregonlive.com/news/index.ssf/2009/03/oregon_students_get_scant_pe_c.html** (January 2012).

vigorous activity and that the quality and quantity of physical education are most deficient in Title I schools.[102] It appears obvious that students are not participating in effective physical-education instruction.

Physical fitness assessments

In an interesting development in 2007, the Texas legislature became the first in the nation to authorize a bill that requires physical-fitness assessments in the public schools in grades 3 through 12. Results from initial assessments of 2.6 million Texas students found that almost "78 percent of fourth-grade students were in the healthy fitness zone for cardiovascular fitness, whereas only 20 percent of high-school seniors reached the healthy fitness zone." Initial findings also suggest that physically fit students are more likely to do well on achievement tests, experience fewer discipline problems, and are less likely to drop out.[103] In a move touted as the future for physical-education instruction, many schools are moving away from an emphasis on team sports and incorporating such fitness activities as riding stationary bicycles, running on treadmills, participating in yoga, and playing video games (for example, DanceDanceRevolution) that require physical activity. Health classes are adding more information about healthy eating habits, and health educators suggest merging nutrition education into regular classes—for example, learning about fractions by slicing fruit.[104] If we want to encourage healthy living habits in our students, curriculum developers must find opportunities for incorporating relevant activities into the school day.

Green Education

Enhancing environmental literacy

Media reports about global warming, skyrocketing energy prices, environmental degradation, and renewable energy sources continually spark debate about important policy decisions that will impact the future of the country and the planet. Schools are responding by expanding offerings that examine such topics, especially through the science curriculum. The National Science Teachers Association (NSTA) strongly endorses the incorporation of environmental education in the PK–16 curriculum to improve **environmental literacy** among students. According to the NSTA, environmental literacy "is the ability of students to master critical-thinking skills that will prepare them to evaluate issues and make informed decisions regarding stewardship of the planet."[105] Students, confronted with environmental issues in daily life, need opportunities to learn scientific content and concepts in a relevant, contemporary curriculum that grapples with real-world issues. Environmental education advocates contend that, in the face of these imminent problems confronting society, we must equip students with the skills necessary to make decisions to prepare them to become citizens of the future.

A survey of environmental literacy in America suggests that students would be well served by learning the content and skills promoted through an environmental education curriculum. Two findings point out that approximately 80 percent of Americans are influenced by incorrect or outdated environmental myths and that only 12 percent

[102]Scott LaFee, "Let's Get Physical! P.E. Struggles to Make the Grade," *The Education Digest* (February 2008), pp. 49–52.

[103]Texas Education Agency, "Physically Fit Students More Likely to Do Well in School, Less Likely to Be Disciplinary Problems," *TEA News* (March 9, 2009) at **www.tea.state.tx.us /fitnessgram_press_release2009.pdf** (January 2012); and Duncan Van Dusen, Steven H. Kelder, Harold W. Kohl, III, Nalini Ranjit, and Cheryl L. Perry, "Associations of Physical Fitness and Academic Performance Among Schoolchildren," *Journal of School Health* (December 2011), pp. 733–740.

[104]"Alternate P.E.," *American School Board Journal* (March 2009), p. 8; and National Association for Sport and Physical Education & American Heart Association, *2010 Shape of the Nation Report: Status of Physical Education in the USA* (Reston, VA: National Association for Sport and Physical Education, 2010).

[105]National Science Teachers Association, *NSTA Position Statement—Environmental Education* (Arlington, VA: NSTA, 2003) at **www.nsta.org/about/positions/environmental.aspx** (January 2012).

blickwinkel/Alamy Limited

Hands-on activities can be integrated into environment-based lessons in order to stimulate students' interests in environmental issues.

can pass a basic quiz on awareness of energy topics.[106] Environmental education advocates point to such findings as evidence that the public must be better educated to deal with environmental issues and that the school is best equipped to do this. The U.S. Department of Education is reacting to these findings by promoting its Green Ribbon Schools program, which is designed to recognize schools that save energy, reduce costs, feature environmentally sustainable learning spaces, protect health, foster wellness, and offer environmental education to boost academic achievement and community engagement. Green Ribbon Schools will spotlight both environmental literacy and healthy living practices.[107]

Student-centered, thematic units

Typically, an environment-based education curriculum tends to consist of student-centered, thematic, interdisciplinary units of instruction incorporated throughout the K–12 curriculum. For example, young children can gain an appreciation for the natural environment through literature-related activities. Interacting with developmentally appropriate books that present accurate information about the natural world around them is likely to instill a fundamental sense of respect for nature.[108] Elementary schools can use environment-based education as a way to integrate subject matter. Hands-on activities that involve inquiry learning can address selected environmental themes. Projects can be developed that incorporate reading and writing skills in language arts classes, measurement skills in math classes, and examination of the political process in social studies classes. As an example, a middle school in New York selected air pollution as a theme and chose to develop a plan to reduce the number of idling cars in front of the school. In groups, students recorded the amount of time cars idled in front of the school and analyzed the data. They also researched how carbon emissions affect children's breathing and produced a publicity campaign to stop the idling cars. Finally, the students organized fund-raisers to purchase trees, which they planted to help

---

[106]Kevin Coyle, *Environmental Literacy in America: What Ten Years of NEETF/Roper Research and Related Studies Say about Environmental Literacy in the U.S.* (Washington, D.C.: The National Environmental Education & Training Foundation, 2005).
[107]*The U.S. Department of Education Green Ribbon Schools* at **www2.ed.gov/programs/green-ribbon-schools/index.html** (February 2102).
[108]Rachel Wells and Pauline Zeece, "My Place in My World: Literature for Place-Based Environmental Education," *Early Childhood Education Journal* (December 2007), pp. 285–291; and R. D. Merritt, "Environmental Education," *Research Starters—Education* (Toledo, OH: Great Neck Publishing, 2008), pp. 1–10.

offset the carbon emissions produced by the cars.[109] Such authentic learning through environment-based education engaged students in critical thinking and encouraged participation in the community.

Infused in the curriculum

Green education has been influencing the curriculum at the high-school level as well, though it, too, has had to compete for curricular space with those subjects that are involved with high-stakes testing. Specific instructional units with environmental themes could be infused into existing biology, chemistry, and physics courses, or separate environmental science courses could be developed.[110] Some schools are creating elective science courses that focus on alternative energy. The state of Maryland became the first state in the nation to require students to be environmentally literate to graduate from high school; environmental content and experiences must be integrated into the existing curriculum framework. There is also a bill pending in the Senate, the No Child Left Inside Act, that would provide states incentives to develop environmental literacy plans.[111]

REFOCUS Which of the trends in this section do you believe will have the strongest influence on your career as a teacher? Why? In what ways will you be affected?

A Final Word on Curriculum

Continuity & Change

Your place on the continuum

Throughout your teaching career, you can expect that the curriculum will continue to evolve to serve a changing society. It also seems certain that the pull from the ends of the curriculum continuum—subject-centered on one side and student-centered on the other—will continue to influence the innovations that are likely to infiltrate the classrooms of the future. As you move forward in your career, consider your own position on this continuum and how your orientation will impact your reaction to new ideas and instructional strategies. Regardless of the approach that influences you most, remember that the ultimate goal of the curriculum is to develop learners willing to participate in a democratic society.

Summing Up

1. In organizing the curriculum, most educators hold to the traditional concept of curriculum as the body of subjects, or subject matter. Nevertheless, progressive educators who are more concerned with the learner's experiences regard the student as the focus of curriculum.

2. Examples of a subject-centered approach include the following types of curriculum: (1) subject area, (2) perennialist and essentialist, (3) back-to-basics, and (4) new core.

3. Examples of a student-centered approach include the following types of curriculum: (1) activity-centered approaches, (2) relevant curriculum, (3) the humanistic approach, (4) alternative or free schools programs, and (5) values-centered curriculum.

4. Recent years have produced significant instructional innovations, including (1) differentiated instruction, (2) cooperative learning, (3) direct instruction, (4) twenty-first century skills, and (5) technology-enhanced instruction.

5. Developing curricular trends include the following: (1) the importance of the arts, (2) education of ELLs, (3) education for healthy youth, and (4) green education.

[109]Kim-Marie Cortez-Riggio, "The Green Footprint Project: How Middle School Students Inspired Their Community and Raised Their Self-Worth," *English Journal* (January 2011), pp. 39–43.
[110]Gilbert Proulx, "Integrating Scientific Method & Critical Thinking in Classroom Debates on Environmental Issues," *The American Biology Teacher* (January 2004), pp. 26–33; and "The Literacy Gap," *Campaign for Environmental Literacy* (2007) at **www.fundee.org/facts/envlit/litgap.htm**.
[111]Erik W. Robelen, "Environment Makes Splash in Curriculum," *Education Week*, October 12, 2011, p. 10; and "Maryland Becomes First State in Country to Require Green Graduates," *No Child Left Inside: Press Release* (June 21, 2011) at **www.edweek.org/media/mdgreengrads-blog.pdf** (January 2012).

Key Terms

The numbers indicate the pages where explanations of the key terms can be found.

curriculum 421
subject-centered curricula 421
subject-area curriculum 422
perennialist-influenced curriculum 422
essentialist-influenced curriculum 422
back-to-basics curriculum 423
new core curriculum (core subjects
    approach) 425
student-centered curricula 426

activity-centered curriculum 426
relevant curriculum 427
humanistic approach to curriculum 427
alternative (free) school 428
values-centered curriculum 428
censorship 433
differentiated instruction 435
cooperative learning 436
jigsaw strategy 437

direct instruction 438
twenty-first century skills 439
technology-enhanced learning 441
Web 2.0 442
blogs 442
Web services 442
environmental literacy 447

Certification Connection Activity

This chapter examines issues related to curriculum and instruction. In the Praxis II: Subject Assessments, you may be required to develop individual lessons or units that demonstrate your ability to effectively plan and teach content from your cho-

sen discipline. After reflecting on the types of curriculum and instructional innovations presented in the chapter, select a common topic from the teaching field, and outline a brief unit that uses two or more of the innovative strategies examined in the chapter.

Discussion Questions

❶ Discuss the benefits and limitations of using a single text-book as the basis for a course curriculum.

❷ Does your teacher-education program seem to favor one curriculum approach over another? Why might this be so? What kind of curriculum approach would you recommend

for a teacher-education program? Relate your approach to your philosophy of education.

❸ Which of the instructional approaches discussed in this chapter best fits your teaching style? Why? Share your thinking with a classmate.

Suggested Projects for Professional Development

❶ How is curriculum organized in the schools you visit? Ask to see a curriculum guide for your subject field or grade level. Is it a general outline of content and activities, or is it a detailed list of standards, objectives, activities, and materials and resources? How are the objectives tied to the state standards/CCSS?

❷ In your visits to schools this semester, talk with teachers about the curriculum they teach. Do they use a subject-centered approach, and, if so, which of the four subject-centered approaches described in this chapter best describes their procedure? If they use a student-centered approach, which of the student-centered approaches best describes what they do? Choose one of the schools you have visited, and explain how its approach best fits your ideas for a curriculum.

❸ Talk with members of the educational faculty at your college. What do they see as the pros and cons of subject-centered versus student-centered curricula?

❹ Use the educational resource database you are most familiar with to conduct a search of current curricular trends in your chosen field of study or level of students you want to teach. Entering the terms "curriculum" and your subject or level (for example, "social studies," "literacy," or "elementary") should produce a number of resources for you to consult. Focus on one relevant trend, and prepare a presentation describing the trend for your classmates.

❺ Using the following Internet Resources section, select a topic or unit of instruction, and develop a portfolio of resources and sample lesson plans to use as a teacher.

Suggested Resources

Internet Resources

The Internet has exponentially expanded teacher access to curriculum resources that will supplement classroom lessons. The Partnership for 21st Century Skills site (**http://p21.org**) provides tools and resources for educators to infuse the framework for twenty-first century learning into a school's program. Toolkits, Twitter feeds, webinars, and downloadable files assist educators in integrating this forwarding-looking approach into teaching and learning. Another site, Thinkfinity (**www.thinkfinity.org**), makes available free lesson plans that incorporate twenty-first century teaching and skills, and incorporates digital sources. Especially interesting are the free professional development webinars that assist in developing curriculum. An example is an online course that teaches how to incorporate twenty-first century skills into classroom instruction.

Curriki (**www.curriki.org**) is another resource that not only provides curriculum materials for the classroom but also encourages contributions and the development of networks. Its blogs, Twitter feeds, and Facebook sites are dedicated to sharing innovative ideas with other teachers. Edutopia (**www.edutopia.org**) also serves as a vast resource for enhancing the curriculum as you create lessons for the classroom. It has videos, blogs, content resource sites, and information about field-tested teaching strategies.

The Association for Supervision and Curriculum Development (ASCD) website (**www.ascd.org**) is an invaluable resource for any educator concerned about effective curriculum development. Membership in the organization allows full access to the site, which provides archived articles from the many publications of the organization, access to blogs from educators from around the world, and podcasts and webinars of discussions with experts on curriculum-related topics.

The Common Core State Standards Initiative (**www.corestandards.org**) is the source for all things related to the standards. Because these will be influencing curriculum and assessment reform in most states for the foreseeable future, you may want to explore the resources at this site.

Publications

Bellanca, James, and Ron Brandt. *21st Century Skills: Rethinking How Students Learn.* Bloomington, IN: Solution Tree, 2010. *Education experts offer ideas for teaching students the skills to succeed in the twenty-first century.*

García Coll, Cynthia T., and Amy Kerivan Mark, eds. *Immigrant Stories: Ethnicity and Academics in Middle Childhood.* New York: Oxford University Press, 2009. *Examines second generation immigrant children's emerging cultural attitudes and identities, academic engagement, and academic achievement.*

Giordano, Gerard. *Twentieth-Century Textbook Wars: A History of Advocacy and Opposition.* New York: Peter Lang Publishing, 2003. *Takes a historical look at the textbook industry and its evolution from the nineteenth century through the end of the twentieth century. Provides a thorough review of the controversies surrounding the industry.*

McDonald, Nan L., and Douglas Fisher. *Teaching Literacy through the Arts.* New York: Guilford Press, 2006. *Reflects the National Standards for Arts Education as incorporated in the enhancement of literacy instruction.*

Noddings, Nell. *Critical Lessons: What Our Schools Should Teach.* New York: Cambridge University Press, 2007. *Challenges teachers to examine issues confronting students in their domestic world, civic lives, and their broader public concerns and how these fit into the curriculum.*

Ornstein, Allan C., and Francis Hunkins. *Curriculum: Foundations, Principles and Issues,* 6th ed. Upper Saddle River, NJ: Prentice Hall, 2012. *An excellent book for researchers, theoreticians, and practitioners of curriculum involved in the development, design, and implementation of elementary- and secondary-school curriculum.*

Richardson, Will. *Blogs, Wikis, Podcasts, and Other Powerful Web Tools for Classrooms,* 3rd ed. Thousand Oaks, CA: Corwin Press, 2010. *Examines the transformation taking place in communication through the use of blogs, wikis, Facebook, and Twitter, which can potentially allow students to learn more, create more, and communicate better.*

Tomlinson, Carol, Kay Brimijoin, and Lane Narvaez. *The Differentiated School: Making Revolutionary Changes in Teaching and Learning.* Alexandria, VA: Association for Supervision and Curriculum Development, 2008. *Provides practical strategies for implementing differentiated instruction on a school-wide basis.*

 Additional resources for this chapter, including the TeachSource Videos, can be found on the Education CourseMate website. Go to **CengageBrain.com** to access the site.

Michael Reynolds/Corbis Wire/Corbis

PART SIX

Effective Education: International and American Perspectives

International Education

Many educational reformers have suggested that the United States could improve its educational system by emulating other countries. Japanese education has received particular attention because it appears to have contributed in large measure to Japan's economic success during the past fifty years. But imitating educational practices from other countries raises questions. Would they work in an American context? Do they mesh with American beliefs and values?

Before beginning to answer such questions, we need to understand the varieties of educational systems other countries employ: how they resemble one another, how they differ, and which particular features are most effective in which contexts. In this chapter, we offer an introduction to that kind of analysis. We then consider education in developing countries and international studies of school improvement. Finally, we offer a brief comment on the accomplishments of U.S. schools in an international context. As you read the chapter, see what answers you formulate to the following basic questions:

FOCUS QUESTIONS

- What do educational systems in various countries have in common? In what respects do they differ?
- How do educational systems differ with respect to the resources they devote to education and the percentage of students they enroll?
- How does the achievement of U.S. students compare with that of students in other countries?
- Which countries provide examples of outstanding educational activities that may be worth emulating elsewhere?
- What should be done to improve education in developing countries?
- How do the purposes and attainments of U.S. schools compare with those of other countries?

*This chapter was revised by Dan Levine.

Commonalities in Educational Systems

At first glance, classrooms around the world may seem to have little in common. Consider a classroom in a rural Sudanese village and one in contemporary Japan, for example. In Sudan, the building has no electricity, and the earthen floor is uncovered. The students are all boys. Few of the teachers have a high-school diploma; the curriculum and teaching, which rely heavily on memorization and recitation, are determined by the country's ministry of education. In highly developed Japan, by way of contrast, modern school buildings house classes of boys and girls, almost all of whom will complete high school. Teachers are highly respected professionals with college degrees. They are given considerable latitude in devising activities and adapting materials that satisfy the national guidelines, which emphasize development of children's thinking and problem-solving skills, as well as social, moral, and physical instruction that benefits the whole person.

Despite the great variety in educational systems worldwide, however, certain commonalities exist. The following sections describe widespread characteristics and problems: the strong relationships between students' social-class origins and their success in school, and the educational challenges posed by multicultural populations. Overview 15.1 summarizes commonalities and differences among educational systems.

OVERVIEW 15.1

Areas of Similarities and Differences among Educational Systems of the World

Commonalities—Many educational systems in the world face the same challenges.

Social Class Origins and School Outcomes	Throughout most of the world, lower-income students are at an educational disadvantage.
Multicultural Populations	Nearly every nation must find ways to effectively educate diverse student populations.

Differences—Many areas of distinction define individual countries' educational systems.

Resources Devoted to Education	The percentage of gross domestic income spent on education varies because of countries' incomes and the priority they give to education. Larger expenditures allow for more student enrollment and a higher level of educational services.
Extent of Centralization	Nations vary widely in how much educational decision making occurs at local and national government levels.
Curriculum Content, Instructional Emphases, and Approaches to Teacher Preparation	The subjects and methods that receive the most attention reflect the culture and priorities of each country.
Vocational versus Academic Education	After the first few years of common schooling, some nations more commonly separate students into academic or vocational educational tracks for further education.
Enrollment in Higher Education	Emphasis on academics in earlier schools, resources devoted to education, and occupational requirements in different countries contribute to wide variations in enrollment and completion of college and university studies.
Nonpublic Schools	Differences in culture and governmental structure contribute to variations in the size and functioning of nonpublic education.
Achievement Levels	U.S. students rank toward the middle on most international achievement tests, which leads many to conclude that U.S. schools need improvement.

Social–Class Origins and School Outcomes

▌ Privileged versus less
    privileged students

As we noted in Chapter 11, Social Class, Race, and School Achievement, various national and international studies have illustrated the strong relationships between students' socioeconomic background and their success in school and in the economic system. For example, World Bank studies have reported that family socioeconomic background is a salient predictor of students' achievement in both industrialized and developing countries. Similarly, Donald Treiman and others have found that individuals' social-class origins and background relate to their educational and occupational attainment regardless of whether their society is rich or poor, politically liberal or conservative.[1] A multitude of studies such as these also demonstrate that the family and home environments of low-income students generate the same kinds of educational disadvantages in other countries as in the United States.[2]

Multicultural Populations

▌ Rising diversity

Except in a few homogeneous countries, nationwide systems of education enroll diverse groups of students who differ significantly with respect to race, ethnicity, religion, native language, and/or cultural practices. (Its geographic isolation and cultural insularity make Japan one of the exceptions to this generalization.) Most large nations historically have included numerous racial/ethnic and cultural subgroups, but the twentieth and twenty-first centuries seem to have greatly accelerated the mixture of diverse groups across and within national boundaries. World and regional wars, global depressions and recessions, migration and immigration to large urban centers that offer expanded economic opportunity, and other destabilizing forces have led some historians to see recent decades as the era of the migrant and the refugee. These forces more or less ensure that you, as a teacher, will have students from other nations in your classes. As the From Preservice to Practice box describes, you might consider using the ease of global travel to your advantage now, to help you prepare for the opportunities and challenges of teaching international students.

▌ Multicultural challenges

Not surprisingly, then, other countries encounter challenges in multicultural education similar to those of the United States: ineffective traditional instruction, providing bilingual education, and desegregating minority students. (See also Chapter 12, Providing Equal Educational Opportunity, and Chapter 13, The Changing Purposes of American Education.) This is partly because minority racial, ethnic, and religious groups in many nations, as in the United States, frequently are low in socioeconomic status. England, France, the Netherlands, and other European countries, for example, have many lower-income students from Africa, Asia, the Caribbean, and other distant locations. Germany is struggling to provide effective education for the children of Romany (Gypsy), Slavic, and Turkish migrants, and most West African nations include students from numerous disadvantaged tribal and minority-language groups.[3]

▌ **REFOCUS** What other characteristics do you believe may be common to schools in many countries? In what other ways, besides those described, might you encounter situations similar to those teachers in other countries encounter?

---

[1]Donald J. Treiman, *Occupational Prestige in Comparative Perspective* (New York: Academic Press, 1977); and Marlaine E. Lockheed, Bruce Fuller, and Ronald Nyirongo, *Family Background and School Achievement* (New York: World Bank, 1988). See also Patrick Heuveline, Honqxing Yang, and Jeffrey M. Timberlake, "It Takes a Village (Perhaps a Nation)," *Journal of Marriage and Family* (October 2010), pp. 1362–1376; Richard Wilkinson and Kate Pickett, "Greater Equality," *American Educator* (Spring 2011), available at **www.aft.org**; and John Ermisch, Jantti Markus, and Timothy M. Smeeding, eds., *From Parents to Children* (New York: Russell Sage, 2012).
[2]Alan C. Purves and Daniel U. Levine, eds., *Educational Policy and International Assessment* (Berkeley, CA: McCutchan, 1975); Emily Beller and Michael Hout, "Intergenerational Social Mobility," *The Future of Children* (Fall 2006), available at **www.futureofchildren.org**; Guillermo Montt, "Cross-National Differences in Educational Achievement Inequality," *Sociology of Education* (January 2011), pp. 49–68; and Laura B. Perry and Andrew McConney, "Does the SES of the School Matter?" January 2012 posting by the Horace Mann League, available at **http://horacemannleague.blogspot.com**.
[3]Nigel Grant, "Some Problems of Identity and Education," *Comparative Education* (March 1997), pp. 9–28; and Eleonora Barbieri-Masini, "Toward Multicultural Societies," *Current Sociology* (Issue 2, 2011), pp. 229–237.

FROM PRESERVICE TO PRACTICE

New Perspectives

Dr. Harris introduced his main topic for the day's discussion to a classroom of education majors: "I'm wondering if any of you know how many languages are spoken in Minneapolis schools, in New York City schools, Houston schools, or Los Angeles schools. Right here in Minneapolis, we have students speaking more than ninety different languages.

"How many of you speak more than one language? How many of you have traveled to other countries to see how children are educated in various parts of the world? Whether or not you have traveled, whether or not you are bilingual, you will be working with students from different cultures and with parents who have differing expectations from educators.

"We have a responsibility to serve all our children well," he continued. "What do you think we can do to help you preservice teachers prepare to deal effectively with students from other countries?"

"One obvious way is to have us read about the different types of schooling and the different approaches to teaching used around the world," suggested Michael Ervin.

"We could research countries on the Internet to get a sense of how their schools are organized and run," commented Sally Newman.

"Why don't we use on-campus resources?" Bob Barrett said. "We could interview international students who we are familiar with about their countries' educational processes."

Tanghe Yu added, "I think the best way to gain an appreciation of the different perspectives would be to actually visit the school site. That way, whether we're students or student teachers, we could immerse ourselves in the educational experiences of the students. I moved here from Taiwan when I was eight years old. I can tell you that my schooling there and here, even in the early years, differed substantially."

Dr. Harris nodded. "Yes, those are all great suggestions. Tanghe, I think your idea has special merit. Since the 9/11 attacks, I have been thinking that we really need to help build more understanding between and among different groups. Who might be interested in traveling and learning about schools in other countries?" About half of the people in the class raised a hand. "Right now, we don't have the funds, but perhaps we can start by looking at grant opportunities that may help us."

Case Questions

1. How are you, as a preservice teacher, preparing yourself to deal with the students and families who come to public schools with languages and cultural backgrounds different from your own?

2. How have the schools you observed in your own community worked with students and families with varying cultural backgrounds? What strategies do you consider most effective?

3. Would you want to participate in a program such as the one suggested by Dr. Harris? If so, to which country would you travel, and why? If not, why not?

Differences in Educational Systems and Outcomes

Each nation's educational system also differs in important ways from other systems. We will discuss some of the most significant differences in the following sections.

Resources Devoted to Education

Expenditures for education

One fundamental way in which nations differ is in the percentage of their resources they devote to education rather than to priorities such as highways, health care, and military forces. As a percentage of gross domestic product (wealth produced annually), public expenditures on K–12 and higher education range from 3 to 4.5 percent in nations low in average income and/or that place relatively little priority on education, to more than 7 percent in nations with high average income and/or that emphasize

Classrooms, schools, and school systems around the world differ in many ways, some obvious as in this picture, others less obvious. Schools also share commonalities, such as the joys most teachers find in working with their students.

© Imagestate Media Partners Limited-Impact Photos/Alamy

education. In some of the world's poorest countries, average per capita expenditures on military forces are nearly one-third greater than per capita spending for education.[4]

Student–Teacher Ratios at the Primary Level   Relatively wealthy nations, as well as nations that allocate many of their resources to education, can provide a higher level of services than poor nations that mobilize relatively few resources for their schools. For example, average primary-level student–teacher ratios tend to be much higher in poorer regions than in wealthier regions. More than half of African nations report an average student–teacher ratio of more than thirty to one, whereas most European and North American nations average twenty to one or fewer. Large differences also emerge, however, when we compare wealthy countries with each other, and when we compare poor countries with other poor countries.[5]

Better student–teacher ratios in wealthy regions

Enrollment Ratios   The resources devoted to education also help determine whether most children and youth attend school and whether they obtain diplomas or degrees. Data collected by UNESCO indicate that in their category of "more developed regions" (Australia, Japan, New Zealand, North America, and most of Western Europe), nearly all children attend elementary schools. In what UNESCO designates as "less developed regions" (including most of Africa, the Arab states, much of Asia, and Latin America), nearly 20 percent of elementary-age children do not attend school. (In underdeveloped nations such as Liberia and Sudan, as many as 60 percent of children are not in school.) Discrepancies in enrollment ratios between developed and less developed nations become even greater at the secondary and higher-education levels.[6]

Higher enrollment in wealthy regions

[4]George Psacharopoulos, *Planning of Education: Where Do We Stand?* (Washington, D.C.: World Bank, 1985); Kevin Martin, et al., *Overcoming Inequality EFA Global Monitoring Report* 2009 (Paris: United Nations Educational, Social and Cultural Organization, 2008), available at **www .unesco.org**; and *The 2011 Statistical Abstract* (Washington, D.C.: U.S. Census Bureau, 2011).
[5]*Education at a Glance 2011* (Paris: Organisation for Economic Co-operation and Development, 2011).
[6]Ewout Fakema, "Comparing the Distribution of Education across the Developing World, 1960–2005," *Social Indicators Research* (September 2008), pp. 437–455; C. Alan Joyce, ed., *The World Almanac and Book of Facts* 2011 (New York: World Almanac Books, 2010); "Out-of-School Children," 2011 Fact Sheet at **www.unesco.org**; Peter Moyi, "Who Goes to School? School Enrollment Patterns in Somalia," *International Journal of Educational Development* (January 2012), pp. 163–171; and numerous other materials available at **www.unesco.org**.

Increasing female enrollment

Male and Female Enrollments   We noted in Chapter 10, Culture, Socialization, and Education, that U.S. girls have higher reading scores than boys and that females have become a majority in higher-education institutions. The same pattern has appeared in other developed nations. With a few exceptions, such as Japan and Turkey, female enrollment in colleges and universities in wealthy nations has been growing to the extent that more women than men obtain first degrees. However, the pattern is different in developing nations, where males frequently outnumber females in higher education, secondary schools, and, sometimes, even elementary schools. Many analysts believe that the low enrollment ratio for girls compared to boys in many low-income countries in Africa and Asia is both a cause and an effect of economic development problems.[7]

The United States among Industrial Nations   For certain purposes, it is instructive to compare wealthy or highly industrialized nations with each other rather than with poor or economically underdeveloped nations. Other factors remaining equal, nations with less wealth and fewer resources have a much harder time supporting education or other government services than do those with a strong economic base. Thus, to analyze how well the United States mobilizes resources for education, we should compare it with other developed countries.[8]

U.S. rank in expenditures

Several controversies have erupted about this subject. Although public-school critics have claimed that American education expenditures are unsurpassed, many researchers disagree. When we subtract funding for higher education, the United States ranks below the top on education expenditures. Figure 15.1 shows such a comparison in graphic form. In terms of public education expenditures for grades 1 through 12 as a percentage of gross domestic product, the United States tied for third-through-fifth among twelve industrial countries.[9]

Comparing teacher salaries

Analysts also debate whether U.S. teacher salaries are high or low in comparison with those of other industrial countries. Data on teacher salary averages indicate that for both beginning and experienced teachers, average salaries in countries such as Ireland and Norway are a good deal lower than in the United States, but in some other countries, they are generally higher.[10]

> **REFOCUS**   How do you think U.S. schools would be affected if the country devoted a greater percentage of its resources to education and children's well-being? What if the United States began to devote fewer resources to these concerns?

Sometimes, the comparisons expand to other types of resources that support children's well-being and development. For example, Timothy Smeeding, comparing the United States with Australia, Canada, Germany, Sweden, and the United Kingdom, found that these five countries average

Comparing social-welfare expenditures

about the same for government expenditures on children's education and health services as a percentage of gross domestic product. However, he also found that U.S. government expenditures to help provide income security for children's families are less than half the average for these countries. Smeeding concluded that high rates of

---

[7]Christopher Colclough, et al., "Gender and Education for All," 2003 paper prepared for the UNESCO Education for All Global Monitoring Report; *Global Education Digest 2010* (Paris: UNESCO, 2010), available at **www.unesco.org**; and *The 2012 Statistical Abstract* (Washington, D.C.: U.S. Census Bureau, 2012).

[8]"Developed" nations as classified by the United Nations Educational, Scientific, and Cultural Organization (UNESCO) include Australia, Canada, most of Europe, Israel, Japan, South Africa, the former USSR, the United States, and New Zealand. All others are classified as "developing" nations.

[9]Ludger Woessman, "Why Students in Some Countries Do Better," *Education Next* (Summer 2001), pp. 67–74, available at **www.educationnext.org**; and Susan Aud et al., *The Condition of Education 2011* (Washington, D.C.: National Center for Education Statistics, 2011), available at **www.nces.ed.gov**.

[10]Daniel U. Levine, "Educational Spending: International Comparisons," *Theory into Practice* (Spring 1994), pp. 126–131; F. Howard Nelson, *How and How Much the U.S. Spends on K–12 Education* (Washington, D.C.: American Federation of Teachers, 1996); David C. Miller et al., *Comparative Indicators of Education in the United States and Other G-8 Countries* (Washington, D.C.: National Center for Education Statistics, 2009); and Liao Maozhong and Shen Hua, "Educational Inequality Analysis," *International Journal of Business and Social Science* (September 2011), available at **www.ijbssnet.com**.

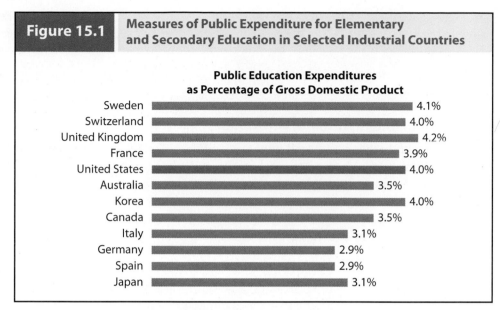

Figure 15.1 | Measures of Public Expenditure for Elementary and Secondary Education in Selected Industrial Countries

Public Education Expenditures as Percentage of Gross Domestic Product

Country	Percentage
Sweden	4.1%
Switzerland	4.0%
United Kingdom	4.2%
France	3.9%
United States	4.0%
Australia	3.5%
Korea	4.0%
Canada	3.5%
Italy	3.1%
Germany	2.9%
Spain	2.9%
Japan	3.1%

Note: Expenditure data are for first grade through high school but exclude capital outlay and debt service. Various adjustments have been made to enhance comparability of the original data.

Source: Adapted from Susan Aud et al., *The Condition of Education 2011* (Washington, D.C.: National Center for Education Statistics, 2011), Table A-38-1.

divorce, out-of-wedlock births, and other social forces are creating a larger urban and rural underclass, making it "increasingly hard to argue that all U.S. children have equal life chances." A later study by the United Nations Children's Fund (UNICEF) supported these conclusions in reporting that the United States stood very near the bottom among twenty-four industrialized nations ranked on various measures of childhood well-being.[11]

Extent of Centralization

✓ Standards & Assessment

▌ Decentralized versus centralized systems

All governments must decide whether to emphasize decentralized decision making, which allows for planning and delivering instruction in accordance with local circumstances, or centralized decision making, which builds accountability up and down a national or regional chain of command. Examples go far in either direction. In the United States, most important decisions are decentralized across thousands of diverse public-school districts. At the other extreme, France, Greece, and Japan, for example, all have highly centralized educational systems and decisions, following nationwide standards concerning acceptable class size and what will be taught in a given subject at a particular grade and time. In some countries, centralization has led to long lines of citizens from all parts of the nation waiting outside the ministry of education for appointments with central school officials who determine what schools children will attend and how students will be treated. We consider centralized versus decentralized systems in the Taking Issue box.

---

[11]Timothy M. Smeeding, "Social Thought and Poor Children," *Focus* (Spring 1990), p. 14. See also Lee Rainwater and Timothy M. Smeeding, *Rich Kids in a Poor Country* (New York: Russell Sage, 2003); Peter Adamson, "The Children Left Behind," *Innocenti Report Card 9*, 2010, available at **www.unicef-irc.org**; and Julis B. Isaacs, "The Recession's Ongoing Impact on America's Children," *First Focus* (December 2011).

TAKING ISSUE

Read the brief introduction below, as well as the Question and the pros and cons list that follows. Then, answer the question using your own words and position.

Establishment of a National Curriculum

Countries with highly centralized public education generally expect teachers to follow a national curriculum that specifies the topics to be taught and the objectives and materials to be emphasized in each subject and grade level. Countries that follow a decentralized pattern primarily relegate decisions about subject matter and materials to a regional group of schools (such as a school district) or individual faculties or teachers. Government officials in some highly decentralized nations such as the United States are considering whether a national curriculum should be established to provide for a more standardized approach in planning and delivering instruction.

Question

Would a U.S. national curriculum be preferable to decentralized policies that allow individual school districts, schools, or teachers to select instructional objectives and materials?

Arguments PRO

1. Availability of a national curriculum is partly responsible for the high achievement levels in Japan, Korea, and other countries.

2. A national curriculum based on the careful deliberation of subject-area specialists and experienced teachers makes it easier to achieve in-depth teaching of well-sequenced objectives and materials.

3. Uniformity in objectives and materials reduces the inefficiencies and learning problems that occur when students move from one classroom, school, or district to another.

4. A national curriculum will improve teacher education because preparation programs can concentrate on objectives and materials that trainees will teach when they obtain jobs.

5. Because it draws on a large base of resources, national curriculum planning can incorporate the best current thinking in each subject area and help prepare technically excellent tests.

Arguments CON

1. Establishment of a national curriculum runs counter to promising trends toward school-based management and professional autonomy for teachers.

2. A national curriculum is undesirable because its objectives and materials will be too difficult for many students and too easy for others.

3. Particularly in large and diverse countries such as the United States, the standardized materials that form the basis for a national curriculum will be uninteresting and unmotivating for many students.

4. Even if the national curriculum allows flexibility in objectives and materials, teachers will be pressured to follow the same path as everyone else, and most likely funds will be unavailable for alternative materials. Therefore, students and classes that might benefit from alternatives will suffer.

5. The extreme difficulty in preparing challenging national curriculum materials appropriate to use across a wide range of classrooms will reinforce tendencies to emphasize low-level skills and uncreative materials.

Question Reprise: What Is Your Stand?

Reflect again on the following question by explaining *your* stand on this issue: Should the federal government encourage or even pressure the states and school districts to adopt national/centralized goals and related practices for the schools?

Curriculum Content, Instructional Emphases, and Approaches to Teacher Preparation

Although much instruction worldwide consists of student seatwork and lectures delivered by poorly trained teachers, nations differ with regard to curriculum content, instructional emphasis, and teacher training. For example, the following well-known practices make New Zealand and Finland distinctive:[12]

■ New Zealand primary schools are known for their systematic emphasis on learning to read through *natural language learning*. Using this approach, children learn to figure out words in context as they read, rather than through phonics and decoding instruction.

■ The education system in Finland has become known for high achievement and attainment at all levels from preschool through higher education (see Table 15.2). Various observers have cited features they believe help account for this success: a national core curriculum that emphasizes thinking and students' active role in learning, school-level (not national) requirements that students perform at high levels, some flexible grouping rather than rigid streaming or tracking, a highly qualified teaching force (see the next paragraph), nearly universal public preschool, significant time in the school day set aside for teacher planning and assessment of students, provision and updating of science laboratory equipment and materials and of computer hardware and software, provision of funds so that schools enrolling many immigrant students can afford such interventions as resource teachers and special-needs classes, and various other interventions to help struggling students in elementary and secondary schools.

■ As noted in the previous bulleted item, observers believe that the quality of teaching and of the teacher workforce helps account for high achievement levels in Finnish schools. Analysts have described notable aspects of Finland's strong teacher preparation as including the following:[13]

■ Entry into teacher training programs is highly selective. Few applicants are accepted initially, and candidates must then do well in a clinical situation before gaining entry.

■ Candidates then must earn at least a two-year master's degree at one of eight well-respected universities.

■ Candidates must spend a significant amount of time in clinical practice in a model classroom associated with the university.

■ Candidates to teach at the elementary level must take at least two subject-area minors in arts or science departments. Candidates for higher grades must participate in a subject-area master's degree program.

■ Candidates who receive a degree in the subject they will teach must receive another master's degree in teaching.

---

[12]Elaine Jarchow, "Ten Ideas Worth Stealing from New Zealand," *Phi Delta Kappan* (January 1992), pp. 394–395; Heather Bell, "Learning to Read in New Zealand," *Reading Today* (April/May 2000), p. 32; Mai K. Lai, et al., "Sustained Acceleration of Achievement in Reading Comprehension," *Reading Research Quarterly* (No. 1, 2009); LynNell Hancock, "Why Are Finland's Schools Successful?" *Smithsonian* (September 2011), available at **www.smithsonianmag.com**; and Stephen Sawchuck, "Teacher Quality, Status Entwined Among Top-Performing Nations," *Education Week* (January 12, 2012).

[13]Alain Jehlen, "How Finland Reached the Top of the Educational Rankings," *NEA Today* (March 4, 2011), available at **www.neatoday.org**; Linda Darling-Hammond, "Soaring Systems," *American Educator* (Winter 2010–2011), available at **www.aft.org**; Robert Rothman and Linda Darling-Hammond, "Teacher and School Leader Effectiveness," *Issue Brief* (March 16, 2011), available at **www.all4ed.org**; Pasi Sahlberg, "Lessons from Finland," *American Educator* (Summer 2011), available from **www.aft.org**; and Mark S. Tucker, "Standing on the Shoulders of Giants," 2011 paper posted by the National Center on Education and the Economy, available at **www.ncee.org**.

Several analysts also emphasize that Finland and other high-performing nations exemplify systemic arrangements involving such coordinated components as a focus on higher-order learning, a well-trained teaching force, collaborative planning and assessment of lessons, and high coordination and articulation of curriculum and instruction across grade levels. Although high-quality teaching seems to be a hallmark of all these nations, student performance also is dependent on correlated arrangements that appear to vary from nation to nation. Analysts also point out that Finland is a small relatively homogeneous nation; some practices that help account for its success in education may not work in much larger and more heterogeneous nations such as the United States.

Vocational versus Academic Education

■ Divergence after primary years

School systems around the world also differ greatly in how they are organized to provide education through the postsecondary level. Although most nations now provide at least four years of first-level education during which all students attend primary or elementary schools, above that level, systems diverge widely. Most students continue in common first-level schools for several more years, but, in many countries, students are divided between academic-track schools and vocational schools after four to eight years of first-level education. This arrangement, which corresponds to the traditional European dual-track pattern described in Chapter 3, Global Origins of American Education, is often known as a **bipartite system**.

■ Wide variations in tracking

The proportion of secondary students enrolled in primarily vocational programs varies from less than one-tenth in industrial countries such as Denmark and the United States to more than one-fifth in others such as Germany. Similar variation appears in academic tracks. Some countries, beginning at the secondary level and extending into postsecondary education, enroll large proportions of students in academic schools designed to produce an elite corps of high-school or college graduates. In others, including Canada and the United States, most secondary students continue to attend common or comprehensive schools, and many enroll in colleges that are relatively nonselective.[14]

Enrollment in Higher Education

■ Factors affecting enrollment in higher education

Countries that channel students into vocational programs tend to have low percentages of youth attending institutions of higher education. By contrast, more youth go on to higher education in countries that provide general academic studies for most high-school students. Other factors that help determine enrollment in higher education include a nation's investment of resources in higher education, emphasis on postsecondary learning rather than job-market entry, traditions regarding the use of higher education to equalize educational opportunities, and the extent to which colleges and universities admit only high-achieving students.

■ Developing versus industrial nations

Developing countries with relatively little funding available for higher education and problems in increasing elementary and secondary enrollment levels predictably have low proportions of youth participating in higher education. Thus, Afghanistan, Ethiopia, Ghana, and many other developing nations enroll less than 20 percent of their young people in higher education. Most industrial countries provide postsecondary education for more than a third of their young adults.

■ Differences among industrial nations

After high-school graduates are enrolled in postsecondary institutions, numerous considerations determine whether they will stay enrolled and eventually gain their degrees: curriculum difficulty, financial aid opportunities, motivation levels, and access

---

[14]Michael McVey, "The Role of Vocational Education and Training in Promoting Lifelong Learning in Germany and England," *International Review of Education* (May 2007), pp. 325–327; and Anita Ratam, "Traditional Occupations in a Modern World," *International Journal for Educational and Vocational Guidance* (No. 2, 2011), pp. 92–109.

Table 15.1	Percentage of Twenty-Five- to Thirty-Four-Year-Olds Who Have Attained Postsecondary (Tertiary) Education, Selected Countries		
Australia	41	Italy	19
Belgium	41	Japan	54
Canada	58	Korea (South)	56
Denmark	40	Netherlands	37
Finland	39	Norway	43
France	41	Spain	39
Germany	23	Sweden	40
Iceland	31	United Kingdom	37
Ireland	44	United States	40

Note: Data are for 2007.

Source: Adapted from *OECD Factbook* 2010 (Paris: Organisation for Economic Co-operation and Development, 2010).

to preferred institutions and courses. Industrial nations differ greatly in the proportion of young people who obtain postsecondary degrees. As shown in Table 15.1, for example, the percentages of young adults who complete postsecondary education in industrial nations varies from 19 percent in Italy to more than 50 in Japan, Korea, and Canada.

Decline in U.S. ranking

Continuity & Change

Decline in U.S. Ranking for College Participation Until the 1990s, the United States generally had higher percentages of young people attending and completing higher-education institutions than any other nation. Only Canada came close. The data in Table 15.1 indicate that this pattern no longer holds. Several nations now surpass the United States in postsecondary participation, and others are gaining rapidly. This change led the author of a study conducted for the Educational Commission of the States to conclude that "if current trends persist and students in the United States continue to enroll in college at the rate they do now, America is likely to slip further behind the growing number of developed nations that have stepped up their efforts over the last decade to increase educational attainment." She further warned of a serious risk "that competing public priorities and shrinking resources will put access to an affordable and high-quality college education further out of reach for more and more Americans."[15]

Nonpublic Schools

Proportion of students in private schools

Depending on their histories, political structures, religious composition, legal frameworks, and other factors, nations differ greatly in the size and functions of their nonpublic education sectors. In a few countries, such as the Netherlands, more than half of elementary and secondary students attend private schools. At the other extreme, governments in Cuba, North Korea, and other nations have prohibited nonpublic schools in order to suppress ideologies different from those supported by the state. In most countries, private-school students constitute less than 10 percent of total enrollment.[16]

---

[15]Sandra S. Ruppert, "Closing the College Participation Gap," 2003 paper prepared for the Education Commission of the States, pp. 6–7. See also "Demography as Destiny," 2006 paper prepared for the Alliance for Excellent Education, available at **www.all4ed.org**; Daniel Gross, "The Education Factor," *Education Next* (Spring 2009), available at **ww.educationnext.org**; and Chandra T. Smith et al., "Developing 20/20 Vision on the 2020 Degree Attainment Goal," 2011 report prepared for The Pell Institute, available at **www.pellinstitute.org**.
[16]Rafak Piwowarski, "The Role of Non-Public Schools in Modern Education Systems," *International Review of Education* (September 2006), pp. 397–407; Michael Omolewa, "Private Schooling in Less Economically Developed Countries," *International Review of Education* (January 2008); Dorian A. Barrow and Samuel Lochan, "Education in a Hidden Marketplace," *Compare* (January 2010), pp. 153–155; and "Private Schools," *PISA in Focus* (August 2011), available at **www.pisa.oecd.org**.

Problems in defining a "private school"

Nations also vary widely in the extent to which they provide public support for nonpublic schools or students. They differ as to government regulation of nonpublic systems, people's perceptions of public and nonpublic schools, and the role that private schools are expected to play in national development. In some countries, nonpublic schools enroll a relatively small, elite group of students who later enter the most prestigious colleges; in others, they serve a more representative sample of the nation's children and youth. In some countries, many private schools are small shoestring operations enrolling poor students in urban slums. Given this variety, it is not possible to cross-nationally define a private school or generalize about policies that encourage or discourage nonpublic schools. Clearly, productive national policies on nonpublic schools must reflect each country's unique mix of circumstances and challenges.[17]

Achievement Levels

Standards & Assessment

Significant studies

Differences in school achievement among nations have received considerable attention since the **International Association for the Evaluation of Educational Achievement (IEA)** began conducting cross-national studies in the 1960s. One of the first major IEA projects collected and analyzed data on the achievement of 258,000 students from nineteen countries in civic education, foreign languages, literature, reading comprehension, and science. This study showed a wide range in average achievement levels across nations. In general, the United States ranked close to the middle among the nations included in the study. Later studies, such as the **Program for International Student Assessment (PISA)**, the **Progress in International Reading Literacy Study (PIRLS)**, and the **Third International Mathematics and Science Study (TIMSS)**, also have found that our students generally rank near the international average (see Table 15.2).[18]

Researchers' conclusions

Analyzing data from these international studies, scholars have reached conclusions that include the following:[19]

- National scores in subjects such as reading, math, and science tend to be highly correlated. For example, seven of the eight nations with the highest reading scores in data collected by PISA also were in the highest eight nations with respect to math and science scores.

More spread in United States

- As shown in Table 15.2, U.S. students' reading scores were well below those of students in the highest-scoring nations. Some nations, including the United States, have a much greater spread between the performances of low- and high-achieving students than do others such as Finland, Japan, and Korea. The performance of high-achieving American students, however, sometimes is comparable to that of the highest performers in other nations. Furthermore, students in U.S. schools with a low percentage of poverty students score as high as students in high-scoring nations. Conversely, U.S. students in high-poverty schools

[17]Pauline Nesdale, "International Perspectives on Government Funding of Non-Government Schools," *Education Forum Briefing Papers* (March 2003), available at **www.educationforum .org.nz**; Karen Evans and Anna Robinson-Pant, "Public-Private Strategies, Regulatory Regimes and Education Systems," *Compare* (February 2009), pp. 1–4; and Lily Tsai, "Friends or Foes?" *Studies in Comparative International Development* (March 2011), pp. 46–69.

[18]Purves and Levine, *Educational Policy and International Assessment;* Justin Baer et al., *The Reading Literacy of Fourth-Grade Students in an International Context* (Washington D.C.: National Center for Education Statistics, 2007); *PISA 2010 at a Glance* (Paris: Organisation for Economic Co-operation and Development, 2011), available at **www.oecd.org**; and Paul E. Peterson et al., "Are U.S. Students Ready to Compete?" 2011 report prepared for the Kern Foundation, available at **www.educationnext.org**.

[19]Iris C. Rotberg, "Why Do Our Myths Matter?" *School Administrator* (April 2007), available at **www.aasa.org**; Cynthia McCabe, "The Economics Behind International Education Rankings," *NEA Today* (December 10, 2010), available at **www.neatoday.org**; and Lori Taylor, "PISA Results Shed New Light on U.S. Education Debate," 2011 interview posted by the Dallas Federal Reserve, available at **www.dallasfed.org**.

Table 15.2	Reading and Math Scores of Fifteen-Year-Olds in Twenty-Two Nations				
Nation	Reading	Math	Nation	Reading	Math
Korea	539	546	France	496	497
Finland	536	541	Denmark	495	503
Canada	524	527	United Kingdom	494	492
New Zealand	521	519	Portugal	489	487
Japan	520	529	Italy	486	483
Australia	515	514	Greece	483	466
Belgium	506	515	Spain	481	483
Iceland	500	507	Russian Federation	459	468
Poland	500	495	Mexico	425	419
United States	500	487	Brazil	412	386
Germany	497	513	Argentina	398	401
Sweden	497	494			
			Average	**493**	**496**

Note: The average score is for OECD nations.

Source: Adapted from *PISA 2009 Results: What Students Know and Can Do—Student Performance in Reading, Mathematics and Science (Volume 1)* (Paris: Organisation for Economic Co-operation and Development, 2010).

score about as low as the average student in the lowest-achieving industrialized countries.

■ Whereas U.S. students generally have reading and science scores near the average for industrialized nations, their mathematics scores are significantly lower.

■ Social class correlates strongly with achievement test scores in nearly all nations. However, the spread between working-class and middle-class students is much greater in nations such as the United States than in others such as Finland and Japan that have high average scores and relatively low spread between high and low achievers.

Emphasis on passive learning

■ Instructional characteristics (including class size, amount of time allocated to instruction, teachers' experience, and amount of homework) generally do not correlate with achievement test scores. For example, many countries studied, including the United States, frequently implement mathematics instruction based on "tell and show" approaches that emphasize passive, rote learning. Because some of these countries had scores considerably higher than U.S. scores, however, such approaches could not account for mediocre U.S. performance levels except in interaction with other variables.

U.S. math curricula lacking

■ Some analysts have concluded that U.S. curricula and instruction, particularly in mathematics, generally are a mile wide and an inch deep and that the mediocre performance resulting from this superficial teaching poses a serious threat to our international competitiveness. Several scholars studying the U.S. math curriculum in an international context concluded that it is *unfocused,* with too many topics in too little depth; *highly repetitive; incoherent,* with little logical order to topics; and *undemanding,* particularly at the middle-school level. In addition, U.S. mathematics curricula, in contrast to many other nations, are highly differentiated. That is, our middle-level students tend to be sorted into mathematics tracks that stress algebra and other advanced topics for high-achieving students and simple arithmetic for low achievers. Thus, many students with low- or medium-achievement levels have little opportunity to proceed beyond basic skills. This is in marked contrast to Finland, Hungary, Japan, and some other locations where most students are challenged to perform at a higher level. Most analysts who have reviewed these patterns believe that action must be taken to reduce this kind of curriculum differentiation.[20]

✓ Standards & Assessment

■ Improvement in U.S. student performance will require systemic change involving setting of standards, assessment of students, teacher preparation, instructional methods, and other aspects of our educational system.

Publication of the PIRLS, PISA, and TIMSS studies has helped ignite emotional controversies. On one side, observers claim that our educational system is more satisfactory than it is often portrayed. While admitting that it needs major improvements, these observers point to such factors as the following:[21]

Defense of U.S. schools

■ Our students generally perform at a relatively high reading level through the fourth grade.

■ Cultural factors, not deficiencies in the schools, may be causing much of the relatively low student performance. For example, the high levels of mathematics achievement reported for Hungary, Japan, and Korea may be attributable primarily to the great value their cultures attach to mathematics performance and to strong family support for achievement.

■ Contrary to critics' statements, achievement in U.S. schools has improved during the past few decades, particularly considering the increased enrollment of minority students from low-income families. These improvements may be attributable in part to the positive effects of compensatory education and school desegregation (see the Chapter 11, Social Class, Race, and School Achievement) and to efforts at educational reform.

Critique of U.S. schools

Critics of U.S. performance have been unappeased by such arguments. Frequently pointing to the particularly low scores that our students register on tests assessing higher-order skills such as math problem solving, they reiterate the importance of improving students' skills in comprehension, geography, math, science, and other subjects. They conclude that the rankings of U.S. students in numerous international achievement studies represent a deplorable performance level that cannot be corrected without radical efforts to reform or even replace our current system of education.[22]

REFOCUS How might your work as a teacher be affected by international comparisons of achievement? How should it be affected?

---

[20]William H. Schmidt, Chi W. Hsing, and Curtis C. McKnight, "Curriculum Coherence," *Journal of Curriculum Studies* (September 2005), pp. 525–559; Xiaoxia Newton, "Reflections on Math Reform in the U.S.," *Phi Delta Kappan* (May 2007), pp. 681–685; Iris C. Rotberg, "Quick Fixes, Test Scores, and the Global Economy," *Education Week* (June 11, 2008); William H. Schmidt, "What's Missing from Math Standards?" *American Educator* (Spring 2008), available at **www .aft.org**; Melinda Burns, "U.S. Middle Schoolers Are Behind in Math," *Miller-McCune*, June 19, 2011, available at **www.miller-mccune.com**; William H. Schmidt et al., "Content Coverage Differences across Districts/States," *American Journal of Education* (May 2011); and Stephen Tung, "How the Finnish School System Outshines U.S. Education," 2012 posting at Physorg.com, available at **www.physorg.com**.
[21]Purves and Levine, *Educational Policy and International Assessment;* Erling E. Boe and Sujie Shin, "Is the United States Really Losing the International Horse Race in Academic Achievement?" *Phi Delta Kappan* (September 2005), pp. 688–695; Gerald W. Bracey, "U.S. School Performance, Through a Glass Darkly (Again)," *Phi Delta Kappan* (January 2009), pp. 386–387; Mike Petrilli, "U.S. Performance on PISA," *Flypaper* (March 15, 2011); and Jay P. Greene and Josh B. McGee, "When the Best is Mediocre," *Education Next* (Winter 2012), available at **www .educationext.org**.
[22]William H. Schmidt, Richard Houang, and Leonard Cogan, "A Coherent Curriculum," *American Educator* (Summer 2002), available at **www.aft.org**; Eric Hanushek et al., "Education and Economic Growth," *Education Next* (Spring 2008), available at **www.educationnext.org**; and William H. Schmidt, Leland S. Cogan, and Curtis C. McKnight, "Equality of Educational Opportunity," *American Educator* (Winter 2010–2011), available at **www.aft.org**.

Problems and Prospects in Developing Countries

Education and economic development

Earlier in this chapter, we saw that educational inadequacies in developing countries are both a cause and a result of poverty. For this reason, national governments and international organizations have strongly supported bolstering the economies of developing countries by expanding and improving their educational systems. Education usually is considered critical for economic development because it can give people the skills and knowledge to compete in international markets and because it can help bring about a more equitable distribution of wealth and power, which in turn contributes to political stability and long-term economic growth.

Problems in upgrading education

However, it has proved exceedingly difficult to achieve widespread, lasting, and balanced improvement of educational systems in many developing countries. For example, extreme poverty in countries such as Rwanda has been partly responsible for restricting the availability of funds to only several hundred dollars per primary student per year. Developing countries such as India and Nigeria also struggle to overcome educational problems associated with the use of dozens or even hundreds of different languages among their multiethnic populations. Numerous developing countries also confront a problem known as **brain drain**: the number of high-school and university graduates increases, but with few well-paid jobs suitable to their level of education, these well-trained people immigrate to wealthier countries with better employment opportunities.

Recommendations for developing countries

To improve education in developing countries, researchers have suggested the following steps:[23]

1. Invest more in primary schools to broaden the base of students who can participate in higher levels of education.
2. Avoid emphasizing higher-education subjects that students will tend to study abroad and perhaps not return.
3. Make private schools an integral part of educational expansion plans.
4. Expand efforts to improve students' cognitive functioning.
5. Work on overcoming obstacles that limit the education of girls and women.
6. Substantially improve teacher preparation.
7. Facilitate private tutoring and other out-of-school skill-building activities.
8. Use online learning courses and systems, laptop networks, and other modern technologies to expand educational opportunities at all levels.

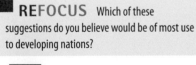
REFOCUS Which of these suggestions do you believe would be of most use to developing nations?

Exemplary Reforms: A Selection

As in the United States, educators in other parts of the world are introducing reforms to make schools more effective. Some of these reforms are based on studies of unusually successful schools and how they function. Most research on these **effective schools** occurred in the United States, but important studies have also taken place in Australia, Canada, the Netherlands, the United Kingdom, and other countries. In this chapter, we are considering substantial reforms many nations have introduced in their educational systems.[24] Some countries have been respected for many decades for the quality

[23]Gary Stix and Paul Wallich, "A Digital Fix for the Third World?" *Scientific American* (October 1993), p. 89; "Drain or Gain?" *Economist* (May 28, 2011); and Stephen P. Heyneman, "Private Tutoring and Social Cohesion," *Peabody Journal of Education* (Issue 2, 2011), pp. 183–188.
[24]David Reynolds, "World Class Schools," *Educational Research & Evaluation* (December 2006), pp. 535–560; Chris James et al., "High Attainment Schools in Disadvantaged Settings," *International Studies in Educational Administration* (No. 2, 2008), pp. 66–79; "Reading by Six," 2010 report posted by the United Kingdom Office of Standards for Education, available at **www.ofsted.gov.uk/publications/100197**; and "Against the Odds," 2011 report prepared for PISA, abstract available at **www.pisa.oecd.org**.

and effectiveness with which they provide early childhood opportunities, mathematics instruction, vocational schooling, or other important educational experiences. In the next chapter, we'll explore in detail characteristics of effective schools, as well as research indicating that systematic change and long-term commitment are the keys to successful schools.

Early Childhood Education in France

Varying child-care arrangements

Recognizing the critical importance of the preschool years in a child's social, physical, and educational development, many countries have taken steps to provide stimulating learning opportunities and positive day-care arrangements for most or all young children. For example, more than 90 percent of three- to five-year-olds in Belgium, Hong Kong, and Italy are enrolled in early childhood education programs, compared with little more than half in the United States. Outstanding child-care arrangements for infants are easily accessible to families throughout Scandinavia. The mix of preschool and day-care programs varies considerably from one country to another, as does the extent to which early childhood educators work with parents and families. Overall, however, early childhood education has become a topic of urgent interest throughout much of the world.

French preschool programs

France has what many observers consider a model approach to preschool services. Nearly all three- to five-year-olds are enrolled in preschool programs, and average salaries of preschool teachers are considerably higher than in the United States or most other countries. Participating children pursue stimulating activities before and after school, during vacation, and at other times when school is out. Equally important, parents have financial incentives to enroll their children in high-quality programs that provide pediatric and other preventive health services. Child-care specialists and civic leaders who examined the French system have reported the following aspects of French programs as worth considering in the United States:[25] ·

Positive features of French programs

- Virtually all children have access to a coordinated system linking early education, day care, and health services.

- Paid parental leave from jobs after childbirth or adoption helps to nurture positive parent–child relationships.

- Good salaries and training for early childhood teachers help to keep turnover low and program quality high.

- Nearly all young children are enrolled in preschool programs.

- The government provides additional resources to ensure high quality at locations enrolling low-income children.

Mathematics and Science Education in Japan

High performance

International achievement studies indicate that Japanese students consistently attain high scores in mathematics, science, and other subject areas. For example, the second International Study of Achievement in Mathematics reported that eighth graders in Japan on average answered 62 percent of the test items correctly, compared with 45 percent in the United States and 47 percent across the eighteen countries included in the study. With respect to science achievement among eighth graders, Japanese students attained an average score of 554, compared with an average of 500 for other nations included in the fourth assessment. However, recent scores for high-school

---

[25]Conn-Powers et al., "The Universal Design of Early Education," *Young Children* (September 2006); and Moncrieff Cochran, "International Perspectives on Early Childhood Education," *Educational Policy* (Issue 1, 2011), pp. 65–91.

TECHNOLOGY @ SCHOOL

An Internet Site Dealing with Achievement and What Influences It Around the World

The Organisation for Economic Co-operation and Development has been publishing numerous documents providing information and analysis based on data regarding student performance in reading, mathematics, and other subjects collected in more than seventy nations as part of the Program for International Student Assessment (PISA). Most of these publications can be downloaded for free at **www.pisa .oecd.org**. (Click on "See More News and Events" at the bottom of the web page.) For example, 2011 reports included the following: "High-Performing Students from Disadvantaged Backgrounds," "Improving Performance: Leading from the Bottom," and "Quality Time for Students: Learning in and out of School." You probably will find that several of the reports are of particular interest to you.

The publication titled "Improving Performance: Leading from the Bottom" has information about thirteen countries

that registered reading gains among fifteen-year-olds between 2000 and 2009. Analysis by PISA staff concluded that success in these countries was due at least in part to the establishment of clear, ambitious policy goals, monitoring of student performance, granting more autonomy to schools, offering the same curriculum to all fifteen-year-olds, and support for low-performing schools and students. Some questions relevant to educators who read this report include the following:

1. To what extent are policies and actions identified in this report transferable to other countries?

2. Where policies and actions are transferable, how might they need to be modified?

3. What kinds of additional support for low-performing students and schools are feasible and desirable?

students have dropped somewhat, leading officials to increase hours in the school week for elementary and junior-high students.[26]

Possible reasons for Japanese success

Certain aspects of Japanese education and society may help account for high achievement levels among Japanese youth. Most of the following characteristics apply to Japanese education in general, not merely to math and science programs. The list of pertinent factors is long, and researchers remain unsure which are important. Perhaps they all are.[27]

■ Outstanding day care helps prepare children for school success. In addition, socialization practices in the family and in early childhood education help students learn to adapt to classroom situations and demands. U.S. schools, in contrast, tend to attain good discipline by making instruction attractive and by bargaining with students to obtain compliance (see Chapter 10, Culture, Socialization, and Education), at great cost to academic standards and rigor.

Parental involvement

■ Intense parental involvement is expected. In particular, mothers feel great responsibility for children's success in school. Families provide much continuing support and motivation, ranging from elaborate celebration of entry into first grade to widespread enrollment of children in supplementary private cram schools (*juku*), which students attend after school and on weekends. Compared with U.S. parents, Japanese parents emphasize effort over ability when asked to identify causes of success or failure in school.

Long school year

■ Students attend school 240 days a year (compared with less than 200 in the United States).

---

[26]Barbara J. Reyes and Robert E. Reyes, "Japanese Mathematics Education," *Teaching Children Mathematics* (April 1995), pp. 474–475; *Before It's Too Late* (Washington, D.C.: America Counts, 2000); and Robert Fish, "Japan," 2011 posting by the Asia Society, available from **www .asiasociety.org**.
[27]Thomas P. Rohlen, "Differences That Make a Difference," *Educational Policy* (June 1995), pp. 129–151; Yalda T. Uhls, "How Is Japan Different Than the U.S.," 2011 posting by Parenting in the Digital Age, available at **www.parentinginthedigitalage.com**; and Harold W. Stevenson and Roberta Nerison-Low, "To Sum It Up," undated paper prepared for the U.S. Department of Education, available at **www.ed.gov/pubs/SumItUp**.

Japanese students consistently attain high scores in mathematics, science, and other subject areas.

AN-PETER KASPER/EPA/Newscom

■ Students are given much responsibility for schoolwork and learning, beginning at an early age.

■ Large amounts of homework correlated with classroom lessons contribute to high student performance.

National curriculum

■ Careful planning and delivery of a national curriculum help students acquire important concepts within a sequential and comprehensive framework.

■ Compared with elementary-school practices in the United States and in many other countries, lessons de-emphasize rote learning.

■ The schools emphasize the development of students' character and sense of responsibility through such practices as assigning students chores and having them help each other in learning.

■ Educators tend to take responsibility for students' learning. For example, many teachers contact parents to recommend homework schedules and curfews.

Status of teachers

■ Prospective teachers must pass rigorous examinations and are intensely supervised when they enter the profession.

■ Japanese educators have relatively high social status, which enhances their authority in working with students and parents. Partly for this reason, there are numerous applicants for teaching positions, thus allowing administrators to select highly qualified candidates.

■ School schedules provide considerable time for counseling students, planning instruction, and engaging in other activities that make teachers more effective.

■ Generous time and support available to slower students helps produce less variability in achievement than in the United States and most other countries. Japanese schools have relatively few extremely low achievers.

Criticisms of Japanese system

Those familiar with the Japanese educational system also point out some apparently negative characteristics:[28]

---

[28]Ken Schoolland, *Shogun's Ghost* (New York: Bergin and Garvey, 1990); Maso Miyamoto, *Straitjacket Society* (Tokyo: Kodansha, 1994); John Nathan, *Japan Unbound* (Boston: Houghton Mifflin, 2004); Sachiko Kitano, "Current Issues in Assessment in Early Childhood Care and Education in Japan," *Early Child Development and Care* (February 2011), pp. 81–87; and Yoshishige Sugiyama, "On Students' Mathematics Achievement in Japan," undated posting by the National Council of Teachers of Mathematics, available at **www.nctm.org**.

■ Emphasis appears relatively slight on divergent thinking. Some observers believe that insufficient emphasis on creativity may severely hamper future social and economic development in Japan.

Class and gender limitations

■ Opportunities for working-class students and women to attend postsecondary institutions and gain high occupational status appear severely limited. For example, one study found that only 11 percent of students in college-prep high schools had fathers who had not completed high school, compared with 32 percent of students in less academic high schools.

✓ Standards & Assessment

■ Partly because of restricted higher-education opportunities, secondary education is exam driven—instruction covers immense quantities of factual information likely to be tested on entrance examinations. In turn, examination pressures further stifle divergent thinking and frequently lead to mental distress and even suicide.

■ Students face relatively few demands after they are admitted to colleges and universities.

Behavioral conformity

■ In accordance with the old Japanese proverb "The nail that sticks out gets hammered down," behavioral standards and expectations in many Japanese schools are so narrow and rigid that some educators believe they generate too much conformity.

■ More than ever before, young people in Japan seem to be rejecting the traditional customs and values on which the educational system is founded.

■ Many students with disabilities receive little help.

■ Bullying appears to be a widespread and growing problem in the schools.

■ Japanese schools have done relatively little to introduce computers and other aspects of modern technology.

Neither ignore nor imitate

In reviewing its various strengths and weaknesses, several thoughtful observers have concluded that we have much to learn from the Japanese educational system, but they add that we should make sure that promising practices from elsewhere are workable and appropriately adapted to our own situation. Likewise, government commissions in Japan have been considering reform proposals that incorporate the more positive aspects of education in the United States (for example, to reduce the emphasis on conformity). A professor of Japanese studies at Harvard University has summarized the situation in this way: "As a mirror showing us our weakness and as a yardstick against which to measure our efforts," Japanese education has great value for us. We should not, however, "allow ourselves either to ignore or to imitate" its approach. Instead, we should "look periodically into the 'Japanese mirror' while we quite independently set out to straighten our schools and our system within our own cultural and social context."[29]

Continuity & Change

Education for Sustainable Development in Wales

Incorporated into national curriculum

Numerous nations are ramping up their educational systems to incorporate learning about energy conservation, environmental education, and other aspects of sustainable development, often in connection with projects of the United Nations, the European

---

[29]Thomas P. Rohlen, "Japanese Education: If They Can Do It, Should We?" *American Scholar* (Winter 1985–1986), p. 43. See also Jackyung Lee, "School Reform Initiatives," *Education Policy Analysis Archives* (April 24, 2001), available at **http://epaa.asu.edu/ojs**; William Jeynes, "What We Should and Should Not Learn from the Japanese and Other East Asian Education Systems," *Educational Policy* (November 2008), pp. 900–927; Heidi Knipprath, "What PISA Tells Us about the Quality and Inequality of Japanese Education in Mathematics and Science," *International Journal of Science and Mathematics Education* (June 2010), pp. 389–408; Yalda T. Uhls, "Japan Education," 2011 posting at Parenting in the Digital Age, available at **www.parentinginthedigitalage.com**; and Yong Zhao, "The Grass is Greener," 2011 posting by Yong Zhao, available at **www.zhaolearning.com**.

Union, and other international organizations and efforts. One of the nations leading the way is Wales—a member of the United Kingdom. The website (**www.esd-wales .org.uk**) that Wales devotes to sustainable development includes sections set aside for elementary and secondary schools, higher education, further education and work-based learning, youth work, and adult and continuing education. The site notes that Wales is one of the "few nations with sustainable development at the heart of government." For elementary and secondary schools, it provides much information on how education about sustainable development can be incorporated in the national curriculum, as well as how teachers can participate in carrying out systematic plans for doing so.

Multicultural Education in Europe and North America

Probably no country has responded adequately to the challenges posed by multicultural populations. However, many nations have made important efforts to deliver educational services suitable for diverse groups of students, particularly minority students who experience racial, ethnic, or religious discrimination or who do not learn the national language at home. Approaches like the following may become future models:[30]

Model multicultural programs

- As we discussed at length in Chapter 12, Providing Equal Educational Opportunity, the United States is trying to provide bilingual education for millions of English Language Learner (ELL) students.

- Canada has implemented sizable bilingual education programs, as well as numerous approaches for promoting multiethnic curriculum and instruction.

▶❚❚ TEACHSOURCE VIDEO ACTIVITY

Bilingual Education: An Elementary Two-Way Immersion Program

After reading this section, go to the Education CourseMate website to access the video entitled, "Bilingual Education: An Elementary Two-Way Immersion Program." In this clip, you'll see how two teachers approach the two-way bilingual program where all students learn to read, write, and communicate both in English and in Spanish for all subject areas. After watching the video, consider the following questions:

❶ In your own words, explain the two-way immersion model depicted in this video, and the pros and cons of this approach.

❷ After reading about the various models of bilingual education and watching this video, where do you stand on this issue? Do you believe that recent immigrants should be immersed in English language instruction or taught for a long period of time in their native language? Use the textbook content to support your argument.

** This video reinforces key concepts found in Section III: Communication Techniques of the Praxis II Exam.**

---

[30]Bruce Carrington and Alastair Bonnett, "The Other Canadian 'Mosaic,'" *Comparative Education* (November 1997), pp. 411–432; Elisabeth Regnault, "Good Practices in Intercultural Education in Europe," *Education and Society* (Issue 1, 2006), pp. 45–56; and Jamie Kowalczyk, "The Immigration Problem and European Education Reforms," *European Education* (Winter 2010–2011), pp. 5–24.

REFOCUS What are the potential benefits of using other nations' educational reforms as models for improving our own schools? What are the drawbacks? What cautions should educators observe in adopting school reforms from other countries?

■ France has provided in-service training nationwide to help teachers learn to teach French as a second language.

■ Belgium provides *reception classes,* in which immigrant children receive up to two years of instruction from both a Belgian teacher and a native-language teacher.

Conclusion: The International Context and the Challenges Facing U.S. Schools

Growing similarities among nations

Continuity & Change

Much to learn, much to offer

Some observers believe that international study of education is becoming increasingly useful because developed societies are growing more alike. Throughout the world, more citizens are becoming middle class, and school systems and other institutions are emphasizing preparation for dealing with advanced technology and rapid social change. Mass media and other technologies exert a common influence across national borders. Even so, no two societies ever will be exactly alike, nor will cultural and social differences disappear entirely. Still, characteristics of social institutions (including the family and the school) will likely converge. For example, Kenichi Ohmae has remarked that Japan's "Nintendo Kids"—youngsters who have grown up with computers, video games, and global media—"have more in common with similar youngsters outside Japan than with other generations within Japan."[31]

If that is true, we have much to learn from studying effective education in other nations. Likewise, other nations can learn from the United States. Despite its many shortcomings described in this book, the United States was long an international leader in striving to educate all students regardless of their social background or previous achievement. Richard Kahlenberg and Bernard Wasow examined educational systems and achievement patterns internationally and reached the following conclusions with respect to implications for the United States: " . . . American public schools have helped make Americans out of wave after wave of immigrants. . . . That said, the public-school system fails a substantial segment of the population, and this failure aligns sharply with class and race." As we noted in this chapter, the achievement of our students is mediocre, and we have fallen behind some other developed nations in college attendance and completion. Recognizing these shortcomings, U.S. Secretary of Education Arne Duncan said soon after taking office that "we used to lead the world, and we have sort of lost our way in the last couple of decades." In pointing to the importance of education components in the American Recovery and Reinvestment Act of 2009, designed partly to promote academic progress in general and students' higher-order skills in particular, he went on to say that we "just have to educate our way to a better economy." Aspects of reform that might help to educate our way to more prosperity and equality will be considered in the next chapter.[32]

REFOCUS Do you believe that increasing similarities between developed nations will eventually lead to increasingly similar educational systems?

[31]Kenichi Ohmae, "China's 600,000 Avon Ladies," *New Perspectives Quarterly* (Winter 1995), p. 15. See also Iris C. Rotberg, "U.S. Education in a Global Context," *Education Week* (February 9, 2005); Cindy Long, "Can We Compete?" *NEA Today* (January 2007), available at **www.nea.org/neatoday**; Craig C. Wiekzorek, "Comparative Analysis of Educational Systems of American and Japanese Schools," *Educational Horizons* (Winter 2008), pp. 99–111; Arne Duncan, "Lessons from High-Performing Countries," 2011 posting by the U.S. Department of Education, available at **www.ed.gov**; and *Lessons from PISA for the United States* (Paris: Organisation for Economic Co-Operation and Development, 2011).
[32]Richard D. Kahlenberg and Bernard Wasow, "What Makes Schools Work?" *Boston Review* (October–November 2003); Yong Zhao, "The Best and Worst of the East and West," *Phi Delta Kappan* (November 2005), pp. 219–222; Stephen Lassonde, "America's Public Schools," *Journal of Social History* (Winter 2008), pp. 522–525; and Robert Manwaring, "School Turnaround Success," *Principal* (March–April 2011), pp. 10–13.

Summing Up

1 Although educational systems differ considerably between nations, they tend to confront the similar problem of providing effective instruction for large numbers of students whose opportunities and performance relate to their social and cultural background.

2 School systems around the world differ greatly in the resources they devote to education, enrollments, student–teacher ratios, male–female student ratios, the extent of centralization or decentralization, curriculum content and instructional emphasis, approaches to teacher preparation, higher education and vocational education opportunities, nonpublic school availability and roles, and student achievement. Among the distinctive practices and arrangements found in various nations are the emphasis on "natural language" learning in New Zealand and the system developed to support high achievement in Finland. Systematic arrangements for attaining high achievement in Finland include a national core curriculum that emphasizes thinking and students' active role in learning, school-level requirements for high levels of student performance, some flexible grouping rather than rigid streaming or tracking, a highly qualified teaching force, nearly universal public preschool, significant time in the school day set aside for teacher planning and assessment of students, provision and updating of science equipment and materials and of computer hardware and software, and various interventions to help struggling students in elementary and secondary schools. Efforts to provide an effective teaching force include emphasis on preparing highly qualified new teachers.

3 Scholars studying education in developing countries advocate an emphasis on improving teacher preparation and primary education, developing student cognitive functioning, and expanding education for girls and women.

4 Educational services or practices appear exemplary in several countries: early childhood education in France, education for sustainable development in Wales, and mathematics and science education in Japan. Canada and the United States seem to be succeeding in some aspects of multicultural education. Researchers can learn much from studying educational systems in other countries, but it is not always easy to identify the reasons for a system's success or failure or its implications for different societies.

5 The United States has been an international leader in the effort to provide equal and effective educational opportunities for all groups of students, but it has been slipping in this regard in comparison with other nations.

Key Terms

The numbers indicate the pages where explanations of the key terms can be found.

bipartite system 463
International Association for the Evaluation of Educational Achievement (IEA) 465
Program for International Student Assessment (PISA) 465
Progress in International Reading Literacy Study (PIRLS) 465
Third International Mathematics and Science Study (TIMSS) 465
brain drain 468
effective schools 468

Certification Connection Activity

This chapter discusses international education. Many countries have a national curriculum. In the United States, each local school district, using state guidelines and national education standards, develops the curriculum for each subject and grade level. As a result, the curriculum may be vastly different. In one state, you might teach multiplication in grade 2, while another state might wait until grade 3. One of the important tasks for a teacher is to understand the curriculum. In your journal, reflect on the curriculum for the grade level or subject that you plan to teach. Remember that it may change to reflect new information or changing standards.

Discussion Questions

1 What are the most important educational problems in developing countries? What policies might be most appropriate in addressing these problems?

2 To what extent should U.S. education policies and practices emulate those in Japan? Which practices might be most transportable, and which may be undesirable?

3 What are the advantages and disadvantages of offering higher-education opportunities for a large proportion of young people? What might or should be done to counteract the disadvantages?

Suggested Projects for Professional Development

1 Use Internet resources to find sources on early childhood education in other counties. (Try searching "early childhood education" plus " international.") What practices elsewhere might be useful here? What kinds of change would be needed to implement them?

2 Examine one or more international studies of educational achievement (such as the ones cited in this chapter) to determine how far the United States ranks from the top or bottom. Has the U.S. position been improving or declining?

3 Research two or three educational policies or approaches used widely in other countries but not in the United States. Do they seem applicable to the United States? If so, what problems might occur in implementing them? How would you prepare a plan to convince school officials to let you try such a policy or approach in your subject or teaching field?

4 What nations stand out with regard to high or low percentages of girls or women enrolled in schools at various levels of education? What seem to be some of the determinants of high or low percentages? What changes appear to be likely in the next few years?

Suggested Resources

Internet Resources

Numerous informative videos about Finnish schools can be found by searching for "Finland" plus "education."

An OECD posting titled "Great Expectations: Girls in Schools Today," available at **www.oecdinsights.org/2011/03/08**, provides links to international analysis and research involving girls and women and education.

PISA 2009 scores in reading, mathematics, and science for more than sixty nations are available at **www.oecd.org /dataoecd/54/12/46643496.pdf**.

Publications

Comparative Education Review. This journal emphasizes such topics as the development of national school systems, education and economic development, comparisons across nations, and international aspects of multicultural education.

International Journal of Educational Research. Recent theme issues have dealt with equal opportunity, giftedness, private education, science education, and other topics of worldwide concern.

Watkins, Kevin, et al. *Overcoming Inequality: EFA Global Monitoring Report 2009*. Paris: UNESCO, 2009. *Dealing with a diversity of subtopics involving inequality in and among nations and regions, this report is available at* **www.unesco.org**.

Additional resources for this chapter, including the TeachSource Videos, can be found on the Education CourseMate website. Go to **CengageBrain.com** to access the site.

School Effectiveness and Reform in the United States

Much of this book is concerned with problems and trends in the reform of elementary and secondary schools. The material in this chapter deals even more explicitly with key selected issues in school effectiveness and reform. After highlighting several major challenges that confront the U.S. educational system, we will examine arguments about and research into the characteristics of effective instruction and effective schools. We will also look at the process of school improvement and reform and other important topics often discussed under the headings of school effectiveness and reform.

Debates about school reform can be resolved partly by analyzing actual research evidence. This chapter cannot discuss or provide comprehensive information about every possible change but instead will examine some of the proposals that seem to hold particular promise or that have received widespread attention. As you read, consider which ideas have solid evidence to support them. Investigate some of the sources in the footnotes to determine whether they report or take account of research, not just provide arguments for or against a particular point of view. Think also about the prerequisites for success, the underlying conditions that may help make each suggested reform appropriate or inappropriate, and how they may affect your career as a teacher. Keep the following basic questions in mind:

FOCUS QUESTIONS

- What are the characteristics of effective teaching and instruction to improve higher-order learning?

- What does research say about unusually effective schools?
- What are some keys to implementing successful school reforms?
- How can we improve instruction across classrooms and at the school level?
- How can schools help special populations of students such as low-income students, rural students, or gifted and talented students?
- Will expansion of school-choice plans improve education?
- What are systemic reforms accomplishing in some states and school districts?

*This chapter was revised by Dan Levine.

Imperatives to Improve the Schools

Underprepared workers

Concern about American schools largely focuses on the need to bolster the nation's international economic competitiveness by teaching students work-related skills and on the related imperative to improve performance among disadvantaged students.

Several major national reports and studies have suggested that American students are leaving school unprepared to participate effectively in jobs that will, in an increasingly sophisticated and technology-based world economy, require them to carry out complicated tasks at a high level. Echoing these reports, President Barack Obama prefaced his proposals for education reform by stating, "The future belongs to the nation that best educates its citizens.... We have everything we need to be that nation ... and yet, despite resources that are unmatched anywhere in the world, we have let our grades slip, our schools crumble, our teacher quality fall short and other nations outpace us."[1]

Compelling need for equity

Nearly all of the recent reports and studies dealing with educational reform also call for improving the performance of economically disadvantaged students to make educational outcomes more equitable. In addition to the desire for fairness, educational equity has also been related to the need for economic competitiveness. Thus, the Forum of Educational Organizational Leaders concluded that "if we wish to maintain or improve our standard of living, we must work smarter ... [but] it is not possible to succeed if only middle-class people from stable families work smarter.... [This capacity] must—for the first time in human history—be characteristic of the mass of our population."

Specific areas of concern for educators working to reform educational opportunities for disadvantaged students include the following:

CCSSO recommendations

- *At-risk students and schools.* Social and economic opportunities have declined rapidly for low-achieving students and those without good postsecondary credentials. Perhaps the farthest reaching set of proposals for helping at-risk and disadvantaged students is in the policy statements of the Council of Chief State School Officers (CCSSO). CCSSO's statements argue that state laws should guarantee educational programs and other services "reasonably calculated to enable all persons to graduate from high school."

Coordinated reform needed to combat declining opportunities

- *Inner-city poverty.* As we pointed out in Chapter 11, Social Class, Race, and School Achievement, and elsewhere in this book, educational problems are particularly severe in inner-city minority neighborhoods of concentrated poverty. A total

---

[1]Paul E. Barton, "The Closing of the Education Frontier," 2002 report prepared for the Education Testing Service, available at **www.ets.org/research/pic**; "The Importance of Schools in Rural Communities," *ASCD Research Brief*, January 18, 2005; Daniel Gross, "The Education Factor," *Education Next* (Spring 2009), available at **www.educationnext.org**; and Emily Richmond, "For School Reform, Is New Investment Enough?" *Atlantic* (April 5, 2012), available at **www.theatlantic.com**.

response to the problems in these neighborhoods will involve improvement of employment, transportation, housing, affirmative action, and social welfare supports; desegregation and deconcentration of poverty populations; reducing crime and delinquency; and other efforts—in which elementary and secondary education must play a pivotal part.

Pockets of rural poverty

■ *Concentrated rural poverty.* Some rural areas have communities of concentrated poverty similar in many respects to those in big cities. Among these are the Appalachian region in the eastern United States and the Ozarks region in the South. Although many poor rural communities have mostly nonminority populations, indicators of social disorganization—high teenage-pregnancy rates, widespread juvenile delinquency, extremely low school achievement, and pervasive feelings of hopelessness—run as high or nearly as high as those in poor minority urban neighborhoods. For the U.S. economy as a whole to work smarter, these rural students, like their inner-city counterparts, need effective education.

REFOCUS What do you believe is the most urgent reason for educational reform?

Many observers believe that our response to these challenges will be of historic importance in determining whether the United States prospers or declines in the twenty-first century.

Characteristics of Effective Classrooms and Schools

The push for greater educational effectiveness became a national growth industry in 1983, and since then it has generated hundreds of research studies as well as thousands of discussion papers and improvement plans. Many studies have been designed to identify the characteristics of effective classroom teaching and **effective schools**.

Classroom Management

Effective classroom practices

Research on classroom management indicates that effective teachers use a variety of techniques to develop productive climates and to motivate students. Effective teachers emphasize practices such as the following: (1) making sure that students know

▶❙❙ TEACHSOURCE VIDEO ACTIVITY

Elementary Classroom Management: Basic Strategies

After reading this section on classroom management, go to the Education CourseMate website to access the video entitled "Elementary Classroom Management: Basic Strategies." The teacher in this video uses trial and error when it comes to classroom management and lets her students play an active role in the rule-making process. After watching the video, answer the following questions:

❶ Which of the twelve classroom-management strategies identified earlier does the teacher use in the video case? Explain which classroom management strategies you find most important.

❷ Explain the ways in which this classroom teacher uses effective questioning strategies with her students.

❸ Briefly explain the relationship between effective questioning strategies and effective classroom management.

** This video reinforces key concepts found in Section III: Communication Techniques of the Praxis II Exam.**

what the teacher expects; (2) letting students know how to obtain help; (3) following through with reminders between activities and rewards to enforce the rules; (4) providing a smooth transition between activities; (5) giving students assignments of sufficient variety to maintain interest; (6) monitoring the class for signs of confusion or inattention; (7) being careful to avoid embarrassing students in front of their classmates; (8) responding flexibly to unexpected developments; (9) designing tasks that draw on students' prior knowledge and experience; (10) helping students develop self-management skills; (11) attending to students' cultural backgrounds; and (12) ensuring that all students are part of a classroom learning community.

Time-on-Task

Time of active engagement

Effective teaching as portrayed in various studies brings about relatively high student **time-on-task**—that is, time engaged in learning activities. As you might expect, students actively engaged in relevant activities learn more than do students not so engaged. Time-on-task studies have pointed out that classrooms can be managed to increase the time students spend on actual learning activities. The school day and the school year can be extended to support academic learning. However, student learning involves more than time spent on academic work. Other variables, such as the suitability of the activities, the students' success or failure in the tasks attempted, and the motivating characteristics of methods and materials, are also important.[2]

Questioning

Skillful questioning and wait time

One way to stimulate student engagement in learning is to ask appropriate questions in a manner that ensures participation and facilitates mastery of academic content. Several studies have identified questioning skills as an important aspect of effective teaching. In particular, research indicates that longer "wait time" (the interval between the posing of a question and selecting or encouraging a student to answer it) significantly improves student participation and learning. Research also indicates that "higher-order" questioning that requires students to mentally manipulate ideas and information is more effective than "lower cognitive" questioning that focuses on verbatim recall of facts.[3]

Direct Instruction and Explicit Teaching

The terms **direct instruction** and **explicit teaching** (frequently used as synonyms) usually refer to teacher-directed instruction that proceeds in small steps. (Direct instruction also is sometimes referred to as "active teaching.") Research has shown a link between this method, properly implemented, and high levels of student achievement. Barak Rosenshine identified the following six teaching steps or functions as central to direct instruction:[4]

Six teaching steps

1. Begin with a review of previous learning and a preview and goal statement.
2. Present new material in steps, with clear explanations and active student practice after each step.

---

[2]Elena Silva, "On the Clock," 2007 paper prepared for Education Sector, available at **www.educationsector.org**; and OECD, *Equity and Quality in Education* (Paris: OECD, 2012).
[3]David Perkins, "Making Thinking Visible," *New Horizons for Learning* (Winter 2004), available at **www.education.jhu.edu/newhorizons**; Abner Oakes and Jon R. Star, "Getting to 'Got It,'" *Center for Comprehensive School Reform and Improvement Newsletter* (March 2008), available at **www.centerforcsri.org**; and Julie Corio, "Talking about Reading as Thinking," *Theory Into Practice* (Issue 2, 2011), pp. 107–115.
[4]Barak Rosenshine, "Explicit Teaching and Teacher Training," *Journal of Teacher Education* (May–June 1987), pp. 34–36. See also John Hollingsworth and Silvia Ybarra, *Explicit Direct Instruction (EDI)* (Thousand Oaks, CA: Corwin, 2008); and Kathy King-Dickman, "Learning to Love Reading in 30 minutes a Day," *Educational Leadership* (June 2011), available at **www.ascd.org**.

Ellen Senisi/The Image Works

Questioning skills—such as ensuring long "wait times" and asking "higher-order" questions—are an important aspect of effective teaching.

3. Guide students in initial practice; ask questions and check for understanding.

4. Provide systematic feedback and corrections.

5. Supervise independent practice; monitor and assist seatwork.

6. Provide weekly and monthly review and testing.

Explicit Comprehension Instruction

 Critique of explicit teaching

Direct instruction has often been criticized for its tendency to neglect important higher-order learning (reasoning, critical thinking, comprehension of concepts) in favor of small-step learning of factual material. In many schools where teachers have been told to follow a prescribed sequence of this kind, the practice emphasizes low-level learning and mindless regurgitation of facts and leaves little room for creativity and analytical thinking.[5]

Higher-order focus

However, direct instruction need not concentrate on low-level learning. Educators have been refining classroom techniques for explicitly teaching comprehension in all subject areas. David Pearson and his colleagues refer to many such approaches as **explicit comprehension instruction**. Barak Rosenshine has characterized the development of this approach since 1970 as an enormous accomplishment in which educators should take great pride.[6]

Continuity & Change

Like explicit teaching, explicit comprehension instruction emphasizes review and preview, feedback and correctives, and guided as well as independent practice, but experts suggest that teachers also systematically model conceptual learning, help

[5]Linda M. McNeil, *Contradictions of School Reform* (New York: Routledge, 2000); Sandra Mathison and Melissa Freeman, "Constraining Elementary Teachers' Work," *Education Policy Analysis Archives*, September 24, 2003, available at **http://epaa.asu.edu/epaa**; Mike Schmoker, "Measuring What Matters," *Educational Leadership* (December 2008/January 2009); and Kyle Huwa, "The Debate within the Classroom," *Stanford Review*, January 18, 2011, available at **www.stanfordreview.org**.
[6]P. David Pearson and Janice A. Dole, "Explicit Comprehension Instruction," *Elementary School Journal* (November 1987), pp. 151–165; Barak Rosenshine, "The Case for Explicit, Teacher-Led, Cognitive Strategy Instruction," 1997 paper available at **www.formapex.com/barak -rosenshine**; Barak Rosenshine, "Principles of Instruction," 2010 booklet prepared for the International Academy of Education, available at **www.formapex.com/barak-rosenshine**; and Shepard Barbash, *Clear Teaching*, 2011 electronic book published by the Education Consumers Foundation, available free at **www.education-consumers.org**.

students link new knowledge to their prior learning, monitor students' comprehension, and train students in summarizing, drawing inferences, and other learning strategies. Techniques and strategies associated with explicit comprehension instruction include the following:[7]

Techniques for explicit comprehension instruction

- Prediction activities in which students infer what will be found in the text based on their prior knowledge
- Reciprocal teaching, student team learning, and other approaches to cooperative learning, through which students learn to take more responsibility for helping each other comprehend material
- Semantic maps and thinking maps that organize information
- Computer simulations designed to develop concepts and thinking skills
- Metacognitive learning strategies through which students monitor and assess their own learning processes

Cognitive Instruction for Low-Achieving Students

Emphasis on passive learning of low-level skills seems particularly pervasive in schools with concentrations of working-class students and low achievers. A change in this pattern will require new approaches for delivering cognitive instruction, as well as fundamental improvements in programming throughout the educational system.[8]

Specific programs aimed at improving the thinking skills of low achievers include the Higher Order Thinking Skills Program (discussed later in this chapter), the Thinking Foundation's programs to help teachers use Thinking Maps, and the Staircase Curriculum developed by Kathryn Au and Taffy Raphael. Research suggests that such approaches have indeed improved performance. However, specific obstacles must be addressed, including the preference many students have developed for low-level learning, teachers' low expectations for low achievers, and the high financial cost of effective instruction that emphasizes cognitive development.[9]

REFOCUS Which of the characteristics of effective teaching are you most confident about demonstrating? Which will you need to work hard to develop?

In summary, research on effective teaching and instruction suggests that successful reform projects should include several changes, including improving teachers' classroom management and questioning skills, increasing time-on-task, expanding the use of direct instruction and explicit comprehension instruction, and introducing cognitive instruction for low-achieving students.

---

[7]Barak Rosenshine and Carla Meister, "Reciprocal Teaching," *Review of Educational Research* (Winter 1994), pp. 479–530; "Interview with Educational Psychologist/Researcher Barak Rosenshine," *Class Notes* (December 2005/January 2006), available at **www.baltimorecp.org**: click on "Newsletter"; Bracken Reed, "Lessons for a Lifetime," *Northwest Education* (Fall 2006), available at **www.educationnorthwest.org/edunw-magazine**; and Bob Kizlik, "Information about Strategic Teaching, Strategic Learning, and Thinking Skills," 2011 posting at the Adprima Internet site, available at **www.adprima.com/strategi.htm.**
[8]Daniel U. Levine, "Teaching Thinking to At-Risk Students," in Barbara Z. Presseisen, ed., *At-Risk Students and Thinking* (Washington, D.C.: National Education Association and Research for Better Schools, 1988); Eric J. Cooper and Daniel U. Levine, "Teaching for Intelligence," in Barbara Presseisen, ed., *Teaching for Intelligence*, 2nd ed. (Thousand Oaks, CA: Corwin, 2007); Ellen O. Keene, "New Horizons in Reading Comprehension," *Educational Leadership* (March 2010), available at **www.ascd.org**; and Bruce Torff, "Teacher Beliefs Shape Learning for All Students," *Phi Delta Kappan* (November 2011), pp. 21–23.
[9]Stanley Pogrow, "Challenging At-Risk Students," *Phi Delta Kappan* (January 1990), pp. 389–397; Stanley Pogrow, "Accelerate the Learning of 4th and 5th Graders Born into Poverty," *Phi Delta Kappan* (February 2009), pp. 408–412; Kathryn Au and Taffy Raphael, "The Staircase Curriculum," 2011 posting by School Rise, available at **www.schoolriseusa.com**, click on "Research," and "Case Studies," undated posting describing schools successfully implementing the Thinking Maps approach to improve cognitive functioning, available at **www.thinkingfoundation.org.**

Effective Schools Research

The preceding sections addressed effective teaching and instruction at the classroom level. However, reformers must also pay attention to the school as an institution and, in the final analysis, to the larger context of the school district and the environment in which schools operate. How effective schools and whole districts are helps determine what happens in each classroom.

Elementary Schools

Most of the research on effective schools focuses on elementary education. Researchers usually define effectiveness at least partly in terms of outstanding student achievement. For example, Ronald Edmonds and others described an effective school as having characteristics such as the following:[10]

1. A *safe and orderly environment* conducive to teaching and learning and not oppressive

2. A *clear school mission* through which the staff shares a commitment to instructional priorities, assessment procedures, and accountability

3. *Instructional leadership* by a principal who understands the characteristics of instructional effectiveness

4. A climate of *high expectations* in which the staff demonstrates that all students can master challenging skills

5. High *time-on-task* brought about when students spend a large percentage of time engaged in planned activities to master basic skills

6. Frequent *monitoring of student progress,* using the results to improve both individual performance and the instructional program

7. Positive *home–school relations* in which parents support the school's basic mission and play an important part in helping to achieve it

Another characteristic that contributes to school effectiveness is **curriculum alignment**—the coordination of instructional planning, methods, materials, and testing. When staff development focuses on such coordination, teachers are less likely to rely solely on textbooks and more likely to select or create materials that are most appropriate for teaching a specific skill to a particular group of students.[11]

According to several research reports, other key features of unusually effective schools are (1) attention to goals involving cultural pluralism and multicultural education; (2) emphasis on responding to students' personal problems and developing their social skills; (3) faculty who strive to improve students' sense of efficacy; (4) continuous concern for making teaching tasks realistic and manageable; (5) targeting interventions on low-performing students; and (6) collaborative problem-solving by the entire faculty. Researchers at the Northwest Regional Educational Laboratory have identified

[10]Joan Shoemaker, "Effective Schools," *Pre-Post Press* (1982), p. 241. See also Ronald Edmonds, "Effective Schools for the Urban Poor," *Educational Leadership* (October 1979), pp. 15–24; Daniel U. Levine, *Unusually Effective Schools* (Bloomington, IN: Phi Delta Kappa, 2004), Karin Chenoweth, "*It's Being Done*" (Cambridge, MA: Harvard Education Press, 2007); J. E. Stone, Guy S. Bruce, and Dan Hursh, "Effective Schools, Common Practices," 2007 paper prepared for the Education Consumers Foundation, available at **www.mosteffectiveschools.org**: click on "About Effective Schooling"; Matthew Lynch, "Examining the Attributes of Effective Schools," *Education News*, July 27, 2011, available at **www.ednews.org**; and William H. Parrett and Kathleen M. Budge, *Turning High-Poverty Schools into High-Performing Schools* (Washington, D.C.: ASCD, 2012).
[11]Daniel U. Levine and Joyce Stark, "Instructional and Organizational Arrangements That Improve Achievement in Inner-City Schools," *Educational Leadership* (December 1982), pp. 41–48. See also Robert A. Martin, "Wake-Up Call," *Journal of Staff Development* (Winter 2006), pp. 53–55; Mike Schmoker, "What Money Can't Buy," *Phi Delta Kappan* (March 2009), pp.524–527; and Douglas B. Reeves, "School Improvement," *American School Board Journal* (May 2011); pp. 38–39.

more than one hundred specific practices, grouped in eighteen categories, that contribute to school effectiveness.[12]

High Schools

Relatively few studies have concentrated solely on the characteristics of unusually effective senior high schools. Because high-school goals and programs are so diverse and complex, it is difficult to conclude that one is more effective than another, particularly when the social class of the student body is taken into account. In addition, hardly any high schools enrolling mostly working-class students stand out as being relatively high in achievement.[13]

Helping low achievers

However, in recent years, researchers have identified and described some high schools that appear unusually effective in educating a broad range of students. In general, these schools heavily emphasize helping low achievers in the entry grade (that is, ninth or tenth grade) and on providing additional support in later grades. They also strive to personalize instruction and avoid rigid grouping into permanent, separate tracks for low, medium, and high achievers. In addition, the following approaches have frequently been successful:[14]

1. *Schools-within-a-school for low achievers.* Students who read more than two or three years below grade level are assigned to a special unit of eighty to one hundred students at the entry grade. If their teachers are selected for ability and willingness to work with low achievers, participating students can make large gains in basic skills and transfer to regular courses.

2. *Career academies.* Functioning as schools-within-a-school that enroll students of various abilities across several grades, career academies focus on such fields as computers, biology or other science, humanities or the arts, or occupational studies such as law enforcement or journalism. Positive data have been reported regarding student engagement and achievement at career academies.

Standards & Assessment

3. *Smaller high-school units in general.* High schools that have low enrollment or have been divided into smaller units such as schools-within-a-school have more student engagement and higher achievement than traditional large high schools with similar students. Assigning students to these smaller schools or units can create a more personalized environment in which the staff provide individual help to students.

Evaluation of Effective Schools Research

Definitions differ

Keep the following points in mind as we evaluate research on effective schools. First, we should recognize the widespread confusion about definitions. There are nearly as

[12]Daniel U. Levine, "Update on Effective Schools," *Journal of Negro Education* (Fall 1990), pp. 577–584; Bracken Reed, "Leaps and Bounds," *Northwest Education* (Winter 2007), available at **www.educationnorthwest.org/edunw-magazine**; "New Approaches to Performance Management and Value-Added in Urban Schools," 2011 posting by the Wisconsin Center for Education Research, available at **www.wcer.wisc.edu**; Michael Siebersma, Sammy Wheeler-Clouse, and Deborah Backus, "School Improvement, Step by Step," *Educational Leadership* (December 2011/January 2012); and descriptions in "Success Stories" at **www.learningfirst.org**, click on "Resources."
[13]Daniel U. Levine and Eugene E. Eubanks, "Organizational Arrangements in Effective Secondary Schools," in John J. Lane and Herbert J. Walberg, eds., *Organizing for Learning* (Reston, VA: National Association of Secondary School Principals, 1988); Victor Kuo, "Transforming American High Schools," *Peabody Journal of Education* (July 2010), pp. 389–410; and Amy Buffenbarger, "Creating a Safe Learning Environment," 2011 posting by the Learning First Alliance, available at **www.learningfirst.org/creating-safe-learning-environment**.
[14]Susan Black, "The Pivotal Year," *American School Board Journal* (February 2004); Gene Bottoms, "10 Strategies for Improving High School Graduation Rates and Student Achievement" and "What Really Works?" 2006 reports prepared for the Southern Regional Education Board, both available at **www.sreb.org**; Janet Quint, *Meeting Five Critical Challenges of High School Reform* (Washington, D.C.: Manpower Demonstration Research Corporation, 2006), available at **www.mdrc.org**; Howard S. Bloom et al., "Transforming the High School Experience" (Washington, D.C.: Manpower Demonstration Research Corporation, 2010), available at **www.mdrc.org**; Carol Ascher and Cindy Maguire, "Beating the Odds," *Education Digest* (January 2011), pp. 13–20; and Joshua Emmet and Dean McGee, "A Farewell to Freshmen," *Clearing House* (March 2012), pp. 74–79.

many definitions of effective schools as there are people discussing them. Whereas some people have in mind a school with high academic achievement (taking account of social class), others are thinking about a self-renewing school that can identify and solve internal problems, a school that promotes students' personal growth, a school that has shown improvement in achievement, or a school that concentrates on developing independent study skills and love for learning.

Research focused on poverty schools

Second, many rigorous studies have focused on high-poverty elementary schools in which academic achievement is higher than at most other schools with similarly disadvantaged students. It is more difficult to identify unusually effective high schools and schools outside the inner city, where high achievement is more common. In addition, the key components of effectiveness outside the inner city may differ somewhat from those at poverty schools.[15]

Problems in research methods

Third, other methodological problems have left much of the research vulnerable to criticism. For example, schools identified as effective in a given subject (say, reading) during a given year may not be effective on other measures or in the next year. In addition, research controls for students' social class and family environment are frequently inadequate. For instance, magnet schools enrolling inner-city students may be judged as unusually effective; but if later research shows that those schools draw their students from highly motivated poverty families dissatisfied with neighborhood schools, the high achievement might be attributable more to the students' background than to school characteristics.[16]

REFOCUS What steps can you take during your teacher-preparation program to help you develop the skills of effective teachers described so far?

Begging the question

Fourth, the literature often tends to beg the question of what teachers and principals should do in the schools. For example, the isolated claim that a school requires good leadership and a productive climate fails to specify what these are or ways to accomplish them.

Characteristics of Successful School Reforms

From analysis of past school improvement efforts, we have some understanding of the steps that will ensure reform efforts of significant and lasting impact. The following list describes lessons learned from past efforts:

Solving day-to-day problems

1. *Adaptive problem solving.* An innovation frequently has little or no effect on students' performance because a host of problems arise to stifle practical application. For example, experts may devise a wonderful new science curriculum for fourth graders, and school districts may purchase large quantities of the new curriculum materials, but teachers may either choose not to use them or not know how to use them. Innovations usually fail unless the organization introducing them is adaptive in the sense that it can identify and solve day-to-day problems.[17]

Focus on individual schools

2. *School-level focus, with external support.* Because the innovating organization must solve day-to-day problems, it must focus at the individual school level, where many problems occur. Conversely, however, a school seeking to improve requires

---

[15]Daniel U. Levine and Robert S. Stephenson, "Are Effective or Meritorious Schools Meretricious?" *Urban Review* (No. 1, 1987), pp. 25–34; David Reynolds et al., "Challenging the Challenged," *School Effectiveness & School Improvement* (December 2006), pp. 425–439; Barry Newstead, Amy Saxton, and Susan J. Colby, "Going for the Gold," *Education Next* (Spring 2008), available at **www.educationnext.org**; and Diane Ravitch, "Waiting for a School Miracle," *New York Times*, May 31, 2011.
[16]David Garcia, "Academic and Racial Segregation in Charter Schools," *Education and Urban Society* (July 2008), pp. 590–612; and Kristina Rizga, "Reforming the Education Reformers," *Mother Jones* (July 2011), available at **www.motherjones.com**.
[17]Craig Jerald, "More Than Maintenance," *CSRI Policy Brief* (September 2005), available at **www.centerforcsri.org**; Martin Haberman, "Victory at Buffalo Creek," *Ed News*, January 22, 2007, available at **www.educationnews.org**; Emily A. Hassel and Bryan C. Hassel, "The Big U-Turn," *Education Next* (Winter 2009), available at **www.educationnext.org**; and David Walters, "One Vision, Many Eyes," *International Journal of Leadership in Education* (January–March 2012).

various kinds of guidance and support from central administrators and/or other external agents.[18]

Compatibility and accessibility

3. *Potential for implementation.* Successful school reform also depends on whether changes can feasibly be implemented in typical schools. Three characteristics that make successful implementation more likely are an innovation's *compatibility* with the context of potential users, its *accessibility* to those who do not already understand the underlying ideas, and its *"doability"* in terms of demands on teachers' time and energy. Levine and Levine have pointed out that many approaches have high "potential for mischief" because they are so difficult to implement.[19]

Sharing a vision

4. *Leadership and shared agreements.* Meaningful innovation requires change in many institutional arrangements, including scheduling of staff and student time, selection and use of instructional methods and materials, and mechanisms for making decisions. The building principal usually is the key person in making these arrangements, but the faculty also must have a shared vision of and must be involved in possible necessary changes. Otherwise, staff members will likely discount proposals that ask them to make significant changes.[20]

Staff development essential

5. *Staff training.* Staff development is a core activity in the school improvement process. In an elementary school, the entire staff should participate; in secondary schools, departments may be the appropriate unit for certain activities. Staff development should be an interactive process in which teachers and administrators work together at every stage. Much of the staff development at unusually effective schools is provided by instructional coaches.[21]

Standards & Assessment

6. *Coherence.* Coherence in school reform efforts has at least two major dimensions. The first refers to coherence across grade levels: teachers in each grade must be willing to help students master the curriculum and standards established for their grade, or students will lack the skills required for success in the next grade. *Coherence* also refers to consistency and compatibility across the instructional programs and approaches used in the school. For example, some students probably will struggle to master reading if their teachers use differing materials that introduce key skills at different times and thus conflict with rather than reinforce each other. Some students will not master social skills if their teachers establish greatly different rules of behavior from one class to another.[22]

---

[18]Daniel U. Levine, "Creating Effective Schools through Site-Level Staff Development, Planning and Improvement of Organizational Cultures," in David H. Hargreaves and David Hopkins, eds., *Development Planning for School Improvement* (London: Cassell, 1994), pp. 37–48; Michael Fullan, *The New Meaning of Educational Change,* 4th ed. (New York: Teachers College Press, 2007); David Kirp, "Audacity in Harlem," *American Prospect* (September 22, 2008), available at **www.prospect.org**; and Jim Parsons and Kelly Harding, "Research Reflections about When Schools Work Well," *e-journal of Organizational Learning and Leadership* (Spring 2011), available at **www.leadingtoday.org**.

[19]Craig Jerald, "The Implementation Trap," *CSRI Policy Brief* (August 2005), available at **www.centerforcsri.org**; Daniel U. Levine and Rayna F. Levine, "Considerations in Introducing Instructional Interventions," in Barbara Presseisen, ed., *Teaching for Intelligence,* 2nd ed. (Thousand Oaks, CA: Corwin, 2007); Jim Knight, "What Can We Do about Teacher Resistance?" *Phi Delta Kappan* (March 2009), pp. 508–513; and Gil-Rey Madrid, "Closing the Math Skills Gap and Boosting Achievement," *eSchool News* (August 29, 2011), available at **www.eschoolnews.com**.

[20]Barbara O. Taylor, "The Effective Schools Process," *Phi Delta Kappan* (January 2002), pp. 375–378; "When the Plan Becomes Part of the Problem," *CSRI Newsletter* (March 2006), available at **www.centerforcsri.org**; Mathew Lynch, "Examining the Attributes of Effective Schools," 2011 posting by Education News, available at **www.educationviews.org**; and Nick Myers and Ed Rafferty, "Moving Up From Mediocre," *School Administrator* (January 2012), available at **www.aasa.org**.

[21]Brian Sims, "Teacher Development Is Key to Closing the Achievement Gap," *Edutopia* (July 22, 2011), available at **www.edutopia.org**; John Rosales, "Oak Hill," 2011 report prepared for the NEA Priority Schools Campaign, available at **www.neapriorityschools.org**; and Corinne van Velzen, et al., "Guided Work-Based Learning," *Teaching & Teacher Education* (February 2012), pp. 229–239.

[22]BetsAnn Smith et al., "Instructional Program Coherence," *Educational Research Reports* (May 2003), available at **http://ed-web3.educ.msu.edu/epc/library/reports.asp**; William H. Schmidt, "What's Missing from Math Standards?" *American Educator* (Spring 2008), available at **www.aft.org**; and Lindsay Fryer and Amy Johnson, "A Coherent Approach to High School Improvement," 2011 report prepared for the National High School Center, available at **www.betterhighschools.org**.

FROM PRESERVICE TO PRACTICE

School Reform

Paul and Jorge are classmates in the college of education at their university and are studying at the library. Paul waves a letter from across the library table. "Jorge, you have to hear about this! My sister Melanie started teaching in this small rural school system last year. You ought to hear some of her stories about how the teachers come together to make things happen for those kids. They don't have much, compared to some of the suburban schools around here, but they do have fine student achievement. I'm thinking that when I graduate, I might want to go that route, too—if they have a teaching position open."

Jorge looks up from his notes. "How do you know that the student achievement is so good, Paul?"

"My sister sent me the results of the statewide exams," says Paul. "Not only is the district rated exemplary, but each of the three schools is rated exemplary, as well. That means that all schools showed 90 percent or more mastery in all the subjects tested. Larger schools have a hard time getting ratings like those. Melanie keeps saying smaller is better."

"You said that they don't have much. What do you mean by that?" Jorge asks.

"Basically, they don't have all the equipment that most schools have," Paul replies. "They don't have extra staff to help with daily routines. The superintendent drives a bus, and each principal drives a bus, too.

"The school libraries have limited books and magazines. The high school has only fifteen computers, all located in the library for instructional purposes. Administrators have computers on their desks, but teachers have to go to the library to use a computer. The other schools have even fewer computers, all in the libraries, too."

"Amazing!" says Jorge. "I don't know what I would do without my laptop! How do they account for the top ratings? Are they still working on the achievement levels?"

"I visited Melanie over the holidays, and actually ended up interviewing her and a friend who teaches with her," Paul answers. "They say the community is close-knit, that faculty members feel like family. It's like moving back in time because everyone knows everyone else. All the students understand that the teachers know their parents, and even grandparents. Melanie says the superintendent and the principals really care. They see each student as a responsible individual. They expect the teachers to pitch in and help each other, to help the students, and yes, to help administrators when they need it. On the other hand, the administrators stand by the teachers, too. It's a team process on each campus. Every teacher who needs training gets it. When they work, they all work hard. When they play, they have fun and enjoy each other's company.

"And, yes," Paul continued. "They are still working to increase achievement levels. Melanie writes that their vision is 100 percent mastery of the statewide tests. They're continually looking for ways to help students."

"Is there any downside to all this?" Jorge laughs.

"Well, the pay is pretty low," Paul admits. Then he brightens. "But there's not much to spend it on around there, either."

Case Questions

1. What characteristics of effective schools does this school district exemplify?
2. How does this district seem to support the process of school improvement and reform?
3. In addition to lower pay, what else might a new teacher consider deterrents to signing on as a team member in this small district?
4. Would you be willing to work in a school such as this? Why or why not?

7. *Professional community.* Schools can ensure that all students learn only if teachers work together, trust their colleagues, and challenge each other to take responsibility for the difficult task of helping low achievers master increasingly challenging material. Analysts refer to this aspect of reform as development of a "professional community."[23]

[23]Mike Schmoker, "A Chance for Change," *American School Board Journal* (April 2007); Donna Ford, "Powerful School Change," *Phi Delta Kappan* (December 2008), pp. 281–284; "New Approaches to Performance Management and Value-Added in Urban Schools," 2011 paper prepared for the Wisconsin Center for Education Research, available at **www.wceruw.org**; and Kimberly K. Hewitt and Daniel K. Weckstein, "Administrative Synergy," *School Administrator* (January 2012), available at **www.aasa.org**.

REFOCUS How might you, as a teacher, participate in implementing reforms at your school? What do you believe teachers can do to best help with successful reform implementations?

The From Preservice to Practice box describes a school improvement plan that features many hallmarks of effectiveness. As you read through it and the rest of this chapter, note which reform programs described seem to exemplify each of these best practices.

Improvement Approaches across Classrooms and Grade Levels

The effective teaching practices cited earlier in this chapter work in individual classrooms, but numerous instructional approaches are designed for use at several or all grade levels in a school. For example, many reading improvement programs often target students in kindergarten and the primary grades. We'll discuss several such improvement efforts in this section.

Higher–Order Thinking Skills (HOTS) Program

■ HOTS components

Developed by Stanley Pogrow and his colleagues, the HOTS program is specifically designed to replace remedial-reading activities in grades 4 through 6. The HOTS approach has four major components: (1) use of computers for problem solving; (2) emphasis on dramatization techniques that require students to verbalize, thereby stimulating language development; (3) Socratic questioning; and (4) a thinking-skills curriculum that stresses metacognitive learning, learning-to-learn, and other comprehension-enhancement techniques of the kinds described earlier. Now used in more than a thousand schools, HOTS frequently has brought about extensive improvements in student performance in both reading and math. According to Pogrow, results of the HOTS program show that at-risk students have "tremendous levels of intellectual and academic potential" but that many do not "understand 'understanding.'" This "fundamental learning problem can be eliminated if enough time and enough resources are made available."[24]

Success for All

■ Comprehensive changes

Possibly the most comprehensive intervention for improving the reading achievement of disadvantaged students, Success for All provides intensive instructional support for students in elementary schools. It also emphasizes cooperative learning and mastery instruction, with technical support and staff development provided by full-time coordinators and resource persons assigned to participating schools. Measurable improvements in student achievement have been documented at numerous low-income schools in both urban and rural districts. According to its developers, Success for All demonstrates that neither exceptional nor extraordinary schools can routinely ensure success for disadvantaged students. However, the program does require a serious commitment to restructure elementary schools and to reconfigure the use of available funds.[25]

---

[24]Stanley Pogrow, "Supermath," *Phi Delta Kappan* (December 2004), pp. 297–303; Stanley Pogrow, "The Missing Element in Reducing the Leaning Gap," 2010 posting by Inside the School, available at **www.insidetheschool.com**; and Bronwyn Cole and Margit McGuire, "Real-World Problems," *Social Studies and the Young Learner* (March–April 2012). Information about the HOTS Program is available at **www.hots.org**.

[25]Robert E. Slavin, "Shame Indeed," *Phi Delta Kappan* (April 2006), pp. 621–623; Betty Chambers, "Technology Infusion in Success for All," *Elementary School Journal* (September 2008), pp. 1–15; Barbara Beatty, "The Dilemma of Scripted Instruction," *Teachers College Record* (March 2011), pp. 395–420; Margarita Caldeon, Robert Slavin, and Marta Sanchez, "Effective Instruction for English Learners," *The Future of Children* (Spring 2011), available at **www.futureofchildren.org**.

Degrees of Reading Power Comprehension Development Approach

Standards & Assessment

Stressing real-life comprehension

Based in part on the Degrees of Reading Power (DRP) test originally developed by the College Board, the DRP approach is being implemented successfully at several urban schools. The test is unlike most other standardized reading measures in that it assesses how well a student actually can comprehend written prose he or she encounters in or out of school, not just whether the student is above or below an abstract grade level. After using the DRP to determine their students' comprehension levels, teachers in all subject areas align their instruction accordingly. For homework and other independent assignments, they select materials that challenge but do not frustrate students; they use classwork materials slightly beyond students' comprehension to help them improve.[26]

Comer School Development Program

Comer's approach

Developed by James Comer and his colleagues at Yale University, the School Development Program aims to improve achievement at inner-city elementary schools through enhanced social and psychological services for students, emphasis on parent involvement, and encouragement and support for active learning. Participating faculties involve parents in all aspects of school operation (including governance), and teachers, parents, psychologists, social workers, and other specialists form "Mental Health Teams" that design and supervise individualized learning arrangements for students with particular problems. Curriculum and instruction are coordinated across subject areas to emphasize language learning and social skills. Schools in various districts have produced improvements in student achievement and behavior after implementing the School Development Program along with other innovations.[27]

The Algebra Project

The Algebra Project involves curriculum interventions that use disadvantaged students' personal experiences and intuitions to help them shift from arithmetic to algebraic thinking. Data collected at multiple sites suggest that students frequently register large gains in mathematics performance and that many are succeeding in algebra and other advanced math courses they otherwise would not be taking.[28]

Knowledge Is Power Program (KIPP)

Emphasis on time for learning and rigorous instruction

KIPP promotional information describes its schools as "open-enrollment public schools where underserved students develop the knowledge, skills, and character traits needed to succeed in top quality high schools, colleges, and the competitive world beyond."

[26]Daniel U. Levine, "Instructional Approaches and Interventions That Can Improve the Academic Performance of African American Students," *Journal of Negro Education* (Winter 1994), pp. 46–63; Daniel U. Levine, Eric J. Cooper, and Asa Hilliard III, "National Urban Alliance for Professional Development," *Journal of Negro Education* (Fall 2000), pp. 305–322; Michael B. Doubek and Eric J. Cooper, "Closing the Gap through Professional Development," *Reading Research Quarterly* (July/August/September 2007); and information available at **www.questarai.com.**
[27]James P. Comer, "Educating Poor Minority Children," *Scientific American* (November 1988), pp. 42–48; James P. Comer, "Child and Adolescent Development," *Phi Delta Kappan* (June 2005), pp. 757–763; Thomas D. Cook and Paul J. Hirschfield, "Comer's School Development in Chicago," *American Educational Research Journal* (March 2008), pp. 38–67; and "When We Know What Works, Why Don't We Do It?" 2011 posting by the Yale Child Study Center, available at **www .childstudycenter.yale.edu**. See also information at **www.info.med.yale.edu/comer**.
[28]Helen M. Kress, "Math as a Civil Right," *American Secondary Education* (Fall 2005), pp. 48–56; Tom Loveless, "The Misplaced Math Student," Brown Center Report on American Education (February 2009), available at **www.brookings.edu**; Ed Dubinsky and Robert P. Moses, "Philosophy, Math Research, Math Ed Research, K–16 Education, and the Civil Rights Movement," 2011 posting by the American Mathematical Society, available at **www.ams.org**; and material at **www.algebra.org**.

▶❚❚ **TEACHSOURCE VIDEO ACTIVITY**

Rethinking How Kids Learn: KIPP Schools Use Effective Schools Correlates

After reading this section on KIPP, go to the Education CourseMate website to access the ABC video entitled "Rethinking How Kids Learn." After viewing the video, answer the following questions:

❶ Identify two or three possible shortcomings in KIPP operations that might have been explored in the video to provide a more balanced treatment.

❷ What are some of the effective schools correlates (described earlier in this chapter) that seem to be important in the functioning of KIPP schools?

Among the central operational themes is more time for learning: KIPP schools typically function from 7:30 a.m. to 5:30 p.m. on weekdays, and students also attend every other Saturday and for three weeks during the summer. KIPP further describes its approach as emphasizing rigorous "college-preparatory instruction...balanced with extracurricular activities, experiential field lessons, and character development."[29]

Careful expansion

Since its first school was opened in 1994, KIPP has expanded to include more than one hundred schools, mostly middle schools but also several high schools and elementary schools. Nearly all are charter schools in big cities. The creators of this model are carefully implementing plans to obtain dedicated staff willing to work long hours with struggling students, and to train and evaluate administrators and teachers, develop networks of supportive KIPP schools nearby, and articulate an effective program ranging from kindergarten through high-school graduation.

Gains for disadvantaged inner-city students

Results to date have been impressive. Most KIPP students graduating to high school are on track to graduate there, and its largely inner-city population of students generally is making good progress. For example, one study indicated that the average student in the fifth grade started near the thirty-fourth percentile in reading and the forty-fourth percentile in math. If completing the seventh grade, that student advanced to about the sixtieth percentile in reading and the eighty-fifth percentile in math. Nearly 90 percent of KIPP graduates eventually attend college. However, some analysts caution that such results might be hard to replicate with other inner-city populations because KIPP students volunteer to attend and because KIPP generally cannot provide much specialized service for students with disabilities or for English Language Learners (ELLs). In addition, dropping out among the weakest students appears to be significant, as is attrition of staff members, who might burn out after several years.

The Harlem Children's Zone (HCZ) and Purpose Built Communities (PBC)

Continuity & Change

As noted previously, KIPP appears to be registering important gains in poverty neighborhoods in big cities, but it does not reach the many students who do not enter or win in the lottery for admission or who leave before completing its difficult curriculum and

---

[29]Jay Matthews, *Work Hard. Be Nice* (Chapel Hill, NC: Algonquin, 2009); Christina C. Tuttle et al., Student Characteristics and Achievement in 22 KIPP Middle Schools," 2010 report prepared for Mathematica Policy Research, available at **www.mathematica-mpr.com**; Jay Mathews, "Does KIPP Shed Too Many Low Performers?" *Washington Post*, January 10, 2011; Ira Nichols-Barrer et al., "Student Selection, Attrition, and Replacement at KIPP Middle Schools," 2011 report prepared for Mathematica Policy Research, available at **www.mathematica-mpr.com**; and information available at **www.kipp.org**.

rigorous schedule. Several projects are trying more comprehensive ecological reforms of the kind advocated in Chapter 12, Providing Equal Educational Opportunity. One of the reform approaches that attempts to improve performance throughout an inner-city community is the Harlem Children's Zone initiated by Geoffrey Canada and his colleagues in New York City. The HCZ approach serves residents of ninety-seven blocks and exemplifies the kind of comprehensive ecological intervention we described in Chapter 12, Providing Equal Educational Opportunity. It includes the following components, among others:[30]

- Early childhood education for all children
- Various forms of family support and counseling
- Health services for children beginning in infancy
- Collaboration with churches, parks, local businesses, and schools to develop a safe, nurturing environment for children and youth
- A variety of services such as employment training and assistance for residents
- Systems for providing psychological support for students
- Establishment of two charter elementary schools, a charter middle school, and a charter high school, all with longer-than-regular school days and school years
- An after-school program for students in regular middle schools
- A fifth-grade institute to help prepare students for middle school
- Coordination of services between charter schools and regular schools
- Best practices for teaching disadvantaged students
- Hiring and supporting talented teachers

Analysts have been reporting impressive outcomes from the first few years of implementation. For example:

- More than 99 percent of four-year-olds who participated in the Harlem Gems preschool in 2009–2010 finished with a school-readiness classification of average or above.
- All students completing third grade at the charter schools in 2009–2010 were at or above grade level in math, and about 90 percent were at or above grade level in English language arts. At the charter middle school, 87 percent of eighth-graders were at or above grade level in math.
- For the 2010–2011, 90 percent of high-school seniors were accepted for entry into post-secondary institutions.

Although some analysts have questioned whether HCZ middle schools are bolstering students' performance to a greater extent than other New York charter schools, the Zone's officials and supporters point out that data on student and community outcomes indicate continuing improvement. In line with these supportive data, states and the federal government have been expanding support for efforts modeled on the Children's

---

[30]Paul Tough, *Whatever It Takes* (Boston: Houghton Mifflin Harcourt, 2008); Geoffrey Canada and Angela G. Blackwell, "The Harlem Children's Zone," 2009 report available at **www.scribd.com**; Paul Tough, "Harlem's Man with the Plan," *Mother Jones* (January–February 2009), available at **www.motherjones.com**; Grover J. Whitehurst and Michelle Croft, "The Harlem Children's Zone, Promise Neighborhoods, and the Bolder, Broader Approach to Education," 2010 report prepared for the Brookings Institution, available at **www.brookings.edu**; Helen Zelon, "Is the Promise Real?" *City Limits*, February 9, 2010, available at **www.citylimits.org**; Will Dobbie and Roland G. Fryer, Jr., "Are High-Quality Schools Enough to Close the Achievement Gap?" 2011 report published by Harvard, available at **www.economics.harvard.edu/faculty/fryer**; Carol Haughton, "Growing Hope, Transforming Lives," 2011 posting by Spotlight on Poverty and Opportunity, available at **www.spotlightonpoverty.org**; and information available at **www.hcz.org**; **www.promiseneighborhoodsinstitute.com**; and **http://purposebuiltcommunites.org**.

Zone. In particular, in 2012, ten school districts were receiving planning grants and six were receiving implementation grants from the federal Promise Neighborhoods Program, and legislators were considering large increases in funding in the future.

In some respects, the Purpose Built Communities (PBC) approach is even more comprehensive than the HCZ approach. In addition to activities of the kind carried out in the Zone, PBC projects involve support for mixed-income housing, coordination with local political allies, and other efforts that program officials describe as involving an educational pipeline "from cradle through college" and constituting "transformative urban revitalization" embracing commercial development, transportation improvements, and other city services. Originally developed and implemented in the East Lake neighborhood in Atlanta, the PBC approach is being considered for implementation in numerous communities throughout the nation.

Advancement via Individual Determination Program (AVID)

Helping middle- to low-performing students

AVID is a support program for grades 5–12 that prepares students for college eligibility and success. Aimed particularly at middle- to low-performing students at schools with significant proportions of disadvantaged students, AVID provides many kinds of support, including help in mastering study skills and learning strategies, personal and career counseling and mentoring, and assistance in enrolling in and completing advanced courses. First developed in San Diego in 1980, AVID is now functioning in more than 3,500 schools internationally and has compiled an impressive record in helping participating students graduate from high school and enter postsecondary institutions. In fact, most AVID students graduate from high school, 75 percent of 2006 AVID graduates were accepted by a four-year college, and more than 60 percent of recent AVID eighth graders enrolled in and passed algebra (compared with about 20 percent nationally).[31]

Response to Intervention with Tiered Instruction

RTI key elements

As we noted in Chapter 12, Providing Equal Educational Opportunity, Response to Intervention (RTI) began as an approach to avoid mistaken labeling and placement of students into special education, but it soon evolved to become a broader approach. Many implementations have involved the identification of three tiers of instruction. The first tier generally consists of 75 or 80 percent of students who are progressing satisfactorily following the school's arrangements for delivering instruction; often these incorporate flexible grouping (see Chapter 11, Social Class, Race, and School Achievement, and Chapter 12, Providing Equal Educational Opportunity) uninterrupted blocks of time for instruction, explicit comprehension instruction, and other improvement strategies we have described elsewhere.

A key element of this approach involves careful monitoring of all students' status and progress, along with assessment of the problems of perhaps 20 or 25 percent of students who are not progressing adequately, resulting in selection and delivery of appropriate additional interventions (for example, tutoring of individuals and providing students with materials at their functional reading levels) for this second tier of students. Only if these more-intensive interventions still fail to help a student meet standards is he or she referred for further help through special education, considered as a third tier.

Most tiered-instruction implementations have aimed to improve reading in elementary schools, but some schools have begun to adapt RTI for other subjects and for high schools and preschools. Many schools also are adapting the approach to address students' behavioral problems, with the first tier involving school-wide policies

---

[31]Jennifer Jacobson, "Focusing on the Forgotten," *American Educator* (Fall 2007), available at **www.aft.org**; Tom Holman, "AVID's Value Proposition," *Access* (Spring 2009), available at **www.avid.org**; and Maria Cobb, "AVID Focuses on Educational Equity," *Access* (Spring 2011), available at **www.avid.org.**

and practices; then individual or small-group interventions are provided for students whose behavior is still unacceptable.[32]

We noted in Chapter 12, Providing Equal Educational Opportunity, that some or many efforts toward inclusion in regular classrooms have failed because the challenge of doing so is very difficult and much must be done to train teachers, introduce appropriate teaching methods, provide a range of suitable materials, or otherwise ensure that teachers can work effectively with heterogeneous groups of students. The same or even greater challenge is present for RTI approaches that aim to provide effective instruction for several tiers of students. Analysts have identified the following components, among others, that should be implemented well for RTI to succeed:[33]

REFOCUS Have you visited any schools that use programs described in this section? Which programs appeal most to you, as a teacher? Why?

Implementation necessities

- Monitor students' progress with technically adequate assessments.
- Choose and implement proven interventions to address students' problems.
- Follow explicit rules to identify students not making sufficient progress.
- Monitor student outcomes with at least biweekly assessments.
- Ensure that the intervention is delivered accurately and consistently.
- Determine the intensity of the support needed for student success.
- Convince parents of children with disabilities that RTI is more effective than traditional special education.

Related Efforts and Aspects Involving Educational Effectiveness

We lack space to describe all of the many activities and proposals related to the innovations discussed so far, but we'll mention several of the more important efforts in the following pages and summarize them in Overview 16.1.

Cooperation and Participation with Business, Community, and Other Institutions

Many schools and school districts are attempting to improve the quality of education by cooperating with other institutions, particularly those in business and industry. Promising efforts include the following:[34]

Type of cooperation

- Partnership or adopt-a-school programs in which a business, church, university, or other community institution works closely with an individual school, providing assistance such as tutors or lecturers, funds or equipment for vocational studies, computer education, or help in curriculum development

---

[32]Laura B. Casey et al., "A Much Delayed Response to *A Nation at Risk*," *Phi Delta Kappan* (April 2008), pp. 593–596; W. David Tilly et al., "Three Tiers of Intervention," *School Administrator* (September 2008), available at **www.aasa.org**; Karen S. Wixson, "A Systemic View of RTI Research," *Elementary School Journal* (May 2011), pp. 503–510; and Mary E. Little, "Action Research and Response to Intervention," *Educational Forum* (No. 1, 2012).

[33]Charles R. Greenwood et al., "The Response to Intervention (RTI) Approach in Early Childhood," *Focus on Exceptional Children* (May 2011), pp. 1–22; John J. Hoover and Emily Love, "Supporting School-Based Response to Intervention," *Teaching Exceptional Children* (January–February 2011), pp. 40–48; Karen S. Wixson and Sheila W. Valencia, "Assessment in RTI," *Reading Teacher* (March 2011), pp. 466–469; and material available from **www.responsetointerventiononline.com** and from the National Center on Response to Intervention, **www.rti4success.org**.

[34]Andrew Sum, "Getting to the Finish Line," 2008 paper prepared for the Boston Private Industry Council and the Boston Public Schools, available at **www.bostonpic.org**; and Kathleen D. Marais et al., "Critical Contributions," 2011 report posted by the University of Georgia and Kromley and Associates, available at **www.giarts.org**.

OVERVIEW 16.1

Examples and Trends Involving Efforts at School Reform or Improvement

Area of Reform or Improvement	Examples and Trends
Business and Community Participation	■ Community and business volunteers, donations, awards for schools ■ Boston Compact
Technology	■ Extensive introduction of computers, increases in Internet access ■ Research that guides effective technology use ■ Schools' efforts to improve equity in technology use ■ Researchers and educators offer cautions and concerns about ineffective use of technology.
Rural Education	■ Research to determine effective improvement programs for rural areas emphasizes that unique approaches are needed, because rural areas are diverse. ■ Distance learning may help rural students.
Gifted and Talented Students	■ Many possible approaches make it hard to determine ways to meet potential of gifted and talented students. ■ Most programs emphasize acceleration through curriculum, enriching curriculum, or a blend of both. ■ Schools must expand efforts to identify disadvantaged and minority gifted and talented students.
Increasing Time for Teaching and Learning	■ Longer school years and year-round schools ■ Longer school days ■ After-school and summer learning programs ■ 21st Century Community Learning Centers

■ Provision of expert help and financial assistance that helps charter schools deal with start-up problems and operating challenges such as evaluation and accounting

■ Funding of student awards for reading books or other positive behaviors

■ Donations of equipment and supplies

■ Substantial financial support for reform efforts such as the Harlem Children's Zone project

Boston Compact   A far-reaching example of cooperation with public schools is the Boston Compact. In forming the Compact in 1982, business leaders agreed to recruit at least two hundred companies that would hire graduates of the Boston public schools, as well as providing employment opportunities for students. In return, school officials agreed to establish competency requirements for graduation, increase placement rates of graduates into higher education as well as into full-time employment, and reduce dropout and absenteeism rates. City students got the message: "If you stay in school, work hard, and master the basics, you will be helped to find a job."

Expansion of the compact   By the early 2000s, more than four hundred companies were participating in the Compact. Activities had expanded to include more than twenty local colleges and universities, and tens of thousands of Boston students had been placed in summer jobs programs or had received help in obtaining full-time jobs after graduation. Data collected by Compact officials indicate that high proportions of high-school graduates in Boston either enter college or are employed full-time, and most college entrants are persisting to graduation.

Support from foundations

The apparent success of the Boston Compact has helped stimulate major corporate and foundation efforts to help improve education. For example, the MacArthur Foundation provided $40 million to support reform efforts in the Chicago public schools, and the Bill and Melinda Gates Foundation and the Annenberg Foundation each have provided hundreds of millions of dollars to improve schools in Chicago, Los Angeles, New York, and many other school districts.[35]

Technology in School Reform

Educators confront many questions and challenges with respect to the introduction of new and emerging technologies as part of school reform efforts. We will consider several major topics, including the effective introduction of new technologies in schools and classrooms, equity and technology use in education, and cautions regarding developments that have occurred during the past decades.[36]

Policies for technology

Effective Introduction of Computers and Other Technologies Analysts have identified many considerations that determine whether the introduction of computer-based technologies will produce or help produce substantial improvements in the performance of elementary and secondary students. State and district decision makers have been considering and often acting on recommendations such as the following:[37]

- Teachers must receive ongoing training and technical support in how to use technologies effectively. Technical support staff should be available at both the district and school levels.

Standards & Assessment

- Teacher licensing standards should include assessment of knowledge and skills involving incorporation of technology in classroom lessons.

Concentration needed

- Computers must be sufficiently concentrated to make a difference. For example, one study found that placing one computer in a classroom did not change student achievement but that providing classrooms with three or more computers did produce better outcomes.

- Training must be sufficiently intensive to make a difference. For example, several studies found that providing teachers with more than ten hours of training results in much more change in instruction than shorter training periods.

- How teachers use computers helps determine student outcomes. For example, one major study using data from hundreds of schools supported the conclusion that eighth graders whose teachers emphasized problem solving and learning of concepts using computers learned significantly more than did those whose teachers emphasized low-level "drill and kill" exercises.

Coordination needed

- Plans for computer use must coordinate with arrangements for scheduling, testing, class size, and other aspects of instruction. If class periods are too short or classes are too large to allow the teacher to deliver a lesson effectively, or if teachers are preoccupied with preparing students for tests or with other urgent tasks, computer availability may make little or no difference.

- Teachers who use technology heavily should not neglect motivational and affective aspects of their instruction.

---

[35]See information at **www.gatesfoundation.org**.
[36]H. McFarlane, "The Laptops Are Coming! The Laptops Are Coming!" *Rethinking Schools* (Summer 2008), available at **www.rethinkingschools.org**; Alexandra Moses, "Tech without Support," *Edutopia* (June 2008), available at **www.edutopia.org**; and Sean McMahon, "Live from Milken," 2011 posting by Smartblogs, available at **www.smartblogs.com/leadership**.
[37]Doug Noon, "What Could Go Wrong?" *Teacher Magazine* (January 1, 2007); Suzie Boss, "Overcoming Technology Barriers," *Edutopia* (August 8, 2008), available at **www.edutopia.org**; Suzie Boss, "Project Engagement," *Northwest Education* (Spring–Summer 2008), available at **www.educationnorthwest.org/edunw-magazine**; and Chris Riedel, "The 4 Keys to a Successful Online School," *THE Journal*, January 27, 2012, available at **www.thejournal.com**.

Training needed

One predominant theme throughout our preceding review of computer-based technologies and successful school reform is that substantial, appropriate teacher training is definitely a prerequisite. The federal government has recognized this imperative in provisions of federal legislation that require states to develop plans to ensure that teachers can use new technologies effectively. Many of these plans focus on training teachers to implement improved technologies in the classroom.[38]

Implementations vary widely

Some studies report large gains

Research on Technology Achievement Effects   Over many decades, thousands of studies have examined one or another effect of a multitude of technologies on a wide variety of aspects of achievement. Given that implementations vary wildly from fragmentary to comprehensive, achievement changes are very difficult to measure, outcomes will be diverse for differing groups of students, and there are numerous other obstacles to valid assessment, it is no surprise that analysts who generalize across many studies report that technology has not been found to substantially boost student achievement across the board. However, some studies of individual projects report large achievement gains when goals are clearly defined and implementation addresses key issues such as meaningful training for teachers and adequate funding.[39]

Analysts disagree about value and success

Success at Online Schools?   In recent years, several projects have involved establishment and operation of virtual schools at which all or almost all of the instruction is delivered by computers and other electronic media. In most cases, these schools are charter schools operated by private organizations, frequently for profit. Inasmuch as many of their students enter as low achievers who were unsuccessful in regular public schools, hardware as well as software vary widely in quality, attention to implementation prerequisites frequently is mostly lacking, and sponsors may not be required to report much in the way of achievement and other outcomes, it is predictable that analysts disagree among themselves as to online schools' value and success. Thus, at the present time, online schools should be viewed as a potentially-important generator of school reform in the future rather than a demonstrated success in practice.[40]

Different approaches to blended learning

Blended Learning Approaches and Flipped Classroom   The term "Blended Learning" refers to approaches that combine computer-mediated activities with person-centered classroom instruction to form an integrated set of activities. In general, students in blended programs learn in supervised school settings at least some of the time. In some cases, the noncomputer segment of instruction involves a teacher-coach who provides assistance and guidance; in other implementations, companion lessons are taught in a traditional manner. Software used in the computer curriculum frequently allows for much individualization and considerable opportunity to draw on students' interests and correct their recurrent learning problems. An analysis funded by the federal government concluded that although there was too little research of K–12 results to support firm conclusions, it appears that blended approaches may produce somewhat better achievement than either totally online instruction or traditional teacher-oriented classrooms.[41]

---

[38]Meris Stansbury, "Program Helps Impart 21st Century Proficiency," *eSchool News* (October 22, 2008), available at **www.eschoolnews.com**; and Doug Johnson, "Stretching Your Technology Dollar," *Educational Leadership* (December 2011/January 2012).
[39]Jon Becker, "Flying Pigs?" 2011 posting by Educational Insanity, available at **www.edinsanity.com**; Rana M. Tamin et al., "What Forty Years of Research Says about the Impact of Technology on Learning," *Review of Educational Research* (March 2011), pp. 4–28.
[40]Jon Becker, "A Critique of the NEPC Report on K–12 Online Learning," 2011 posting by Educational Insanity, available at **www.edinsanity.com**; Gene G. Glass, Kevin G. Welner, and Justin Bathon, "Online K–12 Schooling in the United States," *NEPC Policy Briefs* (October 25, 2011), available at **www.nepc.colorado.edu/publications/policy-briefs**.
[41]Jon Bergmann, Jerry Overmyer, and Brett Willie, "The Flipped Class," 2011 posting by The Daily Riff, available at **www.thedailyriff.com**; Joanne Jacobs, "Flipping Catches On," 2011 posting by Joanne Jacobs, available at **www.joannnejacobs.com**; Susan McLester, "Building a Blended Learning Program," *District Administration* (October 2011), available at **www.districtadministration.com**; Heather Staker et al., "The Rise of K–12 Blended Learning," 2011 posting by the Innosight Institute, available at **www.innosightinstitute.org**; and Bill Tucker, "The Flipped Classroom," *Education Next* (Winter 2012), available at **www.educationnext.org**.

Experience in class and computer learning are flipped

A particular form of blended learning that is receiving considerable attention and support is sometimes referred to as "flipped instruction" or the "flipped classroom." Using this approach, initial instruction is provided by videos or other electronic media studied at home or elsewhere out of class, and class time is devoted to such activities as guided practice, explication of key concepts, and assistance in carrying out what used to be follow-up homework. Several proponents of this approach are developing curricula built around the popular Khan Academy videos on YouTube, but other video-oriented materials used for initial instruction also are being explored.

Computers for every student in select grades

One-to-One Provision of Computers to Students   Some years ago many enthusiasts argued that widespread use of computers in schools would revolutionize instruction and vastly improve achievement. (Before that some reformers said that instructional videos would accomplish this result and before that, several visionaries pointed to instructional television as the agent-to-be of enormous improvement.) Exploring the possibilities, numerous schools provided computers for every student in select grades to determine if major improvements could be registered. The largest efforts involved provision of laptops as part of systematic experiments in Maine and several other states.[42]

One-to-one approaches difficult and frequently disappointing

Unfortunately, the results of these innovative efforts have tended to be disappointing. Some schools have reported gains in some subjects, particularly mathematics, but these gains tended to be small and inconsistent. Even when substantial professional development has been provided, and capable leadership has been present, the massive task of incorporating appropriate computerized instruction throughout a curriculum aligned with other materials and assessment has proven to be very difficult. This has left computers in some classrooms functioning as little more than what one analyst termed "glorified pencils."

Potential advantages of M-Learning

Mobile Learning   One definition for Mobile Learning (or M-Learning) is that it is "any educational technology delivered through mobile technology." M-Learning hardware can include cell phones, smartphones, handheld PCs, netbooks, tablets, E-book readers, and other devices able to run mobile applications. Software can include virtually anything that can be "mobilized" to induce or assist learning. Analysts have identified numerous potential advantages of M-Learning such as capacity for authentic learning, users' constant access to their mobile devices, possibilities for individualizing instruction and drawing on multimedia resources, and ease in updating or otherwise modifying curriculum.[43]

Difficulties and potential disadvantages

There also are serious difficulties and potential disadvantages in designing and delivering M-Learning, such as incompatibilities between mobile devices, lack of sufficient broadband and other carrying capacity, tendencies to be distracted when pursuing learning objectives, and technical complexity of hardware and software. In view of such difficulties, it seems apparent that effective M-Learning may be even more challenging to bring about than other technological approaches discussed in the preceding sections.

[42]Bryan Goodwin, "One-to-One Laptop Programs Are No Silver Bullet," *Educational Leadership* (February 2011), available at **www.ascd.org**; Bridget McCrea, "Measuring 1:1 Results," *The Journal* (November 16, 2011), available at **www.thejournal.com**; Susan McLester, "Lesson Learned from One-to-One," *District Administration* (June 2011), available at **www.districtadministration.com**; and Susan McLester, "Pioneering States in One-to-One Implementations," *District Administration* (June 2011), available at **www.districtadministration.com**.
[43]The quote is from "7 Things You Should Know About Mobile Apps for Learning," 2010 Brief posted by Educause, available at **www.educause.edu**. See also Daniel U. Levine and Rayna F. Levine, "Considerations in Introducing Instructional Interventions," op. cit.; Patricia Wallace, "M-Learning," *New Horizons* (Winter 2011), available at **www.education.jhu.edu**; and Kevin Thomas and Christy McGee, "The Only Thing We Have to Fear is . . . 120 Characters," *Tech Trends* (January 2012).

Peter Cade/Iconica/Getty Images

Many school districts are cooperating with business and industry to improve education quality in their schools. Business partners supply schools with mentors, supplies, funds, and apprenticeship opportunities or guaranteed postsecondary school funding for students.

▍ M-Learning seems to have high Potential for Mischief

REFOCUS Have you had significant experience with any of the technology approaches described in the preceding sections? If yes, to what extent did they assist you in learning?

The pursuit of M-Learning beginning to take place in schools varies from projects at one extreme that allow students to use whatever mobile devices are normally available to them (the BYOD or Bring-Your-Own-Device approach), to provision of the same device for all students at the other extreme. Although the latter approach clearly is much more expensive, both seem to have what Levine and Levine termed high Potential for Mischief, in this case, the temptation for educators to advertise their introduction of the latest innovation without facing up to the grave difficulties involved in effective implementation.

▍ Still an issue at high-poverty schools

Equity and the Use of Technology Another key issue, particularly at the national and state levels, is ensuring equal opportunity for all students to access the benefits of technology improvements. Whether in their schools or homes, low-income students generally have less access to certain computer-based learning opportunities than do middle-income students. Until recently, many low-income families have been unable to afford computers. Schools enrolling high percentages of low-income students usually have computers available, but, in recent years, increasing reliance on Internet and multimedia usage in U.S. schools has bypassed numerous high-poverty schools in big cities.[44]

▍ Silicon snake oil?

Cautions Regarding Computer–Based Technologies in Education As implied previously, not everyone is optimistic about the likelihood that technology will produce productive reforms and widespread improvement in the educational system. Skeptics abound, and their ranks include some of the most knowledgeable analysts of recent developments in the schools and of the evolution of computers in general. For example, Clifford Stoll, widely known for his contributions to Internet development, has written a book titled *Silicon Snake Oil* in which he points out that although computers may be fun to use in the classroom, entertainment is not synonymous with

---

[44]Jonathan D. Becker, "Digital Equity in Education," *Education Policy Analysis Archives,* available at **http://epaa.asu.edu**; Tina Barseghian, "For High-Risk Youth, Is Learning Digital Media a Luxury?" 2011 posting by Mind shift, available at **http://mindshift.kqed.org**; and "Getting Past the Digital Divide," *Teaching Tolerance* (Spring 2011), available at **www.tolerance.org**.

learning. Stoll sees computers as potentially equivalent to the grainy films and the disjointed filmstrips that teachers used years ago mainly to keep their students occupied.[45]

Idle clicking?

Similarly, Jane Healy had become well known as an enthusiast about the computer's potential for opening new worlds to students and then shocked many of her readers with a book in which she questioned the effects of new technologies on children both inside and outside the schools. After two years spent visiting classrooms, she concluded that computers in many classrooms are supervised by ill-prepared teachers whose students engage mostly in mindless drills, games unrelated to coherent learning objectives, "silly surfing," and/or "idle clicking." Other analysts, also on the basis of visits to numerous schools and classrooms, have reached the conclusion that expensive multimedia setups frequently serve more as a medium for classroom control and public relations than as a learning tool. In reaching such conclusions about computer-based technologies in the schools, Healy, Susan Greenfield, and other skeptics typically offer the following cautions and criticisms:[46]

- Research indicating that computers are producing widespread gains in student performance frequently is poorly designed or otherwise invalid.

Creativity reduced?

- Computers too often detract from students' creativity by constraining them within prescribed boundaries of thought and action.

- Schools respond to perceived or real public demands and expectations that classrooms should be loaded with advanced technologies by buying expensive equipment that soon becomes obsolete. This may be happening now with iPads and other tablets.

- Particularly for young children, time on the computer too often replaces time needed to develop motor skills and logical thinking.

Reduced attention span of "screenagers"?

- Even more than television, digital technology is reducing the attention span and depth-of-learning of children and "screenagers" (adolescents growing up in the Internet era). This trend has accelerated with the growing popularity of Web 2.0 sites such as Facebook and Twitter that involve fragmentary contact with people and sources.

Continuity & Change

- Fantasy worlds and other imaginary digitized environments are distorting children's sense of reality.

Scaling up a problem

In reviewing these cautions, we should keep in mind preceding parts of this section as well as earlier parts of this chapter that identified actions associated with the successful implementation of computer-based technologies and other substantial efforts to reform the schools. Will schools and districts provide large-scale and ongoing training and the meaningful technical support required for teachers to use technology effectively? Will educators carefully align the introduction of such technologies and coordinate them with curriculum objectives, testing, and school climate improvements? Fortunately, many educators are working to make this happen.

Rural Education

Rural diversity

About 20 percent of students and 30 percent of schools are located in rural areas, and about one-half of school districts are rural. In trying to improve rural education,

---

[45]Clifford Stoll, *Silicon Snake Oil* (New York: Doubleday, 1995). See also Todd Oppenheimer, "The Computer Delusion," *Atlantic* (July 1997), available at **www.theatlantic.com**; Todd Oppenheimer, *The Flickering Mind* (New York: Random House, 2003); Mark Bauerlein, *The Dumbest Generation* (New York: Tarcher, 2008); and Mark Bauerlein, "Too Dumb for Complex Texts?" *Educational Leadership* (February 2011), available at **www.ascd.org**.
[46]Jane M. Healy, *Failure to Connect* (New York: Simon and Schuster, 1998); Paul Saffo, "Neo-Toys," *Civilization* (November 1998); Colleen Cordes and Edward Miller, eds., "Fool's Gold," 2009 posting by the Alliance for Childhood, available at **www.allianceforchildhood.net**; and Michael B. Horn, "Is There a K–12 Online Learning 'Bubble'?" *Education Next* (April 7, 2011), available at **www.educationnext.org**.

educators must confront the extreme diversity of rural locations, which makes it difficult to generalize across communities. One group of observers defined rural school districts as those that have fewer than one hundred fifty residents per square mile and are located in counties in which at least 60 percent of the population resides in communities with populations under five thousand. Even within this fairly restricted definition, rural communities exemplify hundreds of subcultures that differ in racial and ethnic composition, extent of remoteness, economic structure, and other characteristics.[47]

This diversity is partly why the particular problems of rural schools have received relatively little attention during the past fifty years. Recently, however, a small group of scholars has been trying to determine how to provide high-quality education in a rural setting. They have reached several major conclusions:[48]

Conclusions about rural schools

1. The tremendous diversity in rural America requires similarly diverse school improvement efforts that also address multicultural education goals.

2. The small scale of rural schools offers advantages. Teachers can know students and parents personally, and schools can work closely with community agencies.

3. Teachers in rural schools frequently require substantial technical support.

4. Many rural schools can benefit from distance learning and other advanced technology.

Teacher shortages and distance education

Many rural schools face serious problems in attracting qualified teachers. States have increased certification requirements and reduced the flexibility to employ teachers without proper certification, which has left many rural districts unable either to find or to afford sufficient teaching personnel, particularly in science, math, and foreign languages. But school systems can overcome this problem, in part, by using television, interactive computers, and other forms of **distance education** that deliver cost-effective instruction.[49]

Gifted and Talented Students

Trends in gifted education

Research on the education of gifted and talented students has increased. Widespread program trends include radical acceleration of learning opportunities for gifted and talented students; special mentoring assistance; increased emphasis on independent study and investigative learning; use of individualized education programs (IEPs), as with students with disabilities; opportunities to engage in advanced-level projects; instruction delivery in accordance with students' learning styles; special schools, Saturday programs, and summer schools; increased community resource use; varied instructional approaches to match student interests and abilities; and compacting curriculum to streamline content that students already know and replace it with more challenging material.[50]

Differing approaches

A major issue involving gifted and talented students is the selection of effective approaches to curriculum and instruction. In general, educators have tended to emphasize

---

[47]David Monk, "Recruiting and Retaining High-Quality Teachers in Rural Areas," *The Future of Children* (Spring 2007), available at **www.futureofchildren.org**; and Colleen Heflin and Kathleen Miller, "The Geography of Need," 2011 posting by the Rural Policy Research Institute, available at **www.rupri.org**.

[48]Carrie Aguas, "Rural Elementary School Achieves Gains across All Grades," 2005 description prepared for Houghton Mifflin Beyond the Book site, available at **www.beyond-the-book. com**, click on "Success Stories"; Craig Howley, Jennifer Johnson, and Jennifer Petrie, "Consolidation of Schools and Districts," *Policy Briefs* (February 1, 2011), available at **www.nepc. colorado.edu**; and Dan Gordon, "Off the Beaten Path," *THE Journal* (October 4, 2011), available at **www.thejournal.com**.

[49]Kathy Christie, "The Rural Bellwether," *Phi Delta Kappan* (February 2001), pp. 425–427; Wallace H. Hannum et al., "Distance Education Use in Rural Schools," *Journal of Research in Rural Education* (No. 3, 2009), available at **www.jrre.psu.edu**; and Aimee Howley, Lawrence Wood, and Brian Hough, "Rural Elementary School Teachers' Technology Integration," *Journal of Research in Rural Education* (No. 9, 2011), available at **www.jrre.psu.edu**.

[50]Sally M. Reis, "No Child Left Bored," *School Administrator* (February 2007), available at **www.aasa.org**; Norma Fisher-Dorion and Susan Irvine, "Going Beyond the Basics to Reach All Children," *Principal* (May–June 2009), p. 26; and Joseph S. Renzulli, "What Makes Giftedness?" *Phi Delta Kappan* (May 2011), pp. 81–88.

either acceleration through the regular curriculum or enrichment that provides for greater depth of learning, but some have argued for a confluent approach that combines both. Developing this idea, analysts have advocated combining elements: (1) a "content" model, which emphasizes accelerated study; (2) a "process-product" model, which emphasizes enrichment through independent study and investigation; and (3) an "epistemological" model, which emphasizes understanding and appreciation of systems of knowledge. In general, analysts believe that open-ended, problem-solving approaches should be emphasized for gifted students in any of these or other models.[51]

■ Including more minority students

Much concern has been expressed about the low participation of minority students and economically disadvantaged students in gifted education. Evidence indicates that selection criteria frequently fail to identify disadvantaged students who might benefit from participation. For this reason, many efforts are under way to broaden definitions of giftedness to include indicators such as very strong problem-solving skills, high creativity, high verbal or nonverbal fluency, and unusual artistic accomplishments and abilities.[52]

Increasing Teaching and Learning Time

Several national reports, including *A Nation at Risk* and *Prisoners of Time,* have recommended providing more time for teaching and learning. Possible approaches include extending the school year, lengthening the school day, or offering after-school and summer learning programs.

■ Extending time controversial

Longer School Years or School Days   Numerous school districts have lengthened the school day or the school year. Some offer **year-round schools** that run on rotating schedules so that three-quarters of students attend for nine weeks while the remaining quarter are on vacation for three weeks. Year-round schools have usually been established where schools are seriously overcrowded.

Such moves usually provoke controversy because they require a significant increase in staff costs and may disrupt parents' child-care arrangements. Action to extend time for learning also requires substantial changes in curriculum and instruction if it is to improve student achievement. Massachusetts has begun an effort to help districts and schools restructure their instructional practices and their daily, weekly, and annual schedules to provide students with more time for learning.[53] For a debate on this topic, see the Taking Issue box.

---

[51]Joyce Van Tassel-Baska, "Effective Curriculum and Instructional Models for Talented Students," *Gifted Child Quarterly* (Fall 1980), pp. 162–168. See also Jane Clarenbach, "All Gifted Is Local" and "Defying the Ripple Effects," both in the *School Administrator* (February 2007), available at **www.aasa.org**; Joyce Van Tassel-Baska and Elissa F. Brown, "Toward Best Practice," *Gifted Child Quarterly* (November 2008), pp. 342–358; Saiying Steenbergen and Sydney M. Moone, "The Effects of Acceleration on High-Ability Students," *Gifted Child Quarterly* (Issue 1, 2011), pp. 39–53; and Jack Snowman, Rick McCown, and Robert Biehler, *Psychology Applied to Teaching*, 13th ed. (Belmont, Calif.: 2012).

[52]Julie D. Swanson, "Breaking through Assumptions about Low-Income, Minority Gifted Students," *Gifted Child Quarterly* (Winter 2006), pp. 11–25; Eric Smith, "Weaving the Gifted into the Full Fabric," *School Administrator* (February 2007), available at **www.aasa.org**; Dorothy M. Singleton et al., "Under-Representation of African American Students in Gifted Education Programs," *African American Research Perspectives* (Spring 2008), pp. 11–21; Christine S. Beck, "No More Lost Ground," *Educational Leadership* (April 2011), available at **www.ascd.org**; and Seong-Yong Lee, Paula Olszewski-Kubelius, and George Peternel, "Acceleration for Gifted Minority Students," *Gifted Child Quarterly* (July 2011).

[53]National Education Commission on Time and Learning, *Prisoners of Time* (Washington, D.C.: U.S. Department of Education, 1994); Hilary Pennington, "The Massachusetts Expanding Learning Time to Support Student Success Initiative," 2007 paper prepared for the Center for American Progress, available at **www.americanprogress.org**; Robert M. Stonehill et al., "Enhancing School Reform through Expanded Learning," 2009 paper prepared for Learning Point Associates, available at **www.learningpt.org**; "Learning Time in America," 2011 report posted by the National Center on Time and Learning, available at **www.timeandlearning.org**; "Extended Learning Time Offers Promise in Raising Achievement," *American Teacher* (January/February 2012); and postings at the Summer Matters site, available at **www.summermatters.com**.

TAKING ISSUE

Read the brief introduction below, as well as the Question and the pros and cons list that follows. Then, answer the question using your own words and position.

More Time in School

One suggestion for improving student achievement has been to increase the amount of time students spend in school by lengthening the school day, school year, or both. This idea is based in part on observations of countries such as Japan, where students spend considerably more time in school than do American students. It also reflects research indicating that time-on-task is an important determinant of students' performance.

Question

Should the United States extend the amount of time students spend in school? (Think about this question as you read the PRO and CON arguments listed below. What is *your* take on this issue?)

Arguments PRO

1. Extending the school year or school day will give teachers more contact time and an opportunity to teach students in depth. This is particularly vital for at-risk students, who need special services and remedial work.

2. Experience in countries such as Japan indicates that increased time spent in school can assist in raising achievement scores. Many national task-force reports have also recommended extending time in school.

3. Extending school time can help to solve the problems of latchkey children, who must look after themselves while their parents work. In this way, schools can benefit the family as well as improve education.

4. Lengthening students' time in school will indicate to taxpayers that schools are serious about raising educational standards. Taxpayers will therefore be more willing to support the schools.

5. The present system of school attendance originated in an agrarian period when families needed children's help with farm tasks. In an industrial society, the best use of students' time is to give them additional schooling that prepares them for the world of the twenty-first century.

Arguments CON

1. Extending time in school will not compensate for the poor teaching that takes place in too many schools. The problem is not quantity but quality of schooling, and longer hours could well *reduce* quality.

2. So many social and cultural differences exist between Japan and the United States that simple comparisons are not valid. Little hard evidence indicates that increasing students' time in school will raise achievement levels in the United States.

3. Extending the time children spend in school will add to the growing institutional interference with basic family life. Such interference, however well intentioned, contributes to the fragmentation of the modern family.

4. Extending school time will require major new expenditures to increase salaries and refurbish buildings. Taxpayers will not willingly pay for these expenses.

5. We know too little about the effects of lengthening the school day or year. Do children in our culture need ample breaks from school? Do their originality and creativity suffer when they are kept too long in classes? Until we have answers, we should not make students spend more time in school.

Question Reprise: What Is Your Stand?

Reflect again on the following question by explaining *your* stand about this issue: Should the United States extend the amount of time students spend in school?

21st Century Learning Centers

After-School and Summer Programs Rather than increase the school year or school day for all students, many districts have been initiating or expanding after-school and summer learning programs. After-school and summer programs can provide struggling students with more time for learning or offer safe and educational opportunities for latchkey and other children (see Chapter 10, Culture, Socialization, and Education). These programs have grown rapidly in recent years as the No Child Left Behind Act (NCLB) resulted in the identification of thousands of schools not making adequate yearly progress (AYP). The federal government now provides millions of dollars annually to support them under the **21st Century Community Learning Centers** legislation, and state and local sources provide still more support. The 21st Century Community Learning Centers provide tutoring, after-school classes, summer school, and other academic-enrichment activities for students attending low-performing schools. Analysts and evaluators who have studied the centers and similar efforts have reached several conclusions:[54]

Successful if implemented well

- After-school and summer programs can improve academic performance if implemented well.

- Implementation considerations include selecting and training staff, providing appropriate materials, and making sufficient resources available.

- Progress is difficult to measure because students typically make relatively small gains on tests that assess regular schooling. Therefore officials should assess attendance, parent support, student effort, and other possible correlates of improved attitudes.

- Nonacademic goals such as providing a safe environment, expanding students' interests, and developing social skills are worthwhile and should be addressed in implementing after-school and summer programs.

> **REFOCUS** Would you enjoy teaching in a school or school district that has implemented the reforms described in this section? For example, would you like to teach in a year-round school? How will you prepare to teach gifted and talented students effectively?

School Choice

In recent years, **school choice** plans have been advocated as a way to introduce greater flexibility and accountability into education. The basic idea is to enhance students' opportunities to choose where they will enroll and what they will study. School choice is a broad goal, and many different programs offer students and their families varying levels of choices. Many alternative schools have been established to provide education for students who have been failing in regular public schools. Advocates of school choice point out that parents typically find only one model of education in any given public-school neighborhood. Some advocates argue for creating choices within the public-school system; others contend that the only true alternatives are outside the system. Efforts to increase school choice include the following:[55]

Today's magnet schools

- *Magnet and alternative schools.* Many school districts offer their students the opportunity to choose magnet schools or alternative schools within the district. **Magnet schools**, as described in Chapter 12, Providing Equal Educational Opportunity, are designed to attract voluntary enrollment by offering special programs or curricula that appeal to students from more than one neighborhood. They are often part of a reform effort aimed at decreasing segregation and providing students with opportunities to participate in instructional programs not available in their local schools. More than one thousand magnet schools are now functioning in public-school districts.

[54]Beth Frerking, "A New Learning Day," *Edutopia* (February 2007), available at **www.edutopia .org**; "Aligning Afterschool with the Regular School Day," 2011 posting by the Afterschool Alliance, available at **www.afterschoolalliance.org**; Jane L. David, "After-School Programs Can Pay Off," *Educational Leadership* (May 2011), available at **www.ascd.org**; Chris Gabrieli, "Time—It's Not Always Money," *Educational Leadership* (December 2011/January 2012); and information available at **www.mass2020.org**.
[55]Christine Rossell, "Magnet Schools," *Education Next*, (No. 2 2005), available at **www.educationnext.org**; Peter Tice et al., *Trends in the Use of School Choice* (Washington, D.C.: National Center for Education Statistics, 2006), available at **http://nces.ed.gov**; Erica Frankenberg & Genevieve Siegel-Hawley, "The Forgotten Choice?" 2008 report prepared for Magnet Schools of America, available at **www.civilrightsproject.ucla.edu**; and "Alternative Schooling," 2012 posting available at **http://education.stateuniversity.com**.

Alternative schools provide learning opportunities unavailable in the average public school. From this point of view, magnet schools are a type of alternative school. So, too, are many parochial and other nonpublic schools and institutions such as street academies, storefront schools, and high-school "outposts" designed to make education more relevant for inner-city students. Studies of alternative schools have indicated that they frequently enroll students who have not succeeded in traditional schools.

Compared to traditional schools, alternative schools allow for greater individualization, more independent study, and more openness to the outside community. They tend to offer small class size, high staff morale, freedom from external control, and strong concern for noncognitive goals of education.[56]

- *Charter schools.* As discussed in Chapter 8, Financing Public Education, charter schools funded by public sources also frequently provide opportunities for parents and students to choose among schools. Charter schools can be established by school districts or by other chartering authorities. Some are managed by private profit-making corporations. Charter schools typically have more leeway in spending funds, utilizing faculty, and carrying on other operations than do regular public schools. They also can have their charter revoked if they are not successful. More than forty states now allow for establishment of charter schools, and more than five thousand charter schools are operating nationally, enrolling more than two million students. About a third of charter schools have 75 percent or more low-income students, compared with about one-fifth of other public schools. Many are attended largely by students who have been low achievers susceptible to dropping out of school. In several urban districts, such as Kansas City and Washington, D.C., charter schools enrolled 30 percent or more of public-school students by 2012. President Obama has recognized that many charter schools are functioning successfully and has called on states to "reform their charter rules and lift caps on the number of allowable charter schools, wherever such caps are in place."[57]

- *Open enrollment attendance options.* Several states have also created plans that allow all students the option to transfer to their choice of public schools within, or sometimes outside, their local school district. Colorado laws, for example, require that all districts allow students to transfer freely within their boundaries. Washington's legislation provides students who experience a "special hardship or detrimental condition" with the right to enroll in another school district that has available space; it also requires districts to accept students who transfer to locations close to their parents' place of work or child-care site.

- *Privately funded school choice vouchers.* Philanthropists in numerous locations have provided vouchers to enable students to attend nonpublic schools. After a group of business executives funded scholarships that helped 2,200 New York City students (out of more than 40,000 applicants) to attend nonpublic schools in 1998 and 1999, a larger group raised millions of dollars for a national program to provide

---

[56]Daniel U. Levine, "Educating Alienated Inner City Youth: Lessons from the Street Academies," *Journal of Negro Education* (Spring 1975), pp. 139–148; Thomas Toch, "Invest in Reclaiming High Schools," *Education Sector* (March 14, 2007), available at **www.educationsector.org**; "Alternative High Schools," 2011 posting by Education Portal, available at **www.education-portal.com**; and "Best Practices in Alternative Education," 2012 posting by the Kentucky Center for School Safety," available at **www.kycss.org**.

[57]Joe Williams, "Games Charter Opponents Play," *Education Next* (No. 1, 2007), available at **www.educationnext.org**; Dan Lips, "School Choice," 2008 paper prepared for the Heritage Foundation, available at **www.heritage.org**; Lisa M. Stulberg, *Race, Schools, and Hope* (New York: Teachers College Press, 2008); "Arizona Moves to Increase Tuition Tax Credits," *Education Report* (April 10, 2011), available at **www.educationreport.org**; and *The 2012 Statistical Abstract* (Washington, D.C.: U.S. Bureau of the Census, 2012).

inner-city students with similar scholarships. Thousands of students have received such scholarships.

Arizona tax credits

- *Tuition tax credits.* Initiated in 1997, Arizona's universal tax credit approach allows any taxpayer who pays tuition for a child attending a public or nonpublic school to take a dollar-for-dollar deduction (up to half what the local public schools would have spent) in state tax liability. In addition, taxpayers can receive a credit for donations to "private tuition" charities that spend at least 90 percent of this income for tuition assistance to low-income students. Several other states also have begun to provide this type of assistance. After the U.S. Supreme Court approved Arizona's arrangements in 2011, the state government increased donation limits by 50 percent.

Taxpayer-funded scholarships

- *Taxpayer-funded scholarships.* Choice in Arizona received a further boost in 2006 when the state began paying nonpublic-school tuition for disabled students and foster-care children. Several other states also provide scholarships to help some students attend private elementary or secondary schools.

Government-funded vouchers

- *Publicly funded school choice vouchers.* Although small government-funded voucher programs have been in place in Cleveland and in Colorado, Florida, Maine, Ohio, and Vermont, the best-known voucher project is the sizable program funded by the Wisconsin legislature for low-income students in Milwaukee. Originally initiated to help students attend nonreligious private schools, the Milwaukee program expanded in 1998 to include attendance at religious schools. In 2011, vouchers could be used at more than one hundred private schools, more than eighty of which were religious (mostly Catholic and Lutheran).[58]

Controversy about School Choice

As programs have been implemented to expand school choice, numerous recommendations for and against additional action are being put forward. Those who support choice recommend policies such as enrollment across school district boundaries, vouchers to attend both public and nonpublic schools, magnetization and/or "charterization" of entire school districts and regions, and creation of alternative-school networks. Supporters of choice emphasize the following arguments:[59]

Arguments favoring choice

- Providing choice for disadvantaged students will enable them to escape from poorly functioning schools.
- Achievement, aspirations, and other outcomes will improve for many students because they will be more motivated to succeed at schools they select.
- Both existing public schools and alternative learning institutions (whether public or nonpublic) will provide improved education because their staffs will be competing to attract students.
- Increased opportunities will be available to match school programs and services with students' needs.
- Parents will be empowered to play a larger role in their children's education.

[58]Barbara Miner, "A Brief History of Milwaukee's Voucher Program," *Rethinking Schools* (Spring 2006), available at **www.rethinkingschools.org**; Grace Rubenstein, "Minding the (Achievement) Gap," *Edutopia* (January 9, 2007), available at **www.edutopia.org**; and "Slight Decline in Use of Private School Tuition Vouchers," *Research Briefs* (February 2011), available at **www.publicpolicyforum.org**.
[59]Matthew J. Brouillette, "The Case for Choice in Schooling," 2001 paper posted at the Mackinac Center for Public Policy site, available at **www.mackinac.org**; John E. Chubb, "Ignoring the Market," *Education Next* (No. 2, Spring 2003), available at **www.educationnext.org**; Nelson Smith, "Charters as a Solution?" *Education Next* (No. 1, 2007), available at **www.educationnext.org**; Gene Glass, "Charter Schools," December 3, 2011 posting by the Horace Mann League, available at **http://horacemannleague .blogspot.com**; and Katrina E. Bulkley, "Charter Schools . . . Taking a Closer Look," *Education Digest* (January 2012), pp. 58–62.

Critics of school choice plans question these arguments, particularly in cases that involve public financing of nonpublic schools. The critics maintain the following:[60]

Arguments against choice

- Choice plans will reinforce stratification and segregation because highly motivated or high-achieving white and minority students will be disproportionately likely to transfer out of schools that have a substantial percentage of students with low achievement or low social status.
- Public financial support for nonpublic schools is unconstitutional.
- The opening and closing of numerous schools based on their competitive attractiveness will disrupt the operation of the entire educational system.
- There is little or no reason to believe that most schools that presently enroll relatively few disadvantaged students will be more successful with such students than are their present schools.
- Even if one assumes that schools capable of substantially improving the performance of low achievers are widely available in a choice plan, many students and parents lack the knowledge necessary to select them, and these outstanding schools may not accept many low achievers.
- Although accountability may increase in the sense that unattractive schools will lose students and may even be closed, overall accountability will be reduced because nonpublic schools receiving public funds frequently are not subject to government standards and requirements, such as obligations to enroll special-education students and to administer state tests.
- Public financing of nonpublic institutions will result in the establishment of "cult" schools based on divisive racist or religious ideologies.

Fear of increased separatism

These worries about school choice are shared even by people who have supported proposals to expand student options. For example, John Leo thinks that school choice is "reform's best choice" but also is education's "600-pound gorilla." He believes it may harm education by funding schools that encourage social, racial, and economic separatism. In this context, many analysts have been trying to identify policies that could make choice plans as constructive as possible. They have suggested policies including the following:[61]

Policies for constructive school choice

- Ensure that students and parents receive adequate counseling and information.
- Provide free transportation, scholarships, and other support to make sure that choices are fully available and do not depend on social status.
- Include guidelines to avoid segregation and re-segregation.
- Include provisions to release government-operated schools from regulations not imposed on nonpublic schools.
- Do not ignore other reform necessities and possibilities; instead, treat choice as part of a comprehensive reform agenda that involves systemic reform of the kind described elsewhere in this chapter.

---

[60]Herbert J. Grover, "Private School Choice Is Wrong," *Educational Leadership* (January 1991), p. 51; Luis Benveniste, Martin Carnoy, and Richard Rothstein, *All Else Equal* (New York: Routledge Falmer, 2002); Jay Mathews, "Charter Schools Lag, Study Finds," *Washington Post* (August 23, 2006); Dennis Epple and Richard Romano, "Educational Vouchers and Cream Skimming," *International Economics Review* (November 2008), pp. 1395–1435; Barbara Miner, "Public Studies Puncture the Privatization Bubble," *Rethinking Schools* (Winter 2007/2008), available at **www.rethinkingschools.org**; and Ron Zimmer et al., "Charter Schools in 8 States," 2009 report prepared for the Rand Corporation, available at **www.rand.org**; Joanne Jacobs, "Scores Aren't Higher for Milwaukee Voucher Students," 2011 posting by Joanne Jacobs, available at **www.joannejacobs.com**; and James Harvey, "Privatization," *Educational Leadership* (December 2011/January 2012).
[61]John Leo, "School Reform's Best Choice," *U.S. News and World Report* (January 14, 1991), p. 17; Sol Stern, "School Choice Isn't Enough," *City Journal* (Winter 2008), available at **www.city-journal.org**; Leigh Dingerson et al., "Prophet Motives," *Rethinking Schools* (Summer 2008), available at **www.rethinkingschools.org**; and "Are Charter Schools Models of Reform for Traditional Public Schools?" 2012 posting at Jay P. Greene's Blog, available at **www.jaypgreene.com**.

Research on choice alternatives

Research to date has not conclusively established whether or not students exercising school choice generally achieve at a significantly higher level than comparable students in regular public schools. With some exceptions (such as the KIPP approach described earlier) that either favor schools of choice or report no differences, evaluations of voucher programs, charter schools, and other choice initiatives have tended to conclude that achievement gains generally were small and inconsistent.[62]

Systemic Restructuring and Standards-Based Reform

Improving the entire system

In recent years, many reform efforts have been discussed in terms of **restructuring** all or part of the educational system. Although this term has been interpreted in many different ways, it increasingly is used to indicate the need for **systemic improvement**—that is, reform that simultaneously addresses all or most major components in the overall system. For example, officials of the Education Commission of the States have stated that all parts of the educational system from "schoolhouse to statehouse" must be restructured to bring about systematic improvement in teaching and learning. Systemic restructuring deals with instructional methods; professional development; assessment of student, teacher, and/or school performance; curriculum and materials; school finance; governance; course requirements; and other aspects of education.[63]

 **Standards & Assessment**

Making reforms coherent

When many changes are introduced simultaneously, restructuring and reform activities must be coherent; they must be compatible with and reinforce each other, rather than becoming isolated fragments that divert time and energy from priority goals. Because systemic reforms work for coherence by identifying student performance standards and then aligning testing, instructional methods and materials, professional development, and other aspects of education, they frequently are referred to as "standards-based" reforms.

State-Level Systemic Reform

One of the best examples of state-level systemic reform is in Kentucky, where in 1989, the state supreme court declared the state's system of common schools unconstitutional on the grounds that it was ineffective and inequitable. The court then instructed the legislative and executive branches to improve the "entire sweep of the system—all its parts and parcels." As a result, the following changes, among others, have been phased in as part of the Kentucky Education Reform Act (KERA):[64]

Provisions of Kentucky plan

■ Curriculum, instruction, and student assessment are performance-based, emphasizing mastery-oriented learning and criterion-referenced testing.

■ Parents can transfer their children out of schools they consider unsatisfactory.

■ Faculty members at unsuccessful schools receive help from state-appointed specialists.

■ Youth and family service centers have been established in communities where 20 percent or more of students are from low-income families.

[62]Frances C. Fowler, "School Choice," *Educational Researcher* (March 2003), available at **http://aera.net/publications/?id=331**; Richard D. Kahlenberg, "Back to Class," *American Prospect* (December 2006), available at **http://prospect.org**; Atila Abdulkadiroglu et al., "Informing the Debate," 2009 paper prepared for the Boston Foundation, available at **www.tbf.org**; Julian Betts and Y. E. Tang, "The Effect of Charter Schools on Student Achievement," 2011 posting by the Center on Reinventing Public Education, available at **www.cpre.org**; and Robin Lake and Betheny Gross, "Hopes, Fears, and Reality," 2012 posting by the Center on Reinventing Public Education.
[63]"What Is Systemic Reform?" 2005 posting at the National Academies Internet site, available at **www.nas.edu/rise/backg3.htm**; Ledyard McFadden, "District Learning Tied to Student Learning," *Phi Delta Kappan* (April 2009), pp. 545–553; and Mariana Haynes, "Meeting the Challenge," *Alliance for Excellent Education Policy Brief* (January 2011), available at **www.all4ed.org**.
[64]Thomas R. Guskey and Kent Peterson, "The Road to Classroom Change," *Educational Leadership* (December 1995–January 1996), pp. 10–15; and "Proof of Progress," 2010 statement and "Guidelines for Closing the Gaps for All Students," 2011 posting by the Kentucky Department of Education, available at **www.education.ky.gov/KDE**.

TECHNOLOGY@SCHOOL

Accessing Information on State Assessment and Accountability Practices

State standards for your students' achievement will undoubtedly affect you as a teacher. You'll also encounter the growing movement to hold students, teachers, and schools accountable for their levels of achievement.

Margaret Goertz and Mark Duffy of the Consortium for Policy Research (CPRE) helped conduct a survey of state practices and prepared a report titled "Assessment and Accountability across the 50 States." The report is available at **www.cpre.org/images/stories/cpre_pdfs/rb33.pdf**.

The authors found that all states have "embarked on educational initiatives related to high standards and challenging content" that involve a "common set of academic standards for all students, the assessments that measure student performance, and accountability systems that are at least partially focused on student outcomes." They also reported that all the states publish, or require districts to publish, school or district report cards. But they acknowledge wide variability in how challenging the assessments are, the levels of performance considered proficient, the rewards and punishments in place

based on a school's or district's performance, and the amount and types of assistance made available to low-performing schools. As you saw in Chapter 12, Providing Equal Educational Opportunity, these challenges continue to affect standards-based efforts, including the NCLB laws.

You can obtain information about states' specific standards in various grades and subjects by searching the website of Achieve, Inc., a bipartisan, nonprofit organization established in 1996 by governors and corporate leaders. Search from the home page at **www.achieve.org** to learn, for example, that the first English standard expected of sixth graders in Alaska involves the capacity to "Apply knowledge of word origins, structure, and context clues, and root words, and use dictionaries and glossaries, to determine the meaning of new words and to comprehend text." Another way to learn about state standards is to visit any state's education agency website. Find all such sites at **www.nasbe.org**. What are the English standards for sixth graders in your state?

- All districts offer preschool programs for disadvantaged four-year-olds.
- Taxes have been increased by billions of dollars to pay for the changes.

Standards & Assessment

Gains in Texas

Texas educators and legislators also have been introducing many components of systemic reform. The Texas Assessment of Academic Skills (TAAS) has been used to identify and provide support for modifying instruction in low-performing schools and districts. Particularly large gains have been reported for low-income students and for minority students. Among schools in Brazosport, for example, intensive staff development, tutoring for low achievers, and other reform efforts helped increase the percentage of low-income students passing the mathematics test from 55 percent in 1992 to 96 percent in 2001. In Brownsville, which won a 2008 Broad Foundation award for reducing achievement gaps by income and race/ethnicity and for other improvements, the percentage of fifth graders who met state reading standards increased from 64 percent in 2004 to 83 percent in 2007. For the state as a whole, the percentage of low-income students passing the reading, writing, and math sections of the TAAS increased from 39 percent in 1994 to 68 percent in 2011. In 2011, 90 percent of students passed the state reading tests, and 84 percent passed the math tests. Although some observers complain that too much time is spent preparing students for tests, that the tests are too easy, and that too many low achievers are excluded from testing, many analysts have applauded Texas teachers' efforts to improve the performance of all students.[65] For Internet sources of information on state reforms, see the Technology @ School box.

---

[65]Tyce Palmaffy, "The Gold Star State," *Policy Review* (March–April 1998); Linda Skrla, "Accountability, Equity, and Complexity," *Educational Researcher* (May 2001), available at **aera.net/publications/?id=331**; "Broad Prize Winner," 2008 posting by the Broad Foundation, available at **www.broadprize.org**; and "2011 Comprehensive Annual Report on Texas Public Schools," 2011 report prepared by the staff of the Texas Education Agency. See also Nathan N. Parker, "Urban District Dramatically Increases Reading Achievement," 2006 description prepared for Houghton Mifflin Beyond the Book Internet site, available at **www.beyond-the-book.com**: click on "Success Stories."

District-Level Systemic Reform

Standards & Assessment

High-performing districts

In the preceding section, we cited systemic reforms in Brazosport and Brownsville, Texas. Many other districts throughout the nation also have initiated outstanding reform approaches that are producing large gains on their states' standards-based assessments of student performance. In addition, we are learning much about what districts should do to make their reform plans successful. For example, a study conducted for the Educational Research Service reported that the following practices were characteristic of six districts rated high in performance, based on having brought about substantial achievement improvements while enrolling significant proportions of low-income students:[66]

- The superintendent and other leaders developed widely shared beliefs about the necessity for high expectations.
- Extensive work was done to align curriculum with state tests.
- Regular assessments of student performance helped ensure tutoring for students falling behind.

Districts registering clear gains in student performance on state standards-based assessments include some of the nation's largest districts that enroll disproportionately large percentages of low-income students, minority students, and limited-English learners. The Council of Great City Schools has surveyed its big-city member districts and reported that they have made meaningful gains in math and reading scores on state assessments and on other independent tests such as the National Assessment of Educational Progress, and gaps in achievement between minority and nonminority students are narrowing.[67]

Baltimore gains

Impressive examples of gains in student performance on state assessments and other tests have been particularly evident in Baltimore and several other cities. In Baltimore, students have improved both their reading and math scores at every grade tested by the state. Baltimore elementary students also made major progress on nationally normed tests. The percentages of fifth graders reading at or above the proficient level increased from 44 percent in 2003 to 76 percent in 2011, and comparable scores for third graders improved from 39 percent to 69 percent. Observers have attributed these gains to such coordinated reform initiatives as professional development dealing with balanced literacy; standards-based teaching in reading, writing, and math; increased early childhood, after-school, and summer learning opportunities; and requirements for student promotion from one grade to the next.[68]

Conclusion: The Challenge for Education

Raising performance nationally

We began this chapter by recognizing the need for improved performance on the part of students in our educational systems. This is particularly true with respect to the development of higher-order skills in all segments of the student population and specifically

---

[66]Gordon Cawelti and Nancy Protheroe, *How Six School Districts Changed into High-Performance Systems* (Arlington, VA: Educational Research Service, 2001). See also Jason C. Snipes, Fred Doolittle, and Corinne Herlihy, *Case Studies of How Urban School Systems Improve Student Achievement* (New York: MDRC, 2002), available at **www.mdrc.org/Reports2002/achievementgap /achievement_exsummary.htm**; Rhonda Barton, "What Matters at the District Level," *Northwest Education* (Winter 2007), available at **www.educationnorthwest.org/edunw-magazine**; and Ellen Foley, "Contradictions and Control in Systemic Reform," 2011 report prepared for the Consortium for Policy Research in Education, available at **www.cpre.org**.
[67]Catherine Gewertz, "Urban Schools Continue Test-Score Gains, Reports Finds," *Education Week* (April 5, 2006); and "Large City Schools Improve from 2003 to 2011, Says Nation's Report Card," 2011 report prepared for the Council of the Great Cities Schools.
[68]"Baltimore Builds for Success," *American Teacher* (December 2003–January 2004), available at **www.aft.org**; "2011 Maryland Report Card," 2011 report available at **www.mdreportcrd .org**; and Judy Lightfoot, "What Can We Learn from the Struggles of Baltimore Public Schools?" *Crosscut* (January 24, 2011), available at **www.crosscut.com**.

among disadvantaged students. In Chapter 13, The Changing Purposes of American Education, we described how attention increasingly has focused on national goals. In our chapters dealing with teachers and the teaching profession, we described how emphasis is being placed on preparing and hiring qualified teachers who can function effectively throughout our school systems. In several other chapters, including this one, we have cited successful instructional interventions that can be incorporated into large-scale reform plans. All of these efforts are currently receiving attention in the federal government's educational improvement plans. Among other activities, the government is providing billions of dollars to improve teacher preparation and functioning, encourage and facilitate higher standards that can be implemented on a widespread basis, and identify and support successful reforms to help disadvantaged students.

Closing achievement gaps

With regard to the more specific need to reduce or eliminate achievement gaps by social class and by race and ethnicity, we have described numerous aspects of an overall effort that can help make this goal a reality. Chapter 12, Providing Equal Educational Opportunity, and material in this chapter indicated that comprehensive ecological interventions addressing school, family, and home environments during infancy and early childhood, school arrangements responsive to the particular problems of low-achieving students, and alleviation of disadvantages arising from segregation and concentrated poverty should play important roles in addressing this challenge. Reforms considered in this chapter, such as effective introduction of technology, charter schools specifically serving low-income students in big cities, and systemic plans to implement these or similar components throughout a school district, can generate large performance gains that substantially reduce or eliminate achievement gaps.[69]

Key role for new teachers

Here, too, our school systems and governments are initiating action to meet the challenge. Our federal and state governments are doing much to increase and disseminate research on instructional approaches that work, on procedures to assess higher-order skills, on programs to prepare teachers for urban schools, and on a multitude of other topics involving school reform. We already have learned much about improving educational effectiveness at the district, school, and classroom levels. However, using this knowledge to fundamentally improve the schools is a difficult and complex task. As a teacher, you will face this task because you will play an important part in determining whether the reform effort is successful.

Summing Up

1. The educational system is being challenged to improve achievement to keep the United States internationally competitive and to provide equity for disadvantaged and other at-risk students.

2. Research on effective teaching and instruction provides support for appropriate emphasis on efficient classroom management, direct instruction, high time-on-task, skillful questioning of students, explicit comprehension instruction, and other methods that promote achievement.

3. Research indicates that schools unusually effective in improving student achievement have a clear mission, outstanding leadership, high expectations for students,

positive home–school relations, high time-on-task, frequent monitoring of students' achievement, and an orderly, humane climate. Research also has identified somewhat more specific characteristics such as curriculum alignment and school-wide emphasis on higher-order skills. Regarding high schools, researchers have found that schools-within-a-school, career academies, and smaller units sometimes are effective.

4. It now is possible to create more effective schools, provided educators use what we have learned about the school improvement process.

[69]Greg Anrig; "Building on Success," 2009 report prepared for The Century Foundation, available at **www.tcf.org**; "TAP Research Summary," 2011 report prepared for The System for Teacher and Student Advancement, available at **www.tapsystem.org**; and Diane Ravitch, "Schools We Can Envy," *New York Review of Books* (March 8, 2012), available at **www.nybooks.com**.

⑤ Many efforts, such as the Higher-Order Thinking Skills Program, seek to improve instruction across grade levels. An approach called Response to Intervention is growing in popularity, but it is difficult to implement effectively.

⑥ Research efforts designed to improve whole schools stem from research indicating that the individual school level is crucial in bringing about reform.

⑦ Many school districts and states have undertaken improvement efforts involving cooperation with businesses and other institutions, year-round schooling, and improving rural education and education for gifted and talented students.

⑧ Emerging technologies offer great potential for improving elementary and secondary education, but effective use of technologies will require considerable planning, effort, and resources.

⑨ Many possibilities exist for improving education through expanding school choice, but many potential dangers also exist.

⑩ Promising efforts are now under way to bring about systemic, coherent restructuring and reform. Systemic reforms can do much to meet the challenge of reducing or eliminating achievement gaps by social class and race/ethnicity.

Key Terms

The numbers indicate the pages where explanations of the key terms can be found.

effective schools 479	distance education 500	alternative schools 504
time-on-task 480	year-round school 501	charter schools 504
direct instruction 480	21st Century Community Learning	restructuring 507
explicit teaching 480	Centers 503	systemic improvement 507
explicit comprehension instruction 481	school choice 503	
curriculum alignment 483	magnet schools 503	

Certification Connection Activity

This chapter examines school effectiveness and school reform. An integral part of reform at the local school level is the development of a behavior management plan. In the Praxis II Principles of Learning and Teaching, several questions cover behavior-management topics. In addition, success in behavior management prior to student teaching is often a predictor of first-year teaching success. To prepare for teaching, identify a behavior-management philosophy that is consistent with your teaching philosophy. In your journal, reflect on how you will manage your classroom using consequences, organize your materials, establish classroom rules and routines, and arrange students for successful learning.

Discussion Questions

① Why is school effectiveness so dependent on what happens in the school as a whole, not just in individual classrooms? What are the most important actions a teacher can take to help improve school effectiveness?

② What does research say about the effectiveness of nonpublic schools? Do they produce higher achievement than public schools? If yes, what considerations account for the difference?

③ Why should educators be somewhat cautious in interpreting research on effective schools? What mistakes in interpretation are most likely?

④ Would you be willing to work in a high-poverty school even though teaching there might be more difficult than in a middle-class school? What philosophical commitments might be important in undertaking this assignment?

Suggested Projects for Professional Development

① Collect and analyze information about cooperation between schools and other institutions (such as businesses and colleges) in your community. To what extent has such cooperation helped the schools?

② Visit a nearby school with a high proportion of low-income students. Talk with both teachers and students. Write a description of the school comparing its programs and practices with the characteristics of unusually effective schools discussed in this chapter. Organize your material for inclusion in your personal portfolio.

3 List the first actions you would take to improve the effectiveness of a typical high school. Defend your list. How do your proposals reflect research on school effectiveness? How do they reflect your personal philosophy?

4 In a recent book, journal, or article available on the Internet, find a proposal for a basic reform or restructuring in the public schools. What does the author propose to reform? How? Is the proposal realistic? What philosophic perspectives does it represent? What conditions or resources would be required to implement it successfully? What is the likelihood of success?

Suggested Resources

Internet Resources

The Internet is a treasure trove of places where you can read descriptions and analyses of successful schools and instructional practices as well as other reform topics discussed in this chapter. The following list provides a brief sampling:

- The state of Maryland's "School Improvement" site at **www.mdk12.org/process**

- *The Education Gadfly* available biweekly through a free subscription at **www.edexcellence.net**

- "Improving Schools" from the National Forum to Accelerate Middle-Grades Reform, **www.mgforum.org**

- "Success Stories" at the site of Public School Insights, **www.publicschoolinsights.org**, click on "Resources"

- The Fall 2006 issue of *Northwest Education*, available at **www.educationnorthwest.org/edunw-magazine**, is devoted to the theme "Literacy Coaches." The theme of the Fall 2008 issue is "Response to Intervention," with much attention given to tiered instruction.

- The October 2011 issue of *Educational Leadership* at **www.ascd.org** includes several articles on how coaches help improve teaching and schools.

- The February 2011 issue of *Educational Leadership* at **www.ascd.org** is devoted to the theme "Teaching Screenagers."

- Recent information about school choice has been compiled at **www.schoolchoicewi.org**, **www.ecs.org**, and **www.publiccharters.org**.

Studies opposing school choice approaches are emphasized in analyses at the American Federation of Teachers "Vouchers Home Page," **www.aft.org/issues/schoolchoice/vouchers**. Studies supporting school choice approaches are emphasized at **www.heritage.org/research** and in *School Reform* News available at **www.heartland.org**.

The National Association for Gifted Children (**www.nagc.org**) provides research-based materials for teachers of gifted students.

Material regarding Response to Intervention is available from **www.responsetointerventiononline.com** and from the National Center on Response to Intervention, **www.rti4success.org**.

A film clip of Barak Rosenshine speaking on "Making Instruction Explicit" is available at **www.formapex.com/barak-rosenshine**.

The Thinking Foundation (**www.thinkingfoundation.org**)

provides information about metacognitive strategies in general and Thinking Maps in particular, as well as case studies of schools that have greatly improved instruction using these strategies.

Many of the topics discussed in this chapter are updated frequently in the weekly bulletin *Education Gadfly*, available at **www.edexcellence.net**.

Information on school reform is published regularly at **www.educationsector.org** and is frequently cited at a companion blog, **www.eduwonk.org**.

Thoughtful articles dealing with school reform are presented in the online journals *Education Next*, available at **www.educationnext.org**, and *Education Policy Analysis Archives*, available at **http://epaa.asu.edu**.

Publications

Fullan, Michael. *The New Meaning of Educational Change*, 4th ed. New York: Teachers College Press, 2007. *Analysis of both the theoretical basis and the practical implications of research on the school change process.*

Gradillas, Henry and Jerry Jessness. *Standing and Delivering.* Lanham, MD: Rowman & Littlefield Education, 2010. *A fascinating account of how startling improvements were brought about by improving climate, instruction, and other effective-schools considerations at an inner-city high school in Los Angeles.*

Lake, Robin J. *Hopes, Fears, and Reality*. Seattle, WA: National Charter School Research Project, 2008. Subtitled "*A Balanced Look at American Charter Schools in 2008,*" this publication examines many aspects of the charter school movement and is updated annually at **www.ncsrp.org**.

Stulberg, Lisa M. *Race, Schools, and Hope: African Americans and School Choice after Brown*. New York: Teachers College Press, 2008. *This book explains why some African American leaders have been strong advocates of school choice.*

Additional resources for this chapter, including the TeachSource Videos, can be found on the Education CourseMate website. Go to **CengageBrain.com** to access the site.

Glossary

academic freedom A protection permitting teachers to teach subject matter and choose instructional materials relevant to the course without restriction from administrators or other persons outside the classroom.

academy A type of private or semipublic secondary school dominant in the United States from 1830 through 1870. It was an institutional predecessor of the high school.

accountability Holding teachers, administrators, and/or school board members responsible for student performance or for wise use of educational funds.

activity-centered curriculum A type of student-centered curriculum that emphasizes purposeful and real-life experiences and, more recently, student participation in school and community activities.

adequate yearly progress The regular increments of achievement gain that schools and districts must register to have all students attain academic proficiency in 2013–2014.

aesthetics The branch of axiology that examines questions of beauty and art.

alternative certification Teacher certification obtained without completing a traditional teacher-education program at a school or college of education.

alternative school A school, public or private, that provides learning opportunities different from those in local public schools. Some such schools follow a student-centered curriculum characterized by a great deal of freedom for students and a relative lack of structure.

American Federation of Teachers (AFT) The second largest organization that represents teachers in America. Affiliated with the AFL-CIO, it often is associated with union representation.

Americanization The dominant ideology in public schools imposed on immigrant and minority group children in the nineteenth and

early twentieth centuries. The emphasis was on teaching in English rather than the language the children spoke at home and rejecting the values of the minority child in favor of what was termed American values.

apperceptive mass Herbart's concept that instruction creates a network of ideas in the mind that form a cognitive map on which to relate more ideas, particularly those that are congruent to each other.

a priori ideas Ideas derived from self-evident first principles; they are deductions or conclusions based on reason alone. The theory of *a priori* ideas is associated with realism, Thomism, and perennialism. It is attacked by pragmatists such as Dewey as not being based on experience.

assimilation The strategy that immigrant children should learn to speak and read the English language, learn the values of hard work and punctuality inscribed in the Protestant ethic, and obey the laws of the United States.

axiology The area of philosophy that examines value issues, especially in morality, ethics, and aesthetics.

back-to-basics curriculum A type of subject-centered curriculum that emphasizes the three Rs at the elementary level and academic subjects at the secondary level; also includes a defined minimum level of academic standards.

basic skills testing Testing that examines preservice teachers' basic skills with respect to subjects such as reading, mathematics, and communications.

bilingual education Instruction in their native language provided for students whose first language is not English.

bipartite system A dual-track system consisting of academic schools and vocational schools.

block grants General-purpose funding from the federal government, allowing each state considerable freedom to choose specific programs on which to spend the funds.

blogs A type of personal journal that can provide students a forum to write for an authentic audience and may encourage greater care in writing.

boarding schools Residential institutions where students live and attend school. Boarding schools were used to assimilate Native American children into white culture by insisting they speak only English and study a required industrial training curriculum. In these schools, Native American pupils were not permitted to use their own vernacular languages and engage in tribal customs.

brain drain The emigration of educated people to wealthier nations.

breach of contract What occurs when one side fails to perform as agreed in a contract.

categorical grants Funds designated for specific groups and purposes; the standard method of federal education funding before the 1980s and again more recently.

censorship The suppression of ideas and information that certain persons—individuals, groups, or government officials—find objectionable or dangerous.

central office staff A cadre of supervisors and specialists who work closely with the superintendent to carry out school board policy.

certification State government review and approval that permits a teaching candidate to teach.

character education See *values-centered curriculum.*

charter school A public school governed by a community group granted a special contract (charter) by the state or the local school board. Charter schools often form to offer educational alternatives unavailable in regular public schools.

chief state school officer The chief executive of the state board of education; sometimes called the state superintendent or commissioner of education.

child benefit theory A theory that government aid directly benefits the child rather than a nonpublic institution he or she attends.

child depravity theory A theory that children, because of their sinful nature, tend to be disorderly and lazy and need strict discipline to develop a personal sense of order and civility.

Children's Internet Protection Act (CIPA) An act that went into effect in 2001 in which schools and libraries receiving discounts on electronic equipment and media are required to install a "technology protection measure" preventing minors from using computers with Internet capabilities to access "visual depictions that are obscene, child pornography, or harmful to minors."

classical humanists The leading theory and general method of education during the Renaissance. Refers to the study of the classical Greek and Roman texts with an emphasis on their humanistic (human-centered) meaning.

collective bargaining A procedure for resolving disagreements between employers and employees through negotiation. For teachers, such negotiation pertains to many aspects of their work and salary as well as their relationship with students, supervisors, and the community.

Commission on the Reorganization of Secondary Education A commission appointed by the National Education Association to study and make recommendations for reforming American secondary education. Its 1918 report, *The Cardinal Principles of Secondary Education,* recommended a curriculum based on fundamental personal, social, cultural, and economic needs within a comprehensive institutional setting.

Committee of Ten A committee, chaired by Charles Eliot, appointed by the National Education Association in 1892 to bring greater coherence to secondary education in the United States. It recommended a four-year program and a curriculum that emphasized academic subjects for all students.

Common Core State Standards Standards released by the National Governors Association Center for Best Practices (NGA Center) and the Council of Chief State School Officers (CCSSO) in 2010 to define the knowledge and skills students should gain during their climb of the educational ladder so that by the time they graduate high school, they will be able to succeed in academic college courses and in future career training programs.

common school A publicly supported and locally controlled elementary school.

community control An elected community council or board that shares decision-making power with the local school board.

community education The school serves as a partner or coordinating agency in providing educational, health, social, legal, recreational, and/or cultural activities in the community.

community participation Citizen advisory committees at either the local school or school board level.

community schools When the school is seen as only one of the educational agencies within the community, and the school serves as a partner, or coordinating agency, in providing educational, health, social, family support, recreational, and cultural activities to the community.

compensatory education An attempt to remedy the effects of environmental disadvantages through educational enrichment programs.

concrete-operational period A stage of human development identified by Jean Piaget that occurs from ages seven to eleven years, when children organize their concepts in performing increasingly complex mental operations.

Confucius (551–478 BCE) Chinese philosopher, government official, and educator who devised an ethical system still observed in China and other countries in Asia.

consolidation The combining of small or rural school districts into larger ones.

constructivism A learning theory that emphasizes the ways in which learners actively create meaning by constructing and reconstructing ideas about reality based on their explorations of the environment.

continuing contract An employment contract that is automatically renewed from year to year without need for the teacher's signature.

controlled choice A system in which students can select their school as long as their choices do not result in segregation.

cooperative learning A form of instruction in which teams of students work cooperatively on specific tasks or projects.

copyright A law that gives authors and artists control over the reproduction and distribution of works they create; consequently, permission for reproduction usually must be obtained from the owner.

critical theory (critical pedagogy) A theory of education which contends that some public school systems limit educational opportunities for students marginalized because of race,

class, and gender biases. Proponents argue that teachers should be "transformative intellectuals" who work to change the system. Also known as "critical discourse."

critical thinking Solving problems by means of general concepts or higher-order relationships. Instruction in critical thinking generally emphasizes basic analytical skills applicable to a wide variety of intellectual experiences.

cultural pluralism Acceptance and encouragement of cultural, ethnic, and religious diversity within a larger society.

culture Patterns of acquired behavior and attitudes transmitted among the members of society.

curriculum Planned experiences provided through instruction through which the school meets its goals and objectives.

curriculum alignment Coordination of instructional planning, methods, materials, and testing to accomplish important learning objectives.

deconstruction Critical examination of texts or canons to determine the power relationships embedded in their creation and use. Often used by educators who follow a postmodernist philosophy.

deductive logic The process of thinking by which consequences or applications are drawn out of general principles or assumptions; the process of thought in which conclusions follow from premises.

de facto segregation Segregation associated with and resulting from housing patterns.

de jure segregation Segregation resulting from laws or government action.

deprofessionalization The process of removing from professional status.

desegregation Attendance by students of different racial backgrounds in the same school and classroom.

differentiated instruction A type of instruction based on the premise that all students differ in how they learn, their personal strengths and weaknesses, their backgrounds, and their interests. Differentiated instruction creates learning opportunities in heterogeneous classrooms that capitalize on each student's individuality and uniqueness. When differentiating instruction, teachers adjust the curriculum and classroom instruction to fit the student's preferences.

direct instruction A systematic method of teaching that emphasizes teacher-directed instruction proceeding in small steps, usually in accordance with a six- to eight-part lesson sequence.

distance education Instruction by people or materials distant from the learner in space or time; many distance education projects use interactive television, the Internet, and other modern communication technologies.

dual-track school system The traditional European pattern of separate primary schools for the masses and preparatory and secondary schools for males in the upper socioeconomic classes.

due process A formalized legal procedure with specific and detailed rules and principles designed to protect the rights of individuals.

due process clause A Fourteenth Amendment statement that government shall not deprive any person of life, liberty, or property without due process of law.

Ebonics Frequently used as a synonym for Black English, Ebonics also refers to analysis of a dialect used by many African Americans and of how it might play a part in teaching Standard English.

ecological intervention Comprehensive efforts to improve the environments of young children.

Education for All Handicapped Children Act (Public Law 94–142) A law passed in 1975 that mandated that children with handicaps must have access to a full public education in the least restrictive educational environment.

educational ladder The system of public schooling developed in the United States that begins with kindergarten, proceeds through elementary education, continues through secondary education, and leads to attendance at a college or university.

educational voucher A flat grant or payment representing a child's estimated school cost or portion of the cost. Under a typical voucher plan, the parent or child may choose any school, public or private, and the school is paid for accepting the child.

effective schools Schools that are unusually successful in producing high student performance, compared with other schools that enroll students of similar background; sometimes defined as schools in which working-class students achieve as well as middle-class students.

empiricism An epistemology that relies on human experience, especially sensation and observation, as the source of knowledge about reality. It emphasizes experimentation and the scientific method.

enculturation The process beginning at infancy by which a human being acquires the culture of his or her society.

environmental literacy According to the National Science Teachers Association, environmental literacy "is the ability of students to master critical thinking skills that will prepare them to evaluate issues and make informed decisions regarding stewardship of the planet."

environmentalist view of intelligence The belief that intelligence is mostly determined by environment.

epistemology The area of philosophy that examines knowing and theories of knowledge.

equal protection clause A Fourteenth Amendment statement that government shall not deny any person the equal protection of the law.

essentialism An educational theory that emphasizes basic skills and subject-matter disciplines. Proponents generally favor a curriculum consisting of the three Rs at the elementary level and five major disciplines (English, math, science, history, and foreign language) at the secondary level. Emphasis is on academic competition and excellence.

essentialist-influenced curriculum A subject-centered educational theory based on six major disciplines: English, mathematics, the sciences, history, foreign languages, and geography. Contemporary essentialists also add computer literacy.

establishment clause A constitutional provision that prohibits the establishment of a government-sanctioned religion.

ethical relativism This theory asserts that ideas and values are products of specific cultural groups formulated during a particular historical period. Ideas and values depend on the place, time, circumstances, and situations in which they arise. Ethical relativism denies the existence of universal and eternal truths and values. It is associated with pragmatism, progressivism, social reconstructionism, and critical theory.

ethics The branch of axiology that examines questions of right and wrong and good and bad.

ethnic group A group of people with a distinctive history, culture, and language.

ethnicity A shared cultural background based on identification and membership with an ethnic group.

exclusive product rights Special privileges whereby commercial enterprises pay a fee for the exclusive right to market their product (for example, Pepsi Cola) in the school district.

existentialism A philosophy that examines the way in which humans define themselves by making personal choices.

experience As defined by John Dewey, the interaction of a person with his or her environment.

explicit comprehension instruction Classroom techniques specifically for teaching comprehension.

explicit teaching See *direct instruction*.

fair use A principle allowing use of copyrighted material without permission of the author, under specific, limited conditions.

Family Educational Rights and Privacy Act (Buckley Amendment) A law passed in 1974 to curb possible abuses at institutions receiving federal funds.

first-language maintenance Continued teaching in a language while introducing instruction in another language.

Follow Through A program that concentrated on improving achievement of low-income children in the primary grades.

formal-operational period A stage of child development identified by Jean Piaget that occurs from age eleven through early adulthood, when individuals formulate abstract generalizations and learn how to perform complex problem-solving processes.

free exercise clause A constitutional provision that protects rights of free speech and expression.

gender roles Socially expected behavior patterns for girls and boys, men and women.

goals Broad statements of educational purpose.

Goals 2000 The 1994 revision of the *National Educational Goals* that added two additional goals and updated states' progress on the *National Educational Goals* while providing additional services, programs, and classes as needed.

Head Start A federal government program that provides preschool education for economically disadvantaged four- and five-year-old students.

hereditarian view of intelligence The belief that intelligence is mostly determined by heredity.

hidden curriculum What students learn, other than academic content, from the school milieu or environment.

high school A school for students in the upper secondary grades, commonly serving grades 9 or 10 through 12.

highly qualified teachers An aspect of the No Child Left Behind Act, which specifies that teachers should have (1) a bachelor's degree; (2) full state certification and licensure as defined by the state; and (3) demonstrated competency as defined by the state in each core academic subject he or she teaches.

homogeneous grouping The practice of placing together students with similar achievement levels or ability.

hornbook A single sheet of parchment, containing the Lord's Prayer, letters of the alphabet, and vowels, covered by the translucent, flattened horn of a cow and fastened to a flat wooden board. It was used during the colonial era in primary schools.

humanistic approach to curriculum A student-centered curriculum approach that stresses the personal and social aspects of the student's growth and development. Emphasizes self-actualizing processes and moral, aesthetic, and higher domains of thinking.

hurried children Children highly pressured to excel at an early age.

hypermedia A computer approach that allows learners to browse through an information base to construct their own knowledge relationships and connections.

idealism A philosophy that construes reality to be spiritual or nonmaterial in essence.

inclusion Educating students with disabilities in regular classrooms in their neighborhood schools, with collaborative support services as needed.

individualized education program (IEP) Plans including both long- and short-range goals for educating students with disabilities.

individualized instruction Curriculum content, instructional materials, and activities designed for individual learning. Considers the learner's pace, interests, and abilities.

Individuals with Disabilities Education Act (IDEA) Legislation enacted in 1990.

Individuals with Disabilities Education Improvement Act (IDEIA) A 2004 law which requires that if a child is identified as disabled, school officials must conduct a functional assessment and develop suitable intervention strategies.

induction Providing a supportive environment for novice teachers so they may experience a more methodical entry into the teaching profession; the goal is to enhance the beginning teacher's skills and increase the likelihood they will remain in the profession. Such activities may include reduced teaching loads, special workshops, collaborative planning time, and mentoring.

inductive logic The process of reasoning from particulars to generalities, from the parts to the whole, and from the individual to the general. It is the basis of the scientific method, emphasized by Dewey and the pragmatists.

in loco parentis The idea that schools should act "in place of the parent."

integration The step beyond simple desegregation that includes effective action to develop positive interracial contacts and to improve the performance of low-achieving minority students.

intelligent design The argument that life is too complex to be formed through natural selection as portrayed by Darwin, therefore it must be directed by an "intelligent designer."

intermediate unit An educational unit or agency in the middle position between the state department of education and the local school district; usually created by the state to provide supplementary services and support staff to local school districts. Also known as a regional educational service agency (RESA).

International Association for the Evaluation of Educational Achievement (IEA) A research group that began conducting cross-national studies in the 1960s.

Islam Religion founded by Mohammed (569–632); currently practiced in many Middle Eastern and other countries.

jigsaw strategy A strategy that provides students the opportunity to interact with one another while at the same time learning academic content. This approach necessitates that each student takes responsibility for teaching others in his/her group a specific piece of information (i.e., one piece of a larger puzzle).

Judeo-Christian tradition The Western cultural tradition that has been shaped by Judaism and Christianity.

junior high school A two- or three-year school between elementary and high school, commonly for grades 7–9.

Koran The most sacred book of the Islamic religion and culture.

land grant An arrangement used to found many of today's state universities. The Morrill Act of 1862 granted thirty thousand acres of public land for each senator and representative in Congress, the income from which was to support at least one state college for agricultural and mechanical instruction.

land-grant college A state college or university offering agricultural and mechanical curricula, funded originally by the Morrill Act of 1862.

latchkey children Children unsupervised after school.

Latin grammar school A college preparatory school of the colonial era that emphasized Latin and Greek languages and studies.

learning styles Distinctively different ways students learn, such as emphasis on oral or visual activities.

least restrictive environment A term used in educating students with disabilities to designate a setting that is as normal or regular as possible. Federal law requires that children with disabilities be placed in special or separate classes only for the amount of time necessary to provide appropriate services.

liberation pedagogy An educational theory advanced by Paulo Freire that encourages students to develop a critical consciousness of the conditions that oppress them and to free themselves from this oppression.

litigants Parties in a lawsuit.

local school board A body of citizens, either appointed or elected, who set policy regarding schools in a local school district.

macrocosm The universal whole or entirety. In idealism, it is the most universal, complete, and abstract idea from which all subordinate ideas are derived.

magnet school A type of alternative school that attracts voluntary enrollment from more than one neighborhood by offering special instructional programs or curricula; often established in part for purposes of desegregation.

mainstreaming Placing students with disabilities in regular classes for much or all of the school day, while also providing additional services, programs, and classes as needed.

mastery instruction An approach in which students are tested after initial instruction, and those who fail to master the objectives receive corrective instruction and retesting. Emphasizes short units of instruction and learning defined skills.

mediated entry The practice of inducting persons into a profession through carefully supervised stages.

mental discipline approach Strengthening the mind through mental activities, just as the body is strengthened through exercise.

merit pay A plan that rewards teachers partially or primarily on the basis of performance or objective standards.

metaphysics The area of philosophy that examines issues of a speculative nature dealing with ultimate reality.

microcosm A miniature version of the larger part, the macrocosm, from which it is derived.

middle class Professionals and small-business owners, as well as technicians and sales and clerical workers.

middle school A two- to four-year school between elementary and high school, commonly for grades 6–8.

mill A unit of the local tax rate representing one-thousandth of a dollar.

monitorial method A method of instruction also known as mutual instruction and designed by Andrew Bell and Joseph Lancaster, working independently of each other in the early nineteenth century. It sought to provide an inexpensive form of mass basic schooling by using more advanced students—monitors—to teach less advanced students.

Montessori schools Early childhood institutions that follow Maria Montessori's philosophy and method of instruction. They emphasize that children learn by developing sensory, motor, and intellectual skills by using didactic materials in a structured environment.

multicultural education Education that includes the cultures and cultural contributions of all racial, ethnic, language, and gender groups, especially those marginalized in the tradition curriculum. Many multicultural programs also emphasize positive intergroup and interracial attitudes and contacts.

municipal overburden Severe financial crunch caused by population density and a high proportion of disadvantaged and low-income groups.

National Assessment of Educational Progress (NAEP) A periodic assessment of educational achievement under the jurisdiction of the Educational Testing Service, using nationally representative samples of elementary and secondary students.

National Board for Professional Teaching Standards (NBPTS) A national nonprofit organization that issues certificates to teachers who meet its standards for professional ability and knowledge.

National Council for Accreditation of Teacher Education (NCATE) Prestigious national organization that works closely with state departments of education to review and evaluate teacher-education programs at colleges and universities.

National Education Association (NEA) The largest organization that represents teachers in the United States.

National Education Goals, The A 1990 National Governors' Conference report on education in America that delineated six educational guidelines for state and local education agencies; revised in 1994.

National Education Goals Panel Report A 1998 report that reviewed the progress on the eight goals and twenty-six indicators in *Goals 2000*.

national reports Major reports in the 1980s and 1990s that spurred reform by designating student low performance and other problems as deficiencies in the educational system.

Nation at Risk, A A landmark national report critical of public education in the United States that resulted in raising high-school graduation requirements in most states.

naturalistic theory An educational theory that argues that the natural stages of human development should be the basis of instruction and education.

new core curriculum (core subjects approach) A curriculum of common courses that all students are required to take. Emphasis is usually on academic achievement and traditional subject matter.

No Child Left Behind Act (NCLB) The federal Elementary and Secondary Education Act passed in 2001, which requires states and school districts that receive federal funding to show adequate yearly progress, as measured by standardized tests of students in grades 3–8, and to provide all students with "highly qualified" teachers.

normal school A two-year teacher-education institution popular in the nineteenth century.

norms A social entity's rules of behavior.

nuclear family Mother and father living with their children.

object lesson A method developed by Johann Heinrich Pestalozzi, who used concrete objects as the basis of form, number, and name lessons.

objectives Specific statements of educational purpose, usually written for a particular subject, grade, unit, or lesson; commonly defined in behavioral terms so that student experiences and performance can be observed and measured.

occupational prestige The special status accorded to certain occupations and not to others.

outcomes-based education (OBE) Education guided by the principle that success should be judged by student "outcomes" (generally seen in terms of abilities to function in real-life contexts) rather than by "inputs" such as programs, courses, or funding. Many proponents would revise traditional curricula that fail to produce desired outcomes.

overloaded schools Schools with a high incidence of serious problems that make it difficult for educators to function effectively.

Paideia Proposal, The The *Paideia Proposal*, developed by Mortimer J. Adler, uses the Greek term *paideia*, the total educational formation, or upbringing of a child in the cultural heritage, to assert that all students should pursue the same curriculum consisting of intellectual skills and organized knowledge in language, literature, the arts, sciences, and social studies. It is a modern form of perennialism.

Parent Teacher Association (PTA) A national organization of parents, teachers, and students to promote the welfare of children and youth that has affiliated local groups in school communities.

parent-teacher group An organization of parents and teachers in a local school community.

peer culture Behaviors and attitudes of similar-age children or youth in an institution or society.

perennialism An educational theory that emphasizes rationality as the major purpose of education, asserting that the essential truths are recurring and universally true. Proponents generally favor a curriculum consisting of the three Rs at the elementary level and the classics, especially the "great books" at the secondary level.

perennialist-influenced curriculum A fundamentally subject-centered educational theory that the main purpose of education is the cultivation of the best of the past, the classics.

personal income tax A tax based on a percentage of personal income.

philosophies Fully developed bodies of thought each representing a generalized worldview.

plaintiffs Persons who sue.

Plato's *Republic* Plato's most systematic philosophical statement on politics and education. Using the format of dialogues, it portrays a perfect city ruled by philosopher-kings according to the principle of justice.

postmodernism A philosophy that is highly skeptical
of the truth of metanarratives, the canons that purport to be authoritative statements of universal or objective truth. Rather, postmodernists regard these canons as historical statements that rationalize one group's domination of another.

pragmatism A philosophy that judges the validity of ideas by their consequences in action.

preoperational stage A stage of human development identified by Jean Piaget that occurs from age two to seven years, when children create categories, classify, add to, and reconstruct their conceptions of reality through systematic environmental explorations.

principal The chief administrative officer of the school, responsible for school operation.

profession An occupation that rates high in prestige and requires extensive formal education and mastery of a defined body of knowledge beyond the grasp of laypersons. Members of many professions control licensing standards and have autonomy in their work environment.

professional development Continued education or training of a school district's teaching staff. Such programs often emphasize teacher input as well as collaboration between the school district and a college or university.

professional development school (PDS) An elementary or secondary school operated jointly by a school district and a teacher-training institution that emphasizes thoughtful analysis of teaching and learning. The participants usually include future teachers as well as practicing teachers, administrators, and teacher educators.

Professional Learning Community In collaborative groups, teachers and other colleagues work together to improve instruction for their students. PLCs analyze assessment data and use professional knowledge to develop team-designed lessons and classroom experiences that will assist students in meeting desired learning outcomes.

professional practice board A state or national commission that permits educators to set professional standards and minimal requirements of competency.

Program for International Student Assessment (PISA) Numerous documents published by the Organisation for Economic Co-operation and Development providing information and analysis based on data regarding student performance in reading, mathematics, and other subjects collected in more than seventy nations.

Progress in International Reading Literacy Study (PIRLS) The Progress in International Reading Literacy Study (PIRLS) is an international comparative study of the reading literacy of students at the fourth-grade level. It has been administered periodically since 2001.

progressive taxes Taxes based on the taxpayer's ability to pay, for example, income taxes.

progressivism An antitraditional theory in American education associated with child-centered learning through activities, problem solving, and projects. The Progressive Education Association promoted progressivism as an educational movement.

property tax The main source of revenues for local school districts, based on the value of real property (land and improvements on land).

Protection of Pupil Rights Amendment An amendment to the federal General Education Provisions Act of 1978 specifying that instructional materials used in connection with "any research or experimentation program or project" must be "available for inspection" by participating students' parents and guardians and that no student can be required to participate in testing, psychological examination, or treatments whose "primary purpose is to reveal information" concerning political affiliations, sexual behaviors or attitudes, psychological or mental problems, income, and other personal matters.

pullout approach Taking low achievers out of regular classes for supplementary instruction in reading and math.

race Groups of people with common ancestry and physical characteristics.

Race to the Top An Obama administration education reform program initiated in 2009 to provide competitive grants for projects and approaches to improve K-12 education systems and student achievement.

realism A philosophy, originating with Aristotle, that considers reality to be objective and dualistic in nature. That is, reality has both a material and a formal or structural component.

reflective teaching A style of teaching that emphasizes reflective inquiry and self-awareness. Reflective teachers analyze their own teaching behavior and consider the factors that make their teaching effective or ineffective.

regional educational service agency (RESA) See *intermediate unit.*

regressive taxes Taxes that require lower-income groups to pay relatively more of their income than higher-income groups.

relevant curriculum Curriculum that addresses social change, emphasizing knowledge, skills, and attitudes pertinent to modern society.

reminiscence The recalling or remembering of ideas that Plato asserted were latently present in the mind. Through skilled questioning, the teacher stimulates students to bring these ideas to consciousness.

resistance theory The view that working-class students resist the school in part because a hegemonic traditional curriculum marginalizes their everyday knowledge.

Response to Intervention An approach that dictates leaving a child in the regular school program while providing him or her with suitable interventions; only if that does not work is the child referred for special-education or disability services.

restructuring Multiple changes to bring about systemic improvement in a school or group of schools.

revisionist view of schools The belief that elite groups have channeled disadvantaged students into second-rate schools and inferior jobs.

rhetoric The theory and practice of public speaking, declamation, and oratory in ancient Greece. During the Middle Ages it tended to emphasize written discourse as well as speaking. Along with grammar and logic, rhetoric was part of the *trivium* of the liberal arts.

sales tax A tax based on purchase of taxable goods (generally not food or services).

Scholasticism The intellectual and educational approach used by educators in medieval universities, involving the study of theological and philosophical authorities.

school-based management A system of school governance in which individual schools, rather than the superintendent or board of education, make many important decisions. This system usually gives teachers substantial decision-making responsibility.

school choice A system that allows students or their parents to choose the schools they attend.

school infrastructure The basic physical facilities of the school plant (plumbing, sewer, heat, electric, roof, windows, and so on).

scientific method A systematic approach to inquiry in which hypotheses are tested by replicable empirical verification. Although usually identified with the laboratory method in the natural sciences, the scientific method is also used in philosophy, where it is associated with pragmatism.

sensorimotor stage A stage of child development identified by Jean Piaget that occurs from birth to two years, when children develop their earliest concepts by environmental exploration.

Social Darwinism An ideology that applies Darwin's biological principles of the "survival of the fittest" and competition to individuals in society. During the late nineteenth century, it was a highly influential rationale for unregulated capitalism as the economic system best designed to promote progress.

socialization The process of preparing persons for a social environment.

socialized education The educational philosophy developed by Jane Addams, who advocated that schools emphasize teaching about urbanization, industrialization, technology, and cultural diversity.

social reconstructionism The theory developed by a group of progressive educators who believe schools should deliberately work for social reform and change.

socioeconomic status (SES) Relative ranking of individuals according to economic, social, and occupational prestige and power; usually measured in terms of occupation, education, and income and generally viewed in terms of social-class categories ranging from working class to upper class.

Socratic method An educational method attributed to the Greek philosopher Socrates by which the teacher encourages the student's discovery of truth by asking leading and stimulating questions.

Sophists Members of a group of itinerant educators in ancient Greece during the period from 470–370 BCE who emphasized rhetoric, public speaking, and other practical skills. Their approach contrasts with that of the speculative philosophers Plato and Aristotle.

standards Focused statements on the purposes of education.

state board of education An influential state education agency that advises the state legislature and establishes policies for implementing legislative acts related to education.

state department of education An agency that operates under the direction of the state board of education. Its functions include accrediting schools, certifying teachers, apportioning state school funds, conducting research, issuing reports, and coordinating state education policies with local school districts.

state school code A collection of state laws that establish ways and means of operating schools and conducting education.

state standards Performance indicators showing students have achieved academic mastery at levels set by state boards of education.

student-centered curricula Curricula that focus on the needs and attitudes of the individual student. Emphasizes self-expression and the student's intrinsic motivation.

subject-area curriculum A type of subject-centered curriculum in which each subject is treated as a largely autonomous body of knowledge. Emphasizes traditional subjects that have dominated U.S. education since the late nineteenth century, including English, history, science, and mathematics.

subject-centered curricula Curricula defined in terms of bodies of content or subject matter. Achievement is judged according to defined outcomes such as test scores, correct answers, or responses deemed appropriate.

superintendent of schools The chief executive officer of the local school district, implements policies adopted by the school board.

supply and demand Market conditions that affect salaries such that pay decreases when there is a large supply of teachers and rises when supply is low and teachers are in high demand.

synthesizers' view of intelligence The belief that intelligence is determined by interaction of environment and heredity.

systemic improvement Reform efforts that simultaneously address all or most major components in the overall educational system.

tax base Basis upon which taxes to support public schools are assessed at state and local levels—for example, property tax, sales tax, transportation taxes, and special fees.

taxpayer resistance When taxpayers show reluctance to continue paying increased taxes to support public schools.

teacher empowerment The process of increasing the power of teachers and their role in determining school policies and practices.

technology-enhanced learning Instructional strategies that draw upon technology in a variety of ways.

tenure Permanence of position granted to educators after a probationary period, which prevents their dismissal except for legally specified causes and through formalized due-process procedures.

theories Sets of ideas or beliefs, often based on research findings or generalizations from practice, that guide educational policies or procedures.

Third International Mathematics and Science Study (TIMSS) A research group that has conducted cross-national research since 1996.

time-on-task Classroom time engaged in learning activities.

Title 1 A portion of the federal Elementary and Secondary Education Act that provides funds to improve the education of economically disadvantaged students.

Torah The first five Books of Moses that form the foundation of Hebraic religion, culture, and education.

torts Civil wrongs.

town school The eighteenth- and early-nineteenth-century elementary school of New England that educated children living in a designated area.

traditional view of schools The belief that the educational system provides economically disadvantaged students with meaningful opportunities. Also, the historically based perception that schools should teach basic skills such as reading, writing, spelling, arithmetic, and academic subjects.

transitional bilingual education (TBE) A form of bilingual education in which students are taught in their own language only until they can learn in English.

tuition tax credits Tax reductions offered to parents or guardians of children to offset part of their school tuition payments.

twenty-first century skills Instruction fostering student success in the global job market and problem solving in the modern democratic society that takes place in engaging, flexible, and active environments.

underclass Section of the lower working class subject to intergenerational transmission of poverty.

upper class Wealthy persons with substantial property and investments.

U.S. Department of Education A cabinet-level department in the executive branch of the federal government, in charge of federal educational policy and the promotion of educational programs.

user fees Special fees charged specifically to those who use a facility or service (for example, recreational facilities, bus service, or after-school centers).

utilitarian education The teaching of skills and subjects applicable to daily life, work, and society. Herbert Spencer argued that the subject of most use, or utility, was science. Utilitarian education is often contrasted with the Greek and Latin classical curriculum.

values-centered curriculum Places special emphasis on moral and ethical issues. More popularly known as *character education*.

vernacular schools Primary institutions that provided instruction in students' common language, in contrast to schools that instructed in classical languages such as Greek or Latin.

Web 2.0 The online encyclopedia *Webopedia* defines Web 2.0 as "focused on the ability for people to collaborate and share information online [and] includes open communication with an emphasis on Web-based communities of users, and more open sharing of information. . . . Blogs, wikis, and Web services are all seen as components of Web 2.0."

whole-child concept The view that schools must concern themselves with all aspects of students' growth and development, not mere-ly with cognitive skills or academic learning.

working class Skilled crafts workers and un-skilled manual workers.

year-round schools Rotating schedules that allow students to attend school for three out of four quarters during a chronological year.

21st Century Learning Centers These centers, supported through the No Child Left Behind Act, provide tutoring, after-school classes, summer school, and other academic enrich-ment activities for students attending low-performing schools.

Index

Note: Figures and tables are indicated by *f* and *t* following page numbers.